VICTORY TOGETHER
FOR MARTIN LUTHER KING, JR.

The Story of Dr. Warren H. Stewart, Sr., Governor Evan Mecham and the Historic Battle for a Martin Luther King, Jr. Holiday In Arizona

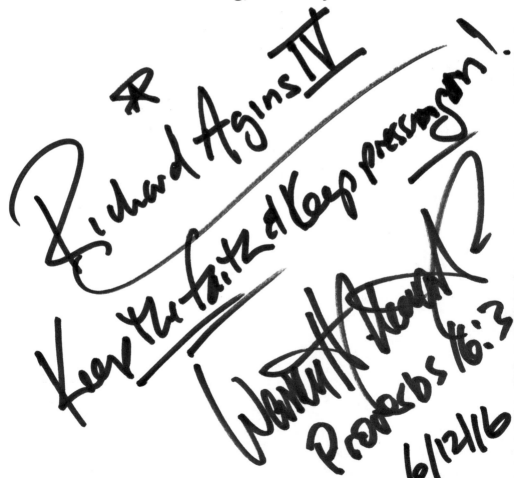

Richard Agins IV

Keep the faith & keep pressing on!

Warren H. Stewart

Proverbs 16:3

6/12/16

VICTORY TOGETHER
FOR MARTIN LUTHER KING, JR.

The Story of Dr. Warren H. Stewart, Sr., Governor Evan Mecham and the Historic Battle for a Martin Luther King, Jr. Holiday In Arizona

Warren H. Stewart, Sr.

A.W.O.L. PUBLICATIONS
ADVOCATES OF WHOLE LIFE
Phoenix, Arizona

VICTORY TOGETHER FOR MARTIN LUTHER KING, JR.
The Story of Dr. Warren H. Stewart, Sr.,
Governor Evan Mecham and the Historic Battle
for a Martin Luther King, Jr. Holiday In Arizona

Published by:
A.W.O.L. Publications
Phoenix, AZ
Phone: (602) 841-6090
Email: info@victorytogetherformlkjr.com
www.victorytogetherformlkjr.com

Warren H. Stewart, Sr., Publisher
Yvonne Rose, Book Packager (www.QualityPress.info)
Printed Page, Interior Designer
Warren H. Stewart, Jr., Cover Designer (www.bigwo.com)
Justin Mitchell Stewart, Cover Layout Consultant

A.W.O.L. Books are available at special discounts for bulk purchases, sales promotions, fund raising, or educational purposes. For information please contact the author at info@victorytogetherformlkjr.com

Dedication

For their enduring love and personal sacrifices during the six and a half years that God allowed me to fight for a Martin Luther King, Jr. holiday in Arizona,

I dedicate this book to my former wife, Ms. Serena Michele Stewart, and our six children, Warren Hampton, Jr., Matthew Christian, Jared Chamberlain, Justin Mitchell, Aaron Frederick Taylor and Jamila Imani.

Acknowledgements

God be praised for the awesome privilege He afforded me to provide leadership for Arizona's historic Martin Luther King, Jr. holiday fight from 1986 to 1992. Without my loving and liberating Lord Jesus Christ as my "Elder Brother" urging and encouraging me on through it all, I never would have made it to experience Victory Together on November 3, 1992, along with millions of other Arizonans. For that I am enthusiastically grateful to Him as my Savior and Lord. Indeed, God is faithful!

I am humbled and honored to acknowledge others who were instrumental in writing this memoir of what was originally titled, *MARTIN, MECHAM AND ME: LEADERSHIP UNDER FIRE—Memoirs of Arizona's Historic MLK Holiday Fight*:

> my partner in marriage and ministry, the Reverend Karen E. Stewart, who has prodded me to publish my manuscript for years now,
>
> the loving people of the First Institutional Baptist Church who afforded me the freedom to lead the King holiday fight while serving as their senior pastor and providing me with a six-month sabbatical to complete the first draft of this manuscript,
>
> my administrative secretary at the time of my writing this book, Janice M. Solomon,
>
> my former administrative secretary who typed my manuscript from hundreds of yellow, legal-size pages of my handwritten manuscript, Sarah L. Alexander,
>
> my current executive assistant who helped me look for key documents for this project, Renette Gutierrez Shaw,

my book packager, production coordinator and editor, Yvonne Rose of Quality Press, who worked with me diligently in detail during the final editing, and publishing for this book,

two of my sons, Pastor Warren H. Stewart, Jr., designer, and Justin Mitchell Stewart, consultant, who worked with me in designing the front and back covers of this book,

to the dozens and dozens of people who worked untiringly alongside me for years to finally win a Martin Luther King, Jr. holiday in Arizona, who are too many to name here but are mentioned in the pages of this book,

and to the late Mrs. Coretta Scott King, the widow of Dr. Martin Luther King, Jr., who victoriously persuaded the United States of America and all 50 states to honor the world's 20th century prophet of God for "liberty and justice for all" as well as who lauded me for my efforts to see that Arizona honored her husband with his day.
                                                            —Warren H. Stewart, Sr.

Contents

Preface

VICTORY TOGETHER FOR MARTIN LUTHER KING, JR.: THE STORY OF DR. WARREN H. STEWART, SR., GOVERNOR EVAN MECHAM AND THE HISTORIC BATTLE FOR A MARTIN LUTHER KING, JR. HOLIDAY IN ARIZONA is the only extensive and personal historical account of Arizona's Martin Luther King, Jr. holiday campaign that records Arizona's metamorphosis as the only state in the Union to have its King holiday rescinded and defeated at the polls to the only state to approve the King holiday by an overwhelming vote of the people in a general election in 1992.

This book's contents journal, through my eyes, mind and heart, a historical and autobiographical account of Arizona's MLKJr. holiday struggle from 1986 to 1993. It deals with the impact and influence of three individuals on an entire state—Dr. Martin Luther King, Jr., former Governor Evan Mecham, and yours truly, born and reared in Coffeyville, Kansas, and sent to the First Institutional Baptist Church in Phoenix, Arizona, in 1977 via Dallas, Texas, and New York City. I believe that my former positions as general chairperson of two of the major MLKJr. holiday coalitions which successfully campaigned for the holiday, namely, ARIZONANS FOR A MARTIN LUTHER KING, JR. STATE HOLIDAY from November 1986 to January 1990, and VICTORY TOGETHER from November 1990 to November 1992, uniquely qualifies me to write this historic book.

From the beginning of our efforts to attempt to persuade Governor-elect Mecham not to rescind the King holiday Governor Bruce Babbitt had declared from the pulpit of the First Institutional Baptist Church on May 18, 1986 to my "thank you" speech in the then-America West Arena on January 15, 1993, just three days prior to Arizona's first official celebration of its Martin Luther King, Jr./Civil Rights Day, I had been preparing to write this book. As a result, over the six and a half years of the campaigns, I kept my personal notes, letters, minutes of meetings, telephone messages, tape recordings, newspaper and magazine clippings, photographs and private recollections of the King holiday fight.

This Story of a Black Baptist Preacher Leading a Fight against Mountainous Odds to Honor the Man who had been to the Mountaintop of "Liberty and Justice for All" details:

- Martin Luther King, Jr.'s Posthumous Influence
- Opposing Factions Working Together
- Leadership under Fire
- African-Americans Making a Difference
- Peculiar Politics Arizona-Style
- Racism and Bigotry Engrained
- Matters of Faith in the Marketplace
- Grassroots Coalition-Building
- Losing and Winning
- "Uneasy Alliance" with Big Business
- A Half-Billion Dollar Holiday Boycott
- Black Lives Matter—Then and Now
- Following God Regardless

Introduction
Martin, Mecham and Me

Martin, Mecham and Me. Who are these three men who made a difference in the history of the State of Arizona?

Martin Luther King, Jr. made it to Arizona only once in the flesh, yet the impact of his life caused a revolution of sorts in this Southwestern state with an African-American population of three percent. How could a Black man in his young adulthood make such a monumental imprint on an entire nation, which imported his ancestors as slaves?

M. L. King, Jr. came forth from the womb of Mrs. Alberta Williams King on January 15, 1929 in the family home in Atlanta, Georgia. Unlike the majority of African-Americans born during the first third of the 20th century, Martin was born into a middle-class family with access to resources of which most people of color only dreamed. His daddy served as the pastor of the prominent Ebenezer Baptist Church of Atlanta where young Martin's maternal grandfather had also served as pastor. Being born into the family of a leading African-American pastor carries its advantages, as it relates to exposure to the best and brightest available to the African-American community. There is little doubt that "M.L." took advantage of his privileged status as being Mike and Alberta King's preacher kid.

Young Martin was thrust into a society that discriminated against him and his people, based solely on the color God chose to make them. A bright young man, he excelled in school, so much so, that he entered Morehouse College at age 15. From there, this young intellectual who was called "M.L." by his family and friends matriculated through seminary and graduated with a Ph.D. from Boston University at age 26. Newly married, Dr. King returned to the South to pastor a small church in Montgomery, Alabama. Providence fixed it so that Martin Luther King, Jr. became the voice and body of the decades-old Civil Rights Movement that would change

America from "Black vs. White" into "living color." From that little city in Alabama the world became Martin's stage.

His undivided devotion, astounding intelligence, golden-tongued eloquence, and refined rage with racism in America catapulted this messianic figure into the spotlight of America's conscience. Martin persuasively utilized America's claim that "all people are created equal under God", his rich Judeo-Christian heritage and acquired Gandhian philosophy of non-violence to convince America that racism and discrimination were not only unrighteous and unchristian, but also unconstitutional! Wherever Martin went, he was the man of the hour.

Being the consistent person that he was, from the Riverside Church pulpit, this modern-day prophet dared to speak out against the violent Vietnam War. Exactly one year later, Dr. King was violently assassinated on a second-floor balcony in Memphis, on April 4, 1968, where he was helping striking garbage collectors.

Today, symbols and signs of Martin Luther King, Jr. are nearly omnipresent in America. Streets, parks, libraries, buildings, boulevards, chapels, schools, classrooms and museums carry Martin's name. T-shirts, sweatshirts, hats, caps, lapel pins, buttons, ties and jackets display the MLK insignia. Scholarships, foundations, commissions, committees and boards are identified by his name. On the third Monday in January, an entire nation, over 100 foreign countries, nearly every major U.S. city, and now, Arizona *stops work* to pay tribute to America's most famous dreamer.

Evan Mecham and Martin Luther King, Jr. mirrored each other in physical stature. Both men evidenced relatively small frames. Each was born in the 1920s to devoutly religious families. But, that is about where their similarities end.

Duchesne, Utah marks the birthplace of Arizona's only impeached governor on May 12, 1924. Evan was reared on a Utah farm along with four brothers. Due to his father's disability, young Evan assumed the task of running the family farm until he went off to Utah State University in 1942 on an agricultural scholarship. Biographer Marianne M. Jennings identified two key characteristics, which Evan Mecham garnered from his family upbringing in the following, words,

His early childhood taught him the value of hard work and persistence: the two qualities that would earn him the state's highest elected office.

Before finishing college, Evan answered Uncle Sam's call to service for the "Red, White and Blue" by entering the Army as an Air Corps pilot during World War II. As a pilot, Evan revealed his ability to fight and win, regardless of the odds. His assignment designated him as a fighter pilot who flew several missions out of England, which won him the coveted Air Medal and Purple Heart. For a short period, Evan became a prisoner of war in Germany. Through it all, this young man from Utah proved that he possessed inner strength to face life's obstacles.

When his military duty was over, Evan Mecham returned to Utah and married his first date for the Altamont High School Prom, Miss Florence Lambert. To that union, seven children came forth, specifically four sons and three daughters. The Mechams pulled up stakes in Utah and moved to Arizona where Evan resumed his college studies at Arizona State University from 1947 to 1950 majoring in management and economics. Just a few credits short of graduating, Mr. Mecham opened a Pontiac and Rambler auto dealership in Ajo, Arizona. According to Mecham's 1986 gubernatorial campaign newspaper, he started "with one mechanic in a two-stall garage adjacent to a service station," and built a successful business as the youngest Pontiac dealer in the nation.

Evan Mecham headlined a two-page life story of himself with the following lines. "My family is my greatest joy....If you want to see what makes me tick—just look at my family." Much of what made Evan Mecham the family man, as well as the person that he was, can be rooted in his Mormon faith. Arizona's former governor unashamedly testified of his lifetime love and allegiance to the Church of Jesus Christ of Latter-day Saints. As an active member of his church, he held several positions of leadership and responsibility. Mormonism comfortably provided Evan Mecham with a religious fervor that transformed his patriotism into a fundamental tenet of his faith. To be a Christian and an American were almost one in the same for Evan.

It is no wonder that the former ward bishop in the Mormon Church launched a career in politics in 1960 when he was elected to a two-year term in the Arizona State Senate. With that victory at age 36, Senator Mecham lifted his voice as a mouthpiece for his religio-political conservatism that could, in his opinion, rescue America. Always willing to challenge the status quo, this businessman-turned-politician proceeded to whet his appetite for political posture and power. In 1962, Mecham won the Republican nomination to run for the U.S. Senate against the then incumbent Senator Carl Hayden. Although he lost, his name gained statewide recognition as a courageous crusader for conservative politics.

The year 1964 inaugurated Evan Mecham's personal quest for the governorship of Arizona. This amazing individual of dogged persistence ran for the highest state office in 1964, 1974, 1978, 1982, 1986 and 1990. In 1978, Mecham amassed 46% of the popular vote in a narrow defeat to the then-appointed incumbent Governor Bruce Babbitt. Finally, as evidence that miracles, fate and/or quirks happen, Evan Mecham won the state office he desired in a three-way race which pitted a woman Democratic nominee, Carolyn Warner, a Democrat-turned Independent by the name of William Schultz and himself, the Republican standard-bearer. Virtually, 60% of the entire state of Arizona suffered from shock the morning after the general election when then, Governor-elect Evan Mecham was declared the winner. Understated, Arizona would never be the same after the 1986 gubernatorial election of Mr. Mecham.

Governor Mecham served less than two years of his elected four-year term of office. During 1987-1988, Evan faced fierce criticism due to his rescinding of Arizona's controversial Martin Luther King, Jr. holiday. A successful statewide recall was launched against him. And he was eventually impeached by the Arizona House of Representatives and convicted by the Arizona State Senate on April 4, 1988, the 20th anniversary of the assassination of Dr. Martin Luther King, Jr. Being one to never give up, former Governor Evan Mecham ran for the Republican nomination for governor in the 1990 primary, and lost.

I missed the blessing of seeing and/or meeting Martin Luther King, Jr. in person. However, do not allow that to make you think I do not *know* the man. Just as plain as if it was happening this very moment, I remember sitting in front of my grandparents' black and white television set as a stocky eleven-year-old glued to the gestures of this giant of a man standing behind a podium on the steps of the Lincoln Memorial proclaiming, "I have a dream!" Maybe it was then that the seed was planted for me to be a crusader for Arizona's Martin Luther King, Jr. holiday even though I was sitting in a living room in Coffeyville, Kansas, a long way from both Arizona and Washington, D.C. That day Dr. King's dream for America became *my* dream!

I am old enough to have experienced the "tail end" of overt, legalized discrimination in America. Although I never attended a segregated school in my life, I know well what it means to be called "nigger" and restricted because of the color of my skin. Once when walking home from elementary school with a friend, we both stopped in Ray's Cafe across from the train station to get a nickel ice cream cone. My friend walked up to the counter and purchased his vanilla ice cream cone. Then, my turn came. The same waitress informed me that I had to exit the front door, go around the building, enter the back door going through the kitchen, come through the hot and dangerous kitchen, walk through the door entering the serving area, stop at the other end of the same counter at which I was standing, and ask for my chocolate ice cream cone, there and then!

One of my most painful encounters with racism hit me broadside in the most unexpected place—my best friend's house! Charles and I hit it off from the first day we met at Longfellow Elementary School located on the westside in Coffeyville, Kansas. We shared homerooms, likes and dislikes, shyness and enjoying being in one another's company. After finally getting permission from my mother to go to his house after school one day, we made it to his place. His mother was home when I walked through the door with him. He gleefully introduced his best friend to his mom. Her returned greeting could not be dismissed simply to the fact that I was a kid and she was a preoccupied adult. No, something else affected her chilly greeting to this little colored boy who had not only invaded her son's inner circle, but who had dared to be standing in her living room. Nevertheless, Charles and I played until my allotted playtime expired and I excitedly rode my second-hand bike home. The next day I asked Charles when I could come back over to his house because we had had such a great time. I should have known something was wrong by the expression on my buddy's face. He painfully responded, "My mom said she didn't want any colored kids in her house. So, you can't come over anymore." Charles and I remained good friends through elementary school, but drifted apart after that. I do not believe I ever went back to Charles' house.

Most of us remember where we were when major life-jolting events shake our worlds. How can I forget driving west on Ninth Street in downtown Coffeyville a little after dusk on April 4, 1968? My grandparents let me drive their 1963 Studebaker Lark for almost any reason. I cannot remember why I was cruising through town, but I will always have imprinted in my memory the very moment that a bulletin announcement interrupted Coffeyville's own KGGF radio programming to shock its listeners. "Dr. Martin Luther King, Jr. was shot by an unknown assassin as he stood on the balcony of a hotel in Memphis, Tennessee where he was supporting striking garbage collectors. He was pronounced dead a few moments ago." Instantaneously I slammed my fist on the red and white dashboard of my folk's car breaking it. Then, I began looking for the first Black person I could find. I saw a familiar face to my right walking near J.J. Newberry's store. I shouted out, "They killed Dr. King!" Filled with anger, pain and despair, I sped home with tears rolling down my cheeks to watch the television news bulletins of the murder of my hero-Martin Luther King Jr..

When it came time to choose a topic for my Master of Divinity thesis in order to graduate from Union Theological Seminary in New York City in 1976, I chose as a subject, "Do Prophets Exist in our Contemporary Culture?" After doing an extensive analysis of the biblical prophets in the Old Testament tradition; I examined the life and writings of Dr. Walter Rauschenbush and Dr. Martin Luther King, Jr. Reading the sermons, speeches and writings of Martin King further provided me with intimate knowledge of my role model- mentor, whom I had never met personally.

On the momentous occasion of the first federal observance of Martin Luther King, Jr.'s birthday as a national holiday, I preached First Institutional's own Martin Luther King, Jr. Memorial Sunday, the third Sunday in January 1986, from the subject, "If Dr. King Were Here Today." That day the Lord was with me in an unusual way. As pastor, I received a rare standing ovation from my own congregation. Little did I know that before 1986 ended, I would make local and national headlines for calling Arizona's newly-elected governor a racist. He pressed forward to keep his campaign promise to rescind Arizona's yet to be celebrated Martin Luther King, Jr. holiday pronounced by executive order on May 18, 1986 from the pulpit of the First Institutional Baptist Church by outgoing Governor Bruce Babbitt.

PART ONE

Chapter One
Thy King Day Come

Friday afternoon May 16, 1986 I was at home in my study, which I renamed "my Sermon Factory". Since two days from then would be Pentecost Sunday my message was "How to Receive the Holy Spirit". When the telephone rang the voice on the other end quite surprisingly informed me to *please hold for the governor*. "*Huh?*", I thought proudly, "*I wonder what he wants, calling me at home?*"

Governor Bruce Babbitt, Arizona's former attorney general, relatively popular governor from 1978 to 1987, unsuccessful but well-respected 1988 Democratic presidential candidate, President Bill Clinton's Secretary of the Interior of the United States, and twice nearly appointed Supreme Court Justice, greeted me with a few perfunctory words of identification, and proceeded to reveal the purpose of his call to me.

"Warren." (*Most White politicians and powerbrokers have this "thing" about calling African-American community leaders by their first names, as if these long-time friendships exist between them and the leaders with whom they never bother to converse, unless it is election time and/or a crisis. Even Evan Mecham, when he was governor asked me if he could call me Warren! As an African-American man whose granddaddy was called by his first name by White co-workers young enough to be his grandchildren, I prefer to be the one to initiate whether "a first-name basis" relationship is desired on my part, especially with a politician of pinkish hue.*) "Warren, I've got this idea about the Martin Luther King, Jr. state holiday, which was defeated in the Arizona State Senate a few days ago by one vote. I believe I have legal precedence to declare a paid state Martin Luther King, Jr. holiday for the executive branch of state government. One of our former attorney generals, Jack LaSota, informed me that former Governor Paul Fanin declared a state holiday a couple of days after President John F. Kennedy was assassinated in November 1963. What do you think? How would the Black community feel about that? I spoke with Art Hamilton in the House of Representatives. He likes the idea."

Still a little bit taken back by the telephone call at my home and the redeeming possibility of Arizona having its own King Day, after over a decade and a half of courageous attempts and degrading defeats in the Arizona State Legislature, my heart responded before my lips spoke words of approval. "Well, Governor, if you think you can do it, then do it. Are you sure you can do it?"

Then the governor popped the question that exposed the real reason he had gotten in touch with *me*. "Warren, I would like to declare Arizona's first Martin Luther King, Jr. paid state holiday from the pulpit of the First Institutional Baptist Church. What do you think about that?"

After having to overcome from that verbal aftershock, I said something like, "We'd be honored!"

He then inquired about the time of our morning worship. I informed him of our two Sunday morning worship services held at 8:00 and 11:00 a.m. He let me know that the 8:00 a.m. worship service would fit his schedule best. In wrapping up our startling conversation, I said I would get the word out among our members and community leaders; and he promised to contact Art Hamilton to be there and get other key leaders to come as well. To say the least, it took the Holy Spirit to calm me down from the content and consequences of that high-level conversation and return my inspiration and energy to my message. Thank the Lord, I did get back to work and finished my preaching Word for Pentecost Sunday.

In 1986, First Institutional's eleven o'clock morning service was our main worship service with the largest attendance of the two. Therefore, I telephoned a few key church leaders and asked my secretary, Sarah Alexander, and other staff members to spread the news that Arizona would have a Martin Luther King, Jr. holiday declared from the pulpit of the First Institutional Baptist Church in less than forty-eight hours on Sunday, May 18, 1986.

The word spread like a late spring brush fire in this Arizona desert. By the call to worship on the third Sunday in May, that early morning service was enjoying an eleven o'clock crowd of members, guests and several news reporters. Always a Christian preacher at heart, I proceeded through the regular order of service with the morning hymn, altar prayer and meditation, selection by the choir, the message, invitation to discipleship and welcome of visitors. That's right! I knew there would be some "big shots" in church that morning who normally slept in on Sundays, so I took full advantage of a captivated audience. However, my message dealing with receiving the Holy Spirit fell on many, many dozens of deaf ears. I mean, I'd dare say that a majority of our members did not come that morning to hear their pastor preach. Their mental prodding probably went something like this, "Hurry up, Pastor! Preach your little message! And let's get on with history!" Unfortunately, those were the vibes I was getting from the people in the pews in the middle of my Spirit-filled, but circumstance-deflated sermon.

Governor Babbitt, an aide and Representative Art Hamilton sat on the second pew, right behind the deacons where most distinguished guests—family, political and religious—sit when we know they are going to share in our worship experience.

After I greeted all visitors, I asked Governor Babbitt, House Minority Leader Art Hamilton, and other key community and political leaders to join me in the pulpit of one of Arizona's leading and largest African-American congregations for the historic proclamation.

Some of those who stood with us that Sunday included the late Reverends L. K. Williams, presiding elder of the African Methodist Episcopal Church and Amos Dudley, executive director of Valley Christian Centers; Gene Blue, executive director of Phoenix Opportunities Industrialization Centers and long-time chair of the Phoenix Martin Luther King, Jr. Celebration Committee; the late Dr. Eugene Grigsby, art professor at Arizona State University; the late Dr. G. Benjamin Brooks, Sr., veteran Arizona pastor and civil rights leader, Clarence Boykins, long-time chair of Tucson's Martin Luther King, Jr. Celebration Committee; as well as several of First Institutional's male and female associate ministers.

My introduction of Governor Babbitt became a prophecy fulfilled, in one sense. After welcoming all special guests, pastors and preachers to the pulpit, I announced, "It just might be providential that two Sundays ago, standing behind the pulpit of the First Institutional Baptist Church was a former contender for the Democratic nomination of the Presidency of the United States by the name of the Reverend Jesse Louis Jackson. He has a message and a declaration to declare, which certainly should endear him and his political philosophy into the hearts, hopefully not only of the Black community and the minority communities of the state and country, but also of all freedom-loving and justice-loving Americans around this nation. I present to you the Honorable Bruce Babbitt, Governor of the State of Arizona." The applause was enthusiastic.

Governor Babbitt stepped up to the pulpit from which God allowed me to begin my pastoral ministry on July 1, 1977. He leaned on that elegantly carved wood-grained pulpit with his left arm and began to utter words that instigated an historic revolution of sorts in the desert southwest.

Reverend Stewart, guests, parishioners, worshippers, you know it's a great pleasure to be here through this wonderful service and all I can say about your pastor, your preacher is *awesome*! (The worshippers responded with an appreciative applause.) I just wish he could *breathe* a little of the Spirit over me. (Those remarks broke up the congregation.) We're going to make a little history together here today. And there are several reasons why I chose this place. I remember coming on a sad day to this church back in 1968 to join with you to mourn the assassination of our leader Martin Luther King, Jr. And I have been back since then and I have listened to your good preacher, taking his advice and counsel, and taking his congratulations when he thought I was doing right and heard his wrath when he thought I was not living up to his expectations.

Now before I get my pen, I'd like to relive with you for just a moment how it is we come to be here. Mr. Hamilton, here, introduced a piece of legislation on behalf of Arizona that Arizona too will honor the birthday and remember officially the memory of Reverend Martin Luther King, Jr. And the debate started on that bill and legislators got up to say, "Martin Luther King may be a hero to Black people, but we don't believe that he is a hero to the United States of America." And echoing through my mind was the remembrance of the day in 1964 (sic) when there were half a million people on that mall in Washington and that leader was talking of the day when all of God's children, Black men and White men, Jews and Gentiles, Protestants and Catholics will be able to join hands together and sing in the words of the old Negro spiritual, "Free at last, Free at last! Thank God Almighty, we're Free at last."

And I heard legislators standing up to say Arizona is not ready to honor Reverend Martin Luther King, Jr. And I heard Mr. Hamilton get up and make an eloquent speech, talking to the hearts of all of Arizona and saying, "This is a time of coming together, of healing, of reconciliation, of redemption for all together."

The bill was defeated by one vote.

And Mr. Hamilton came to me to talk about it and my mind went back to twenty-one years when I was a student and to some news that began coming out of the little town called Selma, Alabama in March 1965. They are events that are now known in history as "Bloody Sunday."…And I remember that young minister saying, "It's time for Americans to come to Selma, Alabama to make a statement about America, about injustice and about oppression." And my heart was touched and I wept and I arrived in Selma, Alabama and I saw the faces of emotions, hatred and love. And I learned during those days that I wasn't safe in a White neighborhood. I learned that I couldn't go into a White restaurant or a White store and that I wasn't welcome to a White church and that you went into a White town at the risk of being killed.

…I was assigned to live with a Black family. They lived in a small three-room tenement house out on the edge of the city. And I slept on the floor and I ate meals with two parents and their children. And we talked and we went down to Brown's Chapel every day and joined hands and consoled each other, sang, talked, and organized a march up to the state capitol. And I remember learning firsthand that the aspirations of the family that I lived with, and that I shared meals with, were exactly the same as mine. And exactly what they wanted for their children was exactly what I would want for mine.

Those days came to a climax and it was like a burst of thunder and lightning because that young minister from Atlanta moved the heart and soul of this nation. And those people in Selma and 20,000 people that had come to help, moved the United States Congress to pass the Voting Rights Act of 1965.

To begin the process of healing and reconciliation, I thought about those things when I was talking to Mr. Hamilton.…And he looked at me and said, "I have an idea. Why don't you just declare it a state holiday?" (The people applauded excitedly.) And I thought for about ten seconds. (Everybody laughed.) I thought of the words of the man we honor, "We will not be satisfied until

justice rolls down like water and righteousness like a mighty
stream." As I sign this proclamation, making the birthday of
Reverend Martin Luther King a state holiday, I admonish. (The
ceiling shook at the thunderous clapping.) I am not done yet.
You've got to hear me a little more. Now I want to tell you just
this. This is yours, this is ours and if you protect and cherish and
fight for this holiday, they're not going to take it away from you!
(The governor's action received a standing ovation.)

And now on behalf of all of the committee, pastors and
the preachers, I am going to deliver this proclamation to your
pastor, the Reverend Warren Stewart, and tell him to keep and
safeguard it. Thank you very much.

I guess it was at that historic high moment I was handed the responsibility for seeing that Arizona would never return to the days when its
citizens did not officially honor Dr. Martin Luther King, Jr. with his day.
There I stood with Executive Order No. 86-5 HOLIDAY HONORING
MARTIN LUTHER KING, JR. in my hands. On it were inscribed, after
the last of five paragraphs paying tribute to Dr. King's contributions to
America, beginning with WHEREAS, the words,

NOW, THEREFORE, I, Bruce Babbitt, Governor of the
State of Arizona do hereby order the third Monday of each
January as a holiday honoring the birthday of Dr. Martin
Luther King, Jr. for all employees of Agencies, Boards and
Commissions within the purview of the Executive Branch of
the State of Arizona.

This Order shall become effective immediately.

Of course, the Great Seal of the State of Arizona was affixed to the
executive order, along with the signatures of two now former Arizona governors, Bruce Babbitt and then secretary of state, Rose Mofford.

Quite ignorantly, I did not know what to do with that priceless
document. I thought the governor would ask for it back after the public
ceremony. But he didn't. And I have kept Executive Order No. 86-85
HOLIDAY HONORING MARTIN LUTHER KING, JR. in my church
office files since May 18, 1986.

Once the tumultuous standing ovation came to a slow end, I asked
Representative Art Hamilton to accept the proclamation on behalf of the

citizens of Arizona. This man of full stature who looks and carries himself like an African tribal chief of a large clan of people of ebony hue and whose intellect and eloquence supersedes any and every politician in Arizona, humbly made the following impromptu acceptance speech,

> "Thank you, Pastor Stewart, Governor, members of the clergy, distinguished ladies and gentlemen, my brothers and sisters; I am pleased to accept this on behalf of us all. But I will tell you now, even as we celebrate and accept this, there are those who will seek to deny it and take this from us. This is not the end of the battle. It is merely the beginning. And we have been given by Governor Babbitt a new opportunity to [fight] this war and to bring Arizona to the fullness of freedom for all God's children. I join you in that battle. I thank you for the honor. And while we may have had a few bumps along the way, it has been a privilege to fight (this) struggle. And God knows I would not exchange a day for it. Thank you." (Those in attendance thanked Art with a grateful applause.)

In his remarks, Governor Babbitt vaguely alluded to the challenge it would be to sustain Arizona's brand-new, governor-declared Martin Luther King, Jr. holiday. However, Art leveled with his brothers and sisters in a way we could clearly understand that Governor Babbitt's declaration of the King holiday was equivalent to a declaration of war with Arizona's perennial King Day opponents. Consequently, May 18, 1986 was a temporary victory for King Day supporters at most, and a pseudo-victory, to say the least.

After Representative Art Hamilton accepted Arizona's First Martin Luther King, Jr. Day declaration, I requested Dr. G. Benjamin Brooks to come and express appreciation for Governor Babbitt's executive order on behalf of the Interdenominational Ministerial Alliance of Phoenix and Vicinity and the overall African-American religious community. Dr. Brooks' measured words captured our rapt attention thusly,

> This church has always been the center of the Civil Rights Movement in the City of Phoenix. I don't know how many of you were around in the old days, when we had meetings and we didn't ask anybody; we just volunteered First Institutional Baptist Church. And I remember the day we had that service, Bruce. I gave the message on that Sunday and I left for Memphis,

Tennessee. And always the preachers were there and you in this congregation were there. The ministers of Phoenix thank you and I thank you as a resident of our community, and the governor for having the kind of tenacity, temerity or any of the other big words that one could conjure up to describe the courage you exemplify this morning. I know that Brother Sossaman and Brother Cooper (anti-King Day state legislators) are not going to like it, but they are going to have to try to undo what you have done. On behalf of the Minister's Alliance, I thank you very much.

With that being said we all stood and sang the battle hymn of the Civil Rights Movement, "We Shall Overcome."

Wow! History had just taken place, as never before, in First Institutional, the state of Arizona, and even our great nation. Little did I know then, that all three speakers on that day *forthtold* like modern-day prophets, as it related to Arizona's Martin Luther King, Jr. Day struggle. Moreover, how naive I was by thinking that my primary responsibility in that King Day inauguration would be to safe keep the piece of paper that Governor Babbitt signed in the pulpit, from which I had been preaching for nearly nine years at the time.

I suppose it can be easy for one to imagine what a "letdown" our eleven o'clock worship service was that Sunday. In the first place, the attendance was less than half of what it normally was. Secondly, the electricity and excitement that had filled the 8:00 a.m. service appeared to have left with our special guests. Nevertheless, as the Apostle Paul instructed his student minister Timothy, it was my lot to "preach in season and out of season." And that I did to the remnant of my eleven o'clock crowd.

◇◇◇◇◇

Even though it was in 1983 when the United States Congress voted to establish a federal holiday on the third Monday of January to commemorate the birth date (which was actually January 15, 1929) of Dr. Martin Luther King, Jr. by a two-thirds majority, the Arizona State Legislature was introduced to its first resolution to create a King Day in 1972 by then Democratic Senator Cloves Campbell, publisher of the *Arizona Informant*, from District 23 in South Phoenix. Regrettably, that historic first try languished and died in the Rules Committee of the Arizona State Senate. Martin Luther King, Jr. Day legislation was introduced in the Arizona State Legislature for several years after Senator Campbell's faithful, but futile attempt. As 1986 approached, the King holiday legislation made it out of House and/or Senate committees only to die on the floor of either chamber, increasingly by fewer and fewer votes. In the spring of 1986, the Arizona State Senate passed the Martin Luther King, Jr. state holiday and forwarded it to the House of Representatives where it went down by one vote.

Less than a month after Governor Babbitt declared Arizona's first Martin Luther King, Jr. Day holiday, the attorney general at that time, the Honorable Robert K. Corbin, responded in writing to an inquiry relative to the "constitutional or statutory authority" of the governor to declare a King Day. The initial letter to Mr. Corbin came from three Arizona State Representatives, namely, Karen R. Mills, Sterling Ridge and Henry H. Haws. Mind you, Governor Babbitt's Office informed the Attorney General's Office that his executive order was intended to cover only state employees of the Executive Department of the State of Arizona. Therefore, from the outset the initial King Day order established only *a piece of a holiday* and not really a statewide paid day off, honoring the American who gave his all for racial equality and justice in America.

The conclusion of the Attorney General's Office read as follows in the letter written to Mills, Ridge and Haws on June 2, 1986.

> We conclude that the Governor has no constitutional or statutory authority to declare a legal holiday that would be observed by closing state offices and giving state employees a paid day off, although he may, of course, publicly give recognition to Dr. Martin Luther King, Jr. by issuing an executive order providing a general observance in honor of Dr. King.

The letter went on to cite cases which legally defined the powers of the governor as well as Arizona Revised Statutes 41-101 which prescribes the powers and duties the governor shall perform, none which includes proclaiming state holidays.

On page 5 of Corbin's letter the following paragraphs were written pertaining to state holidays.

> The only authority the Governor has pertaining to holidays is limited to making a proclamation of Arbor Days. A.R.S. 1-304(B). The statutes provide, however, that "Arbor Day shall not be a legal holiday." A.R.S. 1-304(D).

On the other hand, nothing in the Arizona Constitution prohibits the Legislative Department from declaring state holidays and the hours state offices shall be open for business or closed for observance of holidays. Thus, the Legislature has the power to act in this area, and it has done so.

It appeared that the death knoll to Executive Order No. 86-5 HOLIDAY HONORING MARTIN LUTHER KING, JR. rang loudest on page six of the above-mentioned letter.

The Legislature has set out the state holidays in A.R.S. 1-301(A). The statute includes no holiday on the third Monday of January.

In further stating the *opinion* of the Office of the Attorney General, which was never tested in court, the letter opined,

If Executive Order No. 86-5 was construed to grant time off for state service employees, it would also conflict with applicable administrative rules and regulations promulgated pursuant to the Administrative Procedure Act, A.R.S. 44-1001 40-1015.

Bob Corbin concluded his letter to the "Honorable" King Day opponents with this seemingly defensible paragraph stating:

The power to declare state holidays lies with the Legislature and not with the Governor. Executive Order No. 86-5, therefore, does not have the effect of closing state offices or giving all Executive Department employees a day off with pay. The Governor's executive order must be construed as an executive proclamation of a Dr. Martin Luther King, Jr. Day that is to be observed in ways that serve the public without interfering with the transaction of governmental business.

So, the question shall always remain unresolved by both King Day supporters and opponents, "Did Governor Babbitt have the authority to declare a Martin Luther King, Jr. paid state holiday by executive order?" Based on precedence, *his* counsel answered that question *affirmatively*. In contrast, the King Day detractors who were all Republicans, including the attorney general, responded with a *partisan negative*.

Perhaps, former State Senator Evan Mecham and 1986 Republican gubernatorial candidate got a hold of a copy of Attorney General Corbin's letter to Mills, Ridge and Haws. The evidence existed in black and white in Mecham's pre-election campaign newspaper that was mailed out to thousands of Arizonans in late October 1986. In a four-paragraph article under the bold print headline which read, "Stand on King Holiday", these words were found stating Mecham's official position on the declared holiday,

> Both Democratic candidates for governor, Carolyn Warner and Bill Schulz, have stated that they will try and keep the questionable Babbitt executive order establishing Martin Luther King Day as an official state holiday. Only Ev Mecham, the Republican nominee for governor has said he will rescind it.
>
> Mecham has stated that the Babbitt order probably is not legal. When the Legislature did not pass the bill setting up the holiday for the civil rights leader, Babbitt made a political grandstanding play out of it by declaring the holiday by executive order.
>
> The proposed holiday would be created by combining Washington and Lincoln's birthdays into one holiday and establishing a separate day for King.
>
> Mecham stated that his plan to rescind the questionable order had nothing to do with Dr. King directly. Many outstanding Americans of all races and ethnic background have contributed much to our country and its peoples but so far none have been elevated to the stature of Washington and Lincoln in the minds of most Americans.

If former Governor Mecham had left his comments about Arizona's Martin Luther King, Jr. holiday in his campaign newspaper, he may have never been the subject of a recall and the first governor in America to be impeached in sixty years. Certainly, he would have not caused a national and international maelstrom of negative publicity upon himself and his beloved state. Regardless of what Mecham's intentions were, his vow to rescind Bruce Babbitt's executive order honoring Dr. King left him and this state open to be called *racist*. Granted, by January 1987, there were still several states which had not passed a Martin Luther King, Jr. Day. But *no* state before Arizona (and since) had ever declared a King Day and then crossed it off the calendar. The wrath of the freedom and justice-loving world, warranted or unwarranted, came crashing down upon Arizona as a consequence of Evan Mecham's kept promise and a Republican-controlled Legislature that backed him up by not approving a state holiday honoring Martin Luther King, Jr.

Chapter Two
"Black Folks Don't Need A Holiday"

It was a rainy day in Arizona that Tuesday, November 18, 1986. The political storm clouds had begun to form on Tuesday, November 4, 1986 after Evan Mecham won the gubernatorial election on his fifth try. A group of Martin Luther King, Jr. state holiday supporters from around the state, constituted predominantly of African-American leaders, gathered at the Valley Christian Center's East Washington facility. The late Reverend Amos Dudley, executive director of Valley Christian Centers and long-time civic leader, opened the doors of their facility in order for us to meet with none other than Governor-elect Evan Mecham. In attendance at the meeting were the "Who's Who in Arizona African-American politics," including: Arizona State Representatives Art Hamilton and Representative-elect Sandra Kennedy, Arizona State Senator-elect Carolyn Walker, and longest serving Phoenix City Councilman Calvin Goode. Community activists Mildred Jones of the NAACP and Opal Ellis took their seats around the table. The Reverend T. E. Gantt, II, then pastor of the Mt. Calvary Missionary Baptist Church in Tucson brought along a Jewish friend by the name of Howard Goldwyn. Pastor Hosea Hines from Grace Temple Baptist Church in Tucson also attended. Mr. Steve Harris, an East Valley African-American businessman, came to share the business perspective on the MLK holiday. Mr. Gene Blue, executive director of the Phoenix O.I.C., and chair of the Phoenix MLK, Jr. Celebration Committee, was also there. Pastor Henry L. Barnwell of the First New Life Missionary Baptist Church and Dr. Joseph Parham, community college faculty and administrative member as well as psychologist, worked closely together to get Mr. Mecham to attend our historic meeting. Pastor Barnwell had been befriended by Evan Mecham and had purchased a car from Mecham Pontiac. Dr. Parham gained a reputation as a rare Republican of ebony hue. He eventually attained a position in

Governor Mecham's cabinet. Giving strength to our group was the presence of the relatively new senior pastor of the First Baptist Church of Phoenix, Dr. Paul Eppinger. Somehow, I received the mantle of moderator for this eye-opening meeting with the soon-to-be governor of one of the fastest growing states in the Union.

Although all of Arizona knew Evan Mecham's public position on Arizona's Martin Luther King, Jr. holiday, we assumed that we could reason with him if given the opportunity to discuss with him directly his self-imposed promise to rescind the holiday once he took office in January 1987. A review of my personal notes identified our meeting's purpose—to persuade Mr. Mecham to reconsider his decision to rescind the executive order declaring Arizona's Martin Luther King, Jr. holiday, and/or to wait on the Arizona State Legislature to have the opportunity to vote again on the holiday in the upcoming legislative session *before* he rescinded the holiday.

Prior to Governor-elect Mecham's arrival, several leaders present were assigned as "designated hitters" to address key points on why Mecham should relent on his decision to rescind the holiday. Representative Hamilton accepted the responsibility of explaining the executive order. Jewish layperson Howard Goldwyn would explain to Mecham that the MLK Day could not be pigeonholed as being a "Black" holiday. Businessman Steve Harris awaited the opportunity to explain the minimal cost that the Martin Luther King, Jr. Day would incur for the state. Pastor Gantt would highlight the moral issue surrounding the reasoning for Arizona honoring Dr. King with his day. Mildred Jones stood ready to speak on Mecham's assertion that others were more worthy than King to be honored.

The sky over the Valley of the Sun wept profusely at mid-afternoon that day. As the time of Governor-elect Mecham's arrival approached, excitement mixed with anxiety energized the occupants of the medium-sized conference room. Finally, the moment with destiny appeared on our time clock when Mr. Mecham drove up to the curb on East Washington accompanied by his designated press aide, Mr. Ron Bellus. I think Pastor Barnwell or Dr. Parham greeted Mecham at the door. His apparel included one of his trademark ultra-suede sport coats with coordinating slacks. I wore a recently-purchased dark blue pin-striped Hickey Freeman suit donned over a white-on-white dress shirt with a paisley tie in order to look like I meant business. My greeting with Mecham was strained, but cordial. Most of us in the room proceeded to extend customary handshakes with our two special guests.

Shortly thereafter, each of us took our seats around the makeshift conference table made up of three, long folding tables pushed together. Being the moderator, I sat in the middle of the head table. Pastor Barnwell and Dr. Parham sat at the opposite ends of the table. And guess who sat to my right? None other than Governor-elect Evan Mecham. Official greetings initiated the business at hand. Pastor Hosea Hines offered the invocation. Introductions followed. Then came the purpose of the meeting with Mecham, stated by Dr. Paul Eppinger. "Governor Mecham, we would like you to clarify your position on the Martin Luther King, Jr. state holiday." Then, the next few words that fell from our state's top elected official-to-be shook the foundation of my consciousness as an African-American man.

"I didn't come here to debate or discuss the Martin Luther King, Jr. holiday with you folks. I've made up my mind. It's based on principle and if you folk want to talk about anything else, I'd be glad to talk to you."

A long pause interrupted our few minutes old meeting. In shock and virtually astounded to the point of speechlessness, I could not form words on my lips to respond at that moment. Opal Ellis spoke up in her assertive, articulate way, which restarted the monologue mastered by Mecham.

Continuing, the governor-elect declared that he had other plans for Black people in Arizona. "Black folks don't need a holiday. What you need is jobs."

By that time my blood had surpassed the boiling point. There was some infrequent interchange from members of our group, but Mecham continued to dominate the one-sided dialogue. "Look, I don't have any-thing against Black people. Why, I've got Black friends and friends who are women."

By that time, I had regained my composure enough to speak. I raised the issue about Arizona's tarnished image as a result of Mecham's then nationally publicized promise to cancel King Day in Arizona. "Governor Mecham, I was in Ontario, California yesterday and a local pastor asked me 'How can you still live in a racist state like Arizona?' Governor, aren't you concerned about the negative publicity that your stance on the King holiday is bringing upon our popular, fast growing state?"

His retort reeked with confidence, "It's negative to some and positive to others. The comments I'm getting are mostly positive....Furthermore, I'm used to negative publicity fostered by the liberal media."

Following sparse interchange from our stunned crowd, Mecham acknowledged that he did not support a Martin Luther King, Jr. Day. He opined that Martin Luther King, Jr. did not occupy the lofty status of Presidents George Washington and Abraham Lincoln. We took that as an opening to present our alternative proposal to Mecham. "Governor Mecham, will you hold off rescinding Arizona's Martin Luther King, Jr. Day scheduled for the third Monday in January, 1987 until the newly elected Arizona State Legislature has an opportunity to vote again on the King Day?"

He mused momentarily and appeared to relent on his staid stance, "Well, yes, I'll hold off rescinding the King Day up until the day before it's to go into effect....I must rescind the King Day before then, because the attorney general of Arizona has said that Babbitt's executive order is illegal."

Shortly thereafter, the abbreviated meeting came to an abrupt close. Our disastrous meeting lasted twenty minutes at most. As we stood tensely for a closing prayer offered by the Reverend Amos Dudley, I was forced to clasp the left hand of the man who had just insulted my intelligence as no other White man had ever done, to my face. God empowered me to fulfill that difficult assignment, even though my inner being was infuriated. Our good-byes carried much less cordiality than our half-hour old greetings. When Mecham and Bellus exited the door, our group members stood and looked at one another in absolute amazement. I kept thinking, *Did that really happen? Did that man really say what I thought he said?*

Whatever we discussed at that time remains in a fog to me. However, I remember Dr. Parham saying to me in jest, "Reverend, I'm not a praying man, but as I watched your body language when the governor was talking, I was praying that you wouldn't hit him!"

After we began to disperse, my anger fumed and spouted until it finally erupted as I spoke candidly to my former Bishop College classmate and colleague in the ministry, Theodus Gantt. I must confess I used some multi-syllabic profane words to describe our brand-new governor-to-be. Gantt somewhat effectively calmed me down enough to do an interview with a local television station reporter who was waiting for the meeting to end.

One of our congregation's elderly members saw the news spot on the evening news and called me with some grandmotherly advice. The late Sis. Lucille Reese compassionately counseled, "Now, Reverend Stewart, don't let your anger show in the public like you did. I saw you on T.V. and your countenance was full of anger. You mustn't let anybody make you that angry."

I thanked her, but I knew that Mecham's insensitive remarks to Arizona's key African-American leaders had lit a fire of righteous indignation in me that would not be extinguished for another six years.

In an interview that I had with the Associated Press after the meeting on that day, I summarized my perception of Mecham with these words, "Mr. Mecham has a racist mentality....That's the truth (Mecham saying he has some Black friends); it is the type of jargon that you hear from Whites who are apologetic of being accused of racism and do not want to confront their racist thinking." That statement hit the local and national press, making *The New York Times* on December 1, 1986.

The war was on!

Evan Mecham's obstinate opposition to Arizona observing its own Martin Luther King, Jr. Day did not exist in a vacuum. Hundreds of thousands of Arizonans proudly participated in their own version of a "Just Say No" campaign against honoring Martin Luther King, Jr. with his day. From the state legislature to county seats to city councils to Republican and a few Democrat precincts to churches to neighborhood community activists, King Day bashing held a prominent place in Arizona. Since the early 1970s, legislation to establish a Martin Luther King, Jr. Day was considered in both chambers of the Arizona State Legislature only to be killed in committee, squashed in caucus, and/or defeated on the floor. One needs to remember that most of the legislators making decisions for the entire state came from rural, predominantly Republican-controlled conservative districts. During the 1970s, the mentality of a few of Arizona's right-winged Republican legislators could be characterized by the legislator who opined publicly that abortion should be permissible in the case of rape, only if a Black man rapes and impregnates a White woman. The vast majority of King Day opponents and many of the supporters perceived the holiday as a "Black" holiday.

Once my name became associated with the drive for the King holiday, the fan mail began to arrive at the church and my house. Most of them were comprised of short, scribbled notes with accompanying literature exposing King's alleged Communist connections and flagrant infidelity. A note from a man from St. Petersburg, Florida read, "He's a high quality moral man...."

OK!,??? You better read the *whole* story.

The accompanying article was a review of David J. Garrow's extensive biography of King and the Southern Christian Leadership Conference entitled *Bearing the Cross*. Another letter was addressed "To Good People of Arizona" dated January 14, 1987, and I quote,

> Enclosed is some material that Senator Jesse Helms was able to see out of an F.B.I. file on Martin Luther King, Jr. If we didn't

have a Communist conspiracy well entrenched and doing a good job we would have had this information long ago....The Negro people, who have done a fabulous job in the last 120 years, deserve a better hero than Martin Luther King....Our Governor Evan Mecham, the man of integrity, deserves some support also. So please read the material.

A letter dated November 6, 1987 from a resident of Sun City West carried the following message,

"So, you want a paid holiday in Arizona in honor of Rev. Martin Luther King, Jr. I oppose such a move on the grounds that while the Rev. King did a great service to the Negroes of America, the latter were the sole beneficiaries. I fail to see the validity of Rev. King's actions and its relation to honor him with a paid holiday....In some ways, Rev. King's actions were somewhat in tune with those of the suave, smooth, fast-talking Jesse Jackson. Rev. Jackson went about the Country, even abroad, stirring up controversies and tensions...Rev. Stewart, instead of promoting a paid King holiday, you should stick to preaching the Gospel and leave a civil matter such as this in the hands of the authorities who have already spoken negatively on this matter."

One of my most prolific producers of anti-King Day mail came from a person who always signed his (or her) name illegibly. In a letter postmarked January 17, 1988, are found the following questions.

Dear Rev. *Why* do you waste taxpayers' money calling out the traffic cops for your parades? Don't you know voters do not want tax money used to honor *adultery*? Do you *really* think state legislators who know all about the mistresses will thwart voters' wishes? Is a fornicator (a term from the Bible) whom you endorse as a model for U.S.A.'s youth?...Just quietly withdraw and go back to passing the collection plates!

Perhaps my favorite letter came to me addressed to "BUBBLE-HEAD!"

There's an old saying that every time I read one of your idiotic letters reminds me of you. Better keep your mouth shut and let people think you're stupid than to open it and make them certain of it. Every time I read one of your stupid letters to the editor, I wonder what in hell your neighbors must think of an asshole like you....I have never read such unmitigated hogwash as that contained in your letter. But then you are the valley's unquestioned Bubblehead, liberal, muddleheaded nincompoop...

An anti-King Day pamphlet that showed up quite often during the Arizona campaign was entitled *Abolish The King Holiday*, written by Dr. E. R. Fields, published by *THE THUNDERBOLT* out of Marietta, Georgia. The opening lines inform the reader thusly, "Martin Luther King was a member of 62 Communist fronts. He openly incited violence under the banner of 'nonviolence.' King led a bizarre sex life, which included acts of shocking perversion. Still a cowardly spineless Congress voted to make King's birthday a national holiday. This is the outrage of the century!"

Next to Evan Mecham, Arizona's perennial anti-King holiday crusader was my "new-found friend", Julian Sanders. Julian, a member of the Church of Jesus Christ of Latter-day Saints, would serve as the point man for the successful 1989 and 1990 King Day legislation referendum petition drives. In one of his diatribes blasting Martin King, Sanders pronounced that King "exceeded Lucifer in his ability to deceive the masses with impressive oration and dedication in spite of his addiction to alcohol, tobacco and sex."

Fred Lundin, a board member of the Lake Havasu school district board demanded that King Day not be observed by their district during the 1987-88 school year. According to a newspaper article from *The Lake Havasu City Herald* dated March 13, 1987, Lundin indicated that it had been proven that King was a Communist and that "a colored man, a black man, Smith of St. George, Utah, came to Lake Havasu City and spoke to several groups here about King." Continuing, "The F.B.I.," Lundin said, "had all kinds of evidence that King and his wife wouldn't fly on the same plane. The excuse was that if one of them was killed, the other would survive to be with the kids. But he had 20 concubines -20 different individuals that he sacked up with, and flew with. . ."

A graphic photocopy of a pornographic portrait of a Black man enjoying oral sex from a White woman embarrassed me upon receiving it anonymously in the mail at the church. I am sure glad I opened it before my church secretary did. Scribbled on the margin was the note, "Here's you motherf***ing King!"

Over the years since the Martin Luther King, Jr. state holiday became the topic of discussion in Arizona, it somehow was relegated to "a Black thing." Much discussion in the Legislature centered around the repercussions of honoring a Black hero in light of the fact that the other minorities would want to honor their heroes. In 1986, Representative Bob Hungerford was cited in a *New Times* March 26-April 1 article by Michael Lacey entitled "DREAM DEFERRED AGAIN," with the following words, "Why not have something for the Polish or the Russians?...Let's give them all something. How about Spanish-Mexicans? Let's give them Santa Ana."

As the article continued, the issue of combining the state-observed George Washington and Abraham Lincoln's Days into one day, eliminating an exclusive Lincoln Day to be used for the proposed King Day was addressed by Representative Hungerford like this,

> Lincoln freed them....Now he's to be forgotten. I just can't grasp the thing. You want to put Martin Luther King ahead of a man who put blacks into a position to have a Martin Luther King. It took a hundred years to get a Martin Luther King, but they got one. It's hard for me to grasp.

Yes, I guess it is also hard for me to grasp that most King Day opponents and a few MLK holiday proponents persisted in "Blackenizing" the holiday named after a great American whose non-violent revolution of love over hate changed all of America for the better. Oftentimes, King Day sympathizers would acquiesce that "there shouldn't be a lot of fuss about the holiday that our Black friends want." After all, it was often said, "He did a lot for them." A quick survey of those who attended King Day celebrations which took place in Arizona provided a clear indication that, for most Arizonans, MLK Day meant more to African-Americans other than a few socially-conscious non-African-Americans. On the other hand, I have yet to hear any anti-King Day agitator label Washington or Lincoln Day as a "White" holiday, since both honorees were Caucasian.

To set the record straight, many Arizona municipalities, school and college districts and some private businesses observed Martin Luther King, Jr. Day across Arizona. The Phoenix City Council voted unanimously in 1986 to swap King Day for Columbus Day (and there was no public outcry from the Italian-American community). Of course, Tucson, being the bastion of liberalism in the Copper State, celebrated King's honor with his day.

The Maricopa Community College District gave its faculty, staff administrative and student body time off to join the federal government in setting aside King Day on the third Monday in January. Numerous school districts on the elementary and secondary levels commemorated Dr. Martin Luther King, Jr.'s birthday with a school-free day. In November, 1986, the Arizona Board of Education voted unanimously by resolution to urge the state's 221 school districts to observe King Day on the third Monday in January.

The American Baptists, Roman Catholics, and other progressive religious bodies in Arizona made King Day an additional sabbath day in January for their employees. Before Martin Luther King, Jr. Day became a reality across the nation, the First Institutional Baptist Church added it to our list of employee holidays. A few private businesses recognized King Day, such as Biltmore Properties, Inc., which manages several low-income housing projects, one of which is The Broadway House Apartment Complex, owned and sponsored by First Institutional.

Opposition to King Day surfaced in many places. However, perhaps, the most consistent clue to the holiday's detractors' presence could be found in the letters to the Editor printed in most major Arizona newspapers.

All in all, before the Arizona State Legislature and the state as a whole would willingly laud America's foremost civil rights leader with his day, King Day opponents would have to face and meet the challenge of "Americanizing" the third Monday in January for parochial-minded Arizonans for passage of Martin Luther King, Jr. Day. Their task would be to portray before the public a King painted in "red, white and blue" which would brighten up his "Blackness." What we who supported the day discovered was that that would be a major, monumental challenge, which would last another six long years. And as I think about it, Mecham was partially right and ignorantly prophetic in his condescending pronouncement that "Black folks don't need a holiday…"

My thought was, "Mr. Mecham, Black folks in Arizona did not need a Martin Luther King, Jr. Day as much as you and every other non-African-American did to liberate you from a prejudiced past."

Chapter Three

Arizonans for a Martin Luther King, Jr. State Holiday: The First Grassroots Coalition to Lead the Mlk Day Effort

Mecham must be given credit for inciting the state's slumbering civil rights community, especially African-American Arizonans, to rally in rebellion to his rescission promise. On Sunday, November 9, 1986, just five days after his surprising election victory over two Democratic candidates, an overflow crowd of King Day supporters gathered at the First New Life Missionary Baptist Church, deep in South Phoenix, where people of African and Hispanic descent constitute the majority of residents. The call to converge in that sanctuary of the God of justice went throughout the incensed, socially-conscious community by word-of-mouth.

The rally resulted from members of the Interdenominational Ministerial Alliance of Phoenix and Vicinity, veteran community activists and Arizona's African-American legislators having a rare and quick meeting of the minds to galvanize the community to battle the governor-elect's insensitive assault on a long-awaited, yet to be celebrated King Day. Since Pastor Henry Barnwell served as the president of the Ministerial Alliance, the location of his church edifice was chosen. The size of New Life's sanctuary also became a factor in its selection. The rationale in selecting First New Life revolved around desiring to get an overflow attendance for the hastily called meeting. Had a larger sanctuary been chosen, there might have been difficulty in filling it on a Sunday afternoon. Thank God, our hunch was correct and by the time the meeting got underway the sanctuary was packed with a standing room only crowd, with people spilling outside.

I had not planned to attend that meeting, due to some personal frustrations I was experiencing as an overcommitted pastor. Sure, I wanted to rally against unbridled bigotry boasted by anti-King holiday Arizonans. But, on that Sunday I had been invited to dinner at the home of a couple who were relatively new members of our congregation. Being the *alleged* workaholic that I am labeled, changing my personal schedule for the church and community against my will had reached the protest point that weekend. When I was called by a member of the ad hoc committee to moderate the rally, I offered excuses why I probably would not be able to do it.

First Institutional held its two morning worship services that day. I was tired from preaching both services, as well as mad about having to miss the long-planned dinner invitation between my family and the other family. Nevertheless, as par for the course, I drove to First New Life under protest. Coincidentally, the family to whose home my family and I were invited wanted to attend the rally anyway. Without a doubt, the late Joe and Caryl Terrell, transplanted Chicagoans, evidenced that they were seasoned veterans of the Civil Rights Movement led by King and others. Therefore, everything worked out as far as the postponement of a delightful and delicious Sunday dinner with my new parishioners.

When I walked up the sidewalk to the south entrance of the sanctuary, Opal Ellis hastily approached me with an expression of relief that they were glad I was finally there. She thrust a handwritten agenda in my hand which would supplement the agenda I had outlined on the backs of two copies of Governor Babbitt's Executive Order No. 86-5 ordering Arizona's first MLK Day. The media's presence played in our favor. The packed house looked impressive. Moreover, the presence of a multiracial audience proved a point that Blacks were not the only persons upset about Mecham badmouthing the King Day. Someone ushered me up to the podium and introduced me as the moderator. That day commenced my first public role as a prominent King Day crusader.

The host pastor sat in the pulpit. Other clergy occupied seats in the narrow confines of that holy place. The rally started with opening devotions that included the anthem of the Civil Rights Movement—"We Shall Overcome." Scripture was read from the Old and New Testaments. A Muslim brother offered the prayer followed by a welcome and opening statement by me. Item III on my agenda read, "Business at Hand—Find out what Governor- Elect indeed did say about the MLK, Jr. holiday." That was an easy task in many ways because Evan Mecham had mass-produced and distributed a pre-election campaign newspaper, which explained his position on King Day. I read aloud a few lines from that newspaper which had been sent to my house prior to the election.   Additional business included an identification of challenges facing us, as I saw it. Here's how the list read on my agenda.

- Establish Direct Contact
- Address the Principle of the Holiday,
- not necessarily the Person—Mecham or King
- Change Mecham's Mind
- Get the MLK, Jr. Holiday Bill Passed
- Transform this *PROBLEM* into *PROGRESS*
- Staying Together as a Community
- Soliciting Help from Non-Black Community Leaders/Members

Several speakers trumpeted the call to fight for Arizona's threatened King Day. Arizona's longest serving African-American legislator, Representative Art Hamilton, prophesied that our campaign to celebrate a King holiday in Arizona would be a long one. Former State Senator Carolyn Walker, who at that time served as a Representative in District 23, suggested that upon Mecham's rescission of Babbitt's King Day executive order, Arizona citizens should launch an initiative to put it on the general election ballot in 1988. Dr. Paul Eppinger, the then prophetic pastor of the First Baptist Church of Phoenix, urged people to oppose the plan by Governor-elect Mecham to cancel MLK Day. Pledging critical support from the White community, Eppinger declared, "We dare not let (King's) dream turn into a nightmare." Continuing, my dear friend Paul appeared to speak for the justice-loving majority race in Arizona with these words, "We will pray with you, we will march with you, and, if the time will ever come, we'll go to jail with you." Dr. Mark Reader, an associate professor of political science at Arizona State University, offered the idea of circulating petitions asking the incoming governor and Legislature not to rescind the holiday.

All in all, a cross-section of Arizonans attended that historic rally that eventually gave birth to our state's first broad-based, grassroots coalition in support of King Day. In addition to the "church crowd" which has always provided the home base for America's Civil Rights Movement, groups such as the Black Lawyer's Association, Phoenix Urban League, Phoenix O.I.C., the Rainbow Coalition, Arizona Minority Contractors, the Nation of Islam, Maricopa County Democrats, the National Organization of Women, the

NAACP, and Black Family and Child Services had representatives at that meeting.

The energy and excitement caused by the anger of those in attendance insured that the fire Mecham had ignited by pledging to rescind King Day would hardly die out after the benediction at that rally of righteous rage. In my remarks, I suggested that "direct contact and dialogue" with Governor-elect Mecham were essential if we were to *keep* Arizona's first proclaimed Martin Luther King, Jr. Day. Optimistically, I presented an alternative to protest, saying, "It is one thing to talk here, but we need someone to talk with him (Mecham) face-to-face. We can take this *problem* and turn it into *progress*." Little did I know that my words also were fore telling, even though it did take another six years to win our Martin Luther King, Jr./ Civil Rights Day.

The open and sometimes bitter battle for King Day had begun. The very next day two photographs—one of Dr. Paul Eppinger and the other of me, both addressing the people who had gathered at First New Life on Sunday, November 9, 1986—above the bold print headline "Crowd rallies to back King holiday" plastered the front page of *The Arizona Republic*, Arizona's largest daily newspaper. There was no hiding after that report. Paul and I had been thrust out before the public as "pesky protesters" who had had the nerve to demand a state holiday for a Black man, as well as show disrespect for our newly elected governor by challenging his unpopular position on Martin Luther King, Jr. Day. That was only the second time in my life, up to that point, that I had made the front pages of the newspaper. Twenty years prior to that, I had been anonymously described in a front page article of *The Coffeyville Journal,* after having been shot while burglarizing a house in my immediate neighborhood at age 14. Nevertheless, **both** front-page articles indicated that I was in trouble.

A result of our Sunday rally was a two-page document summarizing the next steps King Day supporters might take in saving the day. First, we would endeavor to "reclaim the holiday" through the Arizona State Legislature bolstered by widespread grassroots support. The grassroots support was to consist of several groups working toward our common goal. The clergy and religious organizations and congregations statewide would have to be mobilized. To be sure, this mobilization of people of faith would be ecumenical and interfaith, including Christians, Muslims, Jews and other religious groups.

Next, we set out to enlist the assistance of community organizations and business leaders to unite with us. Groups such as the Phoenix 40, Arizona Bar Association and Arizona Medical Association filled the list of high-visibility groups to be recruited. Unions, realtors and home finance organizations were sought out. Since several Arizona school districts already recognized King Day, we endeavored to reach out to them to increase King Day support among Arizona's educational community at all levels from elementary to university. The major newspapers in Phoenix and Tucson had already lent strong support to the passage of MLK Day. Therefore, we would seek to meet with their editorial boards to request more of the same.

Another source of support hopefully would come from an increasing number of political leaders. United States Senator-elect John McCain, as a U.S. Representative who voted *against* the federal King holiday, would become a target for King Day conversion. State and municipal leaders, in addition to Native American tribal leaders, would be asked for support. All-in-all, we hoped to have built a broad-based grassroots coalition to cause an overwhelming tide of support when the 38th Session of the Arizona State Legislature convened a week before the Martin Luther King, Jr. holiday in January 1987.

The next major meeting of King Day supporters took place on Sunday, November 23, 1986, in the fellowship hall of the First Institutional Baptist Church. Over 65 citizens gathered that afternoon to proceed to plan strategy to keep our King Day. After calling the meeting to order, Scripture and prayer were offered by a White pastor and a Muslim brother, respectively. Pastor Barnwell welcomed all in attendance, emphasized the importance of moving on with the planned agenda and excused himself to attend another engagement.

Representative-elect Sandra Kennedy reported that during a meeting held on Friday, November 21, Arizona's African-American elected officials from Eloy, Yuma, Casa Grande, Phoenix, Chandler, Florence and other places met and discussed various ways they could send a strong message in support of MLK Day to Governor-elect Mecham. Among their suggestions were the following:

(1) Launch a petition drive with over 50,000 signatures in support of MLK Day; (2) organize a letter writing campaign to state legislators; (3) continue to rally public support; (4) continue to utilize the media to keep this issue before the public;

(5) get local businesses to adopt the holiday for third Monday in January, and (6) plan a press conference with Bruce Babbitt.

Following Representative-elect Kennedy's report and my reminding the group to press forward in transforming our *problem* into *progress*, those in attendance broke up into groups of ten to strategize in smaller discussion groups for forty-five minutes. After reconvening, the groups cumulatively came up with nearly 80 suggestions. Listed below is a sampling of the suggested strategies not previously mentioned:

- Call for special legislative session prior to January 5, 1987
- Exchange Columbus Day for King Day
- Exploit media coverage of Rose Bowl and Fiesta Bowl
- Call for national economic boycott of Arizona
- Hold a MLK rally on Inaugural Day for new governor
- Develop and organize structure for our coalition
- Garner support from labor unions
- Recruit Hispanic and Native American groups to unite with coalition
- Develop strategy to recall Governor Mecham after six months in office
- Picket Mecham Pontiac
- Invite the Reverend Jesse Jackson to Arizona to speak on MLK issue

Before that significant meeting adjourned, a nomination was adopted that I serve as leader of the MLK Day protest and become general chairperson of the newly formed coalition.

The next important meeting that MLK Day supporters held in order to broaden our base of support was with the distinguished Bishops and Executives Roundtable, comprised of religious leaders of Arizona's Christian denominations, which, by the way, included **no** representation from African-American religious bodies operating in the state. It was my lot to state our case before this gathering of influential religious men on November 26, 1986. After providing a brief history of our coalition, Pastors Barnwell and Eppinger outlined the format of the November ninth rally at First New Life. Our delegation left that meeting with the blessings upon our efforts from the Roundtable leaders.

Several key individuals worked behind the scenes to prepare our coalition for our public meetings with the masses as well as various special interest groups. The late Reverend Dudley, who served as chairman of the civic affairs committee of the Interdenominational Ministerial Alliance (IMA), Pastor Barnwell, president of the IMA, Ms. Opal Ellis, City of Phoenix employee and long-time community activist, the Honorable Judge Jean Williams and myself formed the unofficial "executive committee." It was during one of our intensive, productive, creative and sometimes cordially combative meetings when I suggested that the name for our coalition be ARIZONANS FOR A MARTIN LUTHER KING, JR. STATE HOLIDAY. There was some resistance to that nomenclature since a couple of other names had been placed on the table. Nevertheless, due to my strong-willed desire for this particular identifying label, I managed to prevail. We hammered out our statement of purpose, thanks largely in part to the genius of Opal Ellis. It read,

> The purpose of this Ad Hoc Committee is to firmly establish in the state of Arizona the holiday enacted by the United States Congress and signed by the President of the United States honoring Dr. Martin Luther King, Jr.
>
> We solicit the support of all Arizonans who believe in the principles of equality for all Americans-love, peace and non-violence. The celebration of Dr. King's birthday is a reaffirmation of these beliefs and a tribute to America which under Dr. King's leadership achieved its greatest victory and social change. The victory of love over hate.

It is amazing to read our original statement of purpose put together by political novices, which incorporated fundamentally the same themes that the ultimately victorious MLK coalition espoused in 1992 at the expense of several hundred thousand dollars paid to polished political consultants. That proves that packaging oftentimes is more important than the content. Or, perhaps, more accurately, *who* delivers the message takes precedence over the source of the message.

The structure of our ad hoc committee was comprised of a general chairperson, general co-chairpersons including regional chairpersons for the Northern, Central, Western and Southern regions of the state, and a secretary. Initially, ARIZONANS FOR A MARTIN LUTHER KING, JR. STATE HOLIDAY formed six committees, namely (1) executive—to oversee all activities, expenditures and schedule meetings and activities, (2) public relations—to disseminate information and to communicate the purpose of the ad hoc committee, (3) ways and means—to generate operating funds to establish constituency, (4) legal advisory—to advise on legal matters and establish funding sources, (5) Site—to reserve places to meet, and (6) petition drive—to obtain thousands of signatures supporting a state MLK holiday.

In addition to me serving as general chairperson, all of the members of the executive committee served as general co-chairpersons. They were Pastor Barnwell; Mrs. Jennie Cox, Arizona Democratic Party leader; the Reverend Dudley; Ms. Opal Ellis, Dr. Eppinger; Attorney Albert Flores, a leading Mexican-American lawyer; Attorney Chris Johns, our invaluable legal advisor during the early stages of our coalition; Bro. Abdul Malik Muhammad, representative from the Nation of Islam; and Dr. Reader. The late Ms. Mildred Jones, community activist, served as our first secretary. Representing us regionally were the Honorable Mel Hannah, then city councilperson from Flagstaff, for Northern Arizona; Mrs. Caryl Terrell, for Central Arizona; the Honorable James Jefferson, city councilperson from Yuma for Western Arizona; and Pastor Gantt for Southern Arizona.

In an effort to add clout to our infant coalition, we decided to ask a number of high profile Arizonans to serve as honorary chairpersons of ARIZONANS FOR A MARTIN LUTHER KING, JR. STATE HOLIDAY. Our criteria for inviting an individual to serve in such a position in our coalition and have his or her name placed on our letterhead embraced an obvious strong support for a MLK Day in Arizona, proven commitment to civil rights, and respected recognition with a cross-section of constituencies in the community. The task of contacting such prominent persons by telephone, most with whom I had never worked, proved to be anxiety-producing. What if they did not take my calls? What if they said no? Nevertheless, during the second week of December 1986, I began to work through the list of prospective honorary chairpersons.

The response of the majority of those I called left me dumb-founded by their enthusiastic affirmations for our King Day efforts. Prominent attorney Paul Eckstein of the skyscraping Brown & Bain Law Firm quickly consented. The then popular mayor of Phoenix, Terry Goddard, agreed eagerly. After all, under his tenure as Phoenix's mayor, King Day had become a holiday for the ninth largest city in the U.S.A. Long-time community activist and civic leader, Tommie Espinoza, signed on to show solid support from Arizona's Hispanic community. The late Reverend Monsignor Robert J. Donohoe, revered leader in the Roman Catholic Diocese of Phoenix and member of the Phoenix 40, graciously said yes to his name being added to our letterhead. Well-respected and tenured leader of Temple Beth Israel, the late Rabbi Albert Plotkin, accepted our invitation without hesitation. The late Mr. Cloves Campbell, editor of the *Arizona Informant*, Arizona's only weekly African-American newspaper, stood as an automatic yes. Dr. Raymond G. Manker, then pastor of the Unitarian Universalist Church of Phoenix, came highly recommended by several of his members who were vocal and visible King Day supporters. To my surprise, Dr. Paul Elsner, then chancellor of the Maricopa Community College District, returned my call with unwavering support for our efforts and a pledge to solicit support from the business community. His district became the first community college district in Arizona to adopt a paid Martin Luther King, Jr. state holiday. Mr. Peter Fears, then executive director of American Federation of State, County and Municipal Employees, accepted to be an honorary chairperson and served faithfully as an active member of our coalition. The president of the Central Arizona Council, Mr. Mike Bielecki, representing one of Arizona's largest labor groups, united with our campaign as an honorary chairperson. Dr. G. Benjamin Brooks brought a sense of living history to our grassroots organization. Dr. Brooks organized the first and only African-American Presbyterian congregation in Arizona over fifty years ago. Our list of civil rights dignitaries would have been incomplete without him. Providing honorable representation from Southern Arizona was Dr. Charles Ford, Tucson educator and Black then city councilman. Of course, Councilman Calvin C. Goode graced our group by allowing us to place his name among honorary chairpersons. Rounding out our political and civic luminaries were Representatives Hamilton and Earl Wilcox, a longtime Hispanic ally to the African-American community, both of District 22; and Senator-elect Walker and Representative-elect Kennedy of District 23.

A few other persons were contacted to serve as honorary chairpersons, but for one reason or another, they did not return our calls or could not accept. Some of those persons included state superintendent of education, Mrs. C. Diane Bishop, Mr. Peter MacDonald, chairman of the Navajo Tribe and Congressman Bob Stump. I talked personally with popular radio talk show host, Pat MacMahon of KTAR. However, due to his position as a radio personality who had done and would do many talk shows on the MLK Day controversy before the battle was over, he declined our invitation to be named as an honorary chairperson, even though he supported King Day.

Letters were sent to all of those who were asked and consented to serve as a leader on our "Ad Hoc Committee" made up of ARIZONANS FOR

A MARTIN LUTHER KING, JR. STATE HOLIDAY, which brought up another point. Our coalition had no operating monies, no staff, no head-quarters and no office, other than First Institutional Baptist Church. For the duration of our group's existence, the information center was synonymous with the church and staff where I served as pastor. The thousands of letters, phone calls, copies, personnel hours and initial operating income found their source in that church located at 1141 East Jefferson. And, believe me, there never was an official or unofficial complaint for that matter, from the leaders and members of First Institutional Baptist Church concerning utilizing our resources to further the noble cause of ARIZONANS FOR A MARTIN LUTHER KING, JR. STATE HOLIDAY.

By the end of November, Arizona began to receive considerable neg-ative national attention due to Governor-elect Mecham's pledge to rescind the yet-to-be celebrated MLK Day. The Martin Luther King, Jr. Federal Holiday Commission indicated in late November 1986 that only 11 states were without a state holiday honoring King. In addition, some 120 foreign countries celebrated King's birthday in January 1986. Consequently, to rescind King Day in Arizona would buck the national trend.

Taking our lead and advice, the then executive director of the King Commission, Mr. Lloyd Davis, worked on a letter to send to Mecham asking him to either delay his rescinding the holiday until the Legislature could revisit the issue, or to change his mind about canceling the holiday altogether. Davis, like most of us, believed that the Arizona State Legislature, if given another chance, especially in the wake of the negative publicity Mecham's plan for the holiday had caused, would pass King Day legislation. How wrong did we discover we were...

Mecham, through his press aide, Ron Bellus, continued to contend that Governor Bruce Babbitt had declared the holiday illegally and thus he had no other choice than to rescind the MLK Day. But Bellus went a step further on one occasion and suggested that he personally would rather see a holiday named in honor of Brooklyn Dodgers baseball player, Jackie Robinson, who became the first Black major league baseball player in 1947.

Our coalition's next important meeting took place on December 2, 1986, when we adopted our statement of purpose, agreed on a five-point strategy as outlined below, approved the proposed organizational structure, affirmed the names recommended for official and honorary positions, and established a date for a second mass meeting to inform the public on our progress since the November 9, 1986 rally.

Our five-point strategy agreed upon by consensus was outlined thusly:

- Hold a Prayer Service at the same time of the Inauguration of the Governor to be held on Monday, January 5, 1987;

- Lobby the incoming Arizona State Legislature for passage;

- Assign a letter draft for the "letter writing" campaign to the public relations committee;

- Assign the general MLK committee to establish information for the Speaker's Bureau; and

- Assign the public relations committee to solicit support of major corporations, businesses, organizations, churches and educational institutions.

Our first press conference as a newly formed grassroots coalition took place on Friday, December 12, 1986. Its primary purpose served to launch our petition drive to persuade the Legislature to establish a Martin Luther King, Jr. holiday for the slain civil rights leader. Councilman Chuck Ford of Tucson spearheaded that effort, which spread statewide. Our goal was to gather at least 50,000 signatures of Arizonans to put their names, addresses and phone number on our petition that read:

TO THE HONORABLE GOVERNOR AND MEMBERS OF THE LEGISLATURE OF THE STATE OF ARIZONA. We, THE UNDERSIGNED, residents of the State of Arizona do hereby submit and propose to you that action be taken by you to make the third Monday in January of each year as a legal public holiday in the State of Arizona in observance of the birthday of Dr. Martin Luther King, Jr.

Each petition had places for fifteen names and was addressed to be sent to First Institutional Baptist Church by January 7, 1987. Our target date stood at Monday, January 19, 1987, the federal holiday honoring Dr. King, to present our signed petitions to legislative leaders.

During the press conference, we also announced a series of MLK Day celebration activities and demonstrations in support of the holiday. In addition, we called for King Day supporters to wear black ribbons on their lapels as "a statement of mourning" due to Arizona's and Evan Mecham's degrading dealings with the day honoring a great American who gave his life for peace, equality and justice. *The Arizona Republic* gave our press conference front-page coverage the next day, as well as published our schedule of Valley events planned by ARIZONANS FOR A MARTIN LUTHER KING, JR. STATE HOLIDAY and the Martin Luther King, Jr. Celebration Committee, respectively.

Meanwhile, several Arizona legislators speculated on what they could do to quell the controversy brewing to a boiling point as the third Monday in January approached. Representative Jim Green, Republican from Tucson, filed a bill to allow voters in 1988 to decide on MLK Day to be held on a cost-free Sunday. Immediate opposition, both to putting a legislative decision before the voters and moving King Day to a Sunday, arose from within and without the Legislature. Our coalition felt that Representative Green's proposal to solve the King Day controversy was an insult to King and his memory in that it did nothing to provide "a separate but equal" proposal. No other holiday had been referred to the people to decide, and if a paid Monday was acceptable to the United States Congress and a Republican president, why could it not be palatable to the Republican-controlled Arizona State Legislature?

It might be interesting to note that several key national Republican leaders, such as then Congressional Representative Jack Kemp of New York, who also served on the Federal MLK Commission, volunteered to talk with Mecham and try to change his mind about rescinding the King holiday. The incoming governor's press aide responded to such Republican gestures of goodwill with remarks that "President Reagan could talk to Governor Mecham and he would still rescind the holiday because the executive order enacting King Day in Arizona was illegal, according to the attorney general's opinion."

On Tuesday, December 16, 1986, our second Mass Information Community Meeting of ARIZONANS FOR A MARTIN LUTHER KING, JR. STATE HOLIDAY was held at the St. Mary's Episcopal Church in northwest Phoenix. That would be our first King Day gathering in a predominantly White neighborhood and facility. The "Canon", the Reverend Lewis Long, served as pastor to Judge Jean Williams and a few other African-American Episcopalians who were members of that congregation. The attendance turned out to be respectable for a mid-week meeting during the Christmas season. After updating those in attendance of the happenings since formation of our coalition, several ad hoc committee members appealed for a broader base of support and participation in our letter-writing campaign, organized by Ellis and Williams. Speaking of Judge Williams, she worked hard to get the Bishop of the Arizona Episcopal Diocese, the

Dean of Trinity Cathedral, and other Episcopalian clergy and laity actively involved in the King Day struggle through our coalition.

The following are excerpts from a copy of a letter Judge Williams wrote to the Right Reverend Joseph T. Heistand, Bishop, on November 24, 1986.

> During a conversation with my parish priest, the Rev. Lewis H. Long (Rector of St. Mary's Church, Phoenix), I learned of a special action at the recent diocesan convention which tremendously warmed my heart and caused me once again to be proud to be a member of the Episcopal Church. I am referring to the resolution concerning the Martin Luther King holiday. Thank you so much for your courageous Christian leadership....
>
> I am a Black woman who was christened in Grace Cathedral Church (Topeka, Kansas) at the age of three weeks. At the time, Blacks and Caucasians did not worship together. However, my mother was a domestic worker for a very wealthy Caucasian woman who insisted that I should be christened. As my mother told me so many times, she took me to Grace Cathedral on a Monday, *through a back door*, (because on Mondays there would not be too many other Caucasians around to see me), and on that day and in that place (62 years ago) my mother gave me to God. I later worshipped and was confirmed at the mission for Blacks, St. Simon's Episcopal Church (Topeka, Kansas).
>
> Through the years that I have resided in Arizona (17 to be exact), I have questioned the lack of ministerial outreach from the Episcopal Church to the Black community here and in Tucson;...During those periods of conflict, Father Long has quietly consulted with me, and though I have wavered (. . .), I have remained and certainly now intend to remain a member of the Episcopal faith.
>
> While living in Chicago, I became ad hoc chairperson of the legal committee, which Dr. King organized as he began his Southern Christian Leadership Conference campaign in... (Chicago)...Additionally, I had the good fortune of being indoctrinated with his (King's) philosophy of love, peace and justice for all God's children. For this reason, I have also become involved in an effort to ensure that Arizona DOES NOT, lead other states in abolishing that day as a State holiday.

Our letter-writing campaign to legislators and other influential Arizonans shifted into higher gear even though the Christmas season had begun. On Christmas Eve, letters were sent to every Arizona state legislator informing them of our singular goal as a coalition, which was for them to pass a bill that would make the third Monday in January Martin Luther King, Jr. Day in Arizona by modeling the federal government's MLK holiday. In that letter, we reminded the incoming legislators that such a bill failed by one vote in the Arizona House of Representatives earlier in 1986.

By that time, I had an idea for our letterhead, which clearly visualized who we were and what our mission was. I received technical assistance from graphic artists working for *New Times*. The end result was a logo shaped in the form of the State of Arizona with a handsome black and white graphic reproduction of a portrait of Dr. King. To the adjoining right was the name of our coalition. On the left-hand margin the names of our officers and address were listed. The names of our honorary chairpersons were listed in alphabetical order in the right-hand margin. Over the next three years, thousands of letters would go into the mail on our letterhead leaving no doubt in the addressees' minds what our primary goal was.

As mentioned previously, Tucson city councilman, Charles Ford, spearheaded our petition drive. By mail and land, our coalition members distributed petition forms wherever we went. Mrs. Jennie Cox and the Arizona Democratic Party Headquarters provided valuable assistance in allowing us to send out petitions to those on their mailing lists. The number of petition forms sent out by our committee escapes me. However, our numerical goal was to have 50,000 signatures by King Day 1987. Caryl Terrell became the unofficial coordinator for our petition drive for the Phoenix metropolitan area. She utilized her many contacts in the Democratic Party, as well as alliances made when she served as state chairperson of the Reverend Jesse Jackson's 1984 presidential campaign. It goes without saying that Caryl and other members of the First Institutional Baptist Church provided an ever-ready corps of volunteers to advance the cause of King Day, while providing valuable support to their pastor. MLK Day petitioners spread out throughout the state. We exploited mass meeting gatherings, which included weekly religious services, Phoenix Suns' basketball games, public school events, shopping malls, the Fiesta Bowl parade and any other public event that might draw the multitudes. The late Mr. Benjamin Steele, a long-time member of First Institutional, wrote me a note on December 10, 1986, suggesting that we set up petition "tables on both sides of Washington and Jefferson

Streets" downtown. His and many suggestions from interested average John and Jane Doe citizens were what made our grassroots efforts invigorating and worthwhile. Everyday people had been granted the opportunity to participate in affecting history.

The next major event sponsored by ARIZONANS FOR A MARTIN LUTHER KING, JR. STATE HOLIDAY was a Prayer Vigil in support of MLK Day to be held on Monday, January 5, 1987 at 12 noon, the exact same time Evan Mecham would be sworn in as Governor of Arizona. Our group reached the consensus after some other more militant suggestions were laid on the table, one of which was to beat Mecham supporters to his inauguration and fill in all of the unreserved seats with King Day advocates. The decision was for the Prayer Vigil. Thusly, letters of invitation were sent and a program was outlined. There would be prayers—invocations for justice, for the life of Dr. King, for Arizona, for unity and a closing communal prayer at the altar of the First Institutional Baptist Church, where laypersons as well as clergy would lift our petitions to our Creator-God. The Scripture readings came from the Old Testament prophet Micah, who prophesied to his contemporaries about justice and Matthew's Gospel in the New Testament as it relates to prayer. The Negro National Anthem called all in attendance to "Lift Every Voice and Sing." In addition, Mrs. Maxine Jack of First Institutional rendered two specially selected Negro spirituals entitled "Couldn't Hear Nobody Pray" and "Go Down Moses." It was my lot to deliver the statement of purpose, which was an abridged version of a Sunday morning message I preached the Sunday after Mecham was elected governor.

The title was lifted directly from Exodus 1:8, "A New King Who Knew Not Joseph." Within that message, I addressed several issues that proved to be ancient, as well as contemporary. My first point stated, "We ought never to forget the certainty of changes in leadership." Furthermore, I expounded on the fact that Egypt's new Pharaoh "symbolized a radical change from the accustomed and the acceptable. His presence in power pronounced an appalling insensitivity to his predecessor's relationship with Joseph." My second point read thusly, "Look at the consequences of this new king not knowing Joseph." Pressing that point, I preached, "A new course and conduct inconsistent with the previous administration was pursued. Upon his taking office, former alliances between personalities in power were pronounced null and void." Another stinging sub-point that I pronounced came to this conclusion, "I know the Record says, 'Now there arose up a new king over Egypt, who knew not Joseph', but I, personally, don't believe that this new king was *not* knowledgeable of Joseph's legacy. No, no, I believe he deliberately chose to ignore it!" My third point dealt with the challenges facing the people as a result of this new king not knowing Joseph. The three challenges, I identified were (1) the challenge to establish communication with the new king, (2) the challenge to not compromise one's principles, and (3) the challenge of turning a *problem* into *progress*. I further stated, "This new king, in one sense, brought Joseph's people together."

My concluding point theologized the MLK Day struggle for me when I worded it, "In the final analysis, it doesn't matter whether or not the new king knows Joseph or his people…What matters is that the King of kings knows Joseph and his people."

Continuing, I preached, "Picture, if you will, two men about the same age, height and stature standing before the Judgment Throne; one named Martin, and the other named Mecham. The Great Division is about to take place; the sheep to the right, and the goats on the left. The Righteous Judge calls Martin by his first name, and directs him to the right. The Lord smiles, and says to Martin, 'I know you because you fed me when I was hungry….' And Martin raised the question, 'Lord, when did I feed you…?' And the Lord replied, 'In Atlanta, in Montgomery, in Selma, in Detroit, in Washington, D.C., and the last time in Memphis. Come on, Martin, inherit the Kingdom prepared for you before the foundation of the universe.'

Then, Mecham, as he sees Martin heading to the right, asks the Lord, 'Why did that Black man enter the Kingdom ahead of me?' The Lord replied, 'Who are you? I don't know your name, but I know your works. You belonged to a [religion] that discriminated against Martin's people. You became rich by selling cars for much more than they were worth. You defended your wife for associating with the John Birch Society. You bragged about your integrity but refused to give equity. You offended a whole people by canceling Martin's holiday!…Well, all of your life, you thought you were on the right, but throughout eternal damnation you'll suffer on the left! Depart from me…I know you not!'

'Martin, Martin, what's that you're hummin'?' 'Oh, nothing, Lord, just a little song my enslaved foreparents used to sing, "Heabn', Heabn', everybody talkin' 'bout Heabn' ain't goin'!'"

To my amazement, the audience erupted in a standing ovation. Governor Babbitt had arrived from his successor's Inauguration and joined in the applause. When I sat down beside him, he mentioned something to the effect that commended me for my speaking ability. Indeed, it was a high hour in our fight to keep the day that the gentleman sitting beside me had declared from the same pulpit in which we were sitting. Perhaps, my remarks and the response served as a sort of release of built-up tension on the infamous day that Arizona installed a bigot as governor.

Please note that my sermonic statement of purpose sounded rather blunt and brutal. But you must remember that America's racist history and the interpretation of God's Word as liberating as understood in the heart, mind and soul of oppressed African-Americans, especially preachers, give *homiletical license* to be prophetic in our pronouncements against any and all who harbor any remnants of prejudiced philosophy and practice. In addition, in the spirit of the classical prophets of the Old Testament, I exercised my right to utilize *hyperbole*, which is an exaggerated way of speaking to get a point across. Usage of such expression gains few fans from the establishment crowd and the majority race in America. That fact was evidenced when I reluctantly toned down my prophetic pronouncement during the victorious statewide MLK campaign from November 1990 to November 3, 1992.

One of our most civic-minded Hispanic pastors, the late Reverend Reuben Carrico, introduced Governor Babbitt. His remarks were brief, pointed and reminded us that the battle to keep King Day in Arizona would be a major one. Of course, being the political beast that he is, former Governor Babbitt worded his speech cautiously so as not to be politically incorrect in relation to Arizona's brand-new governor. If nothing else, Babbitt's remarks encouraged us. Probably, his being there meant more than what he said.

After his remarks, Gene Blue announced the MLK Celebration activities calendar and led in the distribution of black ribbons which we asked King holiday supporters to wear in protest of Mecham's planned rescission of our holiday. Persons were urged to sign and pass out our petitions to be turned in on King Day 1987. After closing with communal prayer, we all stood to sing the Civil Rights Movement theme song, "We Shall Overcome."

All in all, our prayer vigil proved to be successful. The attendance was commendable for a weekday at noon. The media gave the event broad coverage as it provided a contrast to the happenings down at the State Capitol. Moreover, supporters of a Martin Luther King, Jr. state holiday left First Institutional recharged to press forward.

Speaking of the inauguration of Governor Mecham, Joel Nilsson, a then editorial writer for *The Arizona Republic*, penned an amusing editorial about Blacks in attendance at Mecham's beginning day. During the period after I had suggested that our new governor-elect possessed a "racist mentality," he and/or his press aide countered that accusation by professing that Evan Mecham had Black friends. In clarifying Mecham's statement, "Some of my best friends are Black," he had mentioned three names to reporters. Nilsson used those Black friends as his point of departure for the column he wrote on January 10, 1987.

In the audience at the Capitol for Gov. Evan Mecham's inaugural address, I was struck by the absence of blacks.

The Rev. Henry Barnwell, who gave the opening prayer, was there. That didn't surprise me.

He was, afterall, one of three men Mecham (cited as his Black Friends)…If the other two attended their friend's most celebrated day—his installation as the 17th governor of *all* the people of Arizona—I must have missed them.

> Familiar names were not there. Art Hamilton, the House Democratic Leader, was supposed to be on the dais with Mecham and other dignitaries. He was not. Other black lawmakers and community leaders skipped the festivities as well. I can't blame them. The black community and Arizona's new governor don't have much in common."

For your information, the other two Black friends Mecham identified were the late Lincoln J. Ragsdale, long-time mortician, insurance executive and developer, reputedly identified as Arizona's first Black millionaire (before African-American professional athletes were paid millions for playing sports), and Joseph Parham. A matter of fact, Ragsdale and other African-American leaders sponsored a meeting with Governor-elect Mecham in Ragsdale's Clearwater Hills home on December 13, 1986. Their purpose was to discuss future political and economic participation in Mecham's administration by Blacks, especially business- persons. The strategy of those spearheading the gathering was that since he was going to be the governor, it would be best to try to work with him. It was reported that Mecham and the 50-plus African-American leaders discussed the King holiday, but political and economic development remained first and foremost on that crowd's mind.

The story behind Pastor Barnwell offering one of the prayers at Mecham's Inauguration warrants mentioning at this point. As previously mentioned, Barnwell and Mecham had developed a relationship with one another. It was no secret that Henry was one of the few African-American leaders with whom Mecham communicated. Perhaps, Mecham maintained open lines of communication with Pastor Barnwell because he was not as outspoken regarding the King holiday *and* Evan Mecham, as I was. I guess one could say that Barnwell operated "behind the scenes" and didn't "make waves." Rest assured, our coalition's general co-chairperson wanted a Martin Luther King, Jr. state holiday as much as any one of us did. Without a doubt, Henry served as my "first lieutenant," in spite of our vastly different way in doing politics, especially with ultra-conservative Republicans.

A few days prior to Mecham's big day, Henry called me at my home to seek advice on the governor-elect's request for him to offer the invocation. My immediate reaction was an unequivocal, "No!" I suggested to Pastor Barnwell that Governor-elect Mecham desperately needed a "brother" to be associated closely and visibly with him to take some of the heat off of him that he was getting for vowing to cancel King Day. My belief was that Evan Mecham wanted to use my friend, Henry, to his advantage at this critical time in his political career. Mecham needed a prominently placed African-American leader to stand by him during his "trial." I probably would have consented to stand by Mecham *if* he consented to rescind his promise to rescind our King Day, but that was the only way I would have done so.

But getting back to my conversation with Henry, he countered my unwavering insistence that he *not* accept the invitation to pray at the inauguration with a recitation of a New Testament verse that reads, "Men ought to always pray…" I retorted, "Yea, but, it didn't say *where!*" Our conversation wasn't getting very far. I just kept reminding Barnwell that Mecham needed him at that point, especially, since he was a key leader in ARIZONANS FOR A MARTIN LUTHER KING, JR. STATE HOLIDAY. The debated discussion ended that day with me telling Henry that I would be praying for him to make the right decision (which I sure hoped was for him to decline to do the prayer) and Henry promising that he would do just that. But I kind of knew that when the prayer was offered on January 5, 1987, at the State Capitol, my friend, Pastor Barnwell, would be offering it.

Thank God, I was nearly freezing to death in Rockford, Illinois where I was the guest lecturer for the Winter Christian Life Conference at the Providence Baptist Church when Arizona's new governor rescinded our state's first declared Martin Luther King, Jr. Day. When I heard the news on CNN in my hotel room on Monday afternoon, January 12, 1987, I exploded! I know had I been in Phoenix, our coalition would have called a press conference to blast Evan Mecham for bringing shame to the entire State of Arizona, as well as the legacy of Dr. Martin Luther King, Jr.

The rescission of the executive order making the third Monday in January MLK Day for state employees came in an announcement at the conclusion of Mecham's first State of the State address to Arizona's Republican-controlled Legislature. Ironically, the theme of the new governor's address was "A new beginning for Arizona." That, indeed was an understatement as it related to "new beginning." After canceling the day, the governor challenged the Arizona State Legislature to perform an "act of courage" by putting the King holiday on the 1988 general election ballot. So much for "separate but equal" treatment of a holiday honoring a Black man. Mecham reaffirmed his stance that his predecessor had no legal authority to declare such a holiday; therefore, the holiday had been created illegally.

The responses from legislators and politicians on both sides of the fence provided the governor with very little solace. Art Hamilton responded, "Far from being courageous, I view the governor's act as being somewhat akin to cowardice." Senate Minority Leader Alan Stephens suggested that Mecham's action might "fan the flames of division in this State." Republican Representative Jim Skelly, a very conservative politician from Scottsdale and long-time King Day "no" vote remarked, "That's a lot of crap. We are down here to decide either to have an observance or not to have one." Tucson City Councilman Chuck Ford offered, "During these times when we seem to be slipping into racial unrest…, I think our leaders have to take a more pro-active position so our people can rally around a positive point on race relations. We certainly don't need any more division in the ranks."

Don't think that Governor Mecham did not have his vocal supporters for his biggest political blunder; that was just the beginning of political missteps, which led to his impeachment. Mr. Sanders, now counted as one of my "friends" because of my pro-life position on unborn babies, had launched his own anti-King Day petition drive two weeks prior to the rescission. He rejoiced in the governor's promise kept. The founder of a group called Arizonans for Traditional American Values, Sanders commented, "I just knew that he was going to keep his commitment."

Even though I was out of the state, ARIZONANS FOR A MARTIN LUTHER KING, JR. STATE HOLIDAY had prepared a press release in response to the anticipated gubernatorial cancellation of Babbitt's executive order. We began by reminding the media that the United States Congress, with the approval of Republican President Ronald Reagan, had established a federal Martin Luther King, Jr. Day, as well as thirty-nine states. Following that introduction, these statements were made:

> Despite the clear record of national support for a legal holiday honoring Martin Luther King, Governor Mecham has chosen to rescind the Executive Order established by former Governor Bruce Babbitt, proclaiming a state holiday for Dr. King.
>
> ARIZONANS FOR A MARTIN LUTHER KING, JR. STATE HOLIDAY are disappointed, but not surprised by the action of Governor Mecham. It is consistent with his prior statements regarding the King Holiday that have brought the State of Arizona under national scrutiny. The rescinding of the holiday is a sad day for our Country and Arizona.
>
> …(Our coalition) invite(s) all persons of goodwill to join us in celebrating the Federal legal holiday established to honor the principles of racial equality, justice, love and peace that Dr. King represented and cherished. Despite Governor Mecham's action, we must celebrate and remember the ideals of Dr. King for generations to come, to keep our country strong and free.

Lo, and behold, the day after Evan Mecham cancelled King Day, Martin King's most prominent disciple, the Reverend Jesse Jackson flew into Phoenix to attend the inauguration of then Navajo Tribal Chairman Peter MacDonald. Almost beyond imagination, Jesse and Evan met in the Governor's Office and held a joint press conference on Tuesday, January 13, 1987. Not a whole lot was accomplished other than some intriguing press with two political opposites making the evening news and newspaper headlines. In spite of the Reverend Jackson's appeals to Governor Mecham to reconsider his already "done deal" on rescinding Arizona's first holiday honoring his mentor, Mecham did not budge. The fact that Jackson called the rescission an "attack upon Dr. King's philosophy and approach" left no impressionable impact upon our new governor. The good Reverend also questioned the wisdom of the governor's proposal to put the King holiday issue on the ballot. To counter that proposition, he challenged the Legislature to approve a state holiday honoring Martin Luther King, Jr. and called on the public to push for such a day. For Jackson, the King Day controversy provided Arizonans to "move toward a period of redemption and reconciliation and healing." Nevertheless, the polarization that Mecham's rescission of the holiday was causing between citizens of Arizona did not appear to affect Mecham's steadfast stance.

To deflect criticism from his infamous King Day cancellation, Mecham spoke of his concern for economic equality for African-Americans in his state. Then, to the astonishment of hundreds of thousands of residents living within our state's borders, Governor Mecham declared, "We don't have any problems in Arizona." As evidence, he intimated that Blacks could move into good neighborhoods if they had the money to do so.

Pertaining to Dr. King, Mecham identified King merely as one of the many persons who brought about civil rights advances. A matter of fact, the new governor vowed to be a discrimination opponent and to get "in the trenches" to fight for civil rights. Regardless, civil rights activist Jesse Jackson restated his beliefs that the rescission by Mecham was motivated by more than concerns about the holiday's legality. Yet, he commended Mecham for meeting with him, promised to continue to press the Arizona State Legislature to "do the right thing."

I must confess, my elder brother Jesse, by sitting with "Evan the terrible", accomplished a fete that I was not yet ready to attempt since my November meeting with the then governor-elect. Apparently, I was not by myself with those sentiments, especially after the "no (discrimination) problems in Arizona" remark. The late Junius Bowman, then-longtime president and CEO of the Phoenix Urban League, responded to Mecham's remarks with these words, "If there weren't any racial problems, this whole issue would not be an issue. If there weren't any problems, the state would have accepted this holiday." Further pressing his point, Bowman, who was considered by many as a "moderate, play-it-safe" Black leader, said, "If there was no discrimination in the state there wouldn't be any need for a Civil Rights Commission, there wouldn't be any need for the Equal Employment Opportunity Commission, and there wouldn't be any need for a human-relations office with the City of Phoenix." Mr. Bowman went on to suggest that Mecham was uninformed and needed to get out into the midst of the struggle in order to know what racial problem did exist in Arizona.

The mild-mannered, Phoenix City Councilman Calvin Goode reacted to Governor Mecham's utopian perception of race relations in our state by indicating that the governor must be having a vision problem. Goode was quoted,

There's problems in terms of unemployment and the governor only needs to look at his affirmative-action office, if he doesn't do away with it. There are discrimination cases filed all the time.... If the governor does not really know, there are some of us who will make him aware. It's hard for me to comprehend that he is not aware after living in this state all of these years.

Even former Governor Babbitt, who was in Washington the day after the cancellation of the executive order that he had signed, offered that Mecham's rescinding of the holiday was "an insult" and "a big mistake."

Ironically, Governor Mecham and the Reverend Jackson concluded their joint press conference by agreeing to disagree, shaking hands and flying off to Window Rock to attend the swearing-in ceremonies for Navajo Tribal Chairman Peter MacDonald. To say the least, national and international attention began to focus on Arizona and the man who dared to disrespect the lofty legacy of "Mr. Civil Rights" by erasing Martin Luther King, Jr. Day from Arizona's history books before it could be celebrated. Calls, letters, telegrams and messages from all over the nation and world poured into the state. It didn't help that Governor Mecham rescinded the King Day just one week prior to the federal observance.

As pressure mounted for a showdown on Monday, January 19, 1987, Mecham began to lose his cool and uncover his facade of having simply done what he had to do, due to legal reasons. While speaking before an ultra-conservative breakfast gathering the Friday before King Day in America, the chief executive of the State of Arizona made the following shocking comments,

> I told the press the other day that there was not discrimination in Arizona and if there was, I would wipe it out....But on the other hand, I think we've fought that fight and I think to push it and to have a minority decide that we are all going to pay tribute to a given individual on a given day....For the minority to press that position....and I told Reverend Jackson I'm concerned about you hurting Blacks...because if you continue to push in this manner, if you continue to push people who have willingly said we want equal rights for all people...the time does come when the majority says we're not gonna take it anymore...I fear for what happens to the Blacks and I don't want to see that happen.

Damn! What in the world was Mecham implying would *happen to* us uppity Negroes who simply wanted to honor Martin Luther King, Jr. on the third Monday in January like the entire nation, including almost 40 states? And who was this majority who would "rise up" and "not take it anymore?" In the vernacular of the streets, "Those were some fighting words!" Moreover, they emanated from the top spokesperson for the three million-plus citizens of Arizona in 1987.

Support for Arizona's embattled King Day poured in from all over the nation. In late December, the late Cesar Chavez, courageous leader of the United Farm Workers of America, met with me and Attorney Christopher Johns in the Law Offices of Cordova, Flores, Morales & Inigues, P.C. The purpose of the meeting was twofold, namely (1) sharing Chavez' current issues facing farm workers throughout the country, (2) and our efforts to establish an Arizona holiday honoring King, who like Chavez, fought as an advocate of the rights of the poor, disenfranchised and underpaid laborers of our country. Following that timely meeting in which ARIZONANS FOR A MARTIN LUTHER KING, JR. STATE HOLIDAY received encouragement, as well as invaluable insight from Mr. Chavez, the two of us held a brief press conference, at which time, Chavez pledged his support for our cause and I pledged our support for decent working conditions and fair wages for all workers in our nation. In addition, the United Farm Workers of American drafted a resolution in support of our struggle in Arizona to honor Dr. King, who was in Memphis, Tennessee supporting union garbage collectors when he was assassinated.

Speaking of resolutions, in support of our coalition's efforts, dozens were approved by their respective organizations. The list included the Paradise Missionary Baptist State Convention of Arizona, Inc. and the General Missionary Baptist State Convention of Arizona, representing nearly all Black Baptists in the state, the Phoenix Urban League, Arizona State AFL-CIO, the Martin Luther King, Jr. Committee of Arizona State University, the National Conference of Christians and Jews-Arizona Region, Alpha Phi Alpha Fraternity, Inc., Delta Tau Lambda Chapter, Lowell Elementary School, the American Federation of State, County and Municipal Employees, the 1986 Governor's Conference on Aging, National Operation P.U.S.H., and the N.A.A.C.P.-Maricopa County Branch.

Monday, January 19, 1987 arrived with *no* Martin Luther King, Jr. state holiday! However, by the thousands of King Day supporters who gathered in sub-freezing temperatures at the

Phoenix Civic Plaza on that day, it was crystal clear that the slain civil rights leader had friends in the only state in the Union that had ever had a Martin Luther King, Jr. Day rescinded. We gathered that morning as never before in order to make a statement to our new governor and all of those in the Legislature and elsewhere who shared his ignorance and/or bigotry toward King Day. On that Monday, we had gathered to protest our insensitive governor's rescission of the King holiday in addition to celebrating the life and legacy of the 20th century American hero! Although our blood-thinned Arizona bodies shivered on that cold January winter morning, the warmth of our cause held us together to make an unforgettable statement to Mecham and the world that the fight for King Day had only just begun.

An estimated 15,000 marchers made the two and a half mile walk from Second Street and Adams to the State Capitol. We were of all colors, races, creeds and classes. The young were there as well as the old. Two bus-loads of marchers from Tucson joined the march already in progress. The *Phoenix Gazette Green Streak* edition for that day described those of us who rallied to protest Mecham's action in these words,

> Blacks, Anglos, Hispanics, young and old, people from all walks of life, from punk rockers to union groups, mothers with young children to teenagers and middle-aged couples, joined in the orderly procession, which packed three lanes of Washington Street for more than a half a mile.

I know I will never forget that day. Making up the front line at least at the start, were long-time King Day supporters and community activists and politicians. Of course, Representative Art Hamilton with his imposing physique stood out at the center of the frontline. Senator Walker occupied a prominent position near Art. Dr. Brooks held a well-deserved spot. Former state superintendent of education and Democratic gubernatorial candidate, Carolyn Warner, proudly linked arms with others who were in place. Tommie Espinoza and his pre-teen son shared the slot next to me and my son Matthew who was six years old at that time. Councilman Goode and his wife Georgie took their places. Phoenix Mayor Goddard towered above the rest of us front-liners as he came to march with us. Gene Blue was nearby being his humble self. Many other leaders filled in the second, third and fourth frontlines. However, once the march began the frontline consisted of whoever was there at any given moment.

Several sizes and shapes of signs decorated Arizona's most historic civil rights march. ARIZONANS FOR A MARTIN LUTHER KING, JR. STATE HOLIDAY DAY had transposed our letterhead logo on several large posters nailed to sticks. Other homemade signs read "King Deserves a Holiday", "Live the Dream", "Boycott Mecham Pontiac", and "Mecham for Ex-Governor." Various groups hoisted banners and signs that identified both their organizations and support for King Day in Arizona. The enthusiasm, excitement and intensity of all of the events, good and bad, which had led to that day, generated a comradery among literally thousands of strangers bound together by King's living legacy. The temperature became an afterthought. The nearly three mile hike seemed like a quick stroll down the street. We had come to march to the doorstep of Governor Mecham and the Republican-controlled Legislature to demand that they grant our wish to join the nation in honoring King with his day in our state.

Once we arrived at the Wesley Bolin Plaza, directly in front of the Arizona State Legislature's Senate and House of Representative chambers, word was sent up to House Speaker Joe Lane, an anti-King legislator, that we had a presentation to make to him for the governor and his colleagues in the Legislature. In a low-keyed exchange of words, we presented several boxes of nearly 50,000 signatures on our petitions urging the appropriate state officials to take action to make the third Monday in January a legal public holiday in Arizona honoring King. Speaker Lane appeared somewhat nervous, uttered some words about the legislators' responsibility to hear from their constituents and hastily returned to work, since January 19, 1987 was no day off for state employees. I am not certain where the petitions were taken, but they probably ended up in some cluttered closet in the House of Representatives, if not in the trash.

The rest of the morning, brief speeches in support of King Day were delivered by a variety of community, religious and governmental leaders and representatives. All of the speakers were well-received by the thousands who celebrated King Day anyway, in spite of Mecham's cancellation of Babbitt's executive order.

The governor began his day on NBC's "Today" show debating the Reverend Jesse Jackson by reiterating his myopic stance on the holiday, "Blacks don't need another holiday; what they need is jobs." He further denounced Jesse Jackson and other King Day supporters for trying to make everybody feel guilty for not going along with their push for a King Day. Mecham chided Jackson for trying to force an *honor* on someone when it ought to be *bestowed*. Then, he suggested that the people ought to speak on this controversial issue by letting them decide it at the ballot box. Later that day, he even questioned Art Hamilton in a local interview by suggesting that King Day supporters were afraid to let the people decide this matter in an election.

Never before had so much national and international media attention, been focused on Arizona. Regrettably, thanks to our new governor, it was 99% negative! Nearly every national television and radio network converged on Phoenix the weekend of January 16-19, 1987. News teams from Europe arrived to inquire about the American governor who dared to nix King Day. Representatives from the printed press requested interview after interview from local governmental leaders, Governor Mecham and *yours truly*. I was overwhelmed by the demand for interviews on this historic media event. Every day when I would enter my office, there would be stacks of telephone messages for interviews.

I must confess, I enjoyed this newfound attention locally, nationally and internationally. Friends and family members from all over the country began calling me to inform me that they had seen me on television and to quiz me about our "racist governor what's-his-name." For most media, this was the first time they had given a lot of attention to the King Day struggle in Arizona. But I can say with gratitude that the *ARIZONA INFORMANT*, Arizona's only weekly African-American newspaper, continued to cover Arizona's King Day celebration and holiday struggle as front-page copy as it had always done for years, thanks to long-time publisher and former Senator Campbell.

This matter of calling press conferences was new to me. I was always very nervous about several related matters. One, would the media come? And they did most of the time, especially while the issue was hot. On one occasion, our press conference was covered *live* in Arizona's largest radio news station KTAR. A second thing I discovered was that regardless of the press statement that was prepared and read, usually most of that was not what the reporters included in their articles and/or broadcast reports. It was the impromptu answers to their questions that made the newspapers and newscasts. I had to learn quickly the art of instantaneously interpreting their questions to provide an "appropriate" response that would not be blown out of proportion. Of course, I made mistakes along the way by showing my anger with the way Arizona's "powers that be" had played political football with Dr. King's birthday. For sure, the reporters would try to get me to call Governor Mecham and/or King Day opponents "outright racists" which I learned never to do in public, even though I felt within my heart that many of them were obvious victims of their own racist mentality. A third concern was how much coverage would our press conferences receive. Would we make the evening *and* nightly news? Would we make the front-page, back page, headlines and/or have an accompanying photograph in the paper? How much of *our* message would get out? One other source of mild anxiety dealt with being taken seriously by the reporters. I mean, after all, I was a Black Baptist preacher in mostly White Arizona being covered by mostly White reporters. Would they bring any personal prejudices to the reporting process? Would they respect the efforts of a coalition headed by me, an African-American? For the most part, our presentations before the media commanded respect. Only once was I labeled "a loose cannon" by a columnist for *The Phoenix Gazette* to which I mused, "He doesn't know how restrained I am being for the sake of winning support for King Day in Arizona. Doggone it, if it had been in any other state, we probably wouldn't even be having this acrimonious debate over honoring a Black man who revolutionized America in race relations."

Chapter Four
Inside the Arizona State Capitol

As much as I hate to admit it, the Arizona State Capitol had been off limits to me prior to the King holiday fight. I guess the closest I came to the State Capitol was Wesley Bolin Plaza where the march and festival would end up each year, once we started celebrating the federal observance of King Day.

From hindsight, I know now that there are many, many reasons conscientious and concerned citizens ought to frequent the House and Senate chambers of state legislatures, as well as the executive offices of state government. The legislators, governor and all other elected and appointed governmental employees work for us. Therefore, they need to hear from us, especially when progressive changes need to be made for the welfare of Arizona's citizenry. *Your* representatives and senators should know who *you* are by name. Regardless of the millions of persons, who reside in this state, the governor has a responsibility to recognize you when he or she comes into contact with you. And, in most cases, only *you* can make certain that *you* are more than a vote for, or against, those elected to serve *you*.

To say the least, I did not frequent the Executive Tower while Governor Mecham was in office, as much as I did under Democratic governors. Back in the early 1980s, Governor Babbitt invited the Reverend Jesse Jackson, accompanying civil rights activist/clergy, and a select few local pastors to discuss the Miracle Valley crisis. The Cochise County Sheriff opened fire on members of a Pentecostal sect that migrated to southern Arizona from Chicago, killing and injuring several Black men, which had caused an eruption. Other than that, I had never been to either of the legislative chamber buildings for anything.

My most frequent contact with the Legislature came through the office of Representative Hamilton. He opened his doors to members of our coalition in order that he could keep us abreast on the status of King Day legislation, as well as listen to the strategy we were employing to provide external pressure on the Legislature. No one in the Legislature spoke with more influence or authority relative to the Martin Luther King, Jr. holiday than Art. He called the shots for both Democratic and supportive Republican leadership on this issue. Senator Walker provided leadership on the Senate side, but since she was a freshman senator and the Senate had approved the King holiday legislation in May of 1986, Minority Speaker Hamilton was still the quarterback calling the plays with that political football. Newly elected Representative Kennedy provided solid support, but was also in the process of finding her way around the House. Ironically, my first introduction to the floor of the House of Representatives came from my District 20 Senator, Democrat Lela Alston. She invited me to offer the invocation on Monday, January 19, 1987 in the Senate chambers, the same day thousands of King Day supporters and protestors had converged on Arizona's Capitol. During January through March 1987, I kept in almost daily contact with Art because members of our coalition operated under the illusion that the negative publicity brought down upon Arizona after Mecham's rescission of MLK Day, would have prompted the Republican-controlled Legislature to restore the state's tarnished image by passing legislation for King Day. After all, they had just missed doing that by one vote in 1986. However, we discovered that the Republican leadership had other things in mind.

In an effort to be proactive, our coalition planned and sponsored "Love letters to the Legislature" a working session held on Valentine's Day 1987 from noon to 4:00 p.m. at the Tanner Chapel African Methodist Episcopal Church. Ms. Opal Ellis and Judge Jean Williams were the brainchildren of this event to involve the average Arizona citizens, especially from the Black community in Phoenix, in positively affecting change in state politics. The late Pastor John L. Shaw, Sr. of Tanner Chapel served as the chairperson of our letter-writing and phone-calling campaign. Ministers, politicians, union workers, sorority and lodge sisters and other community organization representatives played active roles in this creative event.

A thoughtful and informative letter-writing kit was prepared for those in attendance. The three-fold purpose for the "letter love-in" was outlined thusly, (1) to maintain support of legislators who supported the 1986 MLK legislation, (2) to persuade legislators who voted against that bill to change their position, and (3) to solicit affirmative votes from new legislators for the new King Day legislation to be introduced.

The names and addresses of all members of the 38th Legislature were included, as well as how each returning legislator had voted on the holiday the year before. Sample letters to senators and representatives constituted part of the packet. Some of the letters invoked the name of former President Ronald Reagan who signed the federal holiday into law. Others highlighted the need for modern-day role models for school-children. Non-violence served as a theme for one sample letter. Several focused on Dr. King helping our nation to reaffirm our belief in peace, liberty and justice for all. Still others provided hope for Arizona's future by having another opportunity to join the nation, other states and many countries in officially honoring Dr. Martin Luther King, Jr. with his day. This event was somewhat successful with the majority of its participants being from the African-American community.

Speaking of letters, it was my assignment to write to Arizona's United States congressional delegation to urge them to write each state legislator to lobby them to support the upcoming MLK Day legislator modeled after the federal holiday. The next to the last paragraph in my January 8, 1987 letter specifically outlined the help we wanted from our elected Congressmen in Washington, D.C.

> Our sole request of you is that you would write a letter in support of our objective to our state representatives and senators before January 19, 1987, if at all possible.

January 19, 1987 was targeted because it was the date of that year's King holiday celebration. As I mentioned before, some of us were unreasonably optimistic that the legislators would rush through a King Day bill prior to the 1987 King Day to crush outside criticism caused by Mecham's rescission of the day.

The most affirmative response came from the late Congressman Morris K. Udall in a letter written to me on February 5, 1987. The letter in its entirety is as follows:

> Dear Dr. Stewart:
> Thank you for your letter urging me to lobby the state lawmakers to pass a bill that would combine Washington's and Lincoln's birthdays into a state President's Day and establish a Martin Luther King, Jr. holiday on the third Monday of January on which the current Federal holiday falls.

As you requested, I sent a copy of the enclosed letter to our state representatives and senators in support of this objective. I hope this effort proves beneficial to your cause.

Thank you for providing me with the opportunity to be of assistance.

> Sincerely,
> Morris K. Udall

Excerpts from Congressman Udall's letter accentuate the forthrightness of his commitment to aid our cause. The first paragraph in his letter to Arizona legislators read,

> During my years in Congress, I have made it a practice not to interfere in matters before the state or local governments. Unfortunately, I must break that silence on the issue of a day to commemorate Dr. Martin Luther King, Jr.'s birthday.

Continuing,

> It is not often that truly great men walk the face of this earth: men who speed us through decades of change in a few short years; men who enlighten our minds and open our hearts-who touch some common thread in all people. Surely, the Reverend Martin Luther King was one of those men....
>
> It is only fitting that we set aside his birthday to honor the man and his dream. We Arizonans share a great deal with Dr. King....I ask you to support legislation to establish a Martin Luther King holiday in the State of Arizona.

We received a response from freshman Republican U.S. Senator John McCain dated March 10, 1987, which exemplified his *negative* response to our specific request.

Dear Dr. Stewart:

> Thank you for your recent correspondence regarding the holiday in remembrance of Dr. Martin Luther King.
>
> ...While no state may change the Federal (King) holiday, each state has the right to decide whether to observe a Federal holiday as a state holiday.
>
> Governor Mecham has chosen to exercise his option to rescind an Executive Order signed by former Governor Bruce

Babbitt that made the Federal holiday a state holiday as well. The Governor has proposed resolving the issue by putting it to a ballot test. As a U.S. Senator, it would not be appropriate for me to interject myself into an issue that can only be resolved at the state government level.

I personally feel, however, that one day should be set aside to honor Dr. King and hope this is the opinion of the majority of the voters of Arizona.

How is that for "straddling the fence?" However, I must say that McCain's last sentence in his letter was a giant step away from his negative vote as a U.S. Congressman from Arizona *against* the federal King Holiday.

Arizona's senior U.S. Senator at that time, the Honorable Dennis DeConcini, complied with our request in a letter directed to our state legislators on February 20, 1987. His letter included the following statements:

I am writing this letter to express my support of the Martin Luther King holiday.

Dr. King was a truly remarkable individual who dedicated his life, through non-violent means, to seeking equal rights and justice for all Americans. For that reason, I supported Congressional efforts to establish a Federal holiday to commemorate the progress of civil rights in the United States.

As the issue comes before the Legislature, I hope you will give the citizens of Arizona the same opportunity to honor the work of Dr. King.

I never received a response to the specific letter from our coalition, ARIZONANS FOR A MARTIN LUTHER KING JR. STATE HOLIDAY, from former U.S. Representative Jay Rhodes and Representatives Bob Stump and Jon Kyl, all Republicans.

On the actual birthday of Dr. King on January 15, 1987, I penned the following letter to Mr. Ronald Reagan in a vain effort to get the "highest" Republican endorsement possible.

Dear President Reagan:

I have just listened to your timely message on the life and contributions of the late Dr. Martin Luther King, Jr., addressed especially to high school students of our nation. Thank God, your words provided a long-awaited healing for me because I was a junior in high school when Dr. King was assassinated and was extremely and bitterly affected by both the actions and attitudes that led to Dr. King's death. As you spoke so truthfully and eloquently, I envisioned myself as a high school student listening to my President speak affirmatively and candidly about the problems, which Dr. Martin Luther King, Jr. both addressed and challenged, and the progress that our nation made in the arena of justice and equality under his leadership. Thank you, Mr. President, for your historic address about America and Dr. Martin Luther King, Jr. on his 58th birthday.

As the General Chairperson of ARIZONANS FOR A MARTIN LUTHER KING, JR. STATE HOLIDAY, I am requesting your support in our efforts to lobby our state Legislature to pass a bill, which would allow all Arizonans to observe a legal state holiday honoring Dr. King and which coincides with the Federal holiday honoring Dr. King on the third Monday in January. My specific and urgent request of you is that you would send a personal letter to each of our state senators and representatives (names and addresses enclosed) urging them to pass a bill honoring Dr. King as mentioned above.

Last year, the Arizona House of Representatives failed to pass such a bill by only two votes. Might I also suggest that in your letter of support for a state holiday in Arizona honoring Dr. King that you would include a copy of your historic address on January 15, 1987.

Thank you in advance for your support of our efforts to join, as a state, the nation in honoring Dr. Martin Luther King, Jr. Also, I would like a copy of your January 15th address for my personal files.

May God continue to bless you, your wife and family.

No response! Absolutely, no response! Of course, I know that any president receives millions of letters. But, his office is staffed with readers who single out mail that needs attention by someone in the President's Office. Surely, his office could have made some kind of response, even if it was a neutral one. However, I discovered this to be the typical Republican presidential response, because I wrote letters to then Vice President George Bush in August 1988 and President George Bush in November 1988 and July 1989 seeking "help from high places" to no avail and no response!

◇◇◇◇◇◇

Our coalition continued to meet, at least twice a month during the winter and early spring of 1987. My tasks, as general chairperson, kept me occupied on nearly a daily basis. During our February 5, 1987 meeting, we discussed the extremely important upcoming Arizona State Senate Government Committee hearing on the newly proposed MLK Day legislation. The subject of the hearing would be Senate Bill #1083 calling for an Arizona version of the federal King Day. We knew we must make a persuasive showing before the majority of Republican Senators on this committee to move forward with realizing King Day in Arizona. One of our objectives was to fill the hearing room as never before with King Day supporters and speakers. We also knew that the opposition would be there *both* in the audience and on the committee. Flyers were sent out to all organizations and persons on our mailing list urging them to attend the public hearing set for Wednesday, February 18, 1987 at 3:30 p.m. at the State Capitol.

The lot fell upon me to contact key individuals from various sectors of our community to speak in support of the Senate version of the King Day legislation at the hearing. I also had to meet with Senator John Mawhinney, chair of the Senate Government Committee, to work out details as to how the King Day supporters would present their appeals for passage. Mr. Mawhinney appeared to be a courteous politician whose politeness tempted me to let my guard down. Had I checked the record of the previous year's King Day vote in the Senate, I would have known that he deserved to be held at a distance, as a King Day nay vote. He even referred to me as "Doctor" in our communicating with one another rather than the typical "Reverend." After meeting with him, facilitated by Senator Carolyn Walker, I discovered that his primary concern was crowd control. He expressed, repeatedly, the need for order throughout the hearing. No doubt, the word had gotten to him that a mass of Black folks was coming to the Capitol to see him and his committee members about Dr. King. I assured him that he had nothing to worry about.

Nearly 36 Arizona citizens were asked to say a word for Senate Bill #1083 on that historic Wednesday afternoon. Among them were: Mr. Tony Mason, Phoenix businessman and former candidate for governor; Dr. Brooks: Attorney Albert Flores: Bishop Heistand of the Episcopal Church of Arizona: Gene Blue; the Reverend Manker; Pastor Gantt, II; Ms. Jones; Representative Kennedy; the Reverend Joedd Miller, then pastor of Central

Presbyterian Church and ardent supporter of King Day; Judge Williams; the Honorable Coy Payne, then councilman of Chandler; Mr. James Kimes, member of AFSCME and prolific letter-writer to local newspaper editors and politicians in support of King Day; the late Reverend Dudley; Mr. Fred Romero, representing labor; Mrs. Brenda Hoskins of the Unitarian Universalist Church; Ms. Cox; Rabbi Plotkin; and yours truly.

The hearing was scheduled for Senate Hearing Room #1. By the time I arrived, there was standing room only, in not one, but three Senate rooms, which had to be improvised into one large room in order to handle the over-capacity crowd. Dozens of news reporters filled the hallway and hearing room, along with television and still-shot cameras, recording devices and note pads. Being both nervous and diplomatic, I strolled up to the head table where the senators were sitting, in order to greet them and give them a list of our scheduled speakers. I politely spoke to each senator and identified myself.

I shall never forget the response I received from the late Senator Hal Runyan, a 70-year-old Republican from Litchfield Park. He had one of his familiar fancy filters holding a cigarette in his mouth. I introduced myself and he responded stoically, "I know who you are." The temperature must have dropped to below freezing at that moment as we faced one another. I proceeded to greet more friendly senators, including our Democrat allies.

The atmosphere in that room was electric and tense. First Institutional Baptist Church members comprised a large number of those present, in addition to people from all walks of life, colors, creeds, persuasions and professions. Pastors Ron Lush and Joel Eidsness, White evangelical members of a small monthly prayer fellowship, of which I was a part, stood along the wall in support of their Black brothers—King and Stewart. At least 500 people were present, waiting for the debate to begin.

The anti-King crowd was few in number. However, they had imported a "star witness" opposed to Arizona making a King Day. His name was Eldridge Cleaver, former Black Panther, ex-Communist, author of *Soul on Ice* and Black Power advocate of the 1960s. In those days, one could not find a more radical and militant Negro. But twenty years later, a "born-again" Cleaver showed up at the Arizona State Capitol as a recent convert to the Mormon faith, member of the Republican party and supporter of Evan Mecham's rescission of the Martin Luther King, Jr. Day. Once again, in an effort to be nice, I walked over to Mr. Cleaver and introduced myself and went back to the front of the hearing room.

Once the meeting got started, each side was allowed to present their speakers alternately. Of course, with the opposition there were the accusations that Dr. King was an adulterer and a Communist, therefore unworthy of a day in his honor. Cleaver stated that he had agreed with Mecham's position on the "illegal" holiday and that King Day proponents were trampling on the grave of Martin Luther King, Jr. The ex-convict also accused me of trying to "intimidate" the legislative process. The supporters trumpeted King's contributions to America through civil rights and non-violent social change. Senator Walker appeared before her colleagues and read a letter from Mrs. Coretta Scott King urging the Arizona legislators to pass the holiday honoring her late husband. Before long, the anti-King Day speakers had depleted their ranks and only pro-King Day speakers were left.

When my time came to speak, toward the beginning of the hearing, I addressed the Senate Government Committee with the following statement in its entirety.

MY STATEMENT IN SUPPORT OF THE MARTIN LUTHER KING, JR. STATE HOLIDAY BILL PRESENTED TO THE SENATE GOVERNMENT COMMITTEE

OF THE SENATE OF THE ARIZONA STATE LEGISLATURE ON WEDNESDAY, FEBRUARY 18, 1987 AT THE STATE CAPITOL IN PHOENIX, ARIZONA

Mr. Chairman and Members of the Government Committee of the Senate of Arizona:

My name is Warren H. Stewart, Sr., Pastor of the First Institutional Baptist Church of Phoenix, Arizona and General Chairperson of **ARIZONANS FOR A MARTIN LUTHER KING, JR. STATE HOLIDAY**, which is an Ad Hoc Committee, made up of citizens of Arizona of all races, creeds, colors, and political persuasions who advocate and support making the third Monday in January a state holiday honoring the life and contributions of that great American, the late Dr. Martin Luther King, Jr. We appreciate this privilege to present our case to you in the hope that when your vote is cast on Senate Bill #1083, establishing a Martin Luther King, Jr. state holiday, which will fall on the third Monday of January by combining Washington's and Lincoln's holidays into President's Day, as the Federal government has done, the majority of you will have voted in favor of the said bill as is.

Mr. Chairman and Members of the Government Committee of the Senate of Arizona, **MARTIN LUTHER KING, JR. IS AMERICA.**

Our nation's first President, George Washington, in 1787, participated in the writing of and served as a signatory on the United States Constitution, which is the supreme law of our land. In the Preamble of our Constitution, the following words were penned by our Founding Fathers,

"We the people of the United States, in order to form a more perfect Union, establish justice, insure domestic tranquility, provide for the common defense, promote the general welfare, and secure the blessings of liberty to ourselves and our posterity, do ordain and establish this Constitution of the United States of America."

Almost two hundred years after those words were written and ratified by the delegates of the first Constitutional Convention, Dr. Martin Luther King, Jr. successfully challenged our great nation to finally live up to the history principles outlined in the Preamble, in that the word "**people**" in "**We the people**" would include **every** native-born and naturalized citizen of the United States regardless of race, creed or color. Dr. King's message and movement sought to do none other than "to form a more perfect Union, establish justice, insure domestic tranquility, provide for the common defense, promote the general welfare, and secure the blessings of liberty to ourselves and our posterity" under the supreme law of the land.

MARTIN LUTHER KING, JR. IS AMERICA

On November 19, 1863, President Abraham Lincoln delivered his most memorable address on a battlefield in Pennsylvania to honor those who had lost their lives in the Civil War battle fought at that location. Please allow me to quote from the introductory paragraph of the Gettysburg Address.

"Four score and seven years ago our fathers brought forth upon this continent, a new nation, conceived in Liberty, and dedicated to the proposition that all men are created equal."

Another great American, who like Lincoln was cut down by an assassin's bullet five score and five years later, lived and died preaching the same principles of our Founding Fathers in an effort to bring forth "a new nation, conceived in Liberty, and dedication to the proposition that all men (and women) are created equal." This new nation which Martin Luther King, Jr. brought forth would soon be virtually free of all its ugly vestiges of racial bigotry and lawful discrimination. And, once and for all, members of the minority races in America could be proud of our new nation devoid of shameful segregation and societal prejudice, "forgetting those things which were behind, and pressing on toward the mark of a higher calling" to equality among all Americans.

MARTIN LUTHER KING, JR. IS AMERICA.

Every American public-school child learns to recite the Pledge of Allegiance to the American Flag, which was instituted under the Presidency of Benjamin Harrison in 1892.

"I pledge allegiance to the flag of the United States of America and to the Republic for which it stands, one Nation under God, indivisible, with liberty and justice for all."

No doubt, the dream of Martin Luther King, Jr. which he shared with both America and the world on the steps of the Lincoln Memorial in Washington, D.C. in 1963; his dream "that one day this nation (would) rise up and live out its creed of justice and liberty for all," could trace its roots to his childhood school days in a segregated school in Atlanta, Georgia as he pledged his allegiance to the flag of the United States of America every morning, even though as a child he knew that those words did not apply to him and the people of color between our shores. Yet, he pledged and he dreamed that the words "liberty and justice for all" would one day be the inalienable right and experiential privilege of every citizen of our nation.

MARTIN LUTHER KING, JR. IS AMERICA

Mr. Chairman and Members of the Government Committee of the Senate of Arizona:

It has been said that Martin Luther King, Jr. is not worthy of a national holiday as Washington and Lincoln are. Lest we forget, our first President lived and died having both supported slavery and owning slaves. President Abraham Lincoln confessed during the Civil War that he did not fight that war to free the slaves, but to save the Union.

Do you remember America *before* the Martin Luther King, Jr. era? I do. *Colored water fountains. Mandated balcony sitting. Back of the bus. Across the tracks. For Whites only. Eating in the kitchen. Carver, Washington, Dunbar and Lincoln Schools. No last names.*

Unequal opportunity. Unequal pay. No right to vote. Segregated institutions of higher learning. Cross-burnings. Nigger Lynchings. White robes and white hoods. Bull Connor's dogs. Stunning fire hoses. Bruising billy clubs. Wallace's Alabama. Maddox's Georgia. Arizona's South Phoenix. And, America's shame.

Tell me, if you can what other American in the 20th Century served as the catalyst to such positive, progressive revolutionary changes which led America to becoming "a more perfect Union?"
MARTIN LUTHER KING, JR. IS AMERICA.

Was Martin Luther King, Jr. a saint? No. Nor was Washington or Lincoln.

Was Martin Luther King, Jr. perfect? No. Is America perfect? No.

Is America closer to becoming "a more perfect Union" since Dr. Martin Luther King, Jr.? The Record speaks for him.

That is why,
MARTIN LUTHER KING, JR. IS AMERICA.

Mr. Chairman and Members of the Government Committee of the Senate of Arizona:

Establishing the third Monday of January as **Martin Luther King, Jr. Day** as outlined in Senate Bill #1083 would bring our popular, progressive and promising state in line with the majority of America. **ARIZONA** needs not *only* the Martin Luther King, Jr. state holiday, but we desperately need a renewed image which is characterized by legislative leadership which is void of any suggestions of racial bigotry and myopic and narrow political viewpoints. **ARIZONA** needs the Martin Luther King, Jr. state holiday to serve as a towering signal to the world that we are ready to move into our second seventy-five years carrying the lighted torch of inclusiveness rather than the burning cross of exclusiveness. **ARIZONA** needs the Martin Luther King, Jr. state holiday because America needs to know that **ARIZONA**

IS AMERICA just as **MARTIN LUTHER KING, JR. IS AMERICA.**

So, my fellow Arizonans, as you consider and reconsider your vote on Senate Bill #1083, be honest with yourselves if you have strongly considered voting **AGAINST** this bill, and admit that the *only* reason that you would not vote **AGAINST** this Martin Luther King, Jr. state holiday bill **is**:

NOT FISCAL, for this bill would not cost our state any more money;

NOT HISTORICAL, for the extent to which you have celebrated Washington's and Lincoln's holidays in the past shows no great allegiance to either of those great Americans;

NOT PARTISAN, for a popular Republican President signed the Federal holiday bill into law after a Republican-controlled United States Senate passed it;

NOT PATRIOTIC, for Martin Luther King, Jr. did more for America than any one of us will ever dream of doing;

NOT MORALISTIC, for the Psalmist evaluated the moral character of every one of us by proclaiming "There is none righteous; no not one."

So, my fellow Arizonans, the only reason that you would vote **AGAINST** this Martin Luther King, Jr. state holiday bill is **RACIAL**, for you are judging the man, his message, his movement and his holiday, based upon "**the color of his skin rather than the content of his character.**"

So, I strongly urge each of you to lay aside any and all un-admitted and un-confessed prejudices you might harbor in your heart, and vote **YES** for Senate Bill #1083 as is.

Thank you very much.

My speech was enthusiastically received by those in attendance. It may have impressed the opposing members of the committee, but, as I discovered later, it did not change their votes in favor of King Day. Once all the public statements for and against Senate Bill #1083 had been given and the crowd had dispersed after three hours, down to the faithful few, Chairman Mawhinney pulled a fast one. He recessed the committee's deliberations until the next day. That following morning the committee voted along party lines to defeat the Senate King Day proposal. What I later became privy to was that the Republican senators had made their minds up to vote against the bill *before* the hearing took place. In one sense, I felt we had been *used* by "Mawhinney and Company." Nevertheless, the public was able to see that the supporters outnumbered the King Day opposition by a seven to one ratio. Our historic appearance proved fruitful for us, if for no one else. We had turned out in full strength before the powers that be, poised and powerful.

Perhaps, as a show of support, the House of Representatives led by Representative Hamilton and other key leaders in the House brought their version of the King Bill to the floor for a vote. Mindful of the previous year's narrow defeat of King Day legislation by one vote, **the Arizona House of Representatives delivered a victorious vote for King Day on Thursday, February 19, 1987.** Thirty-five ayes and twenty-five nays told the story that day. That left the possibility of Arizona's first legislatively approved Martin Luther King, Jr. Day held hostage in the Senate, thanks to Senators Mawhinney, MacDonald, Brewer, Runyan, Sossaman and Stump of the Government Committee and Senate President Karl Kunasek.

Senate President Kunasek, a Republican conservative from Mesa, predicted that the House version of the King Day legislation would be killed, once it made its way from the lower chamber to his side. Furthermore, he spouted that the only acceptable compromise would be a Sunday holiday for King. All in all, Senate Minority Leader Stephens probably was correct in assessing the reason for Mawhinney's committee's defeat of the King legislation sponsored by Tucson Republican Senator Greg Lunn as "protecting the governor" who would have to sign or veto any King Day bill that passed both chambers. True to form, by the end of the 1987 Legislative Session, Arizona's King Day bill never made it to the floor of the Senate. But, rest assured, Arizona would pay out of its pocket for the bigotry of most of the Republican majority who had been elected to do what was best for their state.

On March 4, 1987, I wrote "An Open Letter to the Senate of the Arizona State Legislature." In that letter I reminded the obstinate Senate majority of the statistics *in favor of* the King holiday that they had obviously ignored from January to March of that year. Those statistics included nearly 50,000 signatures calling the governor and Legislature to make the third Monday in January MLK Day; 15,000 Arizonans of all races, creeds and colors marching in support of King Day on Monday, January 19, 1987; over 500 persons voicing their support of an Arizona King holiday in the

February Senate hearing; and the Arizona House of Representatives voting 35 to 25 in favor of the King holiday bill.

◇◇◇◇◇◇

Although the Legislature closed its doors for the remainder of 1987, our King Day coalition continued our quest for victory. In addition to keeping our efforts before the public, which was no major problem with "motor-mouth" Mecham sitting in the governor's chair, ARIZONANS FOR A MARTIN LUTHER KING, JR. STATE HOLIDAY had to make a monumental decision that would have far-reaching economic fall-out on the state that had perennially kicked around King Day. That decision and its ramifications will be discussed at length in the next chapter.

Support from various segments of the non-Black community continued to grow, thanks to the embarrassment "Mecham and Company" caused to many white Arizonans, as well as the threat of economic loss from out of state conventions canceling or not planning meetings in Arizona. However, our coalition was blessed in the early days with the talents of White clergymen, the likes of Paul Eppinger and Joedd Miller who trumpeted MLK Day to their denominational colleagues and constituents and the broader religious community in Arizona. Peter Fears, an experienced labor organizer, proved to be a valuable asset to our cause with local, county, statewide and even national labor union contacts. Professor Mark Reader brought an intense introspective philosophical and political perspective to our deliberations. In many respects, Mark served as our prophetic conscience, warning constantly that "we must take what is ours, rather than wait for someone in authority to give King Day to us." I have already mentioned the late Jennie Cox from the Arizona Democratic Party. James Kimes from labor continued to volunteer hundreds of hours pushing for MLK Day. Although Tommie Espinoza could not make it to a lot of our meetings, he pledged and delivered in garnering support from the Hispanic community. Attorney Flores allowed his law partner, Christopher Johns, to use his time and expertise, as well as their law office's resources to make sure we were within the law, in whatever we did.

Continuing unsolicited publicity spotlighted my leadership role in the King Day fight. I was often puzzled as to the attention directed my way. For example, even though we failed to get Mecham to change his mind about rescinding Babbitt's King Day order and the Senate balked on following the House's lead in March 1987, the news media, especially the newspapers, headlined my actions on various occasions. A case in point was my being given the Roy Wilkins Award on April 10, 1987, by the Maricopa County branch of the NAACP. Very seldom, in the past, had the media highlighted the recipient of that veteran civil rights organization's highest honor. But that year, *The Arizona Republic, The Phoenix Gazette* and a couple of other Valley newspapers did so, with action photos and headlines.

In reviewing one article while writing this book, I was quoted talking about the struggle for liberation in South Africa, where I had first visited on a preaching mission in 1985 sponsored by the National Baptist Convention USA, Inc. In retrospect, it was almost a prophecy when I mused to a *Republic* reporter, "I keep a gold and brown rock, which I picked up in South Africa, near my Bible (in my office). Each day, I look at the rock, and I pray that the people who have suffered so much will own that country again. I have faith that that day will come. When it does, I want to put that rock in my pocket and take it back to South Africa. I want to celebrate with them some day."

Praise God, in 1998 I made my reservations to return to the Republic of South Africa and join Nelson Mandela and 25 million Black South Africans in celebrating their liberation from racist apartheid.

During the latter part of April 1987, one of our meetings raised the question, "Where Do We Go From Here: Celebration, Continuation, or Cessation?" Faithfully, we chose *continuation*. To keep the dream alive, a prayer vigil was held at the MLK Memorial in Wesley Bolin Plaza at the State Capitol on the anniversary of Martin Luther King's assassination. Also, our secretary and neophyte political aspirant herself, Mildred Jones, traveled to Black Mesa in northern Arizona for a Native American- sponsored MLK prayer vigil, held on the same day-April 4, 1987. To aid our cause, the Phoenix Monarchs Alumni Association, a group of African-Americans, who formerly attended the segregated Carver High School in Phoenix, planned a "Freedom Ride" during their annual weekend reunion May 16-17, 1987. Some of the proceeds from their event would be directed our way.

◇◇◇◇◇

Bowing to *pressure* from Mecham's earlier remarks that did *not* exist or were not anything to be worried about, Arizona's embattled chief executive proclaimed a Martin Luther King, Jr.-Civil Rights Day for the third *Sunday* in January, commencing the next year. His press release dated June 18, 1987 read in part:

Martin Luther King, Jr. has become the symbol of a civil rights commitment. All civil rights activists, black and white, past, present and future, are intended to be honored by this proclamation.

A motivation for this proclamation is to remove a major impediment to cooperation in the legislative process between partisan legislators, and a signal that everyone is urged to participate in Arizona's very exciting future.

The words, "very exciting future" were indeed an understatement for what was down the road for Governor Mecham and King Day. Rest assured, for a man who had said in March 1987 in response to convention cancellations due to his rescission of King Day, "Anybody we lose will easily be offset by somebody we'll gain." This was a giant step for Mecham. But, for ARIZONANS FOR A MARTIN LUTHER KING, JR. STATE HOLIDAY, it was a step in the *wrong* direction.

First of all, we had been down that road before with Arizona legislators who wanted King Day supporters to settle for "a separate but unequal" holiday. We told them to "shove it." The whole purpose of the Civil Rights Movement was to win equal rights for persons of color and to make illegal the myth of "separate but equal" laws of discrimination, which had crowded America's legal system for two centuries. Consequently, a *Sunday* King Day was an insult to King's legacy and us.

Secondly, Mr. Mecham's proclamation nowhere mentioned the words "legal holiday." Nor was his proclamation attested to by the secretary of state, as was his predecessor's executive order. A matter of fact, the space on Mecham's June 18, 1987 proclamation for the secretary of state's signature was left blank. And, as most of us know, sitting governors pronounce public relations proclamations for a myriad of special events and causes from "Healthy Heart Week" to "Arizona Ostrich Month."

A precursor to this public relations stunt to still the troubled waters was Mecham's growing impatience with being beat over the head constantly by the media with what his King Day stance was doing to the state's image and tourism industry. In an *Arizona Republic* article dated June 5, 1987, the headline read, "Mecham 'sick' of King furor." The first three paragraphs of that article read:

Gov. Evan Mecham saying he is "totally sick" of the "rhubarb" over his cancellation of a state holiday for the Rev. Dr. Martin Luther

King, Jr., told hotel officials Thursday that it is time for Arizonans to stop allowing outside groups to put pressure on the state.

"It's nobody else's business," Mecham said. "Don't we have guts enough and concern enough in our self-pride that we can determine things for ourself within Arizona?"

"Are we such a bunch of wimps that we listen to people who say, 'We're going to come in from the outside and tell you how to run your political machinery in Arizona?' To me, I find that totally unacceptable."

I guess one could say, "If socially conscious organizations *not* coming to Arizona to hold their meetings was *unacceptable* to Governor Mecham, then his impotent, unattested *Sunday* King Day proclamation proved *unacceptable* to us! Art Hamilton was not impressed and called the move "a slipshod, last-minute political gimmick." Senator Walker gave Mecham a little more credit for trying to put out some of the fire his rescission had ignited.

Mr. Ed Buck, founder of the Mecham Recall Drive, which will be discussed in another chapter, put his reaction to Mecham's proclamation like this, "Mr. Mecham has just created the state's first non-holiday." Of course, the tourism people were cautiously optimistic that this move would end the increasing flight of convention business away from Arizona.

An editorial in the June 19, 1987 issue of *The Arizona Republic* offered subdued commendation for Mecham, at least, doing something to change his mind and do something to patch up the damage already done by his rescinding Arizona's King Day. Thank goodness, though, the editorial echoed our coalition's sentiments that King deserved more than "a middle of the racial bus" holiday. However, no one put it so vividly as Benson, the editorial cartoonist for *The Arizona Republic* in his June 19, 1987 cartoon depicting Mecham driving a 1950s bus for the "Whitehound Lines" with Dr. King sitting in the back of the bus in the Sunday-designated seating.

One thing that Mecham's move did was to renew our commitment to press the 1988 Legislature to pass a state holiday honoring MLK on the third Monday in January. We knew we had much work to do as we went into hibernation for the remaining Arizona summer months until September rolled around.

◇◇◇◇◇

Come September we called together our troops to discuss new and renewed strategies to win a Martin Luther King, Jr. state holiday. Of the many King Day-related events that had taken place throughout the summer of 1987, there were the increasing convention cancellations, a feature story for *JET*, the nation's leading weekly Black magazine, and contributions pledged and/or received from several popular R&B and Rock groups, including Kool & the Gang and BOSTON. As the large contributions began to come to us from entertainers who did not cancel their engagements in Arizona, but rather chose to make a statement in support of our efforts, we took steps to become a non-profit corporation.

Another significant contact came from the Arizona Chamber of Commerce, which finally voted to push for a King holiday. Up until that time and even afterward, the Arizona business community ignored our coalition's efforts. To many of them, King Day was still "a Black thing." I remember writing a letter to every member of the Phoenix 40, a local group of corporate and business leaders who had become known as the most powerful group of "movers and shakers", in Arizona, *and only one* responded that year. *His was a familiar name in Arizona—the late Eddie Basha.* His affirmative response of support was written at the bottom of my letter to him on our coalition's letterhead.

Over the summer, I had done a lot of thinking about what we could do to move this holiday through the Legislature victoriously. Other than those who opposed the King holiday based on racism and bigotry, perhaps, we could remove most major impediments for potentially supportive legislators to convert their nay votes to aye votes. After reviewing the various versions of King Day legislation had sponsored, I came up with what I called "a WIN-WIN COMPROMISE", which eventuated in a slightly revised form that was approved by a vote of the people in 1992. Shortly after this promising proposal hit me, I phoned Art and shared it with him. He became excited about its possibilities and encouraged me to present it to the coalition.

In a nutshell, here is what the "WIN-WIN COMPROMISE" consisted of and the accompanying rationale. My suggestion was that the third Monday in January of every year be designated Martin Luther King, Jr./ Civil Rights Day; and that the third Monday in February be designated as George Washington/Abraham Lincoln Day. By combining MLK Day with Civil Rights Day into one paid state holiday, Arizona would not only join the nation in honoring the monumental contributions of Martin Luther King, Jr. to the advancement of civil rights in America, but we would honor all Americans—local, state, national, past, present and future; regardless of race, creed or color—who advocate civil rights for all persons. By combining

George Washington Day and Abraham Lincoln Day, then celebrated separately in Arizona, into one holiday, we would continue to honor each of these presidents *by name* without the additional costs of establishing a paid state holiday honoring Martin Luther King, Jr. and Civil Rights.

This compromise was fiscally conservative in that it created no additional paid holiday. Dr. King would *share* his day with all advocates of civil rights, and that was different from all other legislative proposals to date. Plus, our two greatest presidents would be remembered by name and not lumped into a generic President's Day as the federal government had done. To me, this proposal eliminated the non-racist and non-bigoted opposition to Martin Luther King, Jr. Day. Once the committee heard my "WIN-WIN COMPROMISE" the coalition adopted it as our official proposal for the 1988 Legislative Session.

By the fall of 1987, ARIZONANS FOR A MARTIN LUTHER KING, JR. STATE HOLIDAY began to join hands with the Phoenix MLK Celebration

Committee to plan for a major King Day March in January 1988. We sent out letters to local, state and national organizations and leaders soliciting their presence and show of support for our battle by participating in our celebration-protest. Our goal was to get 20,000 persons to gather that day and have full participation of city and state organizations. We sent out 236 letters to mostly African-American national organizations and received several responses.

Friday, November 13, 1987 proved *not* to be an unlucky day for Dr. King's cause and our statewide cause. Comedian and movie star, Eddie Murphy, had scheduled a comedy concert at the Veteran's Memorial Coliseum in Phoenix. As a result of the growing entertainer's boycott of Arizona, the Murphy agents had contacted the Martin Luther King, Jr. Center for Non-Violent Social Change in Atlanta about their upcoming appearance. Mrs. King's chief assistant contacted me about Murphy's coming to Arizona and mentioned that he wanted to make a contribution to the King Center and our efforts to win the holiday.

Once the logistics were worked out, I attended the concert with a VIP pass accompanied by our attorney Chris Johns. We had been informed that Martin Luther King, III would be present to receive the donation on behalf of the King Center. All I had to do was pick up a check backstage. As much as I hate to say it, that night Murphy told some of the filthiest jokes I have ever heard. No ethnic group, profession, male or female or sexual orientation was off limits. I am glad I arrived at the concert for its last fifteen minutes, thanks to a warning from a friend. As he finished his risqué routine, Martin III was introduced and escorted on stage. Murphy made a few jokes about Arizona's governor mishandling the MLK Day and then spoke laudably of Dr. King. He then presented Martin Luther King's eldest son with a check.

I later made it to the backstage suite where Murphy and his entourage were doing whatever stars and company do backstage. His strong, muscular Black bodyguards stood alert throughout the several rooms. Martin Luther King, III was in one of the rooms. Several attractive sisters sat around. Mr. Murphy had reclusively moved in his special dressing room. Feeling uncomfortable and slightly anxious, I was glad when one of Eddie's agents sought me out, along with Martin III. To my surprise, he told us both that Eddie wanted to make a contribution for the cause of King in the amount of *$100,000!* Trying desperately not to faint and leap for joy, I looked at Dr. King's namesake son to get a cue from his response. He appeared to be somewhat surprised about the amount. Then the agent said to both of us, "You two decide how you want it split." After conferring a few moments with Mr. King and Christopher, we agreed on a 75/25 split-the King Center would get $75,000 and ARIZONANS FOR A MARTIN LUTHER KING, JR. STATE HOLIDAY would receive $25,000. Until that Friday the 13th, the two largest donations to our coalition had come from First Institutional and the BOSTON Rock Group. Once we told Eddie's agent what we had decided, he hand-wrote a check to our coalition for $25,000. He did likewise for the King Center in the designated amount. As we were leaving, Chris asked me if I had noticed who else was in Murphy's suite. I responded in the negative. He then informed me that he thought Minister Louis Farrakhan and his wife had just walked past me. I felt kind of dumb until Chris informed me that the person who looked like Farrakhan was not dressed in his regular two-piece suit, white shirt and trademark Nation of Islam bow tie. On the other hand, I probably would not have noticed my own father due to the state of shock I was in after receiving $25,000. Thank God, it came at the right time because we were about to retain V&L Enterprises, an African-American public relations media marketing firm, to create a commercial and a newspaper ad for our efforts to gain some King Day votes in the 1988 Legislative Session.

Within four days, I wrote letters of appreciation to Eddie Murphy for his "extremely generous donation" and to Mrs. King, who had suggested that Mr. Murphy share some of his proceeds from his Phoenix concert with ARIZONANS FOR A MARTIN LUTHER KING, JR. STATE HOLIDAY. One line in my appreciation letter to Mrs. King read, "Thank you very much 25,000 times." I also added a P.S. that it was a privilege to meet her son, Martin Luther King, III.

Also, the 1987 Inaugural Martin Luther King, Jr. Prayer Breakfast, sponsored by the Celebration Committee, invited my personal friend and mentor, the Reverend Dr. J. Alfred Smith, Sr., then pastor of the Allen Temple Baptist Church of Oakland and then president of the Progressive National Baptist Convention, which was co-founded by Dr. King. The breakfast was held on December 17, 1987 at the First Baptist Church of Phoenix where Dr. Eppinger served as pastor. The previous Martin Luther King, Jr. Prayer Breakfast had been held at First Institutional Baptist Church. By moving such an event out of the Black community, we hoped to broaden our base of support. After all, Martin Luther King, Jr. had been dually aligned with the Progressive National Baptist Convention, which was predominantly Black, and the American Baptist Churches U.S.A. which was predominantly White. Dr. Smith delivered a thought-provoking, eloquent message, and sent King Day backers away from the North Central Avenue church, recharged for the next year's battle.

As we moved out of 1987 into 1988, I received another honor due to my King Day efforts. The Honorable George Schultz, Secretary of State of the United States, invited me to attend the State Department's reception honoring Dr. Martin Luther King Jr. to be held on Tuesday, January 17, 1988, in Washington, D.C. I accepted. While in D.C., I met Mrs. King who was sitting beside her late husband's sister, Mrs. Christine King Farris, whom I had met on a previous occasion at the Second Baptist Church of Los Angeles. This is where we both had been invited to speak on the same Sunday. Upon seeing me, Mrs. Farris remarked, "We thank you for the great work you're doing in Arizona." Then, as I began to thank Mrs. King for the assistance she and her office had provided us, she interrupted me with these words, "No, no, we thank you, for we can only do so much as outsiders to your state. It is you and your group that must deal first-hand with your governor and legislators in Arizona."

The MLK Time Capsule Ceremony in the nation's capital was held while I was in Washington, D.C. Thousands of names inscribed on a time capsule, including several Arizonans, were lowered into a capsule to be opened on January 15, 2088. I witnessed and/or met several prominent

African-Americans, including: Samuel Pierce, Jr., then Secretary of HUD; former Congressman Walter Fauntnoy; and U.S. Representative John Lewis; former Washington, D.C. Mayor Marion Barry; Dr. Joseph Lowery, President of SCLC[and members of the King family.

Later that evening, at Secretary of State George Schultz's reception, his remarks included a powerful statement that I wish Governor Mecham and our state legislators could have heard directly from him. He said, "Dr. King validated the Constitution of the United States, which had not been in effect before his Civil Rights Movement."

How ironic it was that on January 12, 1988, the nation's leaders, including then President Reagan, stopped to honor a great American by the name of Dr. Martin Luther King, Jr., while one year prior to the day, Governor Mecham became infamous around the world by rescinding the Martin Luther King, Jr. state holiday in Arizona.

◇◇◇◇◇◇

The third federal observance of Dr. King's birthday rolled around and the weather in Arizona was terrible. Wind, rain and cold—all of course, *relatively cold* compared to most of the country. We did not get our 20,000 marchers, but there were thousands who braved the elements to send *another* message to our now beleaguered governor, who unbeknown to him was serving his *last* January in office, and the Legislature, which would have another opportunity to right a wrong that had been done not only to King's legacy but to the entire state. Monday, January 18, 1988 proved to be a great day for King Day proponents. Headlines describing our protest march and King Day celebration read, "Marchers Brave Rain to Honor Martin Luther King", "Wind and rain thrash King procession", and (with) "Wind against their 'sails' King marchers pressed on to the Capitol."

For one reason or another, we did not get the physical presence of the national civil rights leaders we invited to attend, but somehow we felt they were with us. Of those who did come, the list included Bill Lucy, secretary-treasurer of AFSCME International and Norman Hill, executive director of the A. Phillip Randolph Institute. Once we arrived at Wesley Bolin Plaza, the scheduled speakers did their best to speak persuasively in spite of the rain that continued to shower our bodies, but not our spirits. Senator De Concini joined us in the trek as it neared the Capitol. Mayor Goddard kept in step with us, from the beginning to the end, as he had every year from the first march. Tommie Espinoza filled in his *regular* front row spot, along with the King Day veteran warriors—Hamilton, Walker, Goode, Blue, members of the clergy and the parade marshals.

The subject of my remarks that day fell under the title, "An Open Letter to the People of Arizona." Throughout that speech I endeavored to respond to Governor Mecham's recent open confession that he had made some mistakes as governor, for which the citizens of Arizona had reaped the consequences. I particularly said, "We respond by thanking Governor Mecham for placing his handling of the Martin Luther King, Jr. state holiday 'first and foremost' on his list of 'mistakes which may have sparked embarrassing publicity for our state.'"

By that time, in his second year in office; Mecham was facing a recall, calls for his resignation, impeachment, and a possible indictment. Consequently, the pressure upon him had become excruciating and he made some emotional admissions of "political missteps." In that speech, *I* also apologized for statements made by King Day supporters, including myself, reacting in anger to Mecham's words and actions toward Martin Luther King, Jr. From that point, I challenged the governor and Arizona State Legislature to support our "WIN-WIN COMPROMISE", which would honor Washington and Lincoln by name, civil rights, Dr. King—and not cost an extra penny.

As I concluded with a wet sheet of paper in my hand, I proclaimed, "With this proposal, our divided and embarrassed state can unite as brothers and sisters of the same human family, as citizens of a state that advocates 'justice, liberty and equality for all, regardless of race, creed or color.'"

I continued, "In closing, let us join together, Arizona, hand-in-hand and heart-in-heart, building on our past mistakes by establishing a noble present; and charting the course for a brighter and better future for ourselves and our children."

◇◇◇◇◇◇

The time had come to deal with the unyielding Republican members of the Arizona State Senate. Between the closing day of the 1987 session and the opening day of the 1988 session, several alternative King Day bills had been floated. There were those like Senator Peter Kay who wanted to refer the King Day to the voters, as no other holiday had ever been referred. Others promoted the "cafeteria style" where state employees could pick and choose which holidays they wished to observe; and King Day would be one of their choices. The question I kept raising to these senators marching to different drumbeats than the converted House of Representatives was, "Why all the special treatment for the King holiday issue in Arizona?" In the heat of informed "righteous indignation" I answered my own question in a letter to the Editor of *The Arizona Republic* written on December 15, 1987. Excerpts from that letter read,

> The honest answer is that the King holiday honors a *Black* American who confronted the ugliness of this nation's history of racism and discrimination, and effected a positive change that enabled Americans to better live up to the principles espoused in our Constitution.

Continuing, I asked another question,

> Why don't those who label the King holiday issue "very controversial," "artificial and inappropriate"...admit the honest reason they oppose our state's joining more than 40 other states and the nation in honoring Dr. King with a paid holiday?

During the last week of October, I had written all of the legislators a detailed letter outlining our "WIN-WIN COMPROMISE." We also held a press conference that same week to inform the media and public on our desire to offer a proposal that "all parties sincerely interested in restoring the positive and progressive image of Arizona (could) and should unite" around. Once again the news media provided excellent coverage for our announcement. Also, knowing that legislators are known for not formally responding to non-constituents letters, I was surprised to receive a few interesting responses, primarily from King Day opponents. The first was a detailed two-page letter from Senator Jeffrey J. Hill, a Republican conservative from District Nine in Tucson. His letter began, "I received your letter on the "WIN-WIN COMPROMISE" on the Martin Luther King Holiday. Unfortunately, I cannot see how this is a "WIN-WIN" for Arizona and must decline your proposal." He then embarked on a one-sided historical diatribe about Lincoln Day, honoring the Founder of the Republican Party, the Civil War, the Whigs and Abolitionists, Arizona's first Territorial Governor, Presidents Taft and Teddy Roosevelt, and Barry Goldwater. Next, he invited me to visit the Lincoln Memorial in Washington, D.C. and reminded me that "Lincoln graces our pennies", and that he thusly should continue to be honored in Arizona. As he concluded his epistle, he wrote, "Dr. Stewart, as you push for this legislation to outlaw February 12th from our state holiday lists, I urge you to reconsider and invite you to attend each of the three Lincoln Day dinners I try to attend in the three counties I represent, Pima, Santa Cruz and Cochise." His last sentence chastised, "I suggest we stop this nonsense of pitting one group against the other and support the Gubernatorial Proclamation recently signed by Governor Mecham…" Whew!

Senator Kay responded much, much more succinctly by soliciting my support for his legislation to put the King Day issue before the electorate. House of Representative legislator Jim Green returned the original copy of my letter to him with the following note inscribed in felt pen green on it, "I've been an MLK, Jr. day supporter as I'm sure you know. I believe Senator DeLong has a superior WIN/WIN approach that I intend to support." Senator DeLong's proposal was the "cafeteria plan" for the holiday. Representative Mark Killian, a former King Day opponent from ultra-conservative Mesa, wrote an encouraging letter although it was dated "November 18, 1876." He promised to share our proposal with people in his district and in his final sentence, he inscribed, "I appreciate your efforts to mitigate the current situation and I hope for the good of all Arizona we can resolve the current differences." Mark Killian had come a long way. Senator Stephens, a strong King Day supporter, not only thanked me for our proposal, but recommitted to co-sponsoring *our* "WIN-WIN COMPROMISE."

On November 12, 1987, I wrote a letter to President Carl Kunasek in an effort to get him to reason with King Day supporters on this issue and to inquire as to why it was getting such "special treatment." To my amazement, Kunasek responded directly to me in a thoughtful letter dated December 7, 1987. Its second paragraph read thusly,

> To address your question, "Why all the special treatment for the King holiday issue in Arizona?" Specifically, the answer is that there are legislators who are willing to compromise and submit a variation to the proposals that have been offered to the Legislature in the past. Since those past efforts have been unsuccessful, it is my opinion those several legislators you referred to are willing to compromise. It would be my request to you that you approach the table in a spirit of compromise, and Arizona could possibly join the other states in their recognition of Dr. King. It takes both sides to effect a compromise.

The last two sentences of the President of the Senate seemed to open a door that *he* had shut that previous spring by not allowing the House version of the King bill to be voted upon in his chamber. I accepted his invitation on behalf of our coalition, and his office scheduled a meeting for our coalition leaders with him and Senator Robert Usdane, the Senate Majority Leader, on Thursday, January 7, 1988.

In preparation for our promising meeting, I arranged a briefing meeting with Representatives Hamilton and Kennedy, Senator Walker, and Gene Blue. Once getting cued by the "pros in politics", Representative Kennedy, Pastor Eppinger, Mr. Blue and myself met at the Capitol to talk with the two leading men in the Arizona State Senate. After the formalities, we got down to business in reviewing our proposal. Quite honestly, Senator Usdane's "unfamiliarity" with the federal model of our King Day proposal caught me off guard. Even though he had voted for King Day legislation in the past, he stayed on the fence as the bill languished in the Senate a few months before. He claimed that he did not realize that the House-approved legislation would not cost any additional money to taxpayers. He then said before our delegation that he could support our proposal. On the other hand, Senator Kunasek expressed the typical Republican concerns about Abraham Lincoln not retaining a separate day and told us in a respectable tone that his constituents did not support Martin Luther King, Jr. Day; therefore, neither could he. Senator Usdane suggested that we try to meet with Burt Kruglick, state chairman of the Republican Party, to talk about our compromise and the Republican Party's resolution on Lincoln Day. Usdane even offered to arrange such a meeting.

Another senatorial concern came up in that meeting about Dr. King's alleged contact with the Communist Party. My oral and written response to each of the senators was that we did not feel that Congress and the President of the United States would have passed into law such a holiday had sufficient evidence existed to prove that Dr. King was a Communist. In the meantime, Senator Kay's Martin Luther King, Jr. referendum bill was scheduled for a hearing and we were to make contact with Usdane to get him to get Kay to hold his referendum resolution. The Senate eventually decisively voted down Kay's proposal.

Our inside sources informed us that we had thirteen King Day votes in the Senate. Sixteen would be needed to pass the bill already approved by the House of Representatives. We targeted four moderate Republican senators, namely: Jacque Steiner, Bill DeLong, John Mawhinney and Robert

Usdane. Senator Tony West, a pro-life, pro-King Day senator, had to cancel a meeting with us, but I ran into him in the hallway of the Senate, and he said his vote was yes on King Day. Senator DeLong pledged that he had a practice of taking a poll of people in his district and would vote accordingly. Senator Mawhinney reminded us that this issue had to be settled and that he might vote for our compromise bill. Senator Steiner, with ties to the business community, vowed that she would vote her heart, but that her Party was against King Day. We assumed that Senator Usdane was an aye vote after the comments to us in our January seventh meeting with him and Kunasek.

While our politicking was going on in the first month of January, the House of Representatives received a recommendation from their special prosecutor that Governor Evan Mecham be *impeached*. It was a grim Friday afternoon on *January 15, 1988*, the actual birthday of Martin Luther King, Jr. that Evan Mecham heard the bad news. To make matters worse, on *January 18, 1988*, the third national observance of the King holiday, enough signatures were certified by the Secretary of State of Arizona to mandate a *recall* election of Governor Mecham. Shortly thereafter, Mecham had to step down from office temporarily and the secretary of state, Rose Mofford, became Arizona's Acting Governor.

Arizona's first woman governor promised to provide "forceful" gubernatorial leadership, which would head Arizona in a critically needed "healing" process. She stated furthermore that "a resolution to the Martin Luther King, Jr. state holiday issue would be a major objective of hers as Acting Governor. Upon hearing that, I fired her off a letter detailing our "WIN-WIN COMPROMISE." We kept in close contact with her two hastily selected aides, Acting Chief of Staff Andrew Hurwitz and Acting Spokesperson Athia Hardt. Speaking of Athia Hardt, we had gotten wind that her father was wavering on our King Day legislation, even though he was a long-time Democrat. The problem stemmed from opposition to King Day, which he was receiving from some of his rural, conservative constituents from the Globe and Holbrook areas in his District Four. So, Senator Hardt got *another* one of our compromise letters, which buoyed him up to maintain his support on our issue.

With a goal to increase public support for our "WIN-WIN COMPROMISE", our coalition contracted V&L Enterprises, an African-American owned marketing, advertising and promotions agency headed by Vernon L. Bolling, to serve as our agent to produce a 30-second public service announcement for radio and television spots and an ad for local print media.

The money Eddie Murphy and a few other entertainers had donated to ARIZONANS FOR A MARTIN LUTHER KING, JR. STATE HOLIDAY came in handy because none of us realized how expensive producing, airing and/or printing commercials and ads are. Being the civic-minded Black journalist he is, having gained much experience by hosting Phoenix's only weekly television talk show focusing on issues affecting the African-American community on a local news station, Mr. Bolling donated his professional services and was able to produce what we wanted for $10,000.

The main message of our commercials communicated that the Martin Luther King, Jr. Day had been approved by the U.S. Congress, signed by President Reagan, was not a Black holiday, but for all Americans, over 40 states already observed it and our coalition's proposal would honor King, civil rights, our two greatest presidents by name and would not cost us one extra cent. It concluded with a rhetorical statement and question, "The Dream lives across this nation and should live in Arizona, as well. Why not a King Day in Arizona?"

The responses we received from people who saw it during February were positive. Of course, we usually did not hear directly from the anti-King Day forces. With the acting governor coming out in favor of the holiday and getting lots of publicity, the timing of our advertisements could not have been better. Moreover, polls by independent researches tracked an increasing level of support for King Day once people understood our proposal would not cost taxpayers any more money.

The meeting with Republican State Party Chairman Kruglick took place on February 2, 1988, in the former annex of the First Institutional Baptist Church. We had invited Ed Reed, a prominent Black Republican, to join us in our meeting. Our coalition was represented by Christopher Johns, Paul Eppinger, Henry Barnwell, Gene Blue and myself. Kruglick heard our compromise proposal and remarked that he had problems with combining Washington and Lincoln Days into one for the MLK Day. I could understand his concerns, since his Party had voted the previous year that Babbitt's King Day executive order was illegal; that the people of Arizona ought to vote on this issue; and that the Arizona State Legislature must maintain Lincoln's separate holiday. However, Mr. Kruglick said that he would talk our compromise over with Senators Steiner, Mawhinney, DeLong and others, and suggested that we continue our one-on-one conversations.

Arizona's first African-American woman senator, Carolyn Walker, kept us abreast of the King Day movement in the Senate. In spite of the political upheaval the state was going through with former Governor Mecham, the MLK legislation slowly etched its way through the Senate. On April 14, 1988, just ten days after Mecham was convicted on two Articles of Impeachment by the State Senate, the Senate Government Committee *passed* our MLK/Civil Rights Day bill by a five to four vote with Republicans Mawhinney and Carol MacDonald joining the three Democrats—Lela Alston, Jesus Higuera and Alan Stephens—in favor. Miracles still happen!

Next, the challenge to get the entire Senate to say yes to MLK/Civil Rights Day still lingered before us. The Arizona Ecumenical Council sent out a letter urging its delegates to write or call their respective senators to lobby for passage of Senate Bill #1255. Their reasoning was that the King Day would witness appreciation for the MLK legacy on the non-violent civil rights struggle in America, provide a symbol for spiritual and social healing and reconciliation in Arizona, and bring our state into line with the federal government and most other states. By the way, early on, very little, if any support for Arizona's MLK Day came from the evangelical and charismatic communities. I remember, during the holiday struggle, I was asked to guest host the local Trinity Broadcast's Friday "Praise the Lord Program." Upon arriving, I was firmly instructed by the station manager "not to talk politics on the show and to stick to the Savior."

Within days of the Arizona Ecumenical Council letter, the Arizona Chamber of Commerce sent out a letter to its members informing them of the content of Senate Bill #2105. They reminded their constituents that their board of directors had unanimously endorsed a state holiday for Martin Luther King, Jr. modeled after the federal legislation. Their letter expressed belief that "this issue should be settled (that) year by the State Legislature" so all of Arizona could "advance toward the 21st Century." In their significant letter to members statewide, a paragraph of prophecy was included which read,

> The State Senate has taken the first step to address the issue...
> (But Senate Bill 1255) now faces an uncertain fate on its way
> to the Senate floor for a vote. First, the bill must pass the Senate
> Rules Committee and Majority Party Caucus.

To say the least, the dark clouds began to overshadow the rising of a new King Day in Arizona.

Senate President Kunasek single-handedly dashed our hopes for a legislatively-approved King Day in Arizona by pigeonholing the measure in the Senate Rules Committee, which he chaired, on the pretext that it did not have enough votes to forward the bill to the full Senate. One letter to an editor that I saw; summed up Kunasek's maneuvering like this: "The Rules Committee exists to screen bills for their constitutionality and statutory form. The King bill measures up, and King Kunasek ought to step down from his throne."

AFSCME sent out a newsletter to its members urging them to call Kunasek's office and request that "he do the right and proper thing..." for the MLK/Civil Rights Day bill. Arizona's top religious leaders met with Senator Usdane on May 17, 1988, urging Republican Senators to approve the King Holiday. The delegation included Bishop Heistand, Bishop Thomas O'Brien, the Reverends Arthur Harrington, Gary Skinner, Philip Poirier, Raymond Manker and Carl Wallen. They were assured that the King Day legislation "would go through the political process", whatever that meant. Editorials in the state's major newspapers urged the Senate to "let this be the year."

All the positive lobbying would be to no avail. Partisan politics came into play toward the end of the longest ever legislative session in the history of Arizona. The Democrats and Republicans in the Senate squared off at one another over a difficult 202.5 million dollar tax increase and our King Day compromise was killed in the battle by a 16 to 14 vote. Senators MacDonald and Mawhinney, who had voted for the bill in the Government Committee, changed their votes to 'no'. Usdane also joined 13 other Republicans to torpedo the King Day legislation we had worked so hard on. Thank God for Republican Senators Steiner, West and Lunn who united with the eleven Democrats in the Senate to support our bill, even though it was a losing effort.

I was infuriated, especially with Usdane and Mawhinney who, to me, had just become "political jerks" for their betrayal of promises in support of King Day to its supporters! Mawhinney blamed his no vote on his anger with the Democrats who tried to "blackmail" GOP senators. He huffed and puffed that "nobody pushes him around." MacDonald pouted that she did not like the way things happened and changed her vote to a 'no' even though she "still supported the concept" of King Day.

Regrettably, as I told *JET*, after the tragic defeat of King Day once again,

> The Arizona State Senate could have closed the final chapter on the very negative, ugly Mecham era. But now they have begun to

write their own chapter of anti-civil rights, anti-Martin Luther King, anti-minority, by defeating the King bill without having Mecham as a scapegoat.

In haste to express my anger toward Mawhinney, Usdane and Kunasek, I dictated letters to each, with excerpts from the letters provided below.

To Mr. Mawhinney I wrote, "It is with much regret that I witnessed you change your 'yes' vote in support of the Martin Luther King, Jr. state holiday to a 'no' vote…You argued that you were upset with the 'process'. I suppose the late Dr. Martin Luther King, Jr. had problems with the process that allowed, in America, legal discrimination, institutionalized racism, and which ultimately led to his assassination. Nevertheless, he voted 'yes' for civil rights, equality, and justice with his most valuable possession—his life—in spite of the 'process'."

My invective to Mr. Usdane read like this in its entirety. "In our meeting with you and Senator Carl J. Kunasek in his office on January 7, 1988, *you* said that you would support the Martin Luther King, Jr./Civil Rights Day proposal in this session. Regrettably, you voted 'no', thusly not keeping your word.…How tragic!"

Mr. Kunasek was not to be left out as I reminded him of his mentioning of the word compromise on the MLK issue. "Dear Senator Kunasek:…We delivered, but you did not.…Not only did you cancel a second meeting with us this past spring, but it appears that you did nothing to facilitate the process to get the King bill to the Senate floor for a vote.…You and the majority of the Senate Republicans sent a loud and clear message to the minorities of the state and the nation about your commitment to civil rights and equality."

None of the three responded to my letters. However, on the same day I wrote the aforementioned letters, I also sent appreciation letters to Senators Alston, Stephens, Rios, Osborn, Walker, Peña, Henderson, Gabaldon, Hardt, Gutierrez and Higuera for their yes votes on MLK/Civil Rights Day, and wished them all "a blessed summer."

Ironically, one other letter was mailed by me that day to the Editor of the Editorial Pages of *The Arizona Republic*. Being super-sensitive after a shocking loss of a "promised" King Day, I chided the editor for writing in his supportive editorial about "the King Day flip-flop" that "the Senate also stuck its thumb in the eye of Black Arizona, refusing again to commemorate…King…" My point was—the continual reference to the MLK issue as a "black" issue fed into the opposition's hands, which still perceived King Day as "a Black holiday" rather than the American holiday it was. I received a "hot" response from Mr. William P. Cheshire, then Editor, and eventually we met for lunch, talked over our differences, and became regular lunch buddies and friends, agreeing on MLK, a common pro-life position, and a few more issues here and there. Importantly, Bill Cheshire and the Phoenix Newspapers continued to provide unwavering editorial backing for Arizona's Martin Luther King, Jr./Civil Rights Day.

In a press conference called by our coalition on July 11, 1988, ARIZONANS FOR A MARTIN LUTHER KING, JR. STATE HOLIDAY blasted the "turncoat" GOP senators. We also pledged to continue to support conventions, organizations and entertainers who chose to boycott Arizona due to the continued refusal to honor Martin Luther King, Jr. with his day. In addition, we reminded the public that a recent poll revealed that 69% of Phoenix metropolitan residents favored the federal model of King Day, which had just been defeated. The poll further showed that in a little over a year, support for King Day had increased in the Valley by 21% from 48% in February 1987. The sad part about this information is that it had been released on June 20, 1988, several days *prior* to the Senate defeating King Day legislation.

Governor Mofford, in the wake of this first King Day defeat under her administration, explored options she could take to honor King in spite of what happened. She and her staff weighed three options; namely, issuing an executive order like former Governor Babbitt; waiting until the upcoming November elections which might result in the Legislature being more King Day-friendly; or to include the King Day issue in a special legislative session, if she called for one later that year. Wisely, she opted to wait until the 39th Legislature would be called into session in 1989. Yet, Mofford proved successful in getting the Arizona Board of Regents, of which she was a member by virtue of being governor, to vote unanimously to establish Martin Luther King, Jr. Day at our three state universities. That took place in early September 1988.

Chapter Five
Our Most Militant, But Effective Weapon: The Convention Boycott

When you are in a battle to win, there comes a time when you must take risks to reach your ultimate goal. On March 26, 1987, ARIZONANS FOR A MARTIN LUTHER KING, JR. STATE HOLIDAY took a risk that proved effective, although not immediately, but eventually. The final estimated tally of real and potential revenue lost as a consequence of former Governor Evan Mecham and Arizona wrangling over just one day to honor Dr. Martin Luther King, Jr. between 1986 and 1993 approached one-half of a billion dollars. That's right! $500,000,000, if you count the convention and tourism cancellations and organizations, and entertainers who shunned Arizona, as well as the 1993 Super Bowl that had been tentatively scheduled for the Valley of the Sun, but was awarded to Pasadena, California instead. The amount of income from convention visitors that was snatched out of the hands of Arizona's tourism industry dwarfed by more than a hundred-fold the two and a half million dollars that King Day opponents warned was what an outright Martin Luther King, Jr. Day paid state holiday would cost the state.

On the date mentioned above, our coalition announced our support for a convention boycott of Arizona that had begun almost simultaneously by the Democratic National Committee Chairman, Paul Kirk, and the National Newspaper Publishers Association, which aborted their 46th annual mid-winter conference, after arriving in Phoenix amidst the furor created by Mecham's rescission of the King holiday a few days prior to their coming.

The first known national organization to cancel its scheduled meeting in Arizona, in protest of the elimination of Arizona's King Day, came from likely allies to the Civil Rights Movement, namely, the Democratic Party leadership. The Finance Council of the Democratic National Committee had planned a February meeting in Tucson in 1987. Although it would have attracted only about 150 party members who had contributed at least $5,000, the group's chairman utilized his high profile to declare his and the Democratic Party's disdain for Mecham's "intolerance and bigotry." While making the stand against coming to Arizona, Chairman Kirk clarified that his ire was directed toward our brand-new governor, rather than the people of our fast-growing state. No sooner than Kirk's press release of his committee's cancellation of their date in Tucson hit the news, Arizona Democrats directed *their* displeasure with *their* national leader.

Senator Dennis DeConcini felt insulted by Kirk's move to move the Council's meeting away from his hometown of Tucson. He felt that the decision was shortsighted, even though he was a loyal advocate of King Day in Arizona. The late Representative Morris Udall did a verbal dance around the issue by admitting that he empathized with the Finance Council's disgust with Governor Mecham's "extremist views"; nevertheless, Udall was of the opinion that his national party officials had overreacted. Former Governor Bruce Babbitt questioned the moving of the meeting as an effective advocacy position for non-Arizonan King Day supporters. One state Democratic leader called for Kirk to reconsider his decision announced on Tuesday, January 20, 1987. However, taking into consideration that Martin Luther King, Jr. had reached the level of "near patron saint" for Democrats who had enjoyed and needed the nearly 90% African-American voting block for Democratic candidates, Kirk dared not rescind the National Democratic Committee's boycott of "Martin-less and Mecham-full" Arizona.

The very next day, *after* Paul Kirk issued his protest cancellation, the National Newspaper Publishers Association (NNPA), comprised of over 300 newspapers published by Black Americans, held a press conference in their host city of Phoenix to announce their decision to call off their annual mid-winter conference immediately and leave the desert where King Day had been *defamed* by our already infamous governor. The NNPA had not come to Arizona without prior knowledge of the rescission. However, host publisher Cloves Campbell of the *Arizona Informant* had planned long and well to welcome his brothers and sisters of the publishing profession to Phoenix for their meeting, and had not withdrawn his invitation to the group, in spite of several of the publishers' calls for them to boycott Arizona. The officers of NNPA, led by President Christopher Bennett, checked into their head-quarters hotel early to make last minute preparations for their meeting and invited guests, which included the Reverend Jesse Jackson and Dr. Dorothy Height, President of the National Conference of Negro Women.

Word reached me that Bennett and the executive committee of NNPA wanted to meet with members of our coalition, relative to our response to Mecham's actions. By that day, Wednesday, January 21, 1987, the boycott announcement by the Democrats had provided a radical example of con-fronting Mecham. The disadvantage the NNPA leadership had was that they were already in Arizona. The dilemma facing them was to stay or to leave. After intense dialogue between the NNPA and ARIZONANS FOR A MARTIN LUTHER KING, JR. STATE HOLIDAY in a closed session, the publishers of this nation's African-American newspapers unanimously decided to call a news conference that same day to denounce Mecham's rescission and urge organizations throughout the nation to forego Arizona as a meeting place until the Martin Luther King, Jr. Day was reinstated. Gene Blue, Chris Johns and the Reverend Amos Dudley accompanied me to the emergency-called meeting where the far-reaching decision was made. The atmosphere was grim and tense. None of the members of our coalition fully realized the outcome of what was taking place. But, deep down inside, we knew it was right and a sure way to communicate our disgust in Mecham and his crowd of anti-King Day Arizonans.

Even though the press conference was hastily called for Wednesday afternoon; several members of the media showed up to cover the story. Excerpts from the NNPA press release under the caption of "National Newspaper Publishers Association Protests the Rescission of the Martin Luther King, Jr. Holiday" included the following lines:

> The Black Press of American, the National Newspaper Association, denounces the actions taken by Republican Arizona Governor Evan Mecham rescinding the Martin Luther King, Jr. holiday. This action is cowardly, disgraceful and repugnant. It borders on the philosophy of South Africa's apartheid system of government. There is little difference: apartheid there, blatant racism here.
>
> ...It is the decision of the NNPA...to end our 46th Annual Mid-Winter Conference in protest of (Mecham's) action. In addition, NNPA encourages all organizations throughout the

country *not* to come to Arizona until the Martin Luther King, Jr. Holiday is reinstated.

...It appears the Governor has not grasped the true message of Dr. King, that a man should be judged by the content of his character and *not* by the color of his skin.

The Black Press will not be silent. In the coming weeks, Black newspapers across the country will write about this abomination in Arizona and the need for establishing the Martin Luther King, Jr. holiday throughout this nation.

After the statement was read by Publisher Chris Bennett, a local news reporter asked whether or not leaving the city was running from the issue and hurting the Black community. Mr. Bennett referred that question to me and I responded in typical "Warren Stewart fashion", "We want to loudly applaud the decision of NNPA. (And) we hope to show Governor Mecham that he cannot stand before the nation and be a bigot and be proud of it." When local publisher, Cloves Campbell, indicated that he would continue to report on this issue as information unfolds, he further commented chagrinly, "We're not short of news, as long as he (Mecham) keeps talking."

Once these two stories of boycotting Arizona for disrespecting the memory of Dr. King hit the press, the tourism people began to experience anxiety attacks over possible lost business, thanks to Mecham. Prior to the rescission fallout, very few, if any, members of the tourism industry and business at large could have cared less about Arizona's "Black holiday." However, the *Arizona Informant* played the role of prophet by first printing its front page headlines about the NNPA boycott in "red" and three months later in "green" in a follow-up story entitled "KING BOYCOTT GAINING STEAM." To add to their nervousness, the King Day disgrace put in jeopardy the planned 1989 meeting of the National Baptist Convention of America, then the second largest Black Baptist denomination in America, which had scheduled a return visit to the Valley for its 10,000 delegates calculated to bring four to six million dollars to Arizona.

Talk of a King Day boycott also came from another direction—a very prominent entertainer by the name of Stevie Wonder. At least a week prior to the two above-mentioned group protests over King Day, Wonder, America's most popular Martin Luther King, Jr. holiday advocate next to Mrs. King, announced that he would never return to a "King Day-less" Arizona to perform. The end! And when Stevie Wonder talks; his professional peers listen. Jesse Jackson also cancelled a speech to honor King to be held on the

Arizona State University campus the same week of the NNPA conference. However, his office denied that he was boycotting the state, which proved to be true because the Reverend Jackson made his second trip to Phoenix in February, less than a month after Mecham's rescission of the holiday.

All of this unsolicited assistance by way of boycotting the state in which we lived put ARIZONANS FOR A MARTIN LUTHER KING, JR. STATE HOLIDAY in an unprepared position. After all, I do not remember the boycott issue surfacing in our coalition meetings, prior to the NNPA's arrival in Phoenix. Rest assured, though, after the 1987 King Day celebrations and protests quieted down, our coalition's agenda for February 5, 1987 included a "Proposed Convention Boycott Strategy" item. An appointed boycott strategy committee made up of Luther Patton, Mark Reader, Keelan Roberts, Chris Johns and Gerald P. Richard, II, held their first meeting at Arizona State University on January 31, 1987. Their committee report to us recommended that we seek to sponsor a "KING BENEFIT" on April 4, 1987 in Phoenix and Tucson in order to get entertainment groups to donate proceeds to our cause; ask well-known track athletes to boycott the upcoming ASU-Sun Angel Track Meet; draft a list of entertainers who were and/or would boycott the state; and ask Motown Records to make a public statement of support for the Arizona boycott.

On the political front, the committee suggested that we recruit out-of-state speakers who came to Arizona to support the boycott; target anti-King legislators by boycotting their financial interests; persuade prominent national politicians and civil rights leaders and organizations to support our efforts; and win support of Native Americans in the state. As it related to business, we were asked to boycott Pontiac dealerships (since Mecham owned a Glendale Pontiac dealership), as well as businesses which supported Mecham. The committee even dared to target tourism associations for their support of an Arizona boycott.

In that February meeting, we established a two-fold purpose for the boycott, namely, (1) in protest of Arizona not having an MLK Day and (2) to put economic pressure on the state to support a King holiday. We agreed that the Phoenix Mayor's office needed to be consulted and that Phoenix would be a "casualty" even though it had approved a King Day already. Richard, a young, intelligent and gifted African-American attorney, was tabbed as chairperson of the convention boycott strategy committee. Our coalition commenced to writing letters to organizations requesting their support for our militant move begun by "outsiders."

Slowly, but surely, the King Day boycott began to receive more and more publicity and thus pick up steam. It appeared that our most logical support came from African-American organizations, socially-conscious groups, entertainers, and labor unions that had revered the legacy of Dr. Martin Luther King, Jr.

Finally, during our March 17, 1987 meeting, we made the critical decision of calling our own press conference to announce our coalition's support of the spreading convention boycott. For me, this was a very difficult personal decision. It was one thing for outsiders to say, "I'm not coming to your state because I don't like what you did with the King holiday." On the other hand, once we made a public statement in support of the boycott, we would be considered by many Arizonans as "traitors." Moreover, since I was the "point man", as Art called me, I would be the one in the hot seat, getting shot at by the media, politicians, tourism and business leaders and the average John or Jane Doe Arizonan. I remember that the vote was not unanimous, even after lengthy and tension-filled debate and discussion. As general chairperson, I did not have to vote, thank goodness. And, perhaps, I would have been a *no* vote. Whatever the case, the majority of coalition members voted for holding a press conference to address the issue head-on; and as their leader, it was my task to represent our wishes. The D-Day would be Thursday, March 26, 1987 at the Phoenix Press Club, which was housed in a downtown hotel of all places.

Normally, I wrote all of my press statements, but this time I left it up to the boycott committee and its legal and political minds. I was too scared to preach on that subject! Our press release was sent out on March 23, which read in part,

> The press conference will announce details of the organization's (ARIZONANS FOR A MARTIN LUTHER KING, JR. STATE HOLIDAY) efforts to request international, national and local groups to boycott Arizona as a site for conventions with a paid state holiday, like the federal holiday honoring Dr. King, as it is signed into law in Arizona.

The press conference was scheduled for 11:00 a.m. I was very, very nervous. Chris occupied his position to my right for support and guidance. A few of the other "executive members" of our coalition stood nearby. The clock ticked 11:00 a.m. Lights. Cameras. Action. Let's get this show on the road. My first sentence said it all,

THE ARIZONANS FOR A MARTIN LUTHER KING, JR. STATE HOLIDAY ANNOUNCE THEIR SUPPORT FOR A BOYCOTT OF ARIZONA AS A CONVENTION SITE UNTIL A STATE HOLIDAY HONORING DR. KING IS ENACTED AND SIGNED INTO LAW FOR THE THIRD MONDAY IN JANUARY EVERY YEAR.

Yes, I was able to get those words out even though I was shaking on the inside. Continuing, I said,

WE TAKE THIS ACTION NOW BECAUSE IT IS APPARENT THAT THE ARIZONA STATE SENATE HAS DECIDED THAT THE NEARLY 50,000 PEOPLE WHO HAVE SIGNED PETITIONS DELIVERED TO THE STATE LEGISLATURE ARE NON-PERSONS. WE BELIEVE, AND RECENT POLLS DEMONSTRATE, THAT THE MAJORITY OF ARIZONANS FAVOR A HOLIDAY IN THE NAME OF DR. KING.

After reminding the media of the Arizona House of Representatives' passage of King Day legislation and the Senate's ability to bring the King bill to a floor vote and failure to do so, I informed the audience, "WITHOUT OUR ENCOURAGEMENT BUT WITH OUR PRAISE, SEVERAL MAJOR GROUPS HAVE ALREADY CANCELLED THEIR CONVENTIONS IN THE STATE OF ARIZONA." My following words identified nearly a dozen groups that had cancelled or were seriously considering to do so.

Then, I mentioned the name of my nemesis in this sentence,

GOVERNOR MECHAM HAS STATED THAT FOR EVERY CONVENTION LOST BECAUSE OF THE KING HOLIDAY ANOTHER WILL COME; LEADING SOME TO INFER THAT GROUPS WILL COME DUE TO THE RESCINDING OF THE HOLIDAY. WE DO NOT BELIEVE A SINGLE CONVENTION HAS COME TO ARIZONA BECAUSE THERE IS NOT A KING HOLIDAY.

Moving on, my statement deduced that

ARIZONA'S IMAGE HAS BEEN TERRIBLY DAMAGED BY THIS DIVISIVE ISSUE WHICH OUR POLITICAL LEADERS MUST HAVE COURAGE TO ADDRESS

BEFORE THIS LEGISLATIVE SESSION ENDS....WHILE A BOYCOTT IS A HARSH MEASURE TO GET OUR POINT ACROSS, WE BELIEVE IT IS NECESSARY IN ORDER TO SHOW OUR ELECTED LEADERS THE IMPORTANCE OF THIS ISSUE AND ITS MEANING FOR ARIZONANS. THIS IS NOT A BLACK ISSUE....A BOYCOTT IS NOT TOO STRONG A TACTIC TO ENSURE THAT THOSE IDEALS ARE PRACTICED AND REMEMBERED. THAT IS WHAT THE KING HOLIDAY IS ABOUT.

I concluded Chris' well-written press statement thusly,

WE ASK ALL ORGANIZATIONS TO SUPPORT OUR APPEAL BY VOTING ON THIS ISSUE WITH THEIR DOLLARS. WE HOPE ALL CITIZENS OF GOODWILL AND MEMBERS OF ORGANIZATIONS WILL CONTACT THEIR REGIONAL OR NATIONAL OFFICES TO SUPPORT THE BOYCOTT....WE URGE ALL PEOPLE OF GOODWILL TO JOIN US IN THIS ENDEAVOR.

My mind draws a blank as to what questions the press asked me on that day. I am sure I was queried about the possible loss of jobs that a successful boycott could cause, especially to the low-wage laborers who worked as maids, cooks, maintenance people and bellboys. Johns stepped up to the microphones and tactfully answered "technique" questions relative to the boycott. All in all, we got our message out and the rest was yet to come.

No sooner had I arrived back at my office, when there was a call from then Mayor Goddard, one of our honorary chairpersons. He had called to inform me of his resignation from our coalition, due to our support of the King Day boycott against Arizona, which included his city that celebrated a paid King Day. He also had his letter of resignation hand-delivered to me. That same day, before I announced it, he had made his resignation public. It read in part:

It is with deep regret that I am resigning today as an honorary chairperson of Arizonans for a Martin Luther King, Jr. State Holiday committee. I do so because I cannot support the boycott of Arizona as a convention destination. This decision was made without my input. Had I been consulted, I would have argued that this action is incredibly unfair to Phoenix which has celebrated the holiday for two years and been outspoken in advocating State action. The City of Phoenix is critically dependent on the convention and hospitality industry and your action will undoubtedly have widespread and adverse economic impact.

I believe in the Martin Luther King, Jr. holiday...However, I cannot condone an economic boycott of conventions....I have been working with the Valley of the Sun Convention and Visitors Bureau to prevent the loss of any convention business in Phoenix because of Governor Mecham's decision to rescind the state holiday, and I will continue to do so.

In the first place, Mayor Goddard attended only one or two of our coalition's meetings. We took his position for what it was called and what he accepted—honorary chairperson. Anyone knows that honorary chairpersons are asked to be a part of working groups with causes primarily for public relations purposes. Secondly, Chris had written the mayor a letter stating our decision to support the boycott on March 23, 1987, three days prior to our press conference. Moreover, boycotting was nothing new to Goddard. As a liberal Democrat, he had participated in the "grape boycott" to protest unfair treatment of migrant farm workers. He had become Phoenix's youngest mayor as a result of taking on the establishment's at-large city council elections and led the voters to approve district elections for city councilpersons. Plus, he had solicited and received the support of Black clergy in that effort. So, even though Goddard was a privileged, Harvard-educated lawyer, he had had first-hand experience confronting the powers that be where they feel it the most—in their pocketbooks; but, when one becomes a part of the establishment, one's *modus operandi* changes. Then, one must be "politically correct" in all of one's actions. And our coalition members understood that the mayor had to protect his political interests.

When we finally connected on the phone, it was a cordial conversation between two men who understood the dynamics of what was taking place. Terry admitted that he understood our position and I sympathized with his "political" stance. There were no cross words. Tension was absent from the conversation. We really did not agree to disagree because "off the record" there was not much disagreement on the issue and what we had to do to tackle it. Mayor Goddard reiterated his commitment to helping win a King Day in Arizona and honored his word.

After a few days of reflection, I wrote the mayor an "official" response in a letter dated April 19, 1987, which included our rationale for supporting the boycott of the state in which we lived. The first two paragraphs expressed appreciation for his "enthusiastic willingness" for serving as an honorary chairperson and our "regret and understanding" for his resignation due to "a conflict of interest." However, the third paragraph outlined our philosophical rationale for taking the position we did.

The entire third paragraph read,

> Thirdly, *ARIZONANS FOR A MARTIN LUTHER KING, JR. STATE HOLIDAY* wrestled with the idea of a statewide regional and national boycott only after exhausting all other known strategies to persuade the state legislature (particularly the Senate) and governor to pass a Martin Luther King, Jr. state holiday bill. The boycott strategy, which is a nonviolent direct action, was decided upon after raising three of the same questions that the late Dr. Martin Luther King, Jr. raised before he engaged nonviolent direct actions:·
>
> (1) Do we have a just grievance?
> (2) Have we used every form of available means to address the issue by negotiation, petitions, and appropriate appeals to those in authority?
> (3) Having found these efforts unproductive, are we prepared to accept the consequences and criticisms society will inflict?

I concluded my letter to Mayor Goddard with this sentence, "Mr. Mayor, I think you know the honest answer to the above questions as they relate to the Martin Luther King, Jr. holiday issue in our state."

Sure, we knew that our grievance involved a "symbolic" injustice done to MLK Day supporters. But history reminded us that the Legislature had been rejecting a day honoring Dr. King for at least 14 years. Therefore, we agreed that the state's citizens who kept electing anti-King legislators would have to pay.

Another lesson was learned about politics and the media by yours truly after our March 26, 1987 press conference. One of the reporters present took a copy of our press statement typed on our coalition's letterhead and called *every one* of our honorary chairpersons to see if they either knew about and/or supported the boycott strategy. When Senator Walker was contacted, I was told she straddled the fence somewhat by expressing appreciation for our lobbying efforts for King Day, but replied that she could not discourage revenue from coming to Arizona. Paul Eckstein, a "sky-scraper attorney" and Democratic leader responded, in essence, to the reporter that "you have to do what you have to do." Several of our other key honorary chairpersons, including Hamilton, Kennedy, Plotkin, Wilcox and Brelecki all expressed support for our nonviolent direct action. To me, one honorary chairperson's response that especially showed political courage and philosophical courage came from Phoenix's longest serving city councilman, the Honorable Calvin C. Goode, and I quote:

> An economic boycott is a harsh measure to make a point. The group has tried other means and feels that this one is absolutely necessary. I regret that it will negatively affect the city of Phoenix. I hope that the governor and Senate will act positively on the holiday to ensure that we do not lose any more convention business.

Responses also came from everyday Arizona citizens who either supported or opposed the convention boycott. One letter of support was simply addressed, "Dear Friends", and the writer continued,

> I saw firsthand the discrimination against the Negro people (in Virginia in 1953 and 1954). And, I was ashamed. I saw on T.V., this morning that another convention cancelled out, for AZ. This may wake up Gov. Mecham. Hit him in the pocketbook....

The origin of that encouraging handwritten letter came from a lady in nearly all-White Prescott, Arizona. Taking the opposing position, a woman from Mesa opined,

> I am writing as a concerned citizen, regarding your group calling for businesses to boycott Arizona. It is not fair to the innocent people that this calling will hurt....Have you ever been out of a job?...People like myself are pleading with your group to *soften* your boycott. Please do not put us out of a job....Thank you for taking the time to read this letter. I do appreciate it.

The day after our press conference, the national newspaper *USA Today* led its "NATIONLINE" column with the block-print headline, "King Day friends say boycott Arizona." How's that for getting out the word to organizations to cancel or postpone their plans to bring their conventioneers to our sunny state. Then, on April 2, 1987, we got a major endorsement letter from none other than the widow of the late civil rights leader we were fighting to honor. Mrs. King, President of the Martin Luther King, Jr. Center for Nonviolent Social Change, Inc. based in Atlanta, released a statement with the following title, "MRS. CORETTA SCOTT KING… URGES SUPPORT OF ARIZONA BOYCOTT." The leading lady in the post-King Civil Rights Movement went to announce through her office,

> Mrs. Coretta Scott King today supported the call of a group of Arizonans for a boycott of their State. Such a boycott would encourage people not to plan conventions for the state.…Mrs. King said, "By blocking the celebration of the…Federal Holiday as a State Holiday, Governor Mecham and the leadership of the State Senate have done a disservice to the citizens of Arizona.
>
> …Mrs. King praised the nonviolent efforts of "Arizonans for a Martin Luther King, Jr. State Holiday" headed by Dr. Warren H. Stewart, Sr. She said that Dr. Stewart's Committee had met with then Governor-elect Mecham to personally urge his support of the holiday.…
>
> …Mrs. King called upon the good people of Arizona to "see the holiday honoring Dr. King as not simply a day to honor one man, but the cause which he represented and his message of non-violence…"

We were more than ecstatic to receive such support from Mrs. King. Lloyd Davis, the King Center's executive director, and I had conversed over the telephone several times to get the right information into the press release. The fact that we had the King family's blessing put salve on the wounds that we had received from the moment of our announcement.

By the time we held our next press conference on May 5, 1987, I had gotten over my anxiety about the convention boycott and had adopted the strategy as a child of my own. Hoping that external pressure would force some Republican Senators to vote in favor of the King Day, we publicized a list of organizations we were aware of that supported our boycott. Among them were: AFSCME, United Staff Union, Unitarian Universalist Association, National Association of Blacks in Criminal Justice, United Methodist Church-Desert Southwest Conference, American Baptist Churches of the USA and Pacific Southwest, respectively, Progressive National Baptist

Convention, Inc., National Family Planning and Reproductive Health Association, National Baptist Congress of Christian Education, NAACP and National Urban League. Although the Republican majority in the Senate acted out the old Negro Gospel song, "I Shall Not Be Moved," many organizations and groups were indeed moving in our direction.

There is little wonder that I did not become a "VIP" to the local and state tourism executives. A few of them called to "reason" with me about our coalition's boycott call. They were being quoted more frequently in the media about what Mecham's rescission of MLK Day was doing to the image of the state and the hotel and resort business. Behind the scenes they were frantically lobbying the obstinate legislators to change their negative votes to positive votes for their pocketbook's sake, to no avail. According to one source, the estimated dollar value loss to Arizona had reached 20 to 50 million dollars. Mecham began to feel the heat and could not outrun the shadow of Martin Luther King, Jr. that appeared wherever he did. Although he continued to call the King Day fiasco "a non-issue", he was being advised to do something to plug the leak of tourism dollars draining from his beloved Arizona. As mentioned in a previous chapter, the governor was finally forced to declare a non-paid Sunday Day of Commemoration for Dr. King by mid-June 1987. But that proved to be a defective stopgap measure to halt the flood tide of costly protest that his handling of King Day had released.

On May 30, 1987, Mrs. King wired me a message informing our coalition that only seven states had not enacted legislation or issued executive orders recognizing the national holiday honoring Martin. Her message included a forthright indictment which read,

> Arizona remains a national and international embarrassment, with a governor openly in opposition to the national holiday, all Americans of goodwill would find it difficult to understand why the League of Cities would elect to hold its national convention in the state of Arizona. It is regrettable that Phoenix, which celebrates the national holiday, should find itself in such a difficult situation. As president of The Martin Luther King Center for Nonviolent Social Change, I must continue to support Arizonans for a State Holiday and their call for a boycott of that state by those organizations planning conventions.

Who said former Prime Minister of Great Britain was the *first* "Iron Lady?" The reference to the League of Cities had to do with Mayor Goddard and other Phoenix officials and business leaders lobbying for the 1991 annual convention of that organization. When Mrs. King got wind of it, she reiterated her support for our boycott, which proved successful in Phoenix not getting the much sought after national convention that would have brought "Who's Who in municipal government" to the Valley of the Sun, plus over 10,000 delegates and hundreds of media representatives. Before the summer was over the National Basketball Association threatened to move their fall meeting from Scottsdale.

Convention cancellations continued to mount. Added to the list were large meetings, such as: the Council on Social Work Education, the National Intramural Recreational Sports Association, the League of United Latin American Citizens, and the National Head Start Association. Those meetings alone accounted for almost six million dollars in lost revenue for Arizona. Of course, many groups kept their commitments to convene in Arizona, so all was not lost. Mecham, being the "super patriot" that he presented himself to be, reportedly increased the number of a group of Marines that had communicated with his office that they were not canceling their visit to Arizona over the King Day controversy. The governor announced on a radio talk show that 5,000 U.S. Marines were still coming. However, a tourism industry representative placed the official figure at 1,000.

As mentioned earlier, several entertainers followed Stevie Wonder's lead and cancelled engagements in Arizona at the height of the controversy taking money out of their own pockets, in one sense. Stellar names of individuals and groups who boycotted the state included Luther Vandross, the Doobie Brothers, Tina Turner, Whitney Houston and Al Jarreau. Several others who came, as mentioned previously, made statements and/or donations to our efforts to win a King Day or contributed to the Mecham Recall Committee, which will be discussed in the next chapter.

Throughout this period of boycott fever, many of the organizations endeavoring to make a decision whether or not to come to Arizona for their conventions somehow got directed to my church phone number. For the most part, I simply gave them a brief summary of the King Day controversy in Arizona and our coalition's efforts to obtain passage of the holiday in the Legislature. Most of the time once the group's representatives heard our spill; they eventually made the decision not to come. As far as the entertainers were concerned, I only talked to local concert promoters who were concerned about their commissions and a few out-of-town agents who wanted to get the inside scoop on what was going on in Arizona.

The responses toward many of the 300 letters to organizations our coalition sent to the "King-friendly" groups were encouraging and supportive. From the United Methodist Church's letter we learned that "the UMC is willing to cooperate with your group in encouraging a boycott of our national meetings in Arizona." The former president of the National Urban League, Mr. John E. Jacob, wrote, "The NUL fully supports your position, and has already relocated a regional conference to another site." Dr. J. Alfred Smith, Sr. of the Progressive National Baptist Convention informed us, "You may officially announce that I have decided against bringing our PNBC to Arizona...." The General Secretary of American Baptist Churches USA shared with us, "This is to inform you that the ABCUSA can officially be listed as a boycotting organization."

As the fall of 1987 rolled around, more meeting cancellations took place, including the Western Regional Convention of the African Methodist Episcopal Church, the Convention of the Radio-Television News Directors Association and the Alpha Phi Alpha Fraternity annual meeting.

◇◇◇◇◇◇

On July 11, 1988, a week prior to the Democratic National Convention, in response to the Arizona State Senate's second consecutive defeat of the MLK Day legislation in two years, ARIZONANS FOR A MARTIN LUTHER KING, JR. STATE HOLIDAY held a press conference. In our statement to the press, we vowed to keep our word to support a convention boycott of Arizona until we had an official King Day. Furthermore, we planned to send representatives to the Democratic National Convention to distribute our "Honor the Dream...*Boycott Arizona*" badges and garner more national support and publicity from the thousands of attendees and media who would be present in Atlanta, Georgia, Martin King's hometown. Without a doubt that scared the daylight out of Arizona Democrats, tourism officials and business leaders.

Since the Reverend Jesse Jackson was making a second run for the Democratic presidential nomination and would be a key figure at that 1988 Atlanta convention, his Arizona delegates would carry the torch for our boycott strategy once they got there. Tempe resident, Caryl Wade Terrell and Pastor Gantt, of Tucson, both regional co-chairpersons of our coalition, had been elected to serve as Jackson delegates to the convention. Arizona's top state

Democrats, including Governor Mofford, former Governor Babbitt, Mayor Goddard and others planned to speak at a press conference before Arizona's 84 delegates and alternates; trekked to the King Memorial. Several Jackson delegates would wear "Boycott Arizona" buttons at the press conference. When word got out that the boycott buttons could embarrass Arizona over the King holiday rescission and repeated legislative defeats, our boycott strategy fizzled out. Pastor Gantt, being a Jackson delegate, received a lot of criticism from Tucson media about his vow to wear his "boycott button", but being the prophetic pastor he had been since his arrival to Tucson as pastor of Tucson's oldest and largest Black Baptist Church, it did not bother my former Bishop College classmate at all.

Moreover, how ironic it appeared that Arizona Democrats were concerned about *us* tarnishing Arizona's image and scaring off tourism trade. Mecham's ghost and the State Senate's refusal to pass the King Day had already cost the state 25 million dollars. But, the alleged gripe with our coalition's "Boycott Arizona" buttons was that we were "airing our dirty linen in public" a long way from home. Please, couldn't they find a more plausible argument than that? Furthermore, the King Day convention boycott of Arizona was the worst kept secret in the country, especially among socially conscious groups. In addition, at least one of the then Democratic candidates for president had been supportive of our efforts. Michael Dukakis' delegates admitted publicly that he had steered one or two conventions away from Arizona during the Mecham era. His rationale for not supporting the boycott this time around was that Arizona had a Democratic governor who supported the holiday. As far as our coalition was concerned, Mofford or no Mofford, we still saw our goal snatched away from us year-after-year.

As never before, I saw big business and the tourism industry in Arizona getting on board our MLK holiday struggle. I predicted in the hot Arizona summer of 1988 that the next year, 1989, would be the year for passage of the day in honor of King. To let up then, would be a mistake. The business community would be forced to get actively involved as never before if they wanted to stop losing convention revenue, even though many of them saw the King Day controversy by that time as an economic issue. Our group had made a decision based on principle and was willing to take the heat and sacrifice jobs, if necessary, to win King Day. African-Americans are very familiar with ignorant and insensitive criticism, as well as getting the short end of the stick. So, the argument that our boycott would rob minorities in the lower levels of the tourism industry of jobs (where racism and discrimination had kept most Blacks and Hispanic workers for hotels) did not deter us. For that position, one local editorial about our renewed boycott strategy eulogized our coalition and me under the headline "Death of a Dream."

Once in Atlanta and under pressure from the "powers that be" in the Arizona Democratic Party, several of the Jackson delegates decided it was best not to "embarrass" Arizona by urging a boycott at the convention. I had been in constant contact with my friend, Theodus Gantt, urging our coalition Jackson delegates to hold fast to our plan. But, I guess it was too much to stand against the governor and company. The head of the Arizona Jackson delegates, Caryl Wade-Terrell, softened her personal position, and even though she had strongly supported our boycott from its inception, she took part in the official Arizona delegation's tribute to Dr. King and kept her boycott button off her apparel that day. But, it must be noted that the media did not know that the Jackson delegation had already distributed several dozens of our "boycott buttons" prior to the uproar.

The end result of pro-King holiday Arizona Democrats becoming divided over the boycott issue turned out positive for keeping our dream for a holiday before the Arizona public and the appearance of a "backing down" by Black Jackson delegates who were also members of ARIZONANS FOR A MARTIN LUTHER KING, JR. STATE HOLIDAY. Pastor Gantt spoke for our coalition in Atlanta by stating that our decision to back down from pushing the boycott there was "to show solidarity", but that the fight for the Arizona King Day was far from over. However, when asked by a reporter why the boycott supporters were causing problems, Gantt responded, "We didn't cause the problem. Evan Mecham caused the problem." My buddy then pledged to continue the boycott, once he returned to Tucson.

Honestly, I was more than a little disappointed that our coalition members did not follow through as planned with the "Boycott Arizona" strategy. But, I was not there and was not in on the dynamics of the inter-action between our coalition members and our pro-King Day opponents of the boycott. More than that, after conversing with Gantt over the telephone, I reluctantly accepted his revised stance. Afterall, Gantt and I used to double date together in my red 1965 Impala Sport Coupe in college, and I trust him.

◇◇◇◇◇◇

No one will ever be able to convince me that Arizona's Martin Luther King, Jr./Civil Rights Day battle would have been victorious in the

Legislature and by a vote of the people of Arizona *if* the convention boy-cott—a nonviolent direct action—had not been supported and utilized by, not only our coalition, but the numerous organizations, entertainers and professional sports associations and leagues. Money talks; *always* has and *always* will *until* the Second Coming of Christ.

Chapter Six

Mecham's Downfall: The End at the Beginning—Mishandling the Martin Luther King, Jr. State Holiday

Dr. Joseph Parham, Governor Mecham's Director of Affirmative Action and one of the two African Americans in high-level positions in his administration, arranged a post-Christmas meeting between his boss and me. I had not been in Mr. Mecham's company since our "clashing of the minds" meeting on November 18, 1986, and that was no accident on my part. Being Christmastime, the worst of opponents lay aside their weapons to spend time with family and friends and become caught up in the Spirit of Christmas.

Perhaps, the Christ living in me softened my self-imposed boycott of being in the governor's presence. In addition, by December 1987, the same year that Arizona's expected MLK Day was aborted just seven days prior to its due date, Arizona's chief executive faced a possible recall. Mecham was being investigated by a grand jury and about to become the first governor to be impeached in Arizona in over sixty years. As much as I had been seething with anger for the man who denied one of my most significant heroes of his just honor in Arizona, I felt sympathy for Governor Mecham. And, yes, I prayed for him on a daily basis even though my words *to* God about the governor were much kinder than my words *about* him to the press and members of my community.

Therefore, when Joe Parham called me and mentioned that he would like to set up a meeting between the embattled governor and myself, I agreed without hesitation. Because the meeting occurred so close to Christmas, the usual hustle and bustle around the Executive Tower at the State Capitol was conspicuously absent. The meeting took place in the late afternoon. I arrived on time at Parham's office and we exchanged holiday greetings as he led me to a small conference room in his suite of offices. A few minutes later the door opened as the governor's relatively new press aide, Ken Smith, entered first, with Governor Mecham following behind. Dr. Parham and I stood and extended our hands to the two gentlemen. As we sat down at the rectangular table, Smith and Parham moved toward the end of either side of the table and that put the governor and me sitting directly across from one another. The two of us exchanged cordial Christmas greetings and mentioned how our respective Christmas Day was spent with family members. Then, one of us (I cannot remember which one of us) brought up politics. The governor used the Christmas season as his point of departure by saying, "Reverend, I could be really upset with you because you've said some unkind things about me. I could have said some things about you. But, we both accept Jesus Christ as our Lord and Savior. We're Christian brothers, and we can't be saying bad things about one another." A little caught off guard by his response, I hesitated, thought about what he said, and what I had planned to say, and then said to the governor's face what I believed in my heart and had said to others. "Governor, had you not mishandled the King holiday issue I do not believe you would be in the political trouble that you're in." And the Lord knows I was not prepared for the response I received from Evan Mecham.

"Oh, no Reverend, you don't understand. My problems have nothing to do with the King holiday. I know for a fact that the liberal Democrats and a bunch of homosexuals are out to get me."

I do not know what my body language communicated to Mecham, Smith and Parham, but I was flabbergasted! I could tell that the governor sincerely believed what he had just told me. I mean, that was his *heart* talking. Whatever else was discussed at our brief meeting has long since left my memory because I remained in a daze quite awhile after our meeting came to end as a consequence of the governor's remarks. From then on, in my mind, Mecham's political survival was a lost cause. To be honest, I said to myself, "This man is not all here."

Arizona's first Republican governor in twelve years saw *no connection* between his downfall and his mishandling of the Martin Luther King, Jr. state holiday he had rescinded on January 12, 1987. As far as I am concerned, the MLK holiday controversy, which became personalized by the governor, was *the end of the beginning* of the tenure in gubernatorial office that Mecham had fought for and finally won after five tries.

◇◇◇◇◇◇

Arizona, my place of residence since July 1, 1977, had gained its reputation as being *different* for a variety of reasons. After all, what normally came to people's minds when Arizona was brought up as a topic of discussion by most "non-Arizonans *before* the Phoenix Suns and the "fastest-growing state" title became vogue in the 1980s? The scorching 110° summers desert cacti, Wyatt Earp and the wild, wild west. Cowboys and Indians, rattlesnakes and scorpions. Barry Goldwater's 1984 Republican presidential candidacy, conservative politics. The Grand Canyon. And Mexican food. One *other* thing immediately came to *my* mind when I received a letter from the pulpit committee of the First Institutional Baptist Church in the fall of 1976 inquiring if I would send my resumé to them as they searched for a pastor, "Arizona! There ain't no Black people in Arizona!" Well, once I arrived eight months later to shepherd my first flock I discovered that there *were* African-Americans in Arizona—all three percent of us.

Regardless of people's first impressions or thoughts when Arizona was mentioned a few years ago, the mental image surely was not embarrassing. But, thanks to *Mecham on Martin*, all that changed once the votes were tallied the day after the first Tuesday in November in 1986. I have already mentioned that friends of mine from around the country curiously inquired about "our new governor" once the then governor-elect's remark about planning to keep his rescission promise hit the press.

In a speech at the University of Arizona in Tucson early in December 1986, Martin Luther King, III suggested that the new governor-elect's vow to rescind the holiday in his dad's honor was based on racism. Steve Benson, the editorial cartoonist for *The Arizona Republic*, mass-produced original, stinging cartoons caricaturing his fellow Mormon brother's bungling of the MLK Day, one of which portrayed a pint-sized Mecham sitting on Santa Claus' lap with a wish list in his hand which read "No King Holiday" and words appearing from the governor-elect's mouth, "I'm dreaming of a White Christmas." By the week of January 12, 1987, *The Washington Post* described our new governor with this sentence, "Of the 21 new governors being sworn in this month, none is off to a shakier start or shorter honeymoon than Arizona's Evan Mecham, a Republican outsider, who won office on his fifth try." *The Arizona Republic* quoted Mayor Goddard who had just returned from an out-of-state meeting lobbying for the National League of Cities convention as reporting, "The word is out that something is happening, that something is very wrong…Generally, people wanted to know, 'What's going on? What is this we've read about a flat Earth and the Martin Luther King thing?'" Neal Pierce, a columnist for *The Washington Post*, wrote in a March 1987 column, "In a speech to an Arizona utility's political action committee, I had likened Mecham, known nationally for scuttling the Martin Luther King, Jr. holiday in Arizona, to the Audi 5000: a vehicle that seems to take off without control or command, often goes in the wrong direction, may generally wreak havoc on property and people.'" George McEvoy from New Jersey characterized our governor thusly, "There's one thing I have to say for Evan Mecham—just when you think he has gone too far in his political looniness; he goes even further….And in his most recent display of acumen, he chose a commemoration of the U.S. Constitution to proclaim that 'there is too much democracy in America'." *The Boston Globe* commented on Mecham with these words, "Dogged by controversy, a steady decline in popularity and a dubious natural reputation as Arizona's 'shoot-from-the lip' governor, Mecham faces a strong grassroots campaign to remove him." Even popular comedian-actor Eddie Murphy supposedly got in on the joking commentary of Arizona's top leader according to *The New Times*, a Phoenix weekly. In one of their columns in July 1988, the following satire was recorded, "When savvy veteran Hollywood reporters expressed surprise that his first stop was to be Phoenix, Mr. Murphy wasted no time dropping his bombshell. 'Gentlemen, I am going to Phoenix first so I can see my father-Evan Mecham'."

It did not take long for Arizona to feel the brunt of the embarrassment of the new gubernatorial administration. Even loyal Arizonans spouted their frustrations with their new "guv." A caller from Scottsdale, Arizona to one of Governor Mecham's biweekly talk shows on Arizona's largest radio station directed his disappointment to Mecham like this, "We the people of Arizona, are quite the laughingstock due to you on national talk shows and so forth….You're a real embarrassment to the state of Arizona." To which the governor replied, "You, and the people like you, and some elements of the liberal press are actually the only laughingstock." *The Phoenix Gazette* reported a Tucson businessman commenting on Mecham's King Day rescission thusly, "It brings shame and embarrassment to our state."

Rest assured, Governor Mecham had his supporters who jammed the lines on talk shows, cluttered the editorial pages with letters and picketed in front of newspaper buildings demanding a fair hearing for their hero. Nevertheless, the cause of embarrassment for Arizonans came straight from the mouth and actions of the person elected as governor, regardless of the fact that nearly 60% of the voters did *not* cast a vote for him. If you do not believe me, read some of Mecham's own words during his turbulent tenure as governor.

In the *INSIGHT* Magazine in April of 1987, Evan Mecham spoke about himself,

> I'm different. First of all, you have to recognize that I was not the choice of the so-called Establishment. The people that wanted me was the people.

Defending himself against the charge that he was a racist, the same month he rescinded the King Day, he was quoted,

> I'm not a racist. I've got black friends. I employ black people. I don't employ them because they're black. I employ them because they are the best people for the cotton-picking job.

On his infamous "pickaninny" statement, *The Arizona Republic* on March 28, 1987 quoted him as saying,

> As I was a boy growing up, blacks themselves referred to their children as pickaninnies…Mecham, 62, repeated the remark Wednesday and said he "hadn't the foggiest idea" whether the term "pickaninny" is derogatory.

That quote was in reference to a book Mecham endorsed written by W. Cleon Skousen entitled *The Making of America* in which the author makes mention of Negroes as "pickaninnies."

The quote that brings out the governor's true colors on race, in my opinion, was made to reporters in Utah who informed him that the NBA had cancelled its annual meeting set for September 1987 in Scottsdale. Mecham retorted,

> Well, the NBA, I guess they forget how many white people they get coming to watch them play.

The state's largest newspaper ran a story on how Mecham's remarks were making for less than desirable press around the country. On September 27, 1987, *The Arizona Republic* reported,

> On Thursday, Mecham had captured the attention of the *New York Times* with a quick comment to reporters after his radio

show on KTAR-AM. "Golly, I don't know," Mecham replied, "I don't know whether he speaks English or not."

The question that had been asked the governor was how he was planning to greet the Pope who was making a historic visit to Arizona in a day or two. I guess Mecham did not know that the Pope spoke several languages, especially fluent English.

In a heated exchange with reporters at the State Capitol, Governor Mecham shot back at one particular newsman, who dogged his trail throughout his tenure,

Don't ever ask me for a true statement again.

Another statement by Arizona's Utah-born, ex-governor made a month or so before he was removed from office came from remarks he made while recounting his 1987 trip to the Far East to promote Arizona.

Japanese really like to play golf, and their eyes really light up when you say we've got over 200 golf courses in Arizona. My goodness, golf courses. Suddenly, they got round eyes.

Look, I did not make up any of the aforementioned comments and quotes about Evan Mecham. The governor had a very effective way of "putting his foot in his mouth" quite often. Yes, the governor had good qualities. Yes, he appointed two African-Americans to two high-ranking positions in state government. And, yes, he had Black friends (and some women who were his friends, too). But, Evan Mecham probably could have been kept an Arizona secret had it not been for his rescinding the King holiday and some of his commentary on that subject.

Another Arizonan decided to take matters into his own hands, eventually with the help of over 300,000 registered Arizona voters, and deal head-on with the new governor before he took office. Ed Buck, a thirty-two year old, Republican millionaire businessman who openly acknowledged his being a homosexual, launched a recall of the incoming governor in front of the State Capitol in December 1986. At that time, the thing that had incensed Buck enough to buck Mecham was his plans to cancel King Day. Perhaps, the Mecham Recall Movement started as a joke, but thanks to the governor, his actions from the ninth floor of the Executive Building turned would-be jest into a jolt that knocked him out of the governor's chair. Ed Buck's soon-to-be historic campaign started with a militant idea and a handful of amateur-looking "Recall Ev" bumper stickers.

Originally called the Mecham Watchdog Committee, Arizonans from all walks of life united with an *unseemly* leader to unseat another *unseemly* leader. Other than being White, Republican and millionaires, Buck and Mecham faced off at each other from opposite ends of the dusty Arizona "off-the-main-street" politics. In one of their first official mailings, which included their monthly newsletter, an envelope for a contribution and a free "Mecham for Ex-Governor" bumper sticker, the cover letter included the following directed to "My Fellow Arizonan",

> We as concerned citizens of Arizona are horrified about the direction that our state has taken with Evan Mecham as our governor....
>
> Our state has already begun to suffer from the tainted national image painted by Governor Mecham....Adverse economic impact is already evident by the loss of major convention dollars....We are all suffering because of his inability to cooperate and compromise in the legislative process. This is just the beginning.
>
> We need not let ourselves and the State of Arizona fall victim to this governor for four years. The framers of our Constitution saw the potential for this problem and have provided us with the solution: A RECALL. To that end, the Mecham Watchdog Committee has been formed. It is our purpose first to educate the voting public about the recall option, second to send a clear message to the capitol expressing our outrage, and finally, to organize and effectuate a successful recall campaign. We are a non-partisan committee, committed to providing all voters of Arizona with an opportunity to remedy a dangerous situation.
>
> ...Even though a recall cannot formally begin until July, the organizational effort must begin now.

The Arizona Revised Statutes, Title 19 mandated that the governor had to be in office for at least six months. Then, the recall committee would have 120 days to collect 216,747 valid signatures of registered voters signing the recall petition in the presence of the petitioner. At the time of the April 1987 letter from then Chairman Ed Buck of the Mecham Watchdog Committee, neither the Establishment nor the media gave the recallers a chance to attain their goal. However, they had key help from "on high"—like the ninth floor Governor's Office occupied by Evan Mecham. Regional committee contacts were initially set up in Tucson and Flagstaff. Many of the committees' volunteers came from the state universities' campuses, as well as state labor unions. Donations were requested in the amounts of five, ten or more bucks.

By May 1987, the Mecham Recall Committee had elected a new chair to head their effort. Taking everyone by surprise was the physical presence of a little old lady with long silvery-gray hair elegantly rolled into a bun, wearing super-thick glasses and named Naomi Harward. Mind you, Ed Buck was still in charge of the effort, but his biography carried a little excess baggage, if you will, that was becoming a detraction from the recall's target. On the other hand, Naomi was no senile senior for window-dressing. Born in 1907 and moving to Arizona in 1953, Ms. Harward was convener of the Grey Panthers, had traveled to Kenya for the 1985 "Decade of Women" Convention, and earned two Bachelor's degrees in Social Service Administration and Religious Education. She had taught at ASU for 21 years, and in 1976 retired with the honor of Professor Emeritus of ASU.

Thousands of citizens were contacting the "unofficial" recall committee as the May monthly Mecham Recall newsletter described their reason for existence as "A Scandal a Week" in the Mecham administration. Many rallies and recruiting events were held statewide. Buck even telephoned me to see if ARIZONANS FOR A MARTIN LUTHER KING, JR. STATE HOLIDAY would like to become an "official" member of the Mecham Recall Committee, to which I tactfully declined even though Buck had marched with 15,000 King Day supporters that past January. Also, by the spring, pro-Mecham legislators were being targeted for "political harassment" so they might not be reelected next term if they did not distance themselves from Mecham.

July 10, 1987 was the date for the "Mecham Recall Committee Petition Drive Kick-Off Gala" held at the then Adams Hilton Hotel, with tickets being sold at the reasonable price of $25 for couples and $15 for singles. The grassroots effort had located a headquarters on East Northern in Phoenix. What had been considered just a few months ago as a weird rabble-rouser's pipe dream had become reality. That did not stop the naysayers though. One prediction was that the recall drive would never reach its goal because it would be "burned up" by starting in the middle of Arizona's hellish hot summer. Of course, Mecham's disciples brought up Buck's sexual preference. But, it appeared that the more Ed's homosexuality was brought up, the more people united with the Mecham Recall Movement. As a matter of fact, new offices were being set up around the Valley and the state.

Governor Mecham's muted response to the politically hot recall effort was essentially a dare to them to try and recall him for trumped-up charges as to what he had done wrong as governor. One issue that continued to come up from the recall committee was the rescission of King Day and the millions of dollars lost in cancelled conventions, in addition to some apparently inept Mecham appointments.

When the first thirty days of the circulation of the recall petitions rolled around, a whopping 103,379 signatures had been collected—in July! With that many signatures the first month, it was becoming more believable that they would have their 217,000 by November 3, 1987. All of a sudden the governor's advisors suggested that he change his vintage Mecham tactless way of blasting his foes. GOP leaders began to get a little anxious as the numbers kept increasing. He tried for a day, but the old Mecham came to life again.

Even though our King Day coalition never officially aligned with the Mecham Recall Committee because we felt that it could sidetrack our single-purpose mission and possibly rob us of some Republican votes that we had on our side, several of our members were active recall members. After persistent invitations from Virginia Walls, an African-American woman who was very much involved in the Mecham Recall Committee, I consented to offer remarks at a "Salute to Martin" recruiting reception she had put on in the West Phoenix office which the recall committee called their South Phoenix office. The affair was held on August 22, 1987 in an effort to get more Black support for the recall. I suppose Mr. Buck's political and sexual preferences frightened off many anti-Mecham African-Americans. So, Mrs. Walls attempted to make a MLK-Mecham Recall connection. Some of my remarks brought out my belief that "if there had been no Martin Luther King, Jr., perhaps there would be no Mecham Recall." I offered thanks to Ed for supporting the King holiday efforts from the beginning of our struggle. I, then, went on to point out similarities between the Civil Rights and the Mecham Recall Movements. Both were initiated when fundamental principles of respect and equality were not recognized by governmental authorities. Each began as a grassroots coalition and responded to insensitive governmental leadership. The two movements reacted to the consent of the silent majority. For the most part, the coalitions were barely financed, but cost-efficient. The media was no real friend to either cause at first. But, both movements became historic and successful.

As my speech progressed, I stated, "Why I am a supporter of the Mecham Recall." I informed them that I had signed and launched "our" recall petition drive from the pulpit of the First Institutional Baptist Church on July 12, 1987 (which is something I probably would not do now). Next, I shared my list of grievances with the governor under fire. I felt (1) he did not have the genuine welfare of all Arizonans at heart; (2) he had made the MLK holiday a Black issue; (3) he exemplified a racist attitude toward Blacks and other minorities, and (4) he had not been truthful about all he could have done for the King holiday. Lastly, I said that his current actions of dialoguing with various Black, Hispanic and other special interest groups was "too little, too late," kind of like if the captain of the Titanic had recruited passengers after his ship had hit the fatal iceberg. What he failed to realize was that the MLK Day was only the tip of the iceberg that would sink his governorship. After my remarks, I chatted with the few attendees and left a check for $25 for the Mecham Recall Committee.

Toward the end of September, Governor Mecham felt the need to send out a letter to his "fellow conservatives" in an effort to raise 1.2 million dollars to fight for "conservative ideals" under attack by the recall effort. He concluded his lengthy letter with the following P.S.

> If I survive and beat back this attack then maybe, just maybe you might be spared being attacked by the left wingers because of what you believe. But we've got to stick together....

Part of the donations Mecham received must have paid for his September 1987 issue of *The Governor's Report*, a Mecham-published tabloid touting his many accomplishments during his first nine months in office. Besides his full-length color photograph showing off a "Say NO to Drugs" tee shirt, were a list of his accomplishments, including: raising the highway speed limit to 65 m.p.h.; launching an all-out war on drugs; spearheading welfare reform; proclaiming a Sunday MLK/Civil Rights Day; increasing health care to seniors, low-income children and pregnant women; and establishing the Department of Environmental Quality. This was quite impressive, but overshadowed by the MLK Day controversy and other things previously mentioned.

Arizona made history again in 1987 when Buck, Harward and the Mecham Recall Committee turned over 388,988 signatures to Secretary of

State Rose Mofford at a petition-filing ceremony on Monday, November 2, 1987 calling for the recall of the governor. The lead editorial in *The Arizona Republic* on the next day was appropriately entitled "Recall Movement—A Glorious Embarrassment." Over 170,000 *more* signatures than needed made it certain that Governor Mecham would have to run for reelection two years prior to the end of his inaugural term, barring the improbable possibility that less than 217,000 of the signatures collected proved to be invalid. And that would not be the case.

Amidst all of the uproar surrounding Mecham, a breaking news story revealed the governor had received a secret $350,000 loan just prior to his victorious election in 1986. State law requires that, in an annual report filed with the secretary of state, elected officials identify the persons and institutions to which they owe more than $1,000. Records revealed that "the less-than-one-year-serving governor" still owed an east Valley attorney and developer $250,000 on the huge loan that constituted almost one-third of Mecham's entire gubernatorial campaign costs. More investigation turned up a letter in which the governor requested that the loan agreement would "remain confidential" between him and the lender. If indicted, tried and convicted of breaking the campaign law, Mecham would have been found guilty of a class felony and denied the right to hold office. Consequently, Governor Mecham faced increasing criticism, a recall and an attorney general's investigation simultaneously.

Approaching the first anniversary of Mecham's infamous rescission of King Day, Arizona's governor, and his brother Willard, who had served as his campaign Treasurer, were indicted by a state grand jury on several felony accounts linked to his secret $350,000 campaign loan. Included in the six indictments charged against Mecham were alleged crimes of perjury, willful concealment and filing a false campaign contribution and expense report. Although indicted of felonies, the governor was permitted by law to continue to serve. The governor would not be arrested unless he failed to honor the summons to the Maricopa County Superior Court to be fingerprinted and photographed like other criminal defendants.

To make matters worse, Governor Mecham was also under investigation by a special counsel to the Arizona House of Representatives to determine whether or not any of his actions as governor were impeachable. That investigation had been in process since late October 1987. By January

5, 1988, the speaker of the House of Representatives indicated that enough evidence had been gathered to impeach the governor on as many as four counts.

I was contacted by the media in reference to my reaction to the governor's indictment by the grand jury and responded thusly,

> First of all, we need to be in prayer for Governor Mecham, his family, and the State of Arizona. This is not a good time. Had Governor Mecham not rescinded the holiday, I don't believe the recall movement would have had the impetus it had, nor would the news media have searched under every rock, crevice and cranny of the governor's life, in pursuit of some undoing information.

And I sincerely believed that. My sympathy went out to the man who had enraged me a little over a year prior to his indictment. God knows, in spite of all of his idiosyncrasies and imperfections, Mecham possessed a strong constitution. The media and other anti-Mecham detractors attacked every aspect of the governor's life, including his wife and family. I am sure that those were some trying times for his wife of over forty years and their seven grown children. No doubt, a strong sense of family and faith in what they believed granted them the strength to keep pressing on, while being bombarded by negativity from every external source, with the exception of Mecham loyalists who defended their role model through to the end.

The day was Friday, January 15, 1988, the 59th birthday of Dr. Martin Luther King, Jr. I was at home in my study, preparing my Sunday morning message for First Institutional's annual Martin Luther King, Jr. Memorial Sunday. However, that day I made several trips back and forth from my study to the family room to get glimpses of the live coverage of proceedings going on at the Arizona House of Representatives. The special prosecutor, William French, was scheduled to report to that body of 60 legislators dominated by Republicans on whether or not the governor should be recommended for impeachment. It was a not so unusual rainy and dreary January day in Arizona.

At last, Mr. French began to address, not only the House of Representatives, but the entire state. Looking like the professional he was, yet with a sober face, the special prosecutor made his historic report and concluded that Arizona's governor should be recommended to the Senate for an impeachment trial. I guarantee you; there was no rejoicing that took place at that moment; not in my house or in my heart. It was one of the saddest days in Arizona history. Governor Mecham must have sensed something had gone awry in his twelve months of office. Ironically, on the same day of his recommendation for impeachment to the House and Dr. King's birthday, *The Arizona Republic* released a copy of a statement the governor had written to the people of Arizona. Excerpts from the text clearly show that the governor was not oblivious to all that had occurred and was occurring during his tenure. Deep pathos, as well as a sense of regret, helped to word Mecham's message to his constituents as can be discerned from the following lines.

> On New Year's Day, I spent several hours reflecting on the events of 1987. I remembered many enjoyable events and successes, but I also thought about all the turmoil during my first year in office.
>
> Like most Arizonans, I have tried to determine why our state is now so politically divided. I have come to the conclusion that some, but not all the blame rests with me....
>
> I apologize to the people of Arizona for any of my actions or mistakes, which may have sparked embarrassing publicity for our state.
>
> ...I am willing to accept my share of the blame for the contentious atmosphere in Arizona.
>
> First and foremost, if I had it to do over again, I would have disposed of the illegal holiday for Martin Luther King, Jr., last January by immediately declaring a legal Sunday holiday. I would have taken this action instead of canceling the illegal holiday in January and then declaring the legal holiday in May. Under the law, this was the most I could have done and I should have done it as soon as possible.
>
> ...I take total and complete responsibility for the unintentional errors mentioned above.
>
> I hope the people of our great state will balance these errors against the good things, which I have done, accept my apologies and forgive me for my mistakes.
>
> I have always done the best I could and will continue to do so. I hope we can go forward in 1988 in the spirit of good will, new understanding, and a desire to work together to accomplish what is best for Arizona.

Whether or not Governor Mecham actually wrote the above-mentioned statement himself is beside the point. It was attributed to him as governor of Arizona. Words used like "reflect", "blame", "apologize", "mistakes", "embarrassing", "willing", "if", "complete responsibility" and "new understanding" took on trans-forming power coming from Evan Mecham. A change appeared to be taking place. The dogmatic leader that he was softened somewhat to admit that his way was not the only way. Who knows? Had the governor declared a Sunday MLK Day in January, rather than June, he might have not sparked such a raging wildfire that burned him politically. Sure, we who supported the federal model of MLK Day with dogged determination would have rejected his Sunday holiday; but he would have been seen, at least, as a King Day-supporting politician who acted upon the legal opinion he had been given by the state's leading lawyer. Whatever the case, Mecham's message to the people came too late to rescue him from indictment, recall, impeachment, and calls for his resignation from high-profile leaders in his own party.

The irony continued. On Monday, January 18, 1988, the official federal and many states' observances of Dr. King's birthday, the secretary of state of Arizona certified enough signatures to mandate a recall election of Arizona's governor. A recall election would be set for May of that year. Meanwhile, support for an MLK Day in some form appeared to increase in the state. Yet, the mere mention of the words "paid state holiday" brought down the wrath of most Arizonans upon those of us who simply wanted a holiday, like most of the nation.

By the second week in February 1988, Governor Mecham had to step down from his office and Secretary of State Mofford took charge as acting governor to become an instrument in the heading of the state and working for passage of an MLK Day for Arizona. With so much political debris swirling around in the unstable Arizona climate—indictment, recall and impeachment—it was a while before the status of the now-deposed governor was determined. However, Arizona law dictated that once the House of Representatives voted to recommend impeachment, the governor had to vacate his office until the governor's impeachment trial by the State Senate was completed. It would be determined at a later date by the Arizona Supreme Court whether or not the impeachment of the governor would void the recall election.

Candidates began to line up for the recall election. One in particular was former Arizona Congressman John Rhodes, a highly respected statesman, who had served in the United States House of Representatives for 30 years and who had retired in 1982. Although he was 71 years old, the conservative Republican and former minority leader in the House, believed that he was up to facing what would be a bitter recall campaign against Mecham and other candidates. Immediately upon hearing of Rhodes' announcement of his candidacy in the upcoming recall election, I contacted his office to discern his position on the MLK Day in Arizona. I was encouraged to learn that he pledged to sign a paid King holiday bill if it was passed by the Legislature and he was the governor. That was very good news, coming from a Republican leaning to the right. Former super-intendent of public instruction and the Democratic gubernatorial nominee who had been defeated in the three-way governor's race in 1986, Carolyn Warner, joined the race for governor, along with some 87 other individuals who had informed the Secretary of State's Office that they were considering running for the state's highest office on May 17, 1988.

The impeachment trial of Arizona's governor, begun on February 29, proceeded slowly through the Arizona State Senate for a little over a month. The legislative branch of state government had virtually come to a halt throughout the trial. State Supreme Court Chief Justice Frank X. Gordon presided over the historic and unique court proceedings. After hearing the attorneyss representing the case against the governor, the often theatrical defense of Mecham's attorneys, the occasional bizarre testimonies of some put on the witness stand, and the intelligent as well as off-the-wall inquiries by state senators, the day had come to vote on the three articles of impeachment on which Evan Mecham had been charged by the House of Representatives.

On Article I—Obstructing an investigation into an alleged death threat (one of Mecham's aides had been threatened for being a "naughty girl"; it allegedly had been brought to Mecham's attention and he did not report it to the proper authorities), Governor Mecham was convicted by a 21-9 vote. Article II—The charge that Mecham deliberately concealed a $350,000 campaign loan was surprisingly dismissed on March 30, 1988. The third Article, which accused Governor Mecham of misusing $80,000 of his "protocol" fund, received a 26-4 convicting vote. The final vote which failed was labeled the "Dracula clause" and would have prevented Mecham from ever running for political office. Even though a majority of senators voted in favor of this item, it required a two-thirds vote of the 30-member body to penalize the governor as indicated.

Governor Mecham was officially removed from office by the Senate's impeachment convictions, and Acting Governor Mofford immediately became Arizona's first woman governor at the moment of Mecham's conviction. The first impeached governor in the nation in nearly sixty years and one of only seven who had been impeached in this country had sat through the entire impeachment deliberations to the moment of the majority votes cast for his impeachment. After conferring with his attorneys for less than fifteen minutes following his removal from office, he emerged from a conference room, smiled at reporters and commented, "Well, they don't like my politics, so we've finished a political trial. It's as simple as that."

In another ironic twist of history, Governor Evan Mecham's impeachment conviction took place on *the twentieth anniversary of the assassination of Dr. Martin Luther King, Jr. on April 4, 1988.* As a preacher, all that came to my mind was the question, "Was this *coincidence* or *providence?* I raised that same question to the editors of the state's major newspapers and concluded by quoting a couple of passages of Scripture. The first from the Old Testament in Psalm 105:15 which reads "…'Touch not my anointed ones, do my prophets no harm!'" The second came from the Apostle Paul's letter to the Galatians in 6:7, "Do not be deceived, God is not mocked, for whatever a man sows that will he also reap." Then, I mused publicly in the last sentence of my letter to the editors; "I wonder *who* really chose the date for Evan Mecham's conviction." Somebody else mused, "King and Mecham died on the same date."

In her first statement as governor, Rose Mofford called for "binding up the wounds" which had been inflicted upon the state throughout this trying ordeal and "purging our hearts of suspicion and hate." She challenged all Arizonans, regardless of their political affiliations, to "move forward together." Also, the May recall was still scheduled and she had been drafted to run for governor in it. Therefore, she vowed to "not shrink from the job before (her)." The other leading Democrat in the race for governor, Mrs. Warner, dropped out of the race and urged all other Democrats to do the same. The strategy for that announcement was to solidify the Democrats in order to keep Mofford in office.

In hindsight, *I do not think Evan Mecham should have been impeached, at least, not for the articles he was convicted of.* Something told me that the political establishment and most of the members of the Arizona State Legislature did not have enough confidence in the voters of Arizona to remove Mecham and select his successor. Why wouldn't they have recalled the governor? Nearly

400,000 registered voters signed petitions for his recall. Every conscious Arizonan could see and hear for themselves all of the commotion that the former car dealer was causing by his off-the-cuff remarks, less-than-ideal political appointments and suspected campaign dealings. Mecham should have been left to the will of the people to decide on his fate. In many ways, Evan Mecham was a victim of a "political witch-hunt", which he brought upon himself. It is my opinion that the citizens of this state, had they been given a chance, would have democratically brought an early end to Mecham's tenure as governor. But, you can bet your bottom dollar that Warren Stewart was not going to be sending a sympathy card to Arizona's first and only impeached governor; that I could do and did in my daily prayers for him and all governmental authorities.

With Mecham gone (but not forgotten) the questions began to be directed about and toward Arizona's new governor who had been the state's beloved top secretary whose office in the Executive Building was decorated almost everywhere with her personal collection of Kachina dolls. Would she be a caretaker governor? Did she have the political astuteness to govern, especially in the wake of the Mecham era? Would her ties to the Phoenix 40 indicate that she would be their puppet? Could the "grand lady" of the Democratic Party in Arizona really do the job? But a more urgent question probably had to do with how long she would be in the governor's seat, depending on the outcome of the voter-mandated recall election a month-and-a-half away from the day Mecham was kicked out of office.

Thanks to the ruling of the Arizona Supreme Court on April 12th, just eight days after the former governor's impeachment, the gubernatorial recall election was cancelled. The 4-1 ruling was based on the Court's interpretation of the state constitution that outlines what happens in the event of the removal of a governor from office for various reasons. The impeachment made a vacancy in the Governor's Office and the constitution dictated that the secretary of state, if elected to office, becomes governor. Of course, this ruling ruffled the feathers of two groups of Arizonans—the Mecham Recall Committee and the "Mecham Re-election Committee." The ousted governor saw the Court's ruling as the final act to keep him from regaining the governor's seat. The recall workers felt frustrated after all their hard work to follow the constitutional right of recalling a sitting governor. However, many others across Arizona were relieved that the state would not be carried through a certain bitter, nasty and further embarrassing recall election with Mecham being allowed by the Senate to run again. The one individual who was most happy to learn that she would not have to campaign against anyone, especially Mecham, for her newly acquired office was Governor Mofford, an ardent Martin Luther King, Jr. Day advocate.

PART TWO

Chapter Seven
Victory In the Air:
1989 Legislative Seesaw

With Evan Mecham removed from office and a King Day advocate as governor, some of us in ARIZONANS FOR A MARTIN LUTHER KING, JR. STATE HOLIDAY felt that 1989 would be the year that the Arizona State Legislature would pass the MLK Day legislation. After all that Arizona had gone through in 1987 and 1988, our thinking was that the issue that had rocked Arizona and caused it to be viewed as way "off the beaten path" would sail through the legislative process in a jiffy as soon as the 39th Legislature would be seated. Consequently, our coalition regrouped after another hot Arizona summer, which began with a very disappointing and unexpected defeat of the King Day in the Senate.

In mid-September, Gene Blue and I went to Representative Hamilton's office to get some pointers and inside information from him and Brenda Smith, director of the Governor's Office of Affirmative Action, newly appointed by Rose Mofford. Several objectives evolved from our private strategy meeting. As I alluded to already, our initial target was early passage of the MLK legislation once the Legislature opened their session in January 1989. Secondly, we would need personal lobbying by "Rosie" as she had been affectionately called by one of the prominent civic insiders. Because Governor Rose Mofford hailed from Globe, Arizona she had some sway with legislators from rural Arizona—both Democrat and Republican. A third project we would work on would be to get Mrs. Coretta Scott King to make a special visit to Arizona to speak to Governor Mofford, key legislative leaders and, perhaps, even a joint session of both chambers. Fourthly, we planned to hold strategic, positive press conferences with the new governor and key state senators and representatives and promote the new bumper stickers we planned to distribute.

Art informed us that as it related to the new Legislature, it appeared that there was a potential of 15 solid aye votes in the Senate out of 16 needed and 28 certain votes in the House just 3 shy of the 31 needed for majority. We tossed around the idea of including members of the Arizona U.S. Congressional delegation on the program of the annual MLK celebration activities inaugural prayer breakfast coming up in December. One far-fetched notion was to get former Arizona U. S. Senator Barry Goldwater to participate at the MLK breakfast, as well as try to get a personal meeting with the "elder statesman" in Arizona politics. Word had come to Art that one of the owners of a local television station wanted to be involved in the King Day celebration planned for 1989. Possible speakers for the December prayer breakfast included the late Dr. Leon Sullivan, Philadelphia pastor, who was living in the Valley of the Sun, civil rights leader and founder of Opportunities Industrialization Centers; or Bill Cosby.

Another subject addressed in our gathering dealt with arranging a meeting with Governor Mofford and selected members of our coalition. We discussed how large the group should be, preparing a five-minute overview of who we were, and who would be the speakers. The names of Senator Walker and Dr. Eppinger came up to address the legislative and public support concerns, respectively. Representative Kennedy was to be contacted for her input, as well as Tommie Espinoza. We also were given access to a computer printout of the unofficial results of the September 14, 1988 primary election. Art went through each of the 30 legislative districts and attempted to identify pro- and anti-King Day incoming legislators.

Remembering that Senator Usdane, who would be the new president of the Senate, had reneged on his affirmative King Day vote, I wrote some key leaders in the Jewish community to get their help in "converting" Usdane back to the 'yes' vote crowd. I dictated similar letters to Joel Breshin, executive director of the Anti-Defamation League of B'Nai B'rth; Harold Morgan of the Jewish Federation of Greater Phoenix; our friend and honorary chairperson, Rabbi Plotkin; and Don Eagle of the National Conference of Christians and Jews. Don sent me a copy of the letter that he had sent to Usdane urging his support in the next session of the Arizona Legislature. His own words concluded his prompt letter,

Senator Usdane, the past two years have been traumatic, divisive years for Arizona. I strongly urge that adoption of the King Holiday by the Legislature would be one additional step back to a unified citizenry....I hope you will use your considerable influence to these ends.

Rabbi Plotkin responded directly to me in a gracious letter informing me and our coalition that he was "continuing to be [our] ally" in regards to the King Day bill and would "persuade [Usdane] and others to do [support] so." Then, Arizona's most beloved rabbi addressed the following paragraph to me, which still lifts my spirit and causes me to thank God for Rabbi Plotkin and the very few others like him.

It is wonderful to work with you in this great cause and I do want to thank you for the marvelous devotion that you have given to this work and for the dedication it has taken. I know that you are the kind of person who will do your very best to continue whatever we need and however we need it.

I also targeted state senatorial candidate Tom Patterson, a physician, who had won the primary election in District 26. He was portrayed as a moderate candidate and a possible aye vote in a district where the previous senator had voted against the holiday. My letter clarified our "WIN-WIN COMPROMISE" and solicited his support. To my surprise I received a response from Patterson in eight days, in which he informed me that he felt "that a Sunday holiday honoring Dr. King would be most appropriate." He went on to espouse the fiscal argument against an additional paid state holiday (which he had eliminated) and to suggest that King did not deserve "equal footing with Washington and Lincoln." Dr. Patterson concluded his letter by reminding me that "good people may disagree." And then, out of nowhere, he dropped this sentence, "I also believe strongly that, since Dr. King's death, the black community has been ill-served by a well-intentioned but paternalistic government."

Wow! Where did that come from? I mean, he sought to represent a district where most African-Americans seen there until recently were maids, nannies and yard workers.

During our coalition's October 15, 1988 meeting, we updated every-one on the progress made over the summer and early fall. Our bumper sticker had been designed and produced by Annette Driver with its message in English and Spanish, respectively, "Say YES! Arizona—Support a State Holiday—Martin Luther King, Jr. I was excited to inform our group that the Progressive National Baptist Convention in August 1988 had honored me with a leadership award for efforts for the MLK holiday and Mecham recall efforts. (It's amazing how many of my Black colleagues gave me credit for Mecham's ouster as governor.) An extra highlight of traveling to Kansas City, Missouri to receive that award at their annual convention was being the alternate speaker to Dr. Alan Boesak, one of South Africa's leading anti-apartheid activists. I also shared with them about my participation in the Anti-Proposition 106 March and Rally led by Arizona's Hispanic community who protested the upcoming general election proposition, which would outlaw any other language but English, spoken while doing official state government business. Others of our coalition continued to share in the necessary work to attain our goal. For example, Gene continued to plan and coordinate King Day celebration activities; Caryl worked insuring support of Democratic candidates; Brenda Hoskins spoke on our behalf at the National Unitarian Universalists Convention in Palm Springs; and Pastor Miller prayed for Arizona's MLK holiday, while he visited the U.S.S.R. over the summer.

We discussed new and/or renewed strategies on getting free billboard space to state our case. We planned to urge the media agencies to observe the holiday instead of just reporting about it and to recruit churches to celebrate the day by closing their offices. We also discussed garnering support from the Phoenix Suns and the new-in-town Phoenix Cardinals; even the idea of a pray-in and sit-in in the halls of the Arizona State Legislature came up.

Although we had a mailing list of nearly 75 coalition members, after Mecham left office and the King Day was defeated again, many of our meetings consisted of a faithful few, like around a dozen regular committed King Day workers. Pastor Gantt faithfully traveled from Tucson, at least, once a month to attend our meetings and take back information and materials to our "southern branch", which he prophetically and charismatically led. At our October meeting we also removed two names from our letterhead of individuals who had not attended many, if any meetings, and one co-founder, the Reverend Amos Dudley, who had died after a valiant battle against cancer.

By November 20, predictions and projections about the incoming Legislature were being made and the prospects for MLK Day did not look promising. Only one GOP legislator in the Senate, the Honorable Jacque

Steiner, publicly declared her support for King Day. That left the Democratic Caucus in the Senate still in need of two Republican votes to win. The House, under Art's watchful eye, would probably come through once again for a paid state holiday honoring Martin Luther King, Jr. modeled after the federal plan.

By the time we met in late November, plans for the MLK Prayer Breakfast had materialized. The Honorable Rose Mofford would be our guest speaker insuring good press coverage. Our legislative strategy involved meeting with the Democratic Caucus in the Senate, as well as targeting several Republican senators who sources said might be convinced to vote for the MLK Day; namely, Senators Usdane, Mawhinney, Bill DeLong, Leo Corbet, Jacque Steiner and Doug Todd. In spite of Usdane and Mawhinney turning on us in the 1988 session, we decided to let bygones be bygones and get an aye vote in 1989. Senator Todd, though a past no vote, represented Tempe, where Arizona State University is located; so we believed that many of the progressive-minded academics and university students and boosters could move him over to our side. Senator Corbet, considered by some to be an ambitious legislator, who had a leadership post in mind among his senatorial colleagues, would be "a wild card." DeLong of Tucson was considered a practical politician who voted the sentiments of his district's constituents, and with Tucson being more liberal than the Phoenix metropolitan area, he was seen as a long shot, but within reach. As far as Steiner was concerned, we simply wanted to keep her affirmative King Day vote.

Another strategy that we would plan would be to silently fill the galleries in the Senate and House chambers after the 1989 King Day march since the Legislature would be in session. This would be a visible show of strength as the state lawmakers were deliberating on the day most of the nation stopped to honor Dr. King. In addition, our goal was to recruit highly respected Republican leaders, not in the Legislature, to come out in favor of the MLK holiday.

When the state Democratic chairs held their annual meeting in Phoenix earlier in November, we were able to arrange a joint press conference with the president of the Democratic state chairs from around the country, who spoke in favor of Arizona's approving a day honoring King, which mirrored the federal model. Our objective was met—to keep the Martin Luther King, Jr. holiday before the public. Perhaps, if they heard about it enough, the legislators would pass it to keep it out of the news.

Our largest inaugural prayer breakfast to date took place on December 14, 1988 at the First Baptist Church of Phoenix where over 600 King Day supporters from every walk of life overflowed the gym, which seated 400 people tightly. Joedd, Paul, Caryl and others outdid themselves in selling tables of eight to churches, businesses, organizations and the like. The theme for that day was "KEEP THE DREAM ALIVE", and his spirit invigorated all in attendance, even though tables had to be set up in the lobby and outside in the courtyard of First Baptist. Quite encouraging was the "rainbow of races" that packed the auditorium starting at 7:00 a.m. that Wednesday morning. When time came for the governor to speak, my second son, Matthew Christian, made his dad proud by introducing Mrs. Mofford. He did not use a lot of words since he was only eight years old. However, I do remember him telling the audience that Arizona's governor was "the number-one supporter of a paid holiday for the Reverend Martin Luther King, Jr." Ironically, the governor, for some strange reason, did not mention the holiday in her brief remarks, although she did address the breakfast's theme and urged all in attendance "to keep the dream alive within our hearts."

Several other speakers, including Mary Rose Wilcox, Phoenix's first Hispanic vice mayor, Representatives Kennedy and Hamilton, Blue and clergy representing several faiths, lifted up King's contributions to America in praises and prayers. Many who spoke did not shy away from the MLK holiday issue that would be before the Legislature once again in a month. They urged the governor to change some hearts in favor of "the dreamer." We thanked God for that morning.

◇◇◇◇◇

New Year's Day 1989 ushered in both promise and problems for Arizona's nearly two-decade political tug-of-war over King Day. Being the optimists that we were, members of ARIZONANS FOR A MARTIN LUTHER KING, JR. STATE HOLIDAY felt victory in the air, like never before. Ironically, the active support in our coalition had diminished from the 1986-87 era while Mecham was reigning from the Governor's Office. Also, some personality differences had arisen over the course of our elongated campaign among coalition members, which had strained, tested and changed some relationships. Nevertheless, a core of leadership racially, sexually and religiously mixed continued to "fight the good fight of faith." And as I reflect on it, our mission was nothing but an exercise in faith as we waged a campaign of persuading doubting legislators and ill-informed citizens of the merit in honoring the man Martin.

On the fourth day of January I wrote to my ministerial colleagues in the Phoenix area with a two-fold purpose in mind. After thanking my professional peers for their past support of the holiday, I requested them to consider asking their respective denominational or religious bodies to celebrate the third Monday in January 1989 with a paid MLK Day honoring King's life and legacy, if they and/or their denominational or religious groups did not already do so. I was glad to inform them that our congregation had added King Day as an official paid holiday for our church staff and office several years prior to the federal holiday. Certainly, if Arizona's religious bodies honored Dr. King with his day, it would add credibility to the state's religious leaders urging state legislators to pass such legislation for state workers.

I was delighted to receive positive responses from several denominational groups in Arizona who observed a paid holiday honoring their martyred beloved brother. My own area minister, the Reverend Kenneth Kliever, informed me that both the Arizona American Baptist area office and the American Baptists of the Pacific Southwest regional headquarters in California took the Monday day off in memory of American Baptists' most noted 20th century preacher-prophet. In addition, the Arizona Ecumenical Council's office, United Church of Christ, Presbyterian Church, U.S.A., Evangelical Lutheran Synod and Disciples of Christ all observed King Day "in respect and high regard for Martin Luther King." Later on, I learned that the Roman Catholic Diocese of Arizona recognized MLK Day officially by closing its offices on the third Monday in January.

Due to the fact that I could sense a waning of enthusiasm for the holiday, after such a politically and psychologically draining one and a half years the entire state had been through during Mecham's tenure, I wrote a letter to all our coalition's supporters the week before the scheduled Monday, January 16, 1989 MLK Memorial March to make every effort to attend. So emphatic was I in my communiqué that I had my secretary type most of my third paragraph in all capital letters and underlined:

WE MUST NOT ALLOW THE KING HOLIDAY ISSUE TO DISAPPEAR FROM THE FOREFRONT OF THE MINDS OF GOVERNOR MOFFORD, THE STATE LEGISLATURE AND ITS SUPPORTERS! (And I do see that happening.)

Then, I invited each coalition member and supporter to attend our first King Day strategy meeting for 1989 to be held at the place where most MLK Day grassroots meetings had been held since November 1986—First Institutional Baptist Church.

In a welcomed contrast to the prior year's rainy King Day celebration march, the Arizona sunshine greeted about 8,000 marchers with warming rays on a crisp, but bright, January morning. Not quite the 15,000, who angrily protested against Mecham's rescission of King Day two years ago, it was still a crowd to be reckoned with. The march's frontline included the regulars previously mentioned in a description of the 1987 march. There were mixed emotions that could be described as "reserved hope" for a holiday and "ecstatic relief" that the ruler who ruled out Arizona's first MLK Day had been run out of office. Above all, the common cry was "We want a holiday!" and the song sung more than any other of the rhythmic chants we marchers voiced along the two-mile trek echoed Dr. King's Civil Rights days, "We Shall Overcome." Governor Mofford met us at the Wesley Bolin Plaza where the thousands of us had gathered once again. She confessed in her remarks that her "crowding retirement body" would have loved to march all the way with us. Then, she lifted our hopes by indicating, "I am waiting for the Legislature to send over the Martin Luther King bill so I can sign it." Of course, that was nothing that we did not know she would do, but it was just good to hear a sitting governor of Arizona say that, after all we had been through.

As usual, Arizona's three African-American legislators gave the audience a pep talk about the prospects of King Day. Mayor Goddard and Representative Wilcox joined the rally's roster of speakers, with Wilcox pledging the support of the Arizona Hispanic community. Pastor Kenneth Ransfer of the First New Hope Missionary Baptist Church in Sierra Vista, Arizona had traveled over 200 miles from southeastern Arizona to share in our celebration. He was no stranger to Phoenix since he had served as Associate Pastor of First Institutional right out of seminary. He summed up Arizona's King Day dilemma thusly; "We have no more Evan Mecham to use as an excuse not to pass this bill."

For some reason, I did not have the enthusiasm to lead a rallying cry for the holiday at that year's celebration in the shadow of the State Capitol. I cannot remember if I even said anything publicly at Wesley Bolin Plaza. I guess I knew my work would be cut out for me dealing with the new Legislature, particularly the Senate side which had been occupied by several pro-Mecham senators who had unseated some of the Republican senators who voted to impeach Mecham. Therefore, I would reserve my energy for the intense lobbying that would be needed after the once-a-year MLK weekend celebration. Also, after the speeches outdoors, we carried out our plans of silently filling the galleries of both chambers to make our presence known to the legislators in session.

Word came to us that Arizona's second largest city observed their own march honoring King and rallying against the Legislature for failing to pass King Day legislation. Clarence Boykins, long-time King Day celebration leader in Tucson, Pastor Gantt, and the Democratic Mayor Tom Volgy of Tucson, led a thousand King Day supporters on the third Monday in January. The mayor expressed his hope that 1990 would be the year that Arizona would join the nation and 44 other states celebrating the life of Martin Luther King, Jr. as his city, known as "the old Pueblo", already did officially.

Paradoxically, while advocates of King Day were extolling the historic contributions of the world's youngest Nobel Peace Prize winner, the naysayers in the Legislature were predicting that the holiday would be derailed for another year. Senator Mawhinney who had been elevated to Senate Majority Leader spouted that the chances for passage were less in 1989 than the previous year. Of course, he and his partner, Usdane, could change that since they both had voiced support for King Day in previous years. President Usdane strategically assigned the King Day bill to the Government Committee chaired in the 39th Legislature by Wayne Stump, one of the most conservative, right-wing senators in that chamber. Senator Stump, being convinced that damaging information about King was concealed in sealed FBI files, threatened to block a hearing on the legislation. Several of the Democratic legislators felt that when "crunch time" came, conservative Republicans might be willing to make a deal with them on the King Day bill. For some reason, the new governor once again passed up an opportunity to mention the holiday when it was omitted from her first State of the State address delivered the week before national, state and local King Day festivities. Perhaps, her and her advisors' rationale was "You don't mention the obvious and risk ruffling the feathers of the party in power in both chambers." Obviously, several King Day legislators agreed with this new low-keyed strategy; but, to be honest, after being politically double-crossed in the last session, it took me a little getting used to. Venting my frustrations, I remarked to an inquiring reporter concerning the prospects for the holiday in 1989, "We've done everything humanly and rationally possible to get our Republican-controlled Legislature to pass the King bill legislation, short of civil disobedience." Other members of our coalition, like Pastor Barnwell and Blue, espoused patience; remembering the many years it took national King Day leaders to finally win a federal holiday in Dr. King's honor.

The local Public Broadcasting Station affiliate KAET, asked me to be one of their guest commentators during January. The subject matter would be none other than the MLK Day legislation and it would be run during their Horizon news program on January 23, 1989. Their purpose was for me to make my case for the King holiday in Arizona while the 39th Legislature was in its early days. Being rather nervous about doing a commentary that had specific guidelines as it related to time, plus having to use a teleprompter after putting on make-up so I would not project the "spotlight shine", I pre-taped my message to Channel 8's viewers to the best of my "impaired" ability. My commentary is printed below in its entirety.

KAET Commentary on
Martin Luther King, Jr. Holiday

January 23, 1989

COMMENTATOR: Dr. Warren H. Stewart, Sr.

On Monday of last week, over 100 nations around the world, the United States of America, the executive, legislative and judicial branches of our federal government, forty-four states, nearly every urban metropolis in America, the Arizona state university and community college systems, most elementary and secondary school districts and the major cities in Arizona paused to remember respectively and continue conscientiously the life and legacy of the late Dr. Martin Luther King, Jr., America's 20th Century revolutionary who successfully challenged our great nation to finally live up to the historic principles outlined in the Preamble of the United States Constitution. Regrettably, our own 39th Session of the Arizona State Legislature was doing business as usual on that day.

What will it take to move the sincerely stubborn Republican majority in both chambers to enact a paid state holiday honoring Martin Luther King, Jr. on the third Monday of January? When will the legislators assigned the responsibility of leading our state into the mainstream of American politics restore completely Arizona's tarnished image to leadership void of any suggestions of racial bigotry and myopic, narrow political viewpoints?

Times have changed. We now have a Governor who has promised to sign the King holiday bill if it reaches her desk. The additional cost factor for the King holiday has been eliminated. The retaining of the names of Washington and Lincoln on their holiday has been proposed. A recent poll indicated that there is broad-based support for a Martin Luther King, Jr. state holiday in Arizona. And, Arizona needs to unite all of our citizens of every race, creed and color as never before.

The time is now, Arizona State Legislature, in the year that America celebrates the 60th Anniversary of the birth of a red-blooded American citizen whom was to this century what George Washington and Abraham Lincoln were to America in their respective centuries. Before the last gavel is sounded, allow our entire state of Arizona to appropriately celebrate America's foremost dreamer with his day.

On the morning of our February 2, 1989 coalition meeting, the Arizona House of Representatives, under the leadership of its new Speaker, Representative Jane Hull, and guided by the persuasive political savvy of Minority Speaker Hamilton, our "WIN-WIN COMPROMISE" version of King Day passed by 35 ayes to 24 nays and one abstention. That year, our bill was introduced by Representative Kennedy and co-sponsored by several other Democrat and Republican representatives. Our hope was that such quick and decisive passage of the bill would prod the recalcitrant Republican Senate majority to join hands with their Democratic colleagues and do likewise. To our chagrin, we would be reminded that that kind of cooperative mentality did not yet exist on the other side. A matter of fact, *The Arizona Republic* reported that after the House approval of the MLK Day bill, Senator Usdane responded, "You can't count on me (as a yes vote)...." and Senator Mawhinney remarked, "Now, having gone through an election cycle...I'm convinced that a majority of people in my district do not want a paid Martin Luther King holiday...." and further indicated that the only reason he supported the bill in 1988 in committee was to help bring political peace to the state after the impeachment and ouster of Republican Gov. Evan Mecham..."

Between February 2 and February 22, 1989, when our next coalition meeting was held, a lot of politicking by members of ARIZONANS FOR A MARTIN LUTHER KING, JR. STATE HOLIDAY was taking place. Only eight members, five of who were white, showed up to report on the progress that had been made by those of us who had taken lobbying assignments.

Rabbi Robert Kravitz, a newcomer to Arizona and leader of the American Jewish Committee, proved to be a loyal King Day advocate and lobbyist with the many contacts he had made since moving to Arizona in 1988. Shortly after his arrival, Rabbi Kravitz called me to introduce himself and volunteer his time and talents for our common goal. We agreed on having lunch. He met me at First Institutional and we went to the restaurant next to the church housed in Esquire's, one of Phoenix's leading Black barber shops where many of Phoenix star, college and professional athletes get their haircuts. Without a doubt, Bob Kravitz is a faithful Jewish brother. While we were talking and eating chicken, I noticed that he was doing something peculiar with his knife and fork. As I satisfyingly ingested my barbecued dark meat, my new comrade in the King Day struggle had meticulously separated all of the veins and arteries from the "bird" he was eating and piled it neatly to the side of his plate.

As we talked I felt it my obligation to inform the rabbi that I was no darling of the Phoenix Jewish community. In 1980, the Jewish Federation of Phoenix had sent me on one of their public relations tours to Israel along with several other community and civic leaders. *Art, Tommy and I made the trip together along with other distinguished Arizonans.* It was one of the most disturbing junkets I have ever taken because of the apparent discriminatory practices directed towards Palestinians by the Israeli government. Of course, I interpreted what I saw through the eyes of an African-American who has known and experienced discrimination based on race and color since birth. Moreover, I was so unsettled by my observations on the trip that I vowed only to return to the Holy Land for purely Christian faith reasons.

The mistake I had made with the Phoenix Jewish community was to share my reflections, both good and bad, during a Sabbath morning service in one of Phoenix's leading synagogues. As I was leaving a Jewish physician got right into my face and said, "The nerve of you to mention the PLO (Palestinian Liberation Organization) in our synagogue!...You don't know what you saw in Israel!"

I did not mention the PLO, but I did make several references to the conditions of the Palestinians I saw and conversed with, especially in the occupied

territories; and I do know discrimination when I see it! I guess I should have kept
my thoughts to myself and just talked about the Jordan River, the Sea of Galilee,
Golgotha's Hill and the Dead Sea.

I felt incumbent to inform my new Jewish colleague with whom it was
he was having lunch. From hindsight, I am sure Bob had been apprised of
who I was, as it related to the Jewish community. Regardless, the fellowship
was fruitful and Rabbi Kravitz proved to be one of the state's staunchest
supporters of MLK Day.

Quite appropriately, Kravitz had been assigned as "the new kid on
the block" to work on Usdane. To our surprise, the senator suggested that
pro-King Day senators put together a package of civil rights issues, which
included the King Day bill and bring it to the floor all at once, rather than
showcasing the holiday legislation by itself. The rationale behind Usdane's
proposal was that his Republican colleagues would pass the King Day, only
if it was part of a group of civil rights bills. The rabbi was also informed that
"protests" would turn off his GOP colleagues. My response, after skepticism,
was that since "Uzzie" was dealing the cards, our supporters would have to
play by his rules. Bob also had ties to the Phoenix 40 and had been assured
by its chairman that they were now in favor of our King Day bill. What
a difference the loss of a few million dollars had made with the corporate
"powers that be" in Phoenix.

I ran into President Usdane while visiting the Senate on February 21,
1989. It was our first encounter since I had blasted him in our July 1988
press conference for voting against the holiday. He reiterated what he had
told Kravitz about a "civil rights package." Then, he assured me that he
"liked me." Gosh, what a relief!

Paul and I met with "swing" moderate Republican Senator Corbet
in February 1989. Although our meeting was on the record, some of what
we discussed was to be considered off the record. Senator Corbet committed to voting for the King Day bill, but not our version, which would
eliminate Abraham Lincoln Day as a solo holiday in Arizona. However, he
suggested sacrificing Columbus Day instead of Lincoln or Washington Day.
Interestingly, the first time I had heard of that King-Columbus Day swap
came from E. J. Montini, an *Arizona Republic* columnist of Italian-American
heritage, a few days after Mecham's shocking election in November 1986.
Montini's rationale paralleled mine, that if there was any literally *un-American*
holiday, it was Columbus Day. After all, Columbus Day is a racist holiday,
if there ever was one, because it deems non-personhood to the thousands

of people who called this land home for centuries before a lost White man sailed into what he thought was the East Indies.

But, when we discussed Corbet's "off-the-record" suggestion, it was unanimously squashed because we felt it would rile the Italian-American community and cause an unnecessary distraction from our goal. Additionally, by exchanging Columbus Day instead of combining Washington Day and Lincoln Day into a named President's Day, Arizona would still be out of sync with the rest of the nation, particularly the federal government. Also, we found ourselves bargaining for a version of the King Day, other than the one we had agreed upon as a coalition.

As it related to the respective legislative districts of Senators DeLong and Mawhinney who had declared that their constituents did not support MLK Day, which was questionable since the two districts were considered moderate Republican, Peter Fears suggested that our coalition get a highly respected research outfit to poll the two districts. We tossed the idea around and later used it to validate what we speculated.

The last matter we discussed at the late February meeting, was the rumored existence of another King Day group being formed to help pass the holiday, which opposed the boycotting of Arizona. The group in question publicly criticized ARIZONANS FOR A MARTIN LUTHER KING, JR. STATE HOLIDAY for supporting convention and entertainer boycotts. Speaking of the boycott strategy, once Mecham was relieved of his gubernatorial duties in April 1988, no organization had cancelled their annual meeting in Arizona, as far as the tourism industry could tell. On the other hand, it could not even be estimated how many organizations quietly decided to stay away from Arizona until it passed a King Day.

By the end of March, Peter and I met with Dr. Bruce Merrill, a highly respected pollster associated with ASU, who had strong Republican connections. He explained his method of research and his costs. In spite of being a conservative Republican, Dr. Merrill enthusiastically accepted our assignment to conduct surveys in the 12th and 14th Legislative Districts in Tucson, which DeLong and Mawhinney served. We agreed to pay him $3,500 for his professional services.

Within a few days we received very encouraging news from the polls conducted in the two Tucson districts. In Mawhinney's 12th District, Merrill's research showed that the voters supported our version of King Day 59 to 32 percent and on DeLong's terrain in the 14th, MLK Day support was 60 to 31 percent in favor. In summary, our poll results showed that the registered voters in the two Tucson holiday-opposing senators were with us two to one. Quite appropriately, we revealed that news to our coalition members in Room 340 of the Arizona House of Representatives. However, the material was supposed to have been kept confidential until we could get Pastor Gantt and former Senator Greg Lunn of Tucson to meet with Senators DeLong and Mawhinney to "let them down easy" upon hearing that the majority of their constituents voted yes for Martin while they were still voting no. Our hope was that in such a meeting, the two pragmatic-thinking politicians would come out in favor of King Day. This was to be done before our planned press conference announcing the results on April 14, 1989.

Meanwhile, the same day of our 5:30 p.m. coalition meeting at the State Capitol was the 21st anniversary of the assassination of Dr. King. We had sent out a press release announcing a candlelight prayer vigil in memory of Martin Luther King, Jr. and to pray for passage of the King bill by the Senate. In April in Phoenix, the sun set a little before 7:00 p.m., so supporters were asked to bring flashlights or penlights. The prayer vigil idea came out of a meeting I had with Bill Jamieson, a leading Democrat bureaucrat who had headed the Department of Economic Security and was now the major partner in a prominent political consulting firm called Jamieson and Gutierrez. Bill also proposed a larger King Day rally later in April to keep the issue before the slow-moving Senate. What I was to later discover about Jamieson, was that he was a Christian gentleman of depth, warmth and perception.

About 200 faithful supporters of King Day showed up at the State Capitol on Tuesday, April 14, 1989. We sang. We prayed. We talked. We spoke. The regulars spoke—Hamilton, Kennedy and Walker. Josefina Duran of Church Women United and American Baptist prayed that "faith can move mountains." In less than prayerful words, I reminded the audience that "on January 12, 1987, Evan Mecham assassinated all over again the legacy of Martin Luther King, Jr." Then, I reminded them of the first anniversary of Mecham's conviction and removal from office, which took place on April 4, 1988.

Check out the latest irony with Mecham and Martin. *On that same 1989 evening on another side of town, former Governor Evan Mecham was announcing his intentions to run again for governor of the state of Arizona!* "Here we go again!" It must have been on a lot of people's minds that night, much more so than the anniversary of Dr. King's murder or King Day.

Another significant loss occurred for our coalition on April 4, 1989. Chris Johns resigned as a member of our coalition and its corporate board. Chris provided countless hours of free legal services from our inception to incorporation through that day's deliberations. But, he had reached his point of saturation as it related to internal haggling and infighting relative to coalition finances and corporate deliberations. More than anything else, there existed a generational battle between him defending himself and his legal skills and Judge Williams representing the experienced "old guard" with active experience in the historic Civil Rights Movement of the 1960's. I tried to talk him out of leaving us, but he was obviously frustrated at what he considered a distraction from our common cause. That evening he turned all of our corporate papers over to Attorney Gerald Richard, who began to serve as acting statutory agent of our Corporation. Chris was truly missed.

Two days before our scheduled press conference to announce the results from our poll of the two Tucson districts, *Phoenix Gazette* political columnist John Kolbe featured a lengthy column entitled "Playing hard ball wins score for King Day." I began to read his column with great interest because this was the columnist who once labeled yours truly as "a loose cannon." However, our decision to survey two King Day opposing Senators' districts with Bruce Merrill must have impressed the newspaper writer whose articles clearly indicated that *very few people* impressed John Kolbe. He was also the columnist that then Governor Mecham designated as a "non-person" due to his critical columns about him. Nevertheless, some excerpts from his Wednesday, April 12, 1989 column are included below.

> Forget all that high-sounding rhetoric about justice and human rights, the Martin Luther King holiday gang has decided to play old-fashioned, hard ball politics.
> But it probably won't work much better than the rhetoric.

After explaining to his readers that Senators Mawhinney and DeLong had made negative statements and cast negative votes relative to MLK Day legislation, Kolbe commented,

> Both targeted senators say they oppose the King bill because their constituents do. So Stewart saw them and raised them. He hired ASU pollster Bruce Merrill…to find out exactly what the citizens of (their districts) do think about the state holiday.

What he found, Stewart believes, cuts the last props from beneath the opposition rationale.

After revealing the surprisingly favorable poll results, I was quoted in the article,

> "They come up with an excuse every year", Stewart said. "Well, we've eliminated their latest excuse....Now what are they going to say?"

To which Kolbe answered the bare truth, which cast doubt on two individual's political ethics,

> "What they're going to say, apparently is no."
>
> "It doesn't sway me," DeLong said. "I've done polls (in the 14th District) on this for several years, and it always comes up the same, from about 63 or 64 percent against it up into the 70's." He admits his surveys aren't scientific...
>
> Mawhinney's stance seems muddled, but is equally adamant.
>
> "If we're going to start basing all our positions on polls, you can get rid of us and install a button," he said, suggesting there may be reason other than constituent opposition for his position.

Moving to a conclusion of his revealing column, Kolbe addressed Usdane and us,

> Senate President Bob Usdane has predicted the King issue will get a floor vote; but so far, he hasn't lifted a finger to make it possible....
>
> Stewart's brand of hardball is time-honored stuff (although the targets are usually annoyed), and could be effective but for one flaw:
>
> Success depends on lawmakers succumbing to its inherent logic. At the Arizona Capitol, logic is a mighty weak peg on which to hang one's ideological hat.

Kolbe's advance column did not deter our coalition from holding our press conference on the 14th of April. This time we went to the Trinity Cathedral, headquarters of the Episcopal Church in Arizona, to announce our "old" news to the media. I began by stating that **"ARIZONA'S IMAGE IS AT STAKE!"** Then I proceeded to pronounce,

With the resurgence of the gubernatorial candidacy of former Governor Evan Mecham, known nationally and internationally for rescinding Arizona's Martin Luther King, Jr. holiday, there is no better time than now for the Arizona State Senate to pass the **MARTIN LUTHER KING, JR./CIVIL RIGHTS DAY** legislation passed by the Arizona House of Representatives...

> **JUST TWO MORE AYE VOTES ARE NEEDED IN THE STATE SENATE TO REACH THE NEEDED SIXTEEN TO PASS THE KING BILL.**

> Senator John Mawhinney...and Senator Bill De Long... have indicated that their current opposition is based on their legislative constituency **not** supporting the King holiday.

After sharing the poll results of their two districts, I concluded,

> Our request is that you would use your influence in persuading (them) to support King legislation as passed by the Arizona House. ...**this year.** This needs to be done **immediately**...
> **ARIZONA'S RESTORED IMAGE DEPENDS ON YOUR SUPPORT ON THIS ISSUE.**

In Tucson, Pastor Gantt revealed to reporters that the two senators had refused to meet with him to discuss the polls before the results became public. Gantt challenged the Tucson senators to "quit using their constituents as scapegoats."

Understandably, the two targeted lawmakers felt picked upon and threatened that "pressure tactics" very seldom move legislators. One of them even suggested that King Day backers "work to lower the infant mortality and high school dropout rates among blacks."

Another rude awakening to the world of politics was abruptly taught to our grassroots coalition—*two plus two does not always equal four in politics!*

With Evan Mecham's sixth run for Governor of Arizona tripping out of the starting blocks of Arizona's bizarre late 1980s politics, a fortyish multimillionaire developer by the name of J. Fife Symington announced his gubernatorial candidacy with the specific purpose of stopping his fellow Republican former governor. The news media could not withhold their delight in reporting Symington's words describing Mecham as a "schoolyard bully" needing a "poke...in the nose." This new political aspirant's colorful language caught Mecham off guard, perhaps because he was calling for a "kinder, gentler" Arizona and this time around vowed to stick to issues rather than personalities. Fife Symington revealed that he had made his decision to seek the post of governor on *April 4, 1989*, that significant April day that had special meaning to our coalition, Arizona politics, Evan Mecham and now, "the new (rich) kid on the block." Another unusual note about both Republican candidates' announcements was that they occurred 17 months before the 1990 primary elections. Consequently, the Arizona Republican Party, which had not had a GOP in the governor's seat for years prior to Evan Mecham, found itself expending energy just trying to keep from splintering over the resurgence of Mecham's candidacy. Several prominent Republicans declared that they could not support another Mecham run for governor, even if he won the primary. Other GOP possible gubernatorial candidates were not deterred by either announced fellow Republican's candidacy.

Once I saw news clips and sound bites of Fife Syminton's announcement for governor, I wrote him a letter seeking his public support of a state holiday honoring Dr. Martin Luther King Jr. Specifically, I asked him to use his "influence in persuading Senators Mawhinney and DeLong in supporting King legislation as passed by the Arizona House…" that year. I sent him a copy of the poll Dr. Bruce Merrill had done for us in their respective districts. Even though I asked him to let us know if he would contact the two questionable senators, I never received a response, which proved to be the case over half of the time when writing "power brokers." However, in his press conference of April 12, 1989, the soon-to-be governor stated his support for a state MLK Day. Meanwhile, Arizona's then current Governor Mofford "came out of the closet" once again and repeated her call for Arizona to join the rest of the nation in honoring King. She directly challenged Republican legislative leaders to step up their deliberations to make passage of the holiday legislation possible in the *yet to move* Senate. Senator Usdane responded that addressing such an issue too quickly could disintegrate bipartisan agreements between the Republicans and Democrats on other critical issues before their body. Mawhinney dared to spit out what I consider mean-spirited jabs at those of us who simply wanted a vote on King Day. In the governor's remarks, she brought up the money lost, due to convention cancellations, which would remind the lawmakers that the moral issue of the holiday had acquired economic overtones due to its perennial defeats in the state over the past three years.

The reporters continued to inquire if she had considered issuing an executive order establishing MLK Day, like Babbitt had done in 1986.

However, her advisors and our coalition insisted that she shouldn't go that route again. Usdane continued to imply that the King Day would fail if brought to the floor at that time. And Mawhinney challenged holiday supporters to let the Arizona voters hold a referendum on it and then we would see that the will of the people was anti-King Day.

With the Arizona Senate leaders holding the King bill hostage, a coalition of Democrats and moderate Republicans in the House of Representatives considered tying their King Day legislation to Senate bill 1397, which was an economic development package that passed the Senate 25-3, and had been sent over to their chamber for approval. Of course, Senator Mawhinney whined about the "unconstitutionality" of such an attachment since, in his opinion, King Day had nothing to do with economic development. However, one Republican legislator differed with Mawhinney by indicating that state business leaders were being confronted regularly about Arizona's King Day controversy when they sought to woo new businesses to set up shop in Arizona. Senator Walker, the major sponsor of the holiday bill in her chamber, wholeheartedly endorsed the King-economic development tie. Apparently, House Republicans became frightened when legislative attorneys suggested that such a link just might be unconstitutional.

The House Commerce Committee voted 7-6 to attach the holiday to the economic development measure. Once again, the hope for passage of MLK Day by the Arizona State Legislature nearly flickered out by the winds of partisan politics.

Surprisingly, a more confident Governor Mofford came out swinging on behalf of the King Day by speaking at an MLK rally held at the Capitol in front of the Senate on Monday, April 24, 1989. At the gathering of over 400 people around noon, the governor threatened to keep key legislation from becoming law if the "kidnapping" Republican-dominated Senate did not pass the holiday. We were still short of two Republican votes for passage of the holiday, if it ever got to the floor. Usdane, obviously under pressure from his own Jewish community and business leaders, predicted that the holiday would pass in the Senate, even though he still opposed it. Senator Steiner, the Republican from central Phoenix, did not waver on her support from King Day. In addition, our poll and influence from the Tucson business community began to move Senator DeLong in our direction. Could it be that three years of intense public involvement for the Arizona Martin Luther King, Jr. Day was about to pay off? Those of us gathered at the State Capitol believed so.

The April 24, 1989 MLK Day rally was especially important in that it was sponsored officially by the Phoenix Jewish Federation's Community Relations Council chaired by a yuppie Jewish businessman by the name of Arnie Zaler. This name would become very familiar over the next two years as a highly visible pro-King Day advocate. Zaler had come to one of our coalition meetings upon my invitation, after he had made several calls to my church office and home to introduce himself, talk about his willingness to work with ARIZONANS FOR A MARTIN LUTHER KING, JR. STATE HOLIDAY, and find out just who the Reverend Warren Stewart was. To say the least, Arnie, as he became known by all associated with the King Day quest; proved to be one of the most persistent and inquisitive individuals with whom I have ever met and worked. His often-stubborn determination to get the information he wanted could be unnerving at times; but, regardless, we accepted Arnie for who he was and how he was going to operate.

Although the Monday rally was the brainchild of the Community Relations Council of the Jewish Federation, the announcement flyers somehow carried our coalition's logo and name on them without our permission. Nowhere on the flyer was found the names of the two sponsoring organizations-the Jewish Federation and the Black-Jewish Coalition. Mind you, we welcomed the aid of those two well-respected community groups. Moreover, they helped to renew historic links between the African-American civil rights activists and the Jewish community. Nevertheless, in addition to the cover letter attached to some of the flyers, we felt that our permission should have been sought to use our logo on an otherwise unidentified-sponsored publicity piece.

As I mentioned earlier, Governor Mofford appeared on the program shortly after it began, urged the holiday's passing immediately, and left. Blue offered words of optimism, as he always did. Zaler spoke and informed the crowd of his marching in the South during the civil rights demonstrations of the sixties.

It was my turn to speak on behalf of the holiday. Glancing at some notes I had jotted down on the back of two of the flyers, I proclaimed in my preacher-voice,

> The spirit of Martin is smiling today…to see such a broad-based coalition. Thank you, Arnie Zaler. Thank you, Black Jewish Coalition. Thank you, Governor Mofford. Thank you, Brothers and Sisters for being here to make not a color-blind, but **colorful**

statement to all Arizona that "We're Red, Yellow, Black, Brown and White, all precious in God's sight!"

Someone asked, "Why are we here?" **We are here because** 60 years ago, God brought forth a baby boy from the womb of Alberta King. **We are here because** that boy believed in the Pledge of Allegiance, the Constitution of the United States and the Gettysburg Address. **We are here because** that young man Martin had a Dream...**We are here because** Martin Luther King, Jr., like no other American, led this nation in living up to its promises of "justice and liberty for all." **We are here because** in November of 1983, a Republican President by the name of Ronald Wilson Reagan signed into law a bill making the third Monday in January a national holiday honoring the life and legacy of (MLK, Jr.). **We are here because** 44 states, every major city in Arizona, every state university and community college, and nearly every school district celebrate Martin's day. **We are here because** the Arizona House of Representatives has, once again, passed legislation so Arizona can honor America's foremost symbol of civil rights.

AND WE ARE HERE BECAUSE WE WANT THE ARIZONA STATE SENATE TO PASS THE KING HOLIDAY LEGISLATION SO THAT ARIZONA CAN JOIN THIS NATION IN CELEBRATING THE THIRD MONDAY IN JANUARY AS MARTIN LUTHER KING, JR./CIVIL RIGHTS DAY!

THAT'S WHY WE'RE HERE! AND WE AIN'T GOING TO LET NOBODY TURN US AROUND! FOR OUR EYES HAVE SEEN THE GLORY....

THE TIME IS NOW! THE TIME IS NOW! THE TIME IS NOW!

Something in me almost always came alive when I spoke in favor of Arizona MLK Day. That Monday was no different, in spite of experiencing a "blue Monday" as many pastors do after working all day Sunday. Moreover, that seemed to be the case on many of the critical King Day celebrations, protests, rallies and meetings—they often fell on my personal sabbath as a full-time pastor—Monday. But, for six years I would grin and bear it, pooped out or not. My enthusiasm for King Day showed that day, at least to *Republic* columnist E.J. Montini, who wrote,

...The only person, who truly seems to believe that King Holiday legislation will pass, who acts as if he *must* believe it, is the Rev. Warren Stewart, the last speaker at the rally.

Stewart has taken on the role of public conscience over this issue. He reminds us again and again, what we should do. And we ignore him. Just as we ignore our own consciences much of the time....

By the end of his speech, Stewart had the crowd chanting, "The time is now! The time is now!"

It was, ironically, the only time that the crowd could be heard from inside the Senate building. Though it's unclear if anyone there was listening.

Once again, the media provided extensive cover of the King Day supporters' event. Mofford's "threat" made the headlines and the issue was kept very much alive before the public and state senate. So, even though the rally did not get the 2,000 persons Zaler and his supporting groups had hoped for, our efforts paid off in publicity, if nothing else.

Two notes of interest need to be recorded here. The Right Reverend Joseph Heistand, Episcopal Bishop of Arizona, informed the media at our rally that the Episcopal General Convention, which had scheduled its national meeting in Phoenix for 1991 would strongly consider canceling its commitment to the Valley of the Sun due to no King Day in Arizona. Reportedly, its annual meeting ranked third largest in the nation behind the Republican and Democratic National Conventions. Secondly, word leaked out that one of former Governor Mecham's attorneys also represented James Earl Ray, the now deceased, convicted assassin of Dr. King who was serving a 99-year sentence in Tennessee. In spite of all of the above, Arizona's King Day remained "blockaded in the Senate."

On the same day of the rally, the governor wrote her first letter to me as general chairperson of our coalition in response to a letter I had written to her earlier in April about our King Day poll in Mawhinney and DeLong's districts. In her hopeful letter she shared,

Passage of this bill is certainly a priority for me. It would clearly help tourism and economic development, but most importantly, it is the right thing to do. You can count on my full support for passage of this bill in this legislative session.

Reading between the lines, I could sense that the Arizona business community, particularly the Phoenix 40, had given Governor Mofford the "go ahead" to push full force for this holiday with their behind-the-scenes backing. She had definitely made the transition from secretary to chief executive.

The day after the rally in front of the Senate Building, I wrote a letter of appreciation to Arnie thanking him for his enthusiastic leadership in organizing the MLK event which had made a "significant and timely impact." Specifically, I commended him that "…[his] vision of a broad-based coalition of Anglos, Hispanics, African-Americans, Jews, Christians, business persons, politicians and clergy uniting behind a common cause became a visible reality on Monday." I included words of gratitude to other members of the Black-Jewish Coalition who had worked hard and fast putting together the rally, namely, Ida Steele, an active African Methodist Episcopal laywoman; David Frazer, a high-powered, low-keyed corporate attorney who had co-hosted my 1980 trip to Israel; Jeff Santis and Rabbi Kravitz.

ASU experienced some widely publicized racial unrest during the same week of our rally. The university's president at that time, Dr. J. Russell Nelson, made some public commitments to resolve the issues that revolved around alleged racism and bigotry against African-American students on campus. Without missing a chance to plug for King Day votes in the Senate, I wrote Dr. Nelson, commended him for his openness and willingness to provide "rare" leadership on such issues in Arizona, and requested that he "put in a good word" for our King Day legislation to Senator Doug Todd in whose district the 40,000 student state university was located. I requested the same of Mr. Herman Chanen, President of the Arizona Board of Regents, who also was involved in resolving the problems at ASU. In my letter to Miss Tanya Holmes, spokesperson for Students Against Racism at ASU, I saluted her and her fellow Black students for utilizing "courageous and critical nonviolent efforts in fighting against the violence of racism and bigotry on the Arizona State University campus."

Sensing possible victory in the air, our May 9, 1989 coalition meeting addressed corporate matters such as the coalition's financial statement prepared by our auditor, re-activation of a committee for dissolution of our corporation, and allocation of remaining funds on hand at time of dissolution, which totaled $18,600. We also discussed that latest Senate vote count, which had us at 15, and a possible 16th needed for victory. For the first time in a year, we began to discuss a victory celebration once passage occurred.

Judge Williams chaired our committee for an appreciation reception for supporters of an Arizona MLK, Jr. State Holiday. Plans tossed out dealt with a prayer service of thanksgiving to be held at First Baptist Church of Phoenix and a major press conference held at Encanto Park, Eastlake Park or the State Capitol. In case of defeat, we toyed with the ideas of selective patronage of state senators who voted against the holiday and call for a national day of prayer.

Augmenting our efforts to get an aye vote for King Day out of Senator Mawhinney, Danny White, a Phoenician who had moved to Tucson and son of Mrs. White of Phoenix's award-winning Golden Rule Cafe, launched single-handedly a petition drive in District 12 to call upon their senator and two representatives to support Arizona's King Day legislation. Danny wrote me about his efforts and gave me encouraging news relative to the ease he was having at getting the district's mostly White constituents to sign. In response, I sent Danny a copy of our poll for his information. I also saw a copy of Mr. White's letter to his senator, which was a four-page defense, calling for an affirmative vote from Mawhinney. Thank goodness, one of District 12's representatives, Republican Jack Jewett, had already cast his vote in favor of the holiday in the House. Danny, also serving as the *Arizona Informant's* Southern correspondent, wrote a couple of articles, which Editor Cloves Campbell gave front-page coverage.

By the June 6, 1989 meeting of our coalition, plans proceeded to take shape for our long-awaited victory/thanksgiving celebration for the expected senatorial passage of MLK, Jr. /Civil Rights Day. Senators DeLong and Corbet had come over to our side. DeLong had re-polled his 14th District and discovered that a majority of his constituents supported the King Day. We went as far as to plan a candlelight thanksgiving service at the Capitol the Monday after its expected passage, sometime in the middle or latter part of June. Judge Williams and her committee were orchestrating a gala affair to celebrate the attainment of our common goal. All we were waiting for was the call from our legislating honorary chairs to tell us to come witness the victory vote at the Senate.

On June 13th, I received a message from Representative Kennedy at 2:25 p.m., which read, "Very Important. She will call back in about 45 minutes." When she did call back, she informed me that the Senate Republicans who had committed to us were "reneging" on their votes. The inevitable happened! On June 15, 1989, Usdane torpedoed the King Day bill in the Senate by not allowing it to gets the Republican Caucus which could have voted for the bill to get a hearing on the Senate floor, even though the majority of them did not support it. We had the three Republican votes needed to approve the bill—Steiner, DeLong and Corbet. Apparently, some of the conservative Republican senators felt that the pro-Mecham, anti-King voters would make them pay a high "political price" if the King Day passed once they let it get to the floor, like several of the pro-impeachment Republican legislators had paid after kicking Mecham out of office. "Boneless Bob," as one editorial labeled him, had let it happen again. *NO KING DAY FOR ARIZONA!*

You can imagine how lively our July 6, 1989 coalition meeting was. Art was there along with Senator Stephens, minority leader in the Senate, to tell us exactly what happened. Stephens assured us that "we did have the votes for the MLK, Jr. holiday." His story indicated that Mawhinney "threatened" Usdane if he allowed the King bill to go to the floor. According to Alan, Mawhinney, the so-called moderate Republican, had aligned himself with the Republican right-wingers. Art spoke up and said that "Usdane had come up with a new idea, involving exchanging the Columbus holiday to come up with a day for King." Vada Manager, a gifted African-American young man who had served as Governor Babbit's press aide, reported to us that Governor Mofford had discussed calling a special session of the Legislature to address the holiday. She just wanted to be sure that she had the votes before the King Day Special Session was called.

To our advantage there was virtually unanimous statewide criticism of the Senate's latest King Day debacles, especially from the major newspapers, religious organizations, business community, Arizona Democrats and some Republican leaders. By that time, Arnie had a firm grip on his Ad-hoc Committee on MLK, Jr. Holiday. He suggested that we launch a "multipronged attack, take a people's holiday, and urge Arizona businesses to close down on King Day 1990." In an effort to pay back Uzzie and Mawhinney for jerking King Day out of our hands, we discussed renewing our call for support of the convention boycott. Behind the scene, it was suggested to work for Mawhinney's defeat next year. Mark Reader challenged us to exercise our option of nonviolent civil disobedience in protest of the Senate's action. We set a goal of 1,000 participants in that direct action if decided upon to use as a tactic to get our message across. The idea of approaching the NBA and NFL for support was voiced. A concert led by nationally known entertainers was suggested. We were mad!

In a letter I wrote to our supporters, I offered my "words of appreciation" for the president of the Senate with these words,

> As we all know by now the Arizona State Senate under the leadership of...Usdane, denied Arizona the right to celebrate (MLK, Jr. /Civil Rights Day)! Most disheartening about this year's King Holiday Bill defeat was that Senator Carolyn Walker informed us that she had the votes for the King legislation. In my opinion, as it relates to the Martin Luther King Holiday, SENATOR ROBERT USDANE'S WORD IS BANKRUPT!

Both Senator Walker and I wrote letters to Governor Mofford urging her to call a special session on the sole issue of the Martin Luther King state holiday. Another letter that went out to our coalition roster invited them to come to a follow-up strategy meeting to be held on July 20, 1989 to develop the three-pronged strategy, which included soliciting support from (1) the business community and (2) national entertainers, and (3) organizing for a nonviolent direct action protest.

At that meeting, we divided up those present into three committees. Arnie was selected to chair the business involvement sub-committee since he was a small businessperson himself. The chair of the national entertainment sub-committee was Gene, who would work on a major concert to feature major entertainers to raise funds in support of our efforts. I chaired the nonviolent direct action protest subcommittee and we were dead serious about shutting down the right place at the right time to show our disgust with the Senate. Under the political and philosophical guidance of Mark, members of my committee were determined to involve a person with expertise in nonviolent direct action to train our members who volunteered to participate. Arizona had had several such actions in recent history, two of which were the "Sanctuary Movement", in which Arizonans risked arrest and imprisonment for providing sanctuary for illegal aliens and engaging in protests against the building of the Palo Verde Nuclear Power Plant. There were also persons in our state who had experience of the sit-in type of nonviolent civil disobedience.

Because we were extremely serious about such action, we discussed the need for getting lawyers to defend us, once arrested, as well as to advise us about the laws before any action was taken. We would recruit nonviolent protestors and develop a "protestor's pledge card" to get commitments that all protestors would engage in the action, according to our code of ethics and procedures. It was an objective of ours to recruit some local "celebrity" participants to add notoriety to our protests. After much discussion, my sub-committee reported to the broader group that we would plan to shut down the Arizona State Senate on the 1990 Martin Luther King, Jr. federal holiday observance by sitting down in front of the Senate Building's doors. Our preplanning showed us that there would be three double doors to be blocked and one parking lot to obstruct entrances and exits. The press would be notified in advance, as well as the State Capitol police and Phoenix police.

The business subcommittee decided to set October 1989 as a target to get businesses involved in lobbying for King Day and publicly announcing that they would make the third Monday in January a paid holiday for their employees. Dr. Reader suggested a "Business Honor Roll" to list King Day supporting and observing companies.

As it relates to the major concert, Jackie Platt-Jennas and Gene chose Monday, January 15, 1990 as the date for our event. That day the federal holiday observance and King's actual birthday would fall on the same day.

Arizona's summer heat was about to add to our temper over the latest King Day disgrace. Consequently, our coalition decided that our next meeting would be held on August 31, 1989.

ARIZONANS FOR A MARTIN LUTHER KING, JR. STATE HOLIDAY convened the last day of August with an attendance of 24 coalition members, several of whom could be considered as "political and community heavy weights", such as Dr. Paul Elsner, Ed Buck, Carolyn Walker, Alan Stephens and Michael Lacey.

Also, a funny thing happened over the scorching desert summer. A Phoenix Super Bowl '93 Committee had been formed, headed by Mr. Bill Shover, director of public affairs for the Phoenix Newspaper, Inc., which published *The Republic* and *The Gazette*. In the middle of August, appearing in the local newspapers were statements made by Shover; Bill Bidwell, the owner of the Phoenix Cardinals, which had relocated to Phoenix from St. Louis within the last year; and Paul Tagliabue, Commissioner of the National Football League. It became very obvious, from the news reports, that Phoenix would not have a chance to host the 1993 Super Bowl until Arizona passed a paid holiday honoring Dr. King. After all, over half of the players in the NFL were the same color as Martin Luther King, Jr. So, Arizona's fumbling of King Day had not only insulted three and a half percent of its residents (and many others of all races in the state), but it had made this state out of bounds to the lucrative annual Super Bowl extravaganza, which would bring in as much as $250,000,000 to the hosting state. Mind you, the NFL boycotting Arizona was never mentioned "officially" by Commissioner Tagliabue, but it was understood to be a rule for the game.

I was astounded to hear members of Arizona's business community come out from undercover on this issue to talk publicly and unapologetically about the need for a Martin Luther King, Jr. state holiday. Those were some of the guys who never responded to our coalition's letters back in 1986 and 1987 when we solicited their support on purely moral grounds, and eventually in an effort to salvage the image of the state caused by Mecham rescinding the MLK Day. So, I wrote a letter to Shover on August 14, 1989 after reading his comments in an article in *The Phoenix Gazette* on August 10 and again in *The Republic* on the morning of the 14th. In both articles, Shover talked about the upcoming special session, at which time the King holiday might be considered, as well as mentioned that his Phoenix 93 Super Bowl Committee was going to address the King issue in the meeting to be held on September 14, 1989. The second paragraph of my letter read like this.

> Since you chair the Phoenix '93 Super Bowl Committee and both the 1993 Super Bowl and the Martin Luther King, Jr. holiday issue are often mentioned in the same breath, I, as General Chairperson of **ARIZONANS FOR A MARTIN LUTHER KING, JR. STATE HOLIDAY** would welcome the opportunity to meet with you, at your convenience, prior to your September 14th meeting with your group.

Since I was departing on vacation when I wrote Shover the letter, I requested a meeting upon my return to my office on August 29, 1989. Things worked out, where Mr. Shover and I met at First Institutional two hours before our coalition's end of summer meeting. After the normal greetings that strangers go through; we began to converse. My notes reveal that Shover said that he supported the King Day for moral *and economic reasons*. He said, "Normally, I don't get involved in political affairs; but I see that Arizona needs to settle this issue and remove our Alabama of the 80s' image." He went on to inform me that he had convinced several key business leaders to support the holiday, including: Bill Bidwell; John Teets, CEO, of Greyhound-Dial; Jack Pfister, general manager of Salt River Project; as well as several other CEOs of corporations such as, Shamrock Foods, Valley National Bank, and even the chair of the Lincoln Caucus, an ultra-conservative Republican group.

Shover revealed that he had wooed House Speaker Jane Hull into changing her stance against King Day to being supportive of it. He pledged to talk with Senators Usdane, Corbet, DeLong, Mawhinney, Hays and Patterson—all no votes. The Phoenix '93 Super Bowl Committee, according to Shover, was solidly behind the MLK legislation. Realizing the unbreakable connection between his dream to see Phoenix host the Super Bowl and Arizona celebrating King Day as an official paid state holiday, Shover confessed that his committee would abandon their effort if the holiday was not passed soon. To push the day honoring King, he and several business leaders were planning to meet with Governor Mofford to press her to put it on the Special Session's agenda. As our meeting came to an end, Mr. Shover pledged to do all he could to resolve this holiday issue and said he personally supported the King-Columbus Day exchange or the "smorgasbord" MLK Day set-up, where a state employee could choose which holidays out of a pool he or she wished to be off work.

I informed Shover a little bit about who we were and how long our coalition had been working with the Legislature. I am sure he had heard of me and ARIZONANS FOR A MARTIN LUTHER KING, JR. STATE HOLIDAY, as much as we had been in the newspapers that his company owned. He also was a member of the Phoenix 40, to which I had written soliciting their support. But since he ran in a different circle than most of our coalition's members, it did not cross his mind that we *really* existed. That is why it is necessary for grassroots organizations to let the "powers that be" know they are there. If not, they will get about as much attention from them as a pesky fly.

Another significant meeting had taken place during August that would prove fruitful in getting the results we had worked for. Arnie, through his contacts, arranged a meeting with Governor Mofford on August 4, 1989, which I attended reluctantly because I did not know what Arnie was up to. Our working relationship had become strained because I had seen a copy of a press release and a letter of introduction to Mrs. King sent out by Arnie with our coalition logo and name at the top, *with all other names of our chairs, honorary chairs, offices and location removed from the letterhead, and* Zaler's office address at the bottom as well as his name as the sender of both documents. Yes, we were working together, but it would have been proper to get prior permission before altering our letterhead and using our logo. Nevertheless, I attended, upon the advice of some of our coalition members.

The attendees were Rabbi Kravitz, A. J. Miller, Jackie Platt-Jennas, Gene and Zaler, all of whom had met with Mrs. King at the recent 5th Annual Martin Luther King, Jr. Federal Holiday Planning Commission held July 27-29, 1989 in Atlanta; plus Dr. Ed Valenzuela, Richard Zazueta of Senator DeConcini's office and Bill Jamieson. The governor was accompanied by two of her aides, namely Art Othon and Joyce Geyser. Once again, Governor Mofford reiterated her support for the MLK Day. She also reaffirmed her stand that she would "put the MLK Day on the special session agenda only if she was assured that the votes were there to pass it." She also informed us that she would not put the MLK Day issue on the planned special session on solutions to prison overcrowding. Jamieson volunteered to try to get business leaders to support King Day and get some movement out of Usdane. When told of Mrs. King's possible coming to Arizona to speak before a joint session of the Legislature, Mofford advised that any visit by Dr. King's widow should be postponed until the holiday is passed. Then, she could come for the signing ceremony. The "grand lady of Arizona" doled out some other advice to us. "Fight for the King bill with dignity," she said. "You know", she continued, "We need not even mention Evan Mecham's name related to this holiday anymore." Before we left the noontime meeting, Governor Mofford mentioned that she felt Usdane was softening on his preventing the Senate to vote on the holiday. Lastly, she voiced her preference for the federal model of King Day and urged us to stick with that.

In spite of the governor's wishes, by our August 31st coalition meeting, a King bill revision had taken place between the last regular session and the upcoming special one—our "WIN-WIN COMPROMISE" had been replaced by exchanging Columbus Day for King Day. Senator Walker, after conversing with a supportive Republican senator, was now the sponsor of the new King bill. Reluctantly, our group voted to support Senator Walker's Columbus/King Day switch. Personally, I was happy to see Columbus Day get crossed off the calendar. Moreover, the conservative Republicans would have their Founder's Day—Abraham Lincoln Day and George Washington Day—left untouched.

This new version had the full backing of Arizona's business community. Phoenix had utilized such an exchange to honor King when it adopted the holiday a few years back and there was no public outcry. Regardless of the proposal presented by Walker, several Republicans still expressed disdain for the King Day. It had been reported that President Usdane had warned, "…the King Day would pass over his dead body."

On the positive side, Phoenix mayoral candidate Burt Kruglick and chairman of the Arizona Republican Party had now publicly endorsed passage of MLK Day as a state holiday. Also, if needed, we had been in touch with Mrs. King's office and she would consider coming to Arizona to speak before a historic special session on behalf of a day honoring her late husband.

Buck and Arnie were working with Gene trying to set up our 1990 MLK Concert. Their goal was to get Stevie Wonder to return to Arizona to star on the show in support of King Day. A possible agreement was being worked out, where the proceeds from the concert would be split 80-20 between the Atlanta King Center and our coalition; with the King Center getting the larger percentage.

When the possible nonviolent direct action was brought up and the coalition was apprised that we had had two meetings planning a sit-in, Senator Stephens stated that he believed such action would cause us to lose votes in the Senate. Judge Williams and Senator Walker echoed his viewpoint. On the other hand, Buck, now-retired from his cancelled, but successful recall petition drive, spoke up in favor of the protest; indicating that we had already had too many frustrating years and it was time to act radically and militantly.

A new public service announcement committee was suggested by Vernon Bolling to advertise the King holiday effort. Our hope was to revise our commercial and ad that we had previously used to reflect the new proposal.

Before the meeting adjourned, someone remarked that coalition members should urge King supporters to picket in front of institutions where "targeted senators" worked, such as Usdane's employer, Pima Savings. Also, the media had become confused between our coalition and Zaler's Ad-Hoc Committee for an MLK, Jr. Holiday. As a result, ARIZONANS FOR A MARTIN LUTHER KING, JR. STATE HOLIDAY designated one person as our spokesperson—me. As far as Zaler's group, our best hope was to coordinate our activities because Arnie was going to make his public statements whenever necessary.

Eight days after my meeting with Shover, I received a telephone call from Governor Mofford and her press aide, Vada Manager. She had just met with some "heavy hitters" from the Phoenix business community who came to her avowing their support for an MLK Day, based on the federal plan. Her "guests of honor" in her office on September 7, 1989 included Bidwell, Shover and Jerry Colangelo, owner of the Phoenix Suns. She remarked, "I'm very optimistic and I hope to call a special session after the prison overcrowding session if the votes are there." I then suggested, "Governor, you ought to meet with Senator Walker and apprise her of your meeting with the business leaders and inform her of your and the business community's support for the federal holiday plan."

There were two reasons for my making such a request: (1) Senator Walker had not been invited to the governor's meeting, which Arnie Zaler had arranged in early August. *I had gotten wind of her disappointment for not being invited.* (2) Senator Walker had been dealing with Senator Corbet about the Columbus-King Day switch, which was the only version of the holiday bill that he would support.

Also, our coalition had voted to support that version if that was all she could get through. Before she got off the phone, Governor Mofford let me know that the business leaders would be working on several Republican senators.

The next day, Shover called me at my house where I was working on my Sunday's message to inform me about the meeting the governor had told me about the day earlier. Although we had known each other for less than two weeks, it appeared that he intended to be genuine and open in keeping me posted on the King Day movement in the Legislature, particularly on the Senate side. Shover identified Senators Hayes, Corbet, DeLong, Corpstein, Steiner and Todd as their targets for persuasion.

I could have told them they did not need to worry about Senator Steiner. Her decision to support King Day when all her Republican colleagues voted against it in the past year was based on a moral decision that had nothing to do with the Super Bowl or lost convention revenue. Somebody made sure that Mofford's meeting with the business leaders hit the press. The headline of *The Phoenix Gazette* on Friday, September 8, 1989 read, "Heavy Hitters Back King Holiday." After identifying the two sports moguls who were present and Shover, Michael Murphy made a glaring observation in his story on the meeting, "The coalition of 25 business leaders and sports executives has not previously been active on the King Day issue." Later on in Murphy's article, he quoted Shover as commenting, "We're going to contact each of the senators to advise them about the economic factors—primarily the business that we've lost," estimating that nearly 256 million dollars had been lost since 1987 over the MLK holiday. You can be sure that when the anti-King Day senators heard about their new source of pressure, it did not set too well with them.

By September 12, 1989, Mofford had decided to call a second special session of the Legislature the next week to address three economic development issues for the state: (1) to liberalize and clarify credit card laws to benefit Security Pacific Bank of Arizona; (2) to provide tax incentives for a computer-chip corporation called U.S. Memories, Inc. which planned to locate in Arizona and (3) the Martin Luther King, Jr. holiday if the votes were there. Sometime between September 12th and the 15th, the governor removed the *if* and added the MLK Day legislation on the Special Session agenda unconditionally.

The business leaders got their way in a jiffy with the governor this time. After all, the Phoenix '93 Super Bowl Committee met on the 14th of September and unanimously voted to support Arizona's King Day. Shover called me again at my house on Friday, September 15th to inform me that Senator Todd would vote for King Day, if it got to the floor past the Republican Caucus, which could block it a second time in 1989. The pressure was bothering several of the Republican senators and they were threatening to bury the holiday bill in retaliation.

However, later on that same day, Jamieson called me at home to tell me that he "felt good and optimistic" about the holiday's chances. To use his words, "The Republican senators are posturing publicly, but key ones will vote on the holiday if it comes to the floor." Bill committed to getting "others" to persuade Usdane to let the King bill come to the floor without going through the Republican Caucus. Moreover, he was of the same opinion as me—the business leaders had convinced the governor to put MLK Day on the agenda, regardless of the aye vote count. By doing so, Governor Mofford "got the monkey off her back" and the strategy was to "box" in the Senate's Republican leaders.

Senator DeLong did a poll of his constituents on Thursday, September 14, 1989 and his poll showed King Day favored by 51 to 49 per cent. But, he did not reveal how he would vote on the holiday in the upcoming special session. Also, by the middle of September, three more items had been added to the special session agenda; specifically, prison overcrowding, reviewing the state's criminal code, and more money for drug enforcement and education. With the King Day-Super Bowl connection making the headlines nearly every other day, Shover, as chairman of the Phoenix '93

Super Bowl Committee, was making more comments to the media about King Day than anyone else.

I really did not mind because it appeared that our coalition's long-awaited goal was about to become reality. Excitement began to creep its way into my spirit after being disappointed so many times before. However, it was a reserved expression of cautious optimism. Senator Walker, Representatives Hamilton and Kennedy, and Jamieson stayed in close contact with me on the "behind the scenes" politics that took place down at the Capitol.

Unfortunately, the continued mentioning of the Super Bowl invited criticism from both sides of the King Day controversy. For all practical purposes, Arizona would get its King Day, but for the wrong reason—football! Anyone could pick up that King Day was an afterthought to most of the big business crowd. A matter of fact, when it was reported that most of the corporate executives pushing for a King Day for the state did not recognize Dr. King's birthday for their own employees, state senators, newspaper columnists, and members of ARIZONANS FOR A MARTIN LUTHER KING, JR. STATE HOLIDAY were using the adjective hypocritical to describe the new found MLK Day cheering squad. The title of Montini's column on Sunday, September 17th read "State selling spirit of King for football." Tempe Senator Todd challenged the Phoenix 40 crowd, which by and large had ignored King Day until then to "look in the mirror." And the evidence of the hypocrisy of the business community on the King holiday was quite convicting. The list of corporations that were pressuring the Senate to pass King Day, but did not grant the same to their employees, read like the "who's who" in the Greater Phoenix Economic Council, e.g., the Phoenix Newspapers, Inc., Salt River Project, Circle K Corporation, Del Webb Corporation and Woods Development Institute. I felt a conflict of interest. If Dr. King was still alive or even when he was living, some of these corporations would be his targets for perpetuating systemic racism and practicing discrimination, as it related to upward mobility in their companies. *He did not preach and teach, march and rally, sit-in and pray-in, go to jail and eventually lose his life for the Super Bowl.*

Somewhere in Arizona's quest to honor King, we excused others and ourselves for dishonoring him by putting a price tag on why we "must" honor him as soon as possible with his day. Arizona forgot that Martin had paid the ultimate price, which no game, no convention, or no economic development program could match. For that reason, coupled with the post-King America, which had been forced by his nonviolent Civil Rights

Movement to rid itself of discriminatory laws, every legislator in Arizona who enjoyed the benefits of a better Arizona; as a result of the life, legacy and death of that Black American preacher-prophet, should have gladly voted for the King Holiday when it was first introduced. Nevertheless, politics are known for being more practical than philosophical. Therefore, the fact that the King holiday became an economic issue in Arizona will tell historians much more about Arizona's conservative politicians than the legislative records.

As the special session began on September 20, 1989, several Republican legislators tried to throw a curve in the process to vote on our "WIN-WIN COMPROMISE" of the King bill by making a House resolution that a statewide election be held to force a vote on the holiday. The rationale behind such a resolution was that the majority of Arizona voters would defeat such a holiday if given the chance. Minority Speaker Hamilton was able to manhandle that resolution and render it "dead on arrival." The King issue, which had been placed before the legislators would be the federal model combining Washington and Lincoln's Days into one holiday to be called George Washington/Abraham Lincoln Day and allowing the third Monday to become Martin Luther King, Jr./Civil Rights Day.

On the Senate side, three versions, other than the King-Columbus Day switch, were introduced on September 20th; but never made it to the floor. One was our "WIN-WIN COMPROMISE" assigned the number S.B. 1006. Out of somewhere, Senators DeLong and Steiner offered S.B. 1009, which would have made the second Monday in February Civil Rights/ Lincoln Day, completely omitting any holiday bearing Dr. King's name. A third proposal S.B. 1010—was introduced by DeLong alone. His "cafeteria proposal" would have kept the existing paid and unpaid holidays and added King Day, Valentine's Day, St. Patrick's Day, Cinco De Mayo Day and several religious holidays as paid state holidays, from which state employees could choose, as long as the total number of paid holidays selected did not exceed the already legislatively approved number of paid holidays. *Just think of the bureaucratic mess S.B. 1010 would have caused had it been approved.*

After the Senate Judiciary Committee disposed of those three King Day bills, Vada Manager invited me up to Governor Mofford's private office to confer with them about the latest prospects for the MLK Day bill. The meeting was brief, but upbeat. It was 10:00 p.m. We were all tired and a little tense as the last-minute proposals kept popping up. Nevertheless, we departed to our various destinations, knowing that something would happen on the King bill the next day.

The day before the special session began, our coalition had a crucial meeting to update our supporters on the latest happenings with the legislation and we proceeded to devise our plans for protest in case the bill was assassinated again by the Republican senators. Basically, our legislative update paralleled everything being printed in the newspapers and reported over the radio and television. The undecided agenda, which was dealt with, was the nonviolent direct action, which had had its third sub-committee meeting by September 19, 1989. Our recommendation was to use the theme for our civil disobedience-"STAND UP AGAINST BIGOTRY IN ARIZONA BY SITTING-IN AT THE STATE SENATE." If approved by the coalition, we would hire a part-time coordinator to train participants in the action and begin to raise funds for legal defense of those arrested as a result of the action. Due to his protests against the building of nuclear power plants, Ferd Haverly, a local expert in civil disobedience, was recommended by Joedd to become the part-time coordinator. Bolling would handle the necessary publicity, prior, during and after the proposed sit-in at the State Capitol. I think the frustration level had reached a point among our faithful volunteers so that when our subcommittee's recommendations were made for the nonviolent direct action and related-expenses, the vote was unanimous.

Dr. Reader had written our statement to be read at a press conference if the King Day legislation failed in the special session. Excerpts from the first draft read,

> On January 15, 1990, the 61st anniversary of the birth of Martin Luther King, Jr., we shall gather at the State Capitol to nonviolently protest against officially sanctioned bigotry in Arizona.
>
> On that occasion, we shall demand the immediate release and enactment of the Martin Luther King state holiday which has been held hostage by a handful of mean-spirited legislators in the State Senate since the holiday was rescinded by impeached and convicted former Governor Evan Mecham as his first major administrative act....
>
> The failure on the part of the State Senate leadership to permit the holiday bill to come to a vote now stands as the major stumbling block to racial and ethnic harmony in Arizona....

We have made this point repeatedly to officials since the King holiday was rescinded, only to be met with empty promises, unkept commitments, slanderous ridicule and irrational refusal to address this issue affirmatively....

Having exhausted all other traditional means of political discourse for what is our and our children's birthright, we shall gather at the State Senate on January 15, 1990, to declare ourselves a state holiday honoring Dr. King....

We urge all of those who plan to engage in nonviolent direct action on Dr. King's birthday to register for training now.

The mood in the room was solemn when the above-statement was read. But, if the Senate insulted Dr. King's legacy one more time, they left us no choice other than following in his footsteps by "standing up for what was due us by sitting-in" at the culprits' front doors.

In a last ditch effort to win support, I suggested that our coalition send mailgrams to every Republican senator. Upon approval, a brief message was written with these words,

THE MARTIN LUTHER KING, JR. HOLIDAY IS MORALLY RIGHT. A REPUBLICAN-CONTROLLED U.S. SENATE PASSED IT. FORMER PRESIDENT REAGAN SIGNED IT INTO FEDERAL LAW. 46 STATES OBSERVE IT. MANY OF ARIZONA'S LOCAL AND STATE GOVERNMENTAL AND EDUCATIONAL ENTITIES OBSERVE IT. ITS PASSAGE WILL DO NOTHING TO HURT ARIZONA. BRING IT TO THE FLOOR. IT IS THE RIGHT THING TO DO.

On the morning of September 21, 1989, I woke up and read the headlines informing me that the Columbus-King Day switch had been unveiled as the only version of MLK Day that more than one Republican senator would support. The Republican majority still refused to get out of the way of the bill, but this new version would be allowed to get to the floor by President Usdane. A matter of fact, Uzzie appeared on the front page of *The Arizona Republic* smiling at reporters talking about the bill that he reportedly had said "would get to the Senate floor over his dead body!" I guess he had died and rose again. Art indicated that he could go along with the Columbus Day switch. Quite naturally, members of the

Italian-American community in Phoenix cried, "Foul!" Just the day before on the 20th, the Senate Judiciary Committee voted 6-3 to add King Day to the list of paid state holidays by shifting Columbus Day to an unpaid Sunday observance. Even while voting for the switch, Senator Pete Rios, a Democrat from Hayden, chastised what was going on, "It appears we've elected to stick a football in one of Dr. King's hands and a business briefcase in the other."

I was called to come to the Senate Building around 5:00 p.m. late Thursday afternoon on the 21st. A miracle had taken place in the Republican Caucus earlier that day. Nine out of seventeen Republican senators voted to allow the new version of MLK Day to get to the floor. At 5:26 p.m. on September 21, 1989, the following Arizona State Senators voted in favor of the holiday: Democratic Senators Walker, Stephens, Pena, Alston, Arzberger, Bartlett, Higuera, Galbaldon, Henderson, Osborn, Rios, Gutierrez and Hardt and Republican Senators Steiner, Corbet, Todd and Usdane. Usdane? Yep, Uzzie redeemed himself by getting some "King Day religion." "*O Happy Day!*" When asked by a reporter as I rejoiced in the gallery of the Senate over the victory, I replied, "Arizona has finally joined the Union....Our image of being the new Mississippi...a racist redneck state is no more. Arizona has finally come around."

On Friday, September 22, 1989, Governor Rose Mofford signed into law Arizona's *first* legislatively approved Martin Luther King, Jr. Day. *Hallelujah!*

Chapter Eight
Together We Did It!

In my files I ran across a press release dated Thursday, September 21, 1989 on letterhead of ARIZONANS FOR A MARTIN LUTHER KING, JR. STATE HOLIDAY which was to inform the media:

Announcing a Press Conference in Response to the Arizona State Senate's Third Consecutive Defeat of the Martin Luther King, Jr. Holiday Legislation.

What a relief to have been able to scribble the words "Didn't have to use" in the upper left-hand corner of that press release that had been typed. But, we had another press release that we eagerly sent out by fax, mail and hand-delivery that same evening announcing a rally celebrating the passage of the MLK, Jr. state holiday to be held at the Capitol on Monday, September 25, 1989 at 5:30 p.m. under the theme "TOGETHER WE DID IT."

Ours would be the *second* victory celebration in front of the old rotunda, which housed the Arizona State Legislature of yesteryear. I am sure if any of the pioneer Arizona legislators' ghosts were floating around the vicinity of that building, they were frightened to death to hear their grandchildren saluting a Black man with a state holiday. Whatever the case, Governor Mofford, celebrating her most historic political victory next to becoming Arizona's first woman governor, wasted no time in announcing the signing ceremony of Arizona's Martin Luther King, Jr. Day, which would take place 24 hours after its miraculous passage in the Legislature. The date would be Friday, September 22, 1989 at 6:00 p.m., outside, in spite of Arizona's 100-plus degree weather during the first days of fall. Her press aide, Vada Manager, and other members of her staff, worked late into the evening Thursday and nearly all day Friday inviting King Day supporters to the long-awaited event that was "a dream come true" for so many of us.

Contacts had also been made to reach Mrs. King for, at least, a telephone hook-up during the ceremony.

I do not know if I slept at all that Thursday night. I went back down to First Institutional after the vote was taken and shared the great news with church members, who had been King Day advocates for almost three years. Of course, they rejoiced with their pastor. When I finally got home, my then wife Serena and our two oldest sons had already gotten the news and rejoiced with me. They were happy to see me happy. I guess I should say, "They were happy to *see* me." *Maybe, with this victory accomplished with which their husband and dad, respectively, had been obsessed for the last three years, I would be a little more visible around the house and available to them.* Of course, Serena, knowing me like she did after having been married to her hardworking, mission-minded husband for a dozen years, would simply wait for my next mission to be announced; in addition to pastoring, at that time, the state's largest African-American church and preaching all over the country throughout the calendar year.

More than 200 attended Governor Mofford's MLK Day signing ceremony, including former Governor Babbitt, who had signed the *first* Arizona King holiday that never made it off the paper. Senator Walker was up front along with Representatives Hamilton and Kennedy. Senators Jesus Higuera and James Henderson, one of Arizona's Native American legislators representing District 3, stood nearby elated over their state finally honoring the worthy African-American civil rights leader. Jackie Platt-Jennas gleamed as she took her place beside Sandra Kennedy. Arnie Zaler was in the center of the leading King Day advocates, almost directly behind the governor. Gene Blue, was somewhere in the back of the "up-front" crowd. I stood to the right of Senator Walker. People were there from all walks of life, all colors, creeds and classes, as well-wishing MLK Day supporting Arizonans.

The governor's staff had brought out a good-sized table, on which she would sign the brand-new law, making the state she governed the 47th state in the Union to honor Martin Luther King, Jr. I had been asked to deliver the invocation and I took my "good Black Baptist preacherish" time in doing so. It was not a written prayer and from hindsight I regret it for history's sake. But since the ceremony was being covered live on KTAR radio, I am told that the commentator remarked about the length of Reverend Stewart's moving prayer. I do remember invoking a line or two from James Weldon Johnson's prayer-song which is known as the Negro National Anthem, "God of our weary years, God of our silent tears,…" Being thankful for a lot of things in addition, but related to the passage of King Day, I asked for personal and corporate forgiveness for "any mean-spiritedness" or "harsh words" that any of us had spoken during our often intense and contentious war to win King's honor. Governor Mofford lifted our spirits by stating what we all were feeling—something to the effect that Arizonans could stand tall because we had done the right thing in honoring King. After reminding us of Dr. King's dream and drive for justice and equality, Governor Mofford challenged us to keep his dream alive. The primary sponsor of MLK Day in the Senate, the Honorable Carolyn Walker, allowed us to witness and sense her pent-up emotions rising to eye-level to form tears as she rejoiced over our victory. Senator Stephens urged King Day advocates to continue to be involved in legislative issues. Representatives Kennedy and Republican Chris Herstam, extolled our accomplishment as a lofty example of how opposing sides can work together. Then, the "man" was asked to speak, none other than Art Hamilton. Who else but Art would bring up helping "the homeless and helpless" as the most fitting way to honor King's life and philosophy.

Off to the left of the table where the governor signed the new bill was a telephone. Someone from the King family was supposed to call during the short ceremony. As fate would have it, the call was late on that hot evening. Governor Mofford stalled as long as she could waiting for the connection between Arizona and Atlanta to finally be made. Most of the celebrants went their ways after hearing the local King crusaders express our joy over the new day in the state. The governor had become a little fidgety and frustrated waiting for the call from the birthplace of Dr. King. Not too long after the signing ceremony had ended before many had left, the call came. Martin Luther King, III offered his congratulations to Governor Mofford, the State Legislature and even me for the victory that had arrived. What a fitting closure to one the most important 24-hours recorded in the annals of Arizona history.

Conspicuously absent from the ceremony were the business leaders who had applied "heavy-handed pressure" to win the holiday for the sake of their 1993 Super Bowl hopes. Certainly, they were welcome. After all, let us face it, even though the majority of the legislators who supported MLK Day did so for moral reasons, the hard-nosed Republican Senate block did not budge until they heard from the "money men." And speaking of Republican senators, only one showed up for a while that I could notice.

The editorials from Phoenix's two major newspapers eloquently informed their readers that Arizona had done "a good thing." My friend and editor of the editorial page of *The Arizona Republic*, Bill Cheshire wrote:

> For years Arizona's Legislature had refused to acknowledge a fact, all but universally agreed to, even in the Deep South—that the late Martin Luther King, Jr., whatever his human frailties, had given his life for the liberty of black Americans and, as the embodiment of the civil rights revolution, occupied a unique place in the history of our country....
>
> This week all that changed....When the Rev. Warren Stewart, Sr., head of Arizona's King holiday drive, described this sudden breakthrough as 'a miracle', he did not exaggerate.
>
> In some measure, the shift in attitude was brought about through vigorous lobbying by the commercial community....
>
> But as Dr. Stewart noted, such considerations are not without precedent. In the long and choppy history of American race relations, barriers frequently have been toppled by a combination of forces, including self-interest....

The Phoenix Gazette editorialized on September 23, 1989 that the King holiday victory was "A fine moment for Arizona." Explaining what took place, Paul J. Schatt, then editor of that afternoon newspaper's editorial pages wrote,

> Five other GOP senators—Pete Corpstein, John Hays, Tom Patterson, Bill DeLong and John Mawhinney—lent the bill their support in a lengthy majority caucus Thursday morning, even though they did not vote for its passage there....
>
> Cynics might say the King holiday measure was only approved because of pressure from the business community and in anticipation of an Arizona bid for a 1993 Super Bowl. Well, so what?
>
> ...Today, Arizona's blacks like the Rev. Warren Stewart, Sen. Carolyn Walker and House Minority Leader Art Hamilton are standing with white men like Bob Usdane and Doug Todd....

Coincidentally, a weekly feature in *The Republic* called "MOVERS" ran a quarter page article, on Sunday, September 24, 1989, about me and a photo with me and my five sons, Warren, Jr., Matthew, Jared, Justin and

Aaron on bicycles in our front yard. What timing! The writer, Linda Helser, had researched the story several months prior to its being run. I guess it was somewhat accurate to label me a "mover" in Phoenix that weekend for sure.

God help my secretary who worked for me during the King Day campaigns. Oftentimes, like the surprise September 21st victory that came after our church office closing time, I would inform her and any other staff person on church property to volunteer some more time for the King holiday. By the time, I got back to the church after six o'clock on that Thursday; we had to get out press releases, mailgrams, and thank you letters to our supporters, including dozens of churches, informing them of our "Thank You Celebration" to be held four days later on Monday. Poor LeNora Cobbs Hart, a young newly-wed who inherited the position of being my secretary, had to call her hubby, tell him to enjoy his dinner alone and to feed their dogs. Secretaries Rosalyn Ray and Linda Frey, her predecessors, knew how I operated. I guess that is why for my secretaries the survival rate was around two years maximum. But, I can testify that each of my secretaries as well as my other staff members willingly gave hundreds of dedicated hours of time and talent to see Arizona finally honor one of their role models...*and make their pastor happy.*

Our coalition's King Day passage celebration was still two days away once the governor's ended. The theme that kept ringing in my ears was "TOGETHER WE DID IT!" Being the pastor of a multi-talented and multi-gifted African-American Baptist congregation has bountiful benefits. So, I had my secretary to catch up with the Reverend Lee Radford, one of our associate ministers who was a graphic arts designer by profession. I commissioned Lee to make a long rectangular banner in black and white with our logo and coalition name on one end and the above-mentioned theme in bold letters taking up the other three-fourths of the sign. I must say that my preacher-friend did an outstanding job with a day's notice. And he did it at cost.

Excited as I was, the fourth Sunday morning worship services at First Institutional became the Pre-King Day approval celebration a day before September 25, 1989. The joy and enthusiasm was so electric in the 11:00 a.m. worship service that the capacity crowd that filled the pews probably got static shock from one another. People were happy for two reasons. First of all, the King Day that had been declared in their pulpit three years prior had been restored on what they thought was solid ground, so even though they had heard about the Legislature's passage of the day, nothing would take the place of hearing about it, "live" on Sunday morning. After all, throughout the 34-month long struggle, their pastor had kept them updated on the progress and the problems relating to Arizona's getting, losing and trying to get again an MLK Day in both morning worship services, primarily during the pastoral emphases and occasionally referencing the holiday fight in his messages. Secondly, I would like to believe that many members and friends of First Institutional came to witness and share their pastor's jubilation over the "mission-accomplished" which he had led, in addition to shepherding them, as the drafted leader of ARIZONANS FOR A MARTIN LUTHER KING, JR. STATE HOLIDAY. My joy was their joy! They came to join me in the Lord's House in giving glory to the God of M.L. King, Jr. who gave us the victory that was long overdue.

Of course, we all stood and sang, "We Shall Overcome,"

> We shall overcome,
> We shall overcome,
> We shall overcome someday.
> O, deep in our hearts,
> I do believe,
> We shall overcome someday.

In reflection of how we overcame that particular victory the previous Thursday, it was imperative for us to melodiously remind ourselves that "Black and White together, Black and White together, Black and White together" united to get the holiday approved. Then, on the singing of the most familiar verse and chorus that we sang standing with joined hands, I led the hundreds present in changing the chorus from "We *shall* overcome" to "We *did* overcome." There were tears of joy, shouts of thanksgiving, smiles of pride, hugs of hope and laughter of relief that Arizona's "King Day had come," to quote a paraphrase *Arizona Informant* Editor Cloves Campbell suggested as a title for this book.

Sunday, September 24, 1989 would be a holy day, in which no criticism was directed at any of the King Day opponents—past, present and future. Praise was pronounced from the pulpit that day for the governor, state lawmakers, community activists, grassroots volunteers and civic and business leaders who joined together in a rare alliance and garnered a momentous victory. I declared, "TOGETHER WE DID IT!..." It was not any one person, not any one group, but *together* we did it!" I recalled that less than a week earlier I had mentioned publicly that it would take a "miracle" for the conservative Republican Senate Caucus to let the King bill get a vote on the Senate floor. But I guess many of us had forgotten in the heat of the battle that the Christian faith, which King and many of our coalition members professed, had got its start from a Miracle Worker. I had to confess that "something got a hold of those Republican anti-King Day legislators." I testified, "God cannot only change hearts, He can change votes!" After I reiterated our celebration theme, I asked two of our deacons to unfurl in front of the church's altar our victory banner and hold it high. The message of the sign warranted and received a standing ovation.

As mentioned earlier in this chapter, our coalition sent out letters to invite persons who had been critical to our united victory to join us at our thanksgiving rally to be held at the Capitol on Monday, September 25, 1989.

Dear _____:

TOGETHER WE DID IT!

Arizona now has a Martin Luther King, Jr. State Holiday, thanks to the efforts of many thousands of Arizonans, including **you**.

We are inviting you to bring brief remarks at a rally to be held on **Monday, September 25, 1989, 5:30 p.m. at the State Capitol**. Several other speakers also have been invited to share briefly in thanksgiving for Arizona joining the nation and forty-six other states in honoring Dr. Martin Luther King, Jr. and the Civil Rights Movement with a holiday. Our banner theme for the rally will be "**TOGETHER WE DID IT.**"

Thank God, **ARIZONA FINALLY DID THE RIGHT THING.**

Included on our invitation list were: Pastor Gantt, Judge Williams, Dr. Reader, Ms. Ellis, Mike Shea, Mike Lacey, Ms. Carolyn Lowery (a grassroots community activist); Senators Steiner, Pena, Stephens, Walker and Usdane; Representatives Hamilton, Kennedy, Wilcox and Hull; Governor Mofford, Bishop O'Brien, Bishop Heistand, Dr. Arlo Nau, Arnie Zaler, Bill Shover, Bill Jamieson, Gene Blue and Mayor Goddard. We called our gathering "A People's Thank You Rally Celebrating the Passage and Signing into Law of Martin Luther King, Jr. State Holiday." I presided. Joedd Miller brought greetings. Rabbi Robert Kravitz offered the invocation with his *shophar*, a horn used in Jewish celebrations to announce thanksgiving to God. In an effort to be patriotic and true to our heritage we sang "America the Beautiful" and "Lift Ev'ry Voice and Sing." Most of those invited to bring remarks showed up. A few had prior commitments, such as Governor Mofford who was represented by Vada Manager. Unfortunately, Senator Usdane did not make it. But, Bill Shover was there to offer thanks for the opportunity to work with us. Our long-time general co-chairperson, Pastor Barnwell, offered remarks of appreciation to God and the many workers who had labored untiringly to win King Day in Arizona. In addition to presiding, I offered the statement of purpose and the closing prayer (which I thought was my last public prayer for a Martin Luther King, Jr. Day in my adopted home state). In a final victory shout, we sang my modified version of "We Shall Overcome," led by Sis. B.J. Bosley, one of First Institutional's most energetic and powerful songbirds. A cantor from Temple Beth Israel diversified our music to include our Jewish brothers and sisters.

The remarks of most of the speakers stuck with the theme and the gratitude of a job well done on the King Day. Arnie used his slot on the thanksgiving program to announce the forming of the "Grand Coalition", which would become an even more diverse coalition than ARIZONANS FOR A MARTIN LUTHER KING, JR. STATE HOLIDAY to address issues such as: homelessness, substance abuse, job development, repealing the state's "English-only law," and the threatened referendum drive to repeal Arizona's brand-new holiday. The Grand Coalition's political targets would be former Governor Mecham, David Duke—the Ku Klux Klan member running for governor in Louisiana, and the skinheads who had tried to protest at our April 4, 1989 memorial on King's assassination anniversary. Black activist Carolyn Lowery used her time to announce a petition drive to get Buckeye Road in South Phoenix changed to Martin Luther King, Jr. Boulevard, which in my opinion, was and still is not a bad idea, especially in view of the 20-yard radius Martin Luther King, Jr. Circle that is one of the most hard to find streets in central Phoenix.

Opal Ellis, to my surprise, brought up the fact that $18,000 remained in our coalition's coffers, which in her opinion, should be set aside for scholarships.

As the three hundred or so faithful Martin Luther King, Jr. holiday celebrants began to conclude our "official" celebration of thanksgiving, I made mention that "the process for enactment of the holiday had been carried to its completion." Governor Mecham based his rescission of Bruce Babbitt's executive order on the fact that the Legislature is the only authorized governmental entity which could make a paid state holiday. Finally, a

Republican-controlled House and Senate had done so. Thusly, my parting words before my closing prayer voiced, "We would hope this would be the end of the unnecessary controversy surrounding the Martin Luther King, Jr. holiday."

All in all, our hour and a half gathering of regular Arizonans, with the exception of a few "movers and shakers", put a gracious end to an often bitter and contentious clash between diametrically opposed political and philosophical counterparts who squared off on honoring Dr. King. Representatives and supporters from every segment of our community crossing racial, generational, political, educational, economic and religious lines weathered by a steamy, hot evening in Phoenix to thank the Lord and others for a dream come true.

In addition to our "thank you" reception, scores and scores of appreciation letters and mailgrams were sent out under my signature on our letterhead to individuals who had provided key leadership over the three-year span of our struggle. To the First Lady of Arizona, Western Union informed her for us, "You exemplified courageous and wise leadership in placing the Martin Luther King, Jr. holiday on the agenda of the Special Session of the Arizona State Legislature on September 20, 1989. Thank you." To Senate President Usdane, our mailgram read, "Thank you for your historic vote on September 21, 1989 for the Martin Luther King, Jr. state holiday in Arizona. Without your vote it would not have passed. Together we did it." A similar wired message was sent to House Speaker Hull, a previous negative vote on King.

It was my privilege to write to Mrs. King, "...Your husband, Dr. Martin Luther King, Jr., now has his day in Arizona,...Thank you for all of the encouragement and support that you, your family, Lloyd Davis and your staff provided throughout our long and tedious struggle..." To William (Bill) R. Shover, I offered these sincere words of gratitude,

> Thank you for providing critical and strategic leadership in Arizona's long struggle to win a paid state holiday honoring Dr. Martin Luther King, Jr. Without your forthrightness with your colleagues, fellow business and community leaders, legislative leaders and our governor, I do not believe the (MLK) holiday legislation would have thrust its way through the Senate Judiciary Committee, Senate Republican Caucus and onto the Senate floor....

I am deeply grateful for the spirit in which you communicated with me as to the process and progress of your lobbying for the King holiday after our first meeting on August 31, 1989. You did not have to do that.

Lastly, your letter "To the Children of Rev. Warren Stewart" is a document, which...I will preserve and cherish for them...

The following is the full text of Bill Shover's letter to my children:

Dear Kids,

Some day when you are old enough to understand the impact your Father has had on Arizona history I hope you will read this note.

I worked with your Father less than three weeks to enact passage of the bill setting aside a state holiday for the Reverend Martin Luther King, Jr. Your Dad more than anyone else deserves credit for his persistence in getting the bill approved.

If he does nothing more in life than that (but I know he will), your Dad deserves eternal appreciation for bringing the people of Arizona together.

You are fortunate to have a Father who so loves his community that he is willing to sacrifice his time and reputation.

Kindest personal regards,

signed Bill

As much as I was at odds with members of the Phoenix business community for not responding to our coalition's S.O.S. calls in 1986 and 1987, Bill was *different*. There was an openness to establish relationship with others, even if they represented a totally different lifestyle, segment of the broader community and/or political or philosophical *modus operandi* than his. Mind you, Bill was still a WASC—White, Anglo-Saxon Catholic—in the truest sense of the word. But, William R. Shover returned phone calls, responded to letters, kept his commitments to keep all parties involved in the King Day fight abreast, and added a warm personal touch to his politics. Perhaps, a lot of the guys he hung out with in the Phoenix 40 crowd could take a lesson from him. On the other hand, that may be why he held the position of director of public affairs for the Phoenix Newspapers, Inc. and not the CEO's position. I guess I am trying to say that Bill Shover was different than many of his country club golf mates. And that worked to our advantage, even though we would have our moments as the Martin Luther King, Jr. holiday battle lingered on across the years.

Among those who received individual letters from me were movie stars, senior citizens, newspaper reporters, editors and columnists, professionals, pastoral colleagues, community leaders, members of my congregation, academics, people who wrote me letters of congratulations, after watching or reading the news, politicians, prolific letter-writers, like James Kimes, and magazine editors. I must mention the content of two other specific letters that I sent out. The first one went to Ferd Haverly, who was selected to train us in the nonviolent civil disobedience that same day I met Shover:

> ...This was supposed to be a letter of agreement for you to become the Nonviolent Direct Action Coordinator for **ARIZONANS FOR A MARTIN LUTHER KING, JR. STATE HOLIDAY, INC.** However, history both hired and fired you within 48 hours. Amen!

Pastor Joe Eidsness, who at that time, pastored the Trinity Bible Church and was a member of an intimate fellowship of six pastors from diverse Christian denominations, including a Roman
Catholic priest, and myself, sent me a message to which I responded in part,

> Thank you for taking the time to write me a note of congratulations....God knows that He gave me the strength, wisdom, perseverance and boldness to not give up the fight, even when the battles were fierce and intense. I have always believed that we had your support as well as your prayers. Thank you.

Without a doubt, every officer and honorary chairperson of our coalition heard from me, and including the following paragraph and P.S.

> Thank you for the many sacrifices you made to serve on **ARIZONANS FOR A MARTIN LUTHER KING, JR. STATE HOLIDAY.** Your input, participation and wisdom enables us to taste victory. I also appreciate your continued support of my leadership, even when the going got rough...
>
> P.S. Regrettably, it looks like the battle is not over.

The dozens of members of our coalition heard from me in writing. Moreover, I would not think to leave out the majority of the House and Senate members, respectively, who voted for the MLK Day legislation. In a one-sentence paragraph in my letter to them, I stated, "The healing has begun." I also asked Shover to give me a list of business leaders I should thank. Their letter from me offered these words of appreciation.

> Mr. Bill Shover, Chairperson, Super Bowl '93 Committee, shared with me of your critical contributions to the successful lobbying of the Arizona State Senate to approve a (MLK) state holiday. Indeed, the fruits of labor became an historic reality on September 20 and 21, 1989...Thank you.

My letter to the supportive members of the Bishops and

Executives Round Table read in part,

> To God be the glory that...Arizona finally approved and signed into law a paid state holiday honoring Dr. Martin Luther King, Jr.
> Without faith, endurance, courage, hope and love—all Christian virtues—we would not have attained victory.
> Thank you for your prayers and support during this three-year long battle, which proved victorious.

I realized that I could not write every King Day supporter a letter of thanks, especially those who worked with our coalition. But the thought was certainly there to express appreciation, first and foremost, to my wife, Serena, who prayed for her husband and continued to provide tender loving care for our five sons during my absences at breakfast time and dinner time, often in the evenings and on Saturdays as I pressed forward to realize a vision of King Day that had been transferred to me. Four of my boys, although pretty young throughout the 1986-1989 MLK Day controversial campaign, understood on their level what their dad was up to. As I have mentioned, whether learning about Dr. King at home, church or school, or accompanying their dad to annual Martin Luther King, Jr. celebration festivities, especially the annual march, Warren Jr., Matthew, Jared and Justin supported their father's efforts to see Arizona honor the historic efforts of the father of the King children.

What more can I say about the First Institutional Baptist Church at-large and its leaders and officers. Not once to my knowledge did I ever hear a complaint or criticism about the time I was spending on the job trying to win King Day. In actuality, they clearly expected my prophetic involvement in such activities which lift up the African-American church as the unchallenged and unbridled leader in the Black community for causes of justice, liberty and equality for all. I know that the prayers of many of the seasoned saints at First Institutional empowered me to fight on when the going got tough.

God gave me strength to be the "point man" for Arizona's King holiday fight. I know that *His* providence guided and directed me and the coalition every step of the way, even when we took less-than-godly detours reacting to racist and bigoted anti-King crusaders and/or ignorance on the part of the silent majority. I was aware that many coalition members, though men and women of faith; did not actively participate in local churches. Therefore, in an effort to be evangelistic, I always prayed in the name of *my* Savior (and King's too) Jesus Christ, much to the dismay of some of our Jewish and Christian holiday advocates.

We were not the only ones doing the thanking. Calls, cards, telegrams and letters came in from around the state and nation once the word got out that Arizona finally approved King Day. A reporter from the *Mesa Tribune* dropped me a line to my home, "Though I'm a journalist who must remain objective in what I do and write for public consumption at the *Tribune*, I feel compelled to extend to you my highest compliments on your relentless and long quest for the King holiday. . ." Carolyn Walker, another of Arizona's most prominent female politicians at that time, included the following words in her letter to me from her Senate office representing District 23:

> Well we did it! The Martin Luther King, Jr. Holiday is finally reality in Arizona.
>
> I want to thank you for your willingness to give so much of your time and effort to assure passage of the legislation....
>
> It is time for the healing to begin in Arizona and for us to go forward with the positive cultural and economic growth that is so important to all our citizens. Thank you for your leadership in helping to make this possible.

A pastoral colleague from Scottsdale, Dr. Robert Brouwer, penned, "You are a remarkable study in perseverance, but today we celebrate the results of that perseverance...a legal paid holiday in honor of Martin Luther King, Jr...."

A friend who knew me from college days and living in Grand Rapids, Michigan wrote,

> Hi! (smile)…I have been following you and the "King Holiday Committee" in Phoenix, Arizona on the T.V., newspapers, and now in the *Jet* Magazine. I am proud of you and your committee and for the new lady Gov., Honorable Rose Mofford, for signing to make Dr. Martin Luther King's Birthday a holiday in the State of Arizona, finally. God is still in control and He does not come when we want Him to, but He is right on time…."

Two King Day friends took the time to send words of appreciation and prophecy. James Kimes wrote, "I do want you to know that I'm of the opinion there will be enough signatures [from King Day opponents who went into action to petition for a referendum on the newly approved MLK holiday on the day of the signing ceremony] to put the issue to a vote of the people.… Then, a twelve-word letter from Bill Shover dated September 29, 1989 predicted, "Good being on the team. I fear we'll be 'ordered up' again."

As far as I was concerned, the thought of launching *another* King Day campaign to fight off the anti-King holiday vigilantes would *not* be allowed to register in my mind until I had had a chance to relish in our victory, if but for a few days.

Chapter Nine
King for a Day and That's About All

Before Governor Mofford could sign into law Arizona's Martin Luther King, Jr. Day to be observed on the third Monday in January for the first time in 1990, opponents of the new legislation gathered in two camps preparing to attack the day for King. In one camp, the Columbus Day loyalists from Arizona's Italian-American community met to devise a strategy to repeal the new law in order to restore a paid holiday in honor of their lost hero. They claimed to have no beef against Dr. King's day. He just could not be honored at the expense of America's discoverer—Columbus. On the other side of the Valley with headquarters in his residence was Julian Sanders, the little man with the high-pitched voice who was among Evan Mecham's most loyal defending disciples. While we were praying to God thanking Him for our hard-fought victory, Sanders and his anti-King crusaders were playing god by judging, convicting and assassinating Dr. Martin Luther King, Jr's. legacy, portraying him as an unpatriotic, Communist-controlled, philandering anarchist. Sanders, after hearing me offer the invocation at the governor's signing ceremony and concluding my prayer by praying in "the name of the God of Martin Luther King, Jr.," accused me of praying in the name of Dr. King! Obviously, the mere mention of King's name in reference to a holiday caused Arizona's most prominent, ultra-conservative, grassroots activist to "go bananas" and misinterpret plain English.

ARIZONANS FOR A MARTIN LUTHER KING, JR. STATE HOLIDAY predicted that something like this was going to happen when Senator Corbet and his Republican cohorts in the Senate scratched our "WIN-WIN COMPROMISE" in favor of the King-Columbus Day swap. However, none of us thought that the anti-King crowd and the Columbus Day defenders would be able to mobilize so quickly once the bill became law. Within 90 days of either group taking out petitions with the secretary of state, 43,350 valid signatures of registered voters would have to be collected to suspend the legislatively passed holiday until the next general election, at which time its fate would be in the hands of the voters. Ironically, on the same day of our People's "Thank You" Rally, Sanders marched to the State Capitol with a mission to dethrone King. The rationale, if you could call it that, behind Sanders' ranting and raving about the Legislature honoring King with a paid state holiday, was that King Day supporters were hurting the state by forcing all Arizonans to honor a "traitor."

My initial response to Sanders' referendum petition drive was, "What has hurt Arizona is the fight, the controversy over honoring a great American that 46 other states, the entire nation and 110 countries see fit to honor." Moreover, passage of the King bill immediately began a restoration of Arizona's severely tarnished image due to Mecham's rescission of the first King Day. But, that was not something with which the chairman of Arizonans for Traditional American Values could comprehend, let alone agree.

Mr. Sanders, who had led the above-named group for several years, was not new to campaigning against King Day. After then-Governor Bruce Babbitt declared the holiday by executive order in 1986, and Mecham took office, Julian launched an "Arizona vs. King Holiday Petition" Drive petitioning the new governor and Arizona Legislature "to obtain and evaluate all available facts and eye-witness testimonies concerning deceptive UNAMERICAN activities of the late MARTIN LUTHER KING, JR. and his radical supporters—before giving further consideration to the controversial 'state-paid King Holiday'." On the bottom of Sanders' crudely put- together petition form was the well-circulated photo of King supposedly sitting in the front row of a Communist training school in Tennessee. In addition, throughout Mecham's turbulent tenure as governor, Sanders' voice was heard denouncing the "powers that be" for railroading God's gift to Arizona out of office, particularly orchestrated initially by that homosexual Ed Buck.

With no financial backing, the vociferous "Mechamite" who said things publicly about Martin King that even the former governor dared not say carried his banner of hatred for honoring King unashamedly. Sanders had a hunch that if he derided Dr. King's legacy long and loudly enough that he could garner enough support to force a vote on the holiday, which would prove that King was no hero to voting Arizonans, especially red-blooded, flag-waving patriots who espoused pure "traditional American values" upon which this great nation was founded (after it was stolen from the Native Americans and Mexicans by force and economically built up on the backs of African slaves).

I engaged in wishful thinking to hope that someone could talk Sanders out of pursuing his campaign of bigotry. The fact of the matter was that those of us who had had our rejoicing over MLK Day cut short needed to regroup and outline a strategy to keep both upset camps who were mad about the new holiday for different reasons from gathering the necessary amount of signatures to put Arizona's King Day on hold for the 18th consecutive year.

Perhaps, our only hope was to let Sanders self-destruct and focus on reasoning with the Italian-American community, which was upset about the loss of Columbus Day as a paid state holiday. Thank God, their first target was not us or King Day. It was Senator Leo Corbet who endured a tongue-lashing for his co-sponsoring the King-Columbus Day swap. Furthermore, it did not help that Corbet had made some reference to being fitted with "cement shoes" for coming up with the idea of dethroning the Italian-American community's national hero. The leaders of the local Italian-American Club, Center for Italian Culture and Columbus Day Committee held closed-door sessions over the weekend to decide how they planned to attack the Legislature's putting King and the Super Bowl above the explorer from Italy who introduced Western culture to this land.

We got a little help from a King Day ally in the Senate, the Honorable Jesus Higuera, who pledged that he would sponsor a new bill that would restore Columbus Day and keep King Day. Also, on the minds of Arizonans of Italian descent was the upcoming 500th anniversary of Columbus' journey to the New World that he was not even looking for. How in the world could Columbus' descendants join the rest of the nation in honoring him if he only had a Sunday holiday? The bare facts indicated that some members of the Italian-American community made a value judgment that Columbus was more worthy of an American holiday than Dr. King because he discovered America. With the federal observance of Columbus Day a little over two weeks away, the Italian-Americans began to amass their forces to hold a protest march on October 15 in Phoenix.

The news media thrives on controversy, especially anything that has racial and/or ethnic prejudice overtones or evidence. Consequently, the headlines of the newspapers included words like "repeal," "foe," "defeat," and "opponents" whenever mention was made of the separate efforts of

Sanders and the Italian-Americans making headway in removing King Day and restoring Columbus Day, respectively. The radio talk shows buzzed with anti-King sentiment and pro-Columbus Day rhetoric. The healing that we thought had begun on September 21, 1989 had become an enlarged, reopened festering wound by September 25, 1989. Sanders demanded that a vote by the people would be the only way to address the King Day issue democratically. He also questioned the motives of state legislators who seemed to be more concerned about lost convention income and the multi-million dollar Super Bowl prize that was within grasp, since the passage of MLK Day, than with honoring the wishes of the majority of Arizonans. For some reason, the King Day holiday continued to get "separate but unequal" treatment from its opponents. It was not enough for Sanders that the democratically-elected Legislature authorized by its constituents and the state constitution had cast their votes in the interest of the whole state. What was then legal still remained inappropriate, in Sanders' opinion. So, it had to be done away with. It should be noted at that point that the Italian-American community had not definitely decided to launch their own petition drive or unite with Arizonans for Traditional American Values.

In our first meeting after our "Thank You" Rally, our printed agenda was short and listed only three agenda items under old business, namely, (1) furthering planning of an appreciation reception for coalition volunteers, (2) a report from the dissolution committee, which would determine where any remaining fund balance would go once our mission was complete, and (3) a monthly financial report. It was September 27th and our victory was still being digested in spite of the foul smell of Sanders' King-bashing threats. Arnie Zaler's Grand Coalition came up for discussion and our coalition adopted an official position that we would not become a part of it at that time. However, individuals were free to become involved as they saw fit. Then, the anti-King petition drive came up under new business. The matter of how many signatures would be needed by when was discussed. Whether or not their getting enough signatures would prevent Arizona from celebrating its first MLK Day on January 15, 1990 was clarified to our disappointment that any state observance would have to be put on hold until after the election. Mark Reader suggested that we ask the Legislature not to meet on MLK Day in protest of the petition drive by calling in sick. Other than that, the efforts by Sanders did not take up much of our discussion. After three years of hard work, our coalition leadership probably was suffering an acute case of denial. We even voted out $2,000 from our treasury to give to a newly established matching fund scholarship program for minority students at ASU.

By our next meeting held on October 12, 1989, reality coldly cured the leadership of our coalition of any bad case of denial we were experiencing relative to the probable overturning of the King holiday in our state. Julian Sanders touched the nerves of thousands of undercover bigots and racists in Arizona. He and his one-man organization operated out of his Tempe townhouse with a message-recording machine as his secretary had begun to receive a groundswell of support against Martin Luther King Day. As he made his rounds to every indiscriminating, ratings-hungry talk show throughout Arizona, hundreds of Arizonans joined his diminutive-minded movement. Whenever Sanders appeared on the radio, the phone lines jammed with the "good people" of Arizona cheering him for slapping the Legislature on the hand for disgracing the state by voting to honor a man like the Reverend King. Almost as often as the callers would mention King's name they would extol former Governor Mecham who "did what was right by canceling the previous King Day." The callers were equally disgusted that their elected representatives had denied them the right of voting on the Martin Luther King, Jr. holiday, even though they had never in the history of Arizona voted on any state holiday, paid or unpaid, or, for that matter, most of the other laws that governed Arizona.

When the very few pro-King Day supporters could get through to voice admiration for King and disdain for the likes of Sanders, he had to defend himself of charges of being a racist. Of course, his was the typical response of people like him that "he loved everybody because God made us all, therefore, everyone was his brothers and sisters." His opposition to the King Day had nothing to do with racism, so he claimed. Sanders' problem with King revolved around his being a liberal socialist who "wanted every American to be guaranteed an annual income." On the subject of King's alleged unfaithfulness to his wife, Julian demanded that that disqualified King for having a holiday named after him. When King Day advocates would remind Sanders of reports of philandering by Presidents Washington and Jefferson, he would dismiss that as irrelevant since it occurred nearly 200 years ago. To Julian and Company, the King thing was "a current affair," if you please. And the signatures kept coming in. As many as 4,000 petitions had been requested by callers to Sanders' makeshift home office so said the latest "King-buster."

By October 2, 1989, ten days before Columbus' actual birthday, Pat Quaranta, president of the Arizona American-Italian Club, announced their decision to launch a second repeal drive of Arizona's newly approved King Day. The public was assured that this had nothing to do with King, but after many strategy discussions, spearheading a referendum petition drive nearly identical to Sanders' anti-King petition drive would be the easiest way to save Columbus Day. Upon announcing their petition drive, Quaranta attempted to distance his newly founded group called Citizens for the Restoration of Columbus Day from Sanders and Arizonans for Traditional American Values. He alluded to the fact that Sanders' posture had brought up "a question of racism." So, he and his group of proud Italian-Americans pledged to reach their goal of restoring Columbus Day. By that time, Representative Sue Laybe informed the media of her plans to introduce a new bill in the upcoming 1990 session, which would restore Columbus Day by October 1990 and establish a King Day by following the federal model. Sound familiar?

There is a saying, "What a difference a day makes." By the very next day after Quaranta vowed to steer clear of the other referendum petition drive group, the press reported that Sanders and Quaranta and their respective followers had united forces to kill King Day! The motive for such a move was to eliminate an identical effort, which could divide either group's chances of securing 43,350 valid signatures of registered voters by December 21, 1989. The leader of Citizens for the Restoration of Columbus Day claimed that he struck a compromise with Mr. Sanders by getting him to remove any reference to the King holiday from their joint petitions. The top of Sanders' cover sheet read; "Let Arizona Voters Decide Martin Luther King, Jr. Holiday!" The newly agreed upon petition would simply read, "Holiday Referendum Petition." Whatever the case, the two groups had joined hands to lead Arizona through another chapter of ugly, embittered name-calling and character assassinations, just to keep King's Day off the state calendar.

The day after the "wedding" of Quaranta and Sanders' common, yet supposedly uncommon goals, the head of Arizonans for Traditional American Values criticized Dr. King as "exceed(ing) Lucifer in his ability to deceive the masses with impressive oration and dedication, in spite of his addiction to alcohol, tobacco and sex." The remark was part of a letter Sanders had written to Ezra Taft Benson, president of the Church of Jesus Christ of Latter-day Saints, of which both he and Mecham were members.

The letter was prompted by Sanders' complaints about a church spokesman in Mesa being supportive of the King holiday.

Speaking of the devil, all hell broke loose on Sanders when word got out that he equated Dr. King to Satan. Comments of shock, anger and embarrassment generated from the State Capitol to as far away as the King Center in Atlanta. The irony of Sanders' commentary was that they were his interpretation of remarks that current and former Mormon hierarchy had written in the past about Martin Luther King, Jr. and Communism. A somewhat embarrassed Pat Quaranta expressed frustration that such statements were one of the reasons he did not want to hook up with Sanders. The other misfortunate aspect about Sanders' lambasting King was that someone needed to inform faithful Julian who was criticizing a local Mormon brother for commenting on the legal holiday that his own church in Utah gave its employees a paid day off to observe Utah's legislatively-passed King Day that the Mormon Church did not oppose. Nevertheless, the "Lucifer" comments were not enough to sever the politically-expedient relationship between the Italian-Americans and what's-his-name.

As the King Day fight headed to the gutter, state lawmakers tried to reason with Quaranta and his Citizens for the Restoration of Columbus Day to drop their petition drive. However, Quaranta thumb-nosed that suggestion because he felt that was the only way he could keep pressure on the Legislature to pass legislation to reinstate Columbus Day. The calls for new legislation came from the speaker of the House of Representatives, the Honorable Jane Hull as well as Art Hamilton. They saw the issue of restoring Columbus Day as separate from canceling King Day. Moreover, the promises were genuine from key legislators that the mistake would be corrected as soon as the Legislature returned for business in January. But, Pat Quaranta was not about to listen to the governmental body that had taken away his hero's holiday, in the first place, less than a couple of weeks ago.

Community outcry began to be heard that this type of divisive name-calling generated by Sanders in reference to Dr. King, as well as putting the recently adopted King holiday to a public vote would put a halt to any healing that had begun to take place in Arizona. Many felt that the referendum, if mandated by a successful petition drive, would mushroom into a vote about Arizona's stance on civil rights. God forbid, if the election resulted in a defeat of the MLK Day. Who, then, could defend Arizona against accusations of racism and bigotry? With Sanders mouthing off his extremist political, philosophical and distorted theological viewpoints about

America's most recognized prophet of racial harmony, Arizona would bite the dust again politically and economically as espousing the sentiments of its former governor. Speaking of Mecham, he was awfully quiet while this holiday war was erupting again. Was there any communication between him and his disciple Julian? Could it be that most of Sanders' supporters were loyal "Mechamites?" Was there any link between Quaranta and Arizona's only impeached governor? Did Mecham relish the fact that the holiday he rescinded was about to get the electoral test he had campaigned for, which it needed?

Within hours, the word got out across the nation that Arizona's conservatives and Italian-Americans wanted to force a vote on a day to honor the murdered Black American who became a modern-day Moses and led this nation out of two centuries plagued by racism, discrimination and bigotry at its worst. The fastest growing state in the Southwest was on its way to becoming the laughingstock of the nation, and this time Mecham was not even in office.

Columbus Day 1989 was observed on October 9th and it could be understood why a lot more publicity was directed towards that year's parade and festivities. Unless the referendum drive was successful in postponing the King-Columbus Day exchange, that year's observance would be the last time state employees would get a paid day off in his honor. The weekend of festivities also provided numerous opportunities for petition-gatherers to collect hundreds more signatures. However, the woman overseeing the parade promised that it would not be allowed to be transformed into "a political parade." There would be no King-bashing or even lawmaker-lynchings along the parade route. The only hint of politics would be the permitting of a "support Columbus Day" float manned by none other than Pat Quaranta's forces. For the fifth year in a row from its humble beginnings, the Columbus Day parade had featured Miss Black Arizona and Ms. Black Arizona. The 1989 parade would be no different. Coincidentally, that year's Miss Black Arizona, Cecilia Penniston, went on to become one of 1994's top rhythm and blues artists in the nation.

A possible alternative to the petition drive was raised by supporters of paid state holidays honoring King and Columbus. Arnie Zaler called a meeting of the two groups in Tucson on October 10, 1989. Quaranta, accompanied by several of his petitioners, discussed the possibility of persuading Governor Mofford to call a special session for the sole purpose of restoring Columbus Day as a paid state holiday. Members of the Legislature, religious and civic leaders and Arnie's Grand Coalition met for nearly four hours trying to resolve the issue. Those in attendance approved a motion for a 30-day cooling off period, at which time the Citizens for a Restoration of Columbus Day would cease securing signatures on their petitions. However, Quaranta, feeling uneasy about the proposed moratorium, committed only to presenting the proposal to his group at an upcoming meeting in Phoenix. He reiterated that the petition drive was their only weapon to convince the Legislature that they had better do something quickly. Arnie was to be commended for getting Columbus Day advocates to sit down with King Day supporters and to agree that they both wanted the respective days to be honored as paid state holidays.

I had been invited to the meeting, but chose not to attend, because even though I had never set out to eliminate Columbus Day to make room for Dr. King's holiday, I was not a supporter of Columbus Day. My position was since it had been removed, I personally saw no need to restore a day commemorating a European explorer who got lost. I have already mentioned in this book my heartfelt feelings about the erroneous message Columbus Day gives to people of color in America, especially Native Americans and Mexican-Americans.

Fresh on my mind is the trouble I got my oldest son in, in elementary school, when I corrected him on his teacher's history lesson on the "discoverer" of America. Warren, Jr. went to school the next day and told his teacher, "My dad said you were wrong. Columbus didn't discover America because there were people already here before he stumbled upon the place!" For me, it was a "principle-thing" on which I would not compromise, since the Legislature had made the decision to eliminate it from a Monday observance at the suggestion of Corbet. Lest you be too harsh on me, I did keep my sentiments confined to our coalition meetings, until later.

On the other front, Sanders plugged away gathering thousands of signatures by courting the anti-King Day sentiment. He would have nothing to do with a moratorium on collecting referendum petition signatures. His goal was to have collected 45,000 names by early November and another 50,000 by the December 21 deadline. Without the Italian-American community's daily support, it was believed that his efforts alone would be unsuccessful. But that was not to be.

By the time a surprisingly conciliatory Quaranta got back to Phoenix and shared the proposal arising from Zaler's Ad Hoc Committee for the Restoration of Columbus Day, the Citizens for the Restoration of Columbus

Day voted unanimously to eliminate King Day in order to restore Columbus Day. To complicate matters even more, the secretary of state floated the idea that Columbus Day petitioners could circulate a new petition that would call for the restoration of Columbus Day and leave the King Day intact. The same Republican attorney general who had opined that Bruce Babbitt's executive order calling for a King Day was illegal indicated that the Arizona Constitution allows for such a political maneuver to put any portion of a legislative action to the test of the Arizona voters.

ARIZONANS FOR A MARTIN LUTHER KING, JR. STATE HOLIDAY had deliberately stayed out of the divisive fray in order that we could see if enough momentum gathered to really threaten our new-acquired Martin Luther King, Jr. Day. When we met on October 12, 1989, which was the actual birthday of Christopher Columbus, we knew we had to prepare to respond as a coalition to the crazy, cluttered mess which had begun to reek of widespread bigotry and racism. One item on the agenda was my conversing with Mr. Quaranta just before his committee cast 100% of their votes to table King Day. Meeting Mr. Quaranta proved to be interesting. However, the one, first impression that still stands out whenever I think about him was his pronunciation of the name of the renowned civil rights leader who held the nation spell-bound in his "I Have a Dream" speech from the steps of the Lincoln Memorial in 1963. Pat Quaranta did *not* pronounce Dr. King's name properly. I listened closely several times and most of the time when he uttered Dr. King's name defensively, he said "*Martha Luther King*" instead of Martin Luther King. *Doggone it! This man can't even pronounce Dr. King's name! I see why he's trying to put the MLK Day on ice,* I thought to myself. But, getting back to my conversation with Phoenix's most newsworthy Italian-American at that time, I shared with our group that Quaranta had told me he was well aware that our coalition did not push to eliminate Columbus Day for King Day. Nevertheless, he stated that he had no choice other than to continue to gather petition signatures; even if it meant the 1990 King Day would be canceled. In response, I urged him to rally the State Senate to rectify what they had done, by getting them to reinstate Columbus Day, like we had done for three years to get King Day.

Our next and most major agenda item was deciding to hold a press conference to respond as a coalition to the referendum petition drives. The time and place was set for Tuesday, October 17th at 9:00 a.m. in the sanctuary of the First Institutional Baptist Church. Our objective was to urge Arizonans to refrain from signing any of the petitions recalling MLK Day.

To my surprise, the press conference was well-covered by local media with the exception of *The Arizona Republic*, which did not send a reporter because, as I was told, they did not consider it news. KTAR covered it live before the largest radio audience in the state. Of course, I was nervous as usual, but the presence of several religious leaders and Gene Blue gave me courage to state our case and make our appeal to the masses. Our coalition's press statement is provided below in its entirety:

TOGETHER WE DID IT and TOGETHER WE CAN DO IT! ARIZONANS FOR A MARTIN LUTHER KING, JR. STATE HOLIDAY rejoices in the historic victory won after waging a battle for several years to attain the approval of the Arizona State Legislature, finally, on September 21, 1989, and the signature of Governor Rose Mofford on September 22, 1989. Since the announcement of then Governor-elect Evan Mecham in November 1986, of his intentions to rescind the Martin Luther King, Jr. state holiday declared by former Governor Bruce Babbitt on May 18, 1986, and his subsequent rescission of that holiday in January 1987, our broad-based coalition of supporters of the Martin Luther King, Jr. holiday in Arizona lobbied the Arizona State Legislature to approve the third Monday in January as Martin Luther King, Jr. Day in Arizona. After engaging in direct dialogue with gubernatorial and legislative leaders, petitioning the Arizona State Legislature, marching by the thousands in support of the holiday, speaking on behalf of the holiday in legislative hearings, receiving broad-based local, state and national support from prominent civic, political and religious leaders and organizations, and soliciting and receiving the support of the business leaders of our state, Arizona joined 46 other states and the nation in honoring Dr. Martin Luther King, Jr. with his day.

In response to the holiday referendum petition drive launched by Mr. Julian Sanders to place the legislatively-resolved Martin Luther King, Jr. holiday issue on the 1990 General Election Ballot, we offer the following:

1. The Martin Luther King, Jr. holiday will not hurt Arizona. As a matter of fact, its passage has already begun to restore the tarnished image of our state since

former Governor Evan Mecham's rescission of that holiday.

2. The Martin Luther King, Jr. holiday has been approved by the Arizona State Legislature and signed into state law as have all other paid-state holidays. Therefore, our coalition feels that to place the Martin Luther King, Jr. holiday on the ballot would be discriminatory and evidences prejudice toward the only holiday honoring the historic contributions of a Black American to his nation.

3. Our coalition also believes that the spirit in which many proponents of the Sanders' holiday referendum petition drive will advocate their opposition to the Martin Luther King, Jr. state holiday has been and will be divisive, disruptive, detrimental and disadvantageous to the peace and harmony between the various racial, ethnic and political constituencies making up the citizenry of the State of Arizona. We believe further that the holiday referendum petition drives have already cast a shadow over the restoration of Arizona's image which began when the state Legislature and governor approved and signed the King holiday legislation on September 21 and 22, 1989, respectively.

4. It is our personal belief that the people of good-will in Arizona—Black, White, Brown, Yellow, Red, young, old, Republican, Democrat, Third party, Conservative, Moderate, Liberal, lower class, middle class, upper class, laborer, professional, academic, business, religious and non-religious—were relieved to see the long and unnecessary controversy over the Martin Luther King, Jr. state holiday settled, and do not wish to engage in a statewide campaign which will pit White against Black and perhaps, permanently damage the image of our progressive state.

5. Moreover, several poll results on the Martin Luther King, Jr. holiday since 1988 have shown that once Arizonans were informed that the then-proposed and now-approved Martin Luther King, Jr. holiday would

not be an additional paid-state holiday, it received their
support 2 to 1 in favor.

6. We, also, urge all citizens of Arizona who seek the
restoration of Columbus Day in Arizona to lobby the
Arizona State Legislature and Governor Rose Mofford
to restore Columbus Day.

With that being said, **ARIZONANS FOR A MARTIN
LUTHER KING, JR. STATE HOLIDAY** urges all citizens of
good-will in our state to think twice about signing the holiday
referendum petitions to place the Martin Luther King, Jr. state
holiday on the 1990 General Election Ballot.

After I delivered the press statement, I introduced Representative
Laybe who was planning to co-sponsor legislation restoring Columbus Day
to explain her bill. Rabbi Kravitz spoke also and made remarks about the
religious community's support for the need for continued healing after the
long King Day struggle. Monsignor Ed Ryle represented Bishop O'Brien
and stated the diocese's support for both Columbus Day and King Day
and the possibility that the Legislature could resolve this controversy they
created. The press asked a few questions, but basically accepted our statement at face value.

Obviously, the word had leaked to Mr. Sanders that our coalition
would respond to his referendum petition drive because he had a press release
responding to our press conference immediately following our 9:00 a.m.
press conference. I suppose KTAR was providing "equal time" for the man
who compared the Reverend Martin Luther King, Jr. to Lucifer. Excerpts
from Sanders' diatribe are as follows:

**My Dear Fellow Arizonans—Including My Beloved Black
American Brothers and Sisters:**
Only the TRUTH—and NOTHING BUT THE
TRUTH can MAKE US FREE! Reverend Stewart has traded
our American Heroes—WASHINGTON and LINCOLN
for what he proclaims to be our NEW, ONE-WORLD,
MODERN-DAY PROPHET—MARTIN LUTHER KING
JUNIOR!...However, most Americans are NOT going to buy
that TRADE of our HEROES—and that is why this HOLIDAY
REFERENDUM PETITION CAMPAIGN is succeeding here
in Arizona.

What about my response to specific denunciations by Reverend Stewart? NO COMMENTS!

...Before the NOV '90 General Election when Arizonans vote on the STATE-PAID HOLIDAY issues regarding COLUMBUS DAY and KING DAY, **all Arizonans will have a much clearer understanding of THE REAL MARTIN as truth replaces myth!** Recent Associated Press revelations (Reverend Abernathy's eye-witness accounts) of "KING'S SEXUAL LIAISONS" will not be thrust into our campaign...

I love and esteem one BLACK AMERICAN WOMAN in much the same way I love my MOTHER...That BLACK WOMAN was MRS. JULIA BROWN—former disenchanted C.P.U.S.A. member who served a year as undercover agent for the FBI. She testified..."I also believe that Mr. King was one of the worst enemies my people ever had..."

We who choose to accept the whole truth about MLK— both good and bad, have a goal of GOOD WILL to restore both COLUMBUS DAY...and ARIZONA'S CIVIL RIGHTS/ KING DAY on the 3rd Sunday of each January. We feel that is the best compromise for a UNITED ARIZONA!!!

Hopefully, one can get a grasp of the kind of individual Arizona was blessed to have leading its historic anti-King Day referendum petition drive. Moreover, what appeared in his press release was written before he had heard a word from our press conference. I suppose the same one who told him Dr. King was Lucifer's equal allowed him to eavesdrop on me while I wrote that press statement. Regrettably, that was not to be my last close encounter with Julian. However, our coalition's aim was to take the "moral high ground" in fighting the referendum drive and not stoop to Sanders' level.

The same day of our press conference information became public, it was announced that another petition drive would soon be launched to restore Columbus Day and keep King Day. This referendum petition drive would be orchestrated by the Knights of Columbus, a Catholic fraternal organization with 7,500 members in Arizona. With the encouragement of Bishop Thomas O'Brien and Monsignor Ed Ryle, this King Day friendly group wanted to make sure that Italian-American and other supporters of Columbus Day were not thrown in the same wrestling match with Sanders and Quaranta. The reaction to the Legislature's bungled passage of the

King-Columbus Day swap had now led to a three-ring circus providing a "wild, wild West show" for the whole country to witness. There would be little chance that Citizens for the Restoration of Columbus Day would unite with the Knights of Columbus; and absolutely no chance that Sanders would think about doing so. The noble intention of the Catholic organization was to put an end to the divisiveness that the two groups were causing and defuse any hints of racism surrounding the controversy. Leadership for this third resolution attempt was being augmented by Senator Higuera.

Later on that day, the governor, whose ratings in polls signaled a rise in her popularity, announced that she would not call a special session to deal with the King Day confusion, since Arizonans were exercising their right to challenge the legislatively approved law by gathering petition signatures. She indicated that she would wait and see what the outcome of the two referendum petition drives would be before taking any further action. After all, Governor Rose had evidenced her commitment to Arizona's MLK Day on several previous occasions, so even if she did not call a special session at that time, no one could question her support of the holiday.

Amidst all of the increasing tension over Arizona's new day, honoring a major man of the cloth, Democratic veteran and political whiz, Bill Jamieson, entered the ministry of his ordination into the Sacred Order of Deacons at the Trinity Cathedral in downtown Phoenix on October 21, 1989. That was quite a combination for a WASP Democratic powerhouse—preacher and politician. Of course, the Black community is accustomed to such a sacrosanct alignment. One has but to call the honor roll of African-American leaders who fought for and wrought breakthroughs for the oppressed in the land, and I would dare say, the Black preacher and the Black Church have produced the majority of effective revolutionaries, such as Richard Allen, Frederick Douglass, Henry Highland Garnett, Harriet Tubman, Sojourner Truth, Nat Turner, Adam Clayton Powell, Jr., Martin Luther King, Sr. and Jr., Sandy F. Ray, Benjamin Hooks, William Gray, G. Benjamin Brooks, Jesse Jackson and Calvin Butts.

However, for a middle-aged gentleman in Arizona as steeped in Democratic politics as Jamieson, it indeed was newsworthy that a *Republic* political columnist would mention it in her Sunday, October 29, 1989 column. More surprising to me was to see my name listed among her "Who's Who of Arizona politics," along with "an amazing array of political powerhouses" like Mofford, Hamilton, Stephens, Gutierrez, Pfister and Shover. I guess I was just following in the prophetic traditions of my ebony predecessors of the preaching fraternity (and sorority). Reflecting on the occasion, it was a truly spiritual experience to see the men and women who "move and shake" the state's politics stop on a Saturday morning to reverence a friend who accepted a higher calling than "cutting a deal in a political caucus."

Our coalition convened on Halloween to see if any more ghosts of the Ku Klux Klan had removed their white sheets in the desert. Out of the twelve faithfuls attending that meeting of ARIZONANS FOR A MARTIN LUTHER KING, JR. STATE HOLIDAY, nine were of European descent. We evaluated the response to our press conference two weeks prior and discussed my conversations with Quaranta and Senator Higuera, respectively. In spite of my philosophical objections to the celebration of Columbus Day, I queried the group about how we should respond to the new, proposed petition drive seeking just to restore that holiday. I was relieved when Joedd Miller, then-pastor of the Central Presbyterian Church, which is a predominantly Native American congregation, spoke and said, "Let's leave the restoration of Columbus Day in the hands of the Legislature. And those who want a Columbus Day need to get busy like we did and work for it the way we had to do." Joedd is my kind of White brother! Moreover, our constitutional by-laws made reference to one holiday only—the Martin Luther King, Jr. Day. It was never our mission to seek to attain anything else, period. The issue of the involvement of business leaders in *leading* the MLK holiday campaign if the matter would get on the 1990 general election ballot was broached by me. Shover had been in touch with **me** and Jamieson was offering his political advice to key legislative leaders and business leaders on what should be done to counter the anti-King petitioners. Our coalition never envisioned leading a statewide election campaign to win public voter support for King Day. No other state had ever had an election on any holiday, and the Arizona Constitution granted the Legislature the representative authority to designate paid state holidays. Furthermore, to mandate a vote for a holiday honoring a Black American when no other holiday got the same treatment; evidenced for me nothing but outright racism and bigotry. I could not even imagine scores of thousands of freedom-loving citizens, even in Arizona demanding such a vote. But, thanks to Mecham, Sanders, Quaranta and several thousand other Arizona voters who were signing the first referendum petitions, I did not have to *not* imagine what would shortly become a prejudiced reality.

It was at that moment that I shared what had been on my mind a lot the last few days. If the referendum petition drive of Sanders and Quaranta was successful in getting enough signatures to put King Day and Columbus Day on the ballot, there might be an advantage to having an Anglo person to lead the campaign, in order to diffuse the Black against White issue. Dr. Reader responded that collective leadership would be needed. But, I still could not get the leadership issue out of my mind because my bottom-line was to see Arizona honor King with his due day, and if that meant me being removed from the front-pages and evening news sound bites as the leader of the King Day campaign, so be it. After all, I was tired! The meeting adjourned shortly after that discussion, but my mind did not.

A couple of days later I attended a meeting held at Bishop Heistand's office at Trinity Cathedral. It would prove to be the beginning of the next King Day committee that would carry the baton through the election campaign. Hamilton, Kravitz, Shover, Bob Robb, then a Republican public relations/political consultant, and the host, Bishop Heistand were present. It was my first time being in an Episcopal bishop's office. The meeting room was small, warm and aristocratically furnished. Once the meeting began it was obvious that, at least, some in this gathering had met and/or conversed prior to November 2, 1989. After cordial introductions (I really was probably the only one present who had never met Bob Robb), Robb presented his public relations proposal to send out a message to the Arizona electorate who would be voting on King Day. The message—"A Martin Luther King, Jr. Day is the *right* thing to do."

That campaign theme had been the brainchild of the Republican "co-pilot," Robb and the Democratic "co-pilot," Fred DuVal, a success-ful political consultant champion his party's causes and crusaders. Three 60-second commercial spots would be produced, (1) an "I Have a Dream" speech spot, (2) a history of the Civil Rights Movement, and (3) a testimonial of a young Black male who is successful and an older White female with a southern accent praising the Civil Rights Movement. The commercial spots would cost about $50,000. Also, twenty thousand dollars would be earmarked to get the Columbus Day only referendum petition drive qualified and another ten grand would pay for polling on people's feelings about the King holiday.

Robb further informed the group that there was a 40-40 split for and against the MLK Day currently, with 20% undecided. The plan was to develop a coalition of Republicans and Democrats to lead the positive campaign. After being apprised of what had already taken place and what was planned, I was asked to get funds from the pot of ARIZONANS FOR A MARTIN LUTHER KING, JR. STATE HOLIDAY which had around $14,000 left in it. It became very apparent to me in that meeting that the business community planned to "grab the tiger by the tail." A bit amazed at how the money people move forward without missing a half-step when they want something, I also felt relief that King's torch would not be extinguished during an historic statewide election, due to a lack of funds.

I still had my reservations, though, about my political and philosophical rivals *leading* the drive to keep a holiday honoring a man who represented the common folk across the tracks and on the other side of the freeway. Meanwhile, some leaders in Phoenix's African-American community were challenging the business community to finish what they started by pushing the holiday through the Legislature for monetary gain. Even for them, winning a paid state holiday honoring King at the polls would be no cakewalk.

Some good news came across the wire relative to the progress of the Sanders-Quaranta petition drive—halfway through their 90-day time limit they had collected only 30,000 signatures as opposed to the hoped for 45,000 by November 5. Ed Buck, in comparing the number of signatures he had collected in his recall drive against Mecham in about 45 days, expressed his opinion that the anti-King Day forces were in trouble. Sanders certainly would not allow any comment from his gay "brother" to register reality with him. I am sure Buck's comment incited Julian to double his efforts to reach his goal to spite a fellow Republican of non-traditional American values. Quaranta complained about not being able to get enough circulators of petitions from his own ethnic community. Meanwhile, the Knights of Columbus were doing their thing collecting signatures to keep both King and Columbus Days.

Right on the tail end of the good news about the sluggish petition drive, a new poll came out revealing that 60% of Arizonans polled felt the Legislature made a mistake in honoring Martin Luther King, Jr. with a paid holiday. And according to the same *Arizona Republic* poll, 78% believed that Columbus Day should be restored. I am sure both Sanders and Quaranta leaped for joy at such news. It was not too hard to analyze why so many people opposed King Day after it was passed, even though two-thirds of the citizens in Maricopa County had voiced their support for the holiday in 1988. The taking away of Columbus Day had done more damage to sustaining the new legislation than Sanders' anti-King rhetoric.

Perhaps, much more damaging was an external factor which popped into the picture in an untimely manner. The publishing of Dr. Ralph David Abernathy's autobiography entitled *And The Walls Came Tumbling Down* hit the press in mid-October. In that book, Abernathy, who was Martin's right-hand man and successor to the presidency of the Southern Christian Leadership Conference after King's assassination, detailed the alleged activities of himself and Dr. King the night before he was killed in Memphis. The Reverend Abernathy claimed that King spent his last night alive in a bedroom with two women, neither of whom was his wife, and had been physically abusive to a third woman who had come to his motel room, only to find it empty. Upon hearing such allegations, I became upset with two individuals who were critical to my freedom as a Black American and to whom I was indebted for so much.

First, I felt Abernathy had become a modern-day Judas denigrating the memory of his beloved brother who gave his life to change America for the better. Even if his account was true (and it was hotly disputed by others who were with King during those last fateful days), he had broken an unwritten rule by divulging such information for public consumption. Some things are left better unsaid or unwritten. Also, I was a little put out with Dr. King, if it was true. Yes, I had heard of the rumors about his supposed extramarital affairs. Maybe they did take place as the FBI reported. But, I remember unleashing my frustration at Abernathy's revelations in my bathroom, after getting out of the shower. I said to myself in an exasperated, voice, "Martin, why couldn't you be 'Mr. Faithful'. Here I am trying to keep people from signing a petition to cancel your holiday in Arizona, and your buddy makes public, private matters occurring the night before you got killed."

Once I let my pent-up emotions escape, I forgave Abernathy for betraying his dead friend and thanked God for Martin Luther King, Jr., a mortal, fallible human-being, who did not hesitate to lift up the eternal cause of love to win justice, equality and respect for downtrodden Americans, especially people of color, through his historic non-violent philosophy based on fundamental principles arising from his triple heritage—African, American and Christian, mixed with Ghandian teachings. As I would come to respond to inquirers who brought up King's alleged infidelity, "There's only *one* holiday honoring a perfect person, and that's Christmas."

So, the renewed vilifying of King's character from all directions began to pay off for King Day opponents. The honoree would have to pay the price for being honored. Who he was; what he did and who Arizona voters perceived him to be would be destined to stand trial before the court of public opinion, about a year later. Arizonans for Traditional American Values and Citizens for the Restoration of Columbus Day reaped the benefits of Arizona-style slandering of one of God's most gifted leaders in modern-times. I was rather upset with the re-assassination of my role model, not by Sanders and Quaranta, but by the majority of Arizonans polled who wanted to nix the King holiday.

Consequently, on November 13, 1989, I wrote a press release from ARIZONANS FOR A MARTIN LUTHER KING, JR. STATE HOLIDAY, responding to the November 2-5, 1989 *Arizona Republic* poll. It was untypically short but straight to the point.

> If the majority of the White people in Arizona desire to rescind the Martin Luther King, Jr. State Holiday a second time, then that message needs to be communicated loudly and clearly around the world.

For the life of me, I do not know for sure if I sent that press release out over the wire. However, I do know that on November 16, 1989, I sent out the following letter to everyone on the mailing list of our coalition.

> After prayerful consideration, I am tendering my resignation as General Chairperson of **ARIZONANS FOR A MARTIN LUTHER KING, JR. STATE HOLIDAY,** effective January 15, 1990.
>
> The only objective, which we set out to accomplish over three years ago has been attained—the establishment of the third Monday in January as Martin Luther King, Jr. Day in Arizona by the Arizona State Legislature and signed by the Governor of Arizona.
>
> I must now devote more time to my family, the congregation where I have served for over twelve years (and which voted on October 10, 1989 to begin to construct a multi-purpose educational, administrative and outreach building), and to the youth in our drug-laden and crime-infested neighborhoods.
>
> I thank God for sustaining me during this historic struggle for the cause of civil rights, justice and equality to victory in Arizona. Moreover, I will continue to fight to engage in that ongoing struggle.
>
> **TO GOD BE THE GLORY.**

My resignation would be discussed in our November 28th coalition meeting.

It seemed like every day another diversion surfaced to complicate the already confusing and complex chaos surrounding the King-Columbus Day exchange bill. A leak out of the state attorney general's office on November 14, 1989 hinted that the King Day legislation was flawed because it did not specifically mention Columbus Day while identifying the new holiday by name. If the legislation were challenged in court, the King Day portion would not be affected, but Columbus Day would be restored. The governor or the legislators would have to request an opinion from Bob Corbin's office. Either of the King Day or Columbus Day supporting groups could press the governor or legislators to seek the state attorney's opinion on the bill. If the law would be deemed illegal, then questions would be raised whether or not the referendum petitions would become null and void, therefore canceling a popular vote on King Day, even if enough signatures were gathered. In addition, if Columbus Day was restored by the courts and King Day retained, Arizona taxpayers would be saddled with an eleventh paid state holiday which the legislators did not approve.

On November 15th two Phoenix attorneys decided to launch *another* petition drive. This one would be to adopt the federal model of the Martin Luther King, Jr. holiday for Arizona voters to decide upon in November 1990. Because this effort was not a repeal on a law already passed by the Legislature, twice the amount of valid signatures would be required to put this no-cost King Day proposal on the ballot. And the petitioners would have until July 5, 1990 rather than December 21, 1989 to get their names. Ironically, Quaranta did not oppose this move because it would not touch Columbus Day, and both he and the King Day supporters would be happy.

The word had gotten out that there would be a special session of the Legislature called by the governor. Quaranta immediately wrote Governor Mofford and all the senators and representatives citing the *Republic* poll that indicated 60% of the people polled were against King Day and 78% in favor of a paid Columbus holiday. He advised the governor, "To resolve the 'King/Columbus Day' issue and help reunite the citizens of our state, I urge you to add this issue to the agenda on the November 21, Special Session and instruct our legislators to resolve this issue."

The morning of our coalition's November 28, 1989 meeting, the front page of the "Valley & State" section B of *The Arizona Republic* published a small head photo of me under the bold black headlines "King Day group's chief to step down," with a smaller headline beneath the top one reading, "White leader needed, Black preacher says." Off to the right of my portrait was my name and miss-worded quote from me, "I really feel leadership for the board needs to come from the Anglo community." The first paragraph of the article by *Republic* reporter Ed Foster stated,

> The Black Baptist preacher who for three years has led the campaign for a paid state holiday honoring the Rev. Martin Luther King, Jr. said Monday that he is stepping down from the post because the King group needs a white leader "to diffuse" the race issue.

What had apparently happened was someone from within our coalition had "leaked" a copy of my letter to Foster. He was the kind of reporter that could get on one's nerves. A matter of fact, he had called me at home on my day off that Monday bugging me about the letter. He and members of the KFYI radio station had a habit of tracking me down at my house, oftentimes with a call before sunrise to get a sound bite or a news story quote. After he spoke with me, he called some of the more prominent members on our letterhead and Bill Shover for a couple of comments on my letter of resignation, which included nothing about "the need for White leadership." However, Rabbi Plotkin's response to Foster was written thusly,

> Rabbi Albert Plotkin of Temple Beth Israel, who is an honorary chairperson of Stewart's group, agreed that a white leader is probably needed to gain credibility with white voters on the King issue.

Foster, then, wrote about his conversation with Shover.

> However, Bill Shover, who led the business effort to get a King holiday, said a white leader is not necessarily needed.
>
> "We just need a good leader," said Shover... "I don't care what color he is."

I am glad that Foster did quote me accurately when he asked me about my tenure as leader of our coalition,

> "It (the King group) has been a very positive experience," Stewart said. "It has enabled persons from various backgrounds to sit down and work together."

And that is really how I felt. I am a realist/optimist. Without faith, there is no way I could have accepted the leadership of such coalition with a mountaintop goal to reach with a bunch of stubborn, unmoving Republican conservative lawmakers and a right-winged governor in the way. We started as a group of Black ministers and a couple of feisty African-American female community activists responding to an insensitive, condescending newly-elected governor who dared to assault Dr. King. Our coalition began without one red cent and for months depended on contributions from our core leaders and the First Institutional Baptist Church. Thanks to the good Lord and a lot of hard work, we had done all we could do to push and shove the Legislature into passing the King Day.

At the last moment, we were left with no choice other than to "trust" members of the business community who wanted the holiday passed for obvious reasons. As the war raged on, we gained respect and grew in numbers, establishing friendships and relationships with people of all colors, creeds, classes and connections; who normally would never be in the same room together sitting across from one another around a table of brotherhood and sisterhood. *Dr. King did that for us.* It will always remain as one of the most moving and maturing experiences in my life, regardless of the criticisms, cheap shots and exacting toll that such involvement takes on those committed to noble but unpopular causes. But the battlefield had broadened and new troops, tactics and commanders were needed to continue to march forward to keep the prize upon which our eyes were still focused.

Rabbi Kravitz led us in opening prayer on that last Tuesday in November. Several items were covered under the category of progress reports. We spent a little time discussing the *Republic* poll taken at the beginning of the month. After the first experience we had paying for our own poll in 1988, we knew that what questions are asked and how they are asked can pretty much predict the outcome of some polling. Having seen the three questions that the newspaper's pollsters had asked amidst the King-Columbus Day swap controversy, I was surprised Arizona's King Day got as much support as it did.

The next item dealt with the status of the signatures' collection by the pro-Columbus, anti-King coalition. Arnie, who appeared to have been frequently in touch with Quaranta, pointed out the Julian Sanders' group had collected 22,000 signatures and Quaranta and company had amassed nearly 38,000 names. His feeling was that the Legislature would add the King-Columbus Day issue to the agenda of the special session to clean up the mess they had gotten the whole state in. It was then brought up that a few state lawmakers were toying with the idea of approving the following array of holidays: (1) combining Washington and Lincoln Days into one George Washington/Abraham Lincoln Day, (2) making the third Monday in January Martin Luther King, Jr. Day/Human Rights Day, and (3) adding the name of National Heritage Day to Columbus Day. By so doing, every holiday in question in honor of one person would be shared by another person or cause. Of course, that proposal was nearly identical to what was proposed by us and sponsoring legislators in September 1987. On the other hand, if approved during a special session, that solution might eliminate the need for a twelve-month, statewide campaign over the MLK holiday. Everyone was in agreement and authorized me to write letters to the governor, speaker of the House and president of the Senate, stating our coalition's endorsement of the "new" idea.

Questions came up relative to the validation of the referendum petition signatures when they were turned in to the secretary of state. The issue of whether or not the King holiday would be put on hold once the signatures were validated resurfaced. So, I appointed a subcommittee to oversee the petition validation by each county. The matter of the legality of the petitions was referred to one of our honorary chairpersons, Paul Eckstein, for advice, as well as the suggestion that they should be bilingual.

Then, it was my turn to bring up that morning headline story about my resignation. By the way, there were over twenty coalition members present at that meeting, prompted, no doubt, by my resignation letter and the newspaper article. Copies of both the article and my resignation letter lay before everyone in attendance. I then clarified what had actually been said with the following words, "The only references I made, to which I feel Anglo leadership will be needed if the King holiday goes to the ballot have been to the campaign and effort not the board or group." Continuing, I said, "ARIZONANS FOR A MARTIN LUTHER KING, JR. STATE HOLIDAY as a committee and non-profit organization will have to select its own leadership." That was in response to an inquiring member of our corporate board of directors who wondered, after reading the article, how I could determine the racial background of our corporate board, which the article had implied. Mark, in trying to resolve the matter, spoke up, "If we need to go to the ballot, collective leadership will be required with a designated spokesperson." Joedd imputed, "Let's not let the racial tone of this state affect how this group approaches the problem. Color consciousness will not determine our leadership."

Judge Williams brought up the question, "Pastor, are you resigning simply as general chairperson of the coalition and not the corporation, or both?" My immediate response was, "Both, as chairperson and president." Arnie then suggested that the coalition temporarily form a committee to work with me and hopefully, he stated, "If the holiday does not go to the ballot, the matter of Pastor Stewart's dual resignation effective January 15, 1990 will take care of itself."

The matter revolving around my resignation did not end at that moment. Jennie Cox offered a motion that I be asked to reconsider my resignation effective date until after January 30, 1990. The same corporate board member who brought up the previous question about my dual resignation stated that the corporate directors would make that decision. Dr. Reader chimed in and raised the question, "Dr. Stewart, why did you choose January 15?" I responded, "My original letter of resignation was to be effective October 31, 1989, but when I shared my leanings in that direction with King Day advocates in Atlanta, they shared with me the pros and cons about stepping down at this time." Lloyd Davis, Director of the King Center, felt that had I resigned a month earlier on October 31st, it would appear that I was giving up in light of Julian Sanders and Pat Quaranta. So, he had suggested that the 1990 national observance of MLK Day would be a better and more symbolic time to move over for new leadership of the coalition, which could be announced at that time. Then, I said, "It would be unfair to notify you all on January 14th that I would be stepping down the next day. That's why I have given you nearly a two-month notice." With that being said, Jennie withdrew her motion for an extension of my resignation effective date. And a special meeting of the corporate board, which was different from the coalition at large, was scheduled for the next Tuesday to further discuss leadership transition and our financial status. I felt led to close that meeting with prayer and did so.

Within the next three days, Attorney General Corbin came out with his opinion on the King-Columbus Day exchange bill. The portion of the legislation which eliminated Columbus Day was unconstitutional because it did not mention Columbus Day specifically in the bill's title, so announced Corbin. This finding, after researching the Arizona Constitution and Statutes, was called a "non-binding formal opinion." Once his opinion was given, the stage was set for a court challenge to restore Columbus Day without eliminating King Day. To our delight, Arizona Center for Law in the Public Interest, which has a history and philosophy of tackling issues pertaining to justice for the underprivileged, under-represented and unrepresented, and the disadvantaged, was seriously considering filing a lawsuit to test Corbin's opinion. Representative Kennedy had sought the opinion from Corbin. Regrettably, if the lawsuit was to be filed, it would not nullify the efforts of the three groups seeking to put the issue on the 1990 ballot. Of course, the Legislature could have corrected the flaw by adding it to their "annual technical-corrections legislation" in which dozens of minor errors and clarifications were corrected. But, they were not in session.

Kevin Lanigan, Executive Director of the Arizona Center for Law in the Public Interest, contacted me to see if our coalition wanted to formally request that they file a lawsuit on behalf of us on the marred pertain of the King Day legislation. Both Corbin and Lanigan believed that if the law was illegal, Sanders' allies would have to throw out their signatures and start all over, without the aid of the Columbus Day defenders who would have gotten their holiday back. Upon hearing such a humbling possibility, Sanders vowed that his group would then collect four times the number of signatures needed. In addition, as Julian began to boast about having collected 58,000 signatures three weeks prior to the December 21 deadline, a few business leaders began to take him more seriously than when the one-man organization called Arizonans for Traditional American Values began in mid-September. During our December 5 corporate directors meeting, Lanigan attended and reported that the Center was ready to retain us as clients and file the lawsuit. However, he informed us of one area of caution. A judge could find the bill's title in error and throw out both holidays. After hearing that, we voted as a board not to support any effort that might nullify the legislation that we had fought for three long years. However, we welcomed the Center for their interests on our behalf. We later learned that their board president, David Bodney, was so interested in derailing the petition drive that he was considering asking the Center's board to press forward with the lawsuit, even though ARIZONANS FOR A MARTIN LUTHER KING, JR. STATE HOLIDAY decided not to serve as a plaintiff for the lawsuit. Quite interestingly, the Center also said they would not represent the pro-Columbus group because they were not members of "the embattled minority."

Once that issue was disposed of within our December 5, 1989 meeting, Judge Williams made a motion to accept my resignation effective January 15, 1990. The appreciation reception she had been working on was cancelled due to the most probable cancellation of our King Day again. A discussion occurred relative to the Dissolution Committee chaired by Pastor Barnwell, which was assigned in that meeting to oversee my resignation. It was brought up that a member of the clergy should succeed me as general chairperson. There was also wisdom attributed to securing the next general chairperson of our coalition, as soon as possible, in order that he could work closely with me for a smooth transition. The minutes of that meeting indicate that the recommendations relative to my resignation were accepted "with much regret and appreciation." That was reassuring to know that the core of our coalition's leadership, which consisted of Barnwell, Blue, Williams, Fears, Reader, Ellis, Eppinger, Richard and Terrell expressed gratitude for the leadership I had provided for our noble cause in spite of my idiosyncrasies and mistakes. The dissolution committee was assigned the task of finding new leadership within a month.

Arizona got an early Christmas present on December 21, 1989. The less-than dynamic duo of Sanders and Quaranta paraded into the secretary of state's office with 84,700 signatures on their referendum petitions and put on hold Arizona's first Martin Luther King, Jr. Day approved by the Legislature and signed by the governor. Julian, wearing the businessman's trademark outfit—a blue blazer, white shirt, red tie and grey slacks, accompanied by Pat with a two-piece light-colored suit wearing an open-necked shirt hanging slightly over his belt, stood before the media's microphones rambling on about "the will of the people governing the affairs of the state." The Columbus Day crusader tried to distance himself from the man with whom he had just filed twice the number of signatures needed to halt the 1990 MLK Day state observance. Quaranta said, "It's with mixed emotions that I'm here today. I know Mr. Sanders' position on King, and it just goes in one ear and out the other. I can assure you it is not our group's decision to challenge the King issue...We had to take this route."

After the news conference, my church member, and then Representative Kennedy got into a verbal battle with Quaranta, in which the name of "bigot" was tossed back and forth across the room. God forbid, if the heated exchange between that high-level King Day advocate and pro-Columbus Day supporter Quaranta was a prophecy of the divisiveness, which such a holiday campaign would be characterized. As word got out across the nation that nearly 90,000 Arizona voters signed petitions to stop the official celebration of the state's MLK Day, the reputation of Arizona being a state grossly out of touch with civil rights, diversity, and multicultural and interracial awareness, once again, became our embarrassing trademark.

On the other side of Phoenix that same fateful day, former Governor Bruce Babbitt and former Congressman John Rhodes, two wealthy White semi-retired politicians, announced the beginning of their campaign to win the Martin Luther King, Jr. Day at the polls in November 1990, if it was on the ballot. My new comrade in the King Day battle, Bill Shover, obviously had been very busy since I met with them on November 2, 1989.

The knock-out punch for the brand-new MLK Day jolted me into the certainty that Arizona would not observe a King Day in 1990 when I was forwarded a copy of a memorandum sent to all state agency heads from Catherine Eden, Director of Arizona Department of Administration, dated December 28, 1989. The subject was: Martin Luther King, Jr. Holiday. And it read in part:

> On September 22, 1989, the bill establishing the Martin Luther King, Jr. holiday was passed. Under the Arizona Constitution, a law does not become effective until 90 days after the bill has been passed. The Martin Luther King, Jr. holiday would have become effective on December 22, 1989...
>
> On December 21, 1989, referendum petitions opposing the legislative act establishing a Martin Luther King, Jr. holiday were filed with the Secretary of State. Filing of these petitions suspended the Martin Luther King, Jr. holiday until such time as the number of petition signatures prove insufficient or until the vote of the people in the 1990 election.
>
> Please ensure that staff are notified of this change....

As Bugs Bunny used to close his hilarious cartoons, "That's all folks." The new secretary of state, Jim Shumway, inspected the 84,700 signatures turned in a week earlier and found that only about 1,000 had to be rejected. In addition, the revised signature count computed by Shumway's office totaled 78,877, still more than enough to warrant an election in November. Our "petition overseers" learned that, once the secretary of state's office completed their initial verification, they would deliver the petitions to their respective county recorders to check the validity of a 5% random sampling. If the sampling revealed no abnormalities in signatures, the secretary of state would have to notify the public that there would be a referendum on MLK Day. The only option ARIZONANS FOR A MARTIN LUTHER

KING, JR. STATE HOLIDAY had left was to pay for copies of up to 100 of the petitions for our own verification. And we decided that would be a waste of time and money.

The anti-King forces and the pro-Columbus S.W.A.T. team had done their job well. Thanks to their collaborated efforts, the Arizona MLK holiday see-sawed in 1989 with the defeat of the King Day in the regular session of the Legislature, then a compromising and costly victory during the special session in September, and finally, a few days before 1989 became the old year, the waylaying of the would-be paid state holiday honoring the civil rights leader who was ambushed for his work by a lone gunman in 1968. However, the final word had not yet come from the secretary of state that the King-Columbus Day swap would make the ballot. That authoritative word would come in January. And somehow, in my heart, I knew it would come.

Once the good Lord ushered in the new year, anticipation and announcements about Arizona's 1990 MLK celebration could be felt and heard all over the state, especially in Phoenix and Tucson. Although the hopes of thousands had been dashed for the umpteenth time, King Day celebrants moved full speed ahead in lifting up the lofty legacy of our recognized national hero. The annual march would commence from Eastlake Park at 16th Street and Jefferson right in the heart of the historic Booker T. Washington neighborhood across from the residence of Councilman Calvin Goode and his wife Georgie. The King festival would offer an array of cultural and ethnic exhibits, entertainments, food stands and carnival-type games to enjoy. An added component of the 1990 King Day event would be the launching of voter-registration drives to get people eligible to vote in the November election. After all, staunch believers in the life and legacy of Dr. King had never before needed a paid state holiday to give praise and thanksgiving for him, who God had destined to become for America's freedom.

But not every King follower felt like celebrating his contributions in Arizona. Before the brand-new year was seven days old, the National Association of Black Journalists cancelled their plans to hold their annual meeting in our state. They were the first of many more socially conscious, King-friendly organizations who would resurrect Arizona's all-but-dead boycott over the King Day cancellations. Of course, the very public announcement of the National African-American journalist's group sent the somewhat nervous tourism and business leaders into a "tizzie", worrying about the loss of more convention bucks on account of no King Day.

Even the Phoenix Suns organization could not escape the fallout from Sanders and Suns' owner Jerry Colangelo's Italian-American "brother" Quaranta suspending the holiday honoring the Black "elder" brother of the vast majority of NBA professional ballplayers. I have already mentioned the NBA withdrawing its 1987 business meeting from the Valley, thanks to then-Governor Mecham. Well, in addition to working with Shover to get the Super Bowl to Phoenix in 1993, Colangelo was hoping to land the NBA All-Star Game in Phoenix that same year to play in the new arena he and the City of Phoenix were planning to build. However, Mr. Colangelo was astute enough to know that the players association of the NBA would not dare commit a flagrant foul by allowing such a premier show of basketball's best to play in the state that kicked King Day off the court. No way! As much as two of First Institutional's regular worshippers at the time and Phoenix Suns stars, Kevin Johnson and Eddie Johnson, the latter of whom I baptized in 1989, loved Phoenix, they were not about to become a two-man cheerleading squad to persuade their league to dunk millions of dollars into a King-less Arizona.

A.J. Miller, long-time Phoenix police officer and coordinator of the MLK march, announced that he expected a repeat number of people to make the 4-1/2 mile trek from Eastlake Park to the State Capitol—about 8,000. That figure was estimated before the official results were made public from the secretary of state's office, about whether or not the King holiday issue would find a certain spot on the general election ballot. The very next day, Friday, January 12, 1990, the word came that 59,000 of the nearly 85,000 signatures collected passed the test of being from registered Arizona voters. The King Day vote was going to happen for sure.

The opening sentence of a *Phoenix Gazette* front-page article headlined "Businesses plan King Day effort" and sub-headlined "Leaders fear economic losses for state, but legislators wary," read,

> Fearing renewed economic boycotts, including the possible loss
> of the 1993 Super Bowl, Valley business leaders were to declare
> today an all-out effort to settle the prolonged debate over the
> state's Martin Luther King, Jr. holiday.

For goodness sake's, a good place the business moguls could have started was announcing that every one of their corporations would be giving their employees MLK Day as a paid holiday on January 15, 1990! No, what they had in mind was spanking the Legislature for messing up in September and sending them back into their rooms to straighten things out in a hurry. You see, the Phoenix '93 Super Bowl Committee had to make a presentation before the NFL in March to try to win the biggest game in professional football from the other cities that wanted Super Bowl XXVII. Without Martin's Day on an official Arizona calendar, they knew they might as well not waste the airfare traveling to the owners' meeting. So, something had to be done in a hurry again!

While the newcomers to the Martin Luther King Day campaign were "running around like chickens with their heads cut off" (albeit still possessing the ability to lay golden eggs), I presided over my last coalition meeting as general chairperson of ARIZONANS FOR A MARTIN LUTHER KING, JR. STATE HOLIDAY. The date was January 11, 1990. My good friend Paul Eppinger offered the opening prayer after I gave greetings. Then, I shared my opening statement:

> Please know that I have enjoyed serving with you during this historic (and seemingly unending) campaign to win a holiday for Martin Luther King, Jr. in Arizona. In addition to your support, I have been blessed with the loyal love and support of my wife, Serena, our five sons, the First Institutional Baptist Church, and my staff, especially my secretaries, the last being LeNora Hart. To God be the glory, for it was only by His Power and Presence that I have endured this historic experience. I shall continue to support the effort to win yet another paid state holiday honoring Dr. Martin Luther King, Jr. in Arizona, even if it goes to the ballot in November.

TOGETHER WE DID IT and
TOGETHER WE CAN DO IT!

Joedd immediately offered appreciation for my leadership and First Institutional's staff for all of the work we had done since our coalition's campaign began. The person who spoke those words was another divine gift of a noble human spirit to our cause. Hardly no one's enthusiasm equaled Joedd's as he allowed his creative spirit and zeal to push for Arizona to do the right thing by King, illegal aliens, Native Americans and the disadvantaged populating the inner-city neighborhoods of Phoenix. Since my days as leader of two of the King Day coalitions, I have missed attending regular meetings with Pastor Miller. That's the downside of a coalition being successful at attaining its goals—a diaspora takes place.

I shared the latest bits and pieces of information I had heard about what the Legislature had planned to do to rectify the King-Columbus Day controversy. Although they had only been in session for a few days, the House of Representatives was set to restore Columbus Day and keep King Day. As had been the case for the previous three years, the Senate's Republican majority had made up its mind it did not want to deal with the holiday issue anymore. Governor Mofford had announced a couple of weeks earlier that she supported the restoration of Columbus Day and the adoption of the federal model of MLK Day for Arizona, which would combine the two existing Washington and Lincoln Days into one Presidents Day. The Arizona Republican Party had restated their strong opposition to anybody touching Lincoln Day. I reported that the governor's new chief of staff had called my office offering Governor Mofford's continued support and informing me that she would have a representative at the King Day march just four days away.

Bob Kravitz updated our coalition on the formation of the MLK Better America Committee, which was the brainchild of Bob Robb and the Shover group. The new group had set a goal to initially raise $100,000 to launch an effective campaign and recruit supporters from a cross-section of the Arizona community. The rabbi continued that their consultants had arrived at some basic facts about what would be needed to win in November.

The four key messages that would be emphasized by the business-run bipartisan committee were outlined thusly:

We celebrate MLK's birthday to commemorate his singular contribution to making a better America.

There was very little progress made in racial equality in this country from the end of the Civil War until MLK worked to end segregation laws.

It must be remembered that in many parts of the country just 30 years ago, the law required that people discriminate against others on the basis of race. MLK was the catalyst to end that.

MLK ushered in an unprecedented era of social progress without violence. That's an accomplishment America…and Arizona…should celebrate

Several of our veteran coalition members were allowed to surface their defensiveness about another group, especially business leaders, spearheading the common people's holiday by nitpicking at the name of the new coalition. One coalition member voiced, "I think a more appropriate name for that committee would be MLK Better World Committee." Bob Kravitz replied, "All countries may not be in agreement on the King issue." For reasons I will explain in a following chapter, my pro-life stance came up as a possible plus to win over some conservatives to the King Day camp. At that point, Dr. Reader cautioned, "Any publicity emanating from us should make clear that ARIZONANS FOR A MARTIN LUTHER KING, JR. STATE HOLIDAY was composed of various views on the pro-life issue, so that we do not offend any King Day advocates who are pro-choice." I responded, "My involvement in the pro-life movement could possibly be a bridge for some Republicans, especially in the Legislature, and my stance might win some desperately needed votes at the State Capitol."

Later on in the meeting, it was announced that the Arizona Center for Law in the Public Interest had voted not to file a lawsuit against the King/Columbus Day bill because there were too many "ifs" and "risks."

Then, I offered the following suggestions for strategy in winning the King Day at the polls in ten months. It was kind of like a retiring pastor offering his successor helpful advice on leading the congregation to "higher heights and deeper depths." Listed verbatim, they were:

1. Broaden base of supporters of MLK Day in Arizona.
2. Work with MLK Better America Committee.
3. Sustain a positive campaign for MLK Day in spite of obvious and not-so-obvious bigotry and racism on opposing side.
4. Transform vocal support for MLK Day into votes by November.
5. Register new voters
6. Enlist the support of Anglo and Hispanic, Native American and Asian-American church members
7. Raise some funds for campaign.
8. Steer away from economic boycott of state (that will occur on its own).
9. Commit to disagree agreeably and present a united front.
10. Ultimately depend on DIVINE HELP for the cause of Justice, Liberty and Equality.

After I shared my suggestions, other members offered theirs which included developing more deputy registrars; recruiting new voters from high schools; writing letters of support from our coalition to MLK Better America and sending them our mailing list; ask King state workers to come out of their offices at the State Capitol and march with King Day supporters as we marched by their office buildings; call on businesses to close shop on January 15, 1990 and to get busy working in one's own party precinct.

The mood was not somber or fearful because I was stepping down. The decision had been made three months prior to that meeting and the coalition was well aware of it. On the other hand, tension existed as to who would step into my shoes after January 15, 1990. That became evident once the dissolution committee chair, Pastor Barnwell, offered his report. First, he thanked me for my leadership. The two of us had labored side-by-side on many community-related issues, even prior to the King holiday controversy. We had exchanged pulpits and co-hosted a Joint Evangelistic Revival for nearly ten years during the week following the federal observance of MLK Day. However, to my deep regret, the King Day campaign had taken its toll on our relationship. Pastor Barnwell informed us that his committee had not been able to meet, but would be doing so at the next Board of Directors meeting. He reminded all present that the charge of the dissolution committee had been changed from dissolving the organization to transferring leadership. Mark, being a little sensitive about new leadership taking over the reins I had held for 37 months, spoke up. "Well, then, it would seem to me that the name of the committee should be changed."

The next motion sent shock waves bouncing off the walls of this church's then small office annex conference room. "I move," so motioned Dr. Reader, "that we nominate a temporary general chairperson until the board of directors can meet to recommend a new leader, and since Paul Eppinger has worked so closely with Pastor Stewart and Paul has a staff that can continue the work, I recommend Paul."

Almost instantaneously, I felt shock, surprise, hurt, anger, approval, disapproval, betrayal and suspicion filling the space we occupied, and emanating from every individual present. Mind you, I am not saying every one of us felt all of those feelings. What I am saying is that our coalition, which had been dividing into two camps due to a power struggle which had manifested itself into collective personality clashes between the two camps, was beginning the painful process of splitting apart. The person from whom

I felt the most sense of hurt and betrayal was sitting to my right at the head of the table where he always sat in the meetings—Henry Barnwell.

First of all, I was as shocked as most of us present at the recommendation. Yes, I knew that the issue of my successor had been on the minds of all of the coalition faithfuls since October. But, the process to elect a leader had begun. Then, again, since the dissolution committee had not even held a meeting yet and there was no definite line of succession for the coalition, Mark felt that somebody had to be put in charge, since I had only four days left. In a few moments, the motion was seconded and Dr. Paul Eppinger became the temporary general chairperson of ARIZONANS FOR A MARTIN LUTHER KING, JR. STATE HOLIDAY. Paul thanked the members for their vote of confidence and stated that he would need to confer with his deacons before accepting the position, although he felt sure they would not object.

Believe me, after that motion, the meeting was over! Sensing that, I called for adjournment, announced the next corporate board meeting for January 18, and offered the closing prayer. I do not remember what I prayed, but I know that God and I did not talk for long that afternoon. It was time to go.

By Sunday, the day before the federal observance of King Day, over 70% of Arizonans expressed their disapproval with the Legislature's King-Columbus Day exchange through another pre-holiday poll conducted by *The Arizona Republic*. Somewhat encouraging, but still scary, the same poll found that 49% of the persons polled favored a King holiday when it was separated from Columbus Day, with the remaining 51% anti-King or undecided. The latest poll results, the established referendum of King Day, and the cancelled 1990 holiday celebration did not bode well for Arizona's 1993 Super Bowl chances, NBA All-Star game bid, the 1991 Episcopal General Assembly and the League of Cities annual convention prospects for that same year. A hole in the pocket of our state's tourism industry, which had been patched up by the passage of King Day, had begun to quickly unravel and small change had already started getting lost.

The celebration of King was greeted by a beautiful sunshiny Arizona January day and 15,000 marchers in Phoenix! All of the anti-King Day sentiment polluting the air in Arizona prompted thousands to brave the unhealthy political climate for holiday supporters and show state lawmakers, citizens, the nation, the world and Julian Sanders that MLK had a lot of support. As Dr. King's widow proclaimed from Atlanta's Ebenezer Baptist Church that her husband's dream was still unfulfilled, 15,000 Arizonans in Phoenix alone shouted that our dream for a day in MLK's honor would one day become reality, in spite of those who trashed our first legislatively approved holiday. People watched us march, sing, yell and demand justice as the national and international media reported on Arizona's continuing saga over Martin.

I was there for what I thought was my last time as head of a King Day coalition. I was relaxed. I had on a two-piece wool pinstriped suit—the same one I had on when I met with Mecham three years before then. I was going to catch a plane shortly after the march to fly to Washington, D.C. to deliver the King Day celebration address for the Department of Defense. Once we marchers arrived at Wesley Bolin Plaza, they ushered me to the stage. Looking at the sea of thousands of persons "made in the image and likeness of God" was awesome. I had been asked to give brief remarks like the previous years. But this year was different. I had no script, no typed speech and no burden of leading the state to victory in November. So, as we marched to the State Capitol, I decided in my mind what I was going to say.

Gene introduced me as "our leader for three years…" I thanked the people for their support of my leadership and reminded them that we had finally won the holiday last September. Then, I began to pontificate as my friend, William Cheshire, then Editor of the Editorial Pages of the *Republic*, called it as he listened to me "live" over the radio,

> Thanks to the "odd couple" of Julian Sanders and Pat Quaranta, we don't have a Martin Luther King, Jr. state holiday today. So, we've all got to vote in the election in November.…And let me tell you why I am voting for King over Columbus Day. King was an American! Columbus wasn't! Columbus didn't discover America! King worked to liberate those who were enslaved! Columbus enslaved and slaughtered the Indians he stumbled upon when he got lost…The other folk can vote for Columbus Day if they want. But I'm casting my vote for Martin Luther King, Jr. who was born in America, lived in America and died in America!

The crowd went crazy with approval. And when I turned away from the front of the stage, who did I see running beside the stage shouting and demanding an apology from me—Pat Quaranta. Oops! What was he doing there? Between his angry shouts, I replied, "I'm not gonna apologize for telling the truth! You didn't apologize for your referendum drive, even though I tried to get you to wait on the Legislature to restore Columbus Day! I'm sorry; I don't take back anything I said!"

To be honest, if I had known Quaranta was there, I may not have said all that I said about Columbus. But, let's face it. King Day was on the chopping block and 71% of the mostly White voters in Arizona had said that Columbus was their choice over "my man." So, the campaign at that point was going to boil down to King versus Columbus, and do you think I had to think twice about who would get my vote? Furthermore, part of Dr. King's movement had, as its objective, to win people the right to vote. Consequently, even though I felt that the King holiday should have never been on the ballot in the first place, I had to inspire King Day supporters to make their choice at the polls. Also, I felt that the whole Columbus Day issue had given a tree to hide behind to people who really did not want to come out and say that they did not want a King holiday. Whatever the case, I was out of there.

My trip to D.C. was short, but exhilarating. I guess because I was not a big-name speaker I did not receive all of the amenities that people like Jesse Jackson, Martin Luther King, III and Andrew Young get. So I took the clean Washington mass transit to my hotel, spent a nearly sleepless night, and to my liking, I was picked up to travel to where I was speaking the next day. My hostess was gracious. She had heard about me through a former member of our congregation living in Maryland. I was taken to the U.S. Mapping Agency where I would deliver my speech. What I had planned to deliver was a re-worked and elongated version of my "Martin Luther King, Jr. is America" speech, which I had delivered before the Arizona Senate Government Committee in 1987. That was a message written primarily to educate White people who need convincing that Dr. King was "as American as apple pie."

I was ushered into the large meeting room where I was to give the speech. I was introduced to the military commander in charge of that agency, as well as the eminent Dr. Dorothy Height, president of the National Council of Negro Women, who would be the person introducing me on the program. What an honor for a small town boy from Coffeyville, Kansas to be in the nation's capital about to be presented to total strangers by one of America's veteran civil rights leaders! She was very cordial and we chatted for awhile. Dr. Height complimented me on my biographical sketch, to my delight. But, a surprising revelation began to occur for me. As employees of the Defense Department began to trickle in for the program, the overwhelming majority of them were Black. My speech had been written for my American brothers and sisters of "pinkish hue." O Lord, what would I do?

A friend who was studying theology at Howard University had come to hear me speak; so I spontaneously asked my preacher-friend to bring me my briefcase. When I opened it, I took out the handwritten manuscript of a speech, which I had delivered before the Black U.S. West employees, who had invited me to deliver their annual MLK breakfast message a few days earlier. It was entitled "What is the Dream?" based on their theme for their affair. It had been written for Black folks. Hallelujah! Something had told me to bring that speech, just in case. By the time I got up to speak, my nerves had calmed down a little bit. In my introductory remarks, I lambasted then-President George H.W. Bush for being televised golfing on King Day instead of attending a King Day activity on the actual holiday. I forgot about the high-ranking military personnel in my midst who had informed me that my speech was being videotaped to be sent to installations around the world. I am sure if they sent it at all, they "bleeped out" those remarks. Then, I pressed on with my "Warren H. Stewart, Sr." - style sermonic address. To get a gist of its content, the first point was "America, Practice What You Preach!" The audience went wild and gave me a standing ovation.

Afterwards, Dr. Height predicted that I "was going places." She blessed me by uttering, "I knew Dr. King. I traveled with Martin. I watched him mature as a man. And I haven't been moved by a speaker like you moved me today since I last heard Dr. King....The nation will hear from you." I am still waiting for my call for the nation to hear from me, but, thank God, I will never forget the ego boost the outgoing head of Arizona's King Day coalition got from "great Height" that day. Many of the African-Americans in attendance said that my speech touched them, unlike the usual MLK Day message from many accommodating Black Americans who speak for "the other folks" at King Day functions. Me, I do not have any better sense than to preach wherever I speak, unless it is totally out of place. That is a gift from God and I plan on using it to His glory until he takes it or me away.

My last ARIZONANS FOR A MARTIN LUTHER KING, JR. STATE HOLIDAY meeting convened on January 18, 1990, with First Vice President Blue presiding. After going through the preliminaries of greeting, praying, stating the meeting's purpose, which was "to elect new leadership...," and adopting the agenda and minutes of the previous corporate meeting, the agenda called for the report from the nominating committee, i.e., the previously authorized dissolution committee. For some reason, that committee had not met yet. Then, nominations became in order from the floor. Pastor Barnwell was nominated as president of the corporation and general chairperson of the coalition, Pastor Eppinger was recommended as treasurer, the office previously held by Pastor Barnwell, and all other officers of the corporation remained the same. The nominations were unanimously approved. I turned over some materials to Pastor Barnwell and shared a letter I had written to the co-chairs of the MLK Better America Committee on January 12, 1990, which read:

> On Thursday, January 11, 1990, (our coalition) voted unanimously to lend our support to the common goal of winning a paid state holiday in honor of Martin Luther King, Jr. in Arizona.
>
> As soon as our General Chairperson is elected, it is our request that you invite that person to be a part of the Executive Committee of the MLK Better America Committee.
>
> Thanks in advance for your efforts and your consideration of this matter.

I also copied this letter to Bob Robb and Bill Jamieson.

I do not remember when it was, but in a meeting with Shover and the executive committee of the MLK Better America Committee at Trinity Cathedral prior to my last corporate board meeting of ARIZONANS FOR A MARTIN LUTHER KING, JR. STATE HOLIDAY, Shover asked me, "Warren, are you really out of this campaign?" I said, "Yep." And that was unneeded clearance that he and his group would press on without needing to keep in touch with me as Bill had conscientiously done since our first meeting on August 31, 1989.

So, our King Day was gone and so was I.

The Victory Together Journey in Photos

EXECUTIVE ORDER No. 86-5 HOLIDAY HONORING MARTIN LUTHER KING, JR. signed by Governor Bruce Babbitt in the Pulpit of the First Institutional Baptist Church on May 18, 1986

EXECUTIVE ORDER

No. 86-5

HOLIDAY HONORING MARTIN LUTHER KING, JR.

WHEREAS, the Congress of the United States established by Public Law 98-144 the third Monday in January as the official Federal holiday honoring the birthday of Martin Luther King, Jr.; and

WHEREAS, a holiday honoring Martin Luther King, Jr. serves as a time for Arizonans to reflect on the challenges of human equality and nonviolent social change pursued by Martin Luther King, Jr.; and

WHEREAS, Martin Luther King, Jr. rolled away many of the stones of inaction, indifference and injustice; and

WHEREAS, this holiday will encourage the citizens of Arizona to rededicate themselves to the compassionate philosophies by which Martin Luther King, Jr. lived; and

WHEREAS, in honoring Martin Luther King, Jr. each of us reaffirm the ultimate dream of freedom, justice and opportunity for all and his commitment that "we will not be satisfied until justice rolls down like waters and righteousness like a mighty stream";

NOW, THEREFORE, I, Bruce Babbitt, Governor of the State of Arizona do hereby order the third Monday of each January as a holiday honoring the birthday of Dr. Martin Luther King, Jr. for all employees of Agencies, Boards and Commissions within the purview of the Executive Branch of the State of Arizona.

This Order shall become effective immediately.

IN WITNESS WHEREOF, I have hereunto set my hand and caused to be affixed the Great Seal of the State of Arizona

GOVERNOR

DONE in Phoenix, Arizona on this eighteenth day of May in the Year of Our Lord One Thousand Nine Hundred and Eighty-six and of the Independence of the United States of America the Two Hundred and Tenth.

ATTEST:

Secretary of State

Front Line of the Annual Martin Luther King, Jr. March on the Federal Martin Luther King, Jr. Day, January 19, 1987—From left to right: AZ Senator Carolyn Walker, Representative Art Hamilton, Tommy Espinoza and his son, Dr. Warren H. Stewart, Sr. and his son Matthew, Phoenix Mayor Terry Goddard, Pastor Walter Thomas, The Honorable Carolyn Warner, Unknown boy, Dr. G. Benjamin Brooks, Sr. and his wife

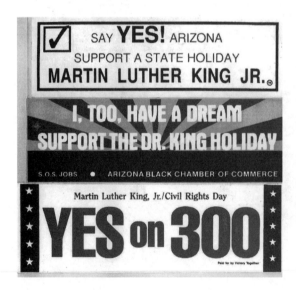

Various Arizona Martin Luther King, Jr. Holiday Campaign Bumper Stickers, 1987 to 1992

Signing of the first Martin Luther King, Jr. Day passed by the Arizona State Legislature on September 22, 1989, signed by Governor Rose Mofford

Victory Banner displayed in the First Institutional Baptist Church on Sunday, September 24, 1989, after passing of first Martin Luther King, Jr. Holiday by the Arizona State Legislature

*Signing of the second Martin Luther King, Jr. Holiday passed by the
Arizona State Legislature on May 16,1990, signed by Governor Rose Mofford*

Cancelling The King Holiday In Arizona Sparks Hot Dispute

Once again, Arizona is at the center of a controversy surrounding the celebration of a holiday to commemorate the Rev. Dr. Martin Luther King, Jr.

This time, it is the entire state that is feeling the brunt of national criticism, after voters defeated a referendum that would have established a state holiday honoring Dr. King.

Reaction to the Nov. 6 vote, which saw a King holiday referendum lose by one percent of the

Rep. Warren Stewart is counting on grass roots support to create a King holiday in Arizona.

vote, was swift.

Arizona, one of only three states that don't honor Dr. King with a holiday—Montana and Vermont are the others—is the only state that has put such a holiday to a statewide vote. Only three percent of the state's voters are Black.

In 1985, outgoing Gov. Bruce Babbitt proclaimed a King holiday as an executive order. His successor, Evan Mecham, rescinded that order in 1987, which, among other things, led to his impeachment. (JET, Nov. 2, 1987). The state Legislature then enacted a King holiday last year, but opponents put the issue on the recent Nov. 6 ballot.

Even before the vote, the National Football League had made it clear that the awarding of the 1993 Super Bowl, which had been approved for Phoenix, hinged upon the vote.

Arizona is one of only three states, joining Wyoming and Montana, that do not have a Martin Luther King holiday.

We estimated the cost of that was about $30 million."

"Potentially, the economic impact has moved into the multimillions of dollars," said Rev. Warren Stewart, pastor of the First Institutional Baptist Church in Phoenix and a leader of the pro-holiday movement. "If the Super Bowl does not come here in 1993, we're talking about a quarter of a billion dollars. We're also talking about a baseball expansion team and the NBA All-Star game."

Gene Blue, director of the Phoenix OIC, said that efforts now are being geared to working out a compromise, possibly combining the Washington and Lincoln holidays into one holiday, President's Day, as is done on the federal level, and make a King Day for the third Monday in January. That would satisfy critics who balked at adding another paid holiday.

"We're uniting under one campaign.

NFL Commissioner Paul Tagliabue said the 1993 Super bowl won't be held in Arizona unless there is a King holiday in place.

NFL Commissioner Paul Tagliabue immediately recommended that the league owners rescind the awarding of the Super Bowl to Phoenix, a recommendation that is almost certain to be approved.

"There was a very negative and divisive message in the Arizona vote," said Tagliabue. "I don't see why we have to give a state a windfall in the wake of that kind of vote. We have no obligation to play our game in any particular state, and they knew that from the outset."

"If history is any indication, we could lose a substantial amount of money," admitted Larry Hilliard, vice-president of the Phoenix Visitors and Convention Bureau. "When Mecham rescinded the holiday in 1987, over the next two years, we had 58 groups cancel, representing about 46,000 people.

NBA Commissioner David Stern won't let the 1993 All-Star game go to Phoenix without a King holiday.

52

JET Magazine Article (Two Pages), December 10, 1990,
"Cancelling The King Holiday In Arizona Sparks Hot Dispute"

Dr. Warren H. Stewart, Sr. attending the first African/African-American Summit, along with Dr. Lincoln J. Ragsdale, Sr., Valley Civil Rights Veteran, Mr. Coretta Scott King, Widow of Dr. King, The Honorable Benjamin Hooks, National President, N.A.A.C.P., April 17-19, 1991, in Ivory Coast, West Africa

AP Laserphoto

ROSA PARKS symbolically rides a city bus from Sky Harbor Airport in Phoenix to her hotel after arriving Thursday night to help honor slain civil rights leader Dr. Martin Luther King Jr. At rights is Phoenix Mayor Paul Johnson, who proclaimed Jan. 16-17 Rosa Parks Days.

Parks Urges Paid MLK Holiday

PHOENIX (AP) — The woman whose refusal to give up her seat on a bus helped spur the civil rights movement more than 35 years ago urged Arizonans today to be courageous and diligent so all people can be at peace with each other.

Rosa Parks said the efforts of Martin Luther King Jr. show that "all of us can make a difference."

Parks, 78, was guest of honor for today's civic breakfast in recognition of King, the slain civil rights activist.

Arizona is the only state without a paid holiday in King's honor. Voters turned down two such proposals in 1990 but will vote on yet another in the November general election.

Parks pledged to keep trying "to make a better world for black people and for our youth."

After arriving in Phoenix Thursday night, she said nonviolence "was the only way we could have made a difference" at the time. We did not want a war, we wanted peace.

She said she will "continue to work tirelessly" to make the King birthday observance a truly national holiday.

But "it's going to be up to the people here to decide what they will to do to bring about justice and good will and freedom for all the people," she said.

A resolution introduced in the House this week by 22 Republican and Democratic representatives seeks broad concurrence in recognizing King's work to end bigotry, racial segregation and discrimination.

The resolution also says his efforts "demonstrate that one individual can make an overwhelming difference to bring about changes that will benefit all people and future generations."

Phoenix established a paid King holiday eight years ago, Mayor Paul Johnson told Parks while giving her a key to the city. Parks gave Johnson a copy of her biography, "Rosa Parks, My Story."

More than 20 other Arizona cit-

ies also observe King Day. The breakfast is one of a number of special events here and in schools, churches, towns and universities throughout the state.

Parks had refused to give up her seat when ordered to do so by a bus driver in Montgomery, Ala., in 1955.

"I felt violated as a human being (under) an unfair and unjust law," she said of that experience. "I decided that would be the last time I would be in that position."

Asked about being jailed, she said she wasn't harmed physically "but it's always a bad feeling to know the doors are locked behind you."

Despite support by Gov. Fife Symington and many other leaders, the King holiday still apparently will face tough sledding in the fall.

A poll conducted by Bruce Merrill of Arizona State University for KAET-TV found 56 percent of those responding would vote for the measure if the election were now, 38 percent would vote against it, and 6 percent were undecided.

The telephone poll conducted Jan. 11-12 questioned 581 Arizona voters and had an error margin of plus or minus 4 percent.

Lack of a paid King holiday cost Arizona the 1993 Super Bowl. Tourism officials say it also has cost the state more than $160 million in lost revenue from canceled conventions.

Most Arizonans Don't Have King Holiday Off

PHOENIX (AP) — While the controversy over a Martin Luther King Jr. holiday continues, a newspaper poll says 70 percent of the people in Arizona who have jobs outside their homes don't get the holiday off and many don't think they should be given a day off.

The *Arizona Republic* survey, released Thursday, was conducted Jan. 9-12 by Winona Market Research Bureau Inc.

According to the 551 jobholders surveyed, 25 percent said they will get Monday off, while the remaining 5 percent weren't sure.

Further, of those who don't get the day off, 67 percent said they don't believe they should get the holiday, 28 percent said they should and 5 percent had no opinion.

The survey's margin of error was plus or minus 4 percentage

points.

Arizona is the only state without a paid holiday honoring King.

Arizona voters narrowly rejected a paid King Day in 1990 and will get another chance to vote on it King Day.

"It's just another paid day off for some people," said poll respondent Craig Scala, who works for a small Phoenix printing firm. "I'm not into holidays. Besides, we don't get into political stuff at work."

Poll participant Sally Steele, who owns a real-estate firm in Sedona, said she probably would give her two employees King Day off with pay if they asked.

"People voted against the holiday because they don't want to be told what to do," she said.

"It's like losing a bit of our good old Western liberty. We have plenty of paid holidays."

Pastor Henry L. Barnwell, Chair, Arizonans for a Martin Luther King, Jr. State Holiday, Mrs. Rosa Parks, "Mother of the Civil Rights Movement" and Phoenix Mayor Paul Johnson taking a Symbolic Bus Ride in Phoenix on January 17, 1992

LUCE PRESS CLIPPINGS

5,000 march for 'the dream'

Thousands march toward the state Capitol to kick off a campaign for the King holiday.

TORU KAWANA/Tribune

State leaders gather at rally urging support of King holiday vote

By Beverly Medlyn
Tribune writer

Edna Stubblefield, a Mesa retiree, rose at 5:30 a.m. Monday to join about 5,000 people who marched through Phoenix to the state Capitol for a rally kicking off a campaign urging voters to pass a Martin Luther King holiday this November.

"He died for it. He has a right to have a holiday — paid," Stubblefield said.

Arizona State University student Jeff Slaton had been up since 5 p.m. Sunday, heading straight from his night job to participate in the 9 a.m. march under drizzly skies commemorating the 63rd anniversary of the civil rights leader's birth.

"I believe in the cause. I believe in the dream," said Slaton, 25. "People look at it from an economic standpoint — that's the wrong reason. You have to look at what he believed in,

VIOLENCE IN DENVER: Fighting breaks out after Klan rally / A8

not in what the state can gain from it."

The state's leaders echoed the marchers' sentiments in speeches that launched the "Victory Together" campaign to promote the November ballot proposition.

The half-day celebration was marred by a mid-afternoon fight among 75 to 100 teenage gang members, said Phoenix police spokesman Kevin Robinson. Six juveniles were arrested on assault and disorderly conduct charges and one officer suffered a sprained back breaking up the scuffles, he said.

Capitol police and the event's organizers decided to close the plaza after the fights. Until then, thousands

Please see **King** / A8

TORU KAWANA/Tribune

Sparkle Sykes, 10, of the Majestic Drill Team, salutes during a ceremony at Wesley Bolin Plaza after the march.

*Annual Martin Luther King, Jr. March, Phoenix, January 20, 1992,
led by VICTORY TOGETHER and Martin Luther King, Jr.
Celebration Committee from the East Valley Tribune*

Grand Opening of the VICTORY TOGETHER Campaign Headquarters in Phoenix, March 15, 1992, Jack Pfister, Member of the Phoenix 40, Dr. Warren H. Stewart, Sr, General Chairperson, VICTORY TOGETHER, and Steve Roman, Bank Vice President

Pastor Benjamin N. Thomas, Sr., Tanner Chapel A.M.E. Church, Phoenix, about to deliver the Invocation at the VICTORY TOGETHER Grand Opening

The Honorable Art Hamilton speaking at the VICTORY TOGETHER Grand Opening

Arizona Representative Ben Arredondo and Monsignor Edward J. Ryle conversing at the VICTORY TOGETHER Grand Opening

Rosie Lopez and other Hispanic Leaders at
VICTORY TOGETHER Grand Opening

Native American Choir from Central Presbyterian Church, Phoenix,
at VICTORY TOGETHER Grand Opening

Attorney Lisa Loo and her son at the VICTORY TOGETHER Grand Opening

A Diverse Group of Persons attending the VICTORY TOGETHER Grand Opening

*Mrs. Rosa J. Edwards greeting Senator John McCain at the
VICTORY TOGETHER Grand Opening*

*The Stewart Family in September 1992—Pastor Warren H. Stewart, Sr., Mrs.
Serena Michele, Warren, Jr., Matthew, Jared, Justin, Aaron and Jamila*

Dr. Paul Eppinger, VICTORY TOGETHER Campaign Director, and Dr. Warren H. Stewart, Sr. announcing the Passage of Proposition 300 establishing a Martin Luther King, Jr./Civil Rights Day in Arizona on election night, November 3, 1992

Dr. Warren H. Stewart, Sr. and Phoenix Mayor Paul Johnson celebrating the 2-to-1 Victory for Proposition 300 at VICTORY TOGETHER Campaign Headquarters, November 4, 1992

USA Today, November 6, 1992, story on the Historic Martin Luther King, Jr. Holiday Victory in Arizona

INSIDE

Astrology	C6	Montini	B1
AzW	C1	Obituaries	CL9
Bombeck	C6	Prayer	A2
Bridge	C6	Puzzles	C5
Business	D1	Short Takes	C3
Chuckle	A2	Solomon	C6
Classified	CL1	Sports	E1
Comics	C7,CL5	Television	C3
+ Dear Abby	C6	Weather	A.10
Editorial	A8	Willey	B2

**Phoenix pastor praised
for role in King holiday**

See Page B1

SECTION **B**

TUESDAY
JANUARY 12, 1993
★★

Photopress

The Rev. Warren Stewart of Phoenix accepts an award from Coretta Scott King, widow of the Rev. Martin Luther King Jr., in Washington on Monday.

VALLEY & STATE

THE ARIZONA REPUBLIC

State praised for King Day

Phoenix pastor honored in D.C. for role in vote

By Jeff Barker
Republic Washington Bureau

WASHINGTON — Civil-rights leaders and politicians singled out Arizona for praise Monday as the Rev. Martin Luther King Jr.'s widow called for a one-day worldwide moratorium on violence to mark her husband's birthday.

Receiving special recognition at a Capitol Hill luncheon was the Rev. Warren Stewart, pastor of Phoenix's First Institutional Baptist Church. He was a key player in voters' November passage of a paid King holiday for state employees.

Stewart was one of six people or groups honored by Coretta Scott King at the luncheon, which was sponsored by the Atlanta-based Martin Luther King Jr. Holiday Commission. The 9-year-old commission coordinates King Day activities nationally.

Coretta King cited Stewart for serving as chairman of Victory Together, a group that registered 75,000 Arizona voters as part of its campaign in behalf of the state holiday, which will be celebrated Monday.

She said her husband's dream of racial harmony lives in the spirits of the honorees, who also included a former Indiana superior-court judge and a Montana YWCA that sponsored King-holiday celebrations.

"The dream is being realized every day one of us becomes more committed and internalizes the philosophy of non-violence and social change," King said.

She called for a one-day moratorium on violence on Monday, the federal and state holiday honoring the civil-rights leader, who was slain

in Memphis, Tenn., in 1968.

She spoke in the same ornate caucus room in which the Senate Judiciary Committee held stormy Supreme Court confirmation hearings for Clarence Thomas last year.

In a Washington interview, Stewart said he never doubted Arizonans' resolve to approve a holiday, even after a pair of rival King Day measures were defeated by state voters in 1990.

"We felt that if there was an effective grass-roots effort that lifted up principles — namely, that all people are created equal under God — that Arizona voters would approve a holiday," Stewart said.

The commission, which King heads, honored Arizona in a newsletter distributed at the luncheon. The quarterly publication featured a complimentary article about the

which it calls the only state without a King holiday. New Hampshire does celebrate a Civil Rights Day on the same day as the federal King holiday.

state and a photograph of Phoenix Mayor Paul Johnson and other holiday supporters.

The commission now has turned its attention to New Hampshire,

*Mrs. Coretta Scott King awarding Dr. Warren H. Stewart, Sr. t
he Making of the King Holiday Award in the United States Capitol Building in
Washington, D.C., on January 11, 1993*

*Stevie Wonder with three of Dr. Warren H. Stewart, Sr.'s young sons
from left to right—Jared Chamberlain, Aaron Frederick Taylor
and Justin Mitchell, on Friday, January 15, 1993, at the City of Phoenix
Martin Luther King, Jr. Holiday Celebration at America West Arena*

*Mrs. Rosa Parks, "Mother of the Civil Rights Movement", addressing the Pastor and
People of the First Institutional Baptist Church, Sunday, January 17, 1993*

Pastor Stewart and Mrs. Coretta Scott King - 1/19/1996

Dr. Warren H. Stewart, Sr. conversing with Mrs. Coretta Scott King at a luncheon on January 19, 1996, in Phoenix where he introduced her, a few days before the 1996 Super Bowl held in the Valley of the Sun

The Rev. Karen E. Stewart, Dr. Stewart's wife (2nd from left), their grandson Joshua Elijah Curry (in the stroller) and Dr. Warren H. Stewart, Sr. (4th from left) on the Front Line of the Annual Martin Luther King, Jr. March, January 19, 2015

PART THREE

It seems that I can hear a voice saying to America: "You started out right. You wrote in your Declaration of Independence that 'all men are created equal and endowed by their Creator with certain inalienable rights. Among these are life, liberty, and the pursuit of happiness.' But, America, you strayed away from that sublime principle.

-Martin Luther King, Jr.

Chapter Ten
Martin Loved The Little Children

The last letter I sent out to the co-workers I had labored with as general chairperson of ARIZONANS FOR A MARTIN LUTHER KING, JR. STATE HOLIDAY on January 15, 1990, Dr. King's 61st birthday and my final day heading our historic coalition, dealt with the *human rights of unborn children*. With mixed emotions of providential privilege and prolonged grief, I offered my last epistle to every individual on our coalition's mailing list as Exhibit A of one of the strongest beliefs I hold as a human and civil rights activist, advocate for the disadvantaged and downtrodden, student of Dr. King's writings and a Scripture- believing Christian.

> In my final letter to you as General Chairperson of **ARIZONANS FOR A MARTIN LUTHER KING, JR. STATE HOLIDAY,** I am taking the liberty to share in writing a deep conviction of mine intricately connected to the principles espoused by the late Dr. Martin Luther King, Jr.
>
> As you know, on November 14, 1989, I was arrested, along with other members of the clergy for engaging in a nonviolent act of civil disobedience in front of a local abortion clinic in protest of unrestricted abortions made legal by the United States

Supreme Court in 1973. Dr. King once wrote of civil disobedience, "If an earthly institution or custom conflicts with God's will, it is your Christian duty to oppose it."

There are those supporting unrestricted abortions who speak of the new life developing inside a mother's womb as "fetal tissue" or not a human being. Is "it" an animal? Is "it" not human life? When does "it" become a baby? Only at the stage of viability? Have you visited any intensive care units or nursing homes lately? If you have, you have seen for yourself many persons who do not possess viability without life support systems. Just a century and a half ago, the Law of the Land determined that the Negro was only to be counted as three-fifths of a person. Sound familiar?

Many who advocate a woman's right to choose to have an abortion often say that abortion is a personal and private matter. Therefore, one should not impose his or her own personal morality on another. God forbid, if 19th Century abolitionists had taken such a position when slave owners defended slavery because enslaved human beings were legally accepted as their personal and private property.

Other pro-choice advocates urge that "morality cannot be legislated." Nevertheless, history has proved time and time again that when all else failed, it took the government, especially in dealing with racism and bigotry to legislate minimum guarantees in order that the moral rights of abused and oppressed humans were granted to them. This is what the Civil Rights Movement was all about.

Some who espouse religious beliefs contend that abortion is basically a religious issue. Thusly, the government should not interfere in a woman's decision to have an abortion and religious persons should not force their religious beliefs on others. Do we so quickly fail to remember that Martin Luther King, Jr.'s dream was first a biblical dream grounded in a strong Judeo-Christian heritage arising from the Old and New Testaments? His movement began in the Church and he organized the Southern Christian Leadership Conference.

As an advocate of nonviolence, I deplore abortion because it is a violent act of the destruction of unborn human life. Therefore, as I oppose capital punishment, child and spousal abuse and violent war, I also oppose abortion on the same principle of nonviolence espoused by Martin Luther King, Jr.

You and I have fought together on various issues of civil rights, human rights, economic development, democracy in Central America and South Africa and of course the Martin Luther King, Jr. state holiday. For those reasons and others, I have come to respect you as a leader who is sensitive and supportive of the oppressed, downtrodden and disadvantaged among us. That is why I felt I **must** write to you to share where I stand on the abortion issue and to ask you to openly consider my position as a position that is **consistent** with the ongoing human rights cause.

Essentially, I am **"WHOLE LIFE"** rather than just **PRO-LIFE**. I believe that we must fight for the rights of every human created in the image and likeness of God "from the womb to the tomb." I am **not** against legalized abortion. I am against the **97%** of abortions performed for reasons other than rape, incest, and life-threatening health reasons to mother and/or child.

Lastly, as a co-worker, I would welcome dialogue with you about my position on abortion as well as yours.

I closed my last letter on our coalition's letterhead differently than the "For the Cause" I had used throughout the three-year campaign. It read, "For THEM." There was also a P.S. I added to my self-explanatory letter which read:

> This letter represents the personal beliefs of Warren H. Stewart, Sr., and not those of **ARIZONANS FOR A MARTIN LUTHER KING, JR. STATE HOLIDAY.** Moreover, this letter was not sent at the expense of (our coalition).

Perhaps the reason none of our coalition's members, even the faithful few making up our core of leadership, took me up on my invitation to dialogue on the abortion issue had to do with the fact that they knew my unwavering conviction on the subject. They remembered vividly I had allowed myself to be arrested for expressing my beliefs while I was still their general chairperson. Or maybe it had more to do with the pro-choice position of the overwhelming majority of King Day advocates both within and without our coalition. Whatever the case, I felt so strongly about the human rights of unborn children that I wanted that to be a human rights cause that I left on their minds, despite their opposing views to mine.

My letter to members of our coalition certainly was not the first letter I have written on that subject. In the summer of 1989, I wrote Arizona's King-supporting, devout Roman Catholic governor shortly after the United States Supreme Court decision in the Webster case gave the power to restrict abortions back into the hands of state Legislatures. Shortly after that July 3, 1989 ruling, the abortion debate began to heat up in Arizona politics. For the first time since 1973, pro-life advocates sensed that a crack might be opening in the door that could lead to the overturning of the Roe versus Wade ruling that legalized abortion on demand. The addition of several conservative Supreme Court justices during the Reagan and Bush administrations had given the defenders of defenseless humans in the womb a glimmer of hope to stop the taking of 1.5 million unborn babies' lives annually since 1973. Please know that I opposed the U.S. Senate confirmation of every one of the Reagan-Bush appointees, based on their civil rights records, especially their opposition to affirmative action and some of their questionable interpretations of laws affecting people of color. However, as excitement began to be generated that the Reagan-Bush Supreme Court might, at least, slow down, if not put a halt to America's own holocaust, I wanted to be a vocal and persuasive proponent of the most fundamental human right—*the right to life*, without which no other human or civil rights can be enjoyed.

Therefore, in my letter to Governor Mofford, dated July 20, 1989, I reminded her,

> You and I have fought together on various issues of civil rights, human rights, economic development, the Martin Luther King, Jr. state holiday and other important political matters. For that reason and others, I have come to respect you as a leader who is sensitive and supportive of the oppressed, downtrodden, and disadvantaged among us. Therefore, I felt that I must write you to inform you where I stand on the ABORTION issue, which will become an intense and emotionally explosive battleground in the months to come.

I proceeded to state my position on abortion in much the same manner that I did in my later letter to members of our King Day coalition. The one prominent difference in my letter to Governor Mofford was that I began by explaining my convictions for unborn children's right to be born based on Scripture. Ironically, I learned from experience in my unrestricted abortion battle that mentioning biblical beliefs supporting unborn babies "made in the image and likeness of God" in front of most politicians and pro-abortion advocates was one of the quickest ways to get them to stop listening to what you have to say. But, actually, since the middle ground in the abortion debate is about as wide as the whitish part of a fingernail, once an individual is identified as pro-life, most pro-choice supporters tune that person out anyway. Moreover, those who attempt to be polite, and reasonable inform pro-lifers, "You are entitled to your own religious beliefs, but this is a civil matter and, you know, our nation built into its Constitution a separation of church and state."

Getting back to my letter to Arizona's first woman governor, I suppose I assumed that her devotion to Catholicism which is unwavering in its pro-life stance would make my appeal, first and foremost based on Scripture, a convincing argument to her. I cited Psalms 139:13-18; 51:5, Job 3:3, Matthew 1:18-20; Luke 1:15, 41-44; and Romans 9:10-13 as Scriptural references substantiating that there is definite theological foundation for recognizing that human life begins at conception.

Daring to share a little of my personal story as to why I am pro-life, I informed the highest state official that *experientially*, I had no choice than to promote giving unborn children a chance at life outside the wombs of their mothers. Specifically, I wrote, "Had abortion been as available in 1951 when I was conceived out of wedlock as it is today, *I JUST MIGHT NOT HAVE BEEN HERE TO WRITE THESE COMMENTS SUPPORTING UNBORN CHILDREN.*" In all respect to my dear mother, I was born to a young, single, physically and mentally unhealthy Black mother after having been fathered by a railroad porter who had layovers in my home town and who was older than my mother's father. To make matters worse, my biological father denied that he had fathered me until after he was arrested and forced to look at his spittin' image son. If *I* got a chance to experience life on this side of the birth canal, then anyone else ought to have that right, *even* children who are the product of rape, incest and prenatal handicaps. (Although I compromised politically for a short while making allowances for abortions to terminate pregnancies resulting from rape and incest as well as congenital birth defects, I later realized that that allowance inflicted inhumane and unjust treatment on a select group of unborn babies. Reluctantly, but thanks to the wisdom of an uneducated Holiness preacher who was a custodian at Bishop College when I was there from 1971-73; my only exception for abortion is to save the life of the mother.)

In concluding my letter to the governor, I invited her to dialogue with me about her position on abortion. A few days later, her office sent me a response under her signature which stated something to the effect that although she agreed with my pro-life position, personally, she could not impose her personal beliefs on others in the matter of abortion. I do not know how much that helps the unborn babies receiving unjust capital punishment, but it does help some politicians keep a few votes among less discerning pro-lifers and a lot more votes from pro-choicers.

I have already mentioned in this book how I wrote both Presidents Ronald Reagan and George H.W. Bush to get them to intervene on behalf of Arizona's Martin Luther King, Jr. holiday between 1987 and 1989; and received no response, not even a form letter. Guess what? I wrote both of those guys about the abortion issue and got letters from a couple of agencies in the executive branch of federal government in little or no time. Hey, what was going on there? Did they *not* get my King letters? I guess their White House letter-readers had been given instructions on which subject matters to forward to high level departments and which ones end up in "File 13."

A similar response to King Day letters versus pro-life letters I wrote came from a U.S. Congressman and Senators and state legislators. Fierce opponents of King Day in the Arizona State Legislature who almost never answered my letters for King Day support wrote me "lovely letters" espousing my pro-life position. On the other hand, a few of the King Day's staunchest legislative sponsors responded to my missives advocating the human rights of the unborn with curt, concise and clear form letters stating their strong, immovable support of a woman's unrestricted right to an abortion.

Speaking of letters related to the abortion issue, I wrote **"AN OPEN LETTER TO THE REVEREND JESSE JACKSON ON ABORTION"** dated January 21, 1990, less than a week after the nation observed his mentor's birthday and also Sanctity of Life Sunday recognized by the pro-life movement nationwide because it was the closest Sunday to the infamous anniversary of Roe versus Wade. The letter in its entirety follows:

Dear Brother Beloved:

I write you this **OPEN LETTER** in **LOVE**. A **LOVE** that would dare to challenge one whom I have admired and respected as one of America's foremost prophetic voices. A **LOVE** that has proven its worth in my vocal, political, financial and theological support of you as a preacher-prophet, civil rights activist, ambassador of global peace and two-time candidate for the Presidency of the United States of America. A **LOVE** that rejoiced when you preached from the pulpit of the First Institutional Baptist Church on **PEACE SUNDAY**, May 4, 1986.

Nevertheless, I write you this **OPEN LETTER** to beg to differ with your **OPEN STAND** for a woman's **unrestricted** right to choose to have an **ABORTION**, which means that for every ABORTION, an unborn baby's life is terminated and kept from being SOMEBODY created in the image and likeness of God.

What has changed your mind since 1977? According to the September 27, 1989 issue of the *Wall Street Journal*, in 1977, at a March for Life rally you said, "The solution to a (crisis pregnancy) is not to kill the innocent baby but to deal with (the mother's) values and her attitudes toward life." Yet, last year during your 1988 presidential campaign, you defended a woman's right, especially poor women, to choose **ABORTION** for any reason. Jesse, that woman's right leads to 1,500,000 unborn babies being **ABORTED** each year.

Your mentor, Dr. Martin Luther King, Jr., espoused a philosophy of nonviolence which you too have advocated. And yet, it appears that you and most other former disciples of Martin ignore the fact that **ABORTION** is the most violent and deadly act which can be perpetrated against an innocent unborn human life developing in his or her mother's womb.

You know that Dr. King quoted the opening lines of Abraham Lincoln's Gettysburg Address in his immortal **"I HAVE A DREAM"** speech, which declared that "this nation (was) dedicated to the proposition that all men (and women) are created equal." Tell me, Jesse, is an unborn child **not** equal until he or she leaves his or her mother's womb?

Last year, you, Andrew Young and Julian Bond, all disciples of the man whose life and legacy we celebrate on the third Monday in January, issued a statement, according to the Wall Street Journal, "denouncing Operation Rescue, comparing those who participate in abortion clinic sit-ins to 'segregationists who fought desperately to block black Americans from access to their rights.'" Well, my Brother, if you haven't heard, on November 14, 1989, I participated in a Project Rescue sit-in in front of a popular Phoenix abortion clinic, was willingly arrested and am awaiting trial. Am I a segregationist? Am I to be castigated by you for engaging in civil disobedience in protest of **unrestricted** legalized **ABORTIONS**, which unjustly deny human rights to precious little children?

Here's what Martin Luther King, Jr. once wrote about civil disobedience. "If any earthly institution or custom conflicts with God's will, it is your Christian duty to oppose it."

Perhaps, you will respond like so many other advocates of the **PRO-CHOICE MOVEMENT** that no other person should impose his or her moral or religious beliefs on a woman and her right to do with **her** body what she chooses. Come on, now, Jesse; you know very well that Martin's dream for justice, liberty and equality in America was first a biblical dream grounded in a strong Judeo-Christian heritage arising from the Old and New Testaments. The Civil Rights Movement was founded on moral principles that acknowledge the God of us all. But, I guess when it becomes **politically expedient,** we go with the votes rather than stay with Eternal Truth.

Lastly, you made famous the esteem-building and culturally-enriching chant in the 1960's, **"I AM SOMEBODY."** "I may be on welfare…I may be uneducated…I may be unwed…I may be Black, **BUT I AM SOMEBODY BECAUSE I'M GOD'S CHILD."**

I guess **UNBORN CHILDREN** ain't nobody in your eyesight no more.

Look, I have got sense enough to know that Jesse Jackson, then the most well-known living African American in the United States, receives hundreds, if not thousands, of letters daily from both friends and foes. Whether or not Jesse ever saw my letter, I do not know. But others saw it, including members of our congregation, selected nationally known newspaper editorial boards and some of my new pro-life friends in the conservative communities. Regrettably, Jesse Jackson's politically expedient position has become the diehard position of virtually every recognized Black civil rights leader in America, much to my dismay.

God forbid, if our enslaved and embattled foreparents had adopted such a self-centered, inhumane, oppressive Euro-centric perspective on the right to life during and after slavery. Rather than bear our future liberators from the wombs of bred and often raped African women, our courageous foremothers would have done what the Hebrew midwives refused to do to the boy-children born to the fertile Hebrew mothers and fathers under Pharaoh's command to kill the infant males. The African-American community has always, until the last two decades, welcomed our little ones taking form in ebony wombs regardless of the circumstances of their conceptions. There were not many orphanages for Black children because we took them in as part of our extended family. To be very frank, abortion was something White folk did, for the most part. Only a few Black families, in spite of their embarrassment and shame surrounding the pregnancy of an unmarried girl or woman, even considered abortion as an acceptable alternative. As a matter of fact, the Reverend Jesse Jackson, like myself and many other prophetic voices proclaiming the unadulterated and liberating Gospel Truth, was the offspring of unwed parents. Tragically, statistics on abortion indicate that African-American women get elective abortions at a higher percentage than any other racial and/or ethnic group in America. For every three Black babies born, two are aborted. And the sisters are complaining about not having enough eligible Black men to marry.

Before I move from discussing some of my letters relating to that issue during the King Day struggle in Arizona, I must note a letter I received from Gloria Feldt, then Executive Director of Planned Parenthood of Central and Northern Arizona on July 1, 1987. Her national agency, the Planned Parenthood Federation of America, had planned their 1988 Annual Meeting in Arizona. However, after the Mecham rescission and the Legislature's failure to reestablish the MLK holiday proclaimed by former Governor Babbitt, her national board adopted a resolution to cancel its contract to convene in Arizona and meet in another state in the Western Region. In my excitement of receiving official word that another socially conscious organization had boycotted its annual convention in our state to protest the aborting of our first King Holiday, I overlooked the following sentence buried in Feldt's paragraph informing me that Planned Parenthood's 1000-plus members would meet in neighboring San Diego rather than Phoenix. It read, "Reproductive rights are the most fundamental of civil rights, as Martin Luther King himself affirmed."

I am sure you are aware that the term "reproductive rights" is a euphemism for *unrestricted abortion on demand*. But, more offensive to me is to put words in Dr. King's mouth that were not even coined when he was living! I have searched extensively the writings of my ministerial role model and have yet to find *one line* written or spoken by Dr. King supporting abortion. Obviously, Mrs. Feldt was speaking anachronistically about Martin King "affirming" abortion as "the most fundamental of civil rights" because Roe versus Wade had not become the Law of the Land, based on the 1973 Supreme Court's interpretation of the Constitution, until five years after Dr. King was violently denied his right to life by an assassin who exercised his freedom of choice to kill him. I guess the only solace I have in not catching the misinterpretation of Dr. King's teaching inscribed in a letter to me back in 1989 is the fact that my response to an executive director of one of the largest abortion providers in the nation was a form letter of appreciation for supporting our boycott.

Sometime during the early summer of 1989, the Reverend John Salvatore, a brave, bold and definitely born-again believer and then director of Project Rescue, the Phoenix arm of Operation Rescue, contacted me through the Reverend Janet Caldwell, the first woman and the only Anglo I have ever licensed to preach at First Institutional as well as our congregation's business manager at the time. She had informed him of my well-known pro-life theology as mentioned occasionally in my Sunday morning messages. Blacks actively involved in the pro-life movement are a rarity because the movement is dominated by White conservative, right-wing Republicans who have traditionally been on the wrong side of Black civil rights issues. That is why my alliance with the pro-life movement as a whole has been somewhat uneasy even though I believe it was genuine on both sides—mine and theirs. Salvatore called for an appointment and when he came, Janet introduced us and we conversed on our commonalties, such as being Christians in the ministry, and unashamedly and unapologetically pro-life.

After several meetings and a growing relationship, he popped the question to me, "Bro. Warren, would you join us in one of our rescues?" A "rescue" is when and where pro-life protestors stage a sit-in modeled after the nonviolent direct actions of the Civil Rights Movement of the late 50s and 60s which helped to integrate schools, restaurants and other public buildings. They take place in front of the entrance(s) of women's health clinics or doctor's offices well-known for primarily being in business to perform numerous first trimester abortions. Some are called "abortion mills" by those advocating the human rights of unborn babies. Once the protesters arrive, they usually sit down in front of the clinic entrance(s) preventing anyone—doctors, nurses, clerical personnel and patients from getting in the building through the blocked entrance(s). This sit-in continues until the pro-lifers leave or the police are called to come and remove and/ or arrest the protesters. The object is to discourage expectant mothers from getting abortions that day, and hopefully change their minds completely, thus saving an unborn baby. Continuing, Brother Salvatore said, "We've had rescues before but never one that involved clergy exclusively. We think that would make a statement. And, well, Warren, as prominent as you are in the community with your leadership in the Martin Luther King holiday effort…, we just feel that you would bring special attention to our common cause. Would you be willing to participate in an all-clergy rescue?"

Without hesitation I asked, "When and where do you want me to be?" Salvatore was speechless for a few moments. He later told me he thought that he was going to have to twist my arm to convince me to take such a costly stand. Noticing his astonishment, I said, "Look, our coalition was making plans to engage in nonviolent civil disobedience at the State Capitol this coming January if they hadn't passed the holiday. So, if I was willing to be arrested for a holiday, how could I say no to being arrested for standing up for the human rights of unborn babies?"

A few weeks later on Tuesday, November 14, 1989 proved to be an unusual day in my life and two of First Institutional's associate ministers, the Reverends Janet Caldwell and Sarahlyn Bristow-Armstrong. We were arrested, by choice, for our convictions that unborn babies "fearfully and wondrously made" by God are entitled to the right not to be aborted against their wills. On that very chilly November morning, several pastors, ministers and spouses arrived at a designated church on the east side of Phoenix at 6:00 a.m. We met one another, many for the first time from various denominations and non-denominational fellowships. We prayed in the parking lot and received last minute instructions. At 6:30 a.m. we drove to the A-Z Women's Center, an abortion clinic that was doing a brisk business.

Once there, about 30 of us gathered in front of the main entrance of the center. Our voices lifted together in singing hymns, praying and reading Scripture. None of us moved when the doctor and workers of the clinic arrived at 7:00 a.m. We just kept singing and praying, even when patients began to arrive. The police were called around 7:30 a.m. Arrests began occurring by 8:30 a.m. Sis. Armstrong, one of my daughters in the ministry, was the first to be arrested in her blue jeans and clergy collar on. Sis. Caldwell was apprehended a little later. Quite nobly, the other clergy gave me the honor of being arrested last.

I knew the officers arresting me because they were members of the Phoenix Police Department's Community Relations Unit and had worked with every Martin Luther King, Jr. march. They included A.J. Miller, Al Madrid, Sebone White and Earl Nelson, all friends of mine. I remember when they came to me, Officers Madrid and Miller, asked, "Now, Reverend Stewart, are you going to get up and walk with us to the paddy wagon?" One of them facetiously complained, "Reverend Stewart, you know I've got a bad back. Come on. Don't make it hard on us." I replied, "Brethren, you all are going to earn your pay today. I'm not going to cooperate at all. You're going to have to pick me up and carry me to wherever you need to take me." And I said it with a smile. Rest assured, when the first uniformed police officers arrived on the scene a little after 7:30 a.m., I got a little nervous because they were big, White and armed. But, the actual police who did the arresting were plainclothes officers and trained in these kinds of arrest. Those guys handled me and my protesting colleagues professionally and gently. I later learned that they felt very embarrassed about having to arrest me.

After deliberately going limp, I was placed on an orange gurney by four struggling policemen trying to lift my limp 215 pound uncooperative body. As I was being carried to the paddy wagon about fifty yards away, I took advantage of the radio, television and print media who were all over the place covering the story. I shouted, "I'm here standing up for the civil rights of unborn children and for nonviolence....I'm a civil rights activist, and a civil rights activist has to be consistent. If you stand up for South Africans and other oppressed people, you must stand up for the unborn children, who are the most oppressed people." One of the reporters asked me something about Jesse Jackson, and I blasted him publicly, as well as all civil rights leaders who had co-opted their civil rights position by not opposing abortion on demand. In a press statement that we had prepared beforehand and passed out to the reporters, we stated our position clearly. The statement declared in part:

> **ABORTION** is worse than capital punishment in that those being executed are guilty of no crime....

We are also here to suggest to persons seeking **ABORTIONS** that we offer alternatives to **ABORTION** through agencies like Crisis Pregnancy Centers, Arizona Life Foundation and our respective congregations....

As advocates of nonviolence and in the spirit of Jesus Christ, Mahatma Ghandi, and Martin Luther King, Jr., we abhor **ABORTION** as one of the most violent and deadly acts against the innocent lives of unborn babies.

After being placed in police vans, we were transported to Sky Harbor Police Station to be processed, fingerprinted and have our personal belongings inventoried, all of which had been removed except our clothing and shoes. From there we were taken to the Madison Street Jail downtown where we went through the same process twice again. There we were body-searched. Then, they placed us in a holding tank with an open toilet, faucet and flat steel mattress-less beds. Then, the men were separated from the women. There we awaited our release, which came about five hours from the time we were arrested.

Our charge was criminal trespassing. The Christian attorney for Project Rescue, John Jacubczyk, secured our release on our own recognizance. Around 2:15 p.m., we were given our personal possessions and released through a back door as men and women with police records and scheduled for trial. Outside the door when I was released were two African-American young mothers, one with a beautiful baby. I introduced myself. One said she had seen me getting arrested on T.V. that morning. She also told me that her mother had tried to get her to abort *her* baby. She said, "Now, my mother just loves my baby." We all got out of jail. But, no aborted baby ever gets out alive.

That afternoon, evening, night and the next morning, our "clergy rescue" made the headlines and news stories with me as the focal point. That afternoon's *Phoenix Gazette* ran the headline, "Clergy held in abortion protest" and in smaller letters "King Day leader arrested." A nearly quarter-page size color photo of the officers placing me on the gurney made the front-page of the *Republic* the next day. As far as accomplishing our goal of lifting up the human rights of unborn babies and linking it, regardless of how loosely, with civil rights and Martin Luther King, Jr., we were successful and I was grateful that my notoriety made a statement on behalf of the babies.

Later on that evening I reported my day's experiences in detail to the pastor-church relations committee of First Institutional Baptist Church. Although, other than the Scriptures, our congregation had not made an official statement on abortion or the human rights of unborn babies, I thank God that they gave their pastor the freedom to exercise his right to advocate his pro-life position, without any official reprisal. However, many in our relatively educated and affluent congregation espouse the pro-choice position, in spite of biblical teachings on the sanctity of life. As it related to various segments of the community, I came under sharp criticism from the more liberal members of the clergy in the Valley and was labeled by, at least, one doctor in the medical profession who is a defiant abortionist as a "terrorist, anarchist and follower of cult leader John Salvatore." But, have no fear, then *Republic* editor of the editorial pages, William Cheshire, a kind friend and frequent lunch partner of mine, came to my defense in two personally written Sunday editorials in the weeks following my arrest.

My trial took place in March 1990, and my co-trespassers and I were found guilty of trespassing. However, to our surprise, the Phoenix Municipal Court judge who handled our case made a strong statement against abortion equating it to "the ultimate cannibalism whereby we destroy our young and consume ourselves." Our sentencing was scheduled for April 12, 1990 which was Maundy Thursday, the same day Christians celebrate the institution of the Lord's Supper and when Jesus was tried all night long before He was crucified the next day for doing what was right. Rather than pay the fine, I opted for jail and spent a day in jail for my convictions.

God allowed me to make a clear connection between Martin Luther King, Jr. and the human rights of unborn children before thousands of people, just six days after I gave my farewell address as general chairperson of ARIZONANS FOR A MARTIN LUTHER KING, JR. STATE HOLIDAY on King's birthday January 15, 1990. Because of my publicized abortion protest and arrest, Arizona's pro-life leaders asked me to deliver the keynote address for their Sanctity of Life Rally and March held on Sunday, January 21, 1990. I accepted readily, primarily for two reasons: (1) due to my unwavering commitment to the human rights of unborn babies, and (2) to try to make the connection between the beliefs and philosophies of Dr. King and the pro-life movement, in order to win some votes for the upcoming King holiday election. I was well aware that many of the conservative, rightwing Republican conservatives who would be in attendance were anti-King Day voters. So, what could I lose? But there was much to be gained. Several pro-life leaders had joined the King Day march for the first time in 1990, including Salvatore, Jackubczyk, Dave Everitt, president of the Crisis Pregnancy Centers and Dr. Carolyn Gerster, physician and long-time leader in Arizona's pro-life movement.

That historic Sunday, I participated and provided leadership in Arizona's largest nonviolent demonstration to that date. The police officials estimated that between 25,000 and 30,000 persons marched, demonstrated and supported either the human rights of unborn children or a woman's legal right to abort her baby for any reason whatsoever. No other issue up to that time, not even the MLK state holiday controversy, had ever drawn that many people to the State Capitol at the same time on the same day. Moreover, to have experienced being there amidst two converging rivers of people on differing sides moving in opposite directions, evoked feelings of excitement, conviction and intensity.

For the second time in a week, the Lord gave me a platform on which to express my strong convictions about human rights, civil rights and Martin Luther King, Jr. directly to several thousands of Arizonans. However, that particular Sunday's crowd was a group, with which I had little in common racially, socially, politically, economically, intellectually, historically and somewhat religiously. Nevertheless, the one key link that we had was our belief in the "Sanctity of Human Life Ethic" which is defined as:

> The reverence for and sacredness of each and every human life based upon its intrinsic worth and equal value, regardless of its stage or condition from conception to natural death.

On that basis I delivered my message entitled "Why Am I Here?" And as I mentioned above, my purpose was to establish a connection between Dr. King's philosophy of human and civil rights, and nonviolence and the human rights of unborn children.

Believe me, when I looked out at that almost all-White audience of thousands, which initially gathered at Encanto Park for the "Celebrate Life" Rally, I asked myself again, "Why Am I Here?" When I looked down in front of the stage and saw former Governor Evan Mecham standing there along with Maricopa County Supervisor Ed Koory, also a King Day opponent and devout pro-lifer, I began to question my sanity for being the invited guest in that crowd. And then, on the program with me was one of the Legislature's most loyal Republican conservatives who was "dead on capital punishment" and "live on no gun control", historically anti-King Day and pro-life, Representative Jim Skelly, who told me later that my arrest for sitting-in at that abortion clinic won his vote on the last King Day bill passed in the House of Representatives. Thank God, a few of our friends, both to me and the King holiday, were present that day, namely, Bishop Thomas O'Brien who offered the invocation and the First Institutional Baptist Church Choir under the direction of Sis. Brenda Hankins, our Minister of Music, who hurried from our 11:00 a.m. worship service once it was over to get ready to sing at the rally at around 1:00 p.m.

Excerpts from my speech reveal that it was packed with rhetoric that worked. Mind you, though, this crowd required a little caressing before they would warm up to this Black preacher who extolled an allegedly adulterous man of God like that rabble-rousing Reverend King.

I began,

WHY AM I HERE?

Just seven days ago at the State Capitol, I stood before a crowd of nearly 15,000 people celebrating the life and contributions of the late Dr. Martin Luther King, Jr. and rallying for a paid state holiday in his honor. Most of you were **not** there. So, **WHY AM I HERE?**

Many of you do not support a Martin Luther King, Jr. holiday and perhaps, the names of some of you are among the 80,000 Arizonans who signed petitions to put the…holiday on the November ballot. So, **WHY AM I HERE?**…

When the words "affirmative action" are mentioned, many of you equate that with "reverse discrimination" in spite of the historical fact that persons of color have been held back for 350 years in America simply because they are not White. So, **WHY AM I HERE?**…

A straw poll taken today would reveal unquestionably that 90% or more of you are Republicans and I am a Democrat. So, **WHY AM I HERE?**

The majority of you gathered here are Euro-Americans and I am an African-American. So, **WHY AM I HERE? I AM HERE TO CELEBRATE LIFE WITH YOU!**

At that moment, the hesitant and skeptical crowd broke out in an applause of relief and acceptance, once they discerned where I was going, and once I answered my self-raised question as to why I was there. Then I launched into my declaration of the human rights of unborn children.

> **I AM HERE** because I believe that all human life is sacred from the womb to the tomb....
>
> **I AM HERE** because I believe that "all men and women are created in the image and likeness of God" and should be guaranteed "life, liberty and the pursuit of happiness."
>
> ...**I AM HERE ALSO** as an advocate of **HUMAN RIGHTS**, especially the human rights of the unborn...**I AM HERE** because I have a record of fighting for the **HUMAN RIGHTS** of the oppressed, the helpless, the disadvantaged and the downtrodden. So, as I have fought for the **RIGHTS** of African-Americans..., persons suffering from AIDS, the handicapped, homeless, women and children, **I AM HERE** fighting for the **RIGHT TO LIFE** of unborn human beings....

As I continued to emphatically state my case, the pro-life crowd quickly became a pro-Stewart crowd also. God anointed once again the gift of preaching that He gave me when He set me apart in my mother's womb to be one of His spokespersons. I could feel His Spirit even though I had already presided twice at First Institutional that Sunday morning. And that feeling of divine assurance gave me the go ahead to move to my next major point dealing with Dr. King's teaching and preaching on human rights.

> An extremely significant and historical reason **I AM HERE** is because I believe that if Martin Luther King, Jr. were alive the **HE WOULD BE HERE.** You see, Dr. King did not limit his civil and human rights beliefs to the awful consequences of racism and bigotry in America perpetrated against persons of his race only. No, Dr. King spoke out against the near-annihilation of the Native-American peoples of this land who were here before the Mayflower. He declared that Hitler's Holocaust of six million Jews stands as a haunting memorial of "man's inhumanity to man." In the early 1960's Martin King denounced the South African government's horrendous system of apartheid.... Although accused of being a Communist, listen to Pastor King's own words on Communism, "Communism and Christianity

are fundamentally incompatible. A true Christian cannot be a Communist...

Then I brought it on home to where I had been heading all along,

And, Martin Luther King, Jr. loved **both** his children and the children of America. For, on the steps of the Lincoln Memorial... in 1963, in his famous "I Have a Dream" speech, he proclaimed, "I have a dream that one day down in Alabama—with its vicious racists—one day right there in Alabama, little black boys and black girls will be able to join hands with little white boys and white girls as brothers and sisters." That's why I **believe** that if Martin were here that **HE WOULD BE HERE** eloquently enunciating the **HUMAN RIGHTS** of unborn children...

Thank you, Martin, for **BEING HERE IN SPIRIT.**

I am sure the thought that Dr. King would *not* be caught amidst a crowd of "cool-on-civil rights" conservatives, if he was living, crossed your mind. But the truth is that most White people who lived during the King era, especially in the South, were conservatives who resisted changes in the discriminatory laws and practices of their day. By and large, Congress was conservative. The state legislatures were conservative. Local governments and politicians were conservative. Businesses, large and small, were conservative. It is so easy to forget that the people in power when Martin Luther King, Jr. came on the scene did not welcome him with open arms. And they certainly did not consider him to be a model American. Yet, he stated his case in pursuit of a dream of justice, equality and liberty for all. For Dr. King to be consistent with his Judeo-Christian heritage and theology, which were rooted in the basic biblical and American principle that "all persons are created equal by God," he would have to acknowledge the human rights of unborn children or else be inconsistent, like most of his activist successors.

Please be advised that I did not conclude my speech with my interpretation of Dr. King's viewpoint on the subject matter. Nope, I brought my message to the masses present, to testimonial climax.

Lastly, **I AM HERE** really for one reason and one reason only. **I AM HERE TO CELEBRATE LIFE**—the **LIVES** of precious little babies who have **A RIGHT TO LIVE**, as much of a **RIGHT** as their mothers did when they were in their mothers' wombs.

I AM HERE TO CELEBRATE THE RIGHTS OF UNBORN CHILDREN to **LIVE** which **negates** the Supreme Court's alleged right of an expectant mother to choose to end the life of the developing human life within her for **any** reason whatsoever.

I have a confession to make. I almost walked away from that "drive in" abortion clinic in November, when the uniformed police officers arrived in several squad cars to arrest us. But, I'll tell you what kept me from walking away.

NO ABORTED BABY EVER WALKS AWAY.

I close with a quote from Father Daniel Berrigan. "When they come for the innocent without crossing over your body, cursed be your religion and your life."

I AM HERE TO CELEBRATE LIFE!

After repeating that last line about a half-dozen times, the crowd which was already standing erupted into applause, cheers, shouts and waving of hands. The Lord had enabled me to get my point across to most of the folk there. I know I did not convince Mecham or Koory to lend their support to a paid state holiday honoring King. I later learned that some of the pro-life, pro-King Day organizers of the rally and march received some criticism about my dealing so heavily with MLK at their pro-life rally. But the way I saw it, "They asked me, knowing full well who I was; and my words were not about to cause them to stop being pro-life, so I had to seize the moment."

Once the speeches were over, the crowd that continued to grow by hundreds, as the afternoon went on, headed toward 15th Avenue to march toward the State Capitol a couple of miles away. As their keynote speaker, I was asked to go to the front line of the marchers to help hold a banner that read "ABORTION STOPS A BEATING HEART." The throng of pro-lifers continued to swell as more supporters arrived in church and school busses from all over the Valley and the state. There was a lot of joy in that demonstration for life. Songs like "Amazing Grace" and "Jesus Loves the Little Children" were sung as we marched. And off to my right and left were several of my police friends who had arrested me two months earlier.

As we headed toward the Wesley Bolin Plaza on Adams, we could see what looked like thousands of people already there. *How did some of our folk get up there ahead of us,* I thought to myself. However, when we got closer we began to see the expressions on some of their faces as they began to jeer and taunt us. Some even called us names. Due to the public address system we could hear their speakers talking about "a woman's right to choose," "reproductive rights" and other familiar pro-abortion messages.

Just before we got to the courtyard in front of the State Capitol, where the pro-life march was to end with a brief prayer service, some hostility began between the pro-lifer marchers and pro-choice advocates. Officer Al Madrid of the Community Relations Unit became very concerned, as the less disciplined protesters on both sides of the issue escalated their insults toward one another. Al came and grabbed me and commandeered an Arizona statue on the west end of Wesley Bolin Plaza. He told me that he did not want to see this number of people amassed in such a small area to begin pushing and shoving, which could easily turn into a nasty, injurious riot. So, he told me anxiously, "Reverend Stewart, get up on this statue and tell your marchers to just keep moving quietly toward the State Capitol mall!" As he held my arm to keep me from slipping off the slanted base of the statue, I shouted with an already strained voice, "Pro-lifers, keep moving! Don't pay attention to the other folks! Just keep moving! Remember this is a nonviolent movement! Remember Dr. King's teaching of nonviolence!" It was a blessing that the word passed down the lines to the marchers still making their way to the Capitol.

Amazingly, once we began the abbreviated prayer service beneath a hand-made cross about 20 feet high—which served as our makeshift altar and focal point—and dismissed fifteen minutes later, other pro-life marchers were still inching their way toward the Capitol by the thousands. Totally awesome! I had never seen, in person, anything like that before. And the fact that I was a participant in the historic mass demonstration for life, made me feel very grateful.

Of course, I was the brunt of criticism from several local civil rights activists and highly visible Democrats. They questioned my "allegiance" with the predominantly Republican "right-wingers" in the pro-life movement. One or two even dared to ask, "How can he (Warren Stewart) side with them?" My response could easily have been "Why would anyone side with supporting the elective extermination of 1,500,000 unborn babies annually in America, in the name of human rights, civil rights and freedom?"

In February of that year I testified before the Judiciary Committee of the Arizona House of Representatives at the request of members of Arizona Right to Life. Legislation that proposed to restrict abortion on demand in Arizona had been introduced in the Legislature. Although I do not remember the exact bill, for which I was asked to speak, I will share the title of my testimony and the first two full paragraphs. My remarks were entitled "My Statement in Support of the Human Right to Life of Unborn Children Presented before the House Judiciary Committee of the Arizona House of Representatives on Wednesday, February 21, 1990 at the Arizona State Capitol in Phoenix, Arizona."

> My name is Warren H. Stewart, Sr., past General Chairperson of **ARIZONANS FOR A MARTIN LUTHER KING, JR. STATE HOLIDAY** and Pastor of the First Institutional Baptist Church of Phoenix. I appreciate this opportunity to stand before you to speak on behalf of the human rights of unborn children. A right that (I believe) is espoused in the Preamble of the Constitution of the United States of America which reads, "We the people of the United States, in order to form a more perfect Union, establish justice, insure domestic tranquility, provide for the common defense, promote the general welfare, and secure the blessings of liberty to ourselves and **OUR POSTERITY,** do ordain and establish this Constitution of the United States of America."
>
> Mr. Chairman and members of the Judiciary Committee of the Arizona House of Representative, the Webster's New World Dictionary, 2nd College Edition published in 1982 defines **POSTERITY** as "all of a person's descendants."

From that point, I share many of the same convictions that I had included in letters and speeches on the human rights of the unborn. I remember vividly, Representative Skelly coming to me that day and commending me for the courage to be arrested for my convictions about the unborn. He continued, "Your courage has made a legislator like me want to join you all in your next rescue. Reverend, I am getting out of the Legislature after this term. Would you contact me if you decide to participate in another protest? I'd be honored to go to jail with you, Reverend." Mr. Skelly later confirmed in a conversation with me that I had caused him to become a pro-King Day vote in the House, after casting nay votes on the holiday for years.

Another transition on my approach to the right to life issue came as I became more acquainted with the law. I changed from advocating the *civil rights* of unborn children to supporting the *human rights* of the unborn. The matter of the law determines one's civil rights, and according to the 1973 landmark Supreme Court ruling, children in the womb have no *civil rights* regardless of the Preamble making reference to *posterity*, which begins in the womb. On the other hand, it is certain that the procreation of a man and woman is human. Therefore, advocating the *human rights* of unborn babies, for me, provides much more solid ground on which to stand.

Finally, by October 1990 I had refined my primary speech on this issue to a message entitled "A Case for Advocating the Human Rights of Unborn Children in the Spirit of Dr. Martin Luther King, Jr." This speech was adapted to be delivered before a luncheon sponsored by NOEL, an Episcopalian pro-life group, which was held during the 70th General Assembly of the Episcopal Church that was in Session in Phoenix in July 1991, even though Arizona still did not have a paid state holiday honoring Dr. King.

In a passing conversation with the wife of Senator Dennis DeConcini, when she and her husband attended worship services at First Institutional in 1991, who like her husband was a rare pro-life Democrat with conservative leanings, I mentioned something about the speech I had delivered at the NOEL luncheon. Mrs. DeConcini requested a copy and I had my secretary to forward one to her. Obviously, she shared the speech with her husband; because I was informed that the Honorable Dennis DeConcini entered my entire speech in the Congressional Record—Senate on September 11, 1991, with the following introductory paragraph under the heading of "DR. WARREN H. STEWART, SR."

> Mr. DeConcini, Mr. President,
>
> I rise to share with my colleagues a speech by Dr. Warren H. Stewart, Sr., pastor of the First Institutional Baptist Church in Phoenix. The speech was delivered at the National Organization of Episcopalians for Life luncheon on July 17, 1991 during the 70th General Assembly of the Episcopal Church in Phoenix, Arizona. Dr. Stewart passionately expresses his views on the human rights of the unborn child and the need to preserve life—views which I share—and I strongly commend his remarks to my colleagues.
>
> I ask that the speech be printed in the Record.

In many ways, with the exception of the Charles Keating Savings and Loan scandal, which tainted Senator DeConcini, he was my kind of moderate Democratic U.S. Senator on many issues such as: civil rights, abortion, the King holiday, taxes, Africa and care for the disadvantaged in our society and around the world. However, I strongly differed with the senator on his confirmation votes for a couple of President Reagan's and Bush's Supreme Court justice appointments, as well as his support for the 1991 Persian Gulf War. Nevertheless, I miss his genre of Democratic leadership, especially being a pro-life Democrat, since he decided not to seek reelection in 1994.

I find it extremely difficult, if not impossible, to cast a vote for a pro-choice politician who is seeking a governmental office in which he or she can cast a vote contributing to or making a decision against unborn children. In many voting boxes beside certain key candidates' names and the offices they seek, my principle on this issue forces me to leave it blank. But, I cannot help it. *A vote for a pro-choice candidate, in most cases, is a vote against unborn babies.* It is a matter of life and death, the way I see it. And there is no in between.

This issue of abortion would enter into Arizona's Martin Luther King, Jr. fight for survival, in both the 1990 and 1992 elections. In both elections I tried to reap benefits from my pro-life, pro-King Day connection with my pro-life friends. I know it worked for many of the leaders in the pro-life movement. Moreover, several persons like Dr. Carolyn Gerster did their part in recruiting their co-workers in the movement to take another look at Martin Luther King, Jr. and the day honoring him. As usual, I had to keep peace with my pro-choice King Day crusaders, even though I did not compromise on my support on the right to life. On a couple of occasions, a mini-war nearly broke out between pro-life and pro-choice advocates who were sitting at the table of brotherhood and sisterhood, trying to win a King Day. Praise the Lord, we got the victory, eventually, without any bloodshed in our nonviolent coalition meetings.

I conclude this chapter on the human rights of the unborn in the spirit of Martin Luther King, Jr. with excerpts from two letters I wrote to the youngest daughter of the late Dr. King. The Reverend Dr. Bernice King is both a preacher and attorney, graduating with a Master of Divinity and Juris Doctorate Degrees in a dual degree program combining theology and law. The first letter was written by me on July 8, 1992 after I had met Dr.

King when she delivered a prophetic message to the American Association of Community and Junior Colleges convening in Phoenix. The third paragraph read,

> I am writing this letter to inquire if you know of any statements that your late father ever made on the issue of abortion and/or unborn children. It will be very helpful for me to know what position, if any, your father held on this issue.

Well, I never heard in writing from Dr. King's baby daughter, nor do I know if she ever saw my letter. But, I do know this—that she answered my letter *in person* when she spoke for the inaugural MLK, Jr. prayer breakfast held in Phoenix on December 10, 1992, the day before my birthday. Her subject was "Celebrating Life." And here is my entire third paragraph to Dr. Bernice King, Esquire, in a thank you letter to her, dated December 15, 1992.

> I do not know if what you said in your subject matter was intentional, but I do know it was providential! Your statements about your father's belief in "the sanctity of life," "that all human life is sacred," and that "the most fundamental human right is the right to life" affirmed my prophetic ministry as an advocate of human rights of the unborn. I feel my belief based on Scripture and the basic American principle that "all people are created equal under God," stands on solid ground. I have been embattled by many of the supporters of the Martin Luther King, Jr./Civil Rights Day in Arizona who said there is no evidence that Dr. Martin Luther King, Jr. believed in the sanctity of life. However, in studying his writings and being a messenger of God myself who utilizes the Word as the ultimate source of authority, in order to be consistent, your father would have had to believe in the sanctity of all human life.

Just to make sure this preacher-daughter of the Reverend M.L. King, Jr. clearly understood my contention, I enclosed a copy of my speech Senator DeConcini had placed in the Congressional Record. I have received no response or rebuttal from Dr. Bernice King or the King Center. But, to tell the truth, I got my response "loud and clear" in front of hundreds of King Day celebrants that second Thursday morning in December 1992. And those who know me and my pro-life position saw a gleam in my eyes and a smile of confirmation on my face that said without speaking a word, "I told you so!" I had to do everything to keep from giving Bernice King a solo standing ovation in the middle of her speech when she talked about her Dad's belief in "the most fundamental human right—the right to life."

Martin loved the little children.

Chapter Eleven
1990: When Voting Rights Went Wrong

I discovered a few days after the 1990 celebration of the life and legacy of Dr. King that my remarks about "King vs. Columbus" which I made before 15,000 marchers had not fallen on deaf ears. A sampling of a few letters to the editors of the *Republic* and *Gazette* indicated that Quaranta was not the only pro-Columbus Day advocate disturbed about my extemporaneous history lesson. Outright, I must confess that I made a mistake in my pro-King Day, anti-Columbus Day rhetoric by linking Captain Columbus to the African slave trade in the Americas. By so doing, one Glendale resident accused me of being "utterly unconcerned that [I] helped fan animosities between the races" in a letter printed in the *Republic* on February 25, 1990. In another letter to the editor of the *Gazette,* which was strategically placed next to the lead editorial on January 26, 1990, lauding Chandler, Arizona for electing Coy Payne, Arizona's first Black mayor of a major city in the state on the fourth Tuesday of January that year, a thoughtful Mesan's letter under the caption "No Warren Stewart fan" read,

> No help wanted: The word on the street reveals that the antics of that loudmouthed character who refers to himself as Warren Stewart is the force most responsible for the swelling of the ranks in opposition to the King Holiday fiasco. Why doesn't he just chill out, go tend to his flock and leave the voting to us, the good people of Arizona?

I admit I had brought such sharp criticism upon myself by stepping out of a diplomatic role, which I had acquired as the King Day war raged on and voicing my personal opinion on Columbus Day in less than grace-ful jargon. Nevertheless, I felt that regardless of what I said about King or Columbus, accurate or inaccurate, the majority of Arizona voters would never choose a Black American over a lost foreigner to celebrate his historic accomplishments. So I called it the way I saw it, with some regret from hindsight.

On the other hand, before I could write a letter to the newspapers correcting my public error in a moment of unleashed political passion, I had a chance to read a letter written in my defense by a Phoenix woman in response to the Mesa man's less than commending letter about me. She wrote,

> In my estimation, Warren Stewart is a man of admirable and deep convictions. He stands up for the right of human life—all human life.

Dr. Stewart's on the right track. If people could have the scales removed from their eyes, they'd see he is tending to his flock. We need someone like Warren Stewart representing the voting "good people" of Arizona! I vote: Martin Luther King holiday and pro-life. I don't think I'm alone.

It appeared that my King-pro-life connection was paying some dividends in the minds of a few Arizonans. And it was nice to be defended publicly by someone I had never met against someone else I would probably never want to meet face-to-face.

Speaking of defense, I penned a letter to the editor of *The Arizona Republic* which was printed on February 14, 1990. In that letter I offered,

> No doubt Mr. Sharp and others are upset by my remarks about Columbus not being an American, not discovering America and engaging in slave trade. Those are historical facts. My mistake was that I linked Columbus to the African slave trade when he was actually involved in enslaving the Arawak Indians of the West Indies, this according to Columbus' own journal. It is my hope that those who object to the Martin Luther King, Jr. state holiday will not use me or Columbus as a scapegoat.

With that being communicated, I closed the last chapter on my activities as leader of ARIZONANS FOR A MARTIN LUTHER KING, JR. STATE HOLIDAY. The rest was in Pastor Barnwell's hands and he certainly had my prayers realizing the monumental task facing him and all other Arizonans providing leadership for a showdown at the ballot box a few months away.

◇◇◇◇◇◇

In the wake of another scheduled MLK Day canceled, tabled or whatever you would like to call it, King Day proponents jockeyed for position to propose ways to make the upcoming election winnable. Zaler announced in a forum held in Paradise Valley a week after the federal observance of the holiday that he would organize an initiative campaign to put the federal model of King Day on the ballot, which would allow voters to decide on King Day totally detached from any Columbus Day baggage. This was Zaler's brainchild waiting to be born if the Legislature did not do what they could in establishing a King Day and restoring Columbus Day to paid holiday status. Julian Sanders who represented the anti-King Day position at the same forum said that he favored an "All Americans' Rights Day" to be observed on the third Monday in January as long as King's name was nowhere attached to it.

Convincingly, Arnie was successful in wooing Quaranta to consider joining forces with him in this new initiative, which could result in making everyone happy except the Sanders' crowd.

Obviously, still stung by my anti-Columbus Day remarks on January 15, 1990, Quaranta reiterated that he had nothing against Martin Luther King and committed to backing Zaler's initiative if it were necessary. He did, however, express concerns about the challenge pursuing another petition drive would be in light of his recent experience in working with Sanders in overturning the King-Columbus Day exchange bill approved in 1989. Pat's faint hope remained within the Legislature, which could straighten out the mess they had made. In the meanwhile, whenever the idea came up of the Legislature negating "the will of the people" of Arizona to vote on this issue by passing another King Day, while simultaneously restoring Columbus Day, threats of voter retaliation could be heard emanating from the Tempe headquarters of Arizonans for Traditional American Values.

Not taking Sander's threat too seriously, the recently convened Legislature had been introduced to two versions of King Day legislation. Representative Kennedy busied herself in gathering co-sponsors for a piece of legislation that would create a George Washington-Abraham Lincoln Day and a second bill that would establish an outright Martin Luther King, Jr. Day. Kennedy's holiday legislation would do what Quaranta and most other Arizona voters wanted—restore Columbus Day. The House of Representatives had been forced to discuss this issue virtually every time their leadership in both parties met together or apart. However, doing anything that would appear to deny the public of their right to vote on this issue in the fall as the Sanders-Quaranta referendum petition drive had mandated caused members of the Legislature to play "political hot potato" with Kennedy's proposals as well as similar bills in the Senate. Once Sanders got wind of the Legislature's latest leaning toward addressing the King holiday issue, he prophesied that his forces would collect another 80,000 signatures in less than two months to overturn any new King Day bill.

On the other side of this issue, the Legislature was being lobbied heavily by the business community to straighten out things because the March meetings of the NFL were less than seven weeks away when the decision for the 1993 Super Bowl was going to be made. The selection committee had narrowed down the sites to Phoenix, San Diego, Los Angeles or San Francisco. Without a King holiday, Valley Super Bowl solicitors knew that their chances were between zero and none to land it. So, Arizona's ninety senators and representatives were being arm-twisted to get the ball moving toward the end zone before it would be intercepted again by anti-King Day opponents.

UNITY, Zaler's successor coalition to ARIZONANS FOR A MARTIN LUTHER KING, JR. STATE HOLIDAY, held its first press conference in the second week of February. Using his undaunted drive to make a difference in winning the King holiday in addition to his business acumen, Zaler pulled together at least three already existing coalitions to bolster the ranks of UNITY. Prior to the official announcement to the media that his new grassroots organization had been formed, Arnie met with Pastor Barnwell at First New Life Missionary Baptist Church to recruit him and ARIZONANS FOR A MARTIN LUTHER KING, JR. STATE HOLIDAY to work with UNITY. After that the Black-Jewish Coalition of which Arnie was a key delegate joined ranks with the growing MLK Coalition. Believe it or not, Quaranta answered the invitation to fight for Arizona's Martin Luther King, Jr. holiday, and it was even reported that the name UNITY came from Quaranta. (I guess everybody can learn from experience, especially after uniting with anti-King activists to suffocate the state's new, never-celebrated King Day.) Their second meeting prior to the press conference was held at Phoenix's oldest African-American church— Tanner Chapel African Methodist Episcopal Church.

In many ways, UNITY, a coalition of labor, business, civic, community and social organizations, was a mirror of the coalition I had led for a little over three years. This time, though, the leadership came from "uptown." Zaler, being an upper class, energetic Jewish businessman, had access to money, staff and time that had been in short supply for much of the earlier years of the King Day struggle since November 1986. Moreover, while the coalition I formerly headed was adjusting to its new general chairperson and monumental challenge thrust upon veteran King Day warriors due to the referendum petition drive, new leadership emerged being welcomed by both those committed to the cause as well as the new leader himself. UNITY'S mission initially would be to ask the Legislature to rectify the mistake it had made relative to King Day and Columbus Day. Furthermore, if that was not done by the end of March, they would ask the Legislature to place the federal model of King Day by combining Washington and Lincoln Days into a generic Presidents Day on the ballot in November to give the electorate a choice. If neither of those goals were attained in due time, UNITY would launch a petition drive to place the federal model option on the ballot. As can be seen, none of these proposals was new, but likewise, none of them had been realized yet in Arizona.

Regardless of what one thought positively or negatively about Arnie, the man was a "go-getter." He was a man on a mission who attracted the yuppie and would-be yuppie crowd to him, including many college-age students who populated his corps of volunteers that tended to multiply rapidly. Thanks to having access to experienced public relations consultants, UNITY quickly became the alter ego to the behind-the-scenes MLK Better America Committee. UNITY's T-shirts and other paraphernalia with the nearly foot-size block letters spelling UNITY became nearly omnipresent in shopping malls, on campuses and at public events around the Valley. Arnie became known by the one-word UNITY logo. Without a doubt, he made his mark on behalf of Martin Luther King, Jr.'s day in his adopted state since 1981.

Amidst all of the Arizona wrangling over a symbolic day to honor America's Nobel Peace Prize-winning champion of justice, liberty and equality, the world witnessed a real-life miracle on Sunday, February 11, 1990. A Black man who had reached cult-like status during his lifetime as he sat in a prison cell 27 years for fighting for the freedom of his South African brothers and sisters was released to new life, new liberty and new leadership that would eventually lift him to become the first Black South African president of a "born-again" nation in 1994. Nelson Mandela walked free from the penitentiary that had held him in bondage as the world's most well-known political prisoner. Although in his younger years as a radical militant attorney who espoused violence to overthrow the inhumanely violent oppressive White South African government, which had profaned God's Word to justify apartheid on theological grounds, Mandela had become a role model to his African National Congress comrades, other Black South African civil rights activists and prophetic clergy, including Bishop Desmond Tutu and Dr. Alan Boesak, White South African governmental officials and the world at large. It is amazing how a person who was imprisoned in virtual isolation from the outside world for nearly three decades could sit down at the table of brotherhood and sisterhood with his former oppressors and insist that they be active participants in the future of a new South Africa.

Knowing that Dr. Martin Luther King, Jr. spoke out against apartheid in South Africa in the 1960s caused me to make the connection between why we were fighting to honor MLK in Arizona and what Mandela's victorious release meant to the majority population in the Republic of South Africa who knew racism, discrimination, poverty and oppression in modes that African-Americans knew not of. I know that is why I got up at around 6:00 a.m. Arizona time to witness live via television satellite the gates of Robben Island prison swing open and see that stately, tall giant of a human being of African heritage walk to freedom before a worldwide audience. I could not wait to get to our Sunday morning worship services to lead our congregation in thanking God for Mandela's liberation. For five years, I had kept a four ounce brownish-red rock on my desk which I had picked up outside of Johannesburg during my first trip to South Africa on a preaching mission there in 1985. That Sunday, I brought it with me to the First Institutional pulpit and declared aloud the promise I had made to myself, "One day, when my South African brothers and sisters are free; I'm going to take this rock back to South Africa and celebrate with my brothers and sisters!"

Thanks to the historic one person-one vote national elections that put the Black South Africans in the driver's seat with President Mandela at the wheel in April 1994, I hoped to make that trip, especially to rejoice with my Christian brothers and sisters of the First Institutional Baptist Church of Soweto, South Africa. God be praised that the prayers of millions of people of all faiths were heard by our God of Justice, Power and Mercy which enabled Nelson Mandela at age 71 to experience the phrase made famous by Dr. Martin Luther King, Jr., "Free at last! Free at last! Thank God Almighty, we're free at last!" And at age 75, the newly elected president of the Republic of South Africa declared those famous words as the widow of Dr. King stood by his side once his victory was assured on May 2, 1994.

◇◇◇◇◇◇

Nelson Mandela might have been "free at last," but Arizona was still shackled with a negative image emerging as a displaced pre-Civil Rights Movement Southern Dixieland state. Reports surfaced that the sports departments of Arizona State University and the University of Arizona; were having to deal with potential athletic recruits shying away from Arizona due to the King Day controversy. With the prospects of a statewide campaign to settle the King Day issue looming eight months away, fears of bitter race-baiting, divisive debates and name-calling caused anxiety in many of the leaders of our state. For goodness sakes, it was not "politically correct" in 1990 to sling mud at the memory of the most well-known African-American hero in American history. The state's already Conservative, "Wild West" image would move more to the extreme right than would be palatable for most progressive-minded Americans.

As movement gradually inched forward in the Legislature, the idea of Arizona voters making a decision on the King holiday became more acceptable through necessity. The Republican speaker of the House, Jane Hull, announced plans to introduce a bill that would put a King Day with no strings attached on the November 6 ballot. She believed that Arizona voters would vote for such a holiday honoring King if given the chance. Even some Democratic legislators who had always shied away from the thought of a public vote on the holiday in the past believed that that might be the best way for the Legislature to resolve the controversy without stirring up the anti-King Day crowd too much. Senator Walker, who had hinted at putting the King Day before the people if necessary back during the early Mecham days, admitted that if that was the best her colleagues could do for her, then so be it. Quite naturally our flip-flopping King Day friend-enemy, Senator Mawhinney, voiced his "I told you so" comments that this was what the Republican majority had supported all along.

Outside the Legislature, such a "less than courageous" proposal was not received enthusiastically by business and civic leaders especially the members of the Phoenix '93 Super Bowl committee. "Shover and Company" had a date with destiny in a few days in Orlando, Florida where the NFL owners would be choosing the city to host the prized 1993 Super Bowl. The last thing they wanted to tell the owner-operators of America's fall past-time entertainment was that they would have to wait until November 1990 to find out if Arizonans would vote to salute King. Moreover, it was the Arizona State Legislature's elected task to lead, not putting the ball back into the voters' laps. So, adding two choices for King Day on the general election ballot did not set too well with those responsible for heavily lobbying our state lawmakers on this issue.

Another reason many did not warm up to Speaker Hull's proposal proved to be that they felt that Sanders, without the aid of the Italian-American community, could not collect the required number of signatures to put a second King Day approved by the Legislature on the ballot. That is why business and civic leaders pushed establishing a King Day free of Columbus Day, and allow Sanders to self-destruct, so they thought. Apparently, the power of the pocketbook overpowered Hull's comfortable solution because word leaked out that the House and Senate were working on their own respective King Day bills to be considered. The lower chamber stuck with its original proposal to combine the two separate Washington and Lincoln Days into one. The more conservative and loyal Republican-controlled Senate floated the fiscally *un-conservative* idea of adding an eleventh holiday honoring King, in order to leave the two President's Days intact. Both chambers would restore Columbus Day. But, it is one thing to propose and quite another to produce the majority votes necessary to enact such laws.

As a retired King Day leader, I continued to do what I was born to do—preach the Gospel. During the second full week that March I conducted a revival in Kingman, Arizona. Trust me, under the circumstances and considering the unwritten history of the Ku Klux Klan, having headquartered itself there, I stretched my faith by accepting an invitation to preach five nights as the guest evangelist of the College Park Southern Baptist Church, a small evangelical, predominantly White congregation in Kingman, which had a grand total of two Black families in the town. The young, daring pastor of that church, the Reverend Charles Wesner, had heard me preach at a Southern Baptist Evangelism Conference in the late 1980s and wanted to expose me to Kingman country. With all of the publicity I had received over the King holiday fight, a few folks up there in those mountains knew of my activities. A little anxious about utilizing my African-American preaching gifts in a rural Anglo conservative setting, I became somewhat more concerned when the host pastor called me a couple days prior to my coming, to inform me that he had gotten calls from Kingman residents criticizing him for inviting "a Communist" to preach Kingman's first citywide revival. To make matters a little more scary, the revival meeting would take place at the Mohave County Fairgrounds. Nevertheless, I put my faith to the test, packed my bags and Bible, and drove my 1982 red Camaro Sport Coupe up "them there hills" to enjoy an inspiring, challenging and uneventful week preaching the Good News to Kingman's citizens who dared to come to hear that "radical, activist Black preacher from the big city who supported a holiday for Reverend King." In addition to enjoying the fellowship of Kingman's relatively new preacher-pastors, I was introduced to the McCourt Family Singers, a traveling family of country Gospel artists, who lived in a trailer that proved to be home away from home, as they put the Good News to that kind of music rural America likes. What an evangelistic team serving Kingman that week!

The same week I was preaching the Gospel in Kingman, the NFL meetings were being held in Orlando. Governor Mofford, Shover, Bidwell and a few other members of the Phoenix '93 Committee had followed the owners there to make their final pitch to win the 1993 Super Bowl. Senators DeConcini and McCain flew to Florida to bolster the support for Phoenix's chance to get the big game. Arizona's delegation would stand shoulder-to-shoulder with bidders from Los Angeles, San Diego and San Francisco. The hour of decision had finally come.

An unexpected Arizonan showed up at the NFL meetings by the name of Art Mobley, a talented African-American gentleman who had worked for several years in the radio industry in the Valley. Art had been a long-time supporter of Arizona's King Day and had formed a group called Arizona "Keep the dream alive" Coalition not long after I resigned as head of ARIZONANS FOR A MARTIN LUTHER KING, JR. STATE HOLIDAY. As Zaler was an Anglo Jewish business- person, Art was an aspiring African-American businessman who dreamed of owning the first Black-owned radio station in Phoenix. Because Arizona had yet to approve MLK Day and keep it, Art felt that the boycott strategy should be kept in place and actually stepped up a notch or two in response to the suspending of the King Day by the referendum petition. Logically, Art was dead set against seeing Arizona win the 1993 Super Bowl void a permanently established King Day. So he paid his own way to Orlando with the intent of persuading the NFL to honor the convention and entertainment boycott initiated in 1987 by *not* selecting Phoenix as the 1993 Super Bowl site.

Just a week or so prior to the NFL meetings, Art wrote a letter to Stevie Wonder informing him that his coalition reaffirmed the entertainment boycott that Wonder had started after Mecham rescinded the holiday in 1987. He further informed Wonder of the convention boycott supported by ARIZONANS FOR A MARTIN LUTHER KING, JR. STATE HOLIDAY and Mrs. Coretta Scott King. Mobley also informed Mr. Wonder of the business community's new-found interest in the day honoring King when it was made crystal clear that Arizona would have no Super Bowl without King Day. In light of the overturning of the holiday by the Sanders-Quaranta coalition, Mobley wrote,

> We will picket and demonstrate against any effort to bring such events or concerts to Arizona.
>
> We have asked the NFL Players Association to also issue a statement to support not playing a Super Bowl in Arizona in defiance of the boycotts.
>
> We are for a King Holiday that follows the guidelines of the federal holiday. When such bill passes in the State of Arizona both boycotts (convention and entertainment) will be immediately lifted.

Art copied this letter to Mrs. King and Gene Upshaw, Executive Director of the NFL Players Association.

Art provided me with a copy of a letter he wrote to Paul Tagliabue, Commissioner of the NFL, and obviously took with him to Florida. After giving pro-football's top executive a one-page summary of our grassroots efforts since 1986 through the referendum drive, Art made it clear what he wanted from Tagliabue in the final paragraph,

> All that we ask is that the 1993 Super Bowl Committee join the more than 50 organizations including the National Basketball Association League Owners, the American Federation of Government Employees and the National Newspaper Publishers Association, to boycott Arizona until a Martin Luther King, Jr. state holiday is passed.

This letter was copied to all of the NFL owners, specifying by name Norman Braman, owner of the Philadelphia Eagles and site selection committee chairman, Mike Brown, Cincinnati Bengals owner, Ralph Wilson of the Buffalo Bills and Jim Steeg, NFL director of special events. Whether or not any of them received and read the letter does not negate the fact that the King holiday see-saw in Arizona would definitely be a factor in the NFL owners' decision to come or not to come in 1993.

The chairman of Arizona "Keep the dream alive" coalition was well-versed in getting the attention of the media since he had worked in that field for years. On March 9, 1990, Mr. Mobley called a press conference in Phoenix informing the public that his group would urge the NFL to select a site other than Phoenix for the much talked about and targeted Super Bowl. It is one thing to write letters and make phone calls to organizational heads and individuals that one wanted them to bypass Arizona for its mishandling of King Day, but Art chose to be up front with the "powers that be" in Phoenix to let them know his strategy in person. Art, who had reunited with First Institutional after being out of the church for years, had conferred with me on his planned activities and I advised him as best I could. I provided him with the press statement and related documents our coalition had used when we announced our support for the Arizona boycott three years earlier that month.

Pastor Barnwell who had been working with UNITY and to some degree with the MLK Better America Committee, called me to express his concern about Mobley's renewing the convention and entertainment boycott. I advised my colleague to stay in communication with Art, but it appeared that Art had made up his mind to press forward in keeping the Super Bowl away from Phoenix. The decision to actively get the NFL to stay away from our state in 1993 was based on two legitimate concerns of Art, me and thousands of other King Day supporters. First of all, what share of the economic bonanza to be reaped from the Super Bowl would wind up benefiting Black folk in Arizona? Were there any African-Americans on the Phoenix '93 Committee, and if so, were they there for themselves and/or for the broader Black community, especially small businesspersons who would jump at the equal opportunity to get a piece of the $200,000,000 pie? Secondly, and probably most fundamentally, Arizona's kicking, tossing and fumbling King Day had become an insult to millions of Americans who continued to be inspired by the preacher-man who gave his life for the fight against racism and discrimination. Consequently, Art espoused the belief that Arizona did not deserve to reap the benefits of the premier championship professional football game whose majority of players were African-Americans. Perhaps, the underlying intent of Mobley's strategy of announcing his intentions to derail the Super Bowl pitch was to get the Legislature off the dime.

Of course, the news of such a strategy sponsored by the "Keep the dream alive" Coalition nearly caused Shover and the Phoenix '93 Committee to have recurring nightmares in broad daylight about losing the game they had worked for, for several months. They sent out a "search and destroy" squad to stifle Mobley's efforts by trying to get some Black leaders to talk him out of going to Florida. Concerned about the professional repercussions such a militant strategy could bring upon Art, I asked him directly if he was aware of all of the consequences he could experience for "messing with the big boys." Without a doubt, he knew what he was doing and proceeded to Orlando.

Once the meetings began, Arizona, led by Governor Mofford, made their appeal to the site selection committee. Ironically, the MLK Day was not mentioned as part of their official presentation. When Mobley showed up at the Hyatt Regency Grand Cyprus, uninvited and planning to pass out literature urging the owners to choose any site but Phoenix, the Phoenix delegation sent their most powerful linemen to block Art's best moves. Governor Mofford and Arizona's two U.S. Senators talked with Art about their commitment to see Arizona pass a King holiday which had nothing to do with the Super Bowl. Those three were about the only ones in the Phoenix delegation who could not have their desire for honoring King linked to a football game. Art publicly backed down from causing a stir in Orlando. However, it was guaranteed that neither the commissioner, nor the owners would allow the 1993 Super Bowl to emanate from the Valley of the Sun minus King's Day in Arizona.

After the Phoenix '93 leaders presented their 15-minute proposal to the selection committee, two of the other cities did the same. Later on that afternoon, Tuesday, March 13, 1990, Paul Tagliabue announced that Phoenix had won the prized game for 1993. The official Arizona delegation went wild. Even without the King Day in place, Arizona had pulled off an upset victory. To be sure, it took five ballots before Phoenix finally won out over Los Angeles and San Diego and the rule requiring the approval of three fourths of the NFL owners had to be suspended. Nevertheless, victory was being celebrated both in Orlando and Phoenix.

Before the cheers could die down, the owner of the Philadelphia Eagles let it be known that if Arizona did not get their King Day act together, he would support an effort to rescind the decision to come to Arizona. Rescind? Wasn't that a familiar word associated with the Martin Luther King, Jr. Day in Arizona? And in spite of assurances by the commissioner of the football league that the awarding of the Super Bowl to Phoenix was *unconditional*, some of us knew that the 1993 showpiece game was *not* a permanent fixture in the desert southwest unless King Day would become a permanent date on the official Arizona calendar. My friend, Art Hamilton, summed up the winning of the Super Bowl that week in the following words,

> I'm hoping that we will demonstrate that we are worthy of this great honor. I'm hoping that we will now continue the effort to make sure that by the time we have a Super Bowl that we have a King holiday to celebrate it.

Perhaps getting the Super Bowl would provide the incentive for the Legislature to approve a Columbus-friendly King Day to diffuse the anti-King Day crusaders who were looking forward to voting no on the King Day proposition in November.

Unfortunately, politics is not a black and white issue. Even though the Legislature was well aware of how they could resolve the King Day powder keg, they hedged for the umpteenth time in doing it. But that was not to say that some leaders in the Legislature were not trying to resolve the King problem. On the Republican side, that is, the far right Republican side, Dr. King's new holiday advocate did everything within his power to get his colleagues in the House to repeal the first King bill and reestablish separate days for King and Columbus. To be sure, once Representative Jim Skelly committed to King Day, there was no wavering on his part. Regrettably, most of his fellow Republican lawmakers thought the political price of interfering with the King Day election was just too high.

Before March ended, the idea of going to court to remove Columbus Day from the King Day ballot proposition surfaced by Bill Stephens, a Democrat attorney who had served in the House of Representatives. The point of reference was Attorney General Corbin's opinion that the King Day legislation had a legal loophole that could invalidate at least a portion of it, if contested in court. The only King Day leader who even commented on it was Arnie Zaler. His contention was that the Legislature ought to pass the new holiday law. And if the state lawmakers did not address the issue, then UNITY would march forward with a petition drive placing the federal model of King Day on the ballot.

By the time April rolled around, evidence that the convention boycott was essentially dead, made the headlines when the hotel industry released their statistics for 1989, as compared to 1987 and 1988. In addition, Dr. Benjamin Hooks, long-time civil rights leader, activist pastor, former federal judge, first African-American appointed to the Federal Communications Commission and prophetic executive director of the NAACP, ended his personal boycott of Arizona by accepting an invitation to serve as the guest speaker for the Maricopa County branch of the National Association for the Advancement of Colored People annual Freedom Fund dinner. According to *The Arizona Republic*, Dr. Hooks met with key legislative leaders and offered his help in any way needed. However, the meeting was essentially a courtesy meeting and not an official request for assistance from the national NAACP. Claiming to be a friend to Arizona, where he once was based at Fort Huachuca, the leader of the oldest and most respected civil rights organization in America commented,

> Arizona was more progressive then than it is now. Don't get me wrong—it was not one of the official Jim Crow states at that time, as far as interstate commerce was concerned. But it's acting more like a Jim Crow state now than it did then....Now I came back to Arizona, but it's not one of the states that I'd have expected to have problems with a King holiday.

The beginning of April also prompted King Day supporters to remember the twenty-second anniversary of the assassination of Dr. King. ARIZONANS FOR A MARTIN LUTHER KING, JR. STATE HOLIDAY, which had been rather quiet since my departure as general chairperson sponsored a prayer vigil at the Pilgrim Rest Baptist Church in Phoenix on April 4, 1990 at 6:00 p.m.

Three hours prior to that service of reflection on the life and sacrifice of Martin Luther King, Jr, Arnie held a press conference at the State Capitol urging the state legislators to pass a new King Day before the Martin Luther King, Jr. Federal Holiday Commission would meet in Phoenix at the end of the month. Gene, Arnie and Jackie Platt-Jennas had been able to convince Mrs. King to bring the holiday commission's annual planning conference to Phoenix when they met with her in 1989. Perhaps, the upcoming presence of the widow of America's most famous twentieth century martyr would move the cold hearts of unmoving Republican lawmakers to pass the day honoring her husband in respect to her. Maybe the coming to Arizona of the Federal King Day Commission would embarrass the Legislature into approving the federal model of the holiday.

But getting back to my former coalition, the prayer vigil was a way for wearied King fans to get in touch with the Higher Power who sustained Dr. King during his most difficult days. Although the church was not packed, God's liberating spirit was there, along with Pilgrim's host pastor, the Reverend Alexis A. Thomas, and several other religious leaders primarily from the African-American community, as well as a few Black civic leaders. They had even asked me to offer the closing prayer, and as I have said before, "It's nice to be remembered."

To my knowledge, our coalition, led by Pastor Barnwell had held two public meetings since I resigned. The first occurred at First New Life on Sunday, February 11th, at which time the "community election" of the new general chairperson took place; and input was received on new strategy and actions. As a show of support of Pastor Barnwell's leadership, I attended. Once again, the numbers were sparse and the presence of Black religious leaders who supported Pastor Barnwell's assuming the leadership, were assured that he would remain as the new leader of the coalition that was started in his church in November 1986. Before the meeting ended I was caught off guard when I was presented an elegant plaque expressing appreciation for my leadership of ARIZONANS FOR A MARTIN LUTHER KING, JR. STATE HOLIDAY. Moreover, after I received my award, the coalition's new head presented a plaque in gratitude of my wife Serena for her support of my leadership in the King holiday struggle. That indeed was rare among social organizations to remember the spouses of the leaders who spend so much time away from family for the betterment of others. Once the ceremonial activities were completed, the Reverend Henry L. Barnwell was unanimously elected as general chairperson of our historic coalition.

As Mrs. King's visit rapidly approached, more talk could be heard buzzing around the Capitol that a new King Day would have to be passed before the Legislature finished its work that session. Art flexed his muscles with his Democratic Caucus that any fiscal matters on the docket would not be passed without the reestablishment of King Day. Governor Mofford, I suppose feeling pressure to get another victory for King Day like she had gotten before with the aid of her "business buddies," let it be known that straightening out the King Day mess was a legacy she wanted to leave in the annals of Arizona history. She even suggested that she would use her veto power if some Republicans did not join ranks with the Democrats to get a new King Day.

The House of Representatives for the fifth consecutive year lined up their majority for the new legislation that would add a free standing Martin Luther King, Jr. Day and restore Columbus Day to paid status. Continuous polls indicated that a King Day separated from Columbus would have a much better chance at winning at the polls than the King-Columbus exchange model. The hold-up in the Legislature was easy to locate in the Senate chambers. However, this time around, the Democrats in the Senate could not boast of a unanimous voting bloc in favor of the holiday bill. Two Democratic senators felt that their constituents would not stand for tampering with the people's right to vote on the issue. As a result, a whopping five Republican votes in the Senate would be needed.

A little outside pressure did not hurt when the news wire reported that two holdout states—Idaho and Wyoming, which had Black populations amounting to a percentage of a percentage point—approved the King holiday that spring. While in Phoenix, a Chinese activist, who had been involved in the 1989 Tiananmen Square demonstration for democracy in Communist China, told King Day supporters that Dr. King's teaching on non-violence had been taught to him as a high school student in China. He confessed "His [Dr. King's] teachings gave us [the Chinese student activists] inspiration in Tiananmen Square; the great achievement of Dr. King in his non-violent ways."

Arizona's hosting of the 1990 Information and Planning Conference of the Martin Luther King, Jr. Federal Holiday Commission took place April 26-28, 1990 at the YWCA Leadership Development Center in northwest Phoenix. The conference moves around the nation annually providing the opportunity for Mrs. King, other civil rights leaders, and members of the Federal Commission to prepare for the national King holiday observances. This commission's officers, members and board of directors constitutes a "Who's Who" in civil rights and political activism, including politicians, clergy, movie stars, congressional leaders, and professional sport executives. Phoenix was blessed beyond measure to land the MLK Federal Commission conference in view of what Mecham, Sanders and the Legislature had done to the one-day observance honoring Dr. King for so long.

As the conference approached and word was confirmed that Mrs. King would spend a day in Phoenix attending the meeting, Mobley directed a letter to Dr. King's widow urging her to personally boycott Arizona. Art's feeling was that the presence of not only the MLK conference, but Mrs. King in Arizona would dilute any remaining pressure that the Legislature might have felt about the holiday. After all, it was Coretta Scott King who sent out a press release endorsing our coalition's boycott in 1987. However, since that time, our first woman governor had met and invited the "First Lady of the Civil Rights Movement" to Arizona in 1988. Then, in 1989, Arizona had finally honored her husband with his day. And local, long-time King Day celebration organizers plus Arnie, had laid out the welcome mat for Mrs. King to come.

Be advised that none of that phased Mr. Mobley at all. In making his appeal for Dr. King's widow to change her plans about visiting the Valley of the Sun on Thursday, April 26, Art wrote a three-page letter with attachments to Mrs. King on April 12, 1990. Excerpts from his letter read as follows:

> It was only the pressure of the boycott that finally forced the state to pass a King Holiday Bill last September....It was the effort to bring the Super Bowl and the fear of the boycott that resulted in action. It was money, not morality....
>
> The boycott has been our only effective weapon. Those of us who believe in the vision of Dr. King respect your ability to have an impact in situations where compromise and mutual respect are possible. However, Arizona is not such a place at this time.
>
> We ask that you please delay or cancel your trip to Arizona. Besides destroying our boycott, we feel that your presence will serve to reward the intransigence of this state and its legislature.

To be honest, I essentially agreed with most of what my church member communicated to Mrs. King, with the exception of what her impact might make on the Arizona State Legislature. Perhaps, having the mother of Dr. King's four children in living color in Phoenix talking about why it is important to honor and celebrate his birthday as well as "keeping the dream alive" would soften the hearts of Republicans in the Senate. On the other hand, the reasons for the heavy lobbying from the business community, which pushed the King Day into the win column, had a whole lot to do with money and very little to do with morality. That is a subject which I would revisit before and after the 1990 general election. But, the reality remained. Mrs. Coretta Scott King and the King Commission were on their way to Arizona.

Her coming created excitement for many loyal King Day supporters. The governor took credit for her being in town. Arnie made the front pages and news sound bites greeting Mrs. King. Phoenix's new, young mayor shared the dais with her. Gene graciously put her and the Commission's being in Phoenix in the most positive light by stating to reporters, "It's a goodwill gesture. We think these people coming here, in spite of the confrontational attitude; is a sign of cooperation." The local King celebration workers had a chance to rub shoulders with *the* lady. Arizona's children, especially those of African descent, could catch glimpses of the real-life widow of a legend in his own time. It was good for her to be in Arizona, regardless.

That Thursday evening, the person most responsible for carrying on the unfinished dream of Martin Luther King, Jr. would speak at a dinner working session on the subject of "The Making of the King Holiday: How Far Have We Come? How Far Must We Go?" About 200 or so persons attended the dinner, in addition to lots of local media representatives. Once again, I was remembered enough to have been asked to bring greetings to Mrs. King and the other conferees. The new general chair of our coalition followed me in doing likewise on the program. I cherished the honor to share the platform with the widow of my hero. When around persons like that of such stature whom you have met before in passing, you kind of wonder if they remember you. I do remember greeting her personally and thanking her for coming.

Mrs. King is a very poised, elegant woman of presence. I have never seen or heard her not to appear to be in control of herself, regardless of the situation. I remember thinking: *Her speech is articulately sophisticated without being snobbish. Her words are pointedly powerful and most often prophetic. Mrs. King's movements are deliberate and distinct. Yet, she possesses a warmth that is rare among persons of such notoriety. And she is gracious in greeting, as well as strong in stature.*

Mrs. King's introductory remarks addressed celebrating her husband's birthday on a national, state and local level. Although she thanked local leaders for working to win a day for Dr. King in Arizona, she did not address directly, and certainly did not attack any of the anti-King Day contingents in our state. She talked about how honoring her husband entailed living out the philosophy and principles he espoused on a year-round basis. The closest she came to directing remarks about Arizona's perennial King Day controversy was when she spoke about the paradox of many King Day detractors still feeling that honoring her husband was "somehow un-American." Then, she proceeded to answer the two questions which her speech's topic raised about how far we have come and how far we must go. Of course, she received a standing ovation and then listened to three responses from Phoenix Mayor Paul Johnson, Monsignor Edward Ryle of the Phoenix Catholic Diocese and John Cox of Atlanta, an assistant vice-president of Delta Airlines.

Before Mrs. King left Phoenix the next morning, she had a breakfast meeting with Governor Mofford, who once again pledged her support to everything within her power to see that Arizona approved another King Day bill while she was still governor. That same morning, Governor Rose Mofford was programmed to address the subject "Passing the King Legacy to our children." In her well-received remarks, Governor Mofford in her own unique politician-style orator's voice declared,

> Ladies and gentlemen, I have eight months, 14 days and two hours left in my administration, and I have a wish. Arizona took pride in 1912 when it joined the Union as the 48th state. It is my wish that we again take pride and join most of the other states in the Union and become the 48th state to have a King holiday.

Those remarks by the "First Lady" of Arizona brought the "First Lady" of the Civil Rights Movement", and everyone else who was in the conference room of the YWCA Leadership Development Center to their feet in joyful applause. The governor had done it again—made it clear where she stood on Arizona's King Day.

All in all, the hosting of Mrs. King and the Commission proved to be a plus for Arizona's efforts to reestablish King Day. The pessimism that had begun to permeate the deliberations of holiday advocates was chased away by optimism that the Legislature would rise to the occasion and alleviate a bitter, ugly and divisive campaign to celebrate Dr. King's life with a paid state holiday.

Whether there was a connection or not, shortly after Coretta King departed from Arizona, two more Republican Senators were leaning heavily toward casting affirmative votes for the new King Day legislation. The president of the Arizona State Senate, none other than Bob Usdane, allowed the word to leak out that he was a strong "yes" vote. The other pro-King, pro-Republican crossover hailed from ASU country in the person of Senator Doug Todd. No doubt, the heavy pro-sports camp persuaded Todd that if the King Day did not get a fair shake, his district might never get to host the 1993 Super Bowl at Sun Devil Stadium.

With the probable addition of Usdane and Todd to the King Day faithful, Republican Senator Jacque Steiner, and eleven solid Democrats in the Senate, only two more votes were needed to gain the majority on the issue. Surprisingly, Senator Corbet who orchestrated the King-Columbus Day swap lined up with the no voters this time around. Democratic Senators Gus Arzberger and Bill Hardt did not feel that they could survive the upcoming election in the rural districts if the voters felt that they interfered with their voting rights by approving another King Day that would kill the referendum. That left three Republican senators from the two major metropolitan areas in Arizona to be courted to come over to the King side. The "Tucson Two" had familiar names as they were the two senators who nixed King Day in the past—DeLong and Mawhinney. The other candidate for conversion was Senator Pete Corpstein, a business-linked legislator from the well-to-do Paradise Valley district. Most of the other Republican senators were so right-wingish, ultra-conservative and anti-King Day that the lobbying experts did not even expend any energy in their direction. Obviously something was in the wind because Senator Walker, who knew her colleagues pretty well, forecasted that the King Day bill would pass.

May had rolled around and the Legislature had not resolved some important tax issues that needed to be addressed before they adjourned and went home. Some legislators were of the mind that it might be best to deal with the King Day issue in a special session called by Governor Mofford just for that matter. By so doing, all other legislative issues could be set aside until that one issue was settled. Additionally, it was critical that before a special session was called on the holiday, the votes for passage had to be close to certain as politics would allow. Another factor facing the holiday proponents was passing the new bill soon enough to give opponents the opportunity to launch a referendum petition drive to set aside the new King Day legislation. The general feeling was that even if a brand-new petition drive were launched, the petitioners would not garner enough valid signatures to put a second King holiday proposition on the ballot for November, particularly because it would be detached from Columbus Day. Moreover, the polls had predicted that standing alone, Arizonans would approve King Day.

Public and private pressure began to mount for the Arizona State Senate to show real leadership on the day to honor America's personal symbol of the Civil Rights Movement that revolutionized America. Editorials by the major newspapers and television and radio stations pressed the Senate to act without any further delay. As the second week in May passed, it was reported that fifteen votes had been committed to the holiday and retiring Senator Hardt was about to become the sixteenth vote.

The thought of passing a new law that would negate the vote of the people, mandated by the Sanders-Quaranta referendum, raised the dander of one particular person *other than* Julian Sanders. Impeached former Governor Mecham threatened to lead the new referendum petition drive himself, if the proposed King Day legislation were approved and blocked the holiday proposition being put on the ballot. On Tuesday, May 8, 1990, Mecham informed every legislator in writing.

> If you bend to the pressure to again take away the people's precious right to vote, I will be just one of a large vanguard in this state to restore the people's right to vote on this issue.

Mecham continued,

> Rest assured, there is ample support to secure the needed signatures to again put this back on the ballot.

Remember, this is the politician who had announced his candidacy to run for the governor's office for the sixth time on the 21st anniversary of Dr. King's assassination. He had made it up in his mind that he would fight Arizona honoring King with every ounce of energy he could muster. On the same day Dr. King's widow was in Phoenix, the maverick gubernatorial candidate announced that if the Legislature passed a King Day while he was governor, he would veto it.

With his hero back in the throe of things, Sanders began to rant and rave more loudly that a second petition drive was imminent. He also put his own Senator Todd on notice that if he voted for the holiday, he would pay a high political price. On May 11, 1990, he journeyed to the State Capitol to voice his threats to the state lawmakers as they busied themselves with doing their jobs and anticipating a special session on King Day to be called within the next three or four days.

D-Day came on Monday, May 14, 1990 when the governor "bit the bullet" and called Arizona's ninety lawmakers into special session to approve a new holiday extolling the life of Martin Luther King, Jr. Each chamber would address four identical bills (1) establishing an MLK paid state holiday on the third Monday in January, (2) reestablishing Columbus Day as a paid state holiday on the second Monday in October, (3) repealing the 1989 King-Columbus Day exchange legislation, and (4) blocking a public vote scheduled for November on the King-Columbus swap. Since the House of Representatives had taken the lead for three consecutive years and knew exactly where they stood on this increasingly controversial issue, they sat back to wait for the Senate to act.

Good news started that historic Monday when Globe Senator Bill Hardt confirmed that he could be counted on as a pro-King Day vote. At the same time, anti-King senators brought up the possibility of passing a resolution to put the new King Day on the ballot, instead of doing away with the referendum as proposed. They began to voice threats of voter retaliation similar to what Mecham and Sanders had predicted. Governor Mofford would not have her voice drowned out by the man she succeeded in office during that special session. *The Phoenix Gazette* reported her using King Day rhetoric similar to what some of us veteran supporters had used in times past, by admitting that she was "embarrassed by Arizona's image as "a racist state.'" She also opined:

> I think it has the greatest effect on Arizona of anything that I
> have ever known, and I've been here 50 years.... We're not taking
> the right to vote (away), in my opinion, because we have never
> voted on any other holiday before.

Now, that was some heavy verbiage coming from the white-haired lady from Globe who fell into the governor's chair. The "guv" came out swinging that day.

The first day of the session witnessed Senator Corbet straddling the fence by proposing a resolution that would provide Arizona state employees with "a cafeteria plan" for 10 state holidays out of a pool of 19 options, including King Day. That resolution went about as high as a lead balloon. Then, he started harping about the $500,000 that an outright King Day would cost taxpayers, according to the *Gazette*.

By the evening of the first day of the special session, Senator Todd waxed eloquent before a group of his district Republicans with these words,

(Arizona's) Berlin Wall of bigotry, fear, hatred and mistrust (must come down)....I had a part of building that wall. I share the responsibility with others...in getting rid of it.

Not stopping with himself, the Tempe senator challenged his fellow Republicans, many of whom he knew did not support King Day.

I will be asked to stand up and be counted...and I want to know will you stand up and be counted with me? Will you stand up with me if you want to tear down Arizona's wall of racism and intolerance? Will you stand up and support me?

What a difference a day makes! And about half of those in attendance rose to their feet and applauded the senator.

It happened! The Arizona State Senate passed the new King holiday at 12:27 p.m. on Tuesday, May 15, 1990, putting it in the Arizona history books. Senators Usdane, Todd, DeLong and Hardt provided leadership for the welfare of their beloved state by setting aside partisan politics, political threats and possible pitfalls on this issue, and helped provide a 16-14 majority vote to approve the state's second legislatively sanctioned MLK Day. The next day, Wednesday, May 16, 1990, the House of Representatives followed suit with a 35-25 Democrat-Republican mixture vote. It was a done deal. At last, that is what King Day supporters thought.

Governor Mofford took no time in signing the brand-new King Day bill in her office. Around dinnertime on the same day the House ratified the legislation, the governor conducted a quickly-called signing ceremony in her office. All of the veteran King Day advocates had been invited. I even received an invitation.

The decision for me to attend the signing ceremony was not as easy as it may sound. First of all, I had not actively lobbied for this particular piece of legislation, so I debated whether or not I had any right to celebrate with those who had pushed hard for this new King Day. After all, I had resigned as general chairperson of ARIZONANS FOR A MARTIN LUTHER KING, JR. STATE HOLIDAY four months prior. I had been out of the thick of things. Additionally, based on principle, I did not support the restoration of Columbus Day which this legislation mandated. So, would my attending the victory celebration be in direct contradiction of my philosophical opposition to what Columbus Day represented, which was at odds with the symbolism of King Day? Thirdly, and of least importance, this new holiday bill carried the liability of adding an eleventh paid sate holiday. Consequently, it was not fiscally conservative and would be an easy target for anti-King Day petitioners to provide voters with a legitimate "bush to hide behind" when they presented a new referendum petition suspending the new King Day until the general election.

Sitting in my office, trying to make a decision after receiving a call from the Governor's Office inviting me to come, I first decided *not* to go to the Capitol that evening; then I thought, "Maybe I should go." Needing advice, I called my wife and asked her opinion. Almost without hesitation she responded, "Aw, Warren, go ahead and go....After all you've done for the holiday, you deserve to be there." So, I finished up the work I was doing and made my way west on Washington, in my 1982 red Camaro, to the Executive Building.

Purposely, I arrived late to avoid the crowds and engaging in a lot of small talk. Even though I had decided to attend the ceremony, I still had my reservations. I was a little concerned about some of the current King Day crusaders thinking I had no business there, since I had watched the 1990 MLK campaign from the spectator's seat. Once I entered the building and took the elevator to the ninth floor, the waiting lobby of the Governor's Office was virtually empty. "What a break", I mumbled to myself in relief. The receptionist directed me to the conference room, where the governors often held media-covered, as well as private meetings with key community, civic, business, legislative and ceremonial briefings. My first visit to that room was over a decade prior to 1990 when I met in a grim-faced meeting with then-Governor Babbitt, the Reverend Jesse Jackson, Bishop H.H. Brookins and DPS officials relative to the Miracle Valley crisis in southern Arizona.

I opened the door to a packed room of King Day victors. I remained near the door as the governor introduced speaker after speaker to comment on Arizona's new MLK holiday. Nothing new was really said about what the passage of that particular King Day meant because most of those present had either given and/or heard the same speeches in September 1989 when the first legislatively-approved King Day occurred. Then, all of a sudden, Governor Mofford called on me to come forward to say something. I was totally shocked! Saying anything at that ceremony was the last thing on my mind. But what could I do?

I had only about ten seconds to come up with something to say, as I made my way through dozens of people crowded into that rather large conference room. Of course, I greeted the governor. Then, I acknowledged the legislators who had led the fight to get the state's second King Day bill through both chambers. At the time I concluded my "off the cuff" remarks by speaking like an amateur auctioneer, "Going once, going twice, going a third time. And I hope that three's a charm." Immediately, I moved away from the podium amidst warm, polite applause. The governor then picked up her black pen and put her signature to her *second* MLK Day law in Arizona fulfilling a dream and a promise to witness the passage of the King holiday before she left office. Before everyone left, Mrs. King called the governor to praise her, the Legislature and "the good people of Arizona" for working to pass the holiday.

The next day, in a prepared statement originating at the Martin Luther King, Jr. Center for Non-Violent Social Change, Mrs. King again praised Arizona state lawmakers for approving the holiday in her husband's honor. Part of her statement read,

> I'm delighted that the Arizona State Legislature has enacted legislation reinstating the Columbus Day holiday and establishing a separate, independent Martin Luther King, Jr. holiday.
>
> I commend Governor Mofford, the members of the state Legislature and all of the concerned citizens who have demonstrated such impressive leadership in this effort.

Regrettably, Mrs. King's remarks of commendation were countered by harsh criticism from Mecham within the same 24-hour period. *The Phoenix Gazette* quoted impeached former Governor Mecham thusly,

> You can't let it heal (referring to the King holiday controversy). There's a festering sore out there. People are mad as hell, quite frankly. The only way to let it heal is let the people vote on it.

In the same conversation with reporters, Governor Mecham announced,

> We've already got a good-sized organization throughout the state, a campaign organization, the Mecham Militia.

That's right! This time around, Second Lieutenant Julian Sanders would have to step aside and allow Major Mecham to rally the troops to get this new referendum drive moving into high gear. There would be an election on Arizona's Martin Luther King, Jr. Day, come hell or high water! Thanks to Mecham, his "Mecham Militia" targeting Martin would be headquartered out of his gubernatorial campaign headquarters in Glendale.

And you could bet your bottom dollar that the same volunteers working feverishly to restore their leader back to the statehouse would double-up to insure that another "M" made it on the general election ballot—the Martin Luther King, Jr. holiday.

Dr. King's widow was not the only outsider commenting on the action of the Arizona State Legislature. Within a day of the signing, all the way from the nation's Capitol, Louisiana State Representative and former Ku Klux Klan leader who nearly won election as governor of the Bayou State, David Duke, supported the efforts of Mecham's planned petition drive. His argument was that Arizona voters and the Americans at-large would defeat a state and national holiday, respectively, honoring King if that got the opportunity. Casting shadows upon the federal observance of King Day, Duke stated,

> I think it is ironic we would have a national holiday for someone whose record is so bad they have to hide it…and yet we don't have a national holiday for George Washington.

Although Arizona once again had an official Martin Luther King, Jr. state holiday (yet to be celebrated), the action of the legislators appeared to awake a sleeping giant of opposition to the King Day. Moreover, with Mecham leading the charge, his solid corps of loyal supporters could be counted upon to take to the streets armed with petitions and pens to guarantee that Arizona voters would make the final decision on King Day. To exasperate matters, the anti-King camp linked the alleged attempt by the state lawmakers to take the people's right to vote away from. You can guess that there was no shortage of verbal firepower being shot by opposing sides of this issue toward one another. On this holiday, there was no middle ground.

The "great divide" had widened by cataclysmic proportions. The second passage of King Day had divided the state. The vote tally in the House and Senate evidenced that legislators were divided over this issue. The Republicans and Democrats essentially remained divided over MLK. Polls indicated that there was a definite generation gap, which drove a wedge between the older anti-King Day crowd and the younger pro-King forces. Most of the affirmative support for the holiday came from the urban areas while the rural counties overwhelmingly lined with the negative block against King Day. The business community cautiously praised their victory for King Day, especially when Philadelphia Eagles owner, Norman Braman, expressed his commendation of Arizona legislators for passing the King bill to remove its absence as a reason for rescission of the already-awarded 1993 Super Bowl. Amazingly, however, a legislative act that was supposed to have settled a years-long battle to honor Martin King appeared to ignite a brush fire that would soon threaten the survival of a state that was entering the 1990s as a more progressive, promising growth state. Thusly, the words "Free at last" hardly seemed apropos for the victory that had just been produced by Governor Mofford's special session of the Legislature on King Day.

Thursday, May 17, 1990 provided a media spectacle with Mecham's name written all over it. The former governor traveled with his militia's chief lieutenants to the Secretary of State's Office just a few floors below the suite which he once occupied as governor. Their purpose was to launch his petition drive to put the new King Day on the November ballot. When they arrived, they were greeted by a couple of individuals they probably had not expected to run into. Arnie Zaler and Pat Quaranta had come to Secretary of State Jim Shumway's office to...Well, I really do not know why they had come, other than to create an exciting photo opportunity for the Arizona civil war over King. I mean, who would believe that they had come to try to convince Mecham not to launch his petition drive?

Whatever the case, I got a kick out of watching on television my former governor "blow his cool" before a dozen or so reporters covering the performance. As Arnie calmly engaged a brown-suit wearing Mecham into conversing about the holiday, Mecham's anger threshold was quickly crossed. The state's previous top leader raised his eyebrows, as well as his voice, and pointed his index finger at Arnie and shouted as he simultaneously pounded his fist on the counter, "If you weren't so damn stupid you would recognize that we've got a King Day, we've got a King Day, we've got a King Day!" Within a moment or two, Mecham turned his ire toward Quaranta and said, "I'm just trying to pound some sense into his stupid head," in response to his supporters urging their irate leader to calm down. Without a doubt, that scene was truly Mecham vintage at its best, or should I say *worst*?

After it was all said and done, Mecham's newly formed Restore the People's Right to Vote on the Holiday Committee officially filed the necessary papers to gather signatures to place King Day II on the ballot alongside King Day I. The "Mecham Militia" had until August 14, 1990 to collect 43,350 signatures of registered voters, the exact same number his disciple, Julian Sanders, aided by Pat Quaranta, had been required to gather. In addition, Mecham boasted of having access to a thousand volunteers who would help him fulfill his mission of heading a successful referendum petition drive. And just for the record's sake, the former governor was not the actual chair of the petition drive. Ms. Brenda High, a short, middle-aged blondish-brunette lady who embarrassingly tried to calm her leader down in the Secretary of State's Office that day, served as the official head of the petition drive, with the abridged name—Restore Our Vote Committee.

Meanwhile, Attorney General Bob Corbin who was no stranger to offering informal legal opinions on Arizona's MLK holiday, declared that if Mecham's army garnered enough signatures to place the 1990 King Day legislation on the ballot, then *both* MLK Day bills—the King-Columbus Day swap and the free-standing King Day—would have to be placed on the November ballot and decided by voters. So, the two holidays, pushed for by the business community to secure a King-Day guarantee for the Super Bowl and to reclaim tourism dollars without going to the people for a vote, would most likely have to be settled at the ballot box anyway.

Zaler, joined by Quaranta, who was working hard to prove his genuine support for Martin's Day and other King Day groups, planned to rise to the challenge and win a Martin Luther King, Jr. Day in the November election. At the same time, Bill Shover immediately restarted the engine of the MLK Better America Committee that had been turned off, while the Legislature drove the holiday through the rough road of partisan and somewhat prejudiced politics to penultimate victory. Even though the King Day proponents publicly remarked that the Mechamites might not be able to get enough valid signatures, since their drive was beginning amidst the scorching late Arizona spring and would hike its way through the average 100° sun-burning days of June, July and part of August, behind the scenes they knew that this holiday issue would face a showdown on election day, the first Tuesday in November. To complicate matters more, King Day advocates would have to dodge bullets aimed at, not one, but two MLK holiday propositions. And to think, all this commotion erupted almost four years to the day former Governor Babbitt declared Arizona's first King Day from the pulpit of the First Institutional Baptist Church.

Speaking of Babbitt, he and his Republican co-chair of the MLK Better America Committee faced the challenge of spearheading a bipartisan coalition that would accomplish what no other state in the Union had dared to try—win a Martin Luther King, Jr. holiday by a vote of the people. There could be no more ultimate test of their beloved state than to find out where its voting citizens stood on the human symbol of civil rights in America. With the Super Bowl supposedly a done deal, regardless of Arizona's handling of King's Day, the business-led campaign to secure a paid state King holiday by the will of the people, hopefully would be based on a sincere belief that honoring King was "the right thing to do," and nothing else.

Within a few weeks after the signing of Arizona's King Day II and the launching of Mecham's referendum petition drive, both opposing sides went underground. The pro-King group spent its time mapping out a winnable strategy. The anti-King Day element commissioned its followers to disperse in the community and get the needed signatures by the deadline.

For a while, the Phoenix Suns' initial success in the NBA playoffs through the end of May, gave Arizonans something positive to cheer about in light of the MLK mess. Governor Mofford was so caught up in the frenzy of Phoenix Suns mania that she suggested out loud that Suns' stars Kevin Johnson and Tom Chambers, a Black and a White, ought to become the King holiday campaign's poster boys. Even though that idea never fully realized, the Phoenix Suns organization would play a vital role in the MLK Better America strategy.

According to *Republic* political columnist, Keven Willey, a closed-door meeting called by Mofford and Shover began to bring together key leaders and groups who shared the common goal of a King Day victory. Along with Babbitt and Rhodes, the business community was well represented as well as local civil rights leaders including Gene Blue and Bob Kravitz. Then, there were the "ethnic types", according to Willey's designation, which included Quaranta and Zaler. A new invitee to sit down with the big boys and the governor was none other than my FIBC member who had trekked to the Orlando NFL owners meeting to urge a Super Bowl boycott—Art Mobley. With that line-up, it appeared that MLK Better America was aiming for a better way to get a majority of votes on November 6, 1990.

◇◇◇◇◇◇

In many ways, Arizona goes into hibernation during the summer months, especially in the arena of statewide politics. The Legislature adjourns. Arizonans who can afford it take extended vacations. Neither of the Valley's professional basketball and football teams make daily headlines. Those of us who cannot afford to leave town, seek relief in refrigerated residences and workplaces every day. Fighting for the King Day in Arizona was no different. Only absolutely necessary politicking takes place, except in an election year, which places the primary state elections in the second week in September.

Summer 1990 had nearly a half dozen Republicans running for governor, including Mecham, Symington and Sam Steiger, Mecham's former top aide. Terry Goddard pressed forward virtually unopposed on the Democratic side. And then, there were the anti-King Day petitioners hitting the public events surrounding the Fourth of July and any other outdoor activity that brought Arizonans together. The East Valley, with its heavy concentration of conservatives, Sun City and Sun City West with its 55 and older King Day-opposition retirees, and the rural areas throughout the state became the hunting ground for referendum signatures. Surprisingly, unlike the nearly daily press conferences called by Sanders when he co-led the first petition drive, Mecham and the Restore Our Vote Committee stayed out of the news while they went about doing what they had formed to do.

Things changed when August began. With two weeks left before the "Mecham Militia" was to file its signatures, Senator McCain had staged a political coup by garnering one signature in support of Arizona's MLK Day. Former President Ronald Reagan wrote a formal statement in support of Arizona's King holiday. McCain's close ties to "the great communicator" reaped a hopefully big dividend for the day honoring King, which Reagan had signed into federal law in 1983. Quite naturally, the leader of the anti-King Day movement did not take too kindly to a former president sticking his nose in Arizona's business. Ironically, Mecham's criticism of President Reagan seemed a bit inconsistent since his 1986 campaign tabloid featured a full-color photograph of Reagan meeting with Mecham, and receiving his endorsement for his candidacy for Arizona's governorship. And why should Mecham care? Unofficial leaks indicated that the King Day foe had amassed 50,000 signatures with fourteen days to go before the deadline.

With the former president adding his John Doe to the pro-King Day element, the question was raised whether or not the sitting president, George H. W. Bush, would say a word or two in way of endorsement of Arizona's King Day drive. Political wisdom mused that he would not dare.

The *New York Times* ran a quarter-page article on Arizona's ex-governor's repeat run for political office and his drive against the state's Martin Luther King, Jr. holiday. In writing a major portion of the article on the controversy Mecham had created by rescinding the King holiday, the writer of the "Special to The New York Times", Dirk Johnson, quoted me under the paragraph caption "A Bigot, Pure and Simple",

If the Martin Luther King holiday is defeated, it will say to black Arizonans and the entire country that Evan Mecham reflects a larger part of society that we have dared to acknowledge....Evan Mecham is a bigot, pure and simple.

The day before the August 14, 1990 deadline for the referendum petition signatures, the "Mecham Militia" ceremoniously carted boxes of their signed petitions to the Secretary of State's Office, at least, temporarily suspending King Day II with 71,055 signatures they claimed were in their boxes. Barring any massive disqualification of signatures, Arizona was going to be given the privilege of voting on *two* MLK propositions in three months. "Whoop-e-doo!" Furthermore, it was announced that the King-Columbus Day exchange bill would be designated Proposition 301, while the 1990 King Day law would be numbered Proposition 302.

On that same day by design, Bruce Babbitt, backed by a host of King Day advocates from nearly every segment of public life, announced MLK Better America's campaign strategy to push Proposition 302. Such a campaign carried a price tag of three-quarters of a million dollars, which would come from the business community. The first big pledges lined up the very next day, namely, the Phoenix Suns and Phoenix Cardinals, both of which had vested financial interests in Arizona winning the holiday at the polls.

As a show of heavy support from every spectrum of Arizona, numerous organizations paid to file statements endorsing the King Day with the Secretary of State's Office to be printed in the publicity pamphlet explaining the propositions submitted to the electors for the general election. Eleven individuals and organizations had their *"ARGUMENT" FOR PROPOSITION 302* endorsements printed in the pamphlet which was mailed to every Arizona voter. The first endorser was former President Ronald Reagan. Among other endorsers were Bidwell; Colangelo; Babbitt; Rhodes; Zaler; Sarah Suggs, state chairman of Arizona Young Republican League; David Radcliffe of the Phoenix & Valley of the Sun Convention & Visitors Bureau; Kravitz; Joel Breshin and Donald Eagle representing three Jewish-related organizations; Gene Blue; and Bishop Heistand.

The sole writer of an *ARGUMENT "AGAINST" PROPOSITION 302* was listed as Evan Mecham, Candidate for Governor. Allow me to provide you with excerpts of Mecham's statement.

I urge you to vote NO on both Proposition 302 and Proposition 301 relating to the establishment of a PAID Martin Luther King, Jr. Holiday.

Arizona already has a day honoring Dr. King....In 1987 I proclaimed this day to be on the third Sunday in January....

There are a few people in Arizona, and some powerful forces outside our state, who claim that 97% of the people in Arizona must pay the state workers (about 30% of the state), to take a day off work in order to honor Dr. King....

I urge all voters to stand firm against the threats and insults which are thrown at us by those who try to intimidate us to vote their way. Time is always on the side of truth and fairness....

Again, I urge you to vote NO on Proposition 302 and Proposition 301.

The reason I did not indicate the pro and con arguments listed for Proposition 301—the King/Columbus Day exchange—was that there was none. Period. Since the MLK Better America Committee had strategically selected to ignore Prop 301, I guess the opponents did too. After all, the polls consistently showed the opposition to Proposition 301 at around 70-75%. I and about 20% of the other voters found ourselves grossly outnumbered in desiring a King Day and wanting to delete Columbus Day. Mecham was the only individual officially mentioning Prop 301 in his diatribe against both King Day propositions.

That brings up a fundamental problem that both Propositions 301 and 302 presented to the would-be voters. Because both propositions called for a King Day, it was believed that some pro-King Day electors might become confused on which one to vote for. Experience had also shown that confused voters are more likely to vote no and be done with it. So, the debate heated up among political strategists, editorial boards, King Day supporters and the average Arizona voter on how the two King Day propositions should be pitched to potential supporters.

Should it be vote no on 301 and yes on 302? Should pro-King Day advocates be urged to vote yes on 301 and 302? What about anti-Columbus Day, pro-King Day voters? Did MLK Better America Committee not want any of their supporters to vote yes on 301? Or how about the fiscally conservative pro-King supporters who did not want an additional paid state holiday, but also desired to keep Columbus Day? And then there were the diehard King holiday advocates who wanted to know if it was all right to vote yes on both propositions.

While the various pro-King Day advocates were trying to decide the best strategy for a victory, Mecham and a guy by the name of Bob Rose, a rotund, self-employed Scottsdale accountant shadowed by his son, Tim, formed the No-No Committee, which made it easy for King Day opponents to cast their double negative vote. Secretary of State Shumway provided their loosely-knit but beehive active committee with the news they wanted to hear. On September 6, it was confirmed that King Day opponents had submitted a total of 57,979 valid signatures, which were more than enough to put the freestanding MLK Day proposition on the ballot. This was a significant victory for the impeached governor. I am sure it affirmed his belief that he was still a force to be reckoned with in Arizona politics. Not only that, by gathering over 71,000 names of anti-King holiday troopers in the heat of the summer, without the comradery of the Italian-American community, Mecham's credibility rose as an effective, but negative influence on Arizona's effort to be recognized as a progressive state.

Still a self-exiled supporter of the long-running struggle to get King his day in my adopted home state, I dared to make some skybox analyses of the major campaign that had begun in late August. Bill Cheshire, at one of our nearly monthly lunches, when either of us hosted the other to chew the fat over Arizona politics, particularly MLK, abortion, conservative leanings, liberal politics and theology, had invited me to write a guest editorial on any subject of my choosing and submit it to be run in the *Republic*. I took him up on it the second week in September, as I observed the maneuvers of the MLK Better America Committee, run behind the scenes, by the Phoenix 40 crowd. In my mind, I knew their intentions were good in the way they chose to go after their goal. But my heart kept telling me that they had better revise some of their campaign strategy, if they expected to win in November.

Consequently, on September 13, 1990, seven days after Proposition 302 became a definite fixture on the general election ballot, I wrote a guest column for Arizona's largest newspaper read statewide. My three-page statement was originally titled "ARIZONA'S KING HOLIDAY IS DOOMED UNLESS…" Once I submitted it to the editor of the editorial pages, he kindly did minor editing which transformed my negative title into a positive heading which read, "What King holiday supporters must do to win the election." Cheshire also honored my right to privacy as to how I was planning to vote on the two propositions by deleting my last underlined sentence in my draft of the column I sent to him for publication. In no uncertain terms, I had declared which proposition would receive my vote. And from hindsight, I am glad he took that liberty.

In the following lines, you can read my Guest Column printed in *The Arizona Republic* on Wednesday, September 19, 1990.

> As immediate past general chairperson of Arizonans for a Martin Luther King, Jr. State Holiday Inc., which began fighting for the Holiday shortly after Gov.-elect Evan Mecham vowed to keep his campaign promise to rescind it, watching the King holiday debate from the sidelines is both frustrating and frightening.
>
> Arizona's protracted struggle over honoring this nation's most prominent symbol of our commitment to civil rights will come to a head in the Nov. 6 General Election, perhaps to the relief of most of us who call Arizona home.
>
> Moreover, the success of holiday opponents in gathering more than enough signatures to challenge the Legislature's reinstatement of Columbus Day and the addition of a King holiday, even in the midst of a record-breaking 122-degree summer, causes just concern. It is my visceral feeling that the MLK Better America Committee and UNITY, up to this point, have been "preaching to the choir."
>
> My analysis leads me to believe that the King holiday is doomed unless holiday advocates do the following.
>
> • Reach the average White Anglo-Saxon "blue-collar worker" and/or spouse. They are suspicious of the "Big Business" push for the King holiday and tend to vote against what business advocates. The threat of losing the 1993 Super Bowl suggests to them that the business establishment's enthusiastic and relatively recent support of the King holiday has more to do with "bucks" than "blacks."
>
> • Enlist the involvement of religious leaders on the basis that Dr. King's dream for America was not only an American dream, but a biblical vision. Without a doubt, Dr. King, a Baptist preacher, developed his inspiration and zeal for equal justice and opportunity from Old and New Testament writings. The Bible evidenced for Dr. King the brotherhood

and sisterhood of the human family and God's continuous involvement in the holistic liberation of humankind. It also influenced his interpretation of the Declaration of Independence, the Constitution of the United States and the Pledge of Allegiance as they relate to race relations. Preachers, pastors, priests, rabbis, imams and other religious leaders and laypersons must spread the word that voting for the holiday is the morally right thing to do.

- Build the case among Arizona's large pro-life constituency that Dr. King's philosophy would require him, if he were alive, to support the human rights of unborn children. Even as Dr. King stood boldly for the rights of black Americans and other oppressed minorities, so I believe he would champion the rights of unborn children, who were an integral part of his American dream.

- Get the Arizona Republican Party to pass a resolution supporting the King holiday. Since the Legislature rejected the George Washington/Abraham Lincoln holiday combination, it is no longer an option, and the Republican Party should urge its members to vote for the King holiday for the good of Arizona. Presidents Ronald Reagan and George Bush both support the King holiday.

- Involve Arizona's largest minority—Hispanics—and its leaders in the King holiday effort. The advances achieved by Dr. King's movement opened the door for Hispanics. Prior to the civil rights revolution, they also were discriminated against because of color. The King holiday is as much a "brown" holiday as it is "black" one.

- Urge every eligible Arizonan 30 and younger to register and vote for the King holiday. If Arizona is not to "shift into reverse" as it relates to the advances in racial harmony made since the 1960's, the young generation must exert progressive leadership.

- Allow Proposition 301, establishing the King holiday on the third Monday in January and making Columbus Day an unpaid holiday, a viable option. As it stands, Proposition

302 adds an additional paid holiday honoring Dr. King. This is not acceptable to many Arizonans, especially in a time of budget deficits, rising inflation and the threat of war in the Middle East. Rather than putting all of the eggs in one basket, supporters of the holiday ought to promote Proposition 301 as an alternative for fiscal conservatives and others who oppose an additional paid state holiday. Furthermore, Proposition 301 is more consistent with Dr. King's philosophy in that it shows respect for the original citizens of this land—Native Americans—who lived here long before Columbus.

My vote in November will be a vote of conscience consistent with the philosophy and principles of Dr. King, whom Life magazine recently named one of the most influential Americans of the 20th Century.

I do not know how the broader public received my analysis of what it would take to win the historic MLK election, but I did get a comment from the MLK Better America Committee chairman. My memory fails me as to where it was, but shortly after my column was printed, I ran into Terry Hudgins, a lobbyist for Arizona Public Service, and Steve Roman, an upward mobile officer of Valley National Bank. These two gentlemen served as the chairman and vice-chairman, respectively, of the MLK Better America Committee, running the day-to-day operation of the campaign. Their respective employer's willingly loaned them to the cause. To say the least, both of these men were talented, committed, well-networked professionals who knew how to get things done and please their CEOs at the same time. I think I am correct in categorizing Hudgins and Roman as advanced yuppies who were involved in upper level corporate management. However, as it related to their awareness of issues affecting the African-American community, both nationally and locally, I doubt whether their grades could have been above average. And yet, history would record them as the player-coaches of MLK Better America's team efforts to honor the 20th century's most prominent Black man.

One of the two men whom I had met for the first time to my recollection remarked to me something like, "We saw your article in the paper.... We didn't have any idea that you were going to write such an article." The inference was that I should have cleared what I had to say with them before I sent the article to the *Republic*. Of course, anyone reading this book or who knows me, can imagine my unspoken response to such a subtle suggestion that I need to clear any comments I had on the King campaign *with them*. Other than that, our conversation revolved around small talk about the campaign and prospects for victory. I left that encounter and commented to some veteran King holiday workers, "I guess those guys didn't think I had sense enough to write an intelligent analysis of what it would take to win the holiday....And to think that they were upset because I hadn't got their permission before I wrote it and sent it to the *Republic.*"

Either at that meeting, my path crossed with Bill Shover who let me know that he had read my column. He did not seem upset about it, as much as I think he was surprised it made it to the papers without his prior knowledge. After all, Bill was the executive in the Phoenix Newspapers, Inc. who had rallied his business buddies to put a full court press on the governor and Legislature, and who was calling the shots in organizing his holiday coalition. But, Bill's reaction to my column did not bother me because the two of us had worked together and both of us press forward when we get our minds set on what needs to be done.

As it relates to the MLK Better America Committee, Babbitt and Rhodes actually served as "honorary chairs." Rhodes was enjoying semi-retirement after serving in the U.S. Congress for years. Babbitt was working for a corporate law firm and pressing environmental and common issues between Mexico and the United States. Neither of the two well-respected politicians had, or maybe took the time, to get involved on a daily basis.

Speaking of a former governor, Evan Mecham lost in the September primary in his efforts to make a sixth run for governor in the general election.

Shover's committee kicked off its MLK campaign on September 14, 1990. The consulting team of DeGraw and Robb would map out the strategy of their campaign. Not being a participant in MLK Better America, I could only observe their activities from the television and newspapers, and get what inside information I could from a few of my former co-workers with ARIZONANS FOR A MARTIN LUTHER KING, JR. STATE HOLIDAY, like Paul Eppinger, Gene Blue, and occasionally, Pastor Barnwell. But, the fact of the matter was that Pastor Barnwell was not an "insider" in MLK Better America, even though he was heading the original King Day grassroots coalition. Arnie would call from time to time. However, he too was an outsider, and considered by some on the MLK Better America Committee as a pain in the posterior.

Jerry Colangelo spearheaded the fund-raising committee for the 1990 campaign. He was highly successful at getting his corporate executive colleagues to contribute big bucks to winning the election. On occasions, the evening news or morning newspaper carried stories of organizations like the Phoenix Cardinals, KTVK-Channel 3, U.S. West and the Phoenix Suns players giving up chunks of money in the tens of thousands to the King campaign. Before September was over, Arizona Public Service, Hudgins' employer, spent several grand on a full-page advertisement in both the *Republic* and *Gazette*, featuring a handsome black and white drawing of Dr. King with the words vertically lined up beneath his image reading "Honor Civil Rights, Help Arizona." In smaller block letters across from the larger word Arizona, the ad read "Vote YES on 302 Nov. 6."

My initial overreacting to the ad was that it would have been perfect if the paper could have left the tiny-print letters at the bottom of the ad which read, "Paid for by Arizona Public Service Company." Although the law required such identification of who paid for the political ad, I felt that the donor of that ad being a big business (and a utilities company at that, which raises rates regularly) would further concretize the average Arizona voter that this holiday was really about dollars more than Dr. King.

As I indicated before, early in August the MLK Better America consultants had convinced their bosses that they should push Proposition 302 and basically ignore Proposition 301. This made Zaler and UNITY very happy since Quaranta was still being courted by Arnie to recruit all his Columbus Day activists to become just as energetic in pushing Proposition 302 as they were in killing the first legislatively approved King Day. In addition, UNITY, joined by a new group led by Vic Washington, who also led the Retired NFL Players Association-Phoenix Chapter, and who formed a group called "MLK/It's The Right Thing To Do" Committee, would provide Shover's coalition with the grassroots links that they desperately needed to diffuse, at least, some of their "fat cats" image.

That same month of September, MLK Better America produced a one-page "Fact Sheet" in English and Spanish entitled "Yes on 302." It explained basic information about Proposition 302, (1) what that proposition would do; (2) what the MLK/Civil Rights Day meant; (3) how not having the holiday had affected Arizona economics, particularly in the tourism industry and the possible forfeiture of the 1993 Super Bowl; (4)

how much the additional holiday would actually cost; and (5) how many nations, states and Arizona cities celebrated a King holiday.

One issue that the 1990 MLK campaigners were clearly told to avoid was the mention of the word *racism*. That was a definite "no, no." The mere suggestion that racism was involved in the often bitter King holiday fight at the State Capitol, which had been taken to the streets, was almost equated to using profanity. MLK Better America volunteers were informed to delete the "R-word" from any discussion about honoring Dr. Martin Luther King, Jr. with his day. No holiday proponent was to confront the opposition. The strategy was to "soft sell" that Black man's holiday. "Don't ruffle any feathers, especially from emissaries of the No-No Committee," MLK supporters were told, in so many words.

Major Lee Hockman in his history of the state's two-decade-long effort to enact the King Day and an analysis of Phoenix Newspapers, Inc. coverage of the struggle, summarized the three messages that Robb and DeGraw developed for the campaign thusly,

> 1) Voting for the King holiday was the most ethical choice because it demonstrated a concern for civil rights. 2) The holiday was important to the state for economic reasons, if stated positively. 3) By voting for Prop. 302, Arizonans would honor civil rights and help Arizona by overcoming the perception that the state was racist and intolerant.

The campaign committee directed by Hudgins and Roman would take several steps to get out their "Honor Civil Rights, Help Arizona— Vote Yes on 302" message. Included to be done were, direct mailing to hundreds of thousands of Arizonans, radio and television ads and public service announcements, in-house solicitations of support by holiday-friendly companies, billboards and phone banks to reach registered voters all over the state. There was even a religious packet devised so Arizona clergy could preach to the pews about passing the King holiday.

The strategy appeared to be working. By October, several polls, conducted among the state's registered voters, showed that a slim majority favored a King Day that did not eliminate Columbus Day. Not surprisingly, Proposition 301 did not get the support of as much as 20% of the voting public, according to early October polling. Anyway, Columbus Day 1990 was just around the corner, so it would not have been kosher to show disrespect for the alleged discoverer of America by voicing support to a pollster for a law banning a paid state holiday honoring him. Now, would it?

With the annual Columbus Day fever filling the air around Phoenix, especially in the year that the 1989 Legislature had voted it *not* to be on a Monday, almost all of the King Day supporting groups joined hands with their Italian-American brothers and sisters to celebrate Captain Christopher for his lucky find. On October 5th, the day before Phoenix's Saturday before the federal observance of Columbus Day Parade, Zaler opened a press conference and introduced his ally, Pat, who publicly endorsed both Columbus Day and King Day. This was a strategic boost that King Day supporters needed. Hopefully, Quaranta's endorsement would win fence-straddling King Day voters and even a few who had decided to vote against Dr. King's day. Of course, UNITY signs, banners, T-shirts, buttons, bumper stickers and literature were nearly omnipresent. Zaler urged everyone, who wanted to see Proposition 302 win, to join UNITY and Quaranta at the big Columbus Day parade, downtown, the very next day.

Watching from afar on my television, I saw several of my colleagues in the ministry, gleefully parading down Central Avenue shouting praises to you-know-who. I just shook my head and said, "Lord, have mercy." But upset, I was not. I knew that my thoughts on Columbus Day were in a minority. I also knew that the only way King Day could be victorious at the polls, was that Columbus Day would have to win too.

Just before the parade, it had been reported that nearly two dozen Valley mayors had come out in support of Proposition 302, as a result of some heavy lobbying by Arnie and UNITY. Phoenix Mayor Paul Johnson rode in the procession, as did Phoenix Suns president, Jerry Colangelo, who served as grand marshal of the parade.

It is interesting to note that Native Americans all over Arizona celebrated that same weekend by hosting a festive Pow-wow, which is a gathering of North American Indians, at the Salt River-Pima Maricopa Indian community. The *Republic* reported the following comments from Native Americans who were asked about the Columbus Day fanfare going on in Phoenix. One Kiowa Indian from Oklahoma stated, "We found him. He didn't find us....We could care less if Columbus Day came and went. We are celebrating our heritage today." A Navajo registrar who explained why the Navajo Nation does not observe Columbus Day as a federal holiday commented, "We don't recognize Columbus Day. We have a tribal holiday instead, and we have the Martin Luther King Day."

◇◇◇◇◇◇

Even though MLK Better America removed "racism" from the vocabulary of its volunteers during the 1990 campaign, others were talking about it in light of several incidents and issues that Arizona and the nation were facing that fall. Continuous claims of racism in every segment of society would not go away by people who got unequal treatment, apparently because of their color. Arizona had dealt with Proposition 106, which outlawed speaking any language other than English on official state governmental business. Hate crimes were on the rise and even the office of Pastor Eppinger of the First Baptist Church had been ransacked. Congress was debating the Civil Rights Act of 1990 that would restore some of the corrective affirmative action laws overturned by a Reagan-Bush conservative Supreme Court. And, then, there was the charge of racism that some believed had catapulted Arizona in the spotlight of the world for demanding a public vote on, not one, but two holiday propositions honoring Martin Luther King, Jr.

Phoenix's local NBC affiliate, Channel 12-KPNX, decided to host an open public forum on racism in Arizona. The panelists included Rabbi Kravitz; Tommy L. Espinoza; Jack Pfister; Lisa Loo, who was chair of the Arizona Asian American Association; then-KPNX anchorwoman Linda Alvarez; Assistant Chief of Police Harold Hurtt; an African-American community leader, Bill Shover; and me. Channel 12's long-time anchor, Kent Dana, moderated the lively discussion.

With so many panelists and limited time allotted for questions and statements from the floor, none of us had a whole lot to say about the hot topic, and maybe that was to our advantage. Again, reminding myself that I was out of the King Day fray, I promised myself that I would deal with racism in general, and not focus on King Day. The forum took place in the North High School auditorium, which faces Phoenix's own version of the Berlin Wall. The nine-foot high block wall on the north side of Thomas Road barricades the Phoenix Country Club home division from the lower income residents who live to the south of Thomas. Mostly Hispanics, lower income and elderly Anglos and a few Blacks live right around North High. Thus, it was not a shock that a majority of those who came to the forum consisted of people of color who had been affected directly by racial prejudice in Arizona.

Once the panelists made our intermittent remarks, the people began to line up at the floor microphones to sound off. That is when the fireworks began. The mention of the death of Ric Rankins, a Black man who died after being subdued by two Smitty's Grocery Store employees as he left their store looking suspicious, raised the tension in the room. People of all colors, but especially African-Americans and Hispanics, spoke angrily about how Whites had discriminated against them in Arizona. Somehow, the King holiday became the target of verbal arrows and Dana directed the audience to me for my comments. I remember saying, "If we back the King holiday overwhelmingly and return to business as usual, we might as well not have a King holiday."

At that point, someone (not me) brought up what they thought was the business community's "hypocritical" leadership in the King Day campaign. The founder of MLK Better America was sitting right next to me and had begun to turn a very fiery red as Bill Shover can do. The criticisms were beginning to get "hot and heavy" when Shover turned to me and said under his breath in indignation, "There wouldn't be a King holiday if it wasn't for the business community." I was caught a little off guard by the way Bill said what he said to me; but, in essence, he was telling the truth.

Speaking of the business community, I was highly impressed by some comments that Jack Pfister, then general manager of the Salt River Project, to whom I have been sending a monthly check for almost forty years now to pay my electric bills. Pfister cited statistics showing that the work force in America, by the first two decades of the 21st century, would be made up of minorities. (I prefer to use the term *people of color* because I do not consider myself a minority in view of the fact that 82% of the world population is not White.) He continued, "It will work to the advantage of corporate America to begin now in investing in recruiting and training minorities who would be making up the majority of America's work force in the future."

Now, that was a smart White man who did not think like most corporate executives! Where in the world did he come from? I was so impressed that I quoted Pfister in my closing arguments attempting to answer the rhetorical question of one of Dr. King's later books, *Where Do We Go From Here?* Pfister, who took an early retirement from Salt River Project, a few months later, would play a larger role in Arizona's King holiday struggle, as well as combating racism by building harmony among people of color residing in Arizona.

On Friday, October 12, 1990, my old coalition raised its head to show that it still existed as the countdown toward November 6 continued. ARIZONANS FOR A MARTIN LUTHER KING, JR. STATE HOLIDAY sponsored a musical that evening featuring several African-American church choirs, local gospel groups and soloists and the South Mountain High School Gospel Choir. The event held at Taylor Memorial Temple gave Black churches and their members a way to plug into the Proposition 302 campaign in a way that was not foreign to them.

On the other side of the Valley, the students of predominantly Anglo Saguaro High School announced that their three year-old project to collect $300,000 worth of pennies to place a permanent memorial to Dr. King's 1963 "I Have a Dream" speech at the Lincoln Memorial in Washington had inched forward. Their instructor, John Calvin, had been in touch with me when the idea first came up and I wholeheartedly endorsed his students' projects before I resigned as chair of ARIZONANS FOR A MARTIN LUTHER KING, JR. STATE HOLIDAY. Even though he and his students had run into a lot of red tape, while lobbying governmental officials and members of Arizona's Congressional delegation, it was a good promotion for the King Day campaign. Once again, the Saguaro students' involvement in a workshop to preserve MLK's dream illustrated that this was not a "Blacks only" issue.

The middle of October would witness King Day supporters pull another almost magical rabbit out of their hat. Arizona's grand ole man of the Republican Party, former U.S. Senator Barry Goldwater, publicly endorsed Proposition 302. That was a remarkable achievement. Everyone knew that there was no love lost by Goldwater for King. Senator Goldwater was "Mr. Conservative" when he served Arizona and especially when he ran as the Republican candidate for president in 1984. His voting record on America's modern Civil Rights Acts while he was in Congress was awful. At 81, it was hard to believe that he would bolt from the ranks of most of his generation of voters and line up with the much younger and liberal King Day supporters. No doubt, his Republican colleague and friend just seven years his junior, former Congressman Rhodes who co-chaired MLK Better America, was instrumental in wooing Goldwater's support.

The Arizona Republic reported the senator as stating,

> "Dr. King and I were not friends. We had differences of opinion, which were strongly held and sometimes strongly expressed. Even so, the civil-rights movement, which could have been accompanied by violence, was not. Mainly because of Dr. King's insistence on non-violence."

The hope was that Goldwater's endorsement would increase the number of Republicans and older Arizona voters whose polls had shown were more likely to vote *and* to vote *no* on both King Day ballot propositions.

With less than a month to go before the election, the media blitz shifted in high gear. Arizonans had to see and hear that voting for Proposition 302 was "the right thing to do." With the TV and radio spots came the immediate need for big business pledges to transform those monetary promises into cold, hard cash to pay the high price of commercial time during an election year. Thank goodness it was not a presidential election year, or else the MLK Better America folks would have needed a couple of hundred thousand more dollars. The attractive logo the coalition had chosen could be seen all over the Valley, along with UNITY paraphernalia. Arnie may not have had but a fraction of the money to campaign with, compared to MLK Better America, but he had the zeal to translate his enthusiasm for King Day into highly visible grassroots support.

And how was the No-No Committee being financed? Basically, by a few dollars here and there from anti-King Day volunteers and Mecham loyalists. The crude commercials urging Arizona voters to vote down both King Day propositions could be seen at sporadic times on the local stations. Even though they were aired at virtually no out-of-pocket expense to their campaign coffers, due to the equal time provision for political ads, I am sure the stations could select at which time slots the "freebies" opposing King Day would be shown. Being basically an evening and night news watcher, I only caught a glimpse of the King Day opponents' ad, once or twice.

To the liking of the pro-King Day team, the NFL kept almost conspicuously quiet about their unofficial position that the Super Bowl XXVII would be pulled, if Arizona did not approve a King Day in the election about three weeks away. Everybody knew that Bidwell had been a key figure in lobbying the Legislature to approve the holiday and was in close contact with Shover and MLK Better America. When the Arizona media contacted NFL Commissioner Tagliabue, for comments, he would always refer them back to Bidwell and Arizona leaders who were leading the campaign. He deliberately stayed out of the personal business of Arizona on MLK and helped to advise NFL owners to keep their mouths shut as November sixth neared, in spite of the boycott hint by the owner of the Philadelphia Eagles.

As I mentioned earlier, one of the issues facing the nation was the political debate over passage of the 1990 Civil Rights Act. That is why I was incensed when it was reported that the Honorable John McCain, who had become a King Day convert, after first voting against the federal MLK Day in 1983 and initially shying away from getting involved in the state debate over King Day in 1987, voted *against* the 1990 Civil Rights Act, which passed Congress that October. I was equally disturbed with the *Republic,* which was meritorious in its support for a King Day in Arizona, after being somewhat wishy-washy when King Day was first introduced in Washington by the Congress, when Bill Cheshire and the editorial board published an editorial opposing the new civil rights legislation.

Both McCain and Cheshire received essentially the same letter from me, which "suggested that (their) support of Arizona's Martin Luther King, Jr. state holiday (had) more to do with symbols than substance." In my October 23, 1990 letter to the two, respectively, I raised the question, "Are you so quick to forget that 'informal hiring quotas' still exist within government, corporations, small business and education?" My wrath did not stop there. I reminded them that institutional racism was alive and well in these United States of America and that the Civil Rights Act of 1990 would move toward eradicating the remnants of pre-MLK discrimination. In a parting shot to the two King Day advocates, I wrote, "Rest assured, however, it appears that you and President Bush are reading one another's notes."

If someone ever tells you that editors and politicians do not read their mail, do not believe it. Cheshire had told me that he read all of the letters to the editor that he received. Of course, members of the Congress who receive thousands of letters each week have to be selective in which letters actually cross their desks in order for them to read them. Moreover, letters dealing with certain topics and issues, as well as the sources of various letters, play a role in which letters are seen in black and white by the addressee.

I said that to say I discovered that Senator McCain received my letter questioning his commitment to civil rights and Arizona's King Day. I was out of the office when my secretary informed me that the *senator himself* had called me from Washington and was pretty upset about what I had suggested in my letter. (McCain is known for having a "short fuse.") Since he could not get me on the telephone (for which I was somewhat relieved), he dictated a two-page response that must have melted the tape on the Dictaphone because it was so hot. In essence, his message was something like "to think you had the nerve to question my commitment to civil rights and the King holiday."

Later on I discovered from his Black aide, Karl Gentles, who was a relatively new member of my congregation, that the senator was pretty bent out of shape by my letter. Karl told me he tried to explain what I was saying about his apparent inconsistencies on the two related issues, but he could not get through the smoke, so to speak. In addition, I was not the only one who was critical of Senator McCain's negative vote on that year's Civil Rights Act. Many others from the nation's noted civil rights and women's rights groups had had harsh words for McCain and his colleagues who turned thumbs down on the legislation. Gentles even told me that he had tried to get his boss to support the 1990 Civil Rights Act, to no avail.

As far as my letter to Editor Cheshire, I cannot remember if he published it like he did most of my other letters. However, I think we discussed our differences over the new anti-discrimination law, at lunch in the Phoenix Country Club, which still remains as a symbol of flashbacks of the time when people of color got into those places only as low-level employees, rather than equal members.

Around that same time, the *USA TODAY* had interviewed me in a feature article they did on Arizona's King holiday ballot measures. It carried an attractive photograph of none other than Arnie and four of his youthful volunteers standing around a table full of campaign literature, buttons, and posters, and wearing UNITY T-shirts. The headline read, "King holiday gains Ariz. momentum", with a smaller headline worded, "But some say support is for wrong reasons." The article quoted many pro- and anti-holiday campaigners including Zaler, Mecham and me. As it related to me, here is how Bill Nichols summed up what I had to say.

> Rev. Warren Stewart, pastor of First Institutional Baptist Church, is upset by the "prostitution" of King's legacy to protect the Super Bowl and interests of wealthy whites.
>
> Some National Football League owners vow to move the Super Bowl from the area if a King Day is defeated—a threat Stewart says has energized Phoenix business barons who've opposed a King Day.
>
> "Across the board—white, black, brown—everybody says off the record that the only reason the holiday will probably win… is because of the Super Bowl. It's the right thing to do, yes, but for the wrong reasons," Stewart says.

I cannot quite put my hands on it, but I was *both* happy and sad that it looked like Arizona voters were going to approve a King Day. I was happy for the just honor King deserved for making Arizona a better place to live. I was sad because it had become such an unnecessary controversy, tarnished by "the almighty dollar." For my benefit if no one else's, I was able to put my thoughts in writing in a bulletin insert I wrote for the Sunday prior to the November sixth election. But among active supporters, I am sure I was very much a loner on the way I felt about what was going down in the name of my hero—Dr. Martin Luther King, Jr.

With Arizona scheduled to elect a governor from three candidates, namely, former Phoenix Mayor Terry Goddard on the Democratic ticket,; Valley land developer Fife Symington representing the GOP; and deposed Mecham cabinet member, Max Hawkins, running as an Independent; a lot of media attention focused on who would lead Arizona into a new era, leaving behind the gubernatorial shuffle board of the eighties. One ray of hope shined on the fact that the nominees for the two major parties both supported Proposition 302.

The stars of professional and college sports in Arizona began to put on a full court press for passage of Proposition 302. Names like Kevin Johnson; Cotton Fitzsimmons; and, of course, Colangelo of the Phoenix Suns; Michael Carbajal, Phoenix's own world champion boxer; and Bill Bidwell; Coach Joe Bugel; and the Phoenix Cardinals; as well as Victor Washington joined the team of pro-302 players. Not only did the Phoenix Suns organization fork over a hunk of cash for the cause, but the players provided a bonus of $25,000 themselves. As far as the big bucks, the Phoenix Cardinal organization donated tens of thousands of dollars to see that Arizona kept the Super Bowl via King Day. Not to be embarrassed by the Suns players, the Cardinal players led by Eric Hill and J.T. Smith, contributed in excess of fourteen grand.

The universities around the state made it their business to educate the voters on why they should vote "yes" on Proposition 302. Between the three presidents of NAU, ASU and UA, about 135,000 letters were sent out to alumni of those institutions. The community colleges in the two major metropolitan areas schooled their students on how they should vote on MLK Day. Even Arizona's "Kids Voting" sponsored by Arizona Public Service, distributed thousands of ballots for kindergartners through high school seniors to cast their votes for the major statewide political offices and several propositions. Coincidentally, on the front page of their ballot, where photos of Goddard, Symington and the two candidates for Superintendent of Public Instruction, Robert Miller, Republican, and C. Diane Bishop, Democrat, filled the top half of the page, was Proposition 302. Almost at the bottom of the back page in much smaller print was Proposition 301. Whatever you make of it, the intent of "Kids Voting" was two-fold: (1) to educate school children on the election process, and (2) to hopefully get the kids' parents out to the polls by seeing the interest level of their children in the 1990 election.

The Hispanic Get-Out-The-Vote Committee, chaired by then-Maricopa County supervisor and later U.S. Congressman who succeeded the Honorable Mo Udall, Ed Pastor, put out a partially bilingual election pamphlet recommending Arizona's largest population of people of color to vote Democratic and for Proposition 302. No mention was made of Prop 301 in the large-size pamphlet paid for by the Democratic Party of Arizona.

A giant step was taken by members of Arizona's Mormon community, of which Mecham and Sanders were members. LaMar Shelley chaired a group called Members of the Mormon Church for Martin Luther King, Jr./Civil Rights Day which distanced themselves from the adversarial antics of their former governor and brother in the faith by stressing passage of Proposition 302. Many of the Mormons for King Day had been embarrassed and falsely labeled, due to the plethora of bad publicity the distracting duo of Mecham and Sanders was bringing upon their beloved Church. With a heavy concentration of members of the Church of Jesus Christ of Latter-day Saints in the East Valley, perhaps this group of avowed Christian conservatives could win some of their younger members, at least, over to supporting Dr. King.

Speaking of religious leaders supporting Proposition 302, none other than the Reverend Dr. Richard Jackson, then-pastor of one of the twenty largest churches in the world, North Phoenix Baptist Church, joined a group of Valley clergy who held a press conference urging Arizona voters to say "Yes" to MLK Day. This was a near-miracle in public relations, because although Pastor Jackson was known worldwide for being an expert in local church evangelism by leading his congregation to a membership roll of over 20,000 persons at its height, he steered clear of public politicking, especially issues that could be considered "social," to say the least, controversial. So, Shover, who told me later that he got Jackson to attend the "religious leaders for Prop 302" press conference, proved he had some faith by arranging for the timely announcement from men (and women) of the cloth.

I was delighted to read a substantive letter to the editor of the *Arizona Republic* on Friday, November 2, 1990 from a woman I had marched and sang arm-in-arm with in Arizona's largest pro-life march in history in January of that same year. Dr. Carolyn F. Gerster did not endeavor to dilute her support for MLK Day by making a statement against abortion. She simply and eloquently stated the case why Arizonans should "go to the polls on Tuesday and reaffirm Dr. King's dream." Reading that letter in the state's largest newspaper made me feel that my previous efforts to make a logical connection between King's human rights philosophy and the right to life had not been in vain in winning some key pro-life leaders to the pro-King Day camp. I only wish I could be as successful in getting pro-King Day and human and civil rights advocates to see that clear connection as it relates to the human rights of the unborn "created equal under God."

By Sunday, November 4, 1990, MLK Better America pulled out all stops in winning support for Proposition 302. They ran a full-page ad in that Sunday's *Republic*. Their television and radio commercial could be seen and/or heard around the clock. The new badge of honor was to wear the Prop 302 button on one's chest. Arnie had creatively got his public relations people to combine the symbols of the MLK Better America campaign and many of his UNITY posters. Vic Washington and his "MLK/It's the Right Thing to Do" Committee joined forces with Pastor Barnwell's ARIZONANS FOR A MARTIN LUTHER KING, JR. STATE HOLIDAY to work the Black community in getting the most natural MLK holiday supporters out to vote. Every group was trying to make simple how to vote for the two King Day propositions on the ballot. Unfortunately, the pro-King groups did not have it as easy to get their message across as the No-No Committee did.

Arizona was on the brink of making history one way or another. The latest polls looked pretty promising. The fate of the King-Columbus Day swap law was almost sealed. It would lose by a landslide. On the other hand, the clean Columbus Day-restoring Martin Luther King, Jr./Civil Rights Day legislation, better known as Proposition 302, showed a slim majority among registered voters being polled by every known pollster in Arizona the weekend before the Tuesday election. Whichever King Day prop won, it would do more to rid Arizona of its acquired "racist image" than any elected official could do. It was no longer in the politicians' hands to make deals. It was on the fingertips of over a million Arizona voters who would exercise the right of suffrage for which Dr. King and the Civil Rights Movement had fought faithfully, and for which many had ultimately given their lives. What would it be? Proposition 301 or 302? Yes, yes? Yes, no? No, yes? Or, no, no?

In First Institutional's Sunday, November 4, 1990 bulletin, I had our church secretary, Bob Russell, who was a sixty-ish single WASP who was hired by FIBC permanently after coming to us as a temporary, to create a one-page, pro-MLK Day mini-flyer to serve as my regular pastoral comments page that Sunday. Up in the left-hand corner we placed the bust photo of Dr. King used on the letterhead of ARIZONANS FOR A MARTIN LUTHER KING, JR. STATE HOLIDAY. Below that, my brief get-out-the-vote message was printed in bold letters—ELECTION DAY, Tuesday, November 6, 1990 DON'T FORGET TO VOTE! YOUR VOTE COUNTS AND YOU **CAN** MAKE A DIFFERENCE. The entire right half of the page from top to bottom sported a reduced facsimile of our coalition's previous bumper sticker reading, "SAY YES, ARIZONA! SUPPORT A STATE HOLIDAY MARTIN LUTHER KING, JR."

As an insert to that bulletin, I spelled out my pastoral comments entitled **"WHY I AM VOTING FOR PROPOSITION 301—A PAID STATE MARTIN LUTHER KING, JR. STATE HOLIDAY."** That documented deliberately printed on green paper read as follows in its entirety and carried my "Pastor Stewart" signature.

FIRST INSTITUTIONAL BAPTIST CHURCH
1141 East Jefferson Street
Phoenix, Arizona 85034

Pastoral Comments   November 4, 1990

WHY I AM VOTING FOR PROPOSITION 301—A PAID STATE MARTIN LUTHER KING, JR. HOLIDAY

There should be no question in any Arizonan's mind about Warren Stewart's unequivocal support for a Martin Luther King, Jr. paid state holiday in Arizona. For years, I have attempted to live, preach, teach and advocate the principles and philosophy of the late Dr. Martin Luther King, Jr. Without a doubt, he has been a key role model for the evolution of my prophetic ministry. From November 1986 to January 15, 1990, I served with vitality, clarity and sometimes audacity as General Chairperson of **ARIZONANS FOR A MARTIN LUTHER KING, JR. STATE HOLIDAY** which fought for and witnessed the passage of Arizona's first legislatively approved holiday honoring Dr. King on September 21, 1989, which is represented in Proposition 301.

Over the past few months, *that* King holiday legislation as well as the second legislatively passed King holiday bill which is represented by Proposition 302 were *both* overturned by more than the minimum required number of Arizona voters displeased with the said legislative actions. On November 6, 1990, Arizona voters will be asked to decide once and for all on a Martin Luther King, Jr. paid state holiday. Ironically, we will have **two** holiday propositions from which to choose.

The Arizona business community saw the "green light" on the King holiday when the NFL players communicated to Arizona's Super Bowl '93 Committee that they would not bring the Super Bowl here unless Arizona had a King holiday. With the prospect of losing the $200,000,000 windfall which the 1993 Super Bowl would bring to our state, in August of last year Phoenix power-brokers began to speak publicly about the **need** for a paid holiday honoring Dr. King in Arizona. Consequently, they formed the MLK Better America Committee to lobby the legislature for the holiday, and now, to win the support of a majority of Arizona voters to pass Proposition 302—Adding a paid state holiday for Dr. King and restoring Columbus Day to paid holiday status. They are also urging voters to **ignore** Proposition 301.

ON TUESDAY, MY VOTE WILL BE FOR PROPOSITION 301, ESSENTIALLY FOR THREE REASONS:

1. **Based on PRINCIPLE.** Honoring Martin Luther King, Jr. with a paid holiday is nothing new for me. Long before Governor Evan Mecham rescinded Arizona's first King holiday, FIBC listed the third Monday in January as one of our paid holidays simply because it was "the right thing to do." In addition, celebrating Columbus Day is **inconsistent** with the principles and philosophy of Dr. King. We all know that Columbus did **not** discover America because the inhabitants who lived here were **not** lost. We all know that Columbus never made it to the shores of what is now known as America. And some of us know that Columbus enslaved some of the "Indians" he found here. Therefore, to vote for a King holiday **and** a Columbus Day is a lesson in contrasts and contradiction! Furthermore, Columbus Day suggests that the people of color who lived here did **not** count until a White man arrived. Now that's racist!

2. **Based on PARENTAGE.** My vote **for** Proposition 301 and **against** Proposition 302 is a vote in solidarity with **my** ancestors. On my mother's side, my great grandfather was part Cherokee Indian. On my father's side, my grandfather was part Indian from one of the tribes that lived in Ohio in the mid-1800s. Therefore, if the Italian-Americans can proudly stick up for their "lost" foreparent who was trying to find a new route to India, then I will boldly vote in the spirit of **my** Native American ancestors.

3. **Based on PROTEST.** My vote **for** Proposition 301 and against Proposition 302 is also a **PROTEST** vote. I have in my files dozens of letters I wrote to several business leaders when we first formed **ARIZONANS FOR A MARTIN LUTHER KING, JR. STATE HOLIDAY.** Only a couple or so bothered to answer my appeals for King holiday support back then. Secondly, a member of the Phoenix 40 whispered to me during the Channel 12 Town Hall on Racism that "if it wasn't for the business community, there would be no King Holiday." He was right! And that's sad commentary on Arizona's commitment to civil rights. Thirdly, most of the "big business" supporters of the King holiday in Arizona do not support the Civil Rights Act of 1990; are cool on affirmative action; do not support a substantial increase in funding for educating our children; and have perpetuated a system of racism and discrimination in their overall business dealings that does not promote equal opportunity for *most* people of color. Fourthly, hardly any big businesses in Arizona, other than banks, currently give their employees a paid holiday honoring Dr. King. *Pure hypocrisy!*

Sure I would like to see Arizona finally celebrate a paid state holiday honoring Dr. Martin Luther King, Jr., **BUT NOT THE "PROSTITUTED" VERSION THAT BIG BUSINESS AND OTHERS ARE PROMOTING WITH PROPOSITION 302.** However, I know that if the King holiday is victorious it will be Proposition 302, thanks to the "BOSS MAN."

But, come November 6th, count on **ONE VOTE** for Proposition 301 based on **PRINCIPLE, PARENTAGE** and

PROTEST. And it will be that of **Warren H. Stewart, Sr.**, a student of the philosophy and principles of the late Dr. Martin Luther King, Jr.

Pastor Stewart

Once again, I had gotten something off my chest that I would not allow to stay there to give me heartburn. I have discovered that other folk do and say what they feel they must do and say, based on their systems of beliefs and codes of ethics. I had become man enough to do likewise. Not surprisingly, I did not receive any negative feedback to my face from any of my parishioners, many of whom were actively involved with the MLK Better America campaign. But, they knew me, and once I had made my mind up based on deeply-held principles, there would be no waffling or wavering on my part. Moreover, I knew that they would vote the way they felt like voting too. It was a kind of mutual understanding.

Unfortunately, my little opinion piece on Prop 301 versus Prop 302 did not amount to a hill of beans in contrast to the few seconds sound bite of CBC sports commentator Greg Gumbel, a Black brother, who mentioned almost in passing that it had been reported that the NFL would move the 1993 Super Bowl from Arizona if the King Day was not passed in the election two days away. Gumbel made his remarks during his regular half-time show between a pro-football game being broadcast that Sunday afternoon.

Well, as history has recorded, "all hell broke loose" in Arizona over those passing comments. The local Sunday evening and night newscasts led their news programs with words like "blackmail" and "threat" as it related to the NFL's plan to transplant Super Bowl XXVII somewhere else if Arizona voters told the King Day where it could go on November 6. The next day's headlines in local Arizona papers fanned the flames surrounding the "un-new" news that the state could very likely lose the lucrative NFL bonanza without a firmly established MLK Day. NFL officials denied that any decision had been made prior to the state's election to pull the Super Bowl if King Day went down. Local news reporters tried to get Gumbel to reveal his sources of such damaging information. He would not do it.

By Monday evening, November 5, 1990, thanks to how the media over-reacted to what was known off the record all along, *Arizona had been threatened by some outside football fat cats whose message was a fair-skinned, overpaid Black guy.* At least, that is the way I imagined many shaky pro-King Day voters, as well as definite anti-King holiday electors felt. Nobody who lived outside the boundaries of this state would be allowed to get away with political extortion. What better gift could the No-No Committee have been given on the eve of Arizona's historic popular vote on the life and legacy of Martin Luther King, Jr.? Mecham, Sanders and the Rose father and son team took full advantage of Gumbel's bringing to the public's remembrance the hidden cost of King Day in Arizona.

The polls still predicted Proposition 302 would win by a small margin. "D-Day" arrived at the polls at 6:00 a.m. on November 6, 1990. I got up around that time to get my three oldest sons off to school. After walking Matthew to the bus stop to catch his 7:04 a.m. bus, I came back to the house and engaged in my morning routine Quiet Time waiting to walk Jared to his first grade classroom. The precinct voting station where my wife and I had voted since living in Phoenix was located in the library of Sevilla Elementary School, where all of our school-aged sons and only daughter attended. So, once I dropped Jared off at Mrs. Bednar's door, I strolled over to the library to mark my general election ballot. After punching holes by the names of some of the election's candidates and bypassing others, I came to the propositions. I quickly found Proposition 301 and punched it on the "yes" box with pride. Then, I moved down to Proposition 302 and hesitated. I began talking to myself and nearly convinced myself to vote "yes" on Prop 302. After all, nobody was in that voting booth with me. I mused, "Who would know?…And what if Proposition 302 was defeated by *one* vote? Maybe, my "yes" vote would win a MLK Day for Arizona." But, I remembered all the comments I had made publicly about Proposition 302, especially my September article in *The Republic* and most recent bulletin insert. Then, I remembered I had to live with me.

I punched "no" on 302.

Once the election polling places closed that Tuesday evening, time came for the anxious election watch. Proposition 302 supporters gathered at a downtown hotel to await election returns. All of them were concerned about to what extent the Greg Gumbel flap turned undecided voters and flaky King Day supporters against Prop 302. The alleged threat might have even brought to the polls "no" voters, who had not planned on even voting that day. Whatever the case, before the polls had closed, over one million Arizonans voted one way or another on MLK Day.

By ten o'clock nightly news, it had been confirmed that my favored proposition, keeping King Day and killing Columbus Day as a paid state holiday was dying a quick death due to its opponents landing three blows to everyone it could strike back. Proposition 301 would hit the canvas by a knockout. However, let it be known that a quarter of a million voters voted *for* Prop 301. So I did not feel all alone in defeat.

Although I had been invited to go down to the MLK Better America Committee's election watch-victory celebration headquarters hotel, I opted to stay at home to observe the election returns in the solitude of my own kitchen. I was experiencing some strange mixed-emotions about what was taking place relative to the holiday honoring my ministerial role model. First of all, I was out of the King Day struggle at the time of the election. Maybe I was feeling some guilt about that. Secondly, White business leaders had run the campaign to honor King and had eagerly donated big bucks to finance the campaign to win a King holiday and a Super Bowl, both of which would be celebrated in January. I still felt that their interests in King Day were not pure and therefore disqualified them from leading such an effort and rightfully claiming credit for the predicted victory. In spite of my feelings, I realized that the King Day campaign had literally come down to being a money issue, but that still disturbed me.

As far as the jolting reaction to Greg Gumbel's remarks, I wondered, "Why was there such an uproar? Everybody who had followed the King Day controversy since the summer of 1989 knew that the Super Bowl's coming to our state for sure was contingent upon the establishment of a Martin Luther King, Jr. Day." I felt that the media jumping on the NFL-King Day connection and inciting people to oppose the holiday was close to unprofessional; but, at least, sensational, without a doubt. The thought also crossed my mind that MLK Better America organizers got what they deserved. I had tried to get them to break the link between the two, in my guest column in September of that year.

So, there I sat watching the returns being displayed on the television screen with Prop 301 being handily defeated and Prop 302 taking an appreciated lead toward the midnight hour. I remember seeing Arnie Zaler being interviewed around 1:00 a.m. Wednesday morning. He was still hopeful and surprisingly energetic for as long a day as he had put in, coupled with leading his UNITY component of the MLK Better America campaign. Shortly thereafter, I went to bed confident, but not excited that it looked like Arizona voters would approve a free-standing MLK Day.

I, along with many Arizonans, woke up Wednesday morning to discover that not only had Proposition 301 been defeated, but so had Proposition 302 in spite of the MLK Better America's campaign slogan that a vote for Proposition

302 was "the right thing to do." Election results showed that 766,387 voted "no" on Proposition 301 to 250,549 who voted "yes." It was the figures on Proposition 302, though, that caused the most pain to King Day supporters. Out of 1,049,784 votes cast on Proposition 302, 516,274 Arizonans voted as if Prop 302 was indeed "the right thing to do." Regrettably, 17,236 *more* Arizonans than the affirmative voters rejected the second proposition to compile a total of 533,510 negative votes against it.

What a narrow margin, by which to become the only state in the history of the United States of America to vote down a holiday honoring the 20th century champion of voting rights for people of color. I guess the only bright side in the narrow defeat was that Proposition 302 had won by close margins in Maricopa and Pima Counties, the two major urban metropolises in Arizona.

Smarting from humiliating national and international embarrassment confirmed by a double-whammy rejection of the two King Day propositions, King Day supporters started pointing fingers at the NFL, CBS and one another. The wrath of an entire state came down on the NFL for committing "economic blackmail" on Arizona. To make matters worse, amidst all the denials by Phoenix Cardinals officials and representatives of the NFL that had begun surrounding Greg Gumbel's report of the NFL planning to take back the Super Bowl if the holiday was rejected, *on November 7, 1990, the day after the election, Paul Tagliabue announced that it would not be "in the best interest" of the NFL to hold the Super Bowl in the state of Arizona as approved by the NFL that previous March.*

Across the Valley emanating from the Mecham headquarters building, leaders of the No-No Committee were celebrating their victory over the powerbrokers in Arizona and boasting of a campaign war chest of around $3,000 compared to the nearly million dollars spent by the MLK Better America Committee.

The 1990 general election in Arizona was a case *when voting rights went wrong. Arizona voters rescinded Arizona's Martin Luther King, Jr. again!*

Chapter Twelve
The 1990 Draft: "Pastor Stewart, This Is Off the Record, But..."

"The fight is over. King Day supporters lost," I told a reporter on the telephone who was sounding out Valley religious leaders on the unexpected defeat of a holiday honoring one of their own. Disappointed that voters had, in a way, affirmed Mecham's and other anti-King Day activists' rejection of a statewide MLK Day, I answered Ben Winton's questions for his Saturday, November 10, 1990 *Phoenix Gazette* Religion section feature story with obvious despair. "Ben, Arizona has rejected the Martin Luther King, Jr. holiday four times. That speaks for itself." I continued, "Yes, there are a lot of freedom-loving citizens who believe in equal rights and human rights. But, you know, I feel sorry for Arizona. Unfortunately, the majority who voted in Tuesday's election have given the 'good people' of Arizona a bad reputation."

From that point, I suggested to Winton that there were more pressing issues that needed to be addressed. Our most valuable human resource—our youth—continued to be ravaged by near-epidemic proportions of drug abuse, teen-age pregnancy, violence and illiteracy. And, particularly, African-American youth face major obstacles in overcoming dysfunctionalities caused by the aforementioned problems directly related to being Black in America. So, I resigned myself to challenging King Day supporters in light of our most recent defeat to redirect our energies and efforts to provide some solutions to the problems plaguing our offspring. In other words, it was time to move on to more important things.

The Sunday after the embarrassing and disparaging defeat of the MLK Day propositions, I had the task of mounting the First Institutional pulpit to provide my Pastoral Emphases and commentary on the politics of the scuttling of King Day at the ballot box. Before a full house of worshippers attending both morning services on November 11, 1990, I began my remarks after greeting those in attendance with the words, "God doesn't like ugly!" Dozens of affirming "Amens" could be heard immediately.

"On Wednesday I needed a 'morning after pill'". I distressfully proceeded. "Please read my Pastoral Comments on page one in the bulletin entitled 'Holiday Shuffle'." Those comments in their entirety read,

> If the events of this past week surrounding Arizona's narrow defeat of a paid state holiday honoring Dr. Martin Luther King, Jr. were not so ridiculous, they would be amusing. No other state in the Union has rescinded any holiday, let alone the Martin Luther King, Jr. holiday, four times in four years. As I have said before—**ONLY IN ARIZONA!**
>
> The tragedy of this unnecessary fiasco is that the philosophy and principles of the late Dr. Martin Luther King, Jr. have been lost amidst Arizona's "HOLIDAY SHUFFLE." The true meaning of the life and legacy of the 20th Century's crusader for justice, liberty and equality has been unjustly misunderstood, bound by selfish business interests and treated unfairly simply because of the color of Martin's skin. A quick glance at some of the headlines of Thursday's major Phoenix newspapers reveals that glaring evidence:
>
> "King loss peril to Super Bowl"
> "King Day defeat backlash rolls in—Fiesta Bowl's
>   plans clouded, NBA not happy"
> "Cards feel heat from 302 defeat"
> "Tourism officials fear loss may cost millions"
> "Defeat likely to strike sour note with artists"
>
> **What about the millions of Americans who suffer from the consequences of racism and discrimination every day perpetuated by the same crowd that is crying over the loss of the Super Bowl!**
>
> Lastly, to quote a former member who called me from back East, "Well, I guess one person's happy—Evan Mecham—because Arizona has **NO** King holiday and **no** governor."
>
> Join me in celebrating the Martin Luther King, Jr. holiday that we've always had!

Next, I identified three problems of Proposition 302. "In my opinion," I criticized, "Proposition 302 had three faults. First, *price*. It was an additional paid state holiday. Second, *power*. It was too closely associated with the Super Bowl and the business leaders who wanted it. And third, *principle*. It would have restored Columbus Day." In a related comment, I referred back to my September 19, 1990 Guest Column in the *Republic* which offered seven steps to win the holiday. I analyzed that some of my suggestions were followed, while others were not.

From there, I raised the question Dr. King made famous, "Where do we go from here?" In answering that timely question, I responded, "Dr. King fought for the right to vote and the people of Arizona have voted. The majority won!" Then I mused, "What if King supporters had won and the anti-King opponents sought to overturn the election?"

But, through the illumination of a glimmer of hope that still resided in me, I spoke to a congregation of disappointed African-American Arizonans these words, "We have only one principled alternative. Let the Legislature pass the federal model of the King holiday that our coalition introduced four years ago and, then, allow the people to vote on that version of the King Day. Furthermore, totally separate the King holiday from the Super Bowl. Then, accept the outcome whatever it is!"

I concluded my lengthy sermonic political comments by reiterating what I had written in my Pastoral Comments, "Let's celebrate the MLK holiday, as we always have." And that statement was received with a hopeful applause.

The days immediately following the defeat of Proposition 302 were filled with frantic and frustrated King Day campaign leaders coming to, from the dizzying side-effects of an unexpected blow to their heads. Plus, Arizona "powers that be" had to cope with the certain losses of the prized Super Bowl XXVII, the NBA All-Star game, several already booked and would-have-booked conventions, entertainers who would "just say no" to Arizona, and possibly even the loss of a bid for a major league baseball expansion team being pushed by Martin Stone, owner of the Phoenix Firebirds, a minor league baseball team.

In addition, Arizona had no governor-elect. Neither Terry Goddard nor Fife Symington attained the necessary 50-plus percentage of votes cast for governor in the general election. Consequently, a run-off election would have to be scheduled between the two gubernatorial candidates early in 1991. Impeached Governor Mecham could get some of the credit for that political logjam because Arizona had approved a law requiring that a gubernatorial candidate get 50% of the votes cast plus one after Mecham was elected governor in 1986 with only 40% of the voters' approval.

Governor Rose, who was ready to turn over the Governor's Office to her successor, whom she hoped would be Democrat Terry Goddard, had to settle back into the hot seat on the ninth floor of the Executive Tower and deal with the holiday which she had signed into law twice (actually three times because as secretary of state she attended then-Governor Babbitt's MLK Day executive order with her signature). What would she do? Declare a King Day by executive order? Call the state lawmakers into special session to deal with MLK Day? Whatever she would or could do, she vowed two days after the election, "I'm going to do everything in my power to get that holiday."

At home in my study, I picked up the telephone after a couple or so rings; and to my surprise, a local television news anchor was on the line. Mind you, I was accustomed to news reporters calling my house, but not a prominent television anchor person. If my memory is correct, it was on Friday, November 9, 1990. A matter of fact, like on so many occasions before as it related to the King Holiday, the caller had interrupted my sermon preparation day. Immediately, the television personality identified himself and said, *"Pastor Stewart, this is off the record, but I need to talk to you about something that has been on my mind."* In a very serious and sincere voice, the man on the other end of the line said, "I'm not calling you as a representative of my station. This is a personal call. And you've been on my mind the last couple of days."

I must admit this particular caller had caught me off guard. I wondered to myself how he got my telephone number (even though it has always been listed). Then, the gentleman began to give his observations of the state of the post-MLK Day defeats. He said, "Pastor Stewart, all we've been hearing since Wednesday is former Governor Mecham and the No-No Committee boasting and bragging about how they defeated the King holiday. And the persons who led the holiday campaign are silent. Everybody is walking around in shock, and the King Day defeat is bringing embarrassment on our state nationally and internationally."

The next statement he made brought forth a defensive response from me. The caller uttered the words I will never forget, words that startled me at first, then challenged me, but also affirmed me.

> *Pastor Stewart, we need to hear from you.... People need to hear a voice that's not tied to the Super Bowl. They need to hear from someone who they could never doubt his motives for wanting the Martin Luther King, Jr. holiday. A lot of people are talking, but we need to hear from you.*

After digesting what the news anchor said, I responded, "Thank you for those kind words, but I'm out of it. I was not involved in this last campaign for some personal reasons based on principle. I even told a newspaper reporter yesterday that we need to move on to more important things.... No, Frank, I'm out of it." To which my challenger responded gently and graciously, "That's why we need to hear from you. People will listen to you because you're not a representative of big business....Pastor Stewart, our state is being torn apart by this King holiday defeat. And I believe if you call some people together they would come. And we could win this thing."

Still resisting, I only agreed to pray about Frank Camacho's astonishing request to a man who had opposed Proposition 302. Frank, who has served as the long-time weekend anchor for KTVK-Channel 3 in Phoenix, is also a deeply spiritual person. The sense of God moving in him could be felt in our telephone conversation. This was definitely no publicity stunt. The man was serious. And his serious comments seriously disturbed my pronounced resignation that Arizona's King Day battles were over and done with. The man disturbed my peace without raising his voice.

When I hung up the phone that Friday I was troubled. *"Why me, Lord?"* After getting a hold of my thoughts somewhat, I decided to call three individuals who had been heavily involved in the King Day battle. The first person was Representative Hamilton whom I reached at his home that weekend. In a nutshell, Art rejoiced and welcomed Frank Camacho's drafting me back into the struggle. Next, I called Paul Eppinger and Joedd Miller. They, too, agreed that my leadership in the MLK holiday saga would be nearly perfect timing. At my request, they consented to pray for me that the Lord would guide me in making a decision whether or not to leave my ten-month hiatus from the cause and give it one more shot.

The next thing I did was to prayerfully select seven members of my own congregation with whom I could share this request to re-enlist in the

MLK Day crusade and get their commitment to pray with me over the weekend for God's guidance and will in this matter. I have this thing about biblical numerology and seven is a number of completion and liberation in the Bible.

Those sincere Christians I called were Deacon Robert L. Williams, who chaired the pulpit committee that brought me to First Institutional in 1977; the late Sister Hazel Bell, a former trustee at FIBC and a praying woman who testifies that I am the only pastor she has ever prayed for; Deacon and Deaconess Charles and Vivian Womack, a couple whom I have grown to love, especially Charles who served as my personal security person on Sundays at church; the Reverend and Mrs. Jerry and Charlotte Hillman, my faithful son in the ministry, friend and then full-time Minister of Youth and Social Service, and his praying wife who serves beside her husband fulfilling her own calling to Christian ministry; and the Reverend William Hogans, a personal friend, pastor, then member of our preaching staff and godfather of my fifth son, Aaron Frederick Taylor Stewart. Each consented to uphold their pastor in prayer the second weekend in November, as I wrestled with the message God had sent to me through a Hispanic news anchor that I had only known primarily from viewing him on Saturday and Sunday nights heading Channel 3's news team. And believe me, it was a wrestling match with God.

It is almost obvious by reading the last point of my Pastoral Emphases I gave on Sunday, November 11, 1990 that I had heard from on High. I mean, as late as Thursday after the election I would not have thought about "one principled alternative." But like Jacob of old, I wrestled and held on to God dealing with my life until He blessed me with an answer.

By Tuesday, November 14th, I had written down nearly 40 names of prospective King Day supporters I would possibly invite to an exploratory meeting to discuss going after the federal model of the MLK Day. Again, dabbling with numbers and having a hunch that, at least, 600,000 Arizonans out of a million had voted for either or both Proposition 301 and 302, I jotted down the following figures:

600,000 Votes for MLK Day
30,000 Signatures on Petitions
60,000 Marchers on MLK Day in Phoenix
30,000 Persons to give $10 each
6,000 Volunteers
300 Organizations to give $100 each

I enlisted my secretary, Ms. Janice Solomon, to get some staff members to help her get the phone numbers of my growing list of names of people I hoped would come to a meeting to discuss making another run for King Day in Arizona. Then, I worked on putting my proposal together to be presented at a meeting with the invitees.

If you have not gathered it yet, God again had given me the go-ahead to pursue the dream of a Martin Luther King, Jr./Civil Rights Day in Arizona. As a result, my creative juices were pumping out ideas faster than a lemonade stand in July. The initial name of this new coalition would be VICTORY '91: 600,000 FOR MLK—"Give Us **ONE** More Chance." Still in love with the bust drawing of Dr. King we had used for the ARIZONANS FOR A MARTIN LUTHER KING, JR. STATE HOLIDAY grassroots organization, I cut it out and placed it in a big **V**, symbolizing **V** for victory. I forwarded my penciled rough draft to FIBC secretary, Bob Russell so he could typeset it. And presto, within hours we had a new logo and letterhead. Also, at the bottom of the letterhead I instructed that a portion of Scripture would be typed in bold print which read,

"LET JUSTICE ROLL DOWN LIKE WATERS..." Amos 5:24a

When that was completed, I informed my secretary and her help that they could tell the invitees we would hold a very important meeting on Wednesday, November 14, 1990 at 8:00 a.m. in the Fellowship Hall of the First Institutional Baptist Church. To my amazement and appreciation, nearly everyone I invited came to hear and see my proposal for:

VICTORY '91: 600,000 FOR MLK
"Give Us ONE More Chance"
CAMPAIGN

After Joedd offered the opening prayer and we went through the process of introducing ourselves to one another, I delivered my statement of purpose from some notes I had jotted down on our new letterhead stationery, hand-made at the First Institutional Baptist Church office. I started out by confessing that "something got a hold of me" after a surprise call from an unnamed television news anchor (who by the way was sitting in the room). I mentioned that I was shocked by what was happening to our state. Then, I shared a skeletal version of my proposal before the actual document was distributed.

"My friends, this proposal is based on *principle*. It is all about the *real* and only real reason for an MLK Day. There is no Super Bowl connection,"

I declared. "Furthermore, the barriers that prevented me from working toward the approval of Proposition 302 have been removed," I said in relief. "Thirdly, we must realize that the people's right to vote cannot be circumvented once a vote has been cast on a particular issue. And I believe that the people of Arizona have a right to vote on a Martin Luther King, Jr. Day, without splitting the vote like we did last week."

Then, before nearly four dozen attentive King holiday advocates, I revealed my layman's analysis of the King Day election results. "Clearly, at least 600,000 different citizens voted for MLK Day in Propositions 301 and 302. 535,000 voted 'No-No' minus a few. 516,000 voted 'Yes' on 302 and 250,000 voted 'Yes' on 301." To press my point further I surmised, "Logic would say that, at least, 100,000 who voted for 301 did not vote for 302....Therefore, 600,000 different voters probably voted for either or both of the propositions—more than the 'No-Nos'."

My next statement was an affirmation of faith in a holiday that had not been observed officially in Arizona statewide, since it was first introduced in 1972. "I believe that with a positive campaign by the grassroots people of Arizona, the majority of voters *will* approve a Martin Luther King, Jr./Civil Rights Day that is not an additional paid holiday, especially in line with what happened to Arizona since the November sixth MLK propositions "defeat."

With that being said, I "opened the door of the church" and started preaching to my captivated audience, "This is a FAITH MOVEMENT! This is a PEOPLE MOVEMENT! This is a PRINCIPLED MOVEMENT! All we want and need is ONE MORE CHANCE at the polls in 1991!" The applause, which followed my remarks, was akin to what was customary of many of the previous King Day rallies. And, maybe that is what the loyal, faithful MLK holiday supporters needed after such a narrow and devastating defeat—a pep rally.

Once I made my statement and things calmed down, I passed out copies of my proposal. It read thusly,

DATE: November 14, 1990

GOAL:

To win a Martin Luther King, Jr./Civil Rights Day for the third Monday in January by the vote of the people of Arizona in a Special Election based on the Federal model which would combine George Washington Day and Abraham Lincoln Day into George Washington/ Abraham Lincoln Day (also known as Presidents Day).

OBJECTIVES:

1. To garner, in a Special Election, in excess of **600,000 votes** in favor of a Martin Luther King, Jr./Civil Rights Day on the third Monday in January by combining George Washington Day and Abraham Lincoln Day into George Washington/ Abraham Lincoln Day. This would not create an **additional** paid state holiday.

2. To obtain **300,000 signatures** on petitions from residents of Arizona requesting the 40th Arizona State Legislature to approve a Special Election to ask Arizona voters to approve or disapprove a Martin Luther King, Jr./Civil Rights Day by combining George Washington and Abraham Lincoln Day into George Washington/Abraham Lincoln Day.

3. To gather **60,000 marchers** in support of a Martin Luther King, Jr./Civil Rights Day to march to the State Capitol in Phoenix on January 21, 1991, the National Observance of the Federal holiday honoring Dr. Martin Luther King, Jr.

4. To seek **30,000 persons** to contribute a maximum individual contribution of $10.00 each toward the expenses of the **VICTORY '91: 600,000 FOR MLK CAMPAIGN.**

5. To recruit **6,000 volunteers** statewide to work for voter approval of a Martin Luther King, Jr./Civil Rights Day.

6. To seek **300 organizations/agencies** to contribute a maximum of $100.00 each toward the expenses of the **VICTORY '91: 600,000 FOR MLK CAMPAIGN.**

NEEDS:

*   Office space and equipment
*   Telephone(s)
*   Campaign Director/Workers
*   Committee and Subcommittee
    1. Public Relations Subcommittee
    2. Legislative Liaison Subcommittee

3. Fund-raising Subcommittee
4. Budget and Finance Subcommittee
5. Volunteer Recruitment and Coordination Subcommittee
6. Religious Liaison Subcommittee
7. MLK Holiday Committees
8. Coordination Subcommittee
9. Get Out To Vote Subcommittee
10. Legal Advisory Subcommittee
11. Education Subcommittee

The discussion of the proposal was very positive. One excellent suggestion was to change the sub-title of our new coalition's name from "Give Us **ONE** More Chance" to "One **CLEAR** Choice." The rationale was that if we only ask for "one more chance" and do not win the holiday if given *one* more chance, it might preclude King Day advocates from trying again. Moreover, since there was believed to have been some confusion in having two King Day propositions on the same ballot so pushing for "one clear choice" on the ballot would get us what we wanted. All of us agreed to the name change.

Also, I brought up the issue of the General Convention of the Episcopal Church scheduled to be held in Phoenix July 10-21, 1991. There were some differences of opinion on whether or not the Episcopalians should come in view of the King Day defeat at the polls. A prominent local Episcopalian priest was dead-set against his brothers and sisters convening in Arizona. On the other hand, Bishop Heistand of Arizona and the Presiding Bishop of the Episcopal Church of America had agreed that they should come and make a prophetic witness in favor of honoring Dr. King. The question I posed in writing on the agenda—should they come as planned or not?—proved to be a moot question because Bishop Heistand informed us that the Episcopalians were definitely not going to cancel their Phoenix Convention. However, the bishop also announced that Bishop Desmond Tutu of South Africa had been invited to address a rally on racism during the convention.

As it related to action items, we needed the question answered, "Can a special election be called for the "clear choice" MLK vote?" Dr. Paul Bender, the former dean of ASU Law School and one of the keenest legal minds on constitutional law, as well as an unwavering King Day supporter, volunteered, along with Art Hamilton, to research that question and inform us if a special election could be called in 1991 on the federal model of MLK Day. It was further mentioned that our coalition could not compromise on "the sanctity of the people's right to vote." Consequently, we would advocate resolution of our "clear choice" only at the ballot box.

The last issue we dealt with was whether or not our newly formed coalition should hold a press conference. The answer was a resounding yes and the orders were to hold the press conference quickly. The date selected was the next day, Thursday, November 15, 1990, 1:30 p.m. at the Valley Christian Center on East Washington. Thank goodness, unlike nearly all of the press statements I made when I led ARIZONANS FOR A MARTIN LUTHER KING, JR. STATE HOLIDAY, I would not have to write this one. A guy by the name of Frank Camacho was drafted to head the "press statement writing committee," which included Gil Tyree, weekend sportscaster for Channel 3 and new member of First Institutional, Art Mobley, and a couple of other able contributors.

My staff would have to re-design the letterhead, send out press releases announcing our press conference, arrange for the meeting at Valley Christian Center, make a large banner with our new logo on it, and type the press statement once the committee completed the rough draft and I edited it. These few assignments would have to be done within the next 24 hours.

Before the birth meeting of VICTORY '91: 600,000 FOR MLK closed with a prayer offered by my pro-life comrade and partner in crime who was arrested with me and several others in our abortion protest, the Reverend John Salvatore, someone recommended that I would serve as the group's spokesperson, and it was unanimously agreed by all present.

We had no problems with getting the press to attend our press conference in spite of the short notice. The small conference was packed with news reporters, accompanied by a battery of audio-visual equipment. Pastor Joedd Miller presided and brought greetings. He also introduced those who would be making statements. Gene had been assigned the responsibility of introducing the organizations which were represented at our press conference. All of the existing King Day groups were present, including representatives of MLK Better America. In addition, the NAACP, Episcopal Church of Arizona, and the Interdenominational Ministerial Alliance of Tucson and Vicinity made their presence known, as well as leaders of the pro-life community who attended.

When it came time for me to speak, I nervously but forcefully read our new coalition's first press statement:

It was nearly four years ago that we came to this center and met with Governor-elect Evan Mecham relative to the Martin Luther King, Jr. holiday. So, we think it only appropriate that we return here to discuss goodwill, healing and peace for our state.

Since November 6th, we have seen our beloved Arizona chastised in the national press. We have seen our citizens unjustly labeled as racists and our beautiful state painted with the broad brush of bigotry. We believe, as men and women of goodwill, that it is time for the healing to begin. Our collective conscience dictates that we extend the hand of friendship and reconciliation. Feelings are bruised and the response throughout the state is indicative of the desire of many people of all genders, all races, all creeds and all ages to find the appropriate forum to do something positive. Those forces have come together in the spirit of brotherhood and sisterhood to present a proposal that reflects the best Arizona has to offer.

November 6th has shown us that Arizona does want a day to honor Martin Luther King, Jr. and Civil Rights. But, not at the cost of another paid holiday. Therefore, we propose that Arizona follow President Reagan's example and that our Legislature follow the federal model that would combine George Washington Day and Abraham Lincoln Day into Washington/ Lincoln Day, while establishing a Martin Luther King, Jr./Civil Rights Day on the third Monday in January. This will not cost our taxpayers any money while extending to each other the courtesy of honoring those three significant persons who have helped make America a great nation.

We believe it is time that Arizona be given a **CLEAR CHOICE**. For too long this issue has been shrouded in the unflattering cloak of politics, commercialism and fear. Now it is time to see it clearly in terms of honoring those who have helped all Americans live in peace and freedom. To do any less is to do them a terrible injustice. They believed in and died protecting the sanctity of the right to vote. We also believe in that principle and we believe the issue should again be placed before the voters providing they are given a **CLEAR CHOICE**. We call upon the Legislature to work toward that end.

One quality found in all great leaders is the ability to persuade us to look at ourselves to chart the course of our destiny.

George Washington did that at our nation's birth. **Abraham Lincoln** did that during a terrible chapter of our nation's history. **Martin Luther King, Jr.** did that when many of our citizens were not yet free of the shackles of discrimination and hate. Each did so in a manner unique to the times during which he lived. Each did so professing the greatest of God's gifts—peace and freedom. They offered us a **CLEAR CHOICE** and we believe that is all Arizona wants today.

We invite anyone and everyone to join us in friendship and charity. Qualities that, in spite of all that has happened, are abundant in Arizona.

With that being said, we present Our Proposal:

VICTORY TOGETHER
"One CLEAR Choice"
CAMPAIGN

Our one goal is:

To win a Martin Luther Rights Day for the third Monday in January by the vote King, Jr./Civil of the people of Arizona in a Special Election based on the Federal model which would combine George Washington Day and Abraham Lincoln Day into George Washington/ Abraham Lincoln Day.

Lastly, I conclude this Press Statement with a poem which was part of my morning devotions today, entitled "Beginning Again" by Frank B. Whitney:

> It matters not what may befall;
> Beyond all else I hear the call
> "You can begin again."
> My courage rises when I hear
> God's voice allay the thought of fear
> And when God whispers gently, near,
> "You can begin again."

That is why we are here. We believe that if Arizona voters are given a **CLEAR CHOICE** on a Martin Luther King, Jr. state holiday on the third Monday in January, which is not an additional paid holiday, the majority of us would vote for its approval. Then, healing in our beloved state can begin again.

On the other side of the MLK issue, Mecham and Bob Rose were ranting and raving about efforts to circumvent the will of the people. The initial suggestions that emanated from the State Capitol hinted that the governor and legislator just might consider approving the federal model of King Day. Upon hearing that, the victorious anti-King Day activists shifted into battle alert to protect the outcome of the historic holiday propositions vote. Their attitude was that no elected officials had better dare try to institute a Martin Luther King, Jr. holiday once the voters had rejected two versions of it. Mecham was also mad because Arizona and he, in particular, had been labeled as "racist" for how they had handled the King holiday. However, when told about our efforts to put a different version of the holiday before the voters, he calmed down enough to state that he and his crowd would not fight such a move.

Our newly forming coalition proved not to be the only gathering of King Day supporters floating ideas to redeem the state's further tarnished image. Representative Hamilton suggested pressing the Legislature to pass a "test drive" MLK Day based on the federal model for January 1991 and then putting that particular holiday before the voters in the 1992 general election. A newcomer to the forefront of the King Day battle, Carl Nicholson, who had worked with UNITY, formed a group called Arizonans for King Recognition and took out initiative petitions to put the federal model MLK Day on the ballot in 1992. The challenge he and his backers faced was to get 105,000 signatures of registered voters on their petitions, even though they had until July 2, 1992. The differences between Nicholson's proposal and ours, in addition to the procedure for getting the federal model on the ballot were the question of when it could be done and more importantly, the naming of Presidents Day. Nicholson chose to go the route of the U.S. Congress and use the generic Presidents Day label. As a result of the insistent Republican leadership demand that we honor Abraham Lincoln, our proposal kept the names of George Washington and Abraham Lincoln. Zaler voiced another suggestion, which would place the federal model before the people to vote at the same time they would go to the polls in the yet to be scheduled runoff between gubernatorial candidates Symington and Goddard.

The legal scholars, both within the Attorney General's Office and in private practice, debated on whether or not the Legislature had the constitutional authority to call a special election. The other matter making a special election unlikely was its estimated three million-dollar cost. More and more, it was looking like another MLK Day election would not take place until the general election in 1992. As it related to adding the MLK issue to the runoff, partisan politics virtually ruled that out because Republican leaders felt such a *liberal* issue would bring out more Democrats to the polls, consequently hurting their Republican candidate's chances for victory.

While discussion was going on about how and when Arizona voters could get another chance to vote on our "one **CLEAR** choice," leaders of MLK Better America were hoping against hope that the Legislature just might dare to buck Mecham's threats and approve a *third* Martin Luther King, Jr. holiday. To do so would have insured the defeat of our version of the King holiday because the anti-King activists would easily gather another 70,000 to 80,000 signatures to put that MLK Day on the ballot. Plus, they would be able to say that their state lawmakers circumvented the will of the voters in the infamous 1990 election.

By the third Sunday in November, I was eating my previous Sunday's words in front of my congregation. After mentioning a peace rally to be held at Wesley Bolin Plaza on Monday, November 19, 1990 to protest strong possibility of the United Nations sanctioning war against Iraq, I announced the formation of "VICTORY '91: 600,000 FOR MLK— "One **CLEAR** Choice" during my pastoral emphases. I told my somewhat surprised church members, "I was drafted by a local television anchorperson...." Then, I went on to share bits and pieces of my conversation with Frank Camacho, whose identity I did not reveal publicly until November 1992. "Even members of the business community attended a meeting I called this past Thursday." Then, I requested from the people God had enabled me to lead for 13 years what I needed most—their prayers for my guidance and protection.

Continuing, "I've received several calls from around the country relative to the King holiday defeat at the polls." (By Friday, November 16th of that week, the hot topic had made the front page of the *U.S.A. Today* and they ran a good-sized column in the sports section of that issue covering our November 15th press conference.) A pastor-friend from Louisville, Kentucky called in reference to whether or not the Black community there should protest the University of Louisville planning to play in the January 1, 1991 Fiesta Bowl in Tempe. Other calls came from New York and Washington, D.C. Jesse Jackson tried to reach me three times on Saturday, inquiring if we wanted him to do anything. He finally got me on his car phone, but I told him to hold off until we could get our strategy developed.

Next, I promised, "This will be a positive campaign if practical....And one thing we need right now is volunteers. Please call the office if you can give us some help...Also, there will be a public hearing at the State Capitol some time in the near future to see if we can get our MLK proposal on the runoff election ballot."

Being one who believes in keeping his parishioners informed, I referred them to the copy of our proposal that we had inserted in the Sunday, November 18, 1990 bulletin.

By the time our coalition held our second meeting on November 28, 1990, a whole lot had taken place. I had promptly written both Fife Symington and Terry Goddard an identical letter informing them of our identity and purpose, enclosing our proposal and press statement, and urging them to contact me at the church office. Letters were sent to key legislative leaders informing them of our new coalition and our request that the Legislature call a special election to allow voters to decide on our "one **CLEAR** choice" MLK Day. They too received a copy of our VICTORY '91 proposal. And I concluded my letter, "Lastly, for the good of our beloved state, we hope that this issue can be settled without having to wait until 1992." Of course, I realized that was wishful thinking, but, after all, what did we have to lose!

I also took pleasure in writing a letter to John Kolbe, Political Columnist for The *Phoenix Gazette* in response to a column he had written on October 26, 1990, which was brought to my attention on November 15th. Excerpts read,

> I was a bit surprised to be labeled a "hard-line black activist" and a "potential loose cannon", simply because, based on the principles of non-violence, mutual respect for all persons regardless of race, creed or color and fiscal responsibility, I supported Proposition 301!
>
> I have taken the liberty to enclose an article written in *The American Baptist* entitled "Columbus: Truth or Consequences?" The American Baptist Churches, USA rejoice that Dr. Martin Luther King, Jr. served as one of its constituents.
>
> Lastly, my contention all along since August was that a "YES-YES" vote was the most logical way to counter a "NO-NO" vote.
>
> I may be a "loose cannon," but, most of the time, I try not to shoot blanks.

Apparently, Kolbe was concerned that I would stand on a soapbox and urge the general public to vote against Proposition 302.

Speaking of the newspaper, the media coverage of the aftermath of Arizona's jolting MLK holiday defeat by the electorate dominated the Arizona daily news. Nearly every front page in the A section, as well as the local and state, sports, entertainment and business sections of Arizona's major newspapers headlined the consequences of saying "NO-NO" to MLK. The radio and television talk shows could find hardly any other topics to argue. Next to Martin Luther King, Jr.'s name, the most printed name to be read in black bold letters in the print was Tagliabue. People were really mad at him for announcing that he would recommend that Arizona's hard-won Super Bowl XXVII would be rescinded; that is, Arizona people. Conversely, NFL owners, civil and human rights leaders and organizations and socially conscious Americans outside of the state supported not only the NFL Commissioner's action, but other groups and individuals who announced cancellations of scheduled conventions and events in a King-less Arizona.

In addition to Carl Nicholson's initiative, a man by the name of Don Marty launched a petition drive to calling the governor and Legislature to declare a MLK Day based on either a count of the "yes" votes from both propositions or call for a special election. Then, there was William Mensch, Jr. of Western Design Center, Inc. who had analyzed the MLK propositions vote by computer and concluded, as I did, by hunch that more individual voters cast "yes" votes for Propositions 301 and 302 than the total number of persons who voted "NO" on both.

Our November 28th meeting was well attended. I had invited Pastor Barnwell to deliver the invocation, but he was late in arriving. Paul Eppinger substituted. In my statement of purpose that day I began by saying, "A lot has transpired since we last met." After reiterating our purpose I rejoicefully proclaimed, "Support for the King holiday is broadening daily! Our goal remains to win the MLK holiday, based on the principle of honoring the Civil Rights Movement under the leadership of Dr. King and civil rights in America....Our goal would also contribute to racial, political, social and economic healing in Arizona."

As I continued to update those present, I shared information I had received about the respective stances of Goddard and Symington. Terry supported the "Hamilton Plan", calling for the "test" King Day in 1991 and referring it to the ballot in 1992. Symington was urging King Day advocates to "wait and let the controversy die down." His fellow Republican, Senator Leo Corbet, was calling for his colleagues to pass the "cafeteria plan" in a special session of the outgoing 39th Session, or perhaps, the incoming 40th Legislature, and refer it to the voters in 1992. Julian Sanders was urging the Legislature to approve an "All-American/Civil Rights Day" without Dr. King's name on it. Amidst all this confusion, the business community wanted another legislative quick-fix so they could get on with business as usual. Still another action circulated was a possible lawsuit calling for a count of the "yes" votes on 301 and 302. This idea had been voiced by Richard Lehman, then president and CEO of Valley National Bank, who was hoping such a count would convince the NFL not to cancel the Super Bowl for Arizona.

I informed our coalition members of a meeting called by Bill Jamieson, which had been held at the Trinity Cathedral on November 25th. Jack Pfister served as the moderator. Several of the CEOs of the major Valley corporations were present at that afternoon meeting. They had gathered to address the MLK disaster and racism in Arizona. Let me tell you, I was very uncomfortable and suspicious of the majority of the individuals there.

In the first place, after I shared Victory '91's proposal before those present, the business leaders moved right into how they saw the problem and what needed to be done, without even commenting on what I had said. In reviewing my personal notes of that meeting, they agreed on four steps to tackle the problem. One, there was no short-term solution. Two, they needed to take control of the agenda. Three, a broad coalition to support the election for 1992 needed to be organized. And four, they needed to address underlying issues such as racism.

If I did not know any better, I would have believed that I was not even in the room with these "fat cats", and certainly that I had not even presented our proposal. I was dumbfounded by the arrogance of that Phoenix 40 crowd! For a moment, I felt like "the spook who sat by the door." But, all would not be lost. Pfister, a member of the Phoenix 40, and as I have mentioned earlier in this book—an unusual White man, spoke up to *his* peers, "Warren has already outlined a proposal that addressing the MLK Day issue and a broad-based coalition has already been formed to prepare for an election....It seems to me that we ought to get behind VICTORY '91."

There was silence and then questions as to who was in our coalition and other condescending inquiries. However, Pfister in his masterful manner, succeeded in getting his colleagues to consent to back VICTORY '91. Believe me, the tension in the room indicated that they did so reluctantly. But, Pfister dispersed much of the tension when he volunteered to be their representative on our coalition, to which I consented. The presence of Hamilton and Espinoza gave me reassurance.

Shortly after, those present, which included Bill Franke, former CEO of America West Airlines; Mark De Michel, head of Arizona Public Service; and Richard Lehmann, volunteered their work forces as people power and financing. Franke also suggested that I contact Jay Stuckey, Jr., a conservative Republican businessman who was promoting a King holiday initiative.

The other outcome of that Sunday afternoon meeting at Trinity was the business leaders' commitment to form a coalition to address racism in Arizona. This would become the personally-guided project of Jack Pfister and become known as Harmony Alliance, Inc.

Getting back to VICTORY '91's second meeting, I threw out to those present that we needed to revise our campaign theme and objectives since it seemed unlikely that we could get the Legislature to approve a special election or attach King Day to the upcoming runoff. After listening to various suggestions, I offered several I had worked on and had Bob, in the church office, to draft a mock up of them. When I presented the new name—VICTORY TOGETHER-ONE CLEAR CHOICE—Pfister smiled and motioned that we adopt that as our identity. Next, we revised our goal by eliminating "Special Election" from our proposal and replacing it simply with "Election."

The third issue we addressed, as it related to one of our objectives, revolved around whether or not we wanted to join an existing petition drive or start a new initiative with our exact wording for both holidays on it. Or, did we wish to launch a "People's Petition" signed by any and all Arizonans who wanted the governor and Legislature to approve that our "one **CLEAR** choice" would be put on the general election ballot for 1992. After much discussion, a motion and a substitute motion, we decided to confer with the governor and legislative leaders before we determined to push an initiative or simply get MLK Day supporters' signatures.

Of utmost importance, we voted to invite every known MLK Day group to unite with VICTORY TOGETHER. We also formed a steering committee to come back with an organizational plan for us. In search of a headquarters, several centrally-located offices were mentioned. Pending selection of a suitable place, I offered First Institutional as a temporary headquarters, since our office was handling all the business of VICTORY TOGETHER anyway.

Before the meeting adjourned, I suggested that each member who could would donate $100 in order that we could have some money to cover current expenses. The target date would be December 12, 1990 for receiving those funds for mailing, printing, telephone calls, etc. The matters of officers, spokespersons, media coordination, structure and strategy would be handled at the December meeting. I also shared a letter from Gordon E. Sellers of Atlanta, an African-American political consultant who had served as national co-chair of the MLK Day march in Atlanta for the past fifteen years. Mr. Sellers offered his assistance to us, by stating in his November 20th letter,

> I believe that a major celebration in the name of Dr. Martin Luther King, Jr. on January 21st in the two largest cities in Arizona will go far to convince the nation that Arizona is not South Africa West.

I also mentioned that Mecham's publicist had contacted me about possibly appearing on the Donahue show with the former governor to debate the King Day controversy in Arizona. Pastor Barnwell had arrived at the meeting late, but was able to lead us in the closing prayer, after a nearly three-hour very productive meeting.

As the organizer and spokesperson of VICTORY TOGETHER, I was able to get an audience with Governor Mofford and key members of her staff on December 4, 1990. Our purposes were to re-introduce ourselves as members of a new MLK Day coalition, to hear the governor's proposals for resolving the King holiday issue, as well as to share our proposal directly with Governor Mofford. Gene, Mark Reader, Jay Stuckey, Art Mobley and myself made up our negotiating team. Once the meeting started and we went through the perfunctory greetings, I got down to the nitty gritty by saying, "Governor, we are concerned about waiting until November 1992 to resolve this issue. It's obvious that a majority of voters supported a King holiday. So, our goal is to contribute to the resolution of this issue and to the healing of our state internally and externally."

Governor Mofford responded, "Gentlemen, I'm pushing for the 39th Legislature to pass the federal model of the holiday *this* year. I'm very optimistic. They ought to do this and have it out of the way for the new governor." Quite impressed and almost taken aback by her enthusiastic belief that the current legislators, many of whom had only about a month remaining in office, would trek back to the Capitol to pass a King holiday, our team smiled politely (and almost facetiously) as the governor continued informing us of her position. "I'll tell you I'm not in favor of this menu plan being proposed by some Republican and Democratic senators. It is a bureaucratic mess."

While nodding our heads in agreement, the governor then made a surprising request of us. "I want you all to hold off on your petition drive in order to let the Legislature do *their* best job of passing this holiday with a referendum attached to it for 1992. You see, if the lawmakers get the idea that you'll take the heat off of them by doing their work for them, they'll sit back and let you do it!" Hesitating a little, we thanked her for her suggestion and let her know that we would have to get back to the coalition on her request.

All in all, it was fruitful to meet once again, face to face with the state's highest official who still played a key role in getting any movement on the holiday. One thing for sure, everyone knew where she stood. After the meeting, she knew where we stood. As usual, she left the lines of communication open between her office and us.

Around that same time, House Speaker Jane Hull responded to the letter I had sent her on November 19th. In no uncertain terms she stated,

> As I am sure you are aware, the MLK issue will *not* appear on the runoff election ballot. I think the Legislature feels it is now far more critical to elect a governor and return some sense of normalcy and progress to our state.

Reading between the lines, I realized that she and other Republican legislators had their hopes on Symington getting into the Governor's Office. But, I also wondered if she was throwing a dig at Governor Mofford when she used the phrase "return some sense of normalcy and progress to our state." Who knew? Probably not.

Later in her letter, she reaffirmed her support for the King holiday the last two years, boasted that her own heavily populated Republican District 18 voted for Proposition 302 by 60% to 40%, but warned that if the Legislature passed another holiday bill in that session, it would be overturned by another referendum petition drive and placed back on the ballot. And she was right.

Her advice, quite different from the other powerful woman in Arizona politics at that time, included, "At this point, I feel it is best to step back from the issue for a while and allow tensions to ease a bit."

I was able to get in touch with Fife Symington on December 5th over the telephone. I had met the "wanna be" governor in my old office before the November election. He and two of his aides of color came by to check in with the pastor of First Institutional, as nearly every candidate running for major statewide and local offices usually did. We had had a nice chat, and before he left I asked him about his position on abortion, which had appeared to have flip-flopped like George Bush's. The pro-life community was upset with him for moving from what they said was pro-life to pro-choice. He answered my question, "Reverend Stewart, I don't think you and I differ much on abortion. I believe that abortion on demand is not right. However, as a practical person, morality cannot be legislated. It would be nearly impossible to enforce a law that restricted abortion." Of course, that was a nice politically safe answer in those days, but it did not help the unborn babies going down the tube, a bit.

Over the telephone candidate Symington said, "I still support the King holiday, in spite of how the television sound bites do not really represent my views accurately." Symington was being portrayed as "hedging" on his support of King Day in the news. "I feel that the incoming Legislature should pass the holiday and then refer it to the people for a vote." As our brief conversation came to a close, the optimistic gubernatorial candidates remarked, "I want to work with you, Reverend, when I become governor."

The conversation I had with Goddard the next day was short and to the point, specifically because his commitment to King Day was never in question. He restated his support for the "Hamilton Plan" and stressed that "we shouldn't wait to do something." In concluding, he stated, "Reverend Stewart, I would like to speak with you later about the governor's race." There was no need in my inquiring of Terry about his position on abortion. He is about as pro-choice as you can be; and that bothered me because I think he is a near-brilliant politician who has a sincere conscience toward civil and human rights.

The week before I made an appearance on the Phil Donahue Show with Evan Mecham, the press did a story on a scheduled appearance in Tucson of the two oldest daughters of the assassinated top African-American leaders in the 1960s, namely Martin King and Malcolm X. Yolanda King and Attallah Shabazz had formed a performing arts and education group called Nucleus, which traveled the country performing their musical play, *Stepping Into Tomorrow*. The story line of the *Republic* article dated December 6, 1990 had to do with the irony of Yolanda King coming to the University of Arizona to perform, while other organizations and entertainers were renewing their boycott of Arizona.

When asked by a reporter how I felt about Miss King coming to the state that had just voted down a holiday honoring her father, I lauded her. My contention was that her coming and presenting a dramatic production about her father and Malcom X could aid in educating potential affirmative voters of the importance of Dr. King. As quoted in the *Republic* article, I said,

What better way can Arizona be made aware of the life, legacy and principles of the late Dr. Martin Luther King than through the dramatic presentation of his gifted and talented daughter, Yolanda.

And, it should be noted anyway that the performance had been booked before the November election.

Dr. King's daughter called me at my home on Monday, December 4th seeking my advice on whether or not she should keep her and Shabazz's engagement. After identifying herself, she informed me that her mother had suggested that she call me since I was heading the King Day struggle again. It was quite evident that pressure was coming from several directions urging her to cancel her engagement, in protest of the disrespect shown to her father by the outcome of the election. I really felt that she sincerely did not know what to do. After informing her that VICTORY TOGETHER had no position on the boycott of the state, she spoke up, "I want to be a positive force for change in Arizona, if I come. I want to help Arizonans understand who my father was." My response was, "Well then, come on to Arizona and contribute to the healing of our state. I mean, the mere fact that Dr. King's daughter would come to Arizona, after what we did to the day honoring your father, would send a powerful message."

Yolanda thanked me for my advice and said that she would have to make a decision very soon. When we hung up, I was certain that she was going to keep her Sunday, December 9, 1990 engagement. However, the day before she was to perform in Tucson, she released a statement canceling her Arizona appearance. Complicating matters more, was the fact that several of the actors in the King-Shabazz musical had already arrived in Tucson to prepare for the performance. According to the *JET*, her reason for reversing her decision had to do with her not wanting boycotting entertainers and organizations to think she opposed their protest actions over the holiday defeat. Part of her statement read,

In time, it became increasingly apparent to me that my presence in Arizona could and would be misconstrued by some to be contrary to the goals and tactics of proponents of the King holiday.

Well, Lord knows I tried. And that was a major move for me to make the jump from supporting a boycott of the state in 1987 through 1989 to urging Dr. King's oldest daughter to come on over and spend some time with us. But, I was in a new position with a whole new set of circumstances that necessitated a different game plan.

By the way, the show did go on without Miss King. Malcom X's daughter Attallah, fulfilled her co-leading role and an understudy substituted for Yolanda.

My next ambassadorial mission involved Anglican Archbishop Desmond Tutu, the outspoken preacher-prophet who castigated the evil system of apartheid in his native South Africa in the name of Christ. He had been invited by the Most Reverend Edmond Browning, presiding bishop of the Episcopal Church of America, to be the special guest at the General Convention to be held in Phoenix July 11-20, 1991. Since the Episcopalians had decided not to boycott the state and keep the commitment to come, Browning used political (and hopefully theological) prowess to get Bishop Tutu to consent to open the General Session with a rally on racism.

Mind you, though, this would have not been the first time a major South African cleric appeared in Arizona to preach about racism and apartheid. I had the privilege of hearing and meeting Dr. Alan Boesak of the Alliance Church preach powerfully on apartheid at the Phoenix Civic Plaza in 1984, when the largest body of American Presbyterians convened in the hot summer of Arizona.

The mere fact that the South African Nobel Peace Prize winner was coming to Phoenix excited me immensely. I revere human and civil rights activists who put their lives on the line and preach against the sins of racism and oppression from a prophetic hermeneutic that believes that "God is actively involved in the holistic liberation of humankind." *The Phoenix Gazette* quoted me rejoicing over Tutu's coming thusly, "He's one of the foremost human rights activists. He's likened to the MLK of the 80s, of South Africa, probably more so than Nelson Mandela. He has a revolutionary, prophetic ministry under the banner of Christ. Tutu will be an honored guest."

On a more personal note, I assumed that since I had worked closely with Bishop Heistand and Bill Jamieson, as well as met and conferred with Bishop Browning on the King Day issue, I would get the opportunity to meet the Right Reverend Desmond Tutu, face-to-face, once he arrived in the Valley of the Sun. Other local leaders, too, were standing in line to greet and meet the short-statured Black man who captured world-wide attention invoking the name of Martin Luther King, Jr. as he led his Anglican Church and other liberated church leaders of South Africa to condemn, without compromise, the institution of apartheid sanctioned by the racist Dutch Reformed Church of South Africa.

Regrettably, within a month of the hopeful announcement, news sent from across the Atlantic Ocean in Capetown, Republic of South Africa dimmed our hopes of Bishop Tutu's possible coming to Arizona. Someone had gotten to him, just like they had gotten to Yolanda King. Ben Winton, religion editor for the *Gazette*, called me to inform me of the press release he had received over the wire. Bishop Tutu was strongly considering canceling his trip to Arizona to lead a rally on racism. The lead paragraph in a December 22, 1990 article by Winton read,

> Fearing that his visit to Arizona may upset supporters of a paid holiday for the Rev. Martin Luther King, Jr., South African Archbishop Desmond Tutu says he may back out of a Phoenix rally against racism.

As I read that paragraph I was trying to identify which Arizona King holiday supporters were upset about Tutu's coming. It certainly was not me or any other members of VICTORY TOGETHER. Continuing to read excerpts from his prepared statement, I became more perplexed,

> The question of having a Martin Luther King, Jr. holiday in Arizona seems to be turning into as emotional an issue in the African-American community as that of apartheid in South Africa. I cannot risk hurting people who have helped us so much in our struggle against injustice.

Huh? Hurting African-Americans in Arizona? What I soon discovered was that Tutu was not referring to Arizona Blacks heavily involved in the King Day fight. *They would welcome his presence.* No, he had reference to groups within the Episcopal Church of America who were against his coming to Arizona in wake of the King Day defeat at the polls. Obviously, those factions who had unsuccessfully urged Browning to cancel their commitment to come to Arizona for their General Convention had communicated directly to Bishop Tutu's office.

What a letdown to think that one of my living role models might not be coming to Phoenix to preach just a few blocks from First Institutional Baptist Church. Not only would his powerful prophetic presence and proclamation have been denied the opportunity to bless Arizona and, perhaps, help us in our holiday campaign, but his boycotting the state would send an alarming announcement worldwide that Arizona is not the place for freedom and justice-loving people to come. On the other hand, I could understand his reasoning since economic boycotts and sanctions had been crucial in breaking the grip of apartheid on the majority of South Africans. My real disappointment was that Browning or somebody had not thought enough of local King Day leaders, particularly African-American leaders like myself, to have us communicate how we felt about his coming or not coming. I guess that is one drawback of being only 3% of the population in the state. Very few "powers that be" take us seriously, both inside and outside of Arizona.

By January 2, 1991, I faxed the Right Reverend Desmond Tutu, Archbishop of Capetown, the following three-page letter.

January 2, 1991
The Right Reverend Desmond Tutu
Archbishop of Capetown
The Anglican Church in South Africa
Capetown, Republic of South Africa

Dear Archbishop Tutu:

Greetings in the Blessed Name of the Prince of Peace, even our Lord Jesus Christ.

Please allow me to introduce myself. I am Warren H. Stewart, Sr., Pastor of the First Institutional Baptist Church of Phoenix, Arizona and a long-time leader in the efforts to win a Martin Luther King, Jr. state holiday on the third Monday in January in Arizona. For over three years I served as General Chairperson of **ARIZONANS FOR A MARTIN LUTHER KING, JR. STATE HOLIDAY** which was instrumental in successfully lobbying the Arizona State Legislature to approve a Martin Luther King, Jr. state holiday in September 1989. Currently, I serve as General Chairperson of a broad-based coalition of Martin Luther King, Jr. state holiday advocates called VICTORY TOGETHER—"One **CLEAR** Choice" whose primary goal is to win a Martin Luther King, Jr./Civil Rights Day by a vote of the people of Arizona, and whose secondary goal is to bring about healing to our State's tarnished image which was a consequence of the narrow November 6, 1990 defeat of the Martin Luther King, Jr. state holiday propositions.

Upon first hearing of your acceptance of Presiding Bishop Edmund Browning's invitation to you to lead a rally against racism in Phoenix on July 10, 1991 in conjunction with the 1991 General Convention of the Episcopal Church in America, I was elated (see enclosed article dated November 15, 1990). I feel that your coming will extol the principles of non-violent social change with which the late Dr. Martin Luther King, Jr. revolutionized America and Arizona for the better in the area of race relations.

On the other hand, your December 21, 1990 press release indicating that you are reconsidering your decision to come to Arizona for the rally against racism causes me much disappointment. And I beg of you, Archbishop Tutu, on behalf of all of those who have advocated a holiday for Dr. King in Arizona, to keep your engagement and come and help us attain our goals (see enclosed newspaper article dated December 22, 1990).

I understand very well the usage of boycotts and economic sanctions as a means of non-violent social change. In March 1987, **ARIZONANS FOR A MARTIN LUTHER KING, JR. STATE HOLIDAY** called for a convention and entertainment boycott of Arizona **after** direct dialogue, negotiations and petitioning then-Governor Evan Mecham and the Arizona State Legislature proved futile. At that time, we received boycott support from national civil rights leaders and organizations, including Mrs. Coretta Scott King. We feel that the economic pressure due to lost convention revenue aided us in winning the King holiday in 1989.

However, our situation now is somewhat different. Polls have revealed that approximately **63%** of the Arizona voters who voted in the November 6th General Election voted **FOR ONE** of the Martin Luther King, Jr. holiday propositions. The defeat resulted in that King holiday voters **SPLIT** their affirmative votes by not voting for both propositions and/or by voting against

ONE of the propositions, while the 37% of opponents of the Martin Luther King, Jr. holiday simply voted against BOTH propositions. Sound confusing? It is, and that is primarily why both Arizona King holiday propositions were defeated.

VICTORY TOGETHER—"One CLEAR Choice" believes that if the Arizona voters are given a CLEAR CHOICE on the Federal model of the Martin Luther King, Jr. holiday which combines George Washington Day and Abraham Lincoln Day into one holiday honoring the, and makes the extra paid holiday Martin Luther King, Jr. Day, they will approve it at the polls. Regrettably, we were not given the opportunity to vote on this model on November 6, 1990.

Therefore, your coming to Arizona can uniquely, prophetically and positively elevate our cause on a statewide, national and international level just as noted African-American civil rights leaders have traveled to South Africa to engage in non-violent activities against apartheid in your country. Indeed, Dr. King traveled to the capital cities of racism and discrimination at its worst in America to preach a gospel of peace, liberty, justice and equality for all persons regardless of race, creed or color.

With that being said, COME TO PHOENIX, ARCHBISHOP TUTU, WITH THE GOSPEL OF PEACE, RACIAL EQUALITY AND JUSTICE. We extend to you "a Macedonian Call."

Please respond affirmatively. Blessings on you and yours in this New Year.

> For the Cause,
> Dr. Warren H. Stewart, Sr.
> General Chairperson
> VICTORY TOGETHER-"One CLEAR Choice"
> 1241 E. Washington Street
> Phoenix, Arizona 85034 USA

WHS: js

cc: Bishop Joseph Heistand, Episcopal Diocese of Arizona
         Presiding Bishop Edmund Browning,
         Episcopal Church of America

Enclosures

Praise the Lord, the Archbishop's secretary acknowledged our faxed communiqué just two days later. Unfortunately, Bishop Tutu was on leave and not expected back in his Capetown office until February 1, 1991. Waiting patiently and prayerfully for a response once Bishop Tutu returned to his office, I was elated to receive a faxed message from Capetown on February 13, 1991 via Bishop Heistand's Trinity Cathedral office.

Once I read it, my *worst* expectations were confirmed. The letter from the Personal Assistant to the Archbishop of Cape Town, the Reverend Mazwi Tisani read:

Dear Dr. Stewart,

His Grace, Archbishop Desmond Tutu, would like to thank you for your very kind and inspiring letter. We apologize for the time it has taken to reply. The reason is that we have all been away on leave.

The Archbishop feels most honoured to have been asked to lend support to the M. L. King-state-holiday-issue. However, after a series of consultations, primarily with the Presiding Bishop, he has decided that the time is not yet right for him to come to Arizona. Nevertheless he remains hopeful that it won't be long before a mutually convenient time can be found for a visit.

He sends you his best wishes and prays for the success of your labors to promote the spirit of togetherness and to fight for the acknowledgement of King's greatness by all.

Kind regards.

Yours sincerely,
Mazwi Tisani

To my surprise, another letter came addressed to me from Bishop Tutu's office dated May 2, 1991. This letter was written by the Reverend Michael Owens, Chaplain to the Most Reverend Desmond M. Tutu. Excerpts from Owens's letter were somewhat more comforting to me than Tisani's February letter. Here are some of his words,

My dear Dr. Stewart,

I am writing on behalf of the Archbishop who is away in Retreat with the other Bishops of this Province. He was quite taken by your very passionate letter we received through Bishop

Heistand…in March. (sic) Blessings upon you and all those who have worked so hard for VICTORY TOGETHER in the State of Arizona.

Your letter was also very helpful in clarifying the results of the November 6 General Election in regard to the Martin Luther King, Jr. holiday propositions.…

He has considered your plea to come to Phoenix in July deeply and prayerfully but feels he cannot change his decision not to come.

…It does appear now that two representatives of the Church of the Province of Southern Africa will be present at (the) General Convention.…Perhaps there would be some opportunity for you to meet with one or both of them during their stay in Arizona.

Again, be assured of the Archbishop's ongoing prayer for all of you working so diligently for peace and reconciliation in that great state.

Oh, well. Nevertheless, I responded to Chaplain Owens's letter with my own letter. Two paragraphs of most significance revealed my thoughts.

I believe I understand the Archbishop's position on deciding against coming to Arizona.…However, to know that we have his prayers and thoughts is encouraging.

Please know that we are continuously praying for the liberation of our brothers and sisters in South Africa.

◇◇◇◇◇

With the acceptance of Frank Camacho's unsolicited draft notice back into the forefront of Arizona's King holiday forces, I acquired essentially another full-time position to be added to my already loaded 60-70 hour work week as pastor of First Institutional. And once again, I would be heading a campaign, for which I would receive no financial remuneration for my efforts, other than the joy that accompanied the expending of my intellect, energy and efforts in leading committed soldiers who refused to give up until the victory was won permanently.

Our congregation was in the middle of erecting an administrative, educational and outreach building in order to provide more space to expand our holistic evangelism and discipleship ministries. We had outgrown our office annex, formerly the old parsonage, which had stood in the parking lot of the church. Thank God, through our desire not to demolish a solidly built house that was constructed when houses were made out of "the real stuff", and with the aid of Councilman Goode, we were able to give that building to the Booker T. Washington Child Development Center located in our neighborhood to provide additional space for their inner-city Head Start program. In the meantime, our temporary church offices had to be located a block and a half away from the church on Washington in an office building, built by a long-time Phoenix Black businessman and realtor, the late Mr. Jackie Berry, Sr. So, when we would have VICTORY TOGETHER meetings at the church, my staff and I would have to transport all necessary materials over to the fellowship hall to facilitate our meetings, and then cart it all back to where we were pilgrimaged.

Any pastor who has ever been involved in a major building program can attest to the extra responsibilities and concerns that accompany such an endeavor, when he or she has nothing else to do but shepherd the flock and make sure the architect and contractors are fulfilling their tasks, according to the specifications that have been agreed upon. I was blessed, however, to have a diligent and dutiful building and renovation committee, which oversaw the construction of our 1.2 million dollar Body Building, as I named it because it would be the key center for "the members of the Body of Christ" known as First Institutional Baptist Church to prepare, train and execute the mission and ministry of the Church of Jesus Christ.

Another challenge that the Lord enabled me not to have to face, while trying to head VICTORY TOGETHER, was raising funds to pay for our new building that was gradually rising from a huge hole dug in the front section of our church parking lot. Through the contributions of tithes, offerings, and a few Property Expansion Fund pledges and special gifts to the building fund, the Body Building was paid for *in full* before the ground was broken in September 1990 to begin construction.

On the other hand, the usual and unusual duties of pastoring did not take a leave while I led VICTORY TOGETHER. Preaching twice, nearly every Sunday, necessitated a major portion of my time weekly for preparation and proclamation. Overseeing the responsibilities of probably one of the most diverse staffs of any leading church in the Valley consisting of persons of three ethnic/racial groups ranging in age from mid-twenties to mid-seventies—men and women, married, single and in transition, various skill levels, different ages in spiritual maturity and dealing in different degrees successfully and/or unsuccessfully with their own personal challenges—tested the ripeness of my own spiritual fruit.

Visiting the sick, burying the dead, winning the lost, teaching the saved and serving the needy constituted divine assignments that I was mandated to do, in addition to trying to get an entire state to approve a holiday they had voted down twice. And, if that was not enough, I had to keep my national and international obligations for ministry intact, particularly financing the erection of the First Institutional Baptist Church of Soweto, Republic of South Africa; working with the late Dr. Leon Sullivan, as he planned the first African/African-American Summit for Abidjan, Ivory Coast, West Africa; conducting a revival for military personnel in Germany; and fulfilling preaching and teaching responsibilities in the National Baptist Convention, USA, Inc.

On the homefront my wife, Serena, was not surprised that I had gotten back involved in another "mission." Being married to a guy with a "Type A" personality, like myself, had made her very acquainted with my absence from sun-up to sundown, taking care of other folks' needs while neglecting my own family's needs. She had resigned herself to not being able to compete with the Lord's work and based her days caring for our five sons, ranging in age from twelve to less than one year old.

I tried my best to keep my weekday ritual of getting our school-age kids up, prompting them to say their "morning altar prayer", and then walking them either to their bus stop or to their classroom door at Sevilla School, respectively. Oftentimes, due to late afternoon or early evening meetings being scheduled out of necessity, prior to my regular evening conferences, the first and last time I would see my boys awake was in the mornings. Regrettably, as the campaign progressed, I would often be denied the privilege of spending a little time with my sons in the mornings because the best time to meet with VICTORY TOGETHER members and busy professionals was in the mornings at meetings beginning at around 7:00 or 7:30 a.m. However, one weekly delight I refused to give up was volunteering in my third son Jared's class on Monday mornings. Although I often felt like a zombie trying to keep my eyes open after a full weekend, usually consisting of three Sunday services, sitting in the little chairs designed for six and seven year olds, I thrived off of helping Mrs. Bednar, my son's teacher, and building relationships with her first grade students who knew me as "Mr. Stewart."

To say the least, the Channel 3 weekend anchorman's conscience prickling statement to me, *"Pastor Stewart, this is off the record…, but we need to hear from you…."* put a lot more on my *record* than can ever be taken off.

PART FOUR

Chapter Thirteen
Competing for Credibility: From Suspect To Respect

Credibility proved to be an immediate problem that MLK Day supporters had to address due, for one, to the defeat at the polls. In addition, the newest coalition that emerged the second week after the November general election was led by a Black preacher. Furthermore, it was common knowledge among MLK Better America Committee members and the media that I was chilly on Proposition 302 and its business crowd proponents during the last fateful campaign. It was obvious that I had no fan club members among the Valley's Italian-Americans. And, perhaps, some could remember that I had been publicly quoted in November 1989 as saying a statewide King Day campaign, which went to the vote of the people, would need a White leader.

A case in point of our coalition's particular initial credibility gap was exemplified by a reporter's evaluation of our coalition the day after our November 15 press conference. Pat Flannery wrote,

> "Stewart, who is backed by a loose coalition of religious and black leaders…"

Maybe we were "loose" at the beginning, but we certainly were comprised of more than "religious and black leaders." I guess Flannery got that myopic impression by observing who attended our press conference. Had he seen who had answered my call to coalesce at our November 14 meeting in First Institutional's fellowship hall, he would have been a little more accurate in his description of the coalition that would make history in honor of Dr. Martin Luther King, Jr.

I cannot remember all of those who met together eight days after the general election, but in addition to most of the former key volunteers from ARIZONANS FOR A MARTIN LUTHER KING, JR. STATE HOLIDAY, the invitation list included Dr. Paul Bender, Pat Quaranta (Can you believe that?), Wilbert Nelson - president of Maricopa NAACP, Michael Kelly, Bishop Heistand, Bill Jamieson, Rosie Lopez, Vernon Bolling, Bishop O'Brien, Senators Alan Stephens and Pete Rios, Lisa Loo, Jackie Berry, Sr., Bill Shover, the Reverend John Salvatore and Dr. Carolyn Gerster. Both Symington and Goddard were invited to attend. And, quite frankly, the diversity of those who showed up to "Keep the dream alive" reflected a rainbow of colors, cultures, classes, careers and community interests, not to mention religious, philosophical and political persuasions. It took a reporter for the *New York Times* to comment on our make-up more accurately than the *Gazette* writer. Robert Reinhold's article in the November 16, 1990 issue of the *Times* described us as,

> "A group of community, political and religious leaders (who) met at the church on Wednesday to devise a new plan" (for the MLK holiday).

Speaking of credibility, Arizona's reputation had taken a big hit. It is one thing to have a unique governor rescind a King holiday and make less than complimentary comments about the honoree's worthiness for such a holiday. But, when a majority of a state's voters turned down the King Day propositions, accusations of Arizona being "a racist state" began to stick.

What could be done in the meantime before Arizona voters would be given another chance to fulfill a twofold purpose: (1) honoring King on the third Monday in January and (2) restoring our "ripped up" reputations? Could the Phil Donahue Show be the answer?

◇◇◇◇◇

Just six days back in the saddle as leader of Arizona's MLK Day struggle, our church receptionist, Patty Davis, took a message from a David Schmidt on November 20, 1990. He identified himself as Evan Mecham's publicist. He told Patty that the Phil Donahue Show had contacted his client for whom he handled public relations (as much as anyone could be a P.R. person for former Governor Mecham). A show coming on the air within a couple of weeks was to feature Mecham speaking on Arizona's MLK holiday situation. The message continued, "At the request of Mecham, your name was referred by former Governor Babbitt and Art Hamilton for you to oppose Mecham on the show." The note went on to say that the

Donahue Show would cover the expenses to fly to New York and to please call Schmidt for further details.

I was quite surprised to receive such a message, as well as skeptical. Who was this David Schmidt? Mecham had a publicist? I did not know he had retained a public relations person to keep himself in the limelight. I just assumed he got the press to cover his stories like I did—by calling them up. Nevertheless, I called Schmidt and got his strange recording on his answering machine. He eventually called back after we played phone tag. He informed me that the offer was for real. He also promised to get back to me as soon as he got more information from New York. He was quite a fast talker and known around the Valley's media community.

One thing I did discover in our telephone conversation was that Babbitt and Hamilton had been the first and second choices, respectively, but both declined the invitation to appear across from Mecham and Donahue before a television audience of 22 million and a studio audience of 150 to 200 picked-at-random talk show visitors. I also called Frank Camacho to seek his advice on whether or not I should go to New York, since he had gotten me into this mess. He affirmed the opportunity for me to get *our* story out! I spoke with Art and he too urged me to say yes to the Donahue Show, in spite of whom I would be appearing with.

Later on Schmidt informed me that I would be allowed to take one person with me since he would be accompanying Mecham. I thought of a couple of people who would be able to coach me and possibly, appear on the show with me. Bill Jamieson was one, since he was a well-respected Democratic political consultant. The other person was my dear friend, Mark Reader, political science professor, author, crusader for environmental issues, peace activist and a remarkably conscientious genius. Between the two, it was Dr. Reader's lot to travel with me to appear on the Donahue Show. It is interesting to note that when Schmidt presented both names to Mecham, he vetoed Jamieson outright.

Within a couple of days, Monday, December 10, 1990 was set for the show's live airing to many of its sponsoring stations and next day showing on most of the other stations. The first Sunday in December I announced to my congregation that "The Ev and the Rev Show" would be appearing before their eyes at 4:00 p.m. on December 10. Of course, I solicited their prayers and uttered in somewhat desperation, "Our state will continue to suffer from a negative racist image, regardless of how true, until we pass the Martin Luther King, Jr. Day. We can't wait until 1992! The governor and Legislature have got to do something!" Once again, First Institutional encouraged their pastor with an enthusiastic round of applause.

My next mission was to prepare to debate Arizona's Martin Luther King, Jr. holiday in nationwide television with a person who had made a reputation for saying anything in public on virtually any subject. I began to compile all of the information I could on both pro-King Day supporters' arguments and anti-King holiday activists' pronouncements against the day. I researched my files and reviewed previous speeches I had written, press statements released and quotable quotes from King and others about him. I imputed into my memory as much as possible, including the ironic dates of King's birthday celebrations and assassination events on which Mecham made the news, mostly negatively, as well as Dr. King's strategy of nonviolent direct action, which we mimicked in launching our 1987 boycott.

The deputy chief of staff of the Phoenix Mayor, former Councilman Barry Starr, sent me a very helpful document of "speaking points" used by the city officials, when trying to keep the League of Cities convention in Phoenix for 1991. I rehearsed the analyzed factors that I and others had determined contributed to the dual defeat of King Day in the general election. I tried to decipher as best I could the contention that a majority of Arizona voters did indeed vote for a paid MLK Day, just not the same one. I got out Phil Jenks' *American Baptist* article about whether or not Christians should celebrate Columbus Day in the event that the Columbus Day issue surfaced before the cameras. About the same time of the election, accusations that Dr. King's allegedly plagiarized substantial parts of his doctoral dissertation surfaced, so I prepared myself to address that issue if it were to come up.

In preparing to confront the "enemy" head-on, I combed through numerous articles quoting Mecham's comments on King Day in Arizona. I especially wrote down a direct quote I read that Mecham had made when he declared the King Day observance in 1987. It read,

> By proclaiming the third Sunday of each January as Martin Luther King, Jr./Civil Rights Day, I act within my power as governor because it is not a state holiday giving paid time off to employees. This makes an official day for all who want to pay tribute to Dr. King's memory and accomplishments...For those who feel the holiday is not justified nor deserved, they are free to ignore it...

That was a quotation that I used on the Donahue Show when Mecham claimed that Arizona had a state holiday honoring King, which he declared. (Even though in my nervousness I misquoted the statement by substituting "Monday" for "Sunday.") I re-examined his official proclamation entitled "Martin Luther King, Jr./Civil Rights Day" and noted in the margin, "The word 'holiday' is nowhere mentioned in the proclamation and it is not an executive order either!" I reviewed the executive order instituted by Babbitt in 1986. All in all, I did everything within my power to get myself ready to represent what many believed were over 600,000 individual voters, out of a million who voted for a paid MLK Day in November. I even read up on the Mormon's position on admitting Blacks into the priesthood, which did not occur until the 1970s.

The Sunday prior to my verbal wrestling match with Mecham I came down with laryngitis, so much so, that I could not even talk above a whisper in either of our Sunday morning worship services. It was a blessing that it was New Members Fellowship Day at First Institutional and my friend, Dr. Walter Malone, Jr. of Kentucky, was our guest preacher for that day. I had to recruit my faithful co-worker in full-time ministry at FIBC, the Reverend Jerry Hillman, to take my handwritten pastoral emphases and read them to the waiting congregation. What made my predicament more frustrating was that I could not even announce that my six-year old son, Jared, had accepted Christ as his personal Savior the prior Sunday at our evening Communion Service after the new pastor of Tanner Chapel A.M.E. Church, Russell Thomas Hill, Jr. had preached mightily. Jerry simply read my remarks urging the people to pray for me at 2:00 p.m. Phoenix time which would be 4:00 p.m. New York time.

Even without a voice, I remained after the benediction at both services on Sunday, December 9th to shake hands with dozens of my parishioners and received their well-wishes, hugs and kisses as I was on my way to meet Phil Donahue and appear before millions of Americans for nearly an hour trying to get a point or two across.

Dr. Reader and I left that same Sunday at 2:25 p.m. heading to LaGuardia Airport. Once we arrived, a limousine met us at the airport and took us to mid-town Manhattan to the posh Drake Hotel where the small rooms, in which we each stayed, rented for $450.00 per night. Once we checked in at the desk, I had three messages. The first was a Western Union Telegram from my church family and three leaders of major ministries there, namely, Sis. Goldye F. Hart, Bro. Robert L. Williams and Bro. Lewis C. Huff. Their words of encouragement exhorted me,

> Tomorrow is not cancelled. May God strengthen you for the task facing you on Monday afternoon. Because of your leadership, Arizona will have a statewide paid King holiday. Keeping you and pastoral family in our prayers. We shall overcome.

Wow! As I looked back over that telegram dated about a month after I started VICTORY TOGETHER, it was definitely prophetic.

The second message was from David Schmidt who had handwritten a note on the hotel's stationery, "Welcome Rev. /Dr. How about breakfast in the morning? Rm: 1463 (Signed) David Schmidt (Your PR Man!) 9:00 a.m. or 10:00 a.m."

And then there was a message from none other than Arnie Zaler. Yep. My friend Arnie had called prior to our late arrival to say, "Good luck and go get 'em!! (P.S.) No need to call unless you want to or you can call to let me know how it went!" That was nice of Arnie to do that. I did not call him, but I felt he was pushing for all of us.

My voice was beginning to return by that night. Mark and I had conversed a little on our nearly six-hour flight to the Big Apple. He spent much of his time reassuring me that I would do well. It had been our hope to have Mark appear with me on the show. However, that next day we discovered that Mecham had nixed that. I bedded down about 11:00 p.m. Phoenix time, talked to the Lord about what I was going to be doing the next day (as if He didn't know), read my evening devotional and called home to let Serena know that we had made it safe and sound.

I nearly lost my appetite, due to shock, when Dr. Reader and I were joined at breakfast on Monday with Schmidt and Mecham. We met in the restaurant and the impeached governor was mild-mannered and cordial as usual. "Good morning, Reverend. How are you doing?" he said. He and Mark exchanged polite greetings and his P.R. man was bursting with unrestrained delight that he was about to witness the biggest public relations accomplishment in his career to have his client on the Phil Donahue Show. I was somewhat more reserved since this was only the third time I had been in Mecham's company, since November 1986. However, I was not really nervous because I was well aware that the former governor had consented to my making the trip to debate him about his beloved Arizona and Dr. King's day.

While ordering breakfast, we all enjoyed small talk about our respective families. I remember Mecham mentioning that he was the father of seven children and asking me, "Don't you have several children, Reverend?"

I swear I saw and heard the former governor speak abruptly to the waiter, who asked him did he want any coffee. Mormons are strict about not intaking any caffeine products. And this small-framed waiter who simply wanted to do his job was rather impolitely brushed away by my Christian brother. I wondered if the fact; that the waiter looked and spoke as if he was from the country of India have anything to do with the way Mecham interacted with him. Our impending debate just came up in passing. After breakfast, we shook hands and went back to our respective rooms. Mark and I had decided to check out before the limousine picked us up, since the Donahue Show began at 4:00 p.m. and our flight left at around 7:00 p.m.

Once we arrived at the ABC Studios where the talk show was produced and aired, we were taken to a dressing room where we could lounge and prepare to go on the air. I was kindly met there by my wife's uncles and aunts who lived in New York and dropped by to wish me well. Without a doubt, the Mitchell clan was well represented. I offered them some of the soda that had been prepared for me. Because the room was so small, Mark stepped out so I could have a little more room to fellowship with my in-laws. As the show time neared, one of Phil Donahue's assistants came in and prepped me on what would take place and confirmed that I would have to go it alone with Dr. Reader sitting only as close as the front row in the talk show studio room. I was then taken around to another larger dressing room, where hors d'oeuvres and other delicious sandwiches and goodies covered the counter. That was Mecham's dressing room, which he had already left. I gathered up some of the leftovers as permitted and took them back to my humble abode to share with my kinfolk.

A few moments before curtain time, Donahue's assistant came and got me so I could meet Mr. Donahue. As we turned the corner heading down a hallway to the entrance to the studio, there was my opponent, standing and waiting. Almost instantaneously, Phil came out and greeted us, made me feel very comfortable and led us into the studio where his show is filmed every week. There was really no stage, just a slightly raised platform. In the middle was a black table with three chairs around. I was directed to the middle seat with Mecham to my right and Donahue to my left. As I peeked into the studio audience, which is much smaller than what it seems on T.V., I searched out the whereabouts of Dr. Reader and located him to my left, off center in the audience. To my amazement, I looked in the audience and saw the brother of Deacon Joseph Bly, one of my beloved lay leaders who, along with his late wife, Gearldine, had hosted my family and me every second Sunday for years. I initially thought that he had come because I was there. However, I discovered that 90% of the audience had simply sent in for tickets weeks in advance to be a member of the studio audience and did not pick and choose an exact date or specific subject matter of personal preference.

I had hoped that two of my former classmates from Union Theological Seminary, who were pastoring in New York City, Dr. Calvin Butts of the Abyssinian Baptist Church and Dr. Marvin Bentley of the Antioch Baptist Church of Corona, could have gotten tickets to be present to give me moral support. My in-laws had to view the show from my little dressing room.

The studio audience was integrated racially, generationally and gender-wise. A moment before the show began they greeted the three of us who would be on the air. I was still a little nervous, but I had brought my own personal security blankets for confidence. I wore my favorite black double-breasted wool suit which, unbeknownst to the 22 million people who watched that program, had a patched inseam from where I had ripped the crotch while doing some "live" and nearly acrobatic preaching at First Institutional the first Sunday in 1990. My son's first grade teacher, Mrs. Bednar, had given me a little gold guardian angel lapel pin, which I had stuck on my tie for a blessing. I wore my Mizpah necklace, which my wife had given me years before. I had my brown pocket Bible in my inside coat pocket, just over my heart, and my FIBC logo lapel pin on my left lapel. *I was ready.*

My nerves calmed down after the first question or two; as I tried to be prepared to answer, respond, rebut, refute and challenge any questions and/or statements that Mecham and Donahue threw my way. My goal in accepting the challenge to debate Mecham before a nationwide television audience was to try to get the facts out about what really happened in the November 6 election and to hopefully restore some of the tarnished image Arizona had suffered by the perennial King Day debate and ultimate defeat at the polls. That proved to be a monumental challenge with Donahue picking and probing Mecham, in particular, trying to accuse him of being a racist in front of his face, before a live studio audience and viewers from every state in the Union. Mecham, in his opening moments, reiterated his paternalistic advice that he had mentioned to King Day supporters four years earlier, a couple of weeks after being elected Arizona governor, "What the Blacks need is more jobs, not more holidays. Now that's a true statement, I don't care whether you like it or whether you don't." Once again, it was obvious that the former governor perceived the MLK Day as "a Black holiday" rather than an American holiday. He also quoted his statistic about the King Day costing the taxpayers $5,000,000, and commended Arizonans for voting on the controversial issue.

When I spoke, I tried to get in the fact that at least 63 percent of Arizona voters voted for a paid state MLK Day in the general election. As a result, by the King Day vote alone, Arizona could not be called a racist state, especially since only 3% of the population was African-American. I spoke about our new effort to get voter approval of the federal model of the King holiday, which would not cost taxpayers one red cent. I tried to convince the audience in responding to Donahue's question about the NFL's interference in Arizona politics by withdrawing the Super Bowl that most King Day supporters have always supported the holiday solely because of his historic contributions to civil rights in America. I further stated that the Martin Luther King, Jr. Day and football and tourism ought to be separated. However, if the NFL chose to express its discontent with what Arizona had done to the legacy of Dr. King, then so be it.

Mecham scored points on the question, "Why should the holiday be paid to honor King?"

A couple of more incidents are worth mentioning. In response to Donahue badgering Mecham about being a racist or, at least, prejudiced like when he said, "Governor Mecham, I bet if you owned the bus company, Rosa Parks would still be sitting in the rear." Mecham responded something like, "I believe God created us all equal...." That is when I could not hold it any longer and interrupted, "Governor Mecham, your Mormon religion didn't even allow Blacks to enter the priesthood until the 1970s." He shot back, "Religion and God are different issues." Then, I said to myself, "Oh, brother, this man is sick." Aloud I said, "How can you say religion and God are separate?" Thank God, a commercial break stopped us before the governor blew his toupee.

During the commercial break, Mecham vented his anger toward me. "Reverend, let's leave religion out of this debate! That's a personal matter." Shocked at what he had just said, I responded, "Governor Mecham, you're the one who brought up religion." He barked back, "No, I didn't. I brought up God." Without a doubt, the Mormon faithful disciple was sizzling. I thought again to myself, *Oh, my God, what have I gotten into?*

Another incident that threw me while doing the show was the former governor of the state of Arizona not coming clean with the facts on nationwide television. The man stated that he had never said that Dr. King was not worthy of a holiday. My thought fired off below my breath, "That man didn't just lie in front of 22 million people." That is when I discovered we were not playing by facts and figures. I had come to New York, naively I guess, to "get the story straight and get the story out." It appeared that the two other major participants had other things in mind.

As the show's hour was almost up, I was concluding by saying something to the effect that "Arizonans wanted another chance to vote on the federal model of the King Day and I was there representing over 600,000 voters." Mecham retaliated, "I speak for more people than you do!" And the theme song of the Phil Donahue show began to signal the end of that once-in-a-lifetime show. Thank goodness!

Mecham grudgingly shook my hand after we went off the air. He was still fuming from my remarks about the former discriminatory practices of his Church. As we walked outside the studio exit, a photographer ran up to snap photos of Mecham, Donahue and myself. It was obvious that he did not care to take any photo with me. After a couple of shots, he headed toward his dressing room and I never saw him in person for months.

Me, I was depressed. The show had moved by so rapidly and Donahue played his role well at instigating and inciting. I felt I had failed in getting my message across. I shared that with Mark and he reassured me that things did not come off to the viewers, as it did to me. Our flight home via Detroit was one of the longest flights I have ever taken. I was glad it was at night and I could sleep off my intellectual and emotional hangover.

As I reflected on my experience, something else that threw me off balance was the reaction of the studio audience to the whole King Day issue, and particularly Mecham's positions on it. Having lived in New York City for four years while attending seminary, I knew New Yorkers to be some of the most liberal people in the world. Surely, I expected, those in attendance that day would be pro-King and anti-Mecham. Wrong! The audience was probably 55% to 45% leaning toward Mecham's positions on MLK, paid holidays and civil rights. So, I had to go through shock at their positive responses to some of what Mecham was spouting out, and then get myself back together quickly or lose it all. I also had to remember that many in the audience were not from New York.

Speaking of my days in New York, Donahue mentioned something about how did I feel as a native Arizonan having my home state accused of being racist. Before I could answer, the Utah-born Arizona transplant interrupted, "He's not from Arizona. He's from New York!" As I was opening my mouth to inform the audience that I was from Kansas, Donahue said, "Reverend, I didn't know you were from New York", and the audience applauded welcoming me back "home." Then, I said in passing, "Yeah, I'm from New York."

You can bet your boots that my relatives, especially my Uncle Gilbert who took Mark and me back to LaGuardia that evening, and friends from Coffeyville, Kansas could not believe their ears when they heard me say I was from New York. But before I could explain that I moved to Arizona from New York where I was going to seminary, Donahue had moved on to another question. Furthermore, it was Mecham who butted in, in the first place, to tell the audience where I was from. How in the devil did he know where I was from? Had he been checking up on me?

The next day, December 11, my 39th birthday, I read some of the local newspaper accounts of "The Ev and the Rev Show." Most were highly critical of Donahue's antics. They tried to salvage what they felt did not help Arizona's image. The headlines read, "Show airs debate over King Day", "Donahue viewers get earful in King Day debate", "Confrontation", "Donahue only fuels fire of King fight", and "Talk show host so bad, he makes Mecham look good."

To take matters in my own hands, I watched the December 10, 1990 Donahue Show for myself on my birthday. My oldest son, Warren, had videotaped it for his *new* television star dad. As I judged the debate, Mecham lost. My score tallied in at nine points for Ev and fourteen points for the Rev. A big boost came to me when Terry Hudgins called my office to say I did a great job. That was a mouthful from the former head of the MLK Better America Committee campaign. Calls began to come in from all over the country, from ministerial colleagues who had witnessed my appearance on the Donahue Show. One pastor, the late Dr. E. J. Jones of Chicago, called to tell me he just wept in joy, as I articulated the reason Arizona should celebrate King Day.

My late pastor-mentor's widow, Mrs. Sandy F. Ray, wrote me a note from New York at 5:30 a.m. on December 11 which read,

> Just a note to let you know that I saw the Phil Donahue Show yesterday. I am exceedingly proud of the way you presented

yourself and the matters concerning the Dr. Martin Luther King, Jr. Holiday!

The former gov. is out of his mind! I never really liked Phil Donahue....He has a way of trying to put you down...under the guise of trying to be fair.

He did not get away with any of his tricks...you were on target with all your responses! (Loved it)

I know your sons are proud, too! Keep up the good fight.... God bless and keep you all.

Of course, I know that those who complimented me on my presentation were biased, but it is always nice when someone takes the time to express appreciation for another's efforts to do well, regardless of how flawed they might be. In addition, several church members and VICTORY TOGETHER supporters commended me. Also, the following excerpts came from letters I received from Dr. Leon H. Sullivan and Arizona Supreme Court Justice Stanley G. Feldman, respectively. First, Dr. Sullivan.

I watched with great satisfaction and pride your presentation on Phil Donahue. You did an exceptional job. You represented our cause in a superb manner. I am sure the results of your presentation will be of great benefit to better human relations in Arizona.

Next, Justice Feldman who wrote me on January 2, 1991.

I recently saw a tape of the Donahue Show. I thought you did an excellent job and were a credit to the state.

Former Governor Mecham was about like I expected him to be, knowing him. I was very upset with Donahue who, I thought, was simply trying to make trouble rather than letting you get to the bottom of the issue....

To be sure, I had my detractors. My favorite anonymous pen pal began his epistle to me,

Dear Rev.

I saw you on the Donahue Show and you were a disgrace to Arizona, as well as to God...

Another letter came from a former local television reporter who had interviewed me on previous occasions. The writer informed me,

I watched your debate Monday on "Donahue", and I was very surprised by your arguments used to debate the…Holiday. For the first time in a long time, I can say, former governor Evan Mecham looked good.

I voted for a paid state holiday, I am Mormon, and I am not prejudice(d)….How can you then, on national television, bring up the subject of blacks and the priesthood and try to parallel that with Mecham and prejudism?

As a former reporter for KPHO-TV 5, I was surprised at your lack of preparation….Please try and rectify your damage to those who are Mormons and those who believe in the Martin Luther King, Jr. cause.

You can't win 'em all, but I do believe that my defending Arizona against the accusation that it was a racist state, due to the November election, enabled VICTORY TOGETHER and me to gain some instant credibility with many skeptical King Day supporters and future voters. Whatever the outcome of my appearance on the Donahue Show, my birthday present to myself was a promise that I would never appear in a debate with Mecham again! Nevertheless, the experience was an exciting, fun, unforgettable and frustrating experience, for which I would trade nothing in this world.

◇◇◇◇◇◇

Much of our credibility came from the members of our coalition. Although, until nearly a year or so later we had no listing of VICTORY TOGETHER steering committee members on our letterhead, not even my name, the word got out in the community that key players representing diverse and often diametrically opposed groups and special interests laid aside their differences for a few hours a week to work for giving Arizona another chance at voting on King Day. We also gained respect by the manner in which we organized ourselves and set up a definite clear-cut structure for developing our statewide broad-based coalition.

Michael Kelly was assigned the task of putting together VICTORY TOGETHER's organizational structure, in order to facilitate our mission. When he presented the first draft of his assignment at the December 12 meeting, we were all very impressed. The gifts and talents of that strong, articulate and intelligent African-American man, who was a new member of First Institutional, proved to be an invaluable asset to the new King Day effort.

One of the key suggestions Mike made was that we needed to establish a steering committee, which would fulfill the week-to-week activities of the larger VICTORY TOGETHER coalition. The steering committee was made up of eight subcommittees to assure broad-based representation. Each subcommittee was co-chaired by individuals representing different constituencies constituting VICTORY TOGETHER. The initial subcommittees were: education/ youth/ecumenical, legal advisory, MLK Holiday statewide coordination, voter registration, public relations, fundraising/ finance, governmental liaison, and volunteer. Moreover, several resource persons, in addition to Michael who represented grassroots organizations, and Kimberly Ovitt who was "on loan" to us from the Public Relations Society-Phoenix Chapter, became vital members of our steering committee, while representing key levels of political office and the tourism industry.

The only position in VICTORY TOGETHER that did not have a co-chair was mine. (And, believe me, that was not by my design.) In the previous coalition, I had led beginning in 1986, there were several general co-chairpersons. From hindsight, it was risky business to devise an organizational structure with no contingency person to preside, in case the general chairperson could not moderate the meeting for whatever reason, even incapacitation or resignation. As I recall, I chaired every meeting of VICTORY TOGETHER from its inception to its dissolution. Furthermore, the responsibilities of the leader of our coalition were far from ceremonial. As described in Kelly's organizational structure piece, first presented on December 12, 1990, I was to assume the following responsibilities:

> **GENERAL CHAIRPERSON**—This person maintains the lines of communication with the steering committee, subcommittee co-chairpersons, regional subcommittee co-chairpersons, calls and leads regularly scheduled meetings, checks on subcommittee progress, conducts planning sessions, maintains direction and resolves problems. This individual is also the primary spokesperson for the organization.

And to think, these responsibilities came from a beloved member of FIBC!

I was appreciative for the foresight of Michael to provide for and define the duties of the regional subcommittee co-chairpersons. The persons fulfilling these positions would guide the efforts of VICTORY TOGETHER in southern, northern and western Arizona. In conjunction with the regional subcommittee, co-chairpersons who would work under my direction, Mike drew a map dividing our state with its fifteen counties, which would illustrate the jurisdiction over which each regional co-chairperson had responsibility to guide the work of VICTORY TOGETHER. The initial idea was to set up several satellite offices around the state, especially in areas where there were major college campuses.

With a few, minor revisions; Michael's masterpiece was adopted unanimously by the entire group present at the December 12 meeting. Next, nominations came from the floor to people the steering committee and names such as Kelly, Tommy Espinoza, Bill Shover, Terry Hudgins, Caryl Terrell and Rosie Lopez were approved. As a sign of genuine sensitivity to separating King Day from the Super Bowl, Shover declined to be added to the steering committee, since he was still the very active chair of the Phoenix Super Bowl Committee.

Caryl Terrell spoke up and offered a motion that Warren Stewart would be approved as the general chairperson and spokesperson of VICTORY TOGETHER. Bill seconded the motion and my name was unanimously approved. Although, I was not all that shocked by what had just taken place, the next motion caught me off guard. Tommy Espinoza recommended that I be given the power to select all of the co-chairpersons of the various subcommittees. Once again, unanimous approval. With that said and done (and much work for General Chairperson Stewart to do at the same time, Pastor Stewart had to prepare to lead his congregation into another celebration of our Lord's Birth as well as put closure on the church's year, and project vision for the new year), Arnie offered our closing prayer and the meeting adjourned after two and a half hours.

◇◇◇◇◇◇

Once we got our organizational structure set up, our next major task would be launching our "People's Petition Drive" in order to get signatures to be presented to the governor and Legislature on King Day 1991 to persuade them to pass a resolution, putting our version of the MLK/Civil Rights Day and Washington and Lincoln Day on the ballot. We still had an astronomical goal of 300,000 signatures, but we thought we might possibly get that many persons to sign, since our "People's Petitions" only required that the signer be a resident of Arizona and was able to sign and print his or her name. That meant even youth could sign it. After all, the Mecham Recall petitioners collected over 300,000 valid signatures from registered voters.

After a few revisions, our "People's Petitions read:

TO THE HONORABLE GOVERNOR AND MEMBERS
OF THE LEGISLATURE OF THE STATE OF ARIZONA:

Whereas,

1) We want to be fiscally conservative and not add any cost or expense to our State, and

2) We want the people of Arizona to have the right to vote on "One **CLEAR** Choice" regarding the Martin Luther King, Jr. Holiday only.

We, the UNDERSIGNED, residents of the State of Arizona do hereby petition you to authorize an Election to ask Arizona voters to approve or disapprove **a Martin Luther King, Jr./Civil Rights Day for the Third Monday in January based on the Federal Model which combines George Washington Day and Abraham Lincoln Day into George Washington/Abraham Lincoln Day and avoids creating an additional paid state holiday.**

That petition's wording stated our cause clearly, and hopefully answered nearly every already asked question about Arizona's proposed King Day that the sincere inquirer could ask.

The press got word of our petition drive and made some mention of it. People began to call my office from around the state seeking petitions to distribute. The first batch was duplicated by First Institutional. As the demand increased for more petitions, Terry Hudgins got his employer, Arizona Public Service, to make 6,000 copies for our use. Meanwhile, plans were discussed for a press conference to officially launch our "People's Petition" Drive and introduce our newly formalized VICTORY TOGETHER "One **CLEAR** Choice" coalition. It appeared that the ideal time would be toward the end of the year after the Christmas holidays and as people looked to the new year with hope. Our hardest task was getting volunteers to circulate our "People's Petitions" while the majority of people were Christmas shopping, enjoying family and friends and/or leaving the state for the holidays.

We added a temporary petition subcommittee to oversee our petition drive. Zaler and Judith Connell, a conservative Republican activist who proved to be one of our most energetic steering committee members and key liaison to right wing Republicans who leaned toward supporting MLK Day, co-chaired that committee.

The first big MLK event, at which time we could pre-announce over "People's Petition Drive" was at the annual Inaugural Martin Luther King, Jr. Prayer Breakfast, which signaled the beginning of another year's King Day festivities in the Phoenix Metropolitan area. First Baptist Church of Phoenix served as the host site, once again. More than 600 persons packed into the Family Life Center of that church, still pastored by Paul Eppinger. During the program, I was given the opportunity to announce our petition drive. Thanks to staff and members of First Institutional Baptist Church and VICTORY TOGETHER volunteers, each table was equipped with the ordinary eating utensils, napkins and our "People's Petitions." I urged those gathered to pray, prayers of thanksgiving to God for lending us Martin King for 39 years. Next, I said, "Let's get these petitions filled out and then deliver them to the governor and Legislature to send a message that Arizona does want a Martin Luther King, Jr. state holiday." My comments were well received.

Of the two gubernatorial candidates still in the running, Goddard showed up, stayed throughout the 7:00 a.m. breakfast, and delivered enthusiastic words of praise for Dr. King, what he stood for, and then urged us to push forward for a holiday honoring such a man. His Republican opponent sent a message via an African-American Symington supporter, which warned us, in so many words, to back off and not urge the Legislature to take matters in their own hands again. How nice for the aspiring politician to preach to the unwavering admirers of the Reverend Doctor M. L. King, Jr.

Actually, Symington's telling us what we ought to be doing was little more than speaking the obvious. The votes were not present in the 39th Legislature, which was quickly moving into history. The much-touted special session to approve a "test drive" MLK Day for 1991 and place it on the '92 ballot, disappeared like steam from an overheated teakettle. As it had for the past four years, the House of Representatives was more apt to tackle the issue, while the cautious Republican senators did not want to touch it. Apparently, the lame duck Legislature had quacked its last official call on the holiday earlier that year.

The sports slant to Arizona's MLK Day fiasco continued to make the headlines. The Phoenix '93 Committee refused to give up on Super Bowl

XXVII. A high-powered delegation from Arizona had traveled to the nation's capitol on December 7 to explain to NFL Commissioner Tagliabue what actually happened during the election. I am sure they informed him that an estimated 60,000 voters changed their affirmative vote for Proposition 302 to a negative vote upon hearing Greg Gumbel's sound bite on the NFL's plan to pull the big game if the King Day went down in defeat.

Whatever they talked about in their two-hour meeting with professional football's chieftain, did not budge Tagliabue. All of the political clout, financial backing and "wings and prayers" of the group from our state consisting of Governor Mofford, Senator DeConcini, Bill Bidwell, Phoenix Mayor Paul Johnson, Tempe Mayor Harry Mitchell, Maricopa County Supervisor Jim Bruner, and Phoenix '93 Committee members C.A. Howlett and Shover could not get the job done. Anyone who saw that evening' local news coverage could tell by the forlorn expressions on their faces, when they appeared before the press immediately following their meeting, that no Super Bowl XXVII was an awful high price to pay for killing King Day at the polls. On the other hand, Tagliabue stuck to his guns and said in essence, "I'm sorry....Maybe another time when Arizona gets their act together and pays just tribute to Dr. King."

The NFL Commissioner's stance on withdrawing the 1993 Super Bowl, the NBA's refusal to let the All-Star game be played in Phoenix that same year, and the awarding of a professional baseball expansion team to a city other than Phoenix easily became top stories in the media around the country. Moreover, the financial loss of the two 1993 NFL and NBA showpiece games totaled $300,000,000 in projected revenue easily. What was going on in Arizona was such a hot news item that *JET* magazine did a three-page feature story entitled "Canceling the King Holiday In Arizona Sparks Hot Dispute" in its December 10, 1990 issue.

The 1991 Fiesta Bowl became the next near-casualty of the MLK Day mess in Arizona. Some of the potential teams to be invited had indicated that they would not come to play, even in one of the nation's top bowl games, because of the King Day defeat. A couple of weeks after the election, the Reverend Jesse Jackson identified Arizona as an example of "race insensitivity" and went further to express his feeling that "(It was) a race-inspired vote, not economic inspired." He did not stop there. As it related to the upcoming Fiesta Bowl, Jackson strongly objected to the game being played in Arizona, at all, and urged sponsors to move it out of Arizona completely. He also found unacceptable the Fiesta Bowl's decision to feature a halftime show during the New Year's Day game, in a tribute to Dr. King and American civil rights.

No small controversy erupted in Louisville, Kentucky where Black football players on the University of Louisville Cardinals team did not want to travel to Arizona, as one of the two invited championship teams to play on the first day of 1991 in Sun Devil Stadium in Tempe. Pastor Walter Malone, Jr. of the Canaan Missionary Baptist Church in Louisville urged the University's protesting African-American faculty representatives and community leaders to get in touch with me, in order to make a more informed decision on whether or not to push the school's officials to cancel their acceptance of the invitation. As was the case with the tourism industry in Arizona, the King Day controversy got tangled up in dollar bills.

Each institution whose team gets invited to a bowl game gets a certain portion of the game's financial receipts. So, while Black players, faculty members and community leaders in Louisville were making a big fuss about playing in "racist Arizona", the University of Louisville administration was fretting about the money they would lose.

The then executive director of the Fiesta Bowl, John Junker, contacted me for advice and came to one of our VICTORY TOGETHER meetings. I explained to him in my office that our coalition had no official position on the boycotting of Arizona. I also made it clear that King Day and sports would remain disconnected from this end. He did pledge to work with our coalition to win a King Day at the polls. The immediate help that he offered was to allow us to solicit signatures for our "People's Petitions" at the entrance of the January 1, 1991 Fiesta Bowl game.

As it related to reaching a compromise with the upset Louisville Cardinal African-American athletes and their activist sympathizers, an agreement was reached by Fiesta Bowl officials and the two institutions which would play one another in the bowl game—University of Louisville and University of Alabama—that each team would receive $100,000 for scholarships for minority students. That appeared to calm down the Kentucky controversy.

However, upon learning about the racially exclusive scholarship monies to be received by both institutions, an over-zealous assistant secretary for Civil Rights in the Bush administration's Education Department ruled that such scholarships were "illegal for federally supported institutions", which were prohibited by Title VI of the 1964 Civil Rights Act from offering any program that discriminated on the basis of race, color or national origin. The real irony was that the Bush official who announced the illegality of the Fiesta Bowl's plan to award the $100,000 for minority scholarship awards was a Black man by the name of Michael L. Williams. In addition, Williams' ruling spelled trouble for any institution of higher learning receiving federal monies for any reason such as research, construction or work study aid. His interpretation meant that any and all scholarships designated specifically for people of color were outlawed by the 1964 Civil Rights Act and consequently had to be halted.

It was embarrassing to believe that Arizona's overturning of Martin Luther King, Jr. Day was indirectly responsible for the potential eradication of scholarships set aside for minorities. Oh brother! However, to the credit of higher up White House officials, Williams' ruling was ignored until further study could be done on the accuracy of his interpretation of the 1964 Civil Rights Act as it related to racially exclusive scholarship funds. President Bush's spokesperson, Marlin Fitzwater, told the press that the president, who had vetoed the Civil Rights Act of 1990 because he said it would have created a quota system of affirmative action in employment hiring, was "very disturbed" about Williams' ruling. A case in point about how much credibility the academic community gave to the declaring of minority scholarships being illegal was the advice of the American Council on Education, which told "its 1,600 member colleges and universities to ignore the department's ruling, saying it (was) not official policy."

How many more far-reaching negative effects would the rejection of MLK Day in Arizona have? It had already divided a state, contributed to the downfall of an impeached governor, cost nearly half a billion dollars in potential and actual revenue, ran off popular socially-conscious entertainers, closed the door on a visit to the desert by Bishop Desmond Tutu, and so on and so forth. When would it stop?

We decided to officially launch our petition drive on December 31, 1990. Symbolically, it was our way of saying good-bye to the defeat of 1990 and hello to the wonderful possibilities of what 1991 held for King Day advocates. We could go no place but up. And that is the same position in which Martin Luther King, Jr. and his contemporaries found themselves in the 1950s and 1960s. Therefore, virtually whatever we did was worth the try.

Joedd and I had the assignment of flying to Flagstaff and Tucson to hold press conferences, announcing our petition drive, after we had held the initial news conference in Phoenix. The opening statements of VICTORY TOGETHER press release read:

Today the people of Arizona claim our right to a paid state holiday honoring Dr. Martin Luther King, Jr. by urging the state's leaders to return this issue to the voters as soon as legally possible so that we can decide on **ONE CLEAR CHOICE**.

Last November 6th, a majority of voters in Arizona clearly intended to pass some form of a King holiday but were split over confusing ballot propositions.

Today we are announcing that our petition drive is well on the way to obtaining thousands of signatures by the King holiday observance on January 21, 1991...

Our Phoenix press conference took place at First Institutional. It was well-received by the local press and put the King Day issue right back where we wanted it—on the front pages of newspapers and on the evening news—stating our pro-holiday, pro-active position.

Unfortunately, our Flagstaff and Tucson press conferences, held at the local airports of each city, did not go well. Flagstaff was freezing, as can be expected on December 31st, but the cold weather was not the problem. Somewhere along the line our public relations link had been broken down. There were no local reporters to meet us at the airport. After waiting for an hour or so, we called back to the church office to see if our public relations co-chairpersons had made prior arrangements for our coming. We eventually ended up calling a representative of the local Flagstaff newspaper, who knew nothing about our scheduled press conference. A half an hour later, the local television reporter who worked for one of the Phoenix stations came out and interviewed us. Joedd called some friends he knew in Flagstaff to see if they would distribute the petitions we brought for our Flagstaff VICTORY TOGETHER volunteers. A couple of students from Northern Arizona University picked up the petitions and promised to solicit signatures for us. Finally, although a little frustrated about not being met by reporters to build a northern Arizona King coalition connection, we felt our trip was not a failure. After grabbing a bite to eat, we flew back to Phoenix on a twin engine propeller plane to make our connection for Tucson.

Due to prior commitments, Joedd had to leave me in Phoenix. However, Art Mobley joined me at Phoenix Sky Harbor International Airport and we flew to Tucson. Once we got there, we found a couple of reporters who had come to the airport to cover our press conference. We were a little more encouraged by our Tucson reception. Clarence Boykins met us at the airport along with a photographer for a Black Tucson newspaper. They committed to distributing the petitions we had brought with us to the Old Pueblo. We said our say to the reporters, conversed about strategy with our Tucson connections, and made our connection flying back to Phoenix, this time on a Boeing 737 jet.

The next day, my three older sons and I covered the entrance to Sun Devil Stadium obtaining signatures from anyone who would sign them. About a dozen or so VICTORY TOGETHER members had volunteered to solicit signatures on that New Year's Day, but I supposed they were sleeping in from the night before. Other than a couple of volunteers that had solicited signatures in another area of the stadium, it was basically me and my sons asking many of the 69,000 fans who attended the 1991 Fiesta Bowl to sign our "People's Petitions."

Only one person turned us down, and the reason stated was that he supported an unpaid Sunday MLK Day. Many game-goers, when they discovered what the petition was for, enthusiastically signed their names and urged friends and family with them to do so. It was encouraging for a few folk to say, "Oh I've already signed one of those....Yeah, I support the King Day." Once the game started, there were very few people left to ask for their signature, so the boys and I took advantage of our "nose-bleed" section seats we had been given free and went to watch the University of Louisville embarrass the University of Alabama 34-7. During the half-time, my sons and I descended to the concession level and got a few more signatures.

It was a fruitful day, as well as fun-filled. I hate to say it, but that was the first college football game I have ever attended, since coming to Phoenix in 1977. I guess I could call it a small fringe benefit of working for King Day in Arizona. Our campaign got plenty of local, state and national publicity by being at the game soliciting signatures. NBC Sports did a live interview with me, a few minutes prior to kick-off. Jamie McFerren, then talk show host for KTAR, had me on for the Fiesta Bowl Pre-game Show, and one of my favorite persons had been contacted, without my knowledge, to provide a brief opposing viewpoint on the King holiday issue. His name was Evan Mecham who spouted his time-worn King-bashing spill. What little I saw of the special half-time show, which originally was supposed to extol the life and legacy of Dr. King had been watered down to celebrate the "red, white and blue" with a dash of mentioning of noted African-American heroes, including Martin Luther King, Jr. The Fiesta Bowl Committee had decided it might backfire to bring too much direct attention to the life and contributions of Dr. King if they had highlighted him exclusively in the firework-popping, band-playing and video-enhanced production. So, their "Celebrate America" showpiece featured the notable contributions of patriot Patrick Henry, Presidents Abraham Lincoln and John F. Kennedy, as well as Dr. King. But, if the purpose was to show the nation Arizona's commitment to the meaning of Martin Luther King, Jr., that goal was not met due to the fact that NBC, which broadcast the Fiesta Bowl, cut away after the Alabama and Kentucky marching bands performed to update New Year's Day "football addicts" on the bowl games played elsewhere.

I do not know how many signatures we received on January 1, 1994. It was a good number. But the highlight for me and my boys was having fun getting them and watching the game for free.

◇◇◇◇◇◇

Our efforts to get Carl Nicholson, who headed the almost phantom Arizonans for King Recognition, proved futile. Since both of our groups were trying to get the federal model of MLK Day on the ballot, the most logical thing to do was to combine forces. The sticking point that needlessly kept us apart was that Nicholson chose to take the initiative route, which would require over 105,000 valid signatures of registered voters while we chose to urge the Legislature to pass a resolution, putting essentially the same holiday proposition on the ballot. In spite of my calling Mr. Nicholson and leaving several phone messages, he simply would not return my phone calls. Furthermore, since he and Zaler had worked together for Proposition 302, it was our original plan for them to co-chair the temporary petition subcommittee.

The second day of the new year, VICTORY TOGETHER held a general meeting to update all interested persons on what had transpired since our last general meeting, the second week in December. Much of what I have already discussed in this chapter was shared with coalition members in my detailed progress report. As busy as we were with our ever-increasing operations, I had to bring up the matter of finance so that we could pay our bills. Thanks to Michael Kelly and Terry Hudgins, our organizational structure booklets and stationary needs were handled by in-kind contributions. Knowing our needs and my congregation's reputation for generosity to key causes, I had asked our members to give, in the special Christmas Offering envelopes, a contribution for VICTORY TOGETHER. In the middle of the Christmas holiday season, First Institutional's members gave

$5,000 to VICTORY TOGETHER. In addition, I had personally loaned our coalition $539 to pay for our travel expenses for the New Year's Eve press conferences in Flagstaff and Tucson. We also got authorization to open a VICTORY TOGETHER-"One **CLEAR** Choice" checking account in order to free the usage of First Institutional's checking account to pay for our political campaign.

Another source of additional income was a requested grant from ARIZONANS FOR A MARTIN LUTHER KING, JR. STATE HOLIDAY. In a letter I wrote to Pastor Barnwell, I requested a contribution in the amount of $3,000. I mentioned in my January 10 letter, "As a member of our coalition of MLK holiday advocates, I am sure you are well aware of VICTORY TOGETHER's lack of income to assist us in attaining our common goal." I went on to inform my colleague in Christian ministry that the MLK Better America Committee, UNITY and First Institutional had contributed in excess of $6,000 in in-kind contributions to the campaign.

I received no immediate and direct response. However, I did get a notice of the annual corporate meeting of ARIZONANS FOR A MARTIN LUTHER KING, JR. STATE HOLIDAY to be held at First New Life a week later. I attended the said meeting on January 17, 1991, and the tension was so thick in the room that it could be cut. Our former coalition had dwindled into two camps—the Barnwell camp consisting of my pastor-friend, Judge Williams and Opal Ellis and the Stewart Camp comprised of Terrell, Reader, Eppinger, Fears and myself. Attorney Gerald Richard and Gene Blue remained neutral and tried to keep peace. During the meeting, the financial report was given, showing cash assets of nearly $16,000. Over $6,500 had been used since I resigned as general chairperson in January, a year before.

VICTORY TOGETHER'S request for $3,000 came up. But, immediately, the issue of who our new coalition was and how ARIZONANS FOR A MARTIN LUTHER KING, JR. STATE HOLIDAY would officially relate to VICTORY TOGETHER surfaced. So, after much discussion that seemed unnecessary and somewhat humiliating to me, I offered to withdraw my request for the time being. The request was officially tabled. After we adjourned with prayer, I was relieved that we had formed a new coalition and I did not have to deal with certain fragile feelings of faithful but frustrated holiday crusaders.

The one thing that salvaged the meeting for me was our prayer for peace in the Middle East, which had erupted in a United Nations-sanctioned war between Allied Forces and Iraq. That very evening, Saddam Hussein, dictator and commander-in-chief of Iraq, had launched SCUD missile attacks on Israel. The threat of the biblically-prophesied Armageddon appeared ominously imminent. On that subject we released our fears and prayed earnestly that the end was not anywhere near.

The 1991 Martin Luther King, Jr. holiday celebration activities were not the only major events that dominated the mindset of our nation. The United States of America, as a member of the Allied Forces, brought together under the auspices of the United Nations, had engaged in war with Iraq. The January 15, 1991 deadline imposed by the Allied Forces had passed without the Iraqi Army pulling out of Kuwait, which they had occupied some weeks prior in a centuries-old territorial dispute. I, for one, was extremely upset that President George H. W. Bush would consent to a deadline for war on the night of the actual birth of America's Nobel Peace Prize Winner—Dr. Martin Luther King, Jr. How insensitive could this nation's leader get?

When the midnight deadline passed, the sky over the capital city of Iraq lit up like a fourth of July firecracker display, except the occasion was not a celebration. Hundreds, if not thousands of "bombs bursting in the air" as fighter jets and missiles from off shore battleships gave Baghdad a very rude and ruinous awakening. War 1990-style had begun, and America's "kinder, gentler" president who had been dropping in the polls instantaneously became the most powerful warrior in the world. Paradoxically, his yearly proclamation calling the nation to celebrate the principles of the life and legacy of Martin Luther King, Jr. was released like clockwork; even though his actions as Commander-in-Chief of U.S. forces engaged in the Persian Gulf War contradicted everything Dr. King stood for.

As a member of the Baptist Peace Fellowship of North America, headed by my former Union Theological Seminary classmate, Ken Sehested, I had been asked to coordinate a prayer vigil/rally for peace in Phoenix before the January 15 deadline. In spite of all the other activities, in which I was heavily involved, my staff shifted into "battle alert" and put flesh on my vision for the program and its participants that I planned.

We held it on Tuesday afternoon of the 15th of January in Wesley Bolin Plaza at the Martin Luther King, Jr. Memorial marker. I invited members of all faiths to participate—Christians, Jews, Muslims, Bahai, Unitarian Universalists and others. We gathered there for a simple and sacred service to earnestly petition God to change the minds of those opposing forces half-way around the world, who had literally drawn a line in the sand in the Middle East and mouthed threats back and forth at one another that each would be the victor in "the Mother of all battles."

Getting a Muslim and a Jew together on the same program that day was a *fait accompli*, especially since Hussein declared that he was engaged in an Allah-sanctioned holy war which would ultimately destroy "Zionist Israel." I also learned a lesson in Muslim-Jewish relations that day when I asked a very prominent Jewish leader to read a prayer that the Baptist Peace Fellowship had written to be used in the prayer services being conducted all over the country. When I handed the typed prayer to my Jewish colleague he quickly read it and handed it back to me saying he could not read it. Quite baffled, I turned to my Muslim ministerial friend and asked him if he would do it, to which we replied affirmatively. Mind you, this interchange took place prior to our beginning the vigil.

After reading over the prayer, the Muslim imam frankly said, "Reverend, I see why he would never read that prayer. It mentioned specifically by name Saddam Hussein in the prayer, and no devout Jew would utter that Arab's name in prayer." I was dumbfounded, but enlightened as to my naiveté. The Muslim leader continued, "Saddam is his enemy and he could never pray for an Arab enemy like Hussein." Ironically, the prayer also mentioned the prime minister of Israel by name. Nevertheless, in adherence to Islam, he read the prayer like it was printed after he prayed to Allah the Beneficent... in English and Arabic.

I left the King Memorial marker on a spiritual and hopeful high. What unity we had all experienced on the eve of a world crisis, yet coming together to pray with one another for *shalom/salaam (peace* in Hebrew and Arabic) in the Middle East. By late that afternoon, my faith in a peaceful resolution in the Iraqi/Kuwait/United Nations conflict was shattered. As I watched the latest news clips coming from overseas, I sank into deep depression.

The next night was Wednesday and First Institutional held its regular mid-week praise and prayer worship service, of course, the prayer focus would be on the brand-new war where lives were being taken by the minute. As I stood in the pulpit to offer the closing prayer, as I customarily do, I broke. I wept. I bowed my head down onto the same pulpit, from which I had preached the peace of Christ the King and cried like a baby. I was hurt deeply that leaders of nations could not find another alternative to working out their differences than killing each other. And to think that the Persian Gulf War commenced on the night of Martin King's birthday.

After I got my pent-up pain out, I could deal with it better. To protest the war, I wore a hand-made yellow paper ribbon that Jared had made in his first grade class that read "Peace in the Middle East." I wore it until the war was over.

One very positive consequence of the Persian Gulf War was evidenced in the largest march ever in Phoenix, in commemoration of the life of the crusader of love, justice, peace and non-violent social change and in a double-directed protest over Arizona's defeat of King Day and the war. Our annual MLK holiday marchers took their places at the march's beginning and along East Washington. But, 1991 saw anti-war activists, Viet Nam era "peace niks", and people of all colors, creeds and causes converging on the State Capitol. By the time we arrived at Wesley Bolin Plaza police estimated the crowd to be more than 25,000. Never before, for a federal observance of King Day, had this happened. Moreover, the celebration spirit was appropriately subdued and an almost sad, sacred sense of solemnity inspired the thousands who honored King and his philosophy of non-violence, more than ever that day.

The program that day consisted of the "regulars" who always spoke about the hope that "this would be the year that Arizona would approve the King Day for keeps." In addition to those persevering African-American legislators, the governor, Phoenix mayor and Attorney General Grant Woods, who was very much a Republican, shared the platform and their hopes for a King Day. The special guests on that day were the most Reverend Edmond L. Browning, whose official title was Presiding Bishop and Chief Pastor of the Episcopal Church of the United States. He was accompanied by his Arizona host, Bishop Heistand, and the Right Reverend Herbert Thompson, Jr., Bishop Coadjutor of the Diocese of Southern Ohio, and a brother of ebony hue. Their presence had been designed to show moral support for our struggle to honor King, and probably to smooth over any ill feelings many Arizona King Day advocates might have had about the Episcopal Church of the USA not canceling its convention here.

The former mayor of Phoenix was right up there, where he had always been. His GOP opponent was "playing it safe" by not showing up. With the gubernatorial run-off coming up in a few weeks, his appearance on the stage with so many radicals and militants might have spelled trouble at the polls. My friend, Tommy Espinoza, was with us on stage as well as Councilman Goode. I was the last speaker on the program and took the opportunity to present about 25,000 signatures on our "People's Petitions." I had Mayor

Johnson's two sons and two of my sons, Matthew and Jared, to stand in front of the podium beside the boxes of petitions while I gave my remarks. There was no need for a rousing speech like I usually had given on behalf of the King Day. The petitions said all that needed to be said to Governor Mofford and the brand new 40th State Legislature.

The 25,000-plus King Day marchers coupled with the 25,000 signatures urging the Legislature to put our MLK/Civil Rights Day to the people for a vote enhanced the credibility of VICTORY TOGETHER's identity and purpose. Also, the fact that community leaders like then President Lattie Coor of ASU, Bishop Heistand and new Secretary of State Richard Mahoney publicly joined in on our celebration caused skeptics to take notice that the new campaign that had started in the fellowship hall of Arizona's leading Black church was headed toward victory.

In spite of the progress VICTORY TOGETHER was making in reaching out to persons from all walks of life and political junkies from both sides of the fence, we had to work at being intentionally broad-based and bipartisan. I often found myself advocating the "rights" of our Republican steering committee members, who were too frequently reminded by our Democratic King Day veterans that the GOP in Arizona had been the party that killed the MLK holiday for the last eighteen years. The late Caryl Terrell and Judith Connell, Democrat and Republican activists, respectively, traded verbal jabs at one another on a regular basis, usually initiated by Caryl. Nevertheless, both women proved to be two of the hardest workers our coalition had, as well as resources for what their respective party machines could and would do for passage of King Day.

One particular partisan mishap, that was no fault of our own, occurred when Goddard sent a letter out to everyone on VICTORY TOGETHER's mailing list advocating passage of the King holiday, while questioning J. Fife Symington, III's commitment to the holiday and soliciting volunteer and financial support for his campaign. A donor/volunteer card and self-addressed envelope were enclosed. All of us knew that politicians get ahold of special interest mailing lists about as easily as getting a phone number out of the directory. That was not what created such a furor among the Republican members of our coalition who, of course, were working to put Symington into office. The explosive issue that almost caused a secession by our Republican members, led by House Minority Whip Chris Herstam, was that Goddard's letter was sent out on his campaign letterhead with our VICTORY TOGETHER logo underneath his name.

Hmmm? That sounded kind of familiar to something that happened in 1989. Could there be a connection? Did one of our coalition members who anxiously wanted to see Goddard take it all somehow give them our mailing list? Whatever the case and at the strong urging of our Republican contingent, I dictated a letter to Mr. Goddard on January 17 after talking with his campaign manager which read,

> VICTORY TOGETHER…from its inception has been a broad-based, bipartisan group of advocates for a Martin Luther King, Jr. state holiday.
>
> Therefore, we strongly object to and request that you and your campaign office NOT use our logo (see above) on any of your stationary or campaign literature….To do so threatens the unity in our cohesive coalition.
>
> Lastly, contrary to what your letter of the 14th of January states, Mr. Fife Symington has come out publicly supporting the Federal model of the Martin Luther King, Jr./Civil Rights Day proposal advocated by VICTORY TOGETHER.
>
> Your immediate compliance with this request will be appreciated.

What had happened that necessitated such a strongly-worded letter to our unwavering King holiday friend was that the press had gotten a hold of Goddard's letter and asked persons in Symington's camp how they felt about VICTORY TOGETHER's support of Goddard. Because of the potential volatility of the controversy surrounding the letter, I had my letter hand-delivered to Goddard's campaign office and he responded in writing that same day by (1) reaffirming his support for the federal model of the King Day and having the Legislature to "test drive" it and put it on the 1992 ballot; (2) explaining that he had asked his campaign workers to put a portrait of Dr. King on the letter he sent out to show his support of the holiday, but did not know they had chosen VICTORY TOGETHER's logo; and (3) disagreeing with my characterization of Symington's position on MLK Day, had renewed his invitation to Symington to make a strong public stance for King Day, as advocated by VICTORY TOGETHER.

Believe it or not, once I shared Goddard's letter with VICTORY TOGETHER Republicans, I received a copy of Symington's position statement on a paid MLK Day which was about "as clear as mud." Goddard had been right. Symington's full-page, typewritten, single-spaced statement entitled "MARTIN LUTHER KING HOLIDAY" was ambiguous, to say the least.

I discovered quickly that a few of the business community's representatives had some doubts about me and my gang. But, persons like Bill Jamieson and Jack Pfister enabled me to lower my guard enough to work effectively with "junior" Phoenix 40 prospective members. Over the two-year period that VICTORY TOGETHER led the campaign, it was safe to say that "we grew on one another." Ironically, though, the three individuals who represented previous grassroots segments supporting the holiday—Pastor Barnwell, Arnie and Carl Nicholson—did not wholeheartedly buy into VICTORY TOGETHER as their organization too. But, the Lord knows that I made several overtures to bring those committed King Day leaders into the fold under my leadership.

And that, too, was a problem. VICTORY TOGETHER's steering committee was made up of leaders in their own right, leaders very different from each other in so many critical ways. But, the key in such a situation is working the best you can with those who will work with you. As far as the holdouts, be cordial, be respectful, keep the door open, if possible, and press on.

◇◇◇◇◇

By the first week in February, the newly-seated 40th Legislature had received communication from VICTORY TOGETHER on what we wanted by way of letter and petitions. Governor Mofford in her last State of the State Address had introduced the "test drive" proposal which made me very nervous. I was concerned about the risks of having the Legislature to pass an interim holiday for 1992 and jeopardize the voter approval of the same version of the holiday in protest later that year. I shared those concerns with the veteran King Day sponsors in the Legislature, namely Art and Carolyn, as well as with business leaders who still were trying to win the 1993 Super Bowl back before the March meetings of the NFL owners. Not being a dictator (to the surprise of many), I put the question of whether or not we should support the "test drive", before our coalition in a general meeting or February 6, and the groups echoed some of my concerns and voted to go for the "permanent" holiday to be decided at the polls in 1992.

I also shared that several Republican legislators still had concerns about the combining of the two separate presidential holidays observed by Arizona into our proposed George Washington/Abraham Lincoln Day. Judith Connell had informed me that placing Lincoln's name in front of Washington's might be more palatable for them and their constituents to accept. By our February meeting, the Senate Government and Public Safety Committee had voted on a resolution for a Martin Luther King, Jr./Civil Rights Day and a Lincoln/Washington President's Day, which was approved 8 to 1. I asked our members, "Do we accept the Senate's modification of Lincoln/Washington/President's Day?" In little time, the slight modification was affirmed by our coalition.

Fife Symington won the run-off election for governor on February 26, 1991. On Monday, March 11, 1991, the new governor appeared before the House of Representatives to urge them to approve House Concurrent Resolution 2011, which would place VICTORY TOGETHER'S King Day proposal before the public with the minor Lincoln/Washington/President's Day modification. It passed by a vote of 40-11, with no Democrats voting no, although, for some reason, four did not vote. The next day, Tuesday, March 12, the Senate voted in favor of the same legislation 25-4, with only one Democrat abstaining. It was a done deal. Our "One **CLEAR** Choice" would be on the 1992 general election ballot.

The gentleman who never returned my calls re-surfaced once the Legislature had made his work easier, and announced that Arizonans for King Recognition would discontinue their initiative drive which, according to Nicholson, had "collected over 30,000 signatures to place an initiative on the 1992 ballot that would allow the citizens of our state to vote straight up to honor civil rights in Arizona through a federal model, tax neutral, Martin Luther King, Jr. holiday." He, then, pledged his group's support for passage of the new referendum to be voted upon in 1992. In his press statement, Nicholson spoke about "believing so strongly in the lessons of cooperation taught to us by Dr. King." Then, he alluded to some changes that were rocking the Legislature, which would call for scrutiny and reform. We never heard from Carl Nicholson and Arizonans for King Recognition again.

◇◇◇◇◇◇

March 12, 1991 proved significant for another reason, other than the confirmation that VICTORY TOGETHER had attained our first major objective by getting our MLK proposal on the election ballot; even though a year later than we had hoped, via the Legislature's overwhelming majority vote in the House and Senate. That is also the day I wrote a detailed letter to Mr. Paul Tagliabue and the NFL Owners Association meeting on Big Island of Hawaii.

No, I had not compromised my principled belief that the MLK Day and Super Bowl should be segregated from one. As I said before, the motivation for the "money men" in Phoenix should have never been the primary catalyst, which converted them into "born again" King holiday disciples. However, I did understand how the power of Dr. King's life and legacy caused socially conscious organizations, at least, superficially so, to use their mouths, means and money to protest the way Arizona, as a state, had disrespected his memory. I was not about to passionately solicit Tagliabue to reconsider his soon-to-be official recommendation to NFL owners to boycott Arizona in 1993 by tossing Super Bowl XXVII out of our bounds, as I had urged Bishop Tutu and Yolanda King to "come on over and give us a hand."

Bill Shover was a risk-taker. He knew how to gamble for what he wanted badly. So, in spite of his knowing my feelings about the Super Bowl-Martin Luther King, Jr. Day connection, he inquired if I would travel with the Phoenix '93 Committee delegation to Hawaii in order to explain to Tagliabue what happened in the 1990 vote and inform him of VICTORY TOGETHER's mission. I could hardly believe my ears when Bill called and propositioned me to make the trip to Hawaii. He even granted me a day or two to think about it.

Trying to be polite and principled, I reminded Shover of my position on the Super Bowl, even though I had never asked the NFL not to come to Arizona. Then, I saw on my calendar where I had a previous engagement of some importance that would not allow me to attend, especially since the NFL owners meetings began on Sunday, March 17. Bill responded, "Oh, Warren, you could miss a Sunday. Your people wouldn't mind too much.…We'd fly you over there at your convenience and fly you right back. Everything would be taken care of…Please think about it, and I'm even going to say a prayer to get you to change your mind."

I really did not have to think twice about going on the final, futile mission to keep Super Bowl XXVII in Phoenix for 1993. However, I waited a day or so and called Bill to inform him that "I just couldn't make it." He was disappointed and even made a last-ditch effort by saying, "Warren, you're the man. If anybody can get Tagliabue to change his mind, it's you." Of course, that was flattering whether it was "b.s." or not. Here was a member of the Phoenix 40 saying that a Black man, and a Black preacher at that, was the most critical person in the state who might be able to convince another

White man who headed a multi-billion dollar organization to change his mind and award Phoenix a two hundred million dollar bonanza. *Now, that's a long way from Coffeyville, Kansas.*

Everybody who was anybody in Arizona politics had been writing and/or talking to the NFL Commissioner. The new governor had been talking to Tagliabue over the telephone trying to get him to look at the business aspects of the bowl game coming to Arizona. Senator DeConcini put poison in his pen by writing a letter which, in essence, called Tagliabue, Norman Braman and the NFL *hypocrites* for threatening to pull the game from Arizona while: (1) The NFL offices celebrated MLK Day on February 15, about a month after the annual third Monday in February observances of the holiday, (2) Braman allowed his auto dealerships to remain open on King Day, (3) only one coach in the NFL was Black in contrast to the race of 60% of the players, (4) there were no African-American owners or general managers, and (5) two of the pro-teams were "culturally insensitive" as a consequence of being named the Washington Redskins and Kansas City Chiefs. DeConcini went on in his letter to blame the television report announcing the league's intention to cancel the Super Bowl bid if the voters turned down the Martin Luther King, Jr. Day which was aired two days prior to the election in 1990 for the defeat of the holiday propositions.

Another testy letter was written to all the NFL owners by Phoenix's youthful mayor and hand-delivered to all the addresses attending the Hawaii meeting. A particularly accusatory letter to Braman was published in the *Arizona Republic* on March 15. Without commentary, I take the liberty to share excerpts:

> ...since your position has been made abundantly clear in the national media, I will reluctantly accept your personal opposition to my community. But I will not accept your hypocrisy (sic).
>
> Mr. Braman, as the apparent moral watchdog of the National Football League, the City of Phoenix will be watching with great interest as you delineate your personal preferences for future Super Bowl sites. Specifically, we are anxious to see if you utilize the same measuring stick on other cities—as fairness ought to dictate.
>
> Will you support Los Angeles, where police recently mutilated a Black man with nightsticks? Or San Diego whose citizens overwhelmingly voted to strip Dr. King's name from a

public street? And will you vote to go back to Louisiana, where David Duke serves in the state legislature—and who received 600,000 votes to serve in the United States Senate? And will you continue to operate your own businesses on Martin Luther King Day, while the cities of Tempe and Phoenix observe the holiday?

I don't hold entire communities responsible for these kinds of injustices…

…Above all, I know that Dr. King stood for fairness.

Many of us will be watching to see if that's where you stand too.

With me declining to make the trip to Hawaii, Shover had to find a Black leader substitute. We tossed around several names, including Pastor Barnwell and Lincoln Ragsdale. Then, Junius Bowman's name came up. After all, he was the long-time CEO of the Phoenix Urban League which had been the *preferred* African-American organization of the White business community. Junius was an articulate, intelligent and obvious Black man who had lived through the Civil Rights Movement and had helped improve Black-White relations upon his arrival to Phoenix in the 1960s. Shover and the Phoenix 40 crowd knew Bowman well and would feel very comfortable with him representing Arizona's 3% African-American population. Surely, we all knew why they needed a Black man from Arizona (other than the Art Mobley-type) to appear before Tagliabue and the "fat cats of football."

In lieu of my joining the Hawaii-based "missionaries" who had added Bowman to their witnessing team, I agreed to write a letter to Tagliabue and the twenty-eight NFL Owners Association. My letter dated 3/12/91 began,

> At the request of Mr. William "Bill" Shover,…and Mr. C.A. Howlett, President, Arizona Chamber of Commerce, I am writing this letter to you to clarify what happened during the November 6, 1990 General Election in Arizona as it relates to the Martin Luther King, Jr. holiday. Hopefully, after reading this letter, it will enable you to make a final decision about the 1993 Super Bowl coming to Arizona.

After that opening paragraph, I explained my analysis of the King holiday defeat and provided information about my leading ARIZONANS FOR A MARTIN LUTHER KING, JR. STATE HOLIDAY and VICTORY TOGETHER up to that point. It was basically the same letter I had written to Bishop Tutu except for the next three paragraphs. Then, I addressed the link of the holiday struggle with the Super Bowl directly.

> I have consistently and publicly said that the Super Bowl '93 and Arizona's Martin Luther King, Jr. holiday efforts should have **never** been connected. Arizonans should support the Martin Luther King, Jr. holiday simply because "it's the right thing to do." Regrettably, Super Bowl '93 and the King holiday became linked and it appears that some 60,000 voters used the link as a reason to *change* their affirmative votes to negative votes last November. God-willing, in November 1992, we will rectify that.

My next to the last paragraph informed Tagliabue and company,

> Lastly, you might want to know that nearly every organization and entertainer who have asked me for clarification on what exactly happened and for advice on whether to keep their engagements to come to Arizona have decided to come and make a strong, public statement in favor of Arizona winning a Martin Luther King, Jr. state holiday.

My last sentence inviting Tagliabue to contact me, if needed, was to no avail because by Tuesday, March 20, 1991 the NFL owners voted to disqualify Arizona for the 1993 Super Bowl, in spite of an impassioned appeal made to the owners by the president/CEO of the Phoenix Urban League. But, to the surprise of the members of the Phoenix '93 delegation who made the six hour flight to Hawaii, the owners awarded Phoenix the 1996 Super Bowl in a "compromise gesture" as a result of the emotional appeal for mercy from the Arizona group. *The Phoenix Gazette* credited Governor Symington with contributing to the "compromise" through several long-distance phone calls to Tagliabue that week. Although it was publicly stated that there was no connection between the passage of King Day in 1992 and the 1996 Super Bowl, everybody knew. So, it was still "No King Day, No Super Bowl." Nevertheless, the flight home for the Arizona Super Bowl fans was relatively an upbeat one. Yes, they missed the longshot by being officially denied Super Bowl XXVII, but they got a multi-million dollar carrot to hang in front of their eyes. And, they assured themselves, as well as the NFL, that Arizona *would* approve its King holiday in 1992 without their help or, probably better said, *interference*.

Back on the home front, another business person, Robert A. Gosnell, Valley developer and builder, was trying to get the Legislature to authorize that the ballots on Propositions 301 and 302 be unsealed and recounted to show that the people of Arizona really voted for a holiday. Probably due to the complicated nature of what he was requesting the Legislature to have done, his idea did not win approval. I met with him once or twice, but did not get a clear picture of how he was going to get the results he desired by the recount. Also, I was chilly on it because he wanted the information in order to prove a point to the NFL owners while meeting in Hawaii.

The Sunday after we got the Legislature to put MLK/Civil Rights Day on the 1992 ballot, I wrote words of encouragement and thanksgiving to my congregation in my Pastoral Comments.

> "Nothing beats a failure but a try." Out of the gloom and shock of the November 6, 1990 defeat of both propositions…, the Lord inspired me to present a proposal to an embarrassed Arizona to win a Martin Luther King, Jr./Civil Rights Day for the third Monday in January by the vote of the people based on the Federal model. Ironically, with the exception of requiring the holiday go before the electorate, it is the same proposal I presented as General Chairperson of **ARIZONANS FOR A MARTIN LUTHER KING, JR. STATE HOLIDAY** to the Arizona State Senate leadership in 1988.
>
> Well, two MLK holiday approvals, two MLK holiday overturnings by referendum petitions, and two MLK propositions being defeated at the polls later, the Arizona State Legislature, this week overwhelmingly approved the proposal I presented on November 14, 1990 under the banner of **"VICTORY '91: 600,000 FOR MLK-"One-CLEAR Choice"**…God-willing, in November 1992 we will vote and approve this ideal version of the MLK holiday. Without your support and helping us present between 25,000 to 30,000 signatures on our "Peoples Petitions", I do not think the Legislature's action would have come so quickly (in spite of others who might get the credit).

The Phoenix '93 Committee may have lost a football game, but VICTORY TOGETHER won some respect.

◇◇◇◇◇

The credibility of King Day advocates was jolted by an unexpected political earthquake that shook the Arizona State Legislature to its core. By early February 1991, the rumors began to surface that several legislators and lobbyists were about to be indicted by a state grand jury on charges ranging from bribery, receiving illegal campaign contributions, money laundering, and even conspiracy to commit murder. An undercover "sting" operation had been conducted under the auspices of the Phoenix Police Department and Maricopa County Attorney's Office, which involved at least eight legislators. The bait was the loaded issue of legalizing casino gambling in the State of Arizona. The authorities created an individual under the assumed name of "J. Anthony Vincent" who threw thousands of dollars at pro-legalized gambling state lawmakers, almost like it was toilet paper. "Vincent" allegedly needed to "buy" a few votes so he could be one of the first to set up his money-making operations in Arizona. This infamous probe, which brought down several lawmakers became known as "AzScam."

Both Republican and Democratic legislators were recorded on video cameras and tape recordings, either asking for and/or receiving money for themselves personally and/or their campaigns. Regrettably, most of the representatives and senators who got caught had been strong supporters of Arizona's Martin Luther King, Jr. Day. Prominent Democrats who would be forced to resign from the state office included one of my then district's representatives, Bobby Raymond, Representative Sue Laybe who had spoken at one of ARIZONANS FOR A MARTIN LUTHER KING, JR. STATE HOLIDAY's press conferences in 1989, Senator Jesus "Chuy" Higuera from Tucson who had cast many strategic votes in committee and on the floor of the Senate for King Day and the foremost MLK Day lawmaker in the Senate and first African-American woman elected to that August body, as well as to serve as majority whip, Ms. Carolyn Walker from District 23 in South Phoenix. Republican lawmakers indicted included three representatives, namely, Jim Hartdegen, Jim Meredith and Don Kenney, whom sources said had pocketed about $60,000.

Ironically, on the same front-page of *The Arizona Republic* dated Wednesday, March 20, 1991, where the bold, black headline read, "NFL pulls Super Bowl", with Tagliabue's photo in the center of the upper portion of page one, there was another headline a little less bold off to the right, upper half of the front page which read: "Ethics panel urges ouster of Walker." Underneath that headline was a photograph of Senator Walker about the same size as Tagliabue's mug shot. That feature story was published on the same day that a shaken, saddened and tarnished Senate body voted 27-0 to expel one of their colleagues and our key King Day sponsor in that chamber.

The woman who had soared from being a freshman representative, speaking and acting on behalf of her constituents in one of the most disadvantaged districts in Phoenix to a nationally recognized, outspoken African-American female success story, for her efforts to win passage of Arizona's MLK Day had refused to resign, as did her other indicted colleagues in the Legislature. Because the Senate Ethics Committee on which a majority of her fellow Democrats sat, as well as the Republicans on the committee, judged that she violated Senate ethics rules and campaign finance laws, there was really no alternative other than expulsion.

Most of our coalition members were shocked at what we saw on television and heard on the radio. "What more would Arizona have to go through?" many of us wondered. Our state was just getting over the national embarrassment caused by impeached Governor Mecham's short, but damaging tenure. Arizona was being compared to Alabama in the 1960s and South Africa in the 1990s due to the perennial defeats of the Martin Luther King, Jr. Day. The two billion dollar debacle surrounding Charles Keating's savings and loans collapse and the linking of both of Arizona's U.S. Senators DeConcini and McCain, to him, further made our state's politics and politicians suspect. And along comes AzScam.

The immediate concern of VICTORY TOGETHER, early in February was, "Would AzScam delay and/or derail our efforts to get the federal model of King Day on the ballot?" As already indicated, it did not. Perhaps, the political scandal in the Legislature might have provided incentive to get something publicly positive accomplished in view of yet another embarrassing episode in Arizona politics. With the national spotlight on Arizona anyway, exposing all of the imperfections at the State Capitol and the polls, passing anything related to MLK Day could be nothing but a plus.

When "AzScam" first became public, I wrote the editors of the major newspapers in the state a short letter, dated February 6, 1991, on First Institutional letterhead which read,

> During these difficult and dark days in our beloved State of Arizona, we need political and civic leadership based on principles rather than politics. With God's help, we shall overcome *even* this latest crisis that has jolted the rank and file of the Arizona State Legislature. But, we must change our ways of doing business for the good of Arizona.

I also wrote a very similar letter to the legislative leadership in both the House and Senate, including the Honorable Senator Carolyn Walker. In my letter to them, I offered my prayers and "any further assistance", if needed.

About three weeks after Senator Walker had been kicked out of the Senate and was facing criminal prosecution, I sat down and dictated a letter to her. She was getting beat up pretty badly in the media. The editorials, cartoons, commentaries, radio talk shows and the like served "shredded Walker" for consumption on a daily basis. I really felt for her and her teen-aged daughter. Carolyn, being a single parent, had been both mother and father to her child. As can be expected, the fall-out did not stop at the Senate. Eventually, she lost her job with US West. But, before that happened I felt I needed to communicate with her.

Thank God, she had the compassionate and caring counsel of her pastor, the Reverend Barnwell. A couple of other Black community activists/ leaders ministered to her in a most meaningful way. But, as is usually the case when a prominent leader falls on hard times, whether guilty or not, friends, associates, supporters and well-wishers thin out quickly. Most of the same people who have been the beneficiaries of the fallen leaders' direct or indirect actions, *contract acute amnesia relative to most or all of the good that that leader has done and join the bandwagon of naysayers and critics in crucifying the reputation of the leader whose help they have received.* Former Senator Walker experienced such unjustified, ungracious and self-righteous ostracism from so many who had walked and worked with her. Believe me, *I* know how she must have felt.

I felt I had an interesting relationship with Senator Walker. I cannot say we were close, but I did support her when she first ran for the House of Representatives, and again when she decided to make the transition to the Senate. I will never forget a small, private meeting that was held at First New Life Missionary Baptist Church and the discussion of Representative Walker came up. The consensus of those present was that she was not the strongest African-American candidate to run against probable South Phoenix Hispanic seekers of state senatorial office. However, I stated her case in that meeting and served as a one-man minority report indicating that she ought to go for it. Those in attendance were all Black males making a "seasoned" judgment on the woman who would run and win the Senate seat in District 23. Although I did not inform her of what took place in the meeting, I sent her a small donation for her soon-to-be victorious campaign.

Of course, we worked together on the King holiday. However, most of my one-on-one contacts were made with Representative Hamilton, the senior African-American legislator in Arizona. But, whenever I called her office or needed to get to her, she made herself available. During her campaign swings, she was welcomed to the pulpit of First Institutional to bring greetings. (And that was something very few politicians of any color were allowed to do during our Sunday morning worship services, even though I have ceased that "seasonal" practice altogether.) It was only until I noticed her liberal view on abortion that I began to feel somewhat distant from her. Before I became actively involved with Arizona's pro-life movement, I really did not pay attention to a politician's stance on abortion. In response to a letter of inquiry that I had written to her about her position on abortion in 1989, she sent me a rather direct letter stating her unwavering position on a woman's right to an abortion. I am almost certain it was a form letter sent out to all inquiries of her position on that subject.

Getting back to the letter I wrote to Ms. Walker on April 10, 1991 during the Easter season, it was sort of confessional and certainly an attempt to be encouraging and compassionate. Some of what I said read,

> This letter is long overdue. But, it has been on my mind for several weeks.
>
> First, I want to thank you personally for your historic leadership in both the Arizona House of Representatives and…Senate. During your years in office you provided strong, courageous and sensitive leadership and representation for not only your constituents in District 23, but the downtrodden and oppressed masses as well as persons of color in Arizona, particularly African-Americans! We are indebted to you for that.
>
> Of course, your forthright advocacy of the Martin Luther King, Jr. state holiday in Arizona will always stand as a testimony to your commitment to civil rights.
>
> My appreciation of your past leadership as one of "our" elected officials is not to deny that you and I differed on certain issues. We did, and that is expected.
>
> Moreover, please know that regardless of what was reported pertaining to my public statements about your alleged AzScam involvement and defense fund, I never once responded to their questions about you as an individual legislator allegedly involved in AzScam. My consistent response was, "It appears that the (indicted) legislators betrayed the public trust. Therefore, I

believe they should apologize, repent and resign." A matter of fact, when the *New Times* reporter asked me about your defense fund, I refused to answer, asked her if she had any more questions and told her that "out of respect and sympathy for Senator Walker, I have nothing to say other than what I said on KTAR."

I have shared the above information with you, simply out of a personal desire of mine.

Our congregation has prayed for you and your family, and I will continue to do so. One of my prayers is that the God of Resurrection will allow a Resurrection experience to occur in your life, in order to give you victory.

As I made a small donation to one or two of your previous campaigns, I would like to make a small personal gift to you for your personal use.

God loves you, Carolyn, and so do I.

Blessings on you and your family.

The reference to "public statements" had to do with me being mis-quoted by a *New Times* reporter. One thing that I clearly remember the Anglo female reporter saying in an exasperated voice, "What's the matter? You don't want to say anything negative about Carolyn Walker because she's Black?...I haven't heard leaders in the Black community say much of anything about Senator Walker....I guess you all are sticking together."

And you know, in a very real sense she was right.

◇◇◇◇◇◇

With a pro-King Day, pro-business Republican governor heading the state, it was a foregone conclusion, that Arizona Republicans would want to be a part of the solution to winning a King Day rather than the problem, as they had been in the past. The same Symington who refused our invitation to march to the State Capitol on the federal observance of King Day in 1991, just a month prior to his victorious run-off election, became a "mover and shaker" prodding the Legislature, Tagliabue and the business community, to get the holiday show on the road. I guess I should not be too harsh on Governor Symington because his support for the holiday would cast his GOP party in a more favorable light than the last Republican governor of the state. Moreover, if he had any ambitions beyond being Arizona's chief executive, his holding that office when the King holiday passed would bring him immediate national attention. Many of us in VICTORY TOGETHER took the position of observing our new governor to see where he really stood on King Day.

During May 1991, I had a revealing meeting with Governor Symington's top African-American aide, Bruce Mayberry. He came to my office in our temporary church offices on East Washington to talk to me about his boss's role in the King Day campaign. Bruce was a bright, progressive Republican "buppie", which is the African-American equivalent to a "yuppie", i.e., a young, upwardly mobile professional who was Black. He was the man who would link the "blue-blooded" J. Fife Symington with the Black community.

Mayberry began his spiel by making reference to all the King holiday groups still floating around the Valley in addition to VICTORY TOGETHER, namely, ARIZONANS FOR A MARTIN LUTHER KING, JR. STATE HOLIDAY, UNITY, Arizonans for King Recognition and the remnants of MLK Better America. He alluded to infighting among the pro-King Day advocates. I am sure he had talked with people who had worked in those coalitions, all of whom had been extended an open invitation to come on board with VICTORY TOGETHER. No doubt, rumors and innuendos about my leadership had been the topic of some of his conversations and discussions about the King Day. At that point, he diagnosed our problem.

"What you guys need to do is set your egos and personal agendas aside. You know you're splintered and divided…" Then, the brother had the nerve to suggest, "How about the governor calling all King holiday advocates together to meet with him. You guys can dissolve your respective groups, and let him lead the King holiday effort."

The Bible speaks about "zeal without knowledge", and Mr. Mayberry certainly was a living example of that shortcoming, when he opened his mouth to suggest that long-time King Day workers step aside for his boss to get the credit. As if the above-mentioned statement was not enough to get him thrown out of my office, Mayberry said, "After all, Fife is the governor of the state and he's the rightful person to head the Martin Luther King Day campaign by virtue of his office." Then, my ebony brother hinted, "A Black man cannot lead a successful campaign of this magnitude in Arizona.…You need the governor. You know some people are saying that you're holding onto the leadership of the MLK campaign so you can run for office."

I suppose I gave the governor's representative one of my noted Warren H. Stewart, Sr. frowns and scowls. I wondered to myself, *Has this young, upstart Black man lost his mind? And where have he and his boss been all those years we were meeting, marching and protesting for a King Day?* I don't even remember how our meeting ended that day, but I do know it ended very shortly after his suggestion.

From hindsight, I can see that he was simply trying to do his job of representing the new governor of Arizona, who had appointed him to a high-paying political payoff job for laboring in his campaign. What better "brownie point" could he make than arranging it so that a White Anglo-Saxon Protestant, multi-millionaire Republican governor could lead the charge in his state, making history by winning MLK Day by a vote of the people? However, at the time of the conversation, I felt that Mayberry had sold out his Black identity to our blond-haired, blue-eyed chief executive of the state. But, thanks to Michael Kelly who had worked closely with Mayberry, he deciphered for me what Mayberry was trying to say, after several telephone calls between the two of them.

In sharing the comments of Mayberry with Art Hamilton, he advised, "As victory looks more apparent, there will be a lot of entities who will want to take the lead of the King holiday campaign. Don't relinquish your leadership, Reverend." Art's words were almost like prophecy. Once the Legislature put it on the ballot in their March 1991 resolution, I started getting shot at regularly from "friendly fire." The verbal assault and under-mining got so bad that I had to express it in a VICTORY TOGETHER steering committee meeting in early June.

A month prior to the June meeting, at which time I unloaded both barrels of pent-up frustration from sneak attacks from several King Day camps, VICTORY TOGETHER held a strategic planning meeting on Saturday, May 4 at the Valley National Bank Building in downtown Phoenix, in, of all places, the corporate board room. Steve Roman had arranged the space for that meeting. It was hard to believe that our grassroots struggle for MLK Day had elevated me and several other veteran holiday activists to one of the "ivory towers of Arizona capitalism." Just being up there, just below the penthouse-level Golden Eagle restaurant, gave me an eerie feeling. Maybe that was because it was Saturday and nobody else was there except the custodians. I looked around at the photographs on the walls of former boards of directors. All of them had basically one common denominator—all White men.

All of our coalition's steering committee members were invited to attend, along with our resource persons and representatives from Governor Symington's and Senator McCain's offices, respectively. Out of our committee of 18 very diverse persons, the core group showed up on that first Saturday in May, namely, Blue, Terrell, Reader, Solomon, Bender, Mobley, Miller, Pfister, Kelly, Roman, Hudgins and Lisa Loo, one of our newest and most committed members. Our special guests at that meeting were two political consultants, a pollster, and Jeff Eldot of the Public Relations Society of America, all of whom had been asked to present their evaluation of what went right and wrong with the last King Day election. In addition, Roman and Hudgins had been asked to share insights from the MLK Better America Committee, and Art Mobley, as a journalist, would provide his analysis of the last campaign. All of the presenters were to advise us on where and how VICTORY TOGETHER needed to be headed. Alfredo Gutierrez had been scheduled to provide his suggestions on what we would do to ensure victory this time, but he had to cancel out.

After providing a welcome and introducing ourselves to one another, I shared an overview of my twice-revised proposal that, by that time, specified winning MLK Day by vote in the general election. Once that was done, Roman and Hudgins analyzed the campaign that they co-coordinated for MLK Better America. Their analysis was very candid, above-board and even self-critical.

They summarized their effort as being basically a ten-week media campaign, which did not have any choice in the selection of the wording of Propositions 301 and 302. How a proposition is worded on the ballot is extremely important to its success or failure. Voters need to know *clearly* what they are voting on. The two suggested that central theme was important for the 1992 campaign. They also admitted that MLK Better America did not run a grassroots effort or reach out in the rural areas of Arizona. Their emphasis had been on Maricopa and Pima counties, the two largest urban metropolitan areas in Arizona, which they had hoped to win by larger margins than they did. Since both of them were working full-time on their regular jobs throughout the campaign; they realized, from experience, that our effort would require a paid, full-time day-to-day campaign manager, at some point. To my embarrassment, they pointed out that the statistics of that election revealed that there was low voter turnout in African-American, Native American and Hispanic precincts. It was also brought out that their polls, which indicated just prior to the election that they would win by nearly 60% were subject to people lying about racial issues. There was no speakers' bureau, and even though they were running the statewide campaign, they had no control on "other" King Day groups and leaders speaking out about the holiday.

The MLK Better America campaign, in their opinion, was run as effective as possible under the circumstances. They were highly commendable of political consultant Bob Robb. Through their big business backers they raised $1,000,000 for the campaign, and for that, they were grateful. In looking to victory in 1992, the two corporate Arizona junior executives recommended that Hispanic involvement be sought, increase phone banks close to the election, and egos must be controlled. In conclusion, they could not over- state the damage that the NFL announcement had done to their prospects for victory the Sunday prior to the election.

Dr. Michael O'Neil opined, based on his experience as a pollster, that one clear central theme was an absolute necessity the next time around. He said that our advantage was that we had a "14-month campaign period." He agreed that the federal model of King Day was a plus for two reasons: (1) no additional cost and (2) it conformed with the rest of the country. Surprisingly, O'Neil felt that "lying about racial" issues to a pollster "was not a major factor in the defeat," and that the economic argument might prove more compelling in the new campaign. However, he was emphatic that we should highlight "King's role in changing America for the better", thusly, utilizing the moral argument. He also felt that the strategy of educating the public on the meaning of civil rights and doing public service announcements on civil rights would be effective in gaining voters.

Judith Connell had introduced me to a young political consultant from the conservative right-wing of the Republican Party. His name was Tim Mooney of Southwest Policy Group. Mooney's strategy suggestions started off by challenging new leadership to emerge in 1992. He believed that voter anger toward the political and business establishments and institutions contributed significantly to the defeat of King Day. He further forecasted that AzScam, redistricting and generational changes would adversely affect the outcome of the 1992 election. Then, he showed transparencies of possible television and radio commercials he would want us to run in the campaign.

It was Bobb Robb's turn to reflect openly about the campaign that he had consulted for, as well as how the new campaign might do what he and MLK Better America almost did. He told us to begin with a "fresh" strategic focus. The situation and circumstances, in which the 1992 election would be held, was much more favorable for victory. It would be a presidential election year that would bring out more "King Day-friendly" voters. Our proposition would be fiscally conservative. He analyzed that almost two-thirds of the electorate possessed a "more complicated view of the holiday issue than the 33% who wanted it for the right reason." Differing from O'Neil, Robb felt that "mini-civic lessons" did not work with many senior citizens. He also felt that our proposition would have a problem with King having his name on a holiday while Washington and Lincoln had to share a day. In his opinion, the "yuppie" crowd did not plug into the "civil rights causes." Moreover, we were going to have to face the "connection" with the Super Bowl. To win, we would need more support from senior citizens and rural communities. We would have to make sure that middle-aged, upper-income voters were with us.

Art's presentation was not long. He simply suggested the need for a central theme. He brought up his favorite subject—the Arizona boycott, as being an example of an effective tool used by Dr. King. He felt that it was working for us in that the NFL refused to hold the Super Bowl in Arizona in 1993. He mentioned that the people who said they changed their votes, after the Sunday NFL sound bite, were no votes anyway. He agreed with O'Neil that Arizona voters needed to be "schooled" in the Civil Rights Movement led by Dr. King.

The last presentation that morning was made by Jack Pfister, which provided a skeletal outline/timetable of what and when we needed to be doing certain things such as fund-raising, refining initial strategy, celebrating the 1992 MLK holiday, conducting the campaign, incorporating and scheduling meetings with political and business leaders.

Our strategic planning meeting lasted for four and a half fruitful hours and we scheduled a follow-up meeting with the entire steering committee for June 8, 1991. Michael Kelly again evidenced why he was such a valuable asset to VICTORY TOGETHER. He, with the cooperative assistance of my secretary, Ms. Solomon, facilitated the critical meeting, which produced the outcome of gaining credibility.

Between the May meeting and the June follow-up meeting, I flew off to Africa to be a participant in the historic First African/African-American Summit held in Abidjan, Ivory Coast, West Africa organized by veteran civil rights activist and pastor, the late Dr. Leon H. Sullivan, who had made Phoenix his home and headquarters for his International Foundation for Education and Self-Help. His vision was to liberate Africa through "building a bridge for the future" between Africa and African-Americans. It was a trip that I will always remember, especially our stop by Goree Island off the west coast of Senegal where we observed and entered the cruel, haunted buildings, which were the last stop for Africans stolen from their native land before they were herded on slave ships headed for fierce oppression as chattel in "America the Beautiful…Land of the Free" and elsewhere.

Arizona's Martin Luther King, Jr. embarrassing holiday battle would travel with me to my motherland. Many of the popular civil rights leaders who had linked hands with Dr. King in the 50s and 60s marches and protest had made the historic trip upon Dr. Sullivan's invitation. Dr. Joseph Lowery, Dr. Dorothy Height, Dick Gregory, Ossie Davis and Ruby Dee, Congressman William Gray, Dr. Benjamin Hooks and Mrs. Coretta Scott King all took part in "building a bridge for the future" between Africa and African-Americans. To my surprise, one evening during a banquet, Dr. Sullivan introduced me to the audience as the key leader working for the Martin Luther King, Jr. holiday in Arizona and an "up and coming" leader to be watched. He asked me, on the spot, to come up and bring greetings. I was so nervous I do not know what I said, but I did receive a round of applause as I left the podium, still shaking on the inside. Dr. Sullivan's introduction of me caused several questions to come my way about what was wrong with Arizona. By the time I got back to the States, my friend Calvin Butts, called me from New York to ask me about being the "heir apparent" to Dr. Sullivan's visionary leadership. I chuckled on the inside about his comments as well as Dr. Sullivan's "prophecy" on my supposed future national leadership. I have heard that before, spoken in reference to me, but the Lord has me still on "desert assignment." I plan to be faithful to His calling on my life, whether I am stuck here for 40 years or I make it to wherever others say I am heading.

During one of the morning general assemblies in the auditorium, I went early to get a seat on the front row, so I could witness close-up the gathering of African heads of states and/or their high-level representatives, as well as African-American national leaders who sat on the multi-tiered platform. That particular morning, I happened to be sitting beside the late Dr. Benjamin Hooks, immediate past executive director of the NAACP, talking about the King holiday, when a brother came up and asked all of us to give up our seats (except Dr. Hooks) for a special guest. A pastor-friend of mine from San Francisco said that he was not going to move, so I joined him in our impromptu sit-in. Anyway, there were a couple of seats available for this dignitary and an aide. Momentarily, everyone was asked to stand as the widow of Dr. King was escorted to the front and was seated in between yours truly and Dr. Hooks. She had just arrived by special jet to the Summit. I nervously greeted her, after we were seated. Several camera persons began to flash several snapshots of her. In one of the special issues of the local Abidjan newspapers, there I was, photographed with Mrs. King and Dr. Hooks. Quite humbling they identified the two of them and mentioned under my photo spot "an unidentified man." Oh, well.

Mrs. King and I talked very briefly about our efforts to honor her husband with his day in Arizona. She gave me encouraging words and said, "I hope the Arizona people will come around and join the nation in honoring Dr. King." So, there I was *in Africa* addressing my state's difficulty in getting an MLK holiday for keeps.

Upon my return from Africa, we added some new persons to our VICTORY TOGETHER steering committee to broaden our base of support: Mike Shea of the Arizona AFL-CIO; Mary Orton, executive director of Central Arizona Shelter Services, Inc.; Rosie Lopez of the State Department of Education; Rabbi Robert Kravitz; Delores Grayam of the Tucson Civil Rights Commission; Ray Clark, executive director of the Tucson Urban League; and a person to be appointed from Flagstaff, all became members of VICTORY TOGETHER by the middle of June. Kimberly Ovitt from Public Relations Society of America joined us as a resource person.

The June follow-up strategy meeting again took place in the Valley National Bank boardroom, courtesy of Steve Roman. That June 8 meeting proved to be critical for several reasons.

First of all, that is when I began each meeting with excerpts from Martin Luther King, Jr. statements, after the opening prayer. On the agenda of each subsequent meeting was the line item entitled "Words from Martin." The first words came from a book written by noted Black theologian, Dr. James H. Cone, who was a former seminary professor of mine. He inspired me to get my doctoral project paper published, which is in its fifth printing as *Interpreting God's Word in Black Preaching*. Dr. Cone's new book was entitled *Malcolm & Martin & America: A Dream or A Nightmare*, in which he compared and contrasted two of the 20th century's most powerful and prophetic African-American leaders, whose lives affected race relations in America, long after their assassinations. Thereafter, I endeavored to select words from Dr. King's prolific writings and speeches, which would keep us on track as to who we were endeavoring to honor.

Secondly, the small campaign strategy committee that had been appointed in the May strategy meeting brought back their report, which recommended that VICTORY TOGETHER begin the selection process for a professional campaign consultant to lead us to victory in 1992. To do so, our coalition would need to raise an initial $100,000 over the next several months with an ultimate goal of $1,000,000. The recommendations were adopted after discussion about structuring the campaign's fundraising so contributors at all levels would be recognized, and not just the "fat cats."

Speaking of "fat cats", the issue of whether or not Governor Symington should be invited to be a part of the steering committee came up. It was unanimously agreed that to have him on the committee would make our coalition appear to be partisan. The compromise was to make room for a representative of Symington, who could keep the Governor's Office informed on correct information about our efforts.

Next, two significant committees were formed. A motion was made to establish a small campaign committee to oversee campaign activities on a weekly basis and to interview and recommend a political consultant to be the steering committee. Jack Pfister, Bill Jamieson, Judith Connell, Caryl Terrell, Art Mobley and I would serve on that committee with Steve Roman providing leadership as a resource person. The other committee that came into being was MLK principles committee, which would develop a set of principles to delineate succinctly our identity and purpose. I was more excited about that committee than the campaign committee. Within the next few days, Dr. Mark Reader, Toni Merchant, Joedd, Caryl and her husband Joe, and I took the responsibilities of developing our principles and philosophy. Once again, the above-mentioned actions were part of our plan to establish credibility, by doing what we were supposed to be doing with excellence.

Jack Pfister updated us on the progress of becoming a non-profit organization and incorporated. We made a few parliamentary motions to move that project along and established a board of directors of no more than twenty-five members. Lisa Loo was named vice-president. Jack Henry was approved as treasurer. (I hate to admit it, but I never met Mr. Henry to my knowledge during the holiday campaign, and he never attended a steering committee meeting. However, it was understood that he was named to that position because his accounting firm agreed to keep all our finances and accounting above board and in line with the laws. Steve Roman recommended him because he had done the same thing for MLK Better America.) My secretary became VICTORY TOGETHER's secretary and I was elected president.

After that business, it was my turn to blow off some steam. As I mentioned previously, I was getting ambushed on a frequent basis, during the spring of 1991. Most of the hits were the "throw and run" type. So, I had Janice type a three-page, single-spaced "general chairperson's comments" for the June 8 meeting, which I had intended to be handed out to all whom were present. But, after second thought that it could fall into the "enemy's hands", or worse yet, the press, I simply read my statement aloud. The statement was read with anger mixed with disappointment that touched the core of my being.

> The ultimate attainment of that goal (VICTORY TOGETHER's) and **VICTORY** for the (MLK/Civil Rights Day) in Arizona will come only, if and when *every* member of our broad-based coalition of (MLK) advocates works **TOGETHER**. Our name— **VICTORY TOGETHER**—can be a self-fulfilling prophecy. On the other hand, **VICTORY DIVIDED** will be virtually impossible as well as harmful to the already tarnished....

> When I was asked to return to provide leadership for the state of Arizona on the King holiday *after* its defeat at the polls on November 6, 1990, I reluctantly and prayerfully consented after "wrestling with God" on the weekend of November 9-11, 1990....

> ...Between November 14, 1990 when **VICTORY TOGETHER**'s first meeting took place, many of us have met with governmental, political, religious, business, civic, academic, community and grassroots leaders and groups....

> We have endeavored to be *inclusive* in the make-up of both our coalition's general and steering committees. It is my estimation that **VICTORY TOGETHER** constitutes one of the most broad-based, diverse coalitions ever organized in Arizona. At every juncture, **VICTORY TOGETHER** has endeavored not to become embroiled in partisan politics...

After making reference to our getting Terry Goddard straight on using our logo, I brought up the *other* party.

> Likewise, we do not expect and will not tolerate Republican partisan politics to dictate or dominate **VICTORY TOGETHER**'s agenda. Moreover, it is a proven fact that Republican support

for the King holiday in the last election was soft and left much to be desired.

Only when Republicans, Democrats and Independents lay aside our respective partisan agendas will we attain *one* goal through **VICTORY TOGETHER**.

Therefore, as we proceed in our historic campaign, it is imperative that **VICTORY TOGETHER** coalition members endeavor to build and earn **MUTUAL RESPECT** and **TRUST** for one another.

My next declaration would "hit the nail on the head" as it related to the cheap shots and rumors that were coming my way. I could feel the tension rising within me and my anger pushing for exit. Somewhat trembling, I proceeded,

Unfortunately, over the past several weeks, our efforts to build mutual respect and trust have been tested by several comments to me coming from various independent sources, which include the following:

I began by mentioning anonymously Mr. Mayberry's suggestion that we close shop and let the governor take over. Then I went on to others, such as,

Warren Stewart has stated strongly that he does not want the governor or big business involved in the King holiday effort at all.

That had been shared with me in a telephone call I received from Bill Shover on May 28.

Continuing the comments I had heard,

Whoever leads the King holiday effort will gain enormous political clout.

Governor Symington and his staff are quietly recruiting members for their own "grassroots" King holiday campaign.

"Warren, why are you stepping down as leader of **VICTORY TOGETHER?**"

"Hey, Warren, I was defending you in a meeting with the governor and…"

Then came the hammer that I slammed down on the table. As I look back at what I had to do that Saturday, I think about Jesus around the Last

Supper Table informing the Twelve that one of them would betray Him and they all would fall away, except it appeared that Jesus kept his cool. "Most regrettably", I said, "some of these comments have been attributed to members of **VICTORY TOGETHER**, whether or not it is true."

At that point, I identified a key group I felt was trying to discredit my leadership.

> From my viewpoint, it appears that "big business" may have some reservations about following the lead of **VICTORY TOGETHER,** in spite of our sincere efforts to include them at every juncture of our planning from November 14, 1990 to today.
>
> …**VICTORY TOGETHER** is a broad-based "grassroots" organization (and by the way, needs to recruit *more* "grassroots" representatives). And **VICTORY TOGETHER** will *remain* a "grassroots" organization which will always take the "moral high ground" on the (MLK/Civil Rights Day) by espousing the principles and philosophy of the person we seek to honor with a holiday in Arizona.

At first, there was silence in the room as people recuperated from what I had just said. Then, Jack Pfister offered a motion that **VICTORY TOGETHER** go on record as supporting me as the "right leader to lead us to Victory in 1992", and Caryl Terrell seconded the motion.

I felt better. I said what I wanted to say and laid things on the table. Among my coalition steering committee members, the issue of mutual respect and trust was dealt with decisively, and we would move on.

And we did!

◇◇◇◇◇

Our next general meeting was set for June 26, 1991 in order that we could update the public on what had taken place, since we last met in February. In the meantime, the campaign committee had much work to do, traveling to Flagstaff, Tucson and possibly Yuma to establish **VICTORY TOGETHER** committees in those places. We also had to develop our principles/philosophy statement and find potential political consultants in the heat of Arizona's summer.

Chapter Fourteen
Victory Together—"One Clear Choice" Coming Into Its Own

A major point in my Master of Divinity thesis entitled "Do Prophets Exist in Our Contemporary Culture?" dealt with the matter of *identity* and *purpose*. An analysis of Israel during the period of the biblical prophets revealed that God's chosen people almost invariably strayed away from their liberating Lord and His Law when they could not answer correctly the following two questions, "Who are we?" and "What are we supposed to do?" *Identity* and *purpose* are absolutely critical for any person and/or group who had been given a mission to fulfill. Further study of Israel during the ancient prophetic times indicated that the Hebrew nation had little problem in reminding themselves of their privileged status of being called out by God. A matter of fact, they boasted in who they were. The problem that led to their nation's conflict, chaos and ultimate defeat could be traced to their failure to complete their God-given *purpose*.

With that theological perspective on *identity* and *purpose*, it can easily be understood why I was excited about the one-and-only meeting on principles and philosophy that took place in my old pastor's study on June 14, 1991. The "sho' nuf" MLK Day faithfuls had been assigned the task of developing VICTORY TOGETHER's *identity* and *purpose*. In opening with prayer, I asked the Lord to guide our thoughts, in order that we could discern who it was He wanted our racially, ethnically, socially, politically, professionally, religiously, philosophically, economically and generationally mixed-up band of King holiday crusaders to be and what would be the guiding principles and philosophy to enable us to attain our clear-cut goal.

Next, I shared ideas from Dr. Cone's book on Martin King and Malcolm X. The three points that I mentioned that my former Black theology professor identified as constituting Dr. King's "frame of reference" included (1) the Judeo-Christian teachings on justice and love, (2) the Declaration of Independence, Pledge of Allegiance and other key constitutional documents and (3) King's personal experience with racism in America. Dr. Reader discussed the important need for our coalition to extol King's philosophy of non-violence and his inclusion of all peoples, regardless of social or economic status into his vision of a world, free of racism and discrimination from any means. The others present—Caryl and Joe, Toni Merchant, Joedd and Mike Kelly—contributed to the meaningful discussion that proved fertile in producing what I consider as one of the key achievements of VICTORY TOGETHER. The principles and philosophy, to which we gave birth that morning, would remind us and inform many who worked with us toward our common goal *who we were*, thanks to God and Martin. The finished product, which was adopted by our coalition in its entirety was as follows:

OUR STATEMENT OF PRINCIPLES

VICTORY TOGETHER is a broad-based coalition of Arizonans dedicated to securing a Martin Luther King, Jr. Day for the third Monday in January as a way of celebrating the principles for which Martin Luther King, Jr. and so many others have lived and died. These guiding principles include:

- A Recognition of the Interrelationship of Justice, Love and Community,

- A Commitment to Human Equality and the Fundamental Worth of All Persons,

- An Awareness of the Historical Importance of Non-Violent Social Change,

- A Dedication to the Empowerment of Peoples in an Interdependent World, and

A Pledge to Fulfill the American Dream of "Life, Liberty and the Pursuit of happiness."

The **VICTORY TOGETHER** campaign will endeavor to reflect and educate ourselves and others through these guiding principles.

This statement would become, for me, if no one else, our "sacred scripture" outlining our *identity* and *purpose*. Although it was simple and succinct, in it could be found principles that, if practiced, would eliminate nearly every human-caused problem society faces in the fifty United States and around the globe. The feeling was that the principles/philosophy committee members had just engaged in an undertaking, which was blessed by the Divine. I guess it could almost be said of what took place that day is often said when the Holy Spirit anoints an African-American worship service, "We had church that day!" The Reverend Joedd Miller dismissed us with a word of prayer.

However, just before we pronounced the benediction at our "service" we felt led to deal with lesser hallowed things, like financing. Mark, who was even more wary than me of the "big business" component serving in our coalition, recommended that "we challenge every contributor to VICTORY TOGETHER to make a matching contribution in the name of Martin Luther King, Jr. to the causes and peoples that reflect the guiding principles of our campaign." Without a doubt, that would be a noble gesture, which could produce a more lasting effect than even King Day.

The day before our principles/philosophy meeting, the campaign committee convened for the first time. We had several items to discuss and/or act upon in the very near future. The agenda items began with the question of how many persons would actually serve on the campaign committee once we "officially" began. The numbers settled on were 11-13, which was a little bulky, but large enough to allow representation from our diverse coalition constituency. The initial ten named were Terrell, Connell, Pfister, Hudgins, Blue, Mobley, Jamieson, David Radcliffe of the tourism bureau, a Hispanic, and me. After completing corporate matters, such as adding potential members to our board of directors, we selected Jack Henry as treasurer to replace Pastor Russell Thomas Hill, who was too busy to serve. Later on that same year, the Reverend Hill died unexpectedly of a heart attack at the same age as Martin Luther King, Jr. Pastor Hill's death at 39 severed a relatively new, but promising friendship between him and me. Shortly after he arrived as pastor of Tanner Chapel A.M.E. Church and began to shake things up with his preaching and administration-style, Russell Hill dubbed the two of us as "The Dream Team on Jefferson Street", since both our congregation's physical plants resided three blocks apart. My beloved brother and friend died in the pulpit, after having preached at a regional African Methodist Episcopal Conference. His death was quite a shock to me, for I had long prayed for prophetic help from another full-time Black pastor who was free enough to confront whoever and whatever needed such in church and community.

A major portion of our meeting involved reviewing and revising Jack Pfister's schedule outline. As it turned out, we were well on our way to adopting a working strategy for May through June, as well as organizing our steering committee and non-Maricopa County groups. We identified high-profile King Day supporters in Flagstaff, Yuma and Sierra Vista, namely and respectively, future Congresswoman Karen English, former Senator Jones Osborne, and would contact the NAACP for a key person in Sierra Vista. It was brought up that we needed more Hispanic VIP support, so our campaign could improve on the amount of support received from the Mexican-American community by the MLK Better America Committee in 1990. Joedd would be asked to recruit more Native American MLK advocates. I brought up the need to reach out to the handicapped, while Caryl said, "Don't forget about the AARP", (which stands for American Association for Retired Persons).

Developing a budget and beginning fundraising was a must. Jack had formulated how VICTORY TOGETHER could raise $180,000 between June and October from three different levels of contributions from $10 to $10,000. It was agreed by consensus that that kind of money was needed ASAP. In addition, we addressed the necessity of meeting with political and business leaders separately.

We also discussed, at length, how we would interview and select a campaign consultant and campaign manager. Believing that VICTORY TOGETHER must exemplify Dr. King's principles, I insisted that we utilize affirmative action in our selection process. Connell and Pfister consented to compile a list of consultants to be interviewed. The creation of an advisory committee came up for discussion, in order to bring on board about 75 people who needed to be in the know. That idea did not go very far.

As is evidenced by what has been written about VICTORY TOGETHER, it should be clear that the general chairperson's responsibilities proved to be more than ceremonial. I was called upon daily to make important decisions about our campaign, which would ultimately determine our success or failure as a coalition. Since the steering committee met monthly and the campaign committee was just getting started, oftentimes I could not call a quick meeting to make key decisions. I leaned on experienced leaders like Jack, Caryl, Mike, Bill and eventually Steve to advise me on calling the shots when I needed collective wisdom. I always got my calls returned because they knew that if they got a message from me, it had to be important. I have never been one to engage in small talk. That is one of my weaknesses in relationships, whether at home or at church. I am constantly on a mission. As I near the end of one endeavor, people who know me closely always wonder, "What next?" *Maybe, the only place, where there will not be a next project for Warren Stewart, will be in Glory.* During the height of the campaign, it was nothing for me to put in 75-80 hours between pastoring and politicking. But, I was driven to give my best to both monumental tasks, in my pursuit of excellence.

All of us, who had been putting in a lot of time developing strategy for VICTORY TOGETHER, agreed that it was time for another general meeting to bring the broader group of King Day supporters up to date on our progress. Even though it was the middle of another scorching, but dry heat Arizona summer, we dared to mail out letters of invitation to the 700-plus persons of our growing mailing list. As much as I hate to say it, I was still the primary letter writer for VICTORY TOGETHER. Unlike the big-time politicians, I had (and still do not have) ghostwriters to articulate their thoughts into mine in letters, press statements and speeches. So, our letter, dated June 17, 1991, went out from the able offices and by the secretarial and clerical staff of First Institutional.

In the first two paragraphs, I used my preaching lingo to make my points as enthusiastically as I could in writing, to get some folk out to the church on Wednesday, June 26 at 8:00 a.m. So, here is how I stated our case.

> **VICTORY TOGETHER** can be self-fulfilling prophecy come November 1992 when our state will vote on a Martin Luther King, Jr./Civil Rights Day for the third Monday in January. **TOGETHER WE CAN DO IT! TOGETHER WE CAN MAKE HISTORY! TOGETHER WE CAN HONOR THE CONTRIBUTIONS OF THE CIVIL RIGHTS MOVEMENT UNDER THE HISTORIC LEADERSHIP OF MARTIN LUTHER KING, JR.!**

Continuing by stating our identity, I wrote,

> **VICTORY TOGETHER** is a broad-based coalition of MLK holiday advocates. Our coalition is comprised of various MLK holiday groups, which worked hard for the passage of the holiday

last November, as well as many MLK holiday supporters, who have joined us since Arizona's infamous MLK holiday defeat at the polls on November 6, 1990. We are every race, both sexes, Democrats, Republicans, Independents, conservatives, liberals, grassroots, business, labor, politicians, Christians, Jews, Muslims, other religions, young, elderly, middle-aged, handicapped, disadvantaged and virtually every other constituency **UNITED** for **VICTORY TOGETHER** on a common goal.

After reciting the initial victories of our "People's Petition" Drive and getting our "One **CLEAR** Choice" on the general election ballot, I urged them to come and hear our progress report and an outline of our campaign strategy.

The June general meeting was attended by nearly 100 King Day advocates. A sampling of the attendance sheets indicated that persons from all walks of life wanted to work toward attaining VICTORY TOGETHER in 1992. Some of those in attendance included Wayne Zink of Hardaway Connections, a public relations firm; Lionel Lyons of the Mayor's Office; Joseph Williams from Prayer Assembly Church of God In Christ; Rae Lynne Chornenky of the Junior League of Phoenix; Monsignor Ed Ryle; Cynthia Tegge, Scottsdale; Deacons Lewis C. Huff and Robert L. Williams, Sr. from First Institutional; Lucia Madrid, KPNX Channel 12; Jay Nenninger, executive director of Arizona Right to Life; Martin Shultz, lobbyist for APS; Brenda Williams of the Black Theatre Troupe; the Reverend Oscar Tillman, president, NAACP; Rosie Lopez; Naomi Harward, Gray Panthers and the United Method Church; Ed Yue, Chinese American Citizens Alliance; Dr. Christine Hall of ASU West; Dr. Bill Starr, founder of Southwest Leadership Foundation; Alvin Lewis, executive director of Valley Christian Centers; and the Reverend Karen Curry, social aide director of the Broadway House Apartment Complex in South Phoenix. Our so-called "loose coalition of community and religious leaders" obviously was tightening up. The press, too, was invited to come and most of the Valley's newspapers had their reporters there to cover the story.

After asking Pastor Eppinger to open with prayer and my reading aloud that meeting's "Words from Martin" which had been extracted from a paper he wrote as a student at Crozer Theological Seminary in 1949 entitled "Autobiography of Religious Development", everyone introduced themselves. Then, it was my turn to preach a little bit in my hand-written statement of purpose. Doing what I was born to do, I proclaimed,

LET'S MAKE HISTORY
THROUGH VICTORY TOGETHER!

Our common goal is obvious....To our "first-timers", thank you
for coming....To our "returnees", thank you for coming....To
our dedicated steering committee members, resource persons
and staff members of FIBC, thank you for providing leadership
and support since our first meeting.

We can celebrate our preliminary **VICTORY TOGETHER**
with our MLK, Jr./Civil Rights Day Proposition being put on
the 1992 ballot...

So, now let's prepare to win the **ultimate VICTORY
TOGETHER** in November 1992!

I continued to describe *who* we were by saying,

Our historical campaign will endeavor to espouse the principles
and philosophy of the person and movement we seek to honor
with a holiday in Arizona. We **will** take "the **moral high
ground**" maintaining **VICTORY** at the polls. We **will** give every
Arizona voter several positive reasons why he or she should
vote for this holiday. We **will** continue to build a **broad-based,
grassroots coalition** whose most valuable contributions will be
the giving of themselves toward the attainment of **VICTORY
TOGETHER**....We **will** endeavor to run a cost-effective,
hopefully low budget "peoples' campaign". We need seed money
now and media money later...but above and beyond every dollar
we receive, we will endeavor to match it with a volunteer....Can
you imagine that? Thousands of volunteers on the streets, in our
schools, on our jobs, in our congregations, in our stadiums and
in our neighborhoods working for **VICTORY TOGETHER!**
With that being said, **"LET'S GET BUSY!"**

To my surprise, applause broke out in response to my sermonic statement of our purpose. Remember, I mentioned that it was in the middle of the
summer, so I had to liven up that crowd to get them ready for the long haul.

I had asked Mike Kelly to provide a summary of activities since our inception in November 1990. Mike did his thing, as only he can do, with dates and
accomplishments in a clearly succinct, yet informative progress report. And this

time, he threw in a one-page introduction to the summary that had homiletic overtones itself, as he praised the vision for VICTORY TOGETHER.

Once that was done, several subcommittee chairs made their way to the podium to share the reports of their respective subcommittees. One of our newest steering committee members, Delores Grayam, had driven from Tucson to report that Tucson would soon have its southern region VICTORY TOGETHER. She and her Tucson Civil Rights Commission would continue to hold meetings around the state and use those opportunities to spread the word about VICTORY TOGETHER. Pfister provided copies of his revised "Work Plan and Schedule" for our coalition. The governmental liaison committee co-chaired by Connell and Jamieson presented a detailed report, which began with the scheduling of a soon-to-take-place meeting with them and Governor Symington. That subcommittee also focused on setting up forums statewide to educate elected officials and their constituents on why the holiday ought to be celebrated in Arizona.

The MLK holiday committee statewide coordination subcommittee reviewed their work with the "People's Petitions" Drive and announced their intention to work to coordinate 1992 King Day celebration activities, beginning with the December inaugural prayer breakfast.

Terry Hudgins read his substantial fundraising and finance subcommittee report, which informed interested MLK supporters that VICTORY TOGETHER had established a checking account at Valley National Bank to protect the "meager" funds that we had that were being spent on mailings, copying and other incidental expenses. Indicating that our coalition would need much larger amounts of cash in our checking account, once the campaign consultant and staff came on board, Terry announced that MLK Better America was about to transfer its left-over funds to VICTORY TOGETHER to the tune of $50,000. Then, he estimated how much would be needed to run our successful campaign—ONE MILLION DOLLARS. The Lord knows I had not seen his report, prior to him giving it. I would have much rather Hudgins not to have mentioned the target for our campaign fundraising, because I figured the reporters would "sensationalize" that multiple of hundreds of thousands of dollars figure. Behind the scenes, the steering committee had debated that amount and I was of the opinion that we would no longer be grassroots if we had to spend $1,000,000 to win the holiday. I was later to learn that grassroots campaigns can be very expensive.

Dr. Reader shared from his volunteer subcommittee report in a philosophically sophisticated manner that is expected of erudite university professors, yet in direct talk that challenged King holiday supporters to adhere to the principles and philosophy of the person for whom we were seeking to honor. His introductory sentence made us confront "the moral destructiveness of the Gulf War and the worsening economic plight of many MLK, Jr. holiday supporters." (Go get'em, Mark!) He further stated that our coalition would need "to restore the authenticity of the MLK…holiday movement in the minds of the voters", which was an obvious reference to the business community's leading the last unsuccessful campaign. After mentioning our statement of principles, he said that their subcommittee suggested "that the campaign to win…be conducted as an above-board, non-manipulative, educational effort designed to remind voters about the values", which the MLK Day calls us to celebrate. Lastly, he brought up his suggestion about campaign donors making matching gifts to causes and organizations which live out King's principles.

The meeting was very well-received. A matter of fact, I believe that many of those who attended, came out of curiosity. However, after such an informative, in-depth presentation, our credibility ratings got bumped up several notches. We even gained some new converts who united with our eight month-old coalition.

The print media, in three major newspapers the next day, were especially kind to us. *The Arizona Republic* wrote a quarter-page article on our meeting, with an action photo of yours truly conducting the meeting. Under my photo, they quoted me saying, "Now is the time for us to win the ultimate victory together." Below the main headline, they typeset the line "Promise grassroots campaign in '92." The only problem I had with the *Republic* article was the bold black headline that read, "Supporters seek $1 million to fund King Day drive."

There was something about the mention of raising and spending that much money for the King holiday that made me uncomfortable. Ironically though, when I mentioned to my parishioners the next Sunday that VICTORY TOGETHER had to raise a million dollars, Sis. Jeannie Williams, a member of FIBC for nearly 70 years, came to me, "Pastor, I don't know why you're concerned about raising a million dollars because you've done it twice…We paid for the educational building in cash and it's not even finished yet, and we raised more than $1,000,000 in church income last year! Why, you can raise a million for the King holiday!"

The Phoenix Gazette headline for their afternoon paper was a little more positive, when it read, "King Day coalition maps plan" subtitled,

"Moral pleas to replace economic arguments." Within the article, Alfredo Azula wrote,

> "We will be taking the moral high ground this time", the Rev. Warren Stewart told a gathering Wednesday of Victory Together, a coalition of community and civic groups spearheading the drive for a King holiday....But in contrast with last year's campaign, which emphasized the economic benefits of a King holiday, Victory Together is hoping to woo voters with philosophical arguments, coalition leaders said.

In an effort to be thorough, the *Gazette* reporter contacted Bob Rose of the all-but-defunct No-No Committee for a response to our meeting and plans to raise a million dollars. Apparently, he criticized us for bringing up the issue that had been settled by the voters in 1990, accused us for being a front for the Establishment, complained about King Day being the only American with a holiday named after an individual and vowed to sell No-No T-shirts and bumper stickers to raise enough funds to defeat the "big money" folk again.

A more troubling article came out in the *Mesa Tribune* which headlined, "King holiday backers remain split; some fear repeat defeat." The reference was to the resurfacing of Carl Nicholson, whom we thought had gone through the necessary procedure to cancel his Arizonans for King Recognition initiative. I had spoken with the secretary of state earlier in June and was informed that if Nicholson's group succeeded in attaining 105,000 valid signatures by July 1992, his office would have no choice but to place that initiative on the ballot after the Legislature's nearly identical resolution proposition. The article indicated that Nicholson "was bitter toward (our) group" when contacted the same day of our general meeting. According to the *Tribune*, he felt that the Legislature only passed the resolution to try at a last chance to save the 1993 Super Bowl, Nicholson was quoted,

> "If they (Victory Together) were really truly concerned, they wouldn't have pushed the Legislature to push this thing right before the Super Bowl. If there happens to be two issues on the ballot, the only ones to blame will be the people who pushed to get this resolution) on the ballot. I don't think we can ever reconcile our differences."

These supposedly were the words of a King Day supporter, to whom I had extended an open hand several times to unite with us for our common cause. He had come to one of our initial VICTORY TOGETHER meetings. I had called him on several occasions and received no response. In March, he had written a statement to the press, announcing his intentions to end his initiative drive since the federal model of MLK Day had been put on the ballot by state lawmakers. He had pledged his support to our efforts. So, where did all this bitterness come from?

Rumor had it that Bob Rose and the No-No Committee had gotten to him and caused him to believe that we were trying to circumvent the hard work that he had begun before we actually formed VICTORY TOGETHER. However, other than his comments in the *Tribune*, we did not hear from him anymore.

I'm so glad that the *Tribune* newspaper redeemed itself in an editorial called, "King holiday: Do the right thing", on July 6, 1991. Much of what they had to say about our coalition lifted my spirits. It began,

> All the big-business types who weep uncontrollably whenever they think of all the money Arizona is losing because we're the only state without a paid Martin Luther King, Jr. holiday should listen to the Rev. Warren Stewart…
>
> …Stewart's message goes beyond confusing ballots, disagreement among King-day sup-porters and arguments about economics and bowl games. In short, Stewart doesn't seem all that much interested in seeing Arizona do the "sensible" thing. Rather, Stewart wants Arizona to do what is right.
>
> This century's foremost civil rights giant deserves a full-fledged, paid holiday in his honor, and in honor of the principles he stood for, Stewart maintains. It's important for the nation— including Arizona—to embrace those principles, he says.
>
> And he's right. He's also to be commended in seeking the "moral high ground" in the upcoming campaign, as opposed to the "good sense" economic arguments….

I am one to know that media reporters and editorial boards can rip you apart at the slightest mistake. That is why I was grateful to receive a "boost" from the same paper which had published an article that implied dissention between King Day groups that really did not exist. Every now and then, the Lord sends an extra blessing to inspire you to "keep on doing what you're doing." Thank you, Lord. And thank you, editorial board of the *Mesa Tribune*.

In our first VICTORY TOGETHER campaign committee meeting held on August 1, I informed the members about my running into former Governor Mecham at his former car dealership, while we both were getting our automobiles repaired. He had seen me in the news after our June 26 general meeting of VICTORY TOGETHER. Quite inconspicuously, he was standing on the curb waiting for his wife to come and pick him up. At first, I saw him and turned away thinking, "I don't want to talk to him." Moreover, that was the first time I had seen him in person, since the Donahue Show. But, then, my spirit said, "Go on over and speak to him." I obeyed. And that is when he told me, "Why don't you folks let the King holiday alone? You know it's going to be defeated again." I responded, "I beg to differ with you, Governor." Just about that time his ride came and he rode off.

In addition to relating to the campaign committee about my encounter with Mecham, I reminded those in attendance that we needed to remain broad-based and grassroots, exemplifying our statement of principles, regardless of who we hired as our campaign consultants. I reiterated our need to make certain that we reflected "visible inclusiveness" of all races, sexes and other various constituencies on the campaign committee in the campaign office and in our coalition, as we progressed. Being the thrifty person I was reared to be by my Kansas grandparents, the late Clarence and Ruby Washington, I urged our coalition to wage "a cost-effective" campaign, endeavoring to spend the least amount of money necessary to win. Related to that, I made it plain that the finance committee would need to reflect our broad-based constituency, and not just the WASP males from Central Avenue.

I left a thought with those present that day that "if every voter who voted for a Martin Luther King, Jr. holiday in November 1990 would simply recruit one new voter for the King holiday election in 1992, we'd win overwhelmingly."

◇◇◇◇◇

In an effort to establish a direct line of communication with Governor Symington, which would clear up a lot of interfering, static mumble-jumble with rumor, innuendo and sarcasm, Judith Connell was able to set up a meeting with me and the governor through her Republican contacts on the ninth floor. The meeting took place on the eve of the Fourth of July 1991. It was actually a two-part meeting—first with just the governor, myself and

Mayberry in his private office; and then with a small delegation of VICTORY TOGETHER steering committee, meeting in his larger ceremonial office.

I had been in the company of the last four Arizona governors, so being in Governor Symington's presence was not a big deal. After all, he was the same guy who had stopped by my office, when he was campaigning prior to the 1990 general election. However, I carried tension with me to the Governor's Office on July third due to the rumors that had been floating around that he wanted to take over the MLK Day campaign. Knowing how I felt about big business's dealing with the holiday and that I considered him to be a bona fide member of their million-dollar club, I entered his office, both skeptical and suspicious of what he would have to say. To his credit, he eased some of my tensions, when he invited me to his private office and shut the door with only the two of us present, and Mayberry.

After exchanging cordialities, he inquired about the progress of the campaign. I updated him on what we had done and informed him that we were almost at the point of interviewing campaign consultants. I, then, shared with him the rumors and innuendos that I had been hearing. Of course, his response was a calm denial of any such intentions on his part to "take over" the campaign for the King holiday. He explained, "I didn't march on the King Day earlier this year because I felt it would have been perceived as purely political, since I had never marched before." He offered his help to me in any way and gave me one of his official business cards, on which he had his secretary to write his direct line. We, then, concluded our brief meeting with a handshake and proceeded to join his top aides and the other members of our delegation to discuss the campaign and where he could best fit in.

By the end of that meeting, Governor Symington committed to working with us and doing whatever we needed and wanted him to do. At that point, he offered a recommendation of a campaign consultant he had worked with, and promised to network VICTORY TOGETHER and the consultant so that we could, at least, talk. It just so happened that the consultant was in town and in the Governor's Office, so the governor introduced us to Joe Shumate who sat in on our public meeting attended by Mobley, Jamieson and Connell from our camp. The governor also advised us that timing was key to a successful campaign and that he would speak with Arizona business leaders to get them to support us. With those promises, our meeting came to a close. After meeting with the chief executive of the

State, our next task as a coalition was to develop our northern and southern Arizona branches of our coalition.

Our first stop was in Flagstaff on July 18 at the third meeting of the Civil Rights Community Task Force that had been organized by Delores Grayam of Tucson. In order to broaden their base of support, they held periodic meetings around the state. She had invited representatives from VICTORY TOGETHER to come and be on the agenda. Several of the state's most active civil rights workers were present. Attorney General Grants Woods and one of his top assistants, former Judge Cecil Patterson provided the majority of the input at that meeting on subjects such as legislative updates on fair housing, hate crimes, human services and future projects relative to civil and equal rights under the jurisdiction of Woods' Office.

Gene and Art accompanied me to Flagstaff. Jack, who was already in Flagstaff attending an Arizona Board of Regents retreat, met us at the City Council Chambers where the meeting was held. After greeting the attendees at the task force meeting and thanking them for allowing us to make a presentation, I went into my presentation explaining our coalition's *identity* and *purpose*. By that time, I had my VICTORY TOGETHER pitch pretty much down pat. I had become hip to why the few times I had spent a day or two with Jesse Jackson on his first presidential campaign I had heard him give basically the same speech over and over again to different audiences. I also came to understand how boring the speeches must become to campaign workers and media representatives who travel with the same candidates, day in and day out on the campaign trail. I guess it is kind of like if you serve chicken all the time because that is what you like. The bulk of the matter to be consumed is always the same. It just may be prepared and served with different trimmings and seasoning, depending on who is going to do the consuming. In other words, most of what I shared with the couple of dozen or so persons in attendance was no different from what I had shared in our June general meeting in Phoenix. However, I did emphasize the need for us to broaden our base and reminded the audience that "people were our greatest resource." I made an appeal for "seed money" and commitments to be active participants in VICTORY TOGETHER. As usual, we were well received. Then, I asked Gene to say some words about the statewide coordination of our efforts, since he was the co-chair of the MLK holiday statewide coordinating committee. We asked for persons from the Flagstaff area who would serve as our contacts and provided them with five VICTORY TOGETHER organizational packets that Mike had put together.

Two weeks later, a group of our coalition's steering committee boarded my 1989 GMC Safari Mini-van and we drove southeast to the Old Pueblo to meet with Tucson MLK Day supporters, in order to organize a southern branch of VICTORY TOGETHER. Significant progress occurred on that day, July 31, 1991, before we even arrived at the Tucson Urban League where the luncheon meeting was hosted by Ray Clarke. In addition to Mike Kelly, Joedd, Caryl and Joe, Steve rode with us. Along the way we conversed about various subject matters such as politics, religion, Arizona, our families and backgrounds, and, of course, our MLK holiday efforts. Relationships had not quite jelled between the Arizona King holiday veterans and latecomers, like Steve from the business community. I suppose that there were still suspicions on both sides of the fence. But, being confined for two hours in a mini-van forces persons suspicious of one another to deal with those feelings, one way or another. What I am saying is that in talking about a wide range of subject matter on our trip to Tucson, we ended up talking about ourselves! In talking about ourselves we discovered the humanity of one another, which caused the suspicions we had toward one another to dissipate. That, for me, was a critical turning point in the togetherness that was required for the core leaders of VICTORY TOGETHER to evidence and experience, if we wanted to win in November 1992. So, if for no other reason, our trip to Tucson on the last day in July 1991 was extremely successful.

Once we arrived, we chatted with Ray, who served as co-presider along with Delores Grayam. The two of them had worked hard to make this initial meeting a success, in spite of being in the middle of the summer. Nearly 30 community leaders showed up at this gathering. Among them were pastoral colleagues of mine, such as Pastor D. Grady Scott of Grace Temple Missionary Baptist Church and Pastor Anthony Moss, then of Mt. Calvary Baptist Church. Mayor Tom Volgy of Tucson came. John Stickler of the Tucson chapter of the Public Relations Society of America was in attendance. Clarence and Deborah Boykins came to share their expertise from many years coordinating the Tucson MLK Celebrations. Dave Rodriguez represented LULAC (League of United Latin American Citizens). Mary Motley of U.S. West Communications attended. The Tucson NAACP was not to be left out, thanks to the presence of David Sanders. Several others took part in that organizational meeting representing other groups including labor, Native-Americans, Asian-Americans and the legal profession.

Our meeting followed the typical VICTORY TOGETHER general meeting format with greetings, opening prayer, words from Martin, introductions, statement of purpose, progress reports, discussion, comments and suggestions, setting of next meeting date and closing prayers. The added feature of that meeting was the establishment of a Southern Arizona Regional VICTORY TOGETHER. Once again, I did my "who we are and what we're are supposed to do" pep talk. Mike presented his latest update of summary of activities of our coalition. We shared our "work plan and schedule" in writing. Joedd commented on VICTORY TOGETHER's statement of principles that we had provided for them to review and keep.

When we got to the discussion part of our agenda, several of the Tucson MLK supporters expressed some frustrations they had had with the 1990 campaign. Clarence Boykins commented, "There was a lack of communication in the last campaign between the MLK Better America coordinators in Phoenix and those of us working with them down here. We had problems getting information, materials and funds to get the word out in Tucson about the campaign." Since Steve was co-coordinating that campaign committee, he responded that he and the Phoenix MLK Better America Committee had been aware of the problems, apologized, explained that they only had about seven weeks to run a statewide campaign, and promised that VICTORY TOGETHER would do better.

In addition, Grayam asked me to come to a larger meeting of King Day supporters she would plan for September. I consented and requested that those present spread the word about our coalition and send me a list of volunteers that we could add to our mailing list. Before the meeting ended, Karl Gentles and Bruce Mayberry stopped by. They had been in Tucson on business for their respective Republican bosses, Senator McCain and Governor Symington. The closing prayer, that day was offered by the late Pastor Robert C. Beatty who was the oldest active pastor in Arizona until his death at 95 in February 2015. He had driven up from Sierra Vista to be a part of this VICTORY TOGETHER organizational meeting. Both Clarke and Grayam were left in charge as our Tucson key contact persons until King Day advocates there could select their own leadership for our coalition's southern branch. Our opinion was that we did not have the knowledge or the right actually to determine who would lead our common effort in their community. So, we left entrusting that decision in their hands.

While many people in Arizona were making their getaway from the monsoon mugginess of the month of August, the majority of the members of the core of the campaign committee of VICTORY TOGETHER were conducting the first sessions of extensive interviews of prospective campaign consultants. That was a learning experience in itself for me. The search committee had compiled a list of thirty different political and media consultants, pollsters and public opinion experts, general communications specialists, and fundraising firms. After sending out letters of inquiry, the list of possible consultants we would interview was narrowed to less than ten. They came from as far away as Washington, D.C., Atlanta, Georgia and West Roxbury, Massachusetts. Two flew in from California. And one was a local political consulting consortium comprised of Tim Mooney of Southwest Policy Group, representing Arizona Republican conservatives and Hardt and Junct Associates, Inc., which was headed by two long-time female Democratic former gubernatorial staff members. The latter consortium could almost be termed "the political odd couple" because on virtually any other issue the two major entities would be fierce political opponents. But Mooney, with the urging of Judith Connell, really wanted to run the 1992 MLK Day campaign.

Gordon Sellers of The Sellers Group had contacted me several months earlier to organize the Arizona King Day celebration in January 1991. He flew in and made a presentation, based primarily on the strength of his involvement in the historic Civil Rights Movement and the work he had done in Atlanta, coordinating the King Day Festivities there. I remember getting a call in my office the day before his interview from Atlanta Mayor Maynard Jackson, highly recommending Sellers as the man who could lead our campaign.

Another notable consulting firm that flew in their key principals to be interviewed by us in our brand-new administrative, educational and outreach building was the Sawyer/Miller Group from the nation's capital. Ed Rollins, a well-known Republican political strategist, came to town in his blue pinstriped suit, accentuated by the trademark Rolex watch. Rollins was kind of a celebrity political consultant as a result of guiding George Bush's 1988 presidential campaign, which had become infamous for its "race-baiting" Willie Horton commercials. I guess I was a little taken aback that such a powerful man was sitting in the conference room of First Institutional. He expressed his enthusiastic interest in running our campaign, which he estimated would cost around 1.5 to 2 million dollars. In spite of his notoriety, the collective wisdom of the campaign consultant selection committee ruled his group out because we were afraid that his possible tactics might exasperate an already "racial" issue, thusly working against our victory. The price tag also caused us to step back from Rollins and company.

All of the selection committee felt that there were definite advantages to selecting the local consortium. Thusly, Mooney, Hardt and Junct made their pitch. Number one, they knew Arizona politics from both sides. Number two, by them being local, we would insure having full-time leadership throughout the campaign that was in the state. Number three, whatever money would be paid to them would remain in the state. Another plus that they brought to the interview was that, up to that point, they were the only consulting group that had women in leadership roles. That caught our attention. On the other hand, one or two of our committee members were uneasy with Tim Mooney. The concern was his relative youthfulness and inexperience in leading such an important campaign. It came to the point that the financial support from the business community would be in jeopardy if we selected the Mooney, Hardt and Junct team. So, even though all three entities were "homegrown", the committee had to continue our search.

Before the first session of interviews we had to iron out a potentially major problem that occurred when Mayberry was not appointed to be on the selection committee. When that did not happen, veiled threats began to be made relative to the governor's continued support of VICTORY TOGETHER. So, in order to keep another controversy from making the news, I appointed Mayberry to the campaign consultant selection committee, as a resource person without vote. After all, the committee had been selected at the beginning of the summer.

Once we got that straightened out, the fact that the governor's recommended political consultant was not on our list of firms to be interviewed, caused another wave of threats of high-level departure. Once again, I had to act to quiet the governor's proxy on our committee. Consequently, the selection committee added Joe Shumate and Associates, Inc. to our second session of interviews, which took place on August 15, 1991. On the day Shumate was interviewed, our team interviewed two other consulting firms. Believe me, these interviews were intensive, exhaustive and lengthy. Between the interviews themselves and our evaluations of those interviewed, each session was the equivalent of an eight-hour day. After the second session of interviews, our selection committee took a vacation break for the rest of the month.

The day after our second session, I had a visitor to my office by the name of Martin Luther King, III, then Fulton County Commissioner. "Marty," as he is affectionately called, was in the city to discuss lobbying for continued funding for the Martin Luther King, Jr. Federal Holiday Commission. Since there was a Republican administration in the White House, King felt that Governor Symington might be able to offer some assistance to getting financial aid from the Congress with the blessings of President Bush, as well as any assistance Arizona could give them. We had met on a previous occasion and he was well aware of my leadership in the King Day fight in Arizona. Our conversation was not long, but Martin King, III was happy to hear of the efforts of VICTORY TOGETHER and repeated his encouragement and support of our efforts. He gave me one of his Fulton County Commissioner business cards, which I keep under the glass on my desk at my church office just below my son Warren, Jr.'s elementary school note that he wanted "to be a minister like his father and Martin Luther King, Jr."

On September 7, 1991, the campaign consultant selection committee reconvened to interview a consulting firm out of Los Angeles that had not been on our original list of potential consulting firms. It had been referred to us because the major principal involved dealt exclusively in ballot propositions and had a winning record of 90%. The firm was actually a conglomerate of two firms called Winner/Wagner & Mandabach Campaigns, headed by Paul Mandabach, and Winner/Bragg, whose representative we interviewed was Ms. Felicia Bragg, an articulate, assertive African-American woman who had worked with several California politicians, one of whom was U.S. Congresswoman Maxine Waters.

First impressions go a long way. Mandabach made the initial presentation to our committee. He was very thorough in extolling the reasons his firm should be selected. But, he was also very lengthy and inanimated in his remarks. On the other hand, when Ms. Bragg spoke, the committee members perked up. As she continued to talk about her involvement in several successful grassroots campaigns, in which she had played a major role as consultant, the members of the committee began to glance at one another using facial expressions and upper body language to communicate, "Hey, this is the team for us!" Mind you, approval was not yet unanimous. A firm from the first session in August called Jack Walsh and Associates had left a favorable impression on us. So, after much discussion and evaluation of all the applicants, we narrowed the finalists down to two—Mandabach and Bragg, and Walsh. Each firm was invited back to Phoenix on September 21. Following the second interview of the two, by a voice vote, we selected Winner/Wagner & Mandabach Campaigns and Winner/Bragg. Our next step was to recommend our selection to the VICTORY TOGETHER steering committee and board of directors, which we did on September 25, 1991.

In a joint letter to Mr. Mandabach and Ms. Bragg dated October 1, 1991, I wrote.

> This letter is to provide written confirmation that the Board of Directors of **VICTORY TOGETHER**, Inc. voted to retain (you) as campaign consultants for…our campaign to win a paid state holiday honoring Martin Luther King, Jr. and Civil Rights in the 1992 General Election, effective immediately. We are confident that after interviewing intensively and comprehensively nearly a dozen campaign consultants that your firms can best guide Arizona to **VICTORY TOGETHER** in 1992.
>
> Welcome to our **winning** team…

In addition to informing them that they had been retained, I listed five items that we had discussed that outlined our expectations of them. I informed them to get back with me on those five items as soon as possible, which were:

1. Develop a campaign strategy that honors the Statement of Principles of **VICTORY TOGETHER,**

2. Be cognizant and sensitive to the "business connection" factor in our campaign,

3. Commitment to not engage in other campaign issues that would cause a negative effect on our campaign, e.g., the abortion issue in Arizona or elsewhere, during our King holiday campaign,

4. Consideration of assistance from other campaign consultants from Arizona and elsewhere who may bring particular and valuable expertise to our campaign, and

5. Forwarding an agreement between your firms and **VICTORY TOGETHER**, Inc., outlining your obligations to us and our obligations to your firms.

In concluding that letter initiating our formal relationship with the California firms, I made it clear that I, as general chairperson, was to be "kept abreast and consulted with about any scheduled, unscheduled and proposed meetings with various MLK holiday supporters and supporting constituencies in Arizona." One of the reasons for such a statement was that Winner/Wagner & Mandabach Campaigns had worked with APS on a previous campaign. The word was out that their firm was pro-big business. Consequently, the antennas of several of us grassroots folk went up high because we did not want a firm that supposedly worked for VICTORY TOGETHER, but, in reality was taking orders from the Phoenix 40. You can believe that we kept our eyes on this out-of-town, high-paid campaign consulting firm consortium that charged us $100,000 for Phase One, which mapped out a plan and another $30,000 a month, plus expenses, including everything down to the tips paid to taxi drivers bringing them from the airport, beginning in January 1992.

Several of us had thought that the local media would make a big deal out of VICTORY TOGETHER hiring an out-of-state political consultant. However, other than a few calls from local politicos, there was not a lot said about it even after a very brief paragraph was printed in the *Arizona Republic,* a day after we voted to hire the firms.

At the same meeting we selected the said firms as our consultants; we also finally formally organized as a corporation known as VICTORY TOGETHER, Inc. This simply was a legal duplication of the constitution and by-laws and corporate officers and directors we had elected in the spring. Two replacements had to be made upon the resignations of Hudgins, whose wife was experiencing a problem pregnancy, and Mark, who co-chaired the volunteer committee. In actuality, I believe that both resignations came as a result of personal frustrations that Hudgins and Reader were experiencing in their labors in VICTORY TOGETHER. Terry had probably gotten a little tired of the "big business bashing" that took place in the media, on the talk shows, and often in our coalition meetings. It was a fact that big business paid Hudgins' salary and financed the 1990 campaign. Moreover, it became obvious that the million-plus dollars that we would need to win the King holiday would come from the corporate giants and mini-giants in the state. He had expressed some of his frustrations with me and in a subtle but non-hostile way, let me know that he did not like some of my remarks about the "fat cats."

Dr. Reader, on the other hand, had become frustrated by big business's involvement in our campaign. He had had to tangle with one or two of the utility corporations over the issue of nuclear power-produced energy for the Phoenix Metropolitan area. So, he reached a point where his principles just would not allow him to continue to work alongside his political counterparts. We had talked about that and I accepted his position. He was very concerned that the corporate moguls would take over and prostitute the name of Dr. King, as they had done in the failed 1990 campaign tied to the Super Bowl.

Both resignations were accepted unanimously, with regrets. Steve was named to replace Terry as co-chair of the finance/fundraising committee. No person was chosen, at that time, to replace Mark. Paul attended our board of directors meeting as my invited guest and was acknowledged for his longtime advocacy of King Day in Arizona.

◇◇◇◇◇◇

Mark and Terry were not the only VICTORY TOGETHER coalition members frustrated with the King holiday-big business connection. For me, the campaign was heading in a direction that I came to describe as "an uneasy alliance." I still was having problems having to deal with the Phoenix 40 crowd, especially after finding out that the kind of money we needed to win the MLK holiday campaign was not going to come from one, five and ten dollar contributions. How in the world was I going to be able to live with myself having to solicit funds from CEOs and their corporations who had gotten involved in Arizona's King Day quest once they saw the *green* light?

I was helped tremendously by a conversation the Lord arranged between Dr. Leon Sullivan and myself in the fall of 1991. At his office earlier that year, in a meeting we had had relative to his Teachers for Africa program, I mentioned that I would like to talk with him about the ministry, prophetic leadership and himself; and get some advice on leading an entire state to win a Martin Luther King, Jr. holiday. One weekday afternoon, he was able to schedule me in, and I made my way to north Scottsdale to his home. Mrs. Grace Sullivan was there and served as a gracious hostess as she served a light snack and left Dr. Sullivan and me to converse.

We talked about a lot of things that afternoon. But, eventually the subject matter got around to Arizona's MLK Day struggle. Dr. Sullivan felt that as long as the King holiday remained unresolved positively, it would remain as an inhibiting blight on our state's being accepted fully as progressive and inclusive in the areas of civil rights, justice, race relations and politics. Being well aware of my presentation on the Donahue Show in 1990 and my evolving leadership role in the King Day campaign, he inquired how our effort was going. After updating him on the *identity* and *purpose* of VICTORY TOGETHER, I began to share with him my frustrations in working with the corporate executives in Arizona to win the holiday, especially since most of them initially viewed the King Day as "a Black issue" until it became an economic issue.

It was then that Dr. Sullivan gave me some seasoned advice that reflected the wisdom he had acquired as a bold and courageous prophetic pastor of Philadelphia's historic Zion Baptist Church, for nearly forty years. One of his books, *Build, Brother Build*, chronicles how he led hundreds of Black clergy in "the City of Brother Love" in boycotting major corporations, which welcomed money from African-Americans for their products, but refused to hire them to work in their profitable enterprises. Since those days in the 1960s, when Dr. Sullivan successfully challenged corporate Philadelphia to engage in profit sharing with the Black community, he had been invited to become a member of the boards of some of the major corporations and financial institutions in America. Until the early 1990s, that towering preacher/civil rights activist from West Virginia still served as one of the senior board members of General Motors. And here is what he said to me.

> Reverend, you've got to remember the veneer of the social consciousness of corporate executives is very thin. They *need* leaders like you to prick their consciences and challenge them to do what's morally right as it relates to justice, equality, the disadvantaged and civil rights....And as far as them contributing money to your campaign, take it, because what you'll receive for your cause is only a drop in the bucket of what they have to give away.

What a revelation! No wonder this man, in whose living room I was sitting, had been about to write "The Sullivan Principles" which guided willing American corporations doing business in South Africa prior to the demise of apartheid to bring about the beginning of economic justice for Black South Africans, especially those working in American companies there. I immediately understood that the Phoenix 40 crowd *owed* VICTORY TOGETHER whatever contributions they would give to the MLK campaign. Their thousands of dollars checks merely constituted a token of the back pay they owed the African-American community as a consequence of their sustaining systemic racism for decades through discriminatory business practices that had affected and continue to adversely affect people of color in the Valley of the Sun, the entire state, and all around the country. So, when I left the home of Dr. and Mrs. Sullivan that afternoon, I left with a new perspective, which enabled me to join in "an uneasy alliance" with the "fat cats" and Super Bowl-catchers who were willing to make an investment in an effort to honor a man who, if he was living, they would probably be trying to run out of town.

Upon the hiring of our campaign consultants, the necessity to get some necessary "start-up" campaign contributions from corporate Arizona became urgent. In the three months remaining in 1991, Mandabach and Bragg, along with their associated polling firm, would incur expenses in the amount of nearly $60,000 in developing a campaign strategy for VICTORY TOGETHER. Consequently, Steve and Jack studied their lists of previous contributors to the 1990 King campaign and expanded their contacts to devise a list of potential corporate donors to our campaign. Once that was done, with the expert assistance of Mandabach's initial fundraising, letters and related materials had to be composed for distribution. Moreover, as general chairperson, I had to make personal visits to key selected corporate executives to appeal for their support. Yuk!

One of those meetings was with Jerry Colangelo of the Phoenix Suns. I went to the Suns' former, surprisingly small, cramped headquarters office on Central Avenue. I parked in the back, where they had very limited parking and walked past Mr. Colangelo's sleek, new Mercedes Benz. I went in the rear entrance, which was the only entrance I could locate, and was guided through a maze of hallways to Colangelo's office. His secretary greeted me and informed him that I was there. He came out and greeted me cordially. It was not the first time we had met. I had been in his company on a previous occasion or two, related to the King holiday. I brought up several of his past and current Phoenix Suns players, who had been members and/or pretty regular attendees of First Institutional. Three of them stood out in my mind, Garfield Heard and Eddie Johnson, both whom I baptized, and Kevin Johnson who, though not a member, came more regularly than any other active Suns players. I also mentioned a mutual friend of ours, Bill Starr, whose Southwest Leadership Foundation had been used by God to perform a miraculous resurrection of the drug-infested, crime-ridden Keys Market in South Phoenix into Keys Community Center, which educates and trains residents for their G.E.D. and other skills to obtain gainful employment.

The Phoenix Suns owner has an unapologetic testimony for being a born-again Christian, so we had common ground on which to converse.

Then, I moved the conversation to the King holiday. Of course, I thanked him for his public support of the holiday in the last campaign and his influence in getting the Phoenix Suns players to make a sizable contribution to that effort. I, then, shared with him about VICTORY TOGETHER's *identity* and *purpose* and dropped the names of Roman and Pfister. He talked genuinely about his support for the MLK holiday, which he said was not linked to the Super Bowl. Quite candidly, he admitted that he knew that the NBA would never bring the All-Star game to Phoenix, until Arizona approved a Martin Luther King, Jr. Day. After that, we discussed the last campaign and the possibilities for victory in 1992. He pledged his support for VICTORY TOGETHER's efforts and said he would be in touch with Steve and Jack, and said that we could count on major assistance from the Phoenix Suns and the corporate community. I was not aware, at that time, that he was the incoming chair of the Phoenix 40, which would go through a name-change and a revival under his activist leadership. *And Mr. Colangelo kept his word.*

At one point in our campaign, after our campaign consultants had developed our strategy for victory, Steve arranged for a meeting with some of the money "movers and shakers" in the boardroom of Valley National Bank. Most of the CEOs of the major Valley corporations were present, including companies like APS, US West, the Phoenix Cardinals, the Phoenix Suns, Bank America Corporation, VNB, Phelps Dodge and the Phoenix Newspapers, Inc. Many of them were still skeptical about putting their cash into our coalition's campaign. At that particular meeting, Steve opened the meeting with introductions of myself and Paul Mandabach. Jack Pfister sat beside me. *Although Steve's official title was co-chair of the finance/fundraising committee, he emerged as the unofficial co-general chairperson of VICTORY TOGETHER without ever having presided at one of our coalition's meetings.* After Mandabach's presentation before those very rich, very powerful decision-makers, some of them obviously became more at ease with the direction, in which we were headed. Not only did some of them have their doubts about the Black Baptist preacher who organized VICTORY TOGETHER, but they were not familiar with the "political brains" we had imported from Los Angeles.

Steve asked me if I had anything to say, which I had really hoped he would not do. A matter of fact, I had asked Steve and Jack prior to our meeting that day if I had to be in attendance when Mandabach made the presentation; and Steve informed them that the campaign would cost about 1.7 million dollars, more than twice the cost of the last campaign. They insisted that my presence was absolutely necessary. In spite of my enlightening conversation with Dr. Sullivan, I still felt uneasy being around those guys who, in my opinion, were part of the Establishment whose biblical and religious equivalents were the targets of the Old Testament prophets. Those were the guys that Dr. King and myself had preached about, who intentionally or unintentionally perpetuated injustice on the "have nots," for the most part. That is why I did not want to be there.

Nevertheless, I was there and I was asked to speak. I began, "Thank you for allowing us to make our presentation to you. We think we can win this election....But in order to do so, we need your support. First Institutional Baptist Church, where I serve as pastor, has contributed in excess of $25,000 in cash and in-kind contributions to this campaign. I want to challenge you to do, at least, that much in order that we can experience VICTORY TOGETHER in 1992." Immediately, Jerry Colangelo spoke up and indicated that his Phoenix Suns had pledged $100,000 to the campaign. Rich Lehmann of VNB, Mark De Michele of APS, and Louis Chip" Weil of the Phoenix Newspapers all matched the Suns' owner's pledge with $100,000 each. Several others chipped in lesser amounts, which still calculated to major bucks for our campaign.

Nevertheless, I will never forget a Friday night call, which I got at my home from one of our members who worked for a major corporation in the Valley. She had been in attendance at a charity golf tournament, where her company's CEO, who had been at that meeting in the boardroom of VNB, had had some disturbing comments about me. It appears that a regional executive of that company who had headed the Phoenix division, at one time, had flown into town for that golf tournament. He, being aware of the King holiday controversy, asked the local CEO if he had been helping in the campaign with some bucks.

My member informed me that the local CEO began to say some unkind and highly critical remarks about the leader of the King Day coalition. She said that he said, in explaining to the regional corporate executive who was a "brother", why he had been reluctant up to that point, to commit to financially backing VICTORY TOGETHER. "The guy heading it, the Reverend is not a leader. He's the wrong guy to be running the show." Immediately, my member interrupted, "The leader is my pastor and I don't appreciate those kinds of remarks about him, which certainly are incorrect!" The regional executive, who knew who I was, because he and his family had attended First Institutional occasionally, when they lived in Phoenix, looked surprised. Then, the local executive tried to explain his criticism of my leadership by saying, according to my member-source, "Well, I've been in a meeting or two with him, and he doesn't say anything. He lets other people take over." At that point, the brother told the local executive to support the King Day coalition with big bucks.

Apparently, the local executive interpreted my allowing Steve to preside over our meetings with the Phoenix 40 group as "weak leadership." To me, it was simply delegation of responsibility to an individual, who had been recommended by me, to use his expertise, contacts and established relationship to handle the financial and fundraising matters of VICTORY TOGETHER. I was shocked that a high-level corporate officer could not recognize that right off. Perhaps, he had some other concerns about my leadership that would not have been "politically correct" to express. Whatever the case, within a few weeks, our campaign received a twenty thousand dollar donation from that company.

I had more favorable meetings with corporate executives at the Phoenix Newspapers, Inc., thanks much to Bill Shover, and at KTVK-Channel 3 in Phoenix. In actuality, a meeting Steve, Jack and I had during lunch hour at the Channel 3 news station was a family gathering. The board of directors and owners of Media Broadcasting, Inc. were members of the Delbert Lewis clan. Even though they were owners of a multi-million dollar media enterprise, you would not know it by the way they looked, dressed and interacted with others. I mean, they carried themselves as just regular people.

We met in a relatively small room, where their monthly board of directors meeting was being conducted. Mr. Delbert Lewis and his wife, their children and perhaps other relatives all sat around the table with assorted sodas and sandwiches. The station's general manager introduced me to the Lewis family. They already knew who Steve was, from the last campaign. I really did not have to say a lot about VICTORY TOGETHER. We had sent them some materials, and being in the media business, they were well aware of our mission. Steve talked a little about finances. Mr. Lewis asked, "How much did we give to the last campaign?" To which Steve replied, "50,000." "Well," Mr. Lewis said, "We'll do better than that this time. We like what we hear and you all need more money, so we can get this holiday passed." Shortly thereafter, we excused ourselves from their family board meeting.

By that afternoon I had a call from Steve, informing me that the Lewis family had voted to give VICTORY TOGETHER a $55,000 contribution.

God can sure work wonders! I received a call from Mr. William R. Hogan, Executive Director of the Phoenix 40, inviting me and Paul Mandabach to make a presentation at their fall retreat at the Wigwam Resort in Litchfield Park. It was at that retreat, held on November 1-2, 1991 that the Phoenix 40 would select 3-4 issues, toward which the group would devote their energies in the following year. Among the invited panelists were Ioanna Morfessis of the Greater Phoenix Economic Council; Jim Marsh, director of State Department of Commerce; Roy Herberger, president of the American Graduate School of International Management; Frank Fairbanks, Phoenix city manager; Charles Cowan, director of the State Department of Transportation; and the kid from Coffeyville, accompanied by our expensive LA campaign consultant. Somehow, Mandabach and I were programmed for late afternoon on Friday, November 1, after five panelists had already spoken that day. We were given fifteen minutes between us to state our case. In that amount of time, I had promised Hogan, in writing, that we would review how our organization came into existence, who our leaders were, and the process to date on how we selected Winner/Wagner & Mandabach Campaigns. Then, Mandabach would present his firm's credentials and a general approach to how they planned to run our campaign.

I was very nervous, upon arrival at that five-star resort hotel, where only "the rich and famous" can afford to chill out. Thank goodness, as I walked into the large conference room, where the group's members were seated, I was glad to see some familiar faces like Tommy Espinoza, Lattie Coor, Paul Elsner, Bill Shover and a brother, George Evans, Esquire. Mandabach was there and we were ushered toward the front. Charles Cowan made his presentation, just before us and talked about the transportation needs of the state, primarily construction of new freeways for the Valley. Then, it was our turn. I began.

> Mr. Mark De Michele, current Chairman, Mr. Jerry Colangelo, incoming Chairman, Mr. William R. Hogan, Executive Director, and members of the Phoenix 40. Good afternoon and thank you for the opportunity to serve as a panelist for your annual retreat, on behalf of **VICTORY TOGETHER,** Inc. and hundreds of thousands of Arizonans who support a Martin Luther King, Jr./ Civil Rights Day.

I then proceeded to give my standard spiel about a brief history and my leadership in the King Day effort, since the Mecham days. Next, thanks to Mike Kelly, I provided a review of our past eleven months of progress. It was helpful that I could also say, "In fact, several members of the Phoenix 40 are active members of our coalition and have provided valuable support and expertise."

Part II of my presentation identified our various sub-committees and their co-chairpersons to evidence our diversity, inclusiveness and organizational structure. Then, came my turn to read our statement of principles which I reveled in declaring before such a group.

I moved from there to Part III, in which I explained the "marathon" selection process through which we conducted nearly a dozen intensive and comprehensive interviews, and arrived at the selection of Winner/Wagner & Mandabach and Winner/Bragg.

My last paragraph climaxed my remarks thusly,

> Lastly, **VICTORY TOGETHER** invites you and all Arizonans who support winning a paid state holiday honoring Martin Luther King, Jr. and Civil Rights on the third Monday in January to become active members of our broad-based coalition, and that includes the Phoenix 40.

Thank you.

I believe they applauded.

Mandabach followed me with a brief statement, indicating that they were currently conducting polls and research to determine what kind of campaign strategy would be needed. He had already informed Steve and me that he could not give them an outline of a definite campaign because he did not have one yet. A permitted addition by the Phoenix 40 was the allowing of Felicia Bragg to talk about the grassroots aspects of the campaign, on which she was working.

The next day I received several calls in my office informing me that the "movers and shakers" had been positively moved by our presentation. The calls came in from inside and outside of the Phoenix 40. Jack informed via telephone that everything he had heard was affirmative, with one editorial comment that "I had tried to preach to the group", to which he responded, "Well, Warren Stewart *is* a preacher after all." Our MLK Day convert even wrote a letter to Jack, which he copied to Mandabach and myself,

Rev. Warren Stewart and Paul Mandabach made a favorable impression in their presentations to Phoenix 40. We didn't count noses or seek commitments, but there is no question that the men and women of Phoenix 40 will strongly support the passage of Martin Luther King, Jr./Civil Rights Days (sic) next year.

Those welcomed words were dictated by William R. Shover.

Before the year was out, in addition to the $45,000 transferred from MLK Better America's account to VICTORY TOGETHER, the Valley National Bank, Phoenix Suns, Bank America Corporation and Del Webb joined over 150 persons and organizations making initial contributions to our effort which all totaled $70,000.

◇◇◇◇◇◇

The remainder of 1991 was spent working closely with Mandabach and Bragg to develop a campaign strategy and budget for 1992 and identify major contributors to our campaign coffers. I let Steve and Jack handle that. In conjunction with fundraising, I nominated a relative newcomer to Arizona, Bettye Jackson, who was an African-American entrepreneur and political activist back in her native South Carolina, to serve as co-chairperson of our finance/fundraising subcommittee, along with Steve. Her assignment was to generate funds from the grassroots community in order that we could diffuse the perception of being "bought and paid for" by the Phoenix 40. She had contacts nationwide with several noted African-American civil rights activists, politicians, entertainers, sport stars, and businesspersons who might be able to lend us a hand in some way.

The last general VICTORY TOGETHER meeting for that year was held in late September, at which time we updated our supporters on all that had been taking place. Since we had not had a meeting for three months, many community leaders had been wondering what was happening with the King Day campaign. Once they heard our progress reports and were introduced to our campaign consultants, they expressed their approval of our work on their behalf throughout the long hot summer.

In October, Dave Radcliffe, informed us that the hospitality industry would engage in its own efforts to "ensure passage of the Holiday Proposition on the November 1992 Ballot." He appeared a little nervous about our consultants' ability to come up with a guaranteed winning strategy. So he secured a campaign strategist to develop an "in house" plan for his industry to get their employees actively involved in a grassroots campaign to win support for the holiday. As a member of our coalition he promised to keep our campaign committee abreast on all of their activities, in order that we could present a united front and attain victory. Mandabach had some serious reservations about the information and subsequent strategy that the consultant for tourism industry came up with. He also felt it could take potential contributions from limited resources for our campaign. But, in time and through candid communication, Radcliffe and the hospitality industry worked with us to the end.

That same month, Phoenix Mayor Paul Johnson decided to do a little tourism boycotting of his own, in protest of the National League of Cities moving their annual meeting from Phoenix to Las Vegas over Arizona's rejection of a paid King Day. Instead of leading the Phoenix delegation of council members and other key municipal workers to Nevada, he announced that he would protest the "make no sense to me" decision to not hold the meeting, which had been scheduled for December 1991. However, six city council members made their plans known that they were going to the 10,000-person convention. Councilman Goode's reasoning was that he needed to be there to represent Arizona on the league's human-development committee, of which he was a member.

In response to the King Day defeat at the polls, as well as what appeared to be increasing incidents of overt ethnic insensitivity, hate crimes and discrimination against people, for simply being different, Jack's brain-child, Harmony Alliance, Inc., began to pull together a diverse group of community, civic, religious, governmental, business and political leaders to promote ethnic and cultural harmony in Arizona. More than a hundred Arizonans from all walks of life met to learn about, from and with one another sharing the goal of spreading harmony through education, economic development and public relations campaigns. He wisely tapped Mrs. Loretta Avent, who later joined the Clinton administration in Washington, to serve as the part-time, practically volunteer executive director.

Beginning the 1992 Martin Luther King, Jr. celebration with the annual inaugural MLK prayer breakfast in December, I was elated to inform those in attendance, which for the first time included Fife Symington, that I was reserved, but expectant that we would be celebrating **VICTORY TOGETHER** in ten months. I declared in faith, "November 3, 1992 is a winnable challenge." The reason I felt confident in saying that, had to do with some information our campaign consultant provided for us a couple of weeks prior to the prayer breakfast.

During the Thanksgiving Day weekend, our new polling firm associated with Mandabach conducted their first poll for us on the King Day issue. The findings of Fairbank, Marilin & Associates revealed that 51% of Arizona voters favored a MLK Day while 40% opposed. In other words, to win in 1992, we had much work to do. Thank goodness, VICTORY TOGETHER had come into its own, which left the pro-King Day voters with "One **CLEAR** Choice" to lead the 1992 campaign—*US*.

Chapter Fifteen
Countdown to Victory: 1992 Was a Very Good Year

The year of decision had arrived for Arizona's Martin Luther King, Jr./Civil Rights Day. With "One **CLEAR** Choice" on the general election ballot, there would be no more opportunities to firmly establish the King holiday in Arizona in the foreseeable future. Our unique version of the holiday proposition which would honor King, civil rights, George Washington and Abraham Lincoln at no additional cost to the taxpayers, while not touching Columbus Day, was to be put before the same voters who narrowly defeated one of the two MLK propositions on the 1990 ballot. The conclusion, after conferring with our campaign consultants, indicated that VICTORY TOGETHER could lead Arizona in a "difficult but winnable" campaign.

In a pre-Christmas special meeting called so that Mandabach and Bragg could present, for the first time, the 1992 VICTORY TOGETHER campaign proposal, our board and steering committee members, resource persons and campaign committee members acted like excited children getting a sneak preview of our asked for Christmas gifts. The December 17, 1991 meeting was closed in order to prevent leaks to the media. A good number of our core VICTORY TOGETHER workers showed up for the presentation held at the church. After opening the meeting with prayer, I called those in attendance to join me in reading the specially chosen "Words From Martin,"

> Rarely do we find men who willingly engage in hard, solid thinking. There is an almost universal quest for easy answers and half-baked solutions. Nothing pains some people more than having to think.

If ever there was a time for our coalition's leaders to "engage in hard, solid thinking," it was on that third Tuesday morning in December.

The first thing we were told by our consultants was that even though the initial polling they had conducted showed Arizona voters favoring the King Day 51% to 40%, with 9% undecided, when the persons who were polled were pushed for their position on the holiday, the figures changed. Richard Maullin, our research analyst, was present to inform us that deeper probing of Arizona's most likely voters revealed that only 29% were definitely affirmative votes and 25% more unwavering negative votes. Furthermore, a whopping 44% were situated in between those two opposing percentages as soft support and opposition. In addition, our campaign was made tougher by three factors, (1) it was a racial issue, (2) the uncontrollability of events, and (3) the need for a "leave no stone overturned" campaign combining grassroots and paid media advertisements.

The actual "CAMPAIGN TO ACHIEVE VICTORY TOGETHER" was a seventeen-page outline divided into seven sections with numerous sub-sections. The abbreviated outline is provided below:

I. THE STRATEGIC CHALLENGE
    A. PUBLIC OPINION
    B. NATURE OF VOTE
    C. ISSUES ENVIRONMENT
    D. OPPOSITION
    E. NATURE OF ELECTION: GENERAL ELECTION IN
       PRESIDENTIAL YEAR
    F. POTENTIAL FOR "UNCONTROLLABLE" OUTSIDE
       EVENTS AFFECTING THE CAMPAIGN
    G. ESTIMATES OF "FOR" VOTES NEEDED FOR VICTORY
       TOGETHER: BETWEEN 650,000 + AND 800,000+
    H. CONCLUSION: DIFFICULT BUT WINNABLE
       CAMPAIGN
II. STRATEGY COMPONENTS: LOW-KEY, HIGH-ROAD
CONSENSUS CAMPAIGN
    A. BROAD MESSAGE FOCUS ON "AMERICAN
       VALUES" RATHER THAN ECONOMIC ISSUES
    B. BALLOT MEASURE DEFINITION FOR GENERAL
       AUDIENCES

C. NON-CONFRONTATIONAL APPROACH TO GENERAL AUDIENCES

D. GRASSROOTS CONSTITUENCY BUILDING CAMPAIGN

E. MULTIPLE SPOKESPERSONS

F. PAID MEDIA CAMPAIGN IN FALL

G. FUNDRAISING

III. FIELD ORGANIZATION - JANUARY-APRIL

A. CAMPAIGN KICKOFF

B. ESTABLISH TUCSON & FLAGSTAFF OFFICES

C. ESTABLISH FOUNDING MEMBERS SUPPORT COMMITTEES, INCLUDING COUNTY COMMITTEES - MARCH-APRIL

D. DEVELOP BASIC FIELD OPERATOR MATERIALS, I.E., FACT SHEETS, KING BID, COMMITMENT/ VOLUNTEER CARD - JANUARY

IV. VOTER REGISTRATION - APRIL-SEPTEMBER

A. TARGET: 100,000 NEW VOTERS

B. AUDIENCE: 18-34 AGE GROUP IDENTIFIED LIKELY SUPPORTERS, FOCUS ON PIMA & MARICOPA COUNTIES

C. CAPITALIZE ON NEW STATE POSTCARD REGISTRATION

D. PERIODIC "PUSH" ACTIVITIES, I.E., RAPID PROMOTION, CELEBRITY SITES, CAMPUS REGISTRATION RALLIES

E. TIE-IN TO COMMITMENT CARD VOTE-BY-MAIL, PHONE BANK, GOTV

V. FIELD ACTIVITY - APRIL-NOVEMBER 3

A. BUILD VOTER/VOLUNTEER SUPPORT

B. GRASSROOTS FUNDRAISERS

VI. VOTE-BY-MAIL - JULY-OCTOBER

A. TARGET: 700,000 VOTERS

B. AUDIENCE: NEW REGISTRANTS, LIKELY SUPPORTERS WHO ARE MEDIUM-LOW PROPENSITY VOTERS, IDENTIFIED SENIOR, SHUT-IN, RURAL SUPPORTERS

C. CAMPAIGN DISTRIBUTION OF REQUEST FOR VOTE-BY-MAIL

        D. MAIL, TELEPHONE FOLLOW-UP
VII.   GOTV - OCTOBER-NOVEMBER
        A. ELECTION DAY WEEKEND PROMOTION
        B. ELECTION DAY TURNOUT - NOVEMBER 3
VIII. BUDGET ($ IN 000'S)
        A. OPINION RESEARCH
        B. GRASSROOTS
        C. ADVERTISING
        D. PROFESSIONAL SERVICES
        E. TOTAL $ 1,730,000

What could we say? All that and more for nearly $100,000 which we had paid to develop our winning strategy. Other than the $1,700,000 price tag, we accepted our long-awaited gift from Martin's helpers-Paul and Felicia, assisted by Richard.

We did our best to discuss it intelligently. Many of us, like myself, were not familiar with a lot of the campaign lingo, e.g., "issues environment," "field organization," or "GOTV," which means "Get-Out-The-Vote." It all sounded good and complicated. But, I believe that one obstacle to our comprehending the detailed campaign plan had a lot to do with our continuing to look at the bottom-line figure of almost two million dollars. I still was having difficulty relating grassroots to that kind of money. And I was not alone. But that was not my worry. Steve Roman had handled his responsibilities meritoriously, up to that point, in getting big bucks whenever we needed some cash. I believed in him to make the necessary contacts and connections with the Phoenix 40 crowd and others yet to be inducted or invited, so that the million dollar-plus would be in the VICTORY TOGETHER bank account at the time it was needed.

In spite of what we had to pay for the plan from Mandabach and Bragg, we felt we got our money's worth. The general consensus was that the campaign strategy we had just had presented to us would work. We were pleased. A couple of days later, we drove down to Tucson to present the plan for their review and feedback. Other than the perennial concern of Tucson political and community activists working on a statewide project that "they be included in the decision-making process and not treated as step-children, as Phoenix leaders often did to them," the Tucsonian VICTORY TOGETHER volunteers united behind the strategy.

◇◇◇◇◇◇

As members of our coalition were preparing for an official VICTORY TOGETHER campaign kickoff, an explosion of sorts on the MLK Day scene in Arizona shattered the peace that we were experiencing. The first week in January, the popular rap group Public Enemy released a video featuring their rap song entitled "*By the Time I Get to Arizona.*" The video and the rap was what Public Enemy's publicist described as "revenge fantasy." Moreover, because Public Enemy and other rap artists are known for making political statements, usually in protest and/or defiance of the Establishment, this particular group selected Arizona's not honoring Martin Luther King, Jr. to be the target for their rancorous ridicule. Some of the words of their piece read,

> I'm countin' down to the day deservn'
> Fittn' for a King
> I'm waitin' for the time when I can
> Get to Arizona
> 'Cause my money's spent on
> The G-ddamn rent
> Neither party is mine not the
> Jackass or the elephant
> 20,000 nig, niggy, nigas in the corner
> Of the cell block but they come
> From California
> Population none in the desert and sun. . .
>   Isn't it odd and unique?
> Seein' people smile wild in the heat
>   120 degree
>   'Cause I wanna be free
>   What's a smilin' fact
> When the whole state's racist
> Why want a holiday F__k it cause I wanna
> So what if I celebrate standin' in a corner...

As if the words of the rap on Arizona dishonoring King Day were not enough, the video took its message to a level of visual volatility which did not extol Dr. King's philosophy of nonviolence one bit. In the opening scene of the video, the actor playing Arizona's governor says, "...as long as

I'm governor and as long as officials support me, Martin Luther King will never be a holiday in this State." At that point, the leader of Public Enemy, Chuck D, detonates a bomb that apparently is attached to the governor's limousine.

The timing for the "revenge fantasy" could not have been more ideal for Public Enemy, which makes millions off the sales of their rap music and videos. On the other hand, making headlines by calling Arizona "a racist state" certainly was not the kind of confrontational publicity that VICTORY TOGETHER needed to launch our winning campaign. As can be expected, local and national media rang my phone off the hook and forced me to take a stand for King Day in Arizona against some young, gifted Black brothers. In addition to calling me, my old buddy Ev got just as many calls inquiring how he felt about being portrayed as a racist governor whose demise came in an explosive assassination. He was quoted by one newspaper as responding, "It sounds like someone trying to make money with trash. It doesn't affect me. I am what I am, and what some trashy people do does not affect me."

First, *Entertainment Tonight* called me to be interviewed on a feature story they were doing on January 8, 1992. I called Mandabach and Felicia to get their opinion on whether or not I should appear. After discussion, we all agreed that Arizona voters needed to hear me take issue with the portrayal of violence in the video, which was certainly antithetical to Dr. King's philosophy of non-violence. To be sure, my cause for consenting to be interviewed for *Entertainment Tonight's* nationwide audience was to remind viewers of King's commitment to non-violent social change and to denounce Public Enemy's "revenge fantasy" video as no way to celebrate the life and legacy of the Black man who was yet to have a legal holiday in Arizona. As much as one can get such a serious message across in a sensationally-oriented entertainment news magazine, I tried.

In a more in-depth response, in an interview I had with the *Mesa Tribune* on the same day, I appeared on *ET.* I was able to say what I wanted to say, and to my surprise, the essence of my comments got published as follows:

> The song is unfortunate. It's regrettable. It does not reflect the spirit of Martin Luther King, Jr. He came out of the Judeo-Christian heritage. He was an advocate of nonviolence. He was a coalition builder. He sought peace and harmony between brothers and sisters who had differences in the past. There's nothing healing in this song. It does a disservice to Martin King

as well as the efforts of thousands of Arizonans trying to honor his life and legacy.

The fallout from Public Enemy's morbid make-believe video, which did include a depiction of Dr. King's tragic assassination as he stood on the balcony of a Memphis hotel, continued to mushroom in the news rooms, locally and nationally. Calls for interviews came in from MTV News, *The New York Times*, WRC Radio in Washington, D.C., *USA Today*, *Time* Magazine, Black Radio Network, *Washington Post* and Black Entertainment Television, as well as nearly every major local newspaper, radio and television station in the Valley. CNBC wanted me to do a live debate with Chuck D of Public Enemy via satellite, which I refused, basically because I did not want to be seen going at it with a brother on nationwide television. Probably, much of that had to do with the fact that "off the record" I could relate to his group's rationale for "fighting fire with fire."

Governor Symington's aides were busy explaining to the national media who were trying to get his reaction to the video, especially the portion depicting the Arizona governor's denouncing of the MLK Day, that he was not the governor who rescinded the King holiday. They were quick to point out that Governor Symington had campaigned on a platform in support of King Day. Symington's basic comment was that the promotional video was "unfortunate."

Within a week of the uproar over the rap against Arizona, ABC's *Nightline* producers called for an interview in order that they could do a story on Arizona's newest enemy. I was interviewed at the church and provided basically the same message that I had given to all the media who called or stopped by. Also, speaking for Arizona were both Governor Symington and impeached Governor Mecham. To my surprise, ABC aired the half-hour program featuring a live interview with Chuck D and an erudite African-American conservative from the Washington, D.C. area who espoused opposing viewpoints on the night of the 1992 MLK federal Holiday, January 20, 1992. They fought it out over the freedom of speech issue and Dr. King's legacy of non-violence, while the Arizona contingent whose interviews were pre-taped disavowed violent talk about our "beloved" state.

Of the many messages I received, as a result of the "*By the Time I Get out Arizona*" rap, two stand out. On Friday, January 10, a gentleman called me. He identified himself by name, which to this day I cannot remember, due to his heavy Brooklyn accent. However, it was clear whose father he was—Chuck D's. He was upset about my comments in the *USA Today* about Public Enemy's video. First off, that was a heck of a father to find my phone number way in Arizona to defend his son. God bless you, Chuck D's Dad. As he continued to express his displeasure over my saying that the "Arizona rap did a disservice to the legacy of Dr. King," his volume level began to rise. I suppose he thought I was some "Uncle Tom" out here in the desert, siding with the White governor and majority of the population, in opposing the King Day. He stated, "Why are you putting down a group of young, gifted Black men who are trying to better themselves by using their intelligence and music to send a message?"

When I finally got him to calm down enough to listen to me, I explained that I was a father too. Then, in brief, I went through the history of what happened in the 1990 election with the two propositions. I shared with him my frustrations with Mecham, when he was governor, and the White businessmen who did not get involved in the holiday fight, until they started losing money. I explained who VICTORY TOGETHER was and what we had been able to accomplish thus far. In addition, I enlightened him on the fact that we needed hundreds of thousands of White voters to vote for our "One **CLEAR** Choice" in the upcoming election. Consequently, my job was to diffuse some of the controversy that his son's video was stirring up.

By the time the conversation was over, his tone and volume had been lowered, and in parting he said optimistically, "You're doing a great job, and you're going to win in November."

The other message of personal significance was from Coffeyville, Kansas from a former Sunday School classmate who was residing in the state penitentiary in Hutchinson, Kansas. Gerry had seen me on *Nightline*. Only knowing that I was in Phoenix, he sent me a letter addressed to: Rev. Warren Stewart, Phoenix Arizona, and it got to me. Gerry will always hold a special place in my heart *because he taught me how to siphon gas, jump cars, joy ride, break into houses, entice unwary girls to be date-and-gang-raped, and so many other un-savoring delinquent juvenile activities*. The blessing I had in getting shot in the chest and arm at age fourteen, after committing burglary, was that I got caught. My friend Gerry did not, and has spent most of his adult life behind bars. One paragraph in my February 4 letter to him read,

> Do you remember that last time I saw you? It was in the late seventies in Wichita, KS. I visited you in the county jail. I'm sorry things haven't worked out better for you. But, please know that

you will always be my "buddy," former Sunday School classmate and "partner in crime."

For a while after that, Gerald and I kept in touch through the mail. He has been moved to another prison. My prayer is that one day he will be truly free of whatever imprisons him.

◇◇◇◇◇◇

The 1992 Martin Luther King, Jr. Holiday Celebration in Phoenix would be truly historic. The "Mother of the Civil Rights Movement," Mrs. Rosa Parks, was coming to Arizona. The City of

Phoenix, which hosted an annual Mayor's Martin Luther King, Jr. Breakfast the Friday before the federal and municipal observances of King Day, had been able to get her to make an official visit as the breakfast's honored guest speaker. Over the years since the King Day recision, that prayer breakfast had continued to grow, as a result of corporate Arizona using it as an "acceptable" event, in which they could show their support for King Day. It had grown in attendance from a few hundred to several thousand. Without a doubt, the presence of Mrs. Rosa Parks guaranteed that the 1992 MLK breakfast would be the largest in attendance and most historic.

The Phoenix Human Relations Commission, which prepared for her coming, utilized creative remembrance to welcome that "working woman who in 1955 refused to give up her seat to a White man on a Montgomery city bus," thus setting in motion her arrest and other events which thrust a young, educated, Black Baptist pastor into the forefront of the revolutionary Civil Rights Movement. A crowd of 200 civic and community leaders, mixed with several children, met her at the Phoenix Sky Harbor International Airport on Thursday, January 16. A city bus had been arranged to take her from the airport to the Hyatt Regency in downtown Phoenix. Several dignitaries rode with her in the symbolic bus ride, while she was flanked on either side by Pastor Barnwell and Mayor Johnson. The next day, over 4,000 persons attended the commemorative breakfast honoring Dr. King, held at the Phoenix Civic Plaza. All of the "big shots" were up front to escort Mrs. Parks—the governor, mayor, city council members, Phoenix Suns basketball team and you name it.

Rosa Parks was a graceful, soft-spoken woman who seemed not at all bothered by her notoriety and all that goes with it. She was 78 at the time she came. When she stood to speak, there was a hush over the auditorium. Mrs. Parks did not speak long. She never did. I listened with rapt attention from my seat literally about a half block or so away from the head table. She thanked the mayor and others for inviting her. She expressed appreciation to her "faithful friend and traveling companion," Elaine Steele for her being by her side. Sergeant Paul Brown, then of the Phoenix Police Community Relations Bureau and member of First Institutional, stood behind her as her personal bodyguard while she spoke. *The Arizona Republic* captured much of what she said to Arizona thusly,

> I'm very hopeful, I will never give up that Dr. Martin Luther King's holiday will be celebrated in this state. I have lived through much change and oppression from my childhood on. I am working to make our world a better place for our young people…I'm so happy to be here. This is a great thing in my life for me to be in Phoenix. I just appreciate everyone who is here.

Then, before you knew it, she turned, was caught by the helping hand of Sergeant Brown, and sat down to a thunderous applause. My, my, my! As I stood clapping my hands with 8,200 other hands, I felt a sense of reverence in that I had just heard and seen a living legend share words of wisdom. I also felt a little sadness because I knew that one day her voice would be hushed by the comforting hand of death, in her case. She, like Martin, would then only be able to be read about or seen in television programs, but no longer touched and felt.

I also remember Mayor Johnson in his remarks before Mrs. Parks, stirring the crowd by saying, "If we don't get the holiday in 1992, we'll be back in 1994…and 1996…And our resolve will be stronger." "Humph!" I said to myself. "He may be back in 1994 and 1996, but if we don't get the holiday this year, he will be the one leading the campaign!"

A reporter for the *USA Today* had asked me to meet her at the press-room after the breakfast, in order to get my photo taken to possibly be used in a front-page article she was working on for the January 20, 1992 issue. She had already interviewed me in my office on Thursday the 16th. I made my way through the departing mass of people and got to where I was supposed to be. Those police officers keeping watch over Mrs. Parks knew who I was and had no problem letting me into the restricted area. There were only a few people in the small room with Mrs. Parks and her protective aide, Mrs. Steele. I stood back away from the lady of grace as photographers continued to snap her photograph. One of the officers urged me to go and greet Mrs. Parks, and I did. I simply welcomed her to the Valley. Finally, the photographer from the *USA Today* came to take my photograph with Mrs. Parks and a young African-American Cub Scout who allegedly had eluded security to meet the Civil Rights Movement celebrity. He took several photographs of the three of us and a couple of just Mrs. Parks and myself. By that time, Paul Brown introduced me to Mrs. Parks and Mrs. Steele as his pastor and "the person leading up the whole 1992 Martin Luther King, Jr. campaign." All of a sudden I became more than a photo opportunist to our two honored guests. Mrs. Parks commended me on our efforts and Mrs. Steele interjected that they both would like to come back to Phoenix when the holiday passed. As I left, Sergeant Brown informed me that he had a gift for me; he would see that I got later-an autographed copy of *Rosa Parks: My Story*, her autobiography, which had just come out and which they had been promoting while in Arizona.

The morning of King Day 1992, I woke up and hurried to my neighborhood convenience store to get a copy of the *USA Today*, and there I was in color on the front page in a cut-out head photograph just below a much larger photograph of Mrs. Parks and Marcus Lytle, the fourth grade Cub Scout. The article's headline used my words to that paper's interviewer under the caption *COVER STORY*, "Today's King holiday 'is for all of us'." That was to be our message to the Arizona voters, if we were to win in ten months. The King holiday had to be seen by a majority of White Arizona voters as "our holiday."

After taking home a couple of copies of the *USA Today* to show my wife and sons, I got them together so we could hop in my van and participate in our annual Family ritual of marching in the King Day parade. When we arrived at 16th Street and Jefferson, after parking the van at the church, we saw Arizona's Republican governor in the front of the line in a light tan jacket and some walking shoes, accompanied by his wife, Ann. He had kept his word, after all. Good for him. The other regulars were there and in due time, Gene and his lieutenants gave us the signal to move forward toward the Capitol.

When we arrived at Wesley Bolin Memorial Plaza and the 10,000 or so marchers formed a sea of people in front of the podium, presider Blue began to introduce the long list of speakers, who would all say the same thing in essence, "Let's pass the MLK holiday this year." We had more Republican speakers than ever before. I guess you could say that the King holiday became the "politically correct" thing to do in Arizona, even for former opposing or lukewarm-supporting GOP politicians. But, one thing remained the same, after most of them gave their speeches, they left.

As usual, I was one of the last speakers. It had been my lot to officially launch the "VICTORY TOGETHER MLK, JR. HOLIDAY CAMPAIGN." It would have been nice for the Republican Party leaders to have stayed to hear my remarks, but, I guess I should have been satisfied that they showed up in the first place. Out of that crowd of thousands had to come some volunteers, new voters, foot soldiers, if you will, to join our fight to victory. So, after briefly rehearsing where we had come from since 1987, I proclaimed,

> Are we frustrated? Are we discouraged? Are we disheartened? Are we tired? Are we defeated? Are we going to give up? No! No! A thousand times **NO**!…Since the 1990 Martin Luther King, Jr. Holiday defeat, **something has happened in Arizona**! The common cause of honoring Dr. Martin Luther King, Jr. with a state holiday…has united hundreds of thousands of Arizonans for **VICTORY TOGETHER** as never before. People from all walks of life, even former "enemies" and those with opposing viewpoints are sitting down at the table of brotherhood and sisterhood. Thanks to Dr. King's dream, persons who would have never joined hands, hearts and minds together on anything are found all over Arizona singing in unison, "We Shall Overcome." "Thank you, Dr. King!"

I continued in my speech to remind and/or inform the audience of our initial victory to get our version of King Day on the ballot. At that point, I brought up the challenges that lay before us.

> …Our campaign is reaching out to all Arizonans who share our common goal. But we've got work to do. We've got to educate all Arizonans that **MARTIN LUTHER KING. JR. IS AMERICA.** And we've got to educate Arizona voters so well that no matter what negative report makes the headlines at the last minute, our "Yes" voters will not think of changing to "No" voters.
>
> We've got to establish **VICTORY TOGETHER** support groups in every county and corner of Arizona. In the rural areas, urban areas, on the reservations, on campuses, among senior citizens, in the barrios, at the country clubs, in the inner cities, in our churches, synagogues and mosques, on the job, in

our social groups and our neighborhoods. We've got to enlist thousands of volunteers for **VICTORY TOGETHER** beginning today. Please fill out a volunteer card before you leave today. We've got to register new voters. We've got to raise some money for **VICTORY TOGETHER** cause "Freedom Ain't Free! Make a donation to **VICTORY TOGETHER** today.

Then, as I headed toward the "mountain top" of African-American preacher-oratory, I tried to get the King Day supporters to envision what could be with these words,

I guarantee you, if we unite as one, become a mighty army of peacemakers, and practice Dr. King's message of freedom, justice and harmony, then **VICTORY TOGETHER** will become a reality in November. **TOGETHER WE CAN DO IT. TOGETHER WE CAN MAKE HISTORY. TOGETHER WE WILL CELEBRATE VICTORY IN NOVEMBER. TOGETHER! TOGETHER! TOGETHER!**

The crowd was into my speech! They shouted a few times, "TOGETHER! TOGETHER! TOGETHER!" Then, the speeches were over. The work began that day. My three oldest sons, Warren, Jr., Matthew and Jared, had been pressured by their father to pass out volunteer cards to everyone they saw. Felicia Bragg had been in Phoenix all that week prior to King Day recruiting and organizing the grassroots efforts of passing out volunteer cards, registering new voters and distributing VICTORY TOGETHER info that would take place that day. She and several other loyal VICTORY TOGETHER steering committee members "peopled" our booth. Paul Mandabach was there at the march for awhile. He liked my speech, but was a little critical of my oratory and how it would be viewed in sound bites on the evening news. All in all, it was a great day for us.

The King Day festivities went on without a hitch, until later in the afternoon. It had rained that weekend and even during our march that morning. The concern was that the water-filled clouds would rain on our annual celebration, before we had a chance to enjoy the day honoring King, by being in the company of the largest gathering of predominantly African-Americans in Arizona. Ironically, the rain held off, but the peace did not.

It seemed that two rival gangs ran into one another in mid-afternoon and began a brawl in the park. I happened to be near the Vietnam Memorial, which is on an elevated human-made slope, and could clearly see the two gangs as they fussed, cussed and fought, while moving toward Jefferson Street simultaneously. All of a sudden, out of nowhere undercover police, dressed like regular King Day marchers, uniformed cops, and police on bicycles began to converge on and around the fighting youth. What I saw was like a human wave of people, moving quickly in the same direction. The police, in an instant, got in between the dozen or so troublemakers. I was astonished as I got closer and witnessed teenage girls dressed in gang garb walking up to police officers who had handcuffed their male comrades, and cursing out the cops, demanding that they let their friends go. And right on time, thanks to "the Man upstairs," the clouds burst and the rain came cooling off several dozen hotheads. The decision had already been made to announce that "the party was over." The police and the MLK Celebration Committee leaders felt that that was in the best interests of the thousands who were still there. The entrepreneurs, who had paid to rent their food and special interest items booths did not like the decision, but that is the way it goes sometimes.

I agreed with the decision to end the festivities earlier than planned. The sad thing about what happened between the two rival gangs was that they did not know any better and maybe did not care that the Martin Luther King, Jr. holiday celebration was all about a Black man who changed America for the better in race relations, through non-violent social change. They took the opportunity to engage in acts of violence toward one another on Dr. King's day. Of course, the media played up the incident on the evening news, but it did not really affect the beginning of a campaign with destiny on its side. VICTORY TOGETHER was on a mission and nothing and nobody was going to get in our way.

Moreover, that weekend, *The Arizona Republic* had released results on its latest King Day poll. In the past, news that the results of one of their polls was going to be released made King Day supporters nervous, especially due to the way they asked some of the polls questions about the holiday. However, that weekend when 808 Arizona adults were asked, "At the present time, knowing that Arizona state employees have 10 paid holidays, would you vote for or against a proposal that would combine the Washington and Lincoln holidays into a Presidents Day, and create a paid holiday honoring the Rev. Martin Luther King, Jr., thereby keeping the number of paid state holidays that same?" Sixty-two (62%) percent said that they would vote for King Day. That was extremely encouraging news for Arizona and for VICTORY TOGETHER leaders.

◇◇◇◇◇◇

The year 1992 was full of a lot of things for me, one of which was meetings, meetings and more meetings. Serving as general chairperson of VICTORY TOGETHER entailed my being present and/or presiding at meetings of the corporation, campaign committee, steering committee, general supporters and various sub-committees. There were the one-one-one meetings with Mandabach, Felicia, Steve, Jack, Bettye, Janice, Judith, Mike and Joedd. Added to the list were my meetings with our Tucson, Casa Grande and Flagstaff workers on their turf. My personal appointment calendar filled-up as VICTORY TOGETHER broadened our base. MLK supporters from various organizations, professions, special interests, generations and virtually every walk of life wanted to offer their assistance, once they found out I was in charge of the King Day campaign. Of course, I attended many of the meetings with the men with the cash, often visiting the plush offices and environs of the Phoenix 40 crowd. As leader, I had to set up tension-filled conferences with disgruntled leaders of other MLK holiday groups. I drove from one elected official's office to another updating each on our progress. My religious colleagues called on me to apprise them of how their denominational bodies and organizations could help VICTORY TOGETHER. Although we had made a deliberate decision not to do radio talk shows, the requests for interviews in person and via telephone became extremely time-consuming.

After our campaign steering committee heard the presentation of our 1992 VICTORY TOGETHER Campaign Proposal and its 1.7 million dollar price tag, I had to address several questions about paying that much money to out-of-town consultants. One of the comments about the consultant's $30,000 a month fee was, "For that much money, we should have a person from the consulting firm in Phoenix throughout the week until the campaign is over!" Another raised the question, "What are we getting for thirty grand a month?"

In a memo to our two consultants, and Art, Steve, Jack and Bettye, I shared the questions raised and offered my own general questions and comments, which included the following:

- VICTORY TOGETHER Campaign should operate in the black, or at least, no more than a month or two in debt at any given time.

- VICTORY TOGETHER should use as many Arizona vendors, firms, agencies, contractors, and employees as possible and feasible.

- VICTORY TOGETHER should utilize as many free and/or in-kind services as possible to keep expenses down.

- VICTORY TOGETHER should set a goal to expend 10%-20% or more for services provided by people of color.

- VICTORY TOGETHER paid-staff should be representative of qualified personnel from various racial, ethnic and gender groups.

- How much will the campaign consultant's fees and commissions increase overall expenses?

- What process will be used to evaluate the performance of the consulting firm?...

We gave the campaign consultants an opportunity to address the meeting and evaluation concerns in our February meeting. From hindsight in view of our historic victory, the $30,000 fee does not seem too exorbitant. Had we lost, I am sure there would have been a lot of "tight jaws" and "finger-pointing." However, I am glad to report that we ran a cost-effective campaign with no outstanding debt when it was all over and our staff in Phoenix, Tucson and Flagstaff met our goal of racial, ethnic and gender diversity. We did not do as well on using Arizona vendors, as a result of already established business relationships Mandabach's firm had with such firms. Moreover, it took a lot of getting used to Mandabach's firms receiving commissions from virtually every product purchased in the campaign, such as printed materials, television and radio time, etc. So, in actuality, the fee we paid to the consultants was $30,000-plus. Mind you, this was customary practice for political consultants. It was just news to some of us grassroots folks, who had been accustomed to doing most of what we do for noble causes, for free.

In order to quell some of the disgruntled campaign steering committee members, Steve and Jack reviewed the proposed campaign budget and got it down to $1,662,000, with a reduction in the professional services payout to $275,000 from $360,000. That budget had been negotiated with our campaign consultants and agreed to after much discussion.

In the meanwhile, our fundraising efforts to get initial campaign contributions from corporate Arizona had brought in $110,000, thanks to Steve and Jack. Feeling moved to provide leadership from the grassroots arena, I asked my congregation to give a special offering for VICTORY TOGETHER on that King holiday weekend, during our Annual Martin Luther King, Jr./ Sanctity of Life Sunday, and the members and friends of First Institutional contributed nearly $5,000 to our campaign. I personally pledged $500 to the campaign and had already paid $200 by February 5, 1992.

◇◇◇◇◇◇

The month of March was significant in that we had begun to hire full-time staff to facilitate the increasing amount of paperwork and correspondence that was required to operate a full-fledged campaign. The First Institutional staff and facilities had reached an overload in trying to keep up with our seven-day-a-week comprehensive holistic Christian ministry and continue to serve as headquarters for VICTORY TOGETHER. A matter of fact, our first full-time employee, Esther Kozinets, had to share office space in First Institutional's administrative offices presenting quite a challenge of finding space and rotating usage of phones, typewriters and coping equipment with church employees.

After conducting marathon interviews for four days, the full-time staff in Phoenix included Esther Kozinets, a Terry Goddard- Democrat, as office manager/volunteer coordinator; DeJarnette Edwards, an African-American Democrat newcomer to Arizona, as office administrator; Mary Beth Swanson, a conservative Republican, as voters registration coordinator; Carlos Sarabia, an Hispanic transplant from Ohio as statewide field coordinator, and Paul Eppinger, recently retired pastor and liberal Republican, as statewide campaign coordinator/director. As far as our Tucson hires, Clarence Boykins, our newly elected regional co-chairperson, recommended Melissa Minerich to coordinate the Tucson VICTORY TOGETHER office and affairs.

With the selection of several staff to conduct VICTORY TOGETHER business, Steve and I had to get busy and locate a headquarters other than First Institutional. We looked at empty office buildings in central downtown Phoenix. After visiting several sites, we settled on an empty office complex located at 1410 North Central Avenue. The price was the drawing card. We got it from one of Steve's competitor financial institutions, Bankwest, for free. All we had to do was clean it up. That was an understatement because it had been vacant for several months and had become a haven for vandalizing vagrants, who had stolen the air-conditioning units, among other things. Nevertheless, miracles still happen because when a crew of volunteers and paid MLK supporters got finished with it, VICTORY TOGETHER had a place to call home, other than First Institutional.

Esther, Dee and Mary Beth spearheaded getting our headquarters ready for our grand opening on Sunday, March 15, 1992 from 2:00 to 6:00 p.m. We scheduled a brief program for 3:00 p.m. Trying to find the best date and time for heavily involved community and religious activists, as well as elected officials, is no easy task. We had to respect the Friday Muslim day of prayer, the Jewish Sabbath, the Christians' Sunday worship, and the non-churchgoer's recreation day. It just so happened that the NFL would be holding their winter owners' meeting in Scottsdale that same weekend; but not wanting to cause any more political upheaval relative Arizona's King Day fight, the only news they were making was that they were not making any news.

The grand opening was attended by a fully racially diverse crowd. People came and went for about three hours. Everyone who entered our doors had to sign in so that we could contact them later for their assistance. Our program participants represented our rainbow coalition. B.J. Bosley from First Institutional sang, "Bless This House." Joedd prayed us in. Some of John Calvin's students from Scottsdale's Saguaro High School led the Pledge of Allegiance. Senator John McCain, Guadalupe Mayor Anna Hernandez, Phoenix Union Superintendent Victor Herbert, Maricopa County Supervisor Ben Arrendondo and Art Hamilton honored their invitations to give brief remarks. Central Presbyterian Church's acapella choir inspired us with their Native American voices. Chuck Huggins came to represent labor's continued support, and Bruce Mayberry spoke on behalf of the governor. I gave remarks. Tanner Chapel's new pastor, the Reverend Benjamin N. Thomas, Sr., offered the closing prayer. Without saying, members of the general chairperson's congregation came and served as hostesses and well wishers, under the direction of Bettye Jackson.

Many other Valley leaders, who had been invited but couldn't come, sent letters of congratulations and regrets. One letter, however, was not exactly a congratulatory missive. It read,

Dear Victory Together,

I do not think it is a good idea to have a Martin Luther King, Jr. Civil Rights Day. I do not support your organization and will try to defeat what you stand for. There is One Clear Choice and you support the Wrong Choice.

Dale Moxon, Councilmember

At least, he was honest. My only regret was his letter did not identify for whom he was a councilmember. Could he possibly have been a councilmember of the Arizona KKK?

Cloves Campbell, Jr. and his *Arizona Informant* were faithful as usual. But, it seems as if the rest of the Valley's media was off chasing fire wagons, which turned out to be the case. A huge explosion in the Valley took place just about the time for our program, which drew the skimpy Sunday afternoon television crews to it. Nevertheless, VICTORY TOGETHER was open for business.

As the campaign progressed, in spite of letters like the one mentioned above, MLK holiday support came from the most unexpected sources. I got a call one day in my office from Hawley Atkinson of Sun City wanting to know what he could do to help VICTORY TOGETHER garner support in Sun City, Arizona's famous senior citizen community, where residents have to be 55 or older to live there permanently. In the 1990 campaign, the King holiday was overwhelmingly rejected by the senior citizen voters in that northwestern section of the Valley. In addition, in his earlier years, Mr. Atkinson gained a reputation as one of the most conservative supervisors serving on the Maricopa County Board of Supervisors. His opposition to many proposals that would have benefited the more disadvantaged residents in Arizona's most populous county, was somewhat notorious. That's why his telephone call to me on March 10 gave me another indication that 1992 was going to be a very good year.

Immediately, I sent him a note of appreciation on VICTORY TOGETHER letterhead, invited him to our headquarters' grand opening and enclosed a couple of information sheets on our coalition's identity and purpose. He wrote me a handwritten response on March 18, and indicated. "I will look forward to hearing from you of specific ways to assist you with VICTORY TOGETHER." The two of us were able to arrange a time when we could meet personally, and he came to my office so we could get acquainted. I do not know if I have ever met a man as genuinely concerned about wanting to make a difference in his particular community on the King issue, as Atkinson. In our conversation, he admitted that he had been on the "other side" of the issue. He spoke a bit apologetically about how the residents of Sun City and Sun City West had made their sentiments known by their negative King Day vote in 1990. But, he felt that things had changed for him and a few other key leaders in his community. He mentioned the Del Webb Corporation, which developed that senior citizen haven as well as an editorial writer for the *Daily Sun News* of Sun City. By May, Dr. Eppinger was speaking at a meeting of the Northwest VICTORY TOGETHER Committee at the home of Carolyn Modeen. In a letter I received from my new-found friend of two generations removed on May 4, his last sentence read, "I await your call to action." That was followed by his closing salutation, "Yours in Victory Together." I must say that establishing relationships and receiving communication like those with the Atkinsons, Pfisters and Hernandezes made the journey more than worthwhile. The end result was that support for the Martin Luther King, Jr./Civil Rights Day increased significantly, by way of advocacy and voter approval in the Sun Cities area. Thanks a whole lot to the Honorable Hawley Atkinson.

An accurate account of our historic 1992 MLK Day campaign must reflect the fact that everyone did not think that our consultants had presented us with a winning strategy. One primary reason had to do with the fact that we stayed out of the news media, as much as possible. VICTORY TOGETHER held no more than a couple of press conferences, once we officially kicked off at the January MLK Day rally at the State Capitol. King Day supporters in Arizona were not accustomed to not being in the news on a regular basis. Thusly, a lot of our supporters became nervous. The question kept coming up, "What's going on with the holiday?" The doubt even plagued long-time members of our coalition, who still had not quite accepted the polished L.A. yuppie consultant and his often outspoken African-American female partner. They were "outsiders." The common thought was "they don't know Arizona." Moreover, the questions about our adopted strategy began to spread, as we met with various segments of our supporters across the state, including Tucson business and community leaders, African-American leaders meeting at Southminster Presbyterian Church in South Phoenix, the Mesa Rotary Club, Valley Hispanic leaders, and certainly, elected officials who had experience in winning campaigns. Those groups are merely examples of the "experts" offering plenty of advice and paying big bucks to our "hired hands from the West Coast".

In cases like that, those in charge have to stick with the well-thought out decisions that have been made, make adjustments where necessary, and trust your intuition that "you're doing the right thing." In light of all the subdued dissension among our diverse coalition, I offered the following "Words from Martin" in our April 8 meeting.

In analyzing our campaign in Albany, Georgia, we decided that one of the principal mistakes we had made there was to scatter our efforts too widely. We had been so involved in attacking segregation in general that we had failed to direct our protest effectively to any one major facet.

It seemed as though I was directed to the right words from the amazing leader we sought to honor at the exact right time. We had to stay focused. After all, the last campaign had failed by a very slim margin. To win in 1992, we could not bank on just getting by with a majority. We had to have a large margin of victory heading into the polls. One of the mistakes that could have affected the outcome of the election could have been a splintered coalition, and that was not going to happen, if I could help it.

In spite of the doubts of sincere King Day backers, our efforts were continuing to pick up steam. The sitting governor, whose Black aide had wanted him to take over the MLK campaign, wrote me a letter on February 14, 1992, which began,

> Congratulations on your role and positive impact on the highly successful Martin Luther King, Jr. Celebration activities!
>
> As we now turn our undivided attention toward our goal of a highly successful election in November '92…, please rest assured that I remain committed to our objective.

I do not know if that letter was a form letter to all of the key King Day leaders. Nevertheless, it was good to have Arizona's chief executive, once again on record, indicating that he was willing to work with us.

Another boost of support came from the Arizona Town Hall, which broke from a thirty-year custom of not endorsing ballot issues, and by a hand vote, cast their organization's name as a proponent for the Martin Luther King, Jr./Civil Rights Day proposition.

Almost the opposite action came from another statewide organization by their tabling a resolution to support a holiday in honor of Dr. King. The Arizona Republican Party, in spite of being led by a King Day-supporting contingent of GOP top brass, such as Governor Symington, Senator McCain, Congressman Kolbe, Speaker of the House Hull and on and on, *refused* to join the growing number of Republican politicos becoming converted King holiday backers. That tabling action, which was tantamount to a negative vote by GOP delegates meeting in their executive committee spring gathering, proved to be a tremendous disappointment to Victor A. Washington.

Mr. Washington is a retired African-American NFL football player who had chosen the Republican Party as his political stomping ground. He had worked with the MLK Better America Committee in the 1990 campaign in some grassroots efforts. As the election loomed ahead, Mr. Washington organized the Republican Coalition for MLK '92 Committee, of which he was the chairman. His committee's logo read "MLK '92-It's Still the Right Thing to Do!...Vote YES..." Washington's efforts were very noble and I'm sure that his influence brought several lesser prominent Republican officials over to the King holiday roster of supporters. The problem that VICTORY TOGETHER encountered with Washington was that he rejected all of our overtures to him to become a leader in our coalition. Regardless of my personal calls, letters, visits and one-on-one meetings with my Black brother, VICTORY TOGETHER was off limits to Victor. I later discovered that he felt Steve Roman and MLK Better America owed him some money for expenditures he personally made to spearhead some grassroots activities in the African-American community during that last campaign. I tried to serve as a mediator between the two 1990 King Day campaign workers, to no avail. I even explained to Victor that I was in charge and Steve took orders from me, but that did not wash with Washington. In addition, I invited him to a VICTORY TOGETHER Board of Directors meeting, but his response to me in writing, on behalf of the Republican Coalition for MLK '92 Committee read,

> Thank you for your invitation...However, we feel it is not advisable to meet with...Victory Together until our steering committee has had a chance to meet to discuss how the Republican Coalition for MLK '92 might successfully work with Victory Together.
>
> We therefore respectfully decline your invitation...

I really regretted Washington's decision not to join us, because virtually every other pre-1990 election coalition had united together with us, at least in a marginal way. The one comforting thought I had was that our relationship, on a personal level, remained cordial and respectful, unlike the "bitterness" exemplified by Carl Nicholson who headed Arizonans for King Day Recognition.

Bettye Jackson's creative juices began to generate ideas for some grass-roots events, which would involve the African-American community in fundraising for VICTORY TOGETHER. Through personal contacts, she was able to secure the presence of veteran actor, the late Ossie Davis, to come to Phoenix on the evening of April 12. The benefit performance was called "An Evening with Ossie Davis." Felicia Bragg teamed up with Bettye to provide assistance for the event held at the Pointe at Squaw Peak. It was an occasion, at which time King Day supporters could dress up in our evening apparel and mingle with a star.

Mr. Davis was personable, charismatic and outstanding, as he stood for nearly an hour, speaking dramatically about his personal relationship to Dr. King and the wonderful undertaking of VICTORY TOGETHER to unite to honor his memory with a holiday, in spite of the many setbacks along the way.

Another effort that our co-chairperson of finance/ fundraising did was to visit several Black churches in Phoenix to solicit contributions for our efforts. I often missed her in our Sunday morning services, but she was out making a pitch for Black dollars for King Day.

In the meantime, one of Phoenix's historic African-American organizations reached out to me to offer assistance to our cause. The Black Theatre Troupe, Inc., the brainchild of the late Mrs. Helen Mason, offered to donate a portion of the proceeds from their preview performance of "The Meeting." The two-man dramatic play was an imagined meeting between Malcolm X and Martin Luther King, Jr., written by Jeff Stetson. Its point was to show that the two men's "lives were linked by a common time period and a uniquely singular goal…to bring about an end to racial discrimination." Debi Mason, the Troupe's executive producer, worked with our VICTORY TOGETHER staff to get the word out that this was a way MLK holiday supporters could witness a unique drama, depicting two of America's most revolutionary and controversial Black men in dialogue about their common goal and different philosophies and methodologies, and at the same time financially support VICTORY TOGETHER. Granted, the April 30 event did not bring in a lot of money, but it was yet another effort by African-Americans in Arizona "putting in our two cents" into making history.

Since I am on the subject of fundraising, the Phoenix 40 crowd was coming through on their commitments to finance our campaign in a big way. Mr. Colangelo had agreed (actually he assumed the role of chief corporate fundraiser for VICTORY TOGETHER) to tap his well-off buddies who ran the Valley's major corporations to give sizable chunks of cash to our coalition's drive for a holiday. And they did.

The exclusive $100,000 club was initiated by the Phoenix Newspapers, Inc. and followed by Roman's Valley National Bank and Hudgin's Arizona Public Service. In a tier all alone was Delbert Lewis of Channel 3-KTVK with $55,000. Right behind Lewis came corporations, such as the Phoenix Suns, Phoenix Cardinals, Dial Corporation, Bank of America and Phelps Dodge, against whom I had once lobbied because they had not divested from South Africa, during the height of the anti-apartheid movement in America. The twenty-five grand group included Salt River Project, which at first, had refused our request for assistance, and UDC Homes. A group of lawyers got together and formed Lawyers for MLK and contributed $13,847. The Valley hotel industry combined to donate over $35,000. Through my contacts with a loyal First Institutional member, Della Smith, who works for Intel, we received a special donation in the amount of $5,000 over and above what her corporate executives gave. Tucson was represented by a $5,000 contribution from the Tucson Newspaper, Inc., plus $1,500 from Sierra Tucson Company and $5,000 from the Westin La Paloma Hotel. Tanner Chapel A.M.E. Church, under the leadership of her new pastor, sent VICTORY TOGETHER a check for five hundred dollars. Pilgrim Rest Baptist Church, located around the corner from First Institutional, received an offering totaling $268.81, which her young pastor, Alexis A. Thomas, forwarded to us. ARIZONANS FOR A MARTIN LUTHER KING, JR. STATE HOLIDAY, headed by Pastor Barnwell, added $3,000 to our coffers.

As the campaign picked up momentum, our coalition employed Janet K. Johnson, one of the most personable women I have ever met and who had worked with Congressman Jon Kyl's campaign, as our part-time finance/special events coordinator, who facilitated the work of Steve Roman and Jerry Colangelo. Ms. Johnson was a person who did not attend a lot of meetings or spend much time around the headquarters, but she could be counted on to shake the bushes and follow-up on potential large donors.

By the first week in April, VICTORY TOGETHER had opened our Tucson headquarters. Paul and I, along with a few other Phoenix Staff, joined Clarence Boykins and his Tucson coalition workers and volunteers in the historic event, which took place in an almost luxurious former Citibank office complex out of which VICTORY TOGETHER's southern Arizona operation would be rung. The MLK Day campaign activities emanating from that spot located at 5151 E. Broadway would encompass Cochise, Graham, Greenlee, Santa Cruz and Pima counties. As Paul and I enviously inspected the spacious and modern facilities, which Clarence had persuasively solicited through his multitudinous contacts in Tucson, we kept wondering, how a branch headquarters could outshine the campaign's central and main headquarters in Phoenix. Whatever the case, we learned to "grin and bear it" every time we visited the southern region headquarters.

Not only could Clarence corral some fancy office space, but he was able to set up a diversely represented VICTORY TOGETHER campaign committee for southern Arizona. Supporters and well- wishers from all walks of life made up their VICTORY TOGETHER campaign committee. He was ably assisted by Larry Hecker, who eventually became the southern regional chairperson, when Clarence surprised us all by taking a leave of absence from his long-time City of Tucson position to become the full-time southern regional campaign coordinator. In addition to Larry, Pastor D. Grady Scott—a friend and colleague of mine, and Dan Eckstrom—a Tucson political leader from the Hispanic community, served as regional co-chairpersons. An energetic African-American sister by the name of Anita Etheridge was hired as office manager for Tucson VICTORY TOGETHER, and Evelyn Urrea fulfilled the responsibilities as voter registration coordinator. The evidence was obvious that Tucson would play a major role in our 1992 Martin Luther King, Jr. holiday campaign.

Northern Arizona was not to be left out. Although we did not need as large an operation in Flagstaff, we felt it necessary to have a presence. Once again, Steve took advantage of his contacts in the financial world and secured a closed branch bank office to house our northern regional headquarters. Paul, Felicia and I traveled to Flagstaff in late July to attend the grand opening of the Flagstaff VICTORY TOGETHER office. Marian Bevins had been hired to coordinate our northern regional campaign. Regrettably, our finances prevented our coalition from hiring any support staff for Ms. Bevins, so she had to depend on volunteers to aid her in her many responsibilities. Believe me, it got quite lonely for Marian, trying to oversee the campaign activities for that vast and sparsely populated northern region, which consisted largely of Native American reservations. Yet, she hung in there as long as she could.

The July 28th grand opening was like a "Who's Who" in Flagstaff. City and county officials, pastors, university faculty and administrators, NAU students, Native American leaders and members of the tiny African-American community in Flagstaff and vicinity showed up in full support of King Day. Dr. Jane Manning, director of Northern Arizona University News and Publications, was recommended by people in Coconino County to become the northern regional chairperson of VICTORY TOGETHER. Since most of us from Phoenix were so surprised to discover a gifted, Black female academician in Flagstaff, we unanimously approved her to be added to our statewide steering committee and appointed her as leader of our efforts up north.

We were blessed to have many other enthusiastic northern Arizonans to comprise our campaign committee in that part of the state. I shall never forget meeting an impressionable fifty-something-Anglo woman from Winslow by the name of Helen Butler. She committed to returning to Winslow after meeting with Dr. Eppinger and myself at the grand opening and, if necessary, becoming a one-woman King holiday campaign commit-tee in her chilly town. Other northern region VICTORY TOGETHER committee members included Ernie Vasquez; Homer Townsend, Flagstaff City Councilman; Rick Lopez; Coconino County Supervisor Paul Babbitt [Chris Bavasi, Mayor of Flagstaff] and Ivan Sidney, special counsel for Native American Programs of NAU. Of course, there were others, just like there were countless numbers of VICTORY TOGETHER volunteers that joined our ranks across this state, as we marched toward victory in November 1992.

The students at ASU in Tempe decided to do something, in addition to hitting the books. Matthew Calpbly became the leader of our ASU VICTORY TOGETHER chapter. He worked diligently to ensure that the leaders of tomorrow would play a vital role in helping Arizona to make history in the second King Day election. Our polls reminded us that 90% of Arizona voters, who were college age, supported our goal. The critical task would be getting a large portion of the 18-25 year olds registered and to the polls on November 3, 1992. I drove to ASU to speak at a sparsely attended rally on April 23 to inspire our ASU VICTORY TOGETHER workers to create a mass movement of students actively involved in our campaign. I challenged those in attendance that their age bracket of voters was desperately needed to offset the 55 and older crowd, who had almost always cast a negative vote for King Day. I reminded them that tens of thousands of university students were in Arizona, and whether or not they knew it, Dr. King's most energetic and enthusiastic supporters during the Civil Rights Movement were students. As a result, the few who attended the ASU VICTORY TOGETHER rally left the auditorium, committed to garnering support throughout their 40,000-plus student body. It also helped to know that President Lattie Coor and the administration of ASU were 100% in support of King Day.

Our grassroots campaign consultant worked feverishly behind the scenes to increase our support among the Native American Communities. Felicia, Carlos Sarabia and I met with several of the Native American legislators in early May to seek their advice on how VICTORY TOGETHER could get out our campaign message to the different Native American communities in Arizona. We believed that their votes were as important as any other special interest Arizona constituency. In pursuing their support, we endeavored to make the connection between the historic Civil Rights Acts, Dr. King and the Civil Rights Movement, and the civil and human rights of Native Americans. One of our steering committee members was the wife of Representative Ben Hanley, as well as a key leader in the Inter-Tribal Council of Arizona, which was made up of twenty-one different Native American tribes and communities. The end result of our meeting was a letter written by three Native American Arizona legislators, namely, Senator James Henderson and Representatives Hanley and Jackson, urging the state's tribal leaders to both support and become involved in the campaign to win voter approval of the King holiday in Arizona. In their letter, at least one quotation was cited from Dr. King, who addressed the plight of the "American Indian" who had endured inhumane racism at the hands of White America, almost to the point of genocide. On a more positive note, the letter included the following paragraph,

> Native American traditions of harmony and respect for all living things are consistent with Dr. King's philosophy of peace, and the dignity and worth of every human being.

To make sure we did not overlook the largest ethnic minority in Arizona, we planned a meeting at our Phoenix headquarters with Hispanic leaders. Rosie Lopez, founder of the Arizona Hispanic Community Forum and board member of VICTORY TOGETHER, co-coordinated our May 20, 1992 meeting with Hispanic community leaders. The attendance at the early morning gathering let us know quickly that the Hispanic leadership stood shoulder-to-shoulder with us on King Day. Breakfast meeting co-sponsors, who allowed their names to go out on the invitation letter included Daniel Ortega of Ortega & Moreno Law Offices; Tommy Espinoza of Espinoza Enterprises; Joe Eddie Lopez, Arizona House of Representatives; and Yolanda Kizer of the Arizona Hispanic Chamber of Commerce. Mandabach flew in to Phoenix to present an overview of the campaign, just as he had done for the Phoenix 40 and the African-American leaders. Quite strategically, Carlos was able to provide a glimpse of our grassroots component of the campaign, which would be critical in winning MLK votes within the Mexican-American communities across Arizona. Father Tony Sotelo who pastored Immaculate Heart Catholic Church, up the street from First Institutional, inspired us with his prayer for unity. Therefore, our 1992 campaign would not duplicate the mistake of the MLK Better America campaign, which did not invest heavily in winning Hispanic support for the King holiday. By the time the meeting was over, we had solidified the backing of our Brown brothers and sisters.

A tragic thing happened toward the end of April that shocked the nation-a jury from Simi Valley, California found four Los Angeles police officers not guilty of police brutality, committed against Rodney King, a Black man who resisted arrest a year before, after he was stopped for speeding, reckless driving and fleeing pursuing patrol cars. When he finally stopped again, he was subsequently beaten by four uniformed police officers, while being unknowingly videotaped by a curious witness who had been disturbed by all the commotion outside his apartment window. The entire nation had seen the public whipping of Mr. King, countless times on the television over that past year. Surely, anyone could clearly see that the officers, caught on film inflicting brutal blows on Rodney King, had to be in the wrong. However, after lengthy deliberations on the trial of the four L.A.P.D. officers, the verdict was read, "Not guilty."

The tragic aftermath of that travesty of justice was one of the most deadly riots in modern-day American history that transformed South Central Los Angeles into a street-level inferno and sad, senseless killing field, where African-Americans wantonly let loose their pent-up, racism-caused anger about such an unjust verdict. When the last fire had been put out, statistics revealed the naked truth—most of the dead were African-Americans, most of the property damage occurred in Black neighborhoods, and the four accused police officers were free.

To my own congregation I reflected in double-sized pastoral comments entitled "KING FEELINGS," on Sunday, May 3, 1992, while L.A. was still smoldering. Three paragraphs of my personal feelings were expressed as follows:

The entire chain of events from Rodney King's fleeing the pursuing police in his car to his brutal beating to "his" trial in Simi Valley to the **NOT GUILTY** verdict to the violent, destructive and deadly rioting in South Central Los Angeles, in my opinion is **A SYMPTOM OF A GRAVE AND GREATER PROBLEM IN AMERICA-VIOLENCE! OUR SOCIETY CELEBRATES LEGAL AND ILLEGAL VIOLENCE** through media, war, capital punishment, violent crime, gang violence, domestic violence, abortion, racism, sexism, militarism and materialism. If the 80's was a decade of greed, then the 90's is rapidly becoming **A DECADE OF VIOLENCE.**

My concern for our **YOUTH** of all colors who are taught that the government is the **guaranteed** purveyor of "justice and liberty for all" and yet, who, in reality, witness regularly the government **meting** out **UNEQUAL JUSTICE,** especially to people of color. The message to them is, **"THE GOVERNING AUTHORITIES CANNOT BE TRUSTED."**

I am equally incensed and outraged by the SENSELESS VIOLENCE perpetrated by rioters in South Central Los Angeles. At least **111** persons have been killed, dozens of innocent people beaten and injured, places of business destroyed and hundreds left jobless by the **VIOLENT REACTION TO THE APPARENT VIOLENCE DONE TO THE PERSONHOOD OF RODNEY KING AND EVERY PERSON OF COLOR IN AMERICA.** Those actions are just as despicable as the jury's!

As it related to VICTORY TOGETHER's quest for a win in November, we were concerned that the riots that could be seen on televisions, in the living and family rooms of hundreds of thousands of Arizona voters, would instigate a brutal beating of our positive position in the polls. Would Arizona voters, most of whom were White, revolt against what they saw on television and vote against MLK Day for the third time?

As much as I intended to stay off the television, as it related to our VICTORY TOGETHER campaign, when the media called me about what was happening in Los Angeles with the trial and the riots, I had to speak as a prophet of God. The local media were not calling me as the King Day coalition leader, but as pastor of the leading African-American church in Arizona. It would have been a sin for me to respond, "No comment." So, being led by the Holy Spirit and informed by knowledge and experience, I tried to make some sense out of the disjointed, but connected train of insane events, which were unfolding in living color before our eyes.

I used every opportunity possible to lift Martin Luther King, Jr.'s message of non-violence, racial harmony and radical love of one's enemies. I spoke at an impromptu press conference with Governor Symington and called for people of all faiths to pray for peace, justice, equality and victory over racism. Upon the suggestion of Pastor Ron Lush, a dear Anglo friend of mine, with whom I have prayed hand-in-hand often, I announced to the media that First Institutional Baptist Church would be one of several Valley churches, serving as gathering spots where Arizonans could bring relief supplies for residents living in riot-torn South Central Los Angeles. People of every color came from across the Phoenix metropolitan area with food, clothing, dry goods, diapers, furniture and money to send some love to Los Angeles. When it was all said and done, Ron had arranged for two Ryder Rental Trucks to transport the goods to our neighbors across the Arizona-California border. We were able to provide an intermission in our quest for a holiday honoring a man of peace in order to *send some peace* to our brothers and sisters.

What about the holiday, though? To the amazement of many of us in VICTORY TOGETHER, a KAET poll showed that the Los Angeles riots improved Arizona's chances for passing a MLK Day! That's right! A press release provided by Dr. Bruce Merrill and KAET carried the following sentence, "Most importantly, 16 percent of Arizona's voters said recent rioting in L.A. made the holiday more needed than before." Therefore, Dr. King's message of nonviolence could not have been more timely for California and Arizona, even though for vastly different reasons. Moreover, the KAET poll showed that overall support for Arizona's King holiday was on the rise. An encouraging 59% of registered voters said they would vote for the holiday.

◇◇◇◇◇

The following week Arizona had a high-profile visitor by the name of Governor Bill Clinton of Arkansas, the leading Democratic presidential candidate at that time. He was in town to bolster his support by appearing at a campaign rally held at the International Brotherhood of Electrical Workers hall and serving as guest of honor at a $500-a-plate private fund-raiser held Friday evening May 8, 1994. I had been asked by a state Democratic Party official to appear on the stage with Mr. Clinton at the afternoon rally. However, I conveniently declined, since it was my Friday sermon preparation day. Honestly, I did not want to share the platform with Clinton, due to his strong support for current abortion laws. His stance, which was the vintage liberal abortion-on-demand position, troubled me. If he would be elected, it would set back some pro-life progress that had been made under the Reagan and Bush presidential administrations. Of course, I knew of his pro-King Day advocacy and expected him to speak in behalf of Arizona's MLK holiday campaign (which by the way, President Bush would not touch with a ten-foot pole on his one stop here, during his campaign).

That brings up another reason I chose not to accept the kind invitation to sit on the stage with the future President of the United States. I did not want to alienate any of our Republican King Day steering committee members. Some tensions had already surfaced among the core leadership of VICTORY TOGETHER as a consequence of the three-way presidential race shaping up between Clinton, Bush and Ross Perot. A few of our hardest workers yielded to the temptation to throw political jabs at one another relative to their opposing preferences for the commander-in-chief. Therefore, somebody had to be neutral, as much as possible. So, I chose to forgo hobnobbing with the local and national Democratic elite.

During his half-day trip to Arizona, Clinton commented on a variety of subjects, two of which were the L.A. riots and MLK Day. *The Phoenix Gazette* reported on his remarks on those two-related subjects by quoting him as saying,

> We have been permitted to be divided by race, man against woman, by income, by age, by region. This country is coming apart when it ought to be coming together. That is one of the lessons of Los Angeles...Arizona can send a good signal by adopting a Martin Luther King holiday. Look at Arizona-native Americans, blacks, Hispanics, whites. Look at Los Angeles-146 different nations in one county. We have to decide, is this going to be a source of our strength, or a source of our undoing?

Even though I did not make it to the podium on Clinton's visit to our state, Arizona African-Americans were well-represented by our newest

Black legislator, veteran pastor and civil rights activist, the Honorable G. Benjamin Brooks, appointed to replace Representative Armando Ruiz who was appointed to replace expelled Senator Carolyn Walker in District 23. Coincidently, I shook Mr. Clinton's hand, later on that year, when he appeared to speak before members of the National Baptist Convention, USA, Inc. meeting in Atlanta, Georgia. I had the mind to tell him of my disapproval of his abortion policy, as he spoke to each of us sitting on the front row of the platform as he passed by. But, I chickened out and protested by not joining in on the customary standing ovation, for which I was criticized by a fellow pastor for disrespecting the presidential candidate. However, the way I figured it, I had to get my "two cents in" one way or another, so I could live with Warren.

Jerry Colangelo did more than raise nearly 1.7 million dollars for our campaign. He lent us the usage of the brand-new America West Arena to hold a VICTORY TOGETHER Valley leadership meeting on June 8, 1992. The purpose of the gathering was to broaden our base of support and recruit volunteers who would constitute our army of thousands to move our grassroots campaign forward. The "Purple Palace," as it had been deemed, since it would become the home of the Phoenix Suns, was the extra incentive to draw King holiday advocates from all over the Valley to downtown Phoenix on a Monday morning—my supposed day off. Felicia and our VICTORY TOGETHER staff and volunteers worked feverishly to get out invitations to nearly 700 persons. They prepared well-stuffed folders with VICTORY TOGETHER paraphernalia, which included an increasing array of our campaign's literature and support forms. The packet contained the following:

- Our premier MLK Jr./Civil Rights Day Pamphlet
- Volume I VICTORY TOGETHER Campaign Bulletin
- MLK VICTORY TOGETHER Campaign Assistance Form
- VICTORY TOGETHER Support/Volunteer Post Cards
- VICTORY TOGETHER Campaign Contribution Envelopes
- VICTORY TOGETHER Ballot Measure Info Sheet
- VICTORY TOGETHER Bio Sheet of Dr. King
- A Chronology of the MLK Holiday Struggle in AZ
- An Arizona 1991 MLK Celebration Booklet
- A Selected Bibliography of Books by and About Dr. King.

- The Agenda for the June 8th Meeting
- Info Sheet and Map of the America West Arena

Our VICTORY TOGETHER logo and purpose would soon become the worst kept secret in Arizona after our "sneak preview" of the most modern professional basketball arena in the country, built in joint partnership by Mr. Colangelo and the City of Phoenix. Nearly 300 people showed up for the meeting, which carried a bonus of a guided tour through the $90,000,000 state of the art facility, which had been sold out for every Phoenix Suns game, since its opening until the turn of the 21st century.

Dr. Eppinger kicked off the meeting with a welcome and introductions. Bishop Heistand led the enthusiastic crowd in prayer. My assignment was to inform and excite the King Day supporters about VICTORY TOGETHER's *identity* and *purpose*. I had scribbled down some notes, from which my remarks would evolve. I began, "Martin Luther King, Jr. was not the only one to have a dream. It's obvious that Mr. Colangelo is a dreamer in his own right..." After I thanked everyone I needed to thank for coming, I reminded the spectating attendees,

> The America West Arena, as magnificent as it is, is not the primary reason we have gathered here on this Monday morn. One common goal has drawn us here from all walks of life... The Martin Luther King, Jr./Civil Rights Day is based on some fundamental American principles that "all persons are created equal under God," basic civil rights are guaranteed by the laws of this Land, Arizona wants to join the nation in honoring Dr. King and civil rights, and this holiday is "as American as apple pie."

Next on the agenda, Mandabach and Bragg provided an audio-visual presentation on what needed to be done between then and November 3, 1992 to attain VICTORY TOGETHER. Mr. Colangelo was strategically placed as the last speaker on the program, in order that he could solidify volunteer and financial support from the 300 or so Valley leaders who were guests in "the house that Jerry built." The title of his speech was "LET'S DO IT!" A fiery speaker he ain't, but as the major "mover and shaker" in the Valley of the Sun, "when Jerry talks, people listen."

One of the justifiable criticisms of the construction of the America West Arena financed by taxpayer dollars revolved around the fact that it was reported that only about $400,000 in construction contracts went to minority contractors. Dr. Lincoln Ragsdale and other African-American community and business leaders had pitched a fit over those disgraceful statistics. I, too, joined in with the verbal protests of "business as usual" concerning minority contractors being ignored when multi-million dollar governmental construction projects were awarded to all-White general contractors. My presence there that morning left one impression on me, as I saw that many of the employees, busily working throughout the arena, were people of color. Seeing several Black brothers and sisters in the uniform on the site provided a little salve for the re-opened wound of racist exclusions where "big bucks" were involved. I even commended Mr. Colangelo for hiring so many persons of color. His reply was that, that was done intentionally, because he had made a commitment to diversify his and the city's employee ranks with people of color who would be working at the America West Arena. Once again, Jerry Colangelo kept his word.

While I am on the subject of Jerry Colangelo and the home of the Phoenix Suns, the June signing of Charles Barkley to become a Phoenix Sun rocked not only Arizona, but the entire sports world. It was hard to believe that the Philadelphia 76er's "bad boy" was on his way to conservative, nearly all-White Arizona to do what he does best—play basketball and make the news with his mouth and/or by hitting someone else in the mouth. The native of Leeds, Alabama had gained a notorious reputation off the court, after engaging in fistfights with bar room patrons. Thinking, eating, drinking, sleeping and leading the King Day campaign, my immediate reaction when I heard Barkley had signed to wear the Suns' purple and gold was, "Oh, my goodness! After a meeting I had with Colangelo relative to campaign fund-raising, I expressed by concern about Charles Barkley coming to town and saying something that would alienate Arizona voters from the MLK holiday. The Phoenix Suns principal owner and president assured me, "Oh, Charles is a very personable guy… "

When he arrived in Phoenix on June 19 to meet the press and tour his new playing ground on Jefferson, the local media popped the question about how he felt coming to play in Arizona where there was no Martin Luther King, Jr. holiday. The *Scottsdale Progress* listed his colorful comments in an inset, which read,

I don't know what the vote was, but I think it was relatively close. But I don't think people voted because it was a black-white thing. It was forced upon them.

When you talk to people about pulling their Super Bowl, not having conventions here and messing with the (college football) bowls…that has nothing to do with the holiday. If you try to force something down someone's throat, they're going to have a problem with it.

If I'm in Phoenix, and I feel like there's racial tension here, I'll address it at that time. But I'm not going to sit here and say, "Phoenix is a racist city." I don't judge anyone like that.

Apparently lost in the *Progress* article was a key sentence which the *Gazette* reported Barkley as adding, "But I think we've got more serious problems in our society other than holidays." *Oh Lord,* I said to myself when I saw that comment reported, *that sounds like something the anti-King Day fighters would mouth off.* So, I decided to take matters in my own hand. I wrote the newest Phoenix Sun a letter. My June 21, 1992 letter to Mr. Barkley addressed to the Phoenix Suns' P.O. Box read,

> Welcome to the Valley of the Sun from another migrant from back East (New York City). I join with others in the excitement that your becoming the newest Phoenix Sun brings to our community.
>
> After reading your comments on Arizona's efforts to observe a Martin Luther King, Jr. holiday, I am taking the liberty to share some background information on the history of the King holiday and **VICTORY TOGETHER**…
>
> Since 1986, I have been one of the leaders in the campaign to win a Martin Luther King, Jr./Civil Rights Day…in Arizona. You already might know that Mr. Jerry Colangelo and the Phoenix Suns have been solidly behind our efforts from the beginning.
>
> If possible, I would like to meet with you personally to welcome you to our city, answer any questions you might have bout the (MLK) campaign, and **REGISTER YOU AS AN ARIZONA VOTER**. Please contact me at my church number… or my home number…, if this meeting can be arranged.
>
> Lastly, moving from Phoenix from back East can be quite a cultural shock for an African-American (it was for me) since we

represent only 3% of the state's population. Several former and current Phoenix Suns, such as Garfield Heard, Eddie Johnson, Larry Nance, Alvin Scott, Kevin Johnson, Mark West and Tim Perry, have either been members or worshipped with the First Institutional Baptist Church...(just 10 blocks from the new America West Arena). Our Sunday morning worship services, which are held at 8:00 and 11:00 a.m., provide one of the largest regular gatherings of African-Americans in Arizona.

As pastor, I invite you to worship with us soon.

I look forward to meeting you personally and offer my friendship to you.

I never heard from Barkley, even though I copied a letter to his boss and had mentioned my letter to Mr. Colangelo. Once he arrived in the Valley later than summer, one of our members became an occasional golfing buddy of his. I told him about my letter and accompanying info on VICTORY TOGETHER to Mr. Barkley, which had received no response. He spoke with Charles who told him he had never received it. So, Bro. Michael Butchee volunteered to hand-deliver a copy of the letter to Barkley the next time they golfed together. I gave him the letter, but still never heard from Phoenix's new NBA star.

It was disappointing to not even receive a form letter from Barkley. Nevertheless, it was obvious that Colangelo and others had briefed him on the King Day struggle and upcoming campaign. The other reason I regretted not getting to meet him was I did not get a chance to witness to him about Christ and the Church. Whatever the case, he kept his cool as much as he could through November 3, 1992.

Thanks to Felicia and our insistence that VICTORY TOGETHER wage a broad-based grassroots campaign, we kept expanding our multi-cultural, interracial, interfaith, non-partisan coalition to the point that thousands of Arizonans were involved. By the first of June we began our *paid* voters' registration drive. I was unaware that individuals could be paid for every citizen they registered to vote. Several aggressive people were added to our payroll to help us in reaching our goal of 100,000 new voters in Arizona. Mary Beth Swanson put in lots of hours as our voter registration coordinator in the Phoenix office and Evelyn Urrea did likewise in Tucson. We particularly targeted younger first- time voters. Nearly every special event, where people would gather in parks, at concerts, in the mall, and after Sunday morning worship services, was covered by someone from VICTORY TOGETHER.

We met with Mormons for MLK in Mesa. Jan Johnson coordinated various special events around the Valley, which could serve as volunteer recruitment and fund-raising functions. Ms. Marion Jones, a recent transplant from upstate New York, was hired as our phone bank coordinator, which would provide critical telephone contact with thousands of known and potential MLK Day holiday supporter in the fall. Jan Williams of First Institutional moonlighted at VICTORY TOGETHER's headquarters inputting countless names and addresses into our computer files. By the middle of August, Abbie Fink was employed as our full-time volunteer coordinator to bring some order and give direction to hundreds of King Day supporters who swelled our ranks as September and October rolled around.

Rest assured, I had no time to supervise our growing staff, which had become a beehive of activity. That was Paul Eppinger's job. Even though he had taken early retirement from First Baptist Church of Phoenix, he was not about to get any rest working for the holiday. A summary of one of his monthly statewide director reports indicated clearly that we were getting our money's worth out of Paul. During July, he attended a series of meetings in Phoenix, Mesa, Sun City, Flagstaff and Tucson. He spoke on behalf of VICTORY TOGETHER at ten organizations, ranging from the Grand Canyon Presbytery to a doctors and spouses wine and cheese party. His responsibilities entailed overseeing full-time campaign staff in Phoenix, Tucson and Flagstaff. His job also required that he identify any needs that the campaign required, as well as keep a check on what the holiday opposition was doing.

Although Dr. Eppinger's immediate supervisor was Paul Mandabach, to whom he was to report, it is safe to say now that he kept me fully apprised of everything that went on. We were not only colleagues, but friends and brothers who had invested our intellect, energy and inspiration into the passage of Arizona's MLK Day, long before any money was ever involved. Furthermore, Paul proved extremely valuable, trying to keep peace in the office among consultants and employees who often butted heads and got on one another's nerves, as deadlines had to be met and critical activities had to be carried out almost instantaneously.

As for me, I would stop by the Phoenix headquarters, as often as possible, usually on my way to the church office. As the general election approached, the demands of the campaign necessitated that I stop by the church office, as often as I could after I had been down at headquarters. Most of my responsibilities involved conferring with Mandabach, Bragg, Jack, Steve and Paul about the latest progress and problems relative to the campaign. Much of that time was spent on conference calls between Los Angeles, Tucson and Phoenix.

By mid-summer Mandabach's big concern was money. He knew that he would need to begin to determine how much television and radio time we would need to purchase to get our message across. In our July 14, 1992 board of directors/campaign committee meeting, Steve and Jack apprised us that we had $700,000 in hard commitments, which only paid for about half of our campaign's total expenses. The minimum amount we needed to reach by that time was $900,000, which left us $200,000 short. Upon analyzing where we were and where we needed to be, Steve, Jack and Jan Johnson went to work shaking the bushes of the corporate executives who were on our list, but had not paid up. For example, Jack singled out the "high tech" executives for a goal of $100,000 to $200,000. Salt River Project, the utility company which Jack had formerly managed, had not committed to give anything. So, Jack made getting, at least $25,000 from SRP's new, hesitating general manager, a priority; and eventually, he got it. The collective wisdom of Jack and Steve estimated that there was, at least $500,000 available from untapped CEOs.

◇◇◇◇◇

The summer was important for another critical reason. Mandabach, Bragg and their respective political consulting firms produced what they were being paid—$30,000 plus expenses monthly—for *a winning theme*. Based on their research, Arizona voters could be convinced to vote for the MLK, Jr./Civil Rights Day, if the following four key campaign strategy points were effectively communicated:

1. The MLK, Jr./Civil Rights Day represents a fundamental American principle that "all people are created equal under God."

2. Dr. King's philosophy of nonviolent social change enables America to live up to our historic principles of liberty and equality.

3. Our proposition provides a practical, sensible and fiscally conservative plan that is patterned after the federal model

of King Day which celebrates Martin Luther King, Jr./ Civil Rights Day and combines the celebration of our great Presidents into one Lincoln/Washington Presidents' Day, at no additional cost to the taxpayer.

4. VICTORY TOGETHER is a broad-based grassroots coalition representing Arizonans from all walks of life.

Our coalition leaders adopted those four points wholeheartedly, especially since most of the foundational information, from which our consultants derived our fourfold theme, came from our statement of principles and seasoned King Day tactics. I guess it just sounded better, after costing the Phoenix 40 crowd hundreds of thousands of dollars. For me, the first point was extremely powerful because it was both patriotic and theological, at the same time. Moreover, to say that the Martin Luther King, Jr. holiday symbolized the one truth that provides the foundation, on which this nation was built; in spite of its hypocritical racism and discrimination against people of color and women, made the King holiday "as American as apple pie." Once I made the connection verbally, I was asked, rhetorically, "What red-blooded American would disagree with that fundamental American principle?"

With our fourfold theme adopted, our consultants went to work with their media experts from Los Angeles to develop new campaign literature, radio and television commercials and suggested speaking points which "Americanized" for Arizona voters the Martin Luther King, Jr./Civil Rights Day. When they got through, only a stubborn, one-track minded bigot refused to comprehend that voting yes for what became known as Proposition 300 on the November 3, 1992 general election ballot was "the right thing to do."

◇◇◇◇◇◇

Speaking of the ballot, another controversial proposition would be listed there for voter approval or disapproval. Proposition 110, which was a citizen's initiative entitled "The Preborn Child Protection Amendment to the Arizona Constitution," was creating quite a stir among the majority pro-choice constituency in Arizona. The proposed amendment, if passed would have done essentially five things, namely,

1. Prohibited the usage of public funds for all abortions except those necessary to save the life of the mother.

2. Guaranteed the right to life to every preborn child at any stage of biological development, except to save the life of the mother. However, the Legislature could expand the exceptions to include abortions for cases of reported sexual assault or incest.

3. No women would be subject to criminal prosecution or civil liability for undergoing an abortion.

4. Any court could appoint counsel and/or guardian for preborn children to protect their right to life guaranteed under the proposed amendment.

5. The proposed amendment would have nothing to do with contraceptives or require any expenditure of public funds.

Let me acknowledge that I agreed in principle with this amendment, which came to be known, popularly (or un-popularly) as "The Common Sense Amendment." To put my money where my mouth was, I made a couple of small contributions to the campaign leaders, even though I felt the timing was bad and the proposition was headed for defeat. I even signed a volunteer card to assist the Proposition 110 folk and made several public statements about my support for it from the pulpit of First Institutional Baptist Church. However, not to cause a mutiny among VICTORY TOGETHER leaders who overwhelmingly opposed the proposition, I did not speak at any of "The Common Sense Amendment" press conferences.

I brought up the amendment's possible effects on the MLK vote in our July 14, 1992 meeting, even though it had not been guaranteed at that time that the initiative would make it on the ballot. Mandabach was somewhat nervous about it bringing out hoards of far right conservatives who usually were anti-MLK Day people. In addition, he was antsy about my public position on the issue. In our coalition's discussion, I brought up Mandabach's first concern about the anti-King voters coming out, and to my surprise, Jack Pfister spoke up and said that conclusion might not be accurate. I, then, informed the steering committee that Mandabach had advised me that my personal position on Proposition 110, if it received media attention, could affect our goal positively and/or negatively.

The campaign co-chairs of Proposition 110 had invited me to a press conference announcing their campaign's progress. I was experiencing quite a struggle trying to decide whether or not to attend. The day before the

July 2, 1992 press conference, I opted *not* to attend. However, the next morning my conscience served as my alarm clock. My soul told me that the abortion issue was a matter of life and death for 1.5 million unborn babies. Consequently, I made my way to the downtown press conference called by "The Common Sense Amendment" supporters and sat quietly in the back as the speakers, who, by the way, were mostly women including an African-American sister, took their turns at the microphone, urging Arizonans to vote for Proposition 110. I felt much better by being there to provide some moral support, spoke to a couple of pro-life, pro-King Day friends, and made my way to the VICTORY TOGETHER headquarters feeling like a person of conviction.

My final contribution to the pro-life amendment campaign took place for a couple of Sundays leading up to the general election. In addition to pastoral comments and bulletin inserts, which re-stated my position on the right to life of "all persons created equal under God" and the Holy Scriptures, I preached a sermon on Sunday, October 25, 1992 entitled "GOD'S WORD ON UNBORN BABIES." If the Scriptures, which clearly substantiate that God forms unborn children in the wombs of their mothers with distinct purposes for each one of them did *not* convince the Christians in our two worship services that day, there was nothing else I could do or say. So, I rested my case.

Coincidentally, I received a second invitation from Mr. Colangelo to visit the America West Arena before the Phoenix Suns played in it. That time the occasion was a dinner meeting Colangelo was hosting for the backers of "The Common Sense Amendment." Being a born-again, evangelical Christian, the chairman of the Phoenix 40 proudly espoused the pro-life position. I suppose I attended the dinner meeting, more out of curiosity than anything else. It was intriguing to me to observe such a powerful man involve himself in issues that most corporate executives would shun. The meeting was held on the suite level of the arena and catered to suit the tastes of the "upper, upper" class crowd who attended. After welcoming his invited guests, Mr. Colangelo turned the microphone over to a representative from Proposition 110's campaign committee. Once he stated his case with homiletic fervor, he prepared those in attendance with a warning about the graphic video that they were about to be shown. It was a very popular film used by the pro-life movement around the country, which shows an awful abortion in the process. I guarantee you, if showing documentaries and photographs of the violently killed corpses of unborn babies to the same extent that they have shown stories on the Holocaust, Persian Gulf War, Africa's trouble spots where lives have been decimated by starvation and civil war, pictorial chronologies of AIDS victims, and the every weekend carnage that sends the death wagons wailing in America's major cities, there would be an uprising about humanity's worse case of inhumanity to defenseless, innocent unborn babies. Throughout the video there was weeping and grimacing faces of women and men as they witnessed second-hand the horrible act of killing, which takes the lives of unborn children equal in number to several smaller states in this nation. Following the film, Mr. Colangelo made an appeal for contributions to support the passage of "The Preborn Child Protection Amendment to the Arizona Constitution." They already had some of my cash.

While I am on Colangelo and his American West Arena, one of the first major events to be held there was the Greater Phoenix Luis Palau Evangelistic Crusade, which took place in late October 1992. Once again, I attended a "support" meeting co-hosted by "Brother Colangelo" and the Crusade leadership.

Out in the East Valley, our Mesa MLK Day supporters were lobbying the Mesa City Council to approve their own King Day in order that they could join the other two major Phoenix metropolitan cities—Phoenix and Glendale-in honoring Dr. King. I had written letters to Mesa's newly elected Mayor Willie Wong, the first Asian-American mayor elected in Arizona, and Councilmember Jerry Boyd, that city's only Black councilman, soliciting their support for VICTORY TOGETHER and offering ours for their efforts. On July 6, 1992, I drove out to Mesa to speak to their City Council on behalf of the passage of a local King holiday. The Mesa City Council Chambers was jam-packed with supporters and opposers of the King Day. After a lengthy public hearing, where various speakers on either side of the issue were jeered and/or cheered, the council members voted 6 to 1 in favor of Mesa's own Martin Luther King, Jr./Civil Rights Day. Regrettably, their victory was short-lived because the opposition launched a petition drive for a referendum on Mesa's King Day, within thirty days and overturned the City Council's action by referring it to the ballot. After much discussion once the holiday was overturned, the Mesa City Council placed the MLK Day proposition in their city election, which was held simultaneously with the November 3, general election. Unfortunately, Mesa voters defeated the King Day in that election.

Although it was hot and humid in Arizona in August, VICTORY TOGETHER moved into high gear as it related to our campaign. We had reached the last three months before "V-Day." Everything that we had done up to that point was preparation for the countdown. At our August fourth board of directors/campaign meeting at VICTORY TOGETHER head-quarters, I selected "Words from Martin" that dealt with faith, which read,

> Faith can give us courage to face the uncertainties of the future. It will give our tired feet new strength as we continue our forward stride toward the city of freedom.

We had come this far by faith and that belief in what could not be seen kept us moving forward to the election.

In addition to Dr. King's words, I wrote a few of my own that I entitled, "WORDS OF ENCOURAGEMENT." They were written to the board of directors, campaign committee and staff. Portions of what I had my committed secretary put into print read like this;

> Allow me to offer a few words of encouragement at this pivotal point in our campaign.
>
> Many of us have been meeting together as VICTORY TOGETHER for the last 21 months. A few of us have served as members of Martin Luther King, Jr. holiday coalitions in Arizona since November 1986. Along the way, we have welcomed new Martin Luther King, Jr. holiday advocates to join us...We are as different as we are diverse. We come from all walks of life. Yet, we are bound together by a common and noble goal. We have progressed from a small closely-knit group of mostly African-Americans to one of the most racially, politically, economically, philosophically, and geographically mixed coalitions in Arizona history...
>
> Please know that VICTORY TOGETHER is approaching a critical and climatic juncture in our historic campaign for Martin Luther King, Jr./Civil Rights Day. August, for us can be compared to "the calm before the storm." Come September, VICTORY TOGETHER will be called upon to make key

decisions, which will determine our success or failure on November 3, 1992. Those decisions will need to be made amidst a very volatile, fluid and frustrated political climate. There will be distractions and diversions from our opponents and probably, even from some of our supporters…

Then, I reminded them of our statement of principles and challenged all of us to make practical application of the same in our campaign. I concluded my page and a half epistle with the exhortation, "Let's keep the faith!"

Several critical issues were on the agenda for that meeting. So much so, that my detailed agenda which included my progress reports stretched to four legal-sized sheets, single-spaced, plus my "WORDS OF ENCOURAGEMENT." But, that much detail is how I operate and administrate the congregation I have pastored since July 1, 1977. My leadership philosophy is "an informed membership is the most effective membership." Moreover, when a leader takes the time to inform those he or she is leading of what is happening, then it curtails a lot of unnecessary and divisive "yakety-yak" and claims that "I don't know what's going on."

A grassroots item that we discussed was a meeting I had had in July with the pastors and delegates of the Paradise Missionary Baptist State Convention of Arizona, Inc., of which our congregation was a member and I was an officer. It was constituted by some 30 African-American Baptist churches from all over the state. Since the annual session was to be held at First Institutional during the week of the general election, beginning with a Pre-Opening Program the night before the election, I suggested to the pastors and delegates that the Pre-Opening Program be cancelled. Rather than having voters from around the state travel to Phoenix that election eve for our Convention, I recommended that VICTORY TOGETHER Prayer and GOTV Rallies be held that same night in Paradise Baptist churches in Phoenix, Winslow, Flagstaff, Sierra Vista/Huachuca City, Tucson, and Yuma. My colleagues in our convention agreed and all we needed from VICTORY TOGETHER was a suggested program format, publicity packet and other guidelines to be sent to designated churches and houses of faith statewide. I asked Joedd and Bob Kravitz to develop the format for the prayer/GOTV rallies.

We also began to talk about the "Election Watch/Victory Celebration" location for Tuesday, November 3, 1992. I offered the Fellowship Hall of First Institutional since it had historical significance to the King holiday fight in Arizona going back to May 18, 1986 when then Governor Babbitt declared the first Martin Luther King, Jr. Day from its pulpit. Nevertheless, I was open to other suggestions. Finally, concerned about being in a central location in close proximity to the media which would be covering the presidential, state and local races at the Democratic, Republican and Independent headquarter hotels downtown, we opted to go for the Hyatt Regency Phoenix. Dave Radcliffe and Steve Roman even worked to get it for us, with hors d'oeuvres, for free. It is nice to have connections.

Our voters' registration efforts had put 15,000 new voters on the county seat record books around Arizona. Dr. Eppinger kept reminding the campaign committee that we needed "volunteers, volunteers, and more volunteers." To get our message out broad and wide we needed our phone banks operating six days a week, building our support base. Also, dozens of volunteers were needed to provide clerical assistance to staff and mail envelopes with campaign literature, which by the last weekend of the campaign totaled half a million pieces of mail. To fill our demands for volunteers, we contacted every organization, church, synagogue, union, association, fraternity, sorority and professional, to which group we could get the address and phone number. Various groups took a night to people the phones and/ or stuff envelopes. They even provided their own refreshments when our supply of day-old donated pastries from a local bakery missed a shipment.

In the middle of the August "hustle and bustle," I dared to take a vacation with my family. All eight of us, including my four-month old, one and only daughter, Jamila Imani (Swahili and Arabic for *beautiful faith*), loaded up our 1989 GMC Safari Mini-Van and trekked to California's beaches only to have our vacation cut short when Justin Mitchell, age five, jumped out of the van in

San Diego and broke his leg. I was not worried about VICTORY TOGETHER because Paul was in charge and there was plenty of work to be done without me standing watch.

Before I departed, however, our political consultants had been in conversation with Secretary of State Dick Mahoney about the wording of the ballot proposition, which was critical to voter understanding of what they were voting on. In view of the two King Day propositions on the 1990 ballot, which fell in defeat, we could not be too cautious to insure that voting for Proposition 300 would entail "no additional paid holiday." Even though Mahoney supported MLK Day, as secretary of state, he had to be impartial in order that supporters and opponents of the holiday would get equal and fair treatment. The end result was the following initial statement printed in the information booklet published by the Secretary of State's Office:

> Proposition 300 establishes a Martin Luther King, Jr./Civil Rights paid state holiday and combines the Lincoln Day holiday and the Washington Day holiday into one holiday known as Lincoln/ Washington President's Day so that there is no increase in the number of paid state legal holidays.

We could live with such a statement, even though the usage of the phrase "paid state legal holiday" made us a little nervous.

To augment the secretary of state's statement, Mandabach's office composed our own argument "for" Proposition 300, which stated in clear terms what a YES vote for Proposition 300 would accomplish, as well as informed the voters on our *identity* and *purpose*. Our statement even dropped some names in its last paragraph found on page 95 in the election information booklet.

It read,

> The Steering Committee is comprised of persons like Rev. Bill Jamieson, Deacon of the Trinity Cathedral; Lisa Loo, of the Arizona Asian-American Association; Jack Pfister, Arizona Civic Leader; Rosie Lopez, of the Arizona Hispanic Community Forum; Larry Hecker, Tucson Civic Leader; Joy Hanley, of the Affiliation of Arizona Indian Centers; Robert Kravitz, a Rabbi; Steve Roman, a businessman; Jane Manning, a Northern Arizona University educator; and Dr. Warren Stewart, an African-American Protestant Clergyman. From around the state, we urge you to vote YES on Proposition 300.

In addition, VICTORY TOGETHER arranged and/or paid for arguments "for" Proposition 300 to be placed in the booklet by Mormons for MLK Day, senior citizens from the Sun City area who supported King Day, and ASU Students for VICTORY TOGETHER.

The only argument "against" Proposition 300 was placed in the state document by an aforementioned father and son team who headed the NO-NO COMMITTEE.

We got a scare from the results of the "focus groups," which were arranged settings where people were paid to gather to discuss a particular issue. In both the over-45 and under-45 focus groups, when pressed on the

King holiday issue, our support became soft. To our discouragement, we found that the focus group participants in Maricopa County were extremely negative toward a paid MLK/Civil Rights Day. If there was a long and protracted public debate about the holiday, the results of the focus groups in August revealed that Proposition 300 would be defeated. On the other hand, it was shown that Dr. King's non-violent philosophy seemed to work to some advantage for us. But, the bottom-line indicated clearly that we would have to go very gently and promote the idea that "we're putting this issue to rest."

VICTORY TOGETHER paid $20,000 for another poll in mid-August and was happy to find that support was gaining for Proposition 300. By August 20, 1992, 57% of Arizona voters favored King Day, 32% opposed it, and 11% did not know how they would vote on it.

On August 31, 1992, Felicia forwarded to me a copy of her "master plan" outlining the campaign field activity for September and October, which would take us to victory. Its four major components were: (1) voter registration, (2) voter ID phone bank, (3) a statewide interfaith network, (4) county and state constituent support groups and the GOTV. When it was all said and done up to and including election day, some 800 paid workers would be on VICTORY TOGETHER's payroll, if but for a day or two, on the GOTV weekend encompassing October 30-November 1, 1992. In order to coordinate the grassroots activities, Ms. Bragg eventually took up temporary residence in Arizona, rather than fly back and forth several times a week between LAX and Phoenix Sky Harbor. Please know that everybody was not accustomed to working with an assertive, vibrant and vocal Black woman from the "big city." On more than one occasion I received a call from one or more of the full-time VICTORY TOGETHER employees complaining about some sharp criticism they had received from Ms. Bragg. As usual, I tried to calm the waters and told the workers to hang in there for the cause. I spoke with Felicia about the complaints when they seemed legitimate. Thank God, we managed to keep the team together, even though we lost a couple of holiday hard workers along the way.

By September 1, we had cracked the one million-dollar mark with $600,000 to go. Our budgetary and accounting process had to become more sophisticated as we were dealing with over a million and a half dollars, operating three regional headquarters, employing nearly twenty full-time staff persons and trying to reach at least 800,000 Arizona voters. Marian Bevins, our northern regional campaign coordinator, had expertise in accounting, so she volunteered to set up an expense statement based on a $1,669,715.00 campaign budget. Additionally, Steve's office via our stealth treasurer, Jack Henry, filled out all of the financial statements required by the Secretary of State's Office, evidencing every contributor, other income, and all expenses.

Just as things were picking up, Evan Mecham announced on August 26, 1992 that he was launching an independent run for United States Senator against the incumbent-fellow Republican John McCain. Mecham claimed to be running to address the nation's number one problem, which he identified as the national debt. But, the rumor mill had it out that the former impeached governor was angry with Arizona's "junior senator" for calling for his resignation during Mecham's turbulent tenure as governor. He made headlines for a couple of days, even in the *USA Today* again. But, the truth of the matter was that his race for John McCain's Senate seat was lost out of the gate.

Early in September, VICTORY TOGETHER hosted another general meeting for our growing army of supporters, to apprise them on our progress and recruit volunteers for all our planned grassroots activities. All the key players heading the campaign were there to give presentations, namely, Mandabach, Bragg, Eppinger and me. The "Words from Martin" that I chose for that gathering planted a fertile seed in those who had gathered to receive marching orders.

> There is amazing power in unity. Where there is unity, every effort to disunite only serves to strengthen the unity.

A couple of weeks after that meeting, Joedd had organized an interfaith gathering of clergy from across the state that met at the Hyatt Regency Phoenix on September 10, 1992. Although I could not attend personally since I was in Dr. King's hometown of Atlanta, Georgia as a delegate to the National Baptist Convention, USA, Inc., I drafted a letter entitled "To My Co-Laborers in
Ministry." In that one-page epistle, I wrote, among other things, that,

> Martin Luther King, Jr. was one of us. He allowed God to use him in spite of his moral frailty to prophetically challenge America to exemplify the principles of "liberty and justice for all" as inscribed in the United States Constitution and taught in the Judeo-Christian heritage of this nation's foreparents. Without a doubt, Arizona's Martin Luther King, Jr./Civil Rights Day

celebrates the fundamental American principle that "all persons are created equal under God."

Next, I wrote our statement of principles and concluded the letter with an appeal for their help.

During our last campaign meeting in September, we announced plans for our "Big Vote Weekend" to take place October 2-4. This would be our last big effort to register new voters before the cut-off date to register passed. Our goal was revised to target 75,000 new voters, and by the deadline, we reached it! Knowing that we would need all kinds of help, the board members present formed a "Special Committee to Get GOTV Volunteers." Of course, I had one big advantage that none of the other board members had—a 2,000-plus congregation, from which to recruit volunteers. First Institutional members responded so well that one would have thought that the VICTORY TOGETHER headquarters was an auxiliary of the church.

In that same meeting, Mandabach informed us that the television commercials would be taped at the end of the week. His strategy involved having experts select "regular" Arizonans to appear on camera, talking about the "American-ness" of the Martin Luther King, Jr./Civil Rights Day. Local stars and celebrities were ruled out. Research had shown that such high profile endorsements turned off the average soft Arizona voter. Our consultant apprised us further on his plans for buying up major blocks of commercial time, during the last two weeks of the campaign. The target group for our television and radio ads would be the swing voters. In the meantime, Paul was trying to gauge what effect Mecham's candidacy would have on the MLK Day, as well as if Ross Perot re-entered the presidential race as an Independent.

A couple of potential problems surfaced during October. The "friendly" rap group from Brooklyn, Public Enemy, came to town to appear as the opening act for the rock group U2, a week before the election. All of us were concerned that, whatever they said, could blow up our low-keyed Proposition 300 Campaign. While our consultants and staff prepared to make a strong statement in case they caused a "political explosion" in the desert, my wife, Serena, got on the phone with a girlfriend of hers in New York who worked for CBS Records in order to get her to contact a friend who was Public Enemy's publicist. The end result of the quick-witted peacekeeping work my "native New York wife" did was that when Public Enemy appeared on the concert stage; they did a couple of numbers and walked off the stage in near-silent protest. Only the Lord knows what the damage would have been, if someone had not told Public Enemy to "chill out" this time around! *Much obliged, Serena.*

The other problem that did not happen the weekend prior to the election was a "repeat performance" by one of the major television network's sportscasters bringing up the connection between the 1996 Super Bowl, promised to Phoenix and the King Day election. Steve got wind that one of the major networks was going to try to link the two again, and got on the phone with network executives in New York and all but threatened to "kick their butts" if they reported anything about our King Day election. Obviously, the vice president of Valley National Bank was convincing (or should I say, threatening enough) because nothing was aired to give shaky King Day voters an excuse in 1992 to change their affirmative votes to negative ones.

Our strategy of running a low-key campaign was so effective that the only news we made from September to Election Day was that we were running a low-key campaign. Of course, that infuriated Bob Rose and the anti-King Day crowd because they could not get free equal time to denounce Dr. King and holiday backers, like they had in the 1990 campaign. Moreover, I refused all requests to appear on radio talk shows, which decreased the opportunities for rancorous debates between recognized pro-King Day leaders and members of the NO-NO Committee. In other words, VICTORY TOGETHER muffled the holiday opposition significantly, which worked to our advantage.

Polls we conducted on October 24 pinpointed our support at the second highest level ever in our campaign—62%. By the next week, MLK voter support peaked at 66%, with 26% in opposition.

Not only did we appear to be on the road to victory this time, but 1.4 million dollars had been contributed to our campaign by October 27, 1992. Even though we had spent $1,331,000.00, *VICTORY TOGETHER WAS NOT IN DEBT!*

A VICTORY TOGETHER Prayer and GOTV Rally for Proposition 300 was planned for the First Institutional Baptist Church on Monday, November 2, 1992 at 7:00 p.m., "Election Eve." And although the vote had not taken place yet (with the exception of absentee ballots which we had targeted also), I led the closing prayer and song at our last pre-election coalition board of directors/ campaign committee meeting. What did we sing? You guessed it! *"We Shall Overcome."*

Chapter Sixteen
Victory Together: A Prophecy Fulfilled On November 3, 1992

By Monday, November 12, 1992, we had done just about all that we could do to win Arizona's Martin Luther King, Jr./Civil Rights Day at the polls. The activities that began with "GOTV Weekend" on Friday, October 30 and continued until the polls closed on Election Day, November 3, 1992 could have been likened to Grand Central Station in the heart of New York City. All weekend, MLK Day supporters were coming and going like crazy. Doorhangers had to be hung. Flyers had to be passed out. The telephone banks had to be in operation. Vans had to be driven to transport volunteers here and there. Media had to be talked to for interviews. Posters had to be put up. Refreshments had to be picked up and replenished. Last minute strategy meetings had to be held at a moment's notice. VICTORY TOGETHER leaders, staff and volunteers had to spread our faith and hope that we would celebrate VICTORY TOGETHER in a few hours.

All of the polls taken over the weekend before the election gave Proposition 300 a twenty point or so lead. But, that was a source of concern for me because the polls had indicated almost the same margin of projected victory in 1990. The fact that I knew people lied on polls dealing with racial issues stayed in the back of my mind. However, our broad-based coalition had done things differently this time around. Nevertheless, I was not about to be premature in my anticipation of victory.

On the other hand, it seemed as if I was the only key player in our coalition who was reserved about the near-certainty that we would win this time, and win big. Paul Eppinger beamed with exuberant faith that we would be celebrating on the night of the election. Paul Mandabach possessed a professional confidence that what he had been hired to do was going to happen. Ms. Bragg would say to me, "Dr. Stewart, don't worry. We're going to win. Just watch and see." Steve was absolutely assured of our victory. (He had better have been after getting 1.5 million from his corporate bosses!) After all, he had been down that path before. The rest of our staff allowed their body language to express their belief that the responsibilities for which they had been hired would be rewarded with a big victory.

First Institutional Baptist Church hosted one of the VICTORY TOGETHER Prayer and GOTV Rallies at 7:00 p.m. on Monday, November 2. All of the VICTORY TOGETHER board and campaign committee members, as well as staff had been invited to attend. I was happy that the MLK Day campaign would come to a symbolic end at the place where the controversy had started. The program for that evening had been collectively put together by Paul, Joedd, Bob Kravitz and myself.

Participants on the program included representatives from Tanner Chapel's Scout Troop who led the Pledge of Allegiance. Music was provided by the combined children's and youth choirs of First Institutional and Gardenia Lacy of the Phoenix Children's Choir, who also was a member of our congregation. The first song was what we called "The Anthem of Praise" which was none other than James Weldon Johnson's "Lift Every Voice and Sing." Bettye Jackson eloquently delivered our committee's statement of purpose. Then, we were led in two litanies, shared by Joedd, which had been originally written in recognition of the Berlin Wall being torn down.

The first was labeled the "Litany of Wall and Unity." Excerpts from it appropriately opened praying to our God of Creation and Justice.

> God of Creation, you made the world and everything in it, you created the human race of one stock....
>
> God of Justice, help us to see and hear the cry of the unemployed person of color, the despair of the migrant worker, the whimper of the hungry child, the fear of the homeless woman, and all of those who are rejected and hurting in our communities.
>
> We pray for the courage to be your hands, your feet, your compassion, even when it is not allowed.
>
> Give to us persistence in undermining unjust structures until they crumble into dust, and give us your grace to exercise a ministry of reconciliation among all people.

That was part of the leader's public prayer in the litany, which was concluded by this statement offered by the people in attendance.

Break down the walls that separate us, and unite us in a single body.

"The Litany for Justice and Unity" followed the above-mentioned communal prayer. One of its most relevant prayer-thoughts that united us together read thusly,

...May we come to see more clearly and surely, not that which divides us, but rather that which unites us. We pray that each hour may bring us closer to that final victory when we shall have learned to be merciful and compassionate, and human beings shall have the courage to love one another....

Those words reminded me that our quest for a holiday was not the ultimate battle for justice-loving activists. The true victory happens when people's lives are transformed by God's love, becoming incarnate in us, and changing people's lives for the better. Our joint prayer was that we could attain our real goal.

Believe it or not, I asked Arnie to read the Old Testament Scripture taken from Amos 5:14-15, 21-24, which contained our Scriptural motto printed at the bottom of our letterhead, "Let justice roll down like waters..." VICTORY TOGETHER's talented and cooperative vice president, Lisa Loo, read "The Beatitudes" found in Matthew 5:1-10. On the program were listed several "Why I'm Voting Yes on Proposition 300" testimonies, which followed the youth challenge of pre-teen Miss Brooke Myatt of our congregation who spoke about "Why Adults Should Vote Yes on Proposition 300." The other speakers who followed Brooke represented different segments of our society, announcing their support for Arizona MLK/Civil Rights Day. Bob Russell, our Anglo church secretary, spoke as a senior citizen. Daniel Ortega represented the large Hispanic community. Steve, impromptu stand-in, inspired all in attendance with his remarks as a businessman.

Steve's remarks began, "We have already won, regardless of what the outcome of the election is...People from all walks of life came together nearly two years ago to fight for a common goal. Initially, there were differences and distrust...But, we're here tonight on election eve already having won the real victory..." The members of the campaign committee that had worked so diligently and deliberately together over the last twenty-three and a half months began to look at one another and at Steve with amazement. "Was that Steve Roman who just *preached* a mini-sermon to us?" I asked myself. Steve was the kind of coalition leader who did not make many public speeches. He simply stated the facts and did what needed to be done, without a lot of unnecessary talking. Yet, there he stood on election eve, in the pulpit of the First Institutional Baptist Church, preaching about the victory that, on a personal level, meant more than winning the King holiday. Unexpected "high" moments like that constitute priceless value on struggles that stress and strain those whose lives have been thrown together to fight for noble causes. I guess I am trying to say, "They make the journey worthwhile."

Before the prayer and GOTV rally concluded, the one hundred and fifty or so in attendance had to read some words from Dr. Martin Luther King, Jr. Of the passages I selected, I cite the following, especially due to their meaning in the context of the campaign.

> For every noted hero, there have been hundreds who have labored humbly and anonymously in the vineyard of freedom.
>
> To become instruments of a great idea is a privilege that history gives only occasionally.

I am certain we need to pray for God's help and guidance in this integration struggle, but we are gravely misled if we think the struggle will be won only in prayer.

The program also allowed for what we called "Open Prayer for Proposition 300," at which time the people were invited from the audience to come to the microphone and petition God about the King Day election. Several persons, both young and old, made their way to pray. However, as that last quotation from Dr. King indicated, once the praying was finished, there were other things that had to be done. That is where Paul came in. He instructed King Day supporters gathered on our final phase of the GOTV plan. Each person present could become a one-person GOTV campaign manager, urging every registered voter within his or her sphere of influence to get-out-to-vote on the next day. After all was said and done, I closed the gathering in prayer and directed us all to stand and sing the "anthem" of the Civil Rights Movement-"We Shall Overcome."

After that, VICTORY TOGETHER co-workers hugged, kissed and congratulated one another realizing that our mission was about to receive the ultimate test. Several of us, no doubt, realized that we would not be meeting together on a regular basis ever, again. So, I experienced mixed emotions, confessing to myself that "something good" was coming to an end. There were no tears on my part, just a sense that special relationships were about to be broken up, due to positive reasons.

Once the holiday well-wishers had left, I gathered up my briefcase and Kangol cap in my office. My family, who had come out in full force to support their husband and dad, respectively, went on home because our four older sons had to go to school the next day. Since it was election eve, VICTORY TOGETHER headquarters was fully lit by the time I drove from East Jefferson to North Central Avenue. Every office in the place was jumping with activity. Most noticeable was the jubilant, even jovial spirit that permeated every room and emanated from every volunteer.

As I walked throughout the office complex, I thanked the staff and volunteers for being a part of our coalition. Several members of First Institutional could be found at the phone bank tables reminding strangers to go to the polls the next day. Their presence made their pastor feel loved and appreciated. Once I checked the schedule of activities for the next day, I said, "Good night," to the staff who were "burning the midnight oil," and went home.

I watched the late news to get the latest on the poll predictions for the presidential election and the King holiday. It looked like Bill Clinton was going to oust the incumbent. The media still predicted a King holiday win. So, there was nothing else for me to do, other than to read my nightly devotional book, say my prayers, and go to bed.

◇◇◇◇◇◇

The morning of Tuesday, November 3, 1992, I awakened at 6:00 a.m. to the sound of the voices of National Public Radio on KJZZ-FM, just as I do every weekday. Once I realized I was no longer asleep, I thanked the Lord for waking me up, recited the Lord's Prayer, John 3:16 and Philippians 4:13, and got up out of the bed to witness history being made. At 6:30 a.m. I knocked on Matthew's bedroom door to awaken him, so he could catch his 7:03 a.m. school bus. After reading my morning devotional, taking a shower and dressing, I made it to the kitchen for my two halves of grapefruit, bowl of Cheerios and glass of orange juice. By 7:00 a.m., my oldest son had begun to stir and my wife was lying in bed nursing Jamila. As is my custom nearly every morning, I got my Bible, Bible study booklet, and whatever Christian book or magazine I was reading a chapter a day at the time from. I transported them from my study to the kitchen table to engage in my second "breakfast." When 7:30 a.m. rolled around it was time to awaken Jared and Justin, so they could get ready for school. Pretty soon, three and a half year old Aaron staggered into the kitchen, half-asleep, and plopped in my lap, as I sat at the kitchen table. Serena had made it to her early morning post, preparing special-to-order breakfasts for the three youngest boys. I admonished Jared, Justin and Aaron to go to the altar in our living room and say their morning prayer. With five minutes to go, before I drove Jared and Justin to Sevilla, I went outside to pick up the morning newspaper in the driveway and glimpsed at the headlines. It was time to go, so I yelled at the two middle boys, "Hurry up! You're gonna be late for school. And I've got to vote this morning. Come on!" Fussing and complaining that he couldn't find his backpack, I had to go back in the house and rush Jared outside. "See you later," I said to Serena, "and don't forget to vote! Bye."

After dropping the guys off at their respective classrooms, I parked my red Camaro near the multi-purpose building at the school, where my precinct's voting booths were. As I headed inside, several of Sevilla's teachers and students spoke to me. I passed the people standing behind the official boundary line for persons passing out campaign literature, urging voters to say yes to their favorite candidates and/or propositions on the ballot. I did not see any VICTORY TOGETHER poll watchers or Proposition 300 signs, so I opened the trunk of my car and taped two of our largest Proposition 300 posters on the schoolyard fence.

Upon entering the auditorium, I did what you have to do to get an official ballot—gave the election workers my name and address, signed the sheet of registered voters next to my name, received the ballot handed to me, and made my way to a vacant booth. Due to the fact that I study the sample election ballot before I get in the voting booth, I basically knew for who and what I would be punching the YES holes. Of late, I vote my convictions, so when it came to President of the United States, I did not have much of a choice. My pro-life stance affects my support for candidates, regardless of their party affiliations. Consequently, I left several offices blank. When I get to the long list of judges, I try to find the names of the very few that I know and/or have heard of, and vote for them. It was a privilege to see the name of one of First Institutional's members on the 1992 list of Superior Court Judge candidates, namely Thomas Dunevant, the past chairperson of our congregation's "African-American Christian Training School Advisory Council. Names I did not know, I did not vote for.

Then, I came to the propositions. Proposition 110 was one of the first listed. Punch. YES. One for the babies. Proposition 300. Punch. YES. One for Dr. King. I was through. Next stop, VICTORY TOGETHER headquarters. Once again, our rent-free office complex was a beehive of activity. "General" Felicia Bragg was giving orders to everybody who crossed her path. Paul E. was in and out checking on the GOTV activities and taking calls, from the press. There really was not a lot for me to do, other than stand around and be in the volunteers' way. I spoke to a few coalition members who had stopped by. Then, I decided I could go on to my place of employment that had paid me on that past Friday.

The staff was busy doing church business and some VICTORY TOGETHER business at the same time. Most of our full-time staff had volunteered to put in, at least, a half-day working with our GOTV efforts. Janet Caldwell, our business manager, had worked out a schedule to have a skeleton crew at FIBC until closing time. My secretary had asked to work at the headquarters all that day, and since she had been doing some computer inputting for the coalition on a part-time basis, I granted her request.

Several telephone messages awaited me when I sat down at my desk in an unusually quiet office. Many of them were from VICTORY TOGETHER members, predicting that everything was going to be all right. I stayed for awhile, made and returned some calls, held a few conversations with my staff who were on the site, and decided to visit some of my sick members. Nervous energy, I guess you could call it.

My radio stayed on, while I drove from one house to another. The midday reports indicated that there was a heavier voter turnout than expected. Our research had informed us that, the larger the turnout, the better our chances were for victory. Of special note was the reported large number of young voters, who were voting in Tempe and around ASU. Several factors were believed to have contributed to the increase in voters, including Clinton's youthful popularity, Bush's poorly managed campaign and plummet at the polls, Perot's independent candidacy, the 70% opposition to the Pro-Life Amendment, *and* the Martin Luther King, Jr./Civil Rights Day proposition. In a nutshell, things were looking good.

I stopped by headquarters again around 5:30 p.m. The "hustle and bustle" of activity had died down because the polls would be closing in an hour or so. Leftover MLK holiday posters, pamphlets, signs and other campaign literature were laid aside on tables and on the floor. Most of the phones were on their hooks. A few staff people and volunteers were still hanging around. But, by that time, attention was being directed toward the Hyatt Regency Phoenix, where our "Election Watch ad Victory Celebration" would take place beginning around 8:00 p.m. Several of the staff had gone to the second floor ballroom to help decorate.

It was about 8:00 p.m. when I made it to the Hyatt. A few folks had begun to gather in addition to the workers. Dee Edwards, Abbie Fink, Marion Jones and Carlos, under the watchful eye of Felicia, evidenced their energetic, creative juices in decorating our room. At my request, our VICTORY TOGETHER banner, which had been unveiled when we launched the campaign officially on King Day in January of that year, was hung as a backdrop to the platform where we hoped to declare victory later on that evening. The hotel provided finger foods and pastries free of charge. A no-host bar was operated by the Hyatt. A few small tables had been set up for well-wishers, while larger rectangular tables were placed around the walls from campaign workers and members of the press.

My family arrived shortly after I did. My boys went wild around all the desserts that were at their fingertips. Serena and they stayed until about nine o'clock. However, once again, it was a school night, so I kissed them "good night" and they went home. The King Day crowd continued to increase in number with coalition members, volunteers, members of First Institutional, politicians and party officials from the Democrats and Republicans, and the media. Television monitors had been set up in our ballroom, in order for us to be able to watch the election reports. That reminded me that not only was Arizona looking at the outcome of our particular campaign, *but so was the nation.*

Whenever the national news coverage would cut into the local coverage they would mention the Martin Luther King holiday election preliminary results in Arizona. The exciting thing about the local and national coverage we were receiving was that *we were winning.* The numbers kept coming in our favor. Yet, I was still cautious. During the practically every quarter-of-an-hour interview from one local station or another, I was asked if I was ready to declare victory. I replied, "I'm elated and encouraged at the preliminary results, but there are still precincts that have not reported yet. It's not time to celebrate yet." Even though we had made inroads into the Sun City area, thanks a lot to Hawley Atkinson, the bulk of their returns did not come in until after 10:00 p.m., and I remembered how their negative majority had turned the tide against the holiday in 1990.

Steve was ready to declare at 10:00 p.m. By 10:30 p.m., Mandabach said it would be virtually impossible for enough NO votes to come in later to turn the tide against. Felicia said, "Dr. Stewart, we've won. You can go ahead and declare." Nope, I still was not for sure. I conferred with Paul Eppinger at 11:00 p.m. He felt it was all right to announce that we had won, but the time had not come for me yet.

As the night grew late, many of the VICTORY TOGETHER crowd had gone home, believing that Arizona had finally passed the Martin Luther King, Jr. Day. Between eleven and about midnight, the margin of our lead stabilized at around 20 points. I talked with Mike Kelly, Art Mobley, Steve, Paul, Joedd and a few others and decided *it was time*. With my dark blue double-breasted suit on, complemented by a paisley tie, a Prop. 300 lapel button, and a white baseball cap accentuated by our black VICTORY TOGETHER logo , I signaled to the core groups of coalition leaders and workers still there to join me on the stage. The media were quickly informed that an announcement was about to be made.

At about 11:45 p.m., clasping and holding high the hand of my brother, Paul Eppinger, I lifted my voice to announce, "Free at last! Free at last! Thank God Almighty, Arizona is free at last! The Martin Luther King, Jr./Civil Rights Day has been overwhelmingly approved by a vote of the people!" Those of us who had gathered on that instantly over-crowded platform naturally turned to one another, congratulating everybody we could get our hands on. After we settled down long enough to join hands again, we sang as never before in Arizona, "We Shall Overcome." We did not stop until we sang the verse, "Black and White Together." On the final go around, I revised the most popular verse of that song Dr. King and the Civil Rights Movement thusly,

> We **have** overcome,
> We **have** overcome,
> We **have** overcome **today**.
> Oh, deep in our hearts,
> We do believe,
> We **have** overcome **today**.

By the next morning it was obvious that our VICTORY TOGETHER announcement had been broadcast nationally, because I began receiving calls from friends, colleagues and relatives all over the country about our historic win and my white cap.

The morning after VICTORY TOGETHER became a prophecy fulfilled. We held a press conference at our headquarters. I read my last press statement as General Chairperson of our historic, broad-based grassroots coalition. My statement is provided below in its entirety.

Arizona can now echo the words of the old Negro spiritual and Dr. Martin Luther King, Jr., "FREE AT LAST! FREE AT LAST! THANK GOD ALMIGHTY! WE'RE FREE AT LAST!" Arizona, by an unprecedented, historic vote of the people, approved the third Monday in January as MARTIN LUTHER KING, JR./CIVIL RIGHTS DAY in the General Election on Tuesday, November 3, 1992. Arizona is the only state in the Union to have attempted such a courageous and challenging endeavor in democracy at its best. Thank God and thank you Arizona voters.

TOGETHER WE DID IT! TOGETHER WE MADE HISTORY! TOGETHER WE CELEBRATE OUR VICTORY! TOGETHER, WE, AS A STATE, WILL OFFICIALLY HONOR THE CONTRIBUTIONS OF THE CIVIL RIGHTS MOVEMENT UNDER THE HISTORIC LEADERSHIP OF DR. MARTIN LUTHER KING, JR. ON MONDAY, JANUARY 18, 1993!

VICTORY TOGETHER, our broad-based, grassroots statewide coalition of Arizonans from all walks of life was established on November 14, 1990 to win a MARTIN LUTHER KING, JR./CIVIL RIGHTS DAY by a vote of the people. Our single common goal both inspired and forged us together over the past twenty-four months in light of our being Red, Yellow, Black, Brown and White. Men, women, boys and girls. Young and old. Republicans, Democrats, Independents, conservatives, liberals, moderates. Christians, Jews, Muslims, other religions and faiths. Business, labor, hospitality, government and grassroots. Rich, poor, handicapped, disadvantaged, employed, and unemployed.

In our first press conference on November 15, 1990, just days after Arizona's infamous defeat of two Martin Luther King, Jr. holiday propositions at the polls, we concluded with this statement of hope. "We believe that if Arizona voters are given a **CLEAR CHOICE** on a Martin Luther King, Jr. State holiday on the third Monday in January, which is not an additional paid holiday, the majority of us would vote for its approval. Then healing in our beloved state can **begin again!**"

VICTORY TOGETHER has become a self-fulfilling prophecy. Arizona voters did make a **CLEAR CHOICE** on Proposition 300 yesterday.

Before VICTORY TOGETHER dissolves as a result of accomplishing our single, common but monumental goal of winning voter approval of Arizona's MARTIN LUTHER KING, JR./CIVIL RIGHTS DAY, we must give thanks to many. First, to our Creator-God, who provides all Arizonans with the fundamental American principle that "all people are created equal under God." That's what the King/Civil Rights Day is all about. Second, to the diverse, but unified members of our VICTORY TOGETHER Steering and Campaign Committee and Board of Directors who have met together regularly for the past two years. Third, to the Arizona State Legislature, its leadership in the House and Senate, former Governor Rose Mofford and Governor Fife Symington, other elected state and municipal officials and thousands of Arizona citizens who have supported VICTORY TOGETHER in putting **our** MARTIN LUTHER KING, JR./CIVIL RIGHT DAY proposition on the ballot and working toward its passage. Fourth, to the VICTORY TOGETHER paid and volunteer staffs who have worked untiringly across this state to win passage of Proposition 300. Fifth, to the Arizona business community who supported our historic campaign not simply with words but with their wallets as our major contributors as well as to the hundreds of individual contributors to VICTORY TOGETHER. Sixth, to our expert and professional political consultants of Winner, Wagner and Mandabach and Winner/Bragg, namely Paul Mandabach and Felicia Bragg, for their successful strategy, which guided our efforts from, defeat to victory. Seventh, to the First Institutional Baptist Church which has served as the headquarters for Arizona's MARTIN LUTHER KING, JR./CIVIL RIGHTS DAY Campaign for years and for its members and staff for supporting their pastor on his "King Day Mission." Eighth, to my wife, Serena, and six children for "eating, sleeping and living with" the King holiday struggle since November 1986. And, lastly, to every Arizona citizen who supported and voted in favor of Proposition 300.

Finally, even though our organization is disbanding, the spirit and the goals of VICTORY TOGETHER will continue to draw people together, continue to inspire them to know their interdependence upon each other, to build trust in each other, and to build for a greater future continuously.

The goal of VICTORY TOGETHER included establishing in Arizona a MARTIN LUTHER KING, JR./CIVIL RIGHTS **spirit**. To that end we commit ourselves. To that end we will work.

TO GOD BE THE GLORY!

To say the least, I had mixed emotions on the morning after the general election because the other proposition-"The Common Sense Amendment"-was defeated overwhelmingly by many of the same voters who gave King Day a two to one victory. God knows, I wish I could have been more involved in packaging the "right" message for the right to life amendments. Maybe another time.

However, what I began to do, even on the day of the election to show my support for the human rights of unborn children was to wear my "Precious Feet" lapel pin. It is a metal, exact-size replica of the perfectly developed feet of a 10-week unborn baby. That was my way of letting others know that Warren Stewart is an unashamed pro-lifer *from the womb to the tomb*. Moreover, since I have been wearing my "Precious Feet," it is amazing at the diverse reaction I get from people-sometimes inquisitive, other times affirming, and often negative body language and/or facial expressions. The opportunity I enjoy most about the wearing of my convictions on my chest is being able to tell a person that these are the size of the feet of a ten-week old "little person" in the womb. Only the Lord knows when Americans will get that through our thick skulls.

◇◇◇◇◇

When it was all said and done, 61% of Arizona voters (nearly 900,000) voted in favor of Proposition 300—Martin Luther King, Jr./Civil Rights Day. A little over 500,000 or 39% said NO to King Day. The campaign raised 1.56 million dollars and spent just about all of that, ending up with a $25,000 surplus. Of special note is the fact that more money was spent statewide on grassroots organization than advertising. Another victorious statistic was that 75,000 new voters were added to voter rolls in our state.

Almost two years to the Sunday that I had informed my worshipping congregation that we needed to "move on to more important issues than the King holiday," I was standing there again commenting on Arizona's MLK/ Civil Rights Day. My words went something like this:

> Thank God for our VICTORY TOGETHER on November 3, 1992! As it pertains to the King holiday, Arizona is now "Free At Last!"
>
> Thank you, First Institutional, for how you've supported your pastor as he has led the King Day fight over the years.
>
> Now, we must challenge Arizona and the "powers that be" that supported Proposition 300 to "MOVE FROM SYMBOL TO SUBSTANCE"!
>
> The one down-side to the King Day victory is the day after the election on KTAR radio's talk show, all they could talk about was the Super Bowl that was sure to come to Arizona now.
>
> I'm going to take Tuesday off, if you don't mind.

Enclosed, as a bulletin insert, was a copy of my original VICTORY '91: 600,000 FOR MLK—"One **CLEAR** Choice proposal, which I had presented to King holiday supporters that I had invited to the First Institutional Baptist Church Fellowship Hall on November 14, 1990. However, I had altered it somewhat. I had circled the date and had placed diagonally across it in red bold-printed letters-MISSION ACCOMPLISHED.

◇◇◇◇◇◇

Congratulatory messages began to pour into my office the day after the election. The first was a news release originating from The King Center in Atlanta, dated November 4, 1992, which read,

STATEMENT BY MRS. CORETTA SCOTT KING REGARDING THE MARTIN LUTHER KING, JR. HOLIDAY IN THE STATE OF ARIZONA

…"The passage of the legislation calling for the statewide observance of the Martin Luther King, Jr. Holiday in Arizona is in compliance with the mandate set forth by the Federal Holiday Commission—for all states to comply with the existing federal holiday observance. On this, the tenth anniversary of the establishment of the Martin Luther King, Jr. Federal Holiday, we are pleased to have Arizona join with 48 other States in carrying out this mandate. Hopefully this will send a message to New Hampshire, the only state remaining that has not passed such legislation."

It was always affirming to receive a word of support and praise from the widow of the man, for whom we fought to honor with his day in the desert.

Telephone messages started tying up the church phone lines, throughout the day, after our victory. From regular First Institutional members like Ron Nicholson and Connie Butchee; to community leaders like George Dean of the Phoenix Urban League, Pastor James Preston and Clarence Boykins from Tucson; to "movers and shakers" in the personages of Jerry Colangelo and Jack Pfister; to a politico by the name of Attorney General Grant Woods; many MLK holiday celebrants took time out of their busy schedules to call and say, "Thank you." As I often tell young preachers and my children, the two words, "thank you," can open doors to opportunities that can lead some of life's most splendid experiences. Take it from someone who knows.

A diverse sampling of written messages recorded commendations from both friends and strangers. Dr. G. Benjamin Brooks who anointed himself as my "father," faxed, "CONGRATULATIONS, SON!! YOU DID IT, AND NOW WE HAVE IT!!" Excerpts from the Western Union message from the leaders of the major ministries at First Institutional read,

> PRAISE THE LORD. IT'S A GREAT DAY FOR ARIZONA…
> THE LONG STRUGGLE IS OVER AT LAST. BECAUSE OF
> YOUR UNTIRING SPIRIT-LED LEADERSHIP, ARIZONA
> VOTERS HAVE OVERWHELMINGLY APPROVED A
> MARTIN LUTHER KING JR HOLIDAY. YOUR CHURCH
> FAMILY HONORS YOU…TO GOD BE THE GLORY.

Kevin Myatt, whose daughter, Brooke, had participated in the Election Eve Prayer and GOTV Rally, wrote his pastor on THE DIAL CORP letterhead, dated November 4, 1992,

> Congratulations on the Victory Together effort. You should feel
> a great sense of relief and joy over this accomplishment. I am

sure you will enjoy your downtime between now and that time that you fill that void in your schedule (I give you 7 days max)...

A one-word letter from an Anglo evangelical pastoral colleague of mine from Mesa saluted me by penning, "Dear Brother Warren, *CONGRATULATIONS!* Your brother in Christ, Gary D. Kinnaman." Another Mesan handwrote the following message on a thank you card,

Dear Rev. Stewart,

Thank you for not giving up & instead so intelligently & thoughtfully led the fight for MLK Day—it was a magnificent campaign & I rejoice in the victory.

I don't pray in political elections but in this case I prayed that the Lord's will would be known—and, as always, He answered—it was God's will!

...From a 60 year old White woman, thank you and God bless,

Mary Jo West, a former local news anchorwoman and active television producer, sent me a thank you card from her and her adopted Honduran daughter, Molly. Two paragraphs warmed by heart thusly,

To this very day I remember so clearly a sermon you delivered on Easter Sunday a few years ago..."Attitude, Aptitude, and Altitude!" On Tues. night a lot of us felt like flying!

You certainly live(d) those words in your fight for MLK Day. I know of the incredible danger you faced and I know of the long days & nights away from your precious Family...

The Phoenix Suns star point guard, Kevin Johnson alias KJ, found some time between playing basketball to dictate,

...I needed to send my appreciation to you for all that you did to make the MLK Day a reality in Arizona.

...Again, I want to say thanks for your efforts and until I see you, God Bless!

In Hope, Kevin Johnson

Congratulations came from around the country, as well as from Dr. Amos Jones, Jr., of the National Baptist Convention, USA, Inc.'s Sunday School Publishing Board who addressed a letter to me, which included the felicitation.

I want to congratulate you on your leadership in achieving a statewide holiday…in the State of Arizona. The coverage in the Friday, November 6, 1992 edition of *USA Today* was tremendous. I am sure Dr. C. N. Adkins, all of us here at the Sunday School Publishing Board, President Jemison and all National Baptists are proud of you and the leadership you are providing in the Valley of the Sun….

The peace of God be with you.

The American Baptist Churches, of which First Institutional is also dually aligned, was not to be left out. Gordon Smith, then Executive Director of the Minister and Missionaries Benefit Board of ABC, worded his epistle of appreciation as follows:

> Congratulations on your success in establishing a King Day in Arizona. I have been following your efforts on behalf of this good cause for several years. You deserved to win—and by a landslide!
>
> We are proud of the fact that Dr. Martin Luther King, Jr. was a member of M&M and we have always believed that his leadership should be appropriately acknowledged by this country.
>
> Thanks for your efforts on behalf of this cause.

The last congratulatory note I will mention was published in *Newsletter From Home—The Alternative to the Alternative*, #20, Nov. 1992. The editor, Nancy Cooper, whom I knew through the fellowship services between First Institutional and First Baptist, noted,

> **A special congratulations to the Victory Together** near-twins Paul Eppinger and Warren Stewart. I believe the energy of their friendship helped to get Prop 300 passed (MLK Day).

◇◇◇◇◇◇

I had to write a few thank you letters myself. In addition to the expressions of appreciation to VICTORY TOGETHER board and statewide staff members, I wrote a few special letters of gratitude to some significant persons who had touched my life personally and powerfully in enabling me to provide leadership in Arizona's historic and victorious campaign.

To Frank Camacho I wrote on November 13,

Thank you for being my "modern day Mordecai" two years ago this week by challenging me to step forth and assume a leadership role in Arizona's historic (MLK, Jr.) holiday campaign...You stepped out of your role as a professional anchorman and spoke from your heart with a message from on High....

For the Honorable Art Hamilton, whom I called for counsel after Frank's recruitment call in November 1990, I expressed myself like this,

Art, those of us who joined this effort late in the game know that you had been carrying the "King ball" for years, often virtually alone. Thank you for those years and the last six in which you have allowed others like myself to help you fight this battle. You're behind the scenes lobbying and politics enabled us to pass the two legislatively approved (MLK, Jr.) holidays as well as put our proposition on the ballot for the 1992 General Election.

I personally thank you for enabling me to make two critical decisions after consulting with you relative to VICTORY TOGETHER's historic campaign. First, for encouraging me to get back in the struggle...Secondly, for encouraging me not to relinquish the leadership of VICTORY TOGETHER when certain powers that be in Arizona wanted to take the lead...for winning Arizona's (MLK/Civil Rights Day).

On Tuesday, November 3, 1992, Arizona won the game in which you've been the "player-coach" for nearly two decades. Thanks, Art.

Our well-paid political consultants got a letter from me, which included the following paragraph to Felicia and Paul:

...Thank you for sharing so generously of your political astuteness and expertise in grassroots campaigns toward attaining our one common goal—winning a MARTIN LUTHER KING, JR./CIVIL RIGHTS DAY in the General Election on November 3, 1992. And who would have ever thought that we would win by a 2 to 1 margin!?!? (You did, I know.). . .

To the First Institutional members that I specifically asked to pray for me daily—the late Hazel Bell, Robert Williams, Jerry and Charlotte Hillman, Charles and Vivian Womack, and William Hogans—I offered these statements of thanksgiving.

To God be the Glory. Together we did it! Thank you so much for being part of the seven persons who prayed specifically for me upon my request in March. I am sure you remember that I asked you to pray for five things on my behalf as the Lord would lead me as the General Chairperson of VICTORY TOGETHER— POWER, PERCEPTION, PROTECTION, PATIENCE and PEACE.

...Please know that I continue to pray for you daily and I will be forever indebted to you for your specific petitions on my behalf over the past nearly eight months...

I called Dollie Heard of our congregation who co-owned a floral shop and instructed her, "I want a very nice plant to be aesthetically arranged for a woman who has sacrificed much during my nearly six-year leadership role in Arizona's King Day fight—Serena Michele Stewart. *Although the two of us as a husband and wife had been experiencing some very difficult days at the time, I had sense enough to show a token of appreciation to Serena for being there through it all.*

Our coalition and staff's final meeting took place at the "high-rent" district's Phoenix Ritz-Carlton Hotel on East Camelback Road on Monday, November 9, 1992 at 12 Noon. It was labeled as the VICTORY TOGETHER Appreciation Luncheon. The program was short and light. For the last time, I had our statement of principles and Amos 5:24a printed inside the cover of the white and blue program. The room was full of VICTORY TOGETHER leaders, workers, staff, volunteers and our consultants. Words of thanks were offered to the steering committee, consultants, financial contributors, and staff and volunteers by myself, Steve, Bettye and Paul E. in that order. Mike Kelly offered special public appreciation to Serena for help in keeping Public Enemy quiet a week before the election. Each coalition leader and campaign staff member received a white paperweight with VICTORY TOGETHER'S logo on it and the date inscribed—November 3, 1992.

In my brief remarks I said,

If I appear a little subdued it's because Steve Roman and Paul Eppinger did it again. They always throughout the campaign scheduled meetings on my day off....

What can I say to a group of so diverse people who have met together in UNITY for 24 months?…Thank you. In a very meaningful and historic way, our steering committee fulfilled our Statement of Principles. I want all of VICTORY TOGETHER's Steering Committee members to stand…I'd also like an *honorary member* to stand—Mrs. Serena Stewart.…

Finally, Dr. King's last full-length book was entitled **WHERE DO WE GO FROM HERE:** Chaos or Community? My challenge to you is that we MOVE FROM SYMBOL TO SUBSTANCE.

God bless you.

Chapter Seventeen
1993: Celebrating Arizona's Voter-Approved Martin Luther King, Jr./Civil Rights Day

With Arizona's 20-year fight for a paid state holiday honoring Dr. Martin Luther King, Jr. won by a knockout blow in the final-round, MLK champions began to celebrate. However, the big party would be held during Arizona's newest *official* holiday weekend, January 15-18, 1993. The magnitude of that upcoming "festival of freedom" was signaled by three major announcements.

First, Stevie Wonder agreed to end his six-year boycott of our state and attend the Mayor's and Phoenix Equal Opportunity Department's annual MLK Breakfast to be held on Dr. King's actual birthday—January 15, 1993. Fatima Halim, a gifted African-American sister who knows she is "black and beautiful" like the sister described in Song of Solomon 1:5, used her contacts as an employee of Phoenix's EOD to telephone Mr. Wonder's office and inform his agent that the election was victorious and the rhythm and blues megastar was invited to come to the breakfast celebration. According to the *ARIZONA INFORMANT*, just before Christmas 1992, Wonder's chief executive officer confirmed that Wonder was coming to Phoenix to join our party. Secondly, Mrs. Rosa Parks had been extended an invitation to return to Phoenix to help Arizonans celebrate the King/Civil Rights holiday. Thirdly, the biggest ever MLK Day breakfast was in the makings as more than 19,000 adults and schoolchildren were expected to fill the America West Arena on Friday, January 15, 1994.

I was relieved to know that the persons planning such a once-in-a-lifetime gala event would not include yours truly. My work on King Day was finished. *Thanks to the good Lord and a lot of hard work, Arizona had moved from the back of the bus due to segregating itself from most of the rest of the nation* by refusing to honor King, to the very front of the bus by becoming the first and only state in the country to approve a King holiday by a vote of the people. It was left up to Gene Blue, Rose Newsome, Pastor Barnwell, Fatima Halim and dozens of other MLK AZ Celebration Committee members to coordinate the celebration activities. My plans were to chill out and enjoy the long and hard fought victory. Anyway, I had a church to pastor, which had generously lent me to the holiday campaign for nearly six years.

Once the historic 1992 became the old year at 12:01, January 1, 1993, I found myself working busily, preparing for preaching a series of sermons on our new year's church theme, establishing goals and objectives for our annual church business meeting, focusing on First Institutional's annual evangelistic revival and fulfilling my multifaceted pastoral responsibilities and community leader. That's why the letter I received on January 4, 1993 caught me off guard. It began,

> It is with much enthusiasm that I am writing to inform you that you have been chosen to receive "The Making of the King Holiday" Award.
>
> Your tireless dedication to securing the passage of Proposition 300 which enabled Arizona to become the 49th state to observe the King Federal Holiday is inspiring. I remember fondly of our meeting in April of 1990 when the Commission held its planning conference in Phoenix....
>
> Again, my congratulations on receiving the award and I look forward to seeing you in Washington on January 11th.

The letter was signed Coretta Scott King, chairperson.

To say the least, I felt extremely honored and humbled to have been selected for such a prestigious award from Mrs. King herself, especially since a cast of thousands joined together to win voter approval of MLK Day. I could not help but reminisce that being invited to travel to Washington, D.C. to receive an award from the hands of the widow of Dr. King had to be light years away from watching Martin Luther King, Jr. deliver his famous "I Have a Dream" speech on a black and white T.V in 1963. My life's motto verse found in Proverbs 16:3 again proved itself for me, "Commit your work to the Lord and he will establish your plans."

Without hesitation, I had my secretary to make air and hotel reservations for my Sunday afternoon trip to the nation's capital and return on the next day after the luncheon. I made the mistake of travelling alone. Such occasions need to be shared with others. Nevertheless, I checked in my hotel late Sunday night and hardly slept a wink. Nervous energy, I'm sure. The next day, I took a cab to the Russell Senate Office Building where The Fourth Annual Recognition Luncheon on the occasion of the Sixty-Fourth Birthday Anniversary and the Eighth National Holiday in Honor of Dr. Martin Luther King, Jr. was to be held.

Washington was buzzing with all kinds of activity getting ready for the inauguration of William Jefferson Clinton as the President of the United States of America. Had the King Recognition Luncheon been scheduled a week later, I probably would not have been able to get a room as the "changing of the parties" was causing a mass exodus of Republicans who had been in power in the White House for twelve years and the onslaught of thousands of Democrat loyalists who would change the political climate of America. Quite interestingly, the luncheon's location-the Russell Caucus Room, Suite 325-was the place where a relatively recent historic event had occurred, which captured the public eye of tens of millions of Americans. I was honored in the same room where the less-than-honorable Supreme Court confirmation hearings were held for America's second African-American associate justice in 1992.

It is amazing how television possesses the ability to magnify the persons and places it flashes across the screen. Watching the confirmation hearings, I got the impression that the jam-packed room of senators, supporters, detractors, media personnel, family and friends of the confirmation candidate, and Mr. Clarence Thomas himself was some huge auditorium. Believe me, the Russell Caucus Room may have been large as it related to the far-reaching effects that took place there, but it was just about the right size to hold the Martin Luther King, Jr. Federal Holiday Commission's annual luncheon gathering of about 125 people.

Prior to the luncheon, all six of the 1993 "Making of the King Holiday" Awardees, as well as the distinguished participants on the program, some of whom included Mrs. Christine King-Farris, the only survivor of Dr. King's siblings; the Reverend Joan Brown Campbell, General Secretary of the National Council of Churches, the Honorable Jack Kemp, outgoing Secretary of HUD; Sharon Pratt Kelly, Mayor of Washington, D.C.; and William Sessions, departing Director of the FBI, gathered in the reception room in the office of none other than Senator Ted Kennedy. That, in itself, was a brief close encounter with a significant era in recent American history. Photographs of Senator Kennedy with famous persons like his late brothers,

President John F. Kennedy and Senator Robert F. Kennedy, in addition to the Pope of the Roman Catholic Church adorned his walls. Moreover, the mere opportunity of rubbing shoulders with prominent newsmakers who wielded, enormous political power in the nation's capital made me want to stop and pinch myself as to my being in their company. I even had a chance to converse with Vada Manager, former press spokesperson for two Arizona governors and then press secretary for Mayor Kelly, who had accompanied her to the luncheon.

Although the luncheon was scheduled to begin at 12 Noon, that did not happen. The coordinators awaited the arrival of Mrs. King and Mrs. Farris who had to fly in from Atlanta. Once they arrived, the luncheon commenced. Following the normal opening portion of most affairs such as that one, lunch was served after which FBI Director Sessions introduced Mrs. King. In her remarks, she gave a mini-"state of the dream" address calling for a one-day moratorium on violence on Monday, January 18, 1993, the federal observance of her husband's sixty-fourth birthday. Next on the program was the presentation of the awards.

It just so happened that I was the last of six award recipients to be called to the head table. Mrs. King was looking as elegant and stately as she always did and was dressed in a black pants suit complemented by a black and white checkered blouse. As my name was called and I walked toward her, she greeted me with a warm smile and outstretched hand. Since Dr. Carole Miller, chair of the Federal Holiday Commission's Award Committee, had already read a citation about the reason for my receiving the award; Mrs. King's words to me were personal and private. She said, "I want to thank you again for all of the wonderful work you did in winning the King holiday in Arizona…" I thanked her on behalf of myself, VICTORY TOGETHER, and all Arizonans. We both paused for the photographer to take a couple of shots of us. Then, in a matter of seconds I was on my way back to my seat holding with both hands the handsome black and clear-glass pyramid-shaped "Making of the King Holiday Award" with my name etched on it. I could not help but to reflect that I was about the same age as Mrs. King's husband when he was tragically assassinated. The next item on the agenda was the closing prayer. Following that, it was time for me to catch a cab to the airport and head home.

Before I left, I was interviewed live by Art Mobley on his Valley KMJK radio station about receiving such a prestigious award. *The Arizona Republic* also had their Washington Bureau reporter to cover the luncheon and interview me in the Russell Senate office building. And to my surprise, my being honored by Mrs. Coretta Scott King made front-page mention in the *Republic* and a feature article on Page B-1 of the Valley & State section of the *Republic* accompanied by a full color photograph of Mrs. King presenting me the award on the next day. The headline and sub-headline read,

State praised for King Day
Phoenix pastor honored in D.C. for role in vote

By Friday, January 15, 1993, excitement had generated to peak levels, as thousands were planning to participate in King Day events in Arizona, particularly in Phoenix. The premier kickoff would be the City of Phoenix extravaganza at the America West Arena. Although selling 19,000 tickets at $20 apiece proved to be a challenge to Rose Newsome's EOD, corporate donors chipped in and purchased 4,000 for schoolchildren to attend the MLK breakfast, beginning at 7:15 a.m. In spite of the slower-than expected ticket sales that caused the city-sponsored function to run in the red for the first time since its inception, the arena was nearly filled to capacity by 8:30 a.m. to celebrate Arizona's brand new holiday.

Everybody who was anybody of note who supported the King holiday was in attendance, including several political, civic and community leaders—Governor Symington, Mayor Johnson, Senator DeConcini and Councilman Goode. The MLK birthday bash turned out to be a non-stop three and a half hour party filled with joy, laughter, tears, dancing and celebrating the life and legacy of Dr. Martin Luther King, Jr. The format of the event included racial, ethnic, cultural and religious presentations from virtually every special interest group in Arizona. I sat in awe as I witnessed the various constituencies proudly and colorfully display their particular gifts and talents God had blessed them with, as distinctive groups of "people created equal" by Him.

Later, the invited guests who came from around the country representing culturally diverse groups which help make America what it is, were escorted to the platform to speak about Dr. King and Arizona's passage of a holiday honoring him. A noted Native American activist voiced his thanksgiving for King, as well as his protest against extant racism in America. Then, came Mrs. Parks and no one held the rapt attention of the 18,000 partygoers like Rosa Parks. Herman Bookbinder, a nationally known Jewish-rights activist, offered his evaluation of the magnanimous festivity by saying, "I've been to a lot of Martin Luther King events, but nothing to match what you did here in Phoenix today. You should be proud." As the celebration progressed, the award-winning contemporary Gospel group-The Winans-got the house rocking with their soulful music, which witnessed loudly and dearly for love and Jesus Christ.

Finally, after a long wait of a couple of hours or so, the announcer alerted the audience that the featured guest, who had flown in from Ghana, West Africa the day before, was about to make his way to the stage-*none other than Stevie Wonder*. When the spotlight illuminated his entry into the main floor of the arena, Wonder was greeted by a thunderous applause and standing ovation. Somehow, the presence of the single-most person who had advocated the passage of the federal MLK Holiday other than Mrs. King and who had sustained a self-imposed six-year boycott of Arizona *concretized* in the minds of those of us in attendance that glorious morning that "King Day had come" to Arizona. Quite appropriately, Stevie Wonder urged the thousands of cheering King and Wonder fans in his remarks, "It is important that you keep the real meaning of that holiday every year it is celebrated." After giving an impromptu speech on what the King holiday meant and cracking jokes about his blindness, Arizona's guest of honor did what everyone had hoped that he would do (even though it had been reported that his music contract would prohibit him from doing it). Wonder utilized the voice that had made him famous to unite Arizona in singing his popular hit, which had melodiously won support for the federal MLK Day, his own version of "Happy Birthday to Martin Luther King, Jr." Everything after that was anti-climatic.

Earlier that morning, somewhere sandwiched between the array of speeches, songs and dances celebrating our VICTORY TOGETHER, I was introduced and ushered upon the stage to stand in the midst of the thousands of King Day supporters. Mayor Johnson and Director Newsome presented me with a plaque of appreciation for my efforts in leading the victorious King Day campaign, and then it was my turn to say a few final, but familiar words on behalf of Dr. King and his long-time coming holiday in Arizona. Although I had a copy of my remarks in my hand, I did not use it. I did not need to, for what I was about to say was in my heart.

Good morning, Arizona. Good morning distinguished guests, officials, honorees, students and all in attendance.

> 1993 is a very significant year as it relates to Dr. Martin Luther King, Jr. It is the 64th Anniversary of his birth; the 30th anniversary of his famous "I Have a Dream" speech; the 25th

anniversary of his tragic assassination; the 10th anniversary of the signing into law of the Martin Luther King, Jr. federal holiday; and the FIRST CELEBRATION OF ARIZONA'S OFFICIAL MARTIN LUTHER KING, JR./CIVIL RIGHTS DAY.

To God be the glory.

Let us never forget that this holiday represents a fundamental American principle that "all people are created equal under God."

Let us never forget that this holiday commemorates Dr. King's philosophy of non-violence that so effectively inspired an historic revolution that changed race relations in America forever.

Let us never forget that **VICTORY TOGETHER** was a historic broad-based grassroots coalition of Arizonans from all walks of life who laid aside differences to work toward the common goal of winning voter approval of the Martin Luther King, Jr./ Civil Rights Day in the general election on November 3, 1992.

Would all former board and campaign committee members, staff and volunteers of **VICTORY TOGETHER** please stand?

As I did on Monday in Washington, D.C., when I received "The Making of the King Holiday" Award from Mrs. Coretta Scott King and The Martin Luther King, Jr. Federal Holiday Commission, I accept this award on behalf of **VICTORY TOGETHER** and all freedom and justice-loving Americans.

Now, let us move **"FROM SYMBOL TO SUBSTANCE"** as it relates to human and civil rights and equal opportunity for "all people created equal under God."

Thank you and God bless you.

Several members of my congregation made their way to the main floor of the arena after the finale to greet me and extend well wishes in the form of words, hugs, kisses and handshakes. Word came to me unofficially that Stevie Wonder was holding a press conference in the pressroom of the arena. Not wanting to miss the opportunity to see Mr. Wonder up close, I made my way up several flights of stairs to the upper level room where the press conference was being held. A crowd of people had filled the small room, where the action was taking place. Being late, I could not get into the room. However, one of the Black Phoenix police officers who knew me beckoned me to make my way through the crowd to stand behind Stevie Wonder as he took questions from reporters about Arizona's King Day.

The press conference concluded in about 20 minutes and one of the national television networks had requested a one-on-one interview with the superstar. Consequently, the security ushered Mr. Wonder through the crowd to another room and took me along with them. Again, one of the African-American bodyguard contingents from the Phoenix P.D. spoke up and introduced me to Stevie Wonder as "the man, who led the King holiday campaign." The guest of honor extended his hand to me and said, "It's a pleasure to meet you, Pastor Stewart. You should have been the one answering all those questions instead of me.... Thank you for your leadership in winning Dr. King's holiday in Arizona." Mr. Wonder will never know how *wonderful* he made my day.

At 12:01 a.m., Monday, January 18, 1993, Arizona joined forty-eight other states in the nation in honoring Dr. Martin Luther King, Jr. on the third Monday in January. VICTORY TOGETHER's prophecy had come to pass with the official paid state holiday labeled Martin Luther King, Jr./ Civil Rights Day. I gathered with thousands of others at Eastlake Park for the beginning of the MLK Day "Victory March" at around 9:00 a.m. No more would our trek to the State Capitol be a protest march demanding, "We want a holiday!" If anything, we should now use the annual celebration to shout in agreement with Mecham, "We need jobs!" I had my sons with me and ended up pushing my three-year- old Aaron in his stroller for the length of the march. That year, I did not make my way to the front of the line to link arms with the other dignitaries. I just stayed a few rows back among the "regular" people and kept up with Jared and Justin Stewart after my two oldest boys had gone to walk with friends. It was time for other folk to take the lead.

The mission had been accomplished. To be honest, I was *weary* that day. For one, it was Monday, my supposed day off. The day before, I had led and preached in our two special Martin Luther King, Jr. Memorial and Sanctity of Life Sunday worship services, at which time Mrs. Rosa Parks was the guest of honor at First Institutional. That same Sunday afternoon I moderated our congregation's annual church business meeting when we approved our goals, recommendations, programs, plans and budget for 1993. Later that evening, I escorted my son, Matthew, to the MLK Candlelight Ceremony held at the Phoenix Civic Plaza where he had been programmed by his godfather, Pastor Barnwell, to read the New Testament Scripture. Plus, some long-term, deep-seated personal problems I had had were coming to a head, draining me of what little energy I had left, after taking care of everybody else's problems, including Arizona's King Day problem, *but my own.*

I was so out of it; I did not go up on the stage at Wesley Bolin Plaza once the crowd of 10,000 had reached our destination. I was not programmed to speak so I sat near the back steps of the stage with my son, Aaron, and chatted with a few friends. After the scheduled speakers had their say, word was sent up to me that they wanted me to come stand with Pastor Barnwell, Victor Washington, Arnie Zaler and a couple of other long-time King Day leaders. I did so, reluctantly. Once on the stage before the crowd sprawled out in front of those on the platform, Mr. Blue informed each of us that we could make a brief statement, but that our time was limited. When it came my turn, I said something, about "thanking God for the sunshine," since it had threatened to rain that morning. Then, I reached in my pocket and asked Gene to come to the podium. My remarks that followed went something like this.

> On behalf of VICTORY TOGETHER, our broad-based, grassroots coalition, I present to you for the Arizona Martin Luther King, Jr. Holiday Celebration Committee a check in the amount of $7,000.
>
> May God bless you.

And I walked off the stage and went home.

The money came from about $25,000 in surplus that the campaign had raised, but did not spend. Steve and I divided it up after approval of the "executive committee" of our coalition, determining to give the money to organizations which fulfill the principles and philosophy of Martin Luther King, Jr. In addition to the $7,000 that went to the MLK Celebration Committee, over $9,000 was donated to two organizations that aid the homeless, and the remaining $7,000 was given to the First Institutional Baptist Church.

Later on that day, I took off my VICTORY TOGETHER cap and T-Shirt, blue jeans and corduroy jacket, packed my bags, and flew to Nashville, Tennessee to attend the Mid-Winter Board Meeting of the National Baptist Convention, USA, Inc.

Conclusion
Leadership Under Fire: Lessons Learned, Places to Go

There is a high cost of leadership. Hopefully, that has been evident throughout this book, whether I was writing *about Martin, Mecham or me,* and others. *LEADERSHIP UNDER FIRE* means that an individual and/or group of persons who have stepped out (or have been pushed out) from the crowd to make a difference in their surroundings must be *on fire* and expect to be *under fire* from those being led and those who do not want to be led by him or her or them. Being *on fire* entails being enthused by a positive force higher than oneself, better known as God, which usually removes the *option* one has *not* to lead in and for a particular cause. Expecting to be *under fire* informs those who lead that they can expect to be the target of criticism-just and unjust, envy and jealousy. from within and outside the ranks, and robbed of precious privacy, even the privacy to make mistakes! It also entails making decisions under pressure, sooner than planned, and amidst frustrations, failure and doubt. Whether a leader is sincere and right, or sincere, but wrong, he or she who affects the lives of those within the sphere of his or her influence must learn to live with *LEADERSHIP UNDER FIRE.*

KEEP FOCUSED

A second lesson I learned from 1986 to 1992 was to *KEEP FOCUSED.* "Keep your eyes on the prize" and do not look back. Know what you want, and finding out how to get it will be more attainable. As I have already indicated in this book, a major challenge of my leadership, especially as general chairperson of VICTORY TOGETHER, was to make certain that our coalition *KEPT FOCUSED* on winning voter approval of the MLK, Jr./Civil Rights Day in the general election.

BROADEN YOUR BASE OF SUPPORT

Another key point in leading people is to *BROADEN YOUR BASE OF SUPPORT*. (But be careful not to dilute your strength.) It goes without saying that the more people a leader can get to join forces with him or her usually works to his or her cause's advantage if the leader can maintain order and keep the group focused on their common goal. Basically, the only criterion for "membership" in both King Day coalitions that I led was uncompromising commitment to the approval of a paid state holiday honoring Dr. Martin Luther King, Jr. to be observed on the third Monday in January, based on the federal model of that holiday. Thank God, we were able to move public opinion from as much as 70% in opposition to our proposal, to a maximum of 66% before the election.

EDUCATE, ENLIGHTEN AND INSPIRE

Fourthly, *EDUCATE, ENLIGHTEN AND INSPIRE*, if possible. Think of the leaders throughout history that you and I remember, whether good of bad. In one way or another, each of them was able to make the mark on others' lives and the broader society by *EDUCATING, ENLIGHTENING AND INSPIRING* persons to their *identity* and *purpose*. Our case in point was that, for most of the two decades that Arizona refused to approve permanently a King Day, the average non-Black Arizonan viewed the observance as a "Black" holiday. Our formidable task necessitated that we engage in *EDUCATING, ENLIGHTENING, and INSPIRING* Arizona voters to understand and support the Martin Luther King, Jr./Civil Rights Day for what it is—*an American holiday.*

STICK WITH PRINCIPLES

A fifth lesson is *STICK WITH PRINCIPLES*. In any worthy endeavor there are principles, upon which the entire cause is founded. There are moral standards based on truth, on which noble causes are built. Moreover, when the principles on which a goal is built are somehow linked to divine truth, those who have adopted such principles are almost always unwavering in their loyalty to what they believe as true. Basic principles do not change and leaders led by principles usually stick with them. That is why VICTORY TOGETHER's statement of principles was so crucial to me and became the source of authority, by which I interpreted and governed everything we did as a coalition. Whenever it appeared that we were veering off course, it was my job as leader to demand that we *STICK WITH PRINCIPLES*.

BUILD A CONSENSUS TO REACH GOALS

A major responsibility of most leaders is to *BUILD A CONSENSUS TO REACH GOALS*. Although this is similar *to BROADENING YOUR BASE OF SUPPORT,* it is not the same. As groups grow, disagreements and differences are bound to arise. Moreover, if the points are in any way contentious, they can disrupt, derail, divide, and/or destroy a coalition, organization, congregation, family and nation. Therefore, *BUILDING A CONSENSUS TO REACH GOALS* becomes imperative to keep the majority of those being led, marching to the same drumbeat. As related to the strategy in both King Day coalitions, whether it was a decision to support the boycott of Arizona or to embrace the strategy proposed by our political consultants, I made sure that we had a consensus of MLK holiday advocates solidly backing the decision that had been made.

DON'T GIVE UP—PERSEVERE

The seventh lesson I offer as a leader to leaders is *DON'T GIVE UP—PERSEVERE.* I deliberately began this principle with a negative because "when the going gets tough," one of the first reactions to roadblocks, detours and obstacles on the way to attaining one's goal(s) is to think about *giving up.* The Lord knows I thought about "calling it quits" on several occasions on the road to VICTORY TOGETHER. However, I was blessed with intimate friends who urged me on, in spite of the difficulties I faced. That prompts me to inform you that a *special* Friend enabled and empowered me to "keep the faith and don't give up" when there was no one else around. That inspiring Intimate was none other than the precious Holy Spirit. God Himself kept me going no matter how tough the task became. There were even several times that I wanted to give up on this writing project, especially during the personally stormy months of 1993 for me, my family, and my ministry, but "a still small voice" constantly whispered in my ear to *persevere.*

BELIEVE THAT GOD IS WITH YOU

Lastly, *BELIEVE THAT GOD IS WITH YOU.* Contrary to what the majority of average citizens might believe, my leadership in Arizona's historic Martin Luther King, Jr. holiday fight was a *ministry for me.* I felt as much called by God to fight for a holiday honoring Dr. King, as I do pastoring First Institutional, engaging in a myriad of justice issues, standing up for the human rights of the unborn, providing food, clothing and shelter for the needy, and loving my family. A matter of fact, I had prayed to God throughout the long King Day struggle, "Lord, let me stay here in Arizona long enough to see this holiday passed." He answered my prayer in a manner I could have never imagined. That is why it was intentional that we opened and closed every coalition meeting of ARIZONANS FOR A MARTIN LUTHER KING, JR. STATE HOLIDAY and VICTORY TOGETHER with prayer. I knew that if we were to win, *we would need God's Presence.*

Whether you are leading a church, political campaign, neighborhood blockwatch club, student body, multi-million dollar corporation or grass-roots movement, be sure that you are in line with divine destiny. You see, if you *BELIEVE GOD IS WITH YOU*, no matter how overwhelming your opposition might appear, *God and you make a majority, regardless of whether you win or not.* Furthermore, you will have His Presence, period!

◇◇◇◇◇

Arizona is better for the process, through which we experienced the agony of defeat over and over again, long before we enjoyed the thrill of victory. Had we not fought over the holiday, we would have not ultimately been forged together to form unity, amidst diversity.

I learned so much from November 1986 to November 1992. I thank God for right decisions, as well as my mistakes as a leader. I was blessed beyond measure with new and renewed friendships, notoriety and infamy, increased influence and political clout, and unexpected exposure to other leaders, from whom I learned by observation and association, not to mention numerous awards and citations which came my way. My relationship with my Lord and Savior Jesus Christ matured to the point that pleasing Him as my Master is the most important goal in my life.

Where do I go from here? I do not know. As I faithfully tell younger aspiring men and women called to preach the Gospel, *"I don't plan. I just prepare."* My definition of faith is—*the trusting belief that my best future is in God's Hands.*

Prophetically and politically, I have toyed with the idea of establishing an activist foundation called *AWOL*, standing for *ADVOCATES OF WHOLE LIFE*. Its four-fold principled platform would address: (1) the *Inalienable Right to Life*, (2) *Educational Initiative, Incentive and Equity*, (3) *Economic Development through Economic Justice*, and (4) *Environmental Sensitivity and Redemption*. Its motto would be *"Policy Based on Principles, Not Politics."* To me, such a foundation could provide *an alternative choice* to partisan politics as usual. Moreover, I would be able to extend the horizons of my prophetic, holistic Christian ministry via a non-sectarian, non-profit coalition of like-minded, non-conformist leaders and workers. In other words, our group would be "absent without official leave" from traditional political parties and special interest groups.

I guess, it can be said of me as Martin said of himself, *"I, too, have a dream."*

Finally, *today's youth*—our most valuable human resource-must become the recipients of the *best* we have to give. Regrettably, as a consequence of our changing society, they can be labeled as *YOUTH UNDER FIRE*, inflamed by decadent demoralizing, devious brush fires and towering infernos, burning out of control while we sit idly by as smoke-dazed arsonists, unaware or uncaring that we are responsible for their promising future going up in smoke in front of all of our eyes.

If Martin Luther King, Jr. was alive, I am certain he would be leading the fight for his grandchildren's and great-grandchildren's survival. That is why we must win that battle for their survival, as well as ours! There is only *ONE CLEAR CHOICE*. And it will take *VICTORY TOGETHER.*

About the Author

Dr. Warren H. Stewart, Sr.

Dr. Warren H. Stewart, Sr., is a native of Coffeyville, Kansas where he was reared in a Christian family and African-American Church environment. He was converted at the age of 16 and preached his Trial Sermon when he was 17 years old. He is married to the Rev. Karen E. (Curry) Stewart and they are the parents of a blended family of five sons, Warren, Jr., Matthew, Jared, Justin, Aaron and two daughters, Jamila Imani and Jessica Elizabeth Curry. He is the grandfather of Warren Josiah, III, Micaiah Lovel, Matthew Christian II, Jonny Angel, Jared Chamberlain II, Kaira Nechee, John Paul Silas, Jase Alexander, Joshua Elijah and Mia Noelai. He is presently the Senior Pastor of the First Institutional Baptist Church of Phoenix, Arizona and has served there since July 1, 1977. Dr. Stewart was appointed Executive Secretary of the Home Mission Board of the National Baptist Convention, USA, Inc., in November 1994 and served through January 2005, and also continued serving as Chair of that Board through January 2010.

Dr. Stewart's academic achievements and awards include an <u>Associate of Arts Degree</u>, 1971, Honor Graduate, Coffeyville Community Junior College, Coffeyville, Kansas; <u>Bachelor of Arts Degree in Religion and</u>

Philosophy, 1973 graduating *Summa Cum Laude*, Bishop College, Dallas, Texas; Master of Divinity Degree, 1976, Union Theological Seminary, New York City; Master of Sacred Theology Degree, 1977, selected to deliver Commencement Address, Union Theological Seminary; Doctor of Ministry Degree, 1982, American Baptist Seminary of the West, Berkeley, California; was recipient of an Honorary Doctor of Divinity Degree from Ottawa University, Ottawa, Kansas, 1994; and the recipient of the Award of Excellence in Black Church Studies, 1982, Ecumenical Center for Black Church Studies, Los Angeles, California. Dr. Stewart has also been the recipient of numerous awards and commendations from churches, colleges, civic and community organizations, locally, statewide and nationally. He was recognized by *The Arizona Republic* newspaper as one of the ten most influential religious leaders in the Valley (Phoenix), October 6, 1985, *The Phoenix Gazette* 1993 Hall of Fame as being "one of ten people whose achievements had the most notable effect on . . . Arizona," the *Arizona Daily Star* (Tucson) as a "Living Legend" on January 20, 2002, 2003 Calvin C. Goode Lifetime Achievement Award by City of Phoenix/MLK, Jr. Celebration, *The Business Journal* as one of 25 "Leaders and Legends" in the business community in 2005, *New Times* "Best Pro-Civil Rights Pastor" and *Arizona Informant* "Faith Community Award", both in 2011.

Dr. Stewart is the author of *INTERPRETING GOD'S WORD IN BLACK PREACHING*, published by Judson Press, 1984 and in its fifth printing, *HOW TO HANDLE GIANTS: Sermons to African-American Youth and Their Mentors*, published by Townsend Press, 1995, *Do Prophets Exist in Contemporary Culture?*, 2009, *Our Values as a Pastor and People: The Bible Study* and *VICTORY TOGETHER FOR MARTIN LUTHER KING, JR.: The Story of Dr. Warren H. Stewart, Sr., Governor Evan Mecham and the Historic Battle for a Martin Luther King, Jr. Holiday in Arizona*, as well as has published articles and sermons in several major publications. He has also served as Adjunct Professor of Ottawa University-Phoenix Campus, Phoenix Seminary and the Doctor of Ministry Program at Fuller Theological Seminary, as well as Chair of the Board of Trustees of the American Baptist Seminary of the West, Berkeley, California.

Dr. Stewart served as Associate Minister of the Cornerstone Baptist Church, Brooklyn, New York, under the pastorate of the late Dr. Sandy F. Ray, in whose honor the Annual Sandy F. Ray Institute for pastors, ministers and lay persons was founded and held annually at First Institutional. At

FIBC, Pastor Stewart has licensed 139 sons and daughters into the Gospel Ministry.

Dr. Stewart has traveled and preached extensively throughout the United States and internationally to include 38 States and Territories, and 51 Countries, including a challenging three-week Preaching Mission, sponsored by the National Baptist Convention, USA, Inc., Foreign Mission Board, to several African countries including South Africa, and attended the First African/African-American Summit held in West Africa in 1991 convened by the late Dr. Leon H. Sullivan. Also, FIBC, under Pastor Stewart, built a new church edifice and parsonage for the First Institutional Baptist Church of Soweto, Republic of South Africa. In April of 2004, he was extended an invitation by Executive Secretary Emile D. E. Sam-Peal to serve as the Guest Preacher during the 90th Annual Session of the Liberia Baptist Missionary and Educational Convention, Inc. Since February 2005, first participating on Baptist World Alliance Mission Team Trip to North-East India, he has been involved in ministry in India. Dr. Stewart's ministry is characterized by an unwavering commitment and Spirit-filled zeal to engage in *Evangelism and Emancipation*, meeting the needs of the whole person. As a result, since 1982, the First Institutional Baptist Church has intentionally BECOME A DISCIPLING FELLOWSHIP THROUGH EVANGELISM AND EMANCIPATION under the leadership of the Holy Spirit through Dr. Stewart's pastoral ministry. In the 1990s, he led FIBC in completing three phases of the VISION 2000 Master Plan which built an educational, administrative and outreach building, acquired additional property, and renovated the worship center at a total cost of nearly four million dollars in cash debt-free. In 2004, a five million dollar family life center was built *completing the VISION 2000 Master Plan, totaling almost $9,000,000.00.* In addition, FIBC has established FIBCO Family Services, Inc., Samaritan House for Homeless Families, Ujima House for Unwed Teenage Mothers and their Infants, and sponsors the Broadway House low-income housing complex and several residential homes for the seriously mentally ill, all of which provide social services to thousands monthly.

Dr. Stewart served as the first General Chairperson for ARIZONANS FOR A MARTIN LUTHER KING, JR. STATE HOLIDAY which contributed significantly to the legislative passage of Arizona's Martin Luther King, Jr. holiday on September 21, 1989. Dr. Stewart also organized and led VICTORY TOGETHER, INC., a broad-based coalition that campaigned for a Martin Luther King, Jr./Civil Rights Day in Arizona which was won by a historic vote of the people in the general election on November 3, 1992. He has also served as the President of the American Baptist Churches of the Pacific Southwest and Paradise Missionary Baptist State Convention of Arizona, Inc. and Congress, respectively. In 2011, he organized an Exploratory Committee for the open U.S. Senate from Arizona in 2012 to consider running on a platform of justice. From 2012-2014, Dr. Stewart served as Chair of the Board of the National Immigration Forum as well as co-organized the Black/Brown Coalition of Arizona. He was drafted and ran for the Phoenix City Council-District 8 seat in 2013. Dr. Stewart is an enthusiastic advocate of the sanctity of life ethic which believes that all human life has intrinsic value from conception to natural death. He is also recognized by others as "a man of conscience, commitment and dedication to the cause of moral leadership, human rights and a soldier of justice and equality."

Revised 3/20/2015